THIS
United Church
OF Ours

THIRD EDITION

OTHER BOOKS BY RALPH MILTON

Radio Broadcasting for Developing Nations

The Gift of Story

Through Rose-colored Bifocals

Commonsense Christianity

Is This Your Idea of a Good Time, God?

God for Beginners

Living God's Way

The Family Story Bible

Man to Man

How to Write and Publish Your Church History

Sermon Seasonings

Angels in Red Suspenders

Julian's Cell

The Essence of Julian

The Great Canadian Improv Bible Study
co-authored with James Taylor

RALPH MILTON

THIS
United
Church
OF
Ours

THIRD EDITION

Includes Study Guide

WOOD LAKE BOOKS

Editor: Michael Schwartzentruber
Cover and interior design: Margaret Kyle
Consulting art director: Robert MacDonald

Unless otherwise noted, all biblical references are from the New Revised Standard Version of
the Bible, copyright © 1989 by the Division of Christian Education of
the National Council of Churches of Christ in the United States of America, and
are used by permission. All rights reserved.

We acknowledge the financial support of the Government of Canada through
the Book Publishing Industry Development Program (BPIDP) for our publishing activities.

At WOOD LAKE BOOKS we practice what we publish, guided by a concern for fairness, justice, and equal
opportunity in all of our relationships with employees and customers.

Wood Lake Books Inc. is committed to caring for the environment and all creation. We recycle, reuse
and compost, and encourage readers to do the same. Resources are printed on recycled paper and
more environmentally friendly groundwood papers (newsprint), whenever possible. A portion of all
profit is donated to charitable organizations.

Canadian Cataloguing in Publication Data
Milton, Ralph.
This United Church of ours
ISBN 1-55145-389-4
1. United Church of Canada. I. Title.
BX9881.M54 2000 287.9'2 C00-910142-X

Published by Wood Lake Books
9025 Jim Bailey Road, Kelowna, BC, Canada, V4V 1R2
PHONE: 250.766.2778   E-MAIL: info@woodlake.com
WEBSITE: www.woodlakebooks.com
Kelowna, British Columbia, Canada

Printing 9 8 7 6 5 4 3 2
Printed in Canada

To the memory of
Robert Hatfield, MD, DD, LLD.
A dear friend and a wise counselor
who shared his gift
of wholeness and laughter

A word to clergy and other church leaders

Please look at the Study Guide, which begins on page 197 of this book. It offers a way to undertake a program of congregational revitalization that you might find very useful. *This United Church of Ours* can be a helpful resource, not just to new people in the church, but to everyone, especially those on boards and committees and in other positions of leadership. Please look at this book as a revitalization tool, as well as a church membership resource.

Contents

Acknowledgments

How this book happened

How do you write a book about the United Church, making it as responsible and accurate as possible, without having all the interesting edges worn off by overzealous committee people?

I stumbled on the answer with the first edition of *This United Church of Ours*. I wrote a draft manuscript, then sent it to a wide cross section of United Church people, and asked for their comments. They responded magnificently. The book became a bestseller in the United Church, as did the second edition.

A similar pattern was followed with the second edition and now with this third edition. I sent copies of the previous version to every division of the national church, to every conference office, to every organized group within the church or related to it that we could find, and to a cross section of folk from coast to coast who we thought might have a particular perspective on the United Church.

In addition to that, we bought an advertisement in *The United Church Observer* and sent out a general request on the Internet, asking anyone who was interested to respond. Many did. Their names are listed below, and their concerns are reflected in the text that follows.

Two people deserve special thanks. Reverend Beverley Milton, my mate of more than 40 years, and Dr. James Taylor, my long-time friend and colleague, who not only helped with the initial review of the second edition, but reviewed and checked the final draft before it was sent off to Wood Lake Books.

As with the first edition of *This United Church of Ours*, so with this third edition; the book is inevitably my personal perspective on a church I love very dearly. Where the book falls short, let me know. Where it succeeds, tell the folks listed on the next page.

Rev. David Allen
Rev. Don Anderson
Dr. Tom Bandy
Dr. Marion Best
Dr. Reg Bibby
Jack Booth
Dr. Rod Booth
Rev. Wendy Bulloch
Rev. Stew Clarke
Shelley Currie
Rev. Foster Freed
Bob Gates
Rev. Doug Goodwin
Julie Graham
Rev. Bruce Gregersen
Dr. Fred Holberton
Rev. Wayne Holst
Rev. Keith Howard
Rev. Alyson Huntley
Rev. George Lavery
Rev. Bill Laurie
Brad Lavenne
Dr. Chris Levan
Elsie Manley-Casimir

Rev. David Martyn
Kari McNair
Dr. Bob Mills
Rev. Bev Milton
Rev. Glenn Morison
Rev. John Moses
Elizabeth Muir
Rev. John Murphy
Rev. Neil Parker
Rt. Rev. Bill Phipps
Barbara Rafuse
Dr. George Rodgers
Mike Schwartzentruber
Rev. Ed Searcy
Rev. Clarence Sellers
Rev. John Shearman
Dr. Victor Shepherd
Dr. Yvonne Stewart
Dr. Jim Taylor
Dr. Brian Thorpe
James Upright
Rev. Bill Wall
Dr. Paul Wilson

1

Nuts and Bolts

—

For just as the body is one and has many members, and all the members of the body, though many, are one body, so it is with Christ. For in the Spirit we were all baptized into one body...

1 Corinthians 12:12–13a

First, the important stuff – things you may need to know the very first time you go to church.

For instance. Why is it that every single Sunday, in every single United Church across Canada, people (especially those who are a bit hard of hearing) fill up the back rows first? Only when there are no more seats available do they sit in the front pew.

Okay, so children will go and sit in the front pews. But they're only kids, so what do you expect. They don't know better.

Let me tell you why this is.

I have no idea. None. I'm told it happens in churches of other denominations too. It ranks among the world's great puzzlers, along with questions such as, "Why do I always get a zit on the end of my nose just before a big meeting?" If you know the answer to either of these questions, please let me know.

What do I wear?

This first chapter is here because my long-time friend and colleague, Jim Taylor, read over the first draft and said, "You're not answering the questions people ask!" Jim was thinking about this kind of thing because he'd just finished writing the United Church chapter in a two-volume set called *How to Be a Perfect Stranger*, which gives this kind of information about a whole spectrum of denominations and faith groups.

"People want practical stuff. Like, what do you wear?" said Jim.

I'd never given that much thought, to tell you the truth. I stumble into the closet Sunday morning and take the first thing that comes into my hand, put it on, stumble out of the closet and Bev says, "You can't wear that!"

So I stumble back in, grab something else, and repeat the process until Bev either gives up or I find myself wearing something she considers suitable. But because of Jim's question, I went to church last Sunday and actually looked at what people had on.

I'm no wiser. I saw everything from blue jeans and sloppy sweatshirts to three-piece suits to hats and white gloves, to…well you name it.

So after that scientific survey, I can report with confidence that you can wear pretty much anything you feel comfortable wearing. There's no such thing as a dress code in the United Church, although if you wear something really weird or skimpy you might get a bit of reaction. Jim says folks are just a tiny bit more formal as you move east in Canada. I'm sure he's right. I never noticed.

After several trips in and out of the closet, I find I'm sometimes wearing my one good suit, which I think should only be worn to funerals. Actually, I don't notice what I have on till we get home and I rush to put my jeans and T-shirt back on. Sometimes I notice I'm wearing a sport coat and slacks. A tie, even.

"What do you wear to church?" I ask Bev.

"You mean you've never noticed?"

"Ah, no. Should I have?" Bev and I have been married to each other for more than 40 years, so she's either given up or become reconciled to the reality of what I notice and don't notice.

"I usually wear a dress or a suit," she sighs. "Sometimes a skirt and blouse or sweater."

"What about hat and gloves? I thought women were supposed to wear hats and gloves to church."

"Ralph. I haven't worn a hat and gloves to church since I was 12." There is just a touch of exasperation in her voice. Then she gives me the short course in appropriate churchly attire. "You and I are old fogies, Ralph. We tend to dress up more than younger people. They're much more casual, often wearing jeans (or shorts in summer) and sweat shirts. Or slacks. Children wear the same sort of thing they wear to school. Some people feel the church is getting entirely too casual, and others think it's still too formal. But I don't think it's much of an issue either way. So wear what's comfortable. Tell your readers not to let any concerns about clothing keep them from going to church! What you wear isn't important."

"What if you came bare naked?"

Bev doesn't seem to consider that a question worthy of response.

Where do we sit?

Well, by now you know that you never sit in the front pew or row of chairs unless there's nowhere else. Kids can sit there. But not adults. That's why it's important to come on time, because otherwise – horrors – you might wind up sitting in the front seats!

We're creatures of habit. A number of years ago, arriving at church with my children, one of them piped up, "Somebody's sitting in our seat!" It wasn't "our seat." It was simply the one we'd gone to every Sunday out of force of habit.

Seriously, you can sit anywhere you like. Some of the more traditional churches have ushers who will give you a bulletin, and then show you to a seat. But if for some reason you want to sit somewhere else, go for it. If you like to sing, go sit with the choir. Most choirs can use another voice or two.

Who's who

The bulletin? You could call it a program. It's a pamphlet that tells you who is who, what things are happening in the church, and how the worship service will proceed. It will tell you the names of the hymns and where to find them in the hymnbook. There will be some prayers in which you join in. If you're not sure what part to read, just listen, or mumble till you know what's going on. Don't worry about when to stand and sit. Just do what the other folks do. We almost never kneel in the United Church.

The bulletin will probably give you the phone number and the office hours of the church. There are many things I can't tell you about in this book because each church is different. Things like the starting time of Sunday services vary from one congregation to the next. The traditional starting time was 11:00 on Sunday morning, but now many churches worship at 10:00 or 10:30. Phone the church and ask. You can call anytime because most churches have an answering machine that tells you when church begins. If you have questions about child care during the service, or Sunday school or parking, call during office hours. In smaller churches, that may only be weekday mornings.

Can you leave early?

Can you leave early? Sure. But it's nice to stay through the whole thing and join the folks for coffee afterwards. The coffee time is, for me, one of the best parts of church. It's important, because that's where we make the connections and build the trust so that we can offer friendship and caring to others.

What do you call "the Rev"?

What do you call the minister? Well, for years I called her "Honey," but I wouldn't recommend that unless you happen to be married to her, as I was. Most of the folks in the congregations she served simply called her "Bev," and a few "Rev. Bev." Some parents insisted that their children call her "Mrs. Milton."

Now that Bev is a member of the congregation like me, we call our minister David. A few people address him as Rev. Martyn, although if you want to be picky about it, that isn't correct. The proper form of address when you are speaking to clergy is Mr. Martyn, or Mrs. Milton. That's if you want to be formal. If you're writing or talking *about* your minister, and you want to be really formal, it would be The Reverend Mr. Martyn, or The Reverend Beverley Milton. Or something like that.

Most United Church people don't bother with any of that. But if you have any doubt, ask.

Singing

Okay, so we've got you dressed, into church on time to get a choice pew halfway between the front and the back, and you know what to call the minister, besides, "Hey, Rev!"

Do you know what a hymn is? No, that is not pronounced, "hy-man." That's something very different. It's pronounced "him" and is simply a song we sing in church. The words are often in the form of a prayer addressed to God, but not necessarily. The old hymns are sometimes a bit slow and draggy, but they have nice harmonies which I like singing bass to. The newer ones often have more zip.

In the United Church, the most common source of hymns is a new resource called *Voices United*, which I think is a really fine collection of the best of the old and the new. In the bulletin, if it says "VU223" the VU refers to *Voices United*. You may also find a supplemental book called *Spirit Anew* which is a collection of easy-to-sing "prayer and praise" songs.

Of course, not every church buys new hymnbooks as soon as they come out. You may find a small green book called *Songs for a Gospel People* or an even older red one called simply *The Hymn Book*.

If you're confused, as I often am, just look sideways at someone nearby and see which book they pick out of the rack. If they're not new or confused, you'll have the right hymnbook. If they are, just remember that the most important thing is to enjoy the singing. So who cares if you start out singing the wrong hymn! Have a good laugh and carry on.

Prayers

When my grandkids say their prayer before a meal (usually called "grace") they sometimes proudly announce, "I closed my eyes." And they get a bit of parental affirmation for that.

The custom of closing your eyes when you pray simply comes from the reality that we can concentrate more easily when we do that. But there's no rule. In fact, you'll notice that in the bulletin there are some prayers that you say along with the minister. So you have to keep your eyes open for that. Except for those prayers, I tend to close my eyes when praying, but I do it simply to keep my mind on the prayer. For me, that's quite a job. My mind tends to wander very easily.

The sermon

Speaking of wandering minds; my mind often wanders during the sermon. That doesn't mean the sermon is dull. It simply means that something the minister says gets me thinking about things in my own life, and so I stay with that for a bit before I rejoin the minister in the sermon.

A sermon is something more than a speech or a lecture. It's not the minister pouring information or ideas into your head out of some kind of a pitcher. I bring my struggles, my life, my fears and hopes into the church. All that connects with the images and ideas in the prayers, hymns, and sermon. And in that mixture, very often the Spirit of God speaks to me.

In other words, a really good sermon is the one that happens in your head, when your life and experience meets the minister's life and experience, and you let God make the connections. You'd be surprised what God can communicate, when you let that happen!

The lectionary

You may notice, as you continue going to church, that there tend to be four Bible readings every Sunday – from the Hebrew Scriptures, the Psalms, the Epistles, and the Christian gospels. If you continue to grow in your faith journey, you'll soon learn what those four sources are about. For now, all you need to know is that those are readings recommended by the lectionary.

Some ministers decide what to preach about, and then find a Bible reading to support that. But most of them use the lectionary. The lectionary is set of suggested readings – four readings for each Sunday of a three-year cycle – so that in the course of three years, you'll have heard all the important parts of the Bible. Most of the major Protestant denominations follow the *Revised Common Lectionary* which is handy because then folks like me can prepare preaching aids knowing what the Bible readings are. And preachers can get together and share ideas about preaching, because they all have the same starting point.

Many congregations have Bible study groups in which they look at the readings coming up the next Sunday. That makes the whole service much more meaningful.

The offering

Then there's the sticky question, "How much do I have to put on the plate when they pass it around?" The answer is easy. Nothing.

Bev and I simply pass the plate along when it comes. We give the church a set of postdated cheques every few months instead. Others arrange to have automatic deductions from their chequing accounts.

So when you are tentatively feeling your way into the church, don't let the offering plate spook you. Anything you put on it will be appreciated, but if you are broke, you won't be the only one who passes it along without putting anything in. But read Chapter 9 on money, because there's a bunch of important stuff to be said about this. Oh, and we never call it the "collection" in the United Church. It's called the "offering."

Holy Communion

You may wonder what is going on the first time they serve communion. Communion is what they call the "Mass" or "Eucharist" in some denominations. Again, there's lots more to be said about this very powerful service (read Chapter 5: Hatched, Matched, and Dispatched), but for now all you need to know is that you are invited.

No exceptions. That doesn't mean you are required to participate. It just means you are welcome if you'd like to.

There are various ways in which this service proceeds, but again, you'll be able to figure that out just by watching folks. You may not understand what it's all about, but if you'd like to participate, please do. You'll learn more about it as you go along.

Baptisms

If you are reading this because you're planning to have a child baptized, then it's important that you read Chapter 5. But in the meantime, you may want to talk to the folks you are inviting to the baptism service. I've seen uncles show up feeling really uncomfortable in suits they haven't worn for years, and aunts feeling a little silly in an old, flowered hat. Tell them things have changed. Sure they can dress up a bit, if they want. It is, after all, a special occasion. But there's no dress code for friends and relatives at a baptism, any more than there is for a regular service. So just tell them to wear whatever is comfortable.

Weddings

If there's a "dress code" at weddings, it comes from the expectations of the bride and groom, and their sense of how formal or informal the wedding may be. If you're reading this because you're planning to get married in the United Church, make sure you read that all-important Chapter 5. But in the meantime, while you are preparing, tell your friends and family that a wedding in a church is a service of worship. People popping up and down taking flash pictures or trying to get it all on video tape don't support the attitude of reverence that should be present in the service of "holy matrimony." Usually the minister will gently tell folks when it's appropriate to take pictures.

Religious language

I'm sure you've run into people who seem to use a lot of words like "Jesus" and "Hallelujah" and "Yes, Lord." You don't have to talk like that in the United Church. Not that there's anything wrong with that kind of speaking, if it is genuine.

United Church people hardly ever use religious words, and I don't mean that as a compliment. We really should learn how to talk about what we believe. That's one of our big weaknesses. But you don't need a specialized vocabulary to do that. We don't need to impress people with how holy we are.

Many United Church folks are refugees from really uptight evangelical churches and they get squirmy when they hear what they sometimes call "Jesus talk." That bothers me. Because somewhere between "Jesus talk" and not talking about your faith at all (which is what mostly happens) there's got to be a happy medium. I've got a lot to say about that in Chapter 6.

What do you have to believe?

You don't have to sign a paper or take a pledge or make any commitments when you come to a United Church.

The United Church is a "non-creedal" church. That means we don't set down on paper that you have to believe this, or you can't believe that. When you boil it right down, it's between you and God. I can tell you what I believe, (which I try hard to do in Chapter 10) but I can't tell you what you should believe.

Eventually, as you begin to feel more comfortable and have a sense of what the church is about, somebody will ask you to help out with some of the many things that happen in the life of a church. You're not *required* to do anything, but we hope that you'll want to help out.

Sunday school

Many people come to church because they want their children to have a religious education. Most congregations in the United Church have Sunday schools. There's usually a program for everyone, from the tiny babies to teenagers.

There are some congregations in the United Church with very small, struggling Sunday schools. They really need new people like you to join and stir things up a little. Congregations grow when people get involved, then tell their friends and family about it. The next thing you know, there's a lively church going. If you want to know more about Sunday schools read Chapter 4.

Laughing in church

Back in the "good old days," people never laughed in church. Or clapped. Now they do it all the time. I don't think a Sunday goes by in our church that we don't have a chuckle over something. Occasionally folks are rolling in the aisles. Ministers often use humor in their sermons. In fact, I trot around the country doing workshops on humor, because I think it really belongs in church, as in all of life.

Not long ago, I was reading the scripture lesson. Halfway through, I realized it was the wrong one. "Whoops!" I said. "I think I've just won the genius award." All of us had a laugh, and I went on to read the correct passage. There is a lot more to say about laughing in church, and you'll find some of that in Chapter 2.

As for clapping – we don't usually clap for things during a service of worship, though there's nothing really wrong with it. When the children's choir sings, we often clap. Or if there's something to celebrate. I've seen people clap at the end of a particularly good sermon, but most ministers don't encourage it. A sermon, or a song by the choir, or anything else is not a performance. It is an offering – a way in which we praise God. And it just doesn't feel right to clap.

Phone and ask

There are lots of questions about the United Church that I can't answer. The funny business of the front pew is just one of them.

The answers to other questions about nursery care, Sunday school, parking, etc., are different in each congregation. Most churches have a secretary who knows more about what is going on than the minister. Phone and ask. The secretary will be delighted to explain things to you.

Even better, if you know someone who already attends the church you are wondering about, buy them a cup of coffee and ask all the questions you like.

Just remember that United Church folks are really just like you. None of us have all the answers. We're all trying to make sense out of life, while we listen hard for God who helps us as we stumble along.

Join us, and learn as you grow!

In the midst of the unprecedented challenges facing Christians in North America at the turn of the millennium, some are beginning to glimpse the stirrings of a renewed church. This emerging church is marked by its recommitment to be a living witness to the gospel of Jesus Christ. It is found in worshipping communities that are moving beyond the old battles between "liberals" and "conservatives." The focus of these renewed congregations is no longer on survival. Instead, they find surprising vitality as they rediscover the mission of God that lies at the heart of the church's reason for being. In the process, such congregations become places where women and men once again find challenge and community.

Ed Searcy – University Hill United Church, Vancouver

———

When we wake up in the middle of the night, convinced that God is trying to tell us something, how do we know it's not the pepperoni pizza we had before bed?

We don't know. That's the problem. Over the centuries, we've discovered that the best thing to do is to take that new insight to the church. Not necessarily to our own little congregation, although that's a good place to start.

That way you can compare your revelation with the insight and perspective of the church through the ages and around the world. The church helps us sort out whether our "revelation" really was God, or an overactive imagination. That's one of the reasons we have a church. None of us is as smart as all of us!

When we speak of a church, we don't mean a building. Or at least, not primarily. We think of the church as God's people or God's family. We're called into the church community to worship God. That worship includes the prayers and liturgy and rites that we undertake there. But worship also includes the way we relate to other people and the way we live our lives.

Ralph Milton – from *God for Beginners* (Northstone Publishing, 1996)

2

I'm Not Religious, But...

The Word became flesh and lived among us.
John 1:14

Having given you a quick look at the "nuts and bolts" of my church, let's back up to the beginning and start all over.

The United Church of Canada is a wonderfully complex organism. Yes, organism. It looks like an organization from the outside, but when you're on the inside you realize there's something living and breathing about the whole thing.

I mostly love the United Church, but sometimes I hate it. It is my church home, and I am describing it from the inside. I'll try to be as objective and as fair as I can, but you might as well know that's going to be hard. For instance, you should know that most often when I go to type "United Church" it comes out as "Untied Cruch." There must be some deep Freudian reason for that.

Let me introduce myself. I'm 65 years old, and just finding out what "retirement" is all about. So far, all I've managed to eliminate is the paycheque, not the work. That's my photo on the last page. I know, I look 70. I've had a hard life.

I'm married to Bev. She looks half my age, but actually she's only a couple of years younger. We had four kids, but now there are three. Lloyd, the youngest, took his own life a few years ago. The other three are all grown and away from home. We have two absolutely wonderful grandchildren. Don't let me get started because I can brag for hours.

Bev is a Rev. She's clergy, though she's not serving a congregation right now. She's on a medical disability. I'm a layperson – a writer and storyteller by trade – a founding partner of Wood Lake Books, Canada's largest and most active religious publishing house of the Protestant variety. Wood Lake publishes books and curriculum and other resources for the whole ecumenical community of Canadian churches, including the United Church. Resources such as this book, for instance.

Wood Lake Books also publishes two international, lectionary-based church-school curricula called *The Best of Whole People of God Online* and *Seasons of the Spirit.* If you want to know more about what they do and what they publish, there's an address, phone number, and e-mail address at the front of the book. Or go directly to www.woodlakebooks.com.

One of the fun things I do each week is write an "e-zine," an online magazine called *Rumors,* which you can find at that same website.

Ticked off

Some of the books Wood Lake publishes are really quite interesting. They don't do that pie-in-the-sky stuff with people predicting the end of the world at 12 noon on Tuesday (12:30 in Newfoundland). Most people in the United Church don't even think about that kind of stuff.

Like me, you probably get a bit squirmy when people start using a bunch of religious words. It may surprise you, but most people in the United Church feel the same way. That's too bad, in a way, because to talk about religious things you need a few religious words. Very few! Not enough to scare anyone off or weigh you down. Some people are really quite afraid of anything that sounds vaguely "religious." They prefer to talk about "spirituality" which of course is pretty much the same thing. For instance, when I go to meetings of writers, and they ask me about the kind of thing I do, they very often reply, "Well, I'm not religious but...."

It sounds as if not being religious is supposed to confer some kind of credibility. I don't mind if they've really thought it through and decided they are not religious, but most of them haven't. They just say it because they think it's expected.

Actually, many of my writer colleagues are really quite religious. But they're too gullible about much of what they see on TV and read in the papers. They think all Christians are like some TV evangelists, selling salvation during the day and sleeping around at night. Or they think of doddering old parsons drinking tea with doddering old ladies.

Or they say something like, "I don't believe in a God who zaps people when they do something wrong, or who hands out treats if you flatter him."

I don't believe in that kind of god either! When my writer friends hear that, we usually have a very different conversation. It often turns out they're hungry for something to believe in. But they've bought all the silly, sometimes insulting portrayals of religious people they see on TV. The only experience they've had of church and Christianity goes back 30 years to Sunday school, and all they can remember is being constantly told to be quiet and sit still. They don't realize that, just like the rest of the world, the church has changed. Dramatically! That's why I'm updating this book for the second time in 20 years.

If you get the conversation going far enough, you often find people wanting to do something significant with their lives, and not just for bucks or prestige. Deep inside them there's a kind of hunger. They're not atheists. They just haven't taken the time to think through what kind of god they believe in.

The fact is, genuine atheists are pretty scarce. Most of us have something, vague as it may be, in that little compartment labeled "religion" or "spirituality." Actually, more people go to church on a Sunday than go to sports events during the week. Check the yellow pages of your phone book. You'll be surprised how many churches there are. More people go to church on one Sunday than watch the Blue Jays in a whole year. About 20 percent of Canadians are in church on any given Sunday. Can you think of anything else 20 percent of the population does every week? Just because the popular media spend great gobs of time and money on sports and hardly any on religion simply means there's more money in sports.

Which is not to say that all those people going to church know why they go, or that the people who stay home are not very religious. Going to church and having an active, meaningful faith are not necessarily the same thing. Going to church doesn't make you a Christian any more than going to a garage makes you a car.

It's true that organized religion has plenty to answer for. All religious groups, including my own United Church, have done some rotten things. Pointing the finger at religious leaders who have turned out to be crooks or charlatans is sometimes necessary.

A little thought would help

But the fact that religious groups contain a few deadbeats doesn't discredit religion any more than deadbeats in politics discredit the whole democratic process, or that some irresponsible journalists prove all media to be unreliable.

Some of my friends in the writing business assume that if you close the door on religion you step into a wider world. You free yourself up for something better. Baloney! (I had a stronger word but the editor took it out.)

Okay, there's *some* truth in that charge. Some religious groups put their people into emotional and intellectual straightjackets, just as some political systems have done. The only way to be human is to break free. But those groups and systems are aberrations. Political systems and religious structures should serve people, not the other way around. That's a basic principle behind all the world's great religions. In Christianity, it was expressed by Jesus who said, "I came that you might have life, in all its fullness."

The late Margaret Laurence (a Canadian novelist of international renown) was a strong supporter and mentor to the Wood Lake Books publishing ministry. "Keep telling the story without all the crap that usually gets attached to it," she wrote to me, "because then I can give your books to my literary friends. They've got their lives all screwed up because the only thing they believe in is themselves, and that's just not enough." Margaret was a long-time member and supporter of the United Church.

I ache for Margaret's friends and for a number of my own friends who have the same attitude. So many, especially the high-profile personalities, are terribly lonely people with lots of acquaintances but no real friends.

So often, they are hungering for the friendship and sense of personal meaning that a Christian faith can give. Or, at least, the Christian faith as it's expressed in denominations like the United Church, where they don't expect you to park your brains outside when you come in the front door.

Too many people have thrown their religion out because of something negative they vaguely remember from long ago, or because they think high-pressure TV evangelists represent all denominations.

Freedom!

Genuine religion frees you up. A cult ties you down. Some well-established and respectable groups are cults, I think.

The religious perspective that everything we do has meaning is certainly more liberating than the atheist's view of life. For them, if life has any meaning, it's so abstract and philosophical that it makes no practical difference.

To believe that humans are infinitely precious to a loving God is no harder than believing humans are simply organisms that function for a few years and then die. "You're born, you thrash around, then you die," is the way one cynic put it. True, maybe. But that kind of thinking puts no gas in my tank.

I respect people who thoughtfully and honestly reject religion. I also feel sorry for them. To abandon religion may be honest and honorable, but it isn't exactly leaping a prison wall.

If the kind of religion I'm talking about is a delusion, at least it's a delusion of grandeur. If a lively faith is a delusion, at least it's a dynamic delusion, one that puts the spice, the zip, the fun into life.

If you know how to laugh

That's where I've ended up. That's not where I began. I began my adult life as a semi-militant atheist who would have begun conversations with, "I'm not religious myself, but..."

I worked as a news reporter. I was sent to cover an event at a local United Church. I was to do a story on a speaker, a "name" of some sort. The topic was of interest to church people presumably, though I couldn't have cared less.

Slowly, pushing past the green fog of my cynicism, the speaker got through. I remember him well. Not his name, but his jokes. They were good, spicy, gutsy stories and we all laughed until we literally ached. Then just as the laughter reached a peak, he burned a sentence into my consciousness.

"If we know how to laugh, then we also know how to pray. Let us pray!"

That man shattered my image of Christians. To suggest that laughter belonged in the church – that at some level it was like praying – didn't correspond at all with what I thought these people believed.

I was convinced Christians worshipped a stuffy Grandfather in the sky whose chief joy was saying "Thou Shalt Not!" to just about anything that was fun.

That church basement event wasn't what you'd call a "conversion experience." But it was a tiny crack in my armor of distaste for anything vaguely connected with the church. From that point on, I listened just a bit more openly.

Over the years, I began to realize I was operating on ideas about the church that had gone out with the *Ed Sullivan Show*. Since I had hardly ever gone to church as a child, I had little firsthand experience to go on. I do remember what I thought was a photograph (it looked so real!) of God in an old Bible. God was sitting on a cloud, zapping sinners with thunderbolts.

Hidden back in my childhood memory were feelings of anger at a church that wanted my dad to stand up and make a public confession of his "sin," because he had grown a mustache. Apparently there's some obscure phrase in the Bible about that.

I also remember an evangelist coming to town. I must have been very small, but I can remember being afraid because he kept yelling and shouting.

What's going on around here?

I came into the United Church as an adult without any real church background. Within a year, I found myself an "elder." I was often terribly confused. Things everybody else seemed to know, I didn't. And I was too embarrassed to ask.

Since then, I've found that a great many people who join the church as adults are in the same situation. I worship at First United in Kelowna, in British Columbia's beautiful Okanagan Valley. About half, maybe two-thirds of the congregation, is made up of older persons. Many urban churches are like that. But many, such as Westbank United where Bev ministered a number of years ago, have a majority of younger families. About a third of them grew up in the United Church. Another third came from some other denomination. For the rest, this is their first church experience. Most United Churches across Canada are like one of those two congregations.

The covenant community

When I first joined the church I found two things, and I have no idea which came first. I discovered some people who took an interest in me, who liked me even when I acted like a cocky, smart-ass kid. And more importantly, I encountered God in the flesh and blood person of Jesus Christ, who could see right through my "attitude" and who loved me anyway.

There were no shattering "born again" experiences. Changes happened slowly over several years. But they happened. From a sense of aimlessness and frustration, I found a sense of knowing what life was about and what I should be doing with mine.

In other words, I found myself being part of a special kind of community called the church. This community has a history that goes back thousands of years. It includes people from almost every country in the world, yet it takes a very special form in a little faith community known as a congregation. My congregation and the church as a whole has its "warts" just as I have. There are a few "saints" and a few "s.o.b.s" but the vast majority of us simply have strengths and weaknesses, good days and bad days. We're human.

Living in that human community, I experienced (which is different from learning or understanding) the truth that God loves us and yearns for us to love back.

Morning sickness

There was very little church life in my growing up years. But in my late teens I did join a choir at a United Church in Lethbridge, Alberta, mainly because of a beautiful blond soprano. When that romance faded, so did my "commitment."

A romance that *hasn't* faded is the one with Bev. She grew up in church. Well, sort of. Her parents went mostly at Christmas and Easter. Shortly after we were married, she got talked into teaching Sunday school. (She wasn't a "Rev" then.)

Not many months later, she began suffering a not uncommon malady called morning sickness. She felt miserable till near noon. After that, she looked absolutely glorious. Since I had some responsibility for that morning sickness, I "volunteered" to substitute in the Sunday school.

I had a problem. I considered myself an atheist. Well, at least an agnostic. There I was, in that dingy furnace room that doubled as a classroom, teaching an unruly gang of eight-year-old boys what I only half believed myself.

Actually, I had three problems. One was integrity. How do you teach stuff you don't believe? Another was sheer ignorance. I had never gone to Sunday school. Or church. Now, here I was teaching the stuff. My third problem was utter terror. Have you ever been alone in a furnace room with a gang of eight-year-old boys?

Dave Stone was our minister. "Why don't you join a Bible study group?" he asked. "Find out about that God you don't believe in."

I can't tell you the exact point at which it happened, but one day I knew I was a Christian. One day it started to make sense.

I'd always thought that religion would shut down my life. It would give me a bunch of rules that would take most of the fun out of living. Religion meant running away from real life.

Instead, it opened life up. The more I understood about that tiny seed of faith that seemed to be sprouting inside me, the more I felt open. Liberated. Free to look at my life and see what I wanted to do with it.

Not my grandchild!

"Mom," I said on the phone. "Sit down."

"What's wrong, Ralph?" she wanted to know. In those days you didn't phone long-distance unless there was a disaster.

"Nothing's wrong, Mom," I said. "Bev and I are going to the Philippines as missionaries."

A long pause. "Are you crazy?"

"Yes, Mom, a little. But that's what we're doing. We're convinced that's what God wants us to do."

"With a small baby? You're not taking my grandchild to some god-forsaken jungle!"

"Oh, that's the other thing, Mom."

"What!" Mom sounded a fair bit concerned.

"Bev's pregnant again."

I won't tell you the rest of what Mom said, but let's just say she wasn't enthusiastic. We had similar conversations with most of our family and many of our friends.

We went to the Philippines and spent five wonderful, growing years there. Bev studied theology at the university where we lived (it was anything but a "god-forsaken jungle") though she didn't become an ordained minister till many years later.

This new "opening up" of our lives then took us to live in an African American community in New Jersey, and to work for the National Council of Churches in a huge office building in New York City.

Coming home

After ten years of living in other people's countries, we moved back "home." The first Sunday, we went to church. I remember thinking, "Canada may not be the best country and the United Church may not be the best church. But, it's my country and my church." And I felt a deep sense of love for both.

On the other hand, the experience of living and traveling abroad also gave us a deep appreciation for many kinds of people and cultures, for different traditions and denominations. As people shared the beauty of what God had given them, Bev and I learned to appreciate our own roots even more.

We moved often in those early years. Each time we moved, we headed for a church where we knew we'd find friendship and acceptance, a place to belong.

Sometimes the Christian life seemed like such a long pilgrimage. We got fed up or angry at the way the church did some things and didn't do others. There were people in the church who let us down and people we let down.

But, when I look around, I can't see a better way. My Christian faith gives me a deep sense of joy and fulfillment. Life would be drab and meaningless without it. I don't know of any family in which I'd rather express this faith, than the United Church of Canada.

A very Canadian church

Many times in the Philippines and in the U.S. people asked me questions about the United Church of Canada. I couldn't always answer them. It would have been much easier for me to describe a Catholic or a Presbyterian.

It's hard to pin down what the United Church is. It doesn't have a clear-cut identity, but it certainly has some definite characteristics.

It's a *Canadian* church. A number of years ago, author John Robert Colombo said "the two most Canadian of institutions are the National Hockey League and the United Church of Canada." I'm not sure if he intended that as a compliment or an insult, but regardless, it's not true any longer, for either the NHL or the United Church.

The United Church is Canadian in the way it sprang out of our desire to cooperate rather than to compete on the harsh western frontier. The settlers, especially in those tiny western communities, knew it was either one church together or no church at all.

Certainly, the United Church has become a distinct denomination. That isn't the way it was planned.

When the Methodist, Presbyterian, Congregational, and community churches came together in 1925 to form the United Church of Canada, they were looking for a looser kind of arrangement, one in which many denominations might feel at home.

The Evangelical United Brethren became part of our fellowship in 1968. For a while, we had discussions with the Christian Church (Disciples) toward some kind of union, but nothing came of that. We had a courtship going with the Anglicans too, but that didn't work out either.

We have certain distinct characteristics. Words I'd use to describe them include freedom, openness, warmth, diversity, courage, and integrity.

That's on good days. On bad days I think we're really a few opinionated do-gooders mixed in with a large batch of wishy-washy Charlie Brown fence-sitters.

Our greatest strength and our greatest weakness is the variety of viewpoints in one denomination. If the United Church can be true to its heritage, the right and left wing of the church will learn to fly together. We won't always feel comfortable, but we'll listen to each other. With respect! If we don't learn to do that, the United Church will lose one of its distinctive and, for me, essential characteristics. In fact, I think if we don't learn how to do that, we're lost.

We are also an ecumenical church. "Ecumenical" is a Greek word we use when we're talking about the whole Christian church – all the denominations. The United Church has a long history of putting lots of time, energy, and money into ecumenical ventures, especially in working for justice here in Canada and overseas. I was very proud of my church in that regard. But recently, with budget constraints, the United Church found it easiest to cut back on their ecumenical commitments.

An open church

We are not a "confessional church." Although we have a creed, it's not something you have to say or sign before you can become a member. Nor do we demand that you use a certain set of religious words, or pray in a certain way, or believe in a particular interpretation of the Bible.

We do have convictions! We just don't believe in formulas. Faith is a living thing. If you try to nail it down, you kill it.

Our Creed (which you can find in our new hymnbook *Voices United*, page 918) expresses much of what our church people believe. We say it often together. But it's just a statement. It's already been changed as the church changes. The most recent change was the addition of the line, "to live with respect in Creation," a line that was included at the suggestion of some of our First Nations members. The creed will be changed again as our understanding of God keeps growing.

More and more, we are trying to be an inclusive church, a community where everyone is valued and appreciated. That's why we also use the traditional creeds from time to time. You can find them in *Voices United* – the Apostles' Creed (VU918) and the Nicene Creed (VU920).

We do believe in a God who was revealed to us in the person of Jesus of Nazareth, and who is still revealed to us by the Holy Spirit. That part doesn't change.

Middle-class diversity

We are a middle-class church, both economically and educationally. Some people object when I say that, and I agree it may not be a good thing. But, it's true anyway.

The majority of United Church members are white, middle class, and complain about high taxes. But there are more and more non-Anglo-Saxons in our church. There are people of every variety you could imagine.

One of our most beloved leaders during the 1980s was Sang Chul Lee, our Moderator from 1988-1990, who was a refugee from Korea; and before that (1974) Wilbur Howard, who is an African Canadian. Stan McKay, a First Nations leader, was chosen as our Moderator in 1992. There have been a number of women who followed Lois Wilson. In 1980, she was the first woman to be elected as head of a major Canadian church. The first time I was on a church board, we had two members who both worked for the city. One collected garbage. The other was the mayor.

The diversity of the United Church is a strength when we see the church as a colorful mosaic, each different piece contributing to the beauty of the whole.

Not only in our church, but in our country, we've simply got to learn to live with diversity. Unfortunately, some people become so passionate in their convictions they slide over into arrogance. They forget that Jesus emphasized a "suffering love," a genuine love for those who have different traditions or ways of worshipping God. The challenge is to learn to live Jesus' words, "love your neighbor" and "love your enemy." Sometimes, they're the same people and often they sit next to us in church.

Part of the problem is our sentimentalizing of "love." Love, as projected by our culture, is two people gazing into each other's eyes and finding there a perfect reflection of themselves. Those of us who have struggled with the problems of love within a marriage, family, and church know that real love means living creatively with the differences. Real love always means commitment, conflict, forgiveness, and reconciliation. And respect! That's hardest and most important with the people closest to us.

Many kinds of people

Because we have such a variety of people in the United Church, there's a real temptation to set up categories. By sticking labels on them, we feel we've got people identified so we can deal with them more easily.

One group is often called the "social activists" or "liberals." They don't use many religious-sounding words, but claim their faith should be evident in the way they live. They are very critical of the social scene; of large corporations, governments, and trading practices that discriminate against poor people. These social justice Christians are often criticized for being entirely too comfortable with society's general beliefs on such matters as sex. They can be very judgmental, sometimes arrogant, about people who don't agree with them.

Others get tagged as "fundamentalists" or "conservatives." They often quote from the Bible and are very concerned about personal morality, especially matters related to sex. They are quite comfortable using religious language and showing enthusiasm in worship. They're often faulted for accepting the social order uncritically and failing to see their part in the sin of an oppressive world order. They, too, can be very judgmental, sometimes arrogant, about people who don't agree with them.

There are some who emphasize meditative prayer. Others have a strong appreciation for the sacraments and symbols of worship. (United Church people have learned much from the Anglican and Roman Catholic traditions about this.)

There are those who bring together their understanding of Christianity and psychology in order to understand themselves and others better. Some have looked toward the New Age movement for ways to enrich their Christian understanding.

There are many people in our church who simply want to get along with everybody. Their motto is "don't rock the boat," avoid troublesome questions, and let's just all get along.

Personal and social

Every group in the church, like every group anywhere, has its strengths and weaknesses. In some circles of the United Church, there are people willing to look beyond the labels, beyond the caricatures, and recognize they have the most to learn from people with whom they disagree. The church has an almost desperate need for more such people.

More of us are trying to take *both* our personal faith and social morality more seriously. We're trying to be more enthusiastic and open in the expression of our faith. And we want to be more conscious of how this faith is lived in the social and political world.

We'd like to think of ourselves as "evangelical" in the sense that we're enthusiastic about telling others the good news, and "fundamentalist" in that we try to focus on biblical fundamentals, the essentials of faith. We'd like to be "liberal" in the sense of being open to new ideas; and "social radicals" in that we don't walk away from tough issues of justice, liberation, and the care of God's creation.

Unfortunately, some United Church members are not very clear what their faith stance is. What's worse, they're not motivated to do the work involved in finding out.

On the brighter side of things, there seems to be a new interest in Bible study in the United Church. That's good, but it does present another problem.

The Bible can be trusted

It's all very well to say, "The Bible is our authority. I'll read it and I'll know which way to go." But people interpret the Bible in so many ways. Every little sect and all the many denominations find their justification in the Bible. Even in the Bible study group that meets in our church every week, there are as many ways of looking at scripture as there are people.

Nevertheless, the Bible can be trusted, provided we see it whole and don't pick out a phrase here and a sentence there to justify what we've already decided. Many of us would like to see the church spend more time with the Bible, especially learning some of the delightful and rich stories that are in it.

The United Church is constantly examining itself, its mission, and what it believes. We invite people from other denominations and from other parts of the world to come and tell us what they see. Their comments at times have been less than flattering and difficult to accept.

On the other hand, sometimes we're really flattered. Not long after the United Nations said Canada was the best country in the world in which to live, Bishop John Shelby Spong (a very controversial figure in the U.S. Episcopal Church) said the United Church was the best denomination in North America. Some were delighted. Others, considering where the remark came from, felt it was less than a compliment.

Shalom

There's no single word that describes United Church people. Sometimes, we are simply a pious do-gooder non-profit organization and we really have very little reason for being. When that happens, we have no way to justify our tax-free status.

But when we are what God calls us to be, the only word that comes close is borrowed from the Hebrew.

Shalom.

Shalom is often translated as "peace" but it's a far richer word. It means more than peace as the absence of conflict. *Shalom* has within it the concept of wholeness, of a yearning for justice, of hope, of unity, of common purpose. It's a very rich word and you'll find it used often by United Church people.

The word *shalom* helps us know we are not alone. Others have been on this journey before us – centuries of searching people stumbling along life's journey: Abraham and Sarah, Mary and Joseph, Nellie McClung, Desmond Tutu, Sang Chul Lee, Marion Best, Nelson Mandela, and Anna Williamson.

Anna Williamson? She's a person in our congregation who very quietly, in a hundred different ways, simply does what needs doing. Anna would be surprised and very embarrassed to see her name in this book because she's not doing "anything special." So that's not her real name, but she is a very real person.

In the church as a whole, there are thousands like Anna. We call them the "company of saints." They're not a group of "perfect" people. But, through the centuries, they are the ones who have discovered a pathway.

A pathway

We begin our journey of faith expecting to be alone on the road, sort of hoping for a little "divine guidance" along the way. Then, we find that most of our "divine guidance" comes through very ordinary folk we find walking beside us. These are the saints in blue jeans and sneakers who help us over the rocks and who bandage our bruised knees; people we call "the church."

We walk together with others in our shalom community, which extends way beyond the United Church and includes people from other faiths.

Perhaps most important, we discover Jesus there too, walking among us, walking beside us.

The tough decades are far from over. But we confidently declare that the church will be reborn, and that the new birth will start with local congregations. Sometimes the church that is arriving will look a lot like the old one, and other times will be unrecognizable. If it survives the trauma of its birth (and we believe it will), it will be more whole. It will know its weaknesses and will not be frightened by them. Above all, in a society that often seems devoted to the pursuit of individual gain, it will recognize its own value as the carrier of memory and compassion, mystery and love, song and prayer.

Donna Sinclair and Christopher White – from *Jacob's Blessing: Dreams, Hopes, & Visions for the Church* (Wood Lake Books, 1999)

3

Sunday Morning

⬛

They devoted themselves to the apostles' teaching and fellowship, to the breaking of bread and the prayers.

Acts 2:42

So what do they actually do in a typical United Church on Sunday morning? Well, there's no such thing as a typical United Church. If I tried to explain all the variations and combinations of Sunday worship, I'd write an encyclopedia, and a dull one at that. What follows is the compromise.

Exceptions

No matter what I might say about the United Church, there are always exceptions. A number of congregations are feeling their way into this new millennium by experimenting with different forms of music, different kinds of music. What follows are descriptions of several United Churches. None of them actually exist. Each is an amalgam of several congregations. Any real congregation would combine features of several of these, plus a few that are uniquely its own. And you may find yourself in a United Church that is trying something totally new, which could be really wonderful or sensationally awful. Try not to jump to conclusions on the basis of one single church service.

Just as business and industry have developed consultants who study and make recommendations on "company culture," organization, method, personality, etc., the ecumenical churches have spawned a variety of folks who try to help us become more relevant to the changing needs of our society. They travel around doing various workshops, which sometimes are very helpful and sometimes simply raise our anxiety levels. I mention this because there's a good possibility you'll encounter some experiments in worship at any church you go to. If they ask for feedback, and you have some feelings about it, express them.

But don't expect the church to be like the one you may remember in your childhood. Don't expect old, old hymns and long, long prayers. Things have changed!

In fact, things have been changing more rapidly in the last few years than ever before. It is my impression that there is more diversity between various congregations than ever. No two are exactly alike. But these descriptions might help.

Dover Park United

There are two services each Sunday at Dover Park United. The first one is at 9:30, the second at 11:00. They are identical, except that the people tend to be younger at the first service and there are more kids around. The church is full but not packed, and there are a lot of young families. If there's a typical suburban congregation, this is it.

The Rev. Dawson Peterson is 40ish, with graying hair. He and the choir walk casually into the sanctuary, which is buzzing with muted conversation behind the quiet music of a large electric organ. Nobody pays too much attention.

The choir sits down in the pews, Peterson pins a small lapel mike to his tie, tucks the cord behind the jacket of his three-piece suit, looks up at the congregation and says, "Hi." Many people in the pews respond with "Hi," or "Good morning."

"Does anybody have a song or hymn they'd like to sing this morning?" he asks.

"Number 509" comes a quick response from someone who was obviously ready. Everyone stands to sing *I, the Lord of Sea and Sky* (also known as *Here I Am, Lord*) from *Voices United* a brand new United Church hymnbook. That's not surprising. According to *The United Church Observer*, it's at the top of our denominational hit parade.

Peterson then talks about events coming up in the congregation that week. The United Church Women had a garage sale and Elena Dowds stands up to tell people the sale was a success. She's given a round of applause. Then several committee meetings are announced.

There are always half a dozen visitors and new people at the services, so Peterson asks them to identify themselves and he welcomes them. The couple who were greeting at the door pin a small rosebud on each of the visitors and newcomers.

The children are beginning to get fidgety, but the service is ready to begin.

There's a "Call to Worship," followed by another hymn. This time it's VU232, one of the all-time favorites: *Joyful, Joyful, We Adore Thee!*

That's followed by a prayer and a reading from one of the psalms from *Voices United*, in which the congregation reads the lines printed in bold and sings the response when the bold letter "R" comes up.

As the psalm ends, the children begin to move to the front of the church. Peterson leaves the pulpit and motions to the rest of the children to follow. Soon they're all sitting together on the steps leading up to the chancel.

Sometimes Peterson has a story for them. Sometimes he asks them questions. Unlike the adults in the church, the children don't hesitate. If they have something to say, they say it. Peterson used to treat the youngsters as "adults in training," but he doesn't anymore.

Peterson's change in attitude came through church school curricula such as *The Whole People of God* and *Seasons of the Spirit*. These curricula encourage congregations to see children as full participating members of the church with their own gifts and talents to share. It makes quite a difference to the style and content of the service.

These curricula base their lessons on the Bible readings assigned for that day from the lectionary, the same lessons as are recommended for the morning worship service.

The lectionary (used by many denominations) is a schedule of readings, spanning three years. Over that three-year period, the people at Dover Park will hear most of the major readings from the Bible. Peterson bases his sermons on those readings because "it keeps me from riding my own hobby horses. Besides," he adds with a grin, "there are really good preaching resources that have all kinds of neat stories and ideas to go with the lectionary. Sermon preparation time is cut in half."

All together now!

After the children's "theme conversation" comes a hymn. It's "intergenerational," which means that it's meaningful to people of all ages. This morning it's number 87 in *Voices United, I Am the Light of the World,* a bouncy tune which the organist drags a little. There's a very mild disagreement between the organist and some people in the choir who would like the hymns sung much faster.

The children leave during the last verse of the song. And the church looks strangely empty without them.

Marj Cornelson also leaves her seat and by the time the last child has left she's ready to read the day's scriptures. Marj has two children in the church school. She knows they'll hear the same Bible readings in their classes.

Now it's time for the choir. There are about 20 members, wearing bright maroon robes. No one is paid except the organist, who is also the choir director. She gets a small honorarium. The choir sings an anthem called *The Lord Is My Shepherd,* based on Psalm 23. Musically, that would probably be in the category of a "popular classic."

The choir sits and the minister stands up. It's time for the sermon. Twenty minutes.

If there is such a thing as a "typical" United Church sermon, Peterson preaches it. It's not what you'd call "evangelical," though he talks often of spiritual growth and the "life in Christ." It's not what you'd call a social justice sermon either, though he often relates some of the scripture to current issues of justice and equality. It's a well-crafted meditation, and the people find it interesting, and very often useful and relevant to the things they face in daily life.

The sermon ends with a short prayer and a hymn. That's followed by the "pastoral prayer" in which Peterson tries to express some of the concerns he has been hearing from people through the week. He also puts in some of the things that bug him personally.

When the plates are passed around for the offering (never call it a "collection" in the United Church), it is not just a matter of gathering money so the church can operate. The offering is the congregation's response to the Word of God. It's a special way for them to take part in the service, though some people in the pews don't make the connection. That's followed by a final hymn and the benediction, which is the final blessing before people leave.

Peterson stands at the door shaking hands with everyone. He doesn't particularly like doing this, because so many people all at once turn into a blur for him. He's told them many times, "Don't say anything to me on the way out on Sunday morning that you expect me to remember." They do anyway.

Dover Park has a good-looking building with a high, vaulted, laminated beam roof and lots of windows. People admire the architecture, but those who sit on the Committee of Stewards know what it costs to heat all that space up there. They also know about the horrendous interest on the mortgage. Sometimes they find themselves resenting the heavy financial burden and wonder out loud if they aren't "overbuilt."

The building went up in the late 1950s when it was assumed that Dover Park would be serving a huge area and financing would not be a problem. Old-timers in the church remember the high morale and enthusiasm that went with the building program and feel a little hurt by newcomers who can only see the mortgage.

During the 1960s the congregation went into a slump. But with a recent housing boom attendance is up and the church's future looks bright.

Southhill United

Six kilometers south of Peterson's church another congregation meets in a school gymnasium. There are no pews. People sit on folding chairs. There seem to be kids everywhere. Some are sitting quietly, others are just being kids.

Except for two large banners near the front of the gym and the portable pulpit, it looks more like parents' day at the elementary school than a Sunday morning at church. But it's a regular congregation that calls itself Southhill United Church.

Joyce Reynolds is the minister. She wears a bright golden, ankle-length gown and a liturgical stole, both hand-woven by a member of her congregation. She moves around the hall, talking to this person and that. When she sees that the choir has settled itself in the group of chairs near the front, she moves in that direction.

She flicks the switch of an overhead projector and the "Call to Worship" appears on the wall. Everyone says it together.

Doing things together seems to be a major characteristic of this congregation. A teenager reads the scripture. The "sermon" is a dialogue and a poem prepared by the young adults group. The announcements are made by people popping up here and there. In fact, Reynolds is more like an emcee or coordinator than a minister. She likes having people involved.

There is no organ in this church, but there is a piano and a small instrumental group that plays soft rock versions of some of the hymns, and most Sundays performs a contemporary piece. The teenagers think it's great. Some of the older folks think it's loud, but they're glad it's there. "Not everything has to be geared to our tastes," says gray-haired Angus Tuttle. "There's something for everyone, but not everything is for everyone."

"The traditional word for worship is 'liturgy,' which means 'the work of the people'," says Joyce. "It's something we all do together."

The choir doesn't wear gowns. They've talked about that occasionally, but nobody wants them badly enough. There always seem to be more important things to spend their money on. When they stand up to sing, a child leaves her mom in the fifth row to join her dad in the choir. She stays there for the rest of the service and nobody seems to notice. A young mother opens her blouse and nurses her baby. Nobody pays attention to that either.

Like Dover Park, Southhill emphasizes small groups in the church. Both Reynolds and Peterson feel the Sunday morning worship is a bringing together – a "celebration" of what happens during the week. And plenty happens during the week.

A connected sermon

There are study groups of all sorts. One of the more important in both Dover Park and Southhill is a Bible study group that looks at the lectionary readings coming up each Sunday. "We get so much more out of the worship service when we do this," they say.

"People who don't get involved in the midweek groups just don't get as much out of church," says Reynolds. "The Sunday morning group is too big and there's no way you can feel you're a part of what's happening if that's all you plug into."

It's definitely a middle-class church. Most of the Southhill people own homes or condominiums, though they are heavily mortgaged. Many are business or professional people. They are generally well-educated and ambitious.

Most of the people at Southhill have little church background or experience. In fact, about half the board are not even United Church members. They have little knowledge of the church and its traditions, and even less about the Bible and what it teaches. Their biggest asset is their eagerness to ask questions.

"I'm not worried about the lack of tradition," says Reynolds. "We're building traditions of our own. But I am worried about the lack of understanding of what their faith is all about. They're an easy mark for any crackpot who comes along and spouts a good, sincere sounding line. We need to do far more Bible study, and I don't just mean learning a few verses here and there. I mean some solid, in-depth stuff. There are lots of people around who can quote scripture, but there aren't too many who know what the whole Bible really says."

A continuing discussion (sometimes an argument) at Southhill is whether they should put up their own building. One committee drew up elaborate plans for a high-rise that would be a senior citizens' villa, a daycare center, a community center, and a church all rolled into one. They claimed they could get provincial and federal funding for such a venture, pointing to other congregations which have done this. They are the ones who feel that worshipping in a school just doesn't "feel like church."

Other members of the congregation point to the mind-boggling expense of building. "Let's buy a house or something," they say, "just so we can have an office for the minister and a place for small groups. But let's not get ourselves tied down by all the expense and fuss of a building."

The minister is very much on the side of the second group. "We can be the church without a building," she says. "It lets the church be the church. The people of God. We can respond to the needs of each other and the community, instead of taking care of facilities."

Riverside United

Riverside United Church has a slightly older building than Dover Park. It's about the same size, with about the same number and kinds of people as at Peterson's church.

Harold Murphy, the minister, wears a white robe with a green stole. He's among the congregation while they gather, smiling, laughing and hugging. Murphy makes a fuss over newcomers, asking where they're from, introducing them to people next to them in the pews. And he says a short prayer for them.

When he gets up into the pulpit, he begins immediately into a long, fervent prayer. Very soon, a few hands are raised, palms upward.

The Bible never leaves Murphy's hands while he's preaching. He refers to it often and quotes from it. His sermons are emotional and usually last about 35 minutes, which is long for the United Church.

During the prayer following the sermon, Murphy leaves time for others to pray out loud, and several do. The singing is lively, and includes a number of "choruses," songs specifically designed for easy group singing, which are shown with an overhead projector. The congregation clearly enjoys these. The hymnbook in the pew is not *Voices United,* but one from a more conservative denomination.

The service is longer than at most United Churches, but few people complain. There's much handshaking at the door as people leave. Folks seem to be very friendly.

Riverside and Murphy represent the evangelical side of our United Church. They sometimes feel shut out of other parts of the church. Unfortunately, there's some reality behind that feeling. It's much easier to be inclusive with folks on the other side of the world, than with members of your own family.

When he arrived two years ago, Murphy appeared to have instant success. Many new people were joining the church. Still, in spite of newcomers, the congregation grew very little. Many of the old members had drifted to other congregations because they simply didn't feel comfortable with his emotional style of ministry. But Murphy attracted people from other United Church congregations and even other denominations – people who found something they needed in his highly charged preaching.

First United

In the center of town, you'll find First United Church. A few blocks away is Central United. Both are imposing structures that can seat many people. Both have large pipe organs. Their choirs wear deep maroon gowns and their soloists, four in each church, are all paid an honorarium.

There are two ministers at First United. The "senior" minister preaches the sermons. That's Dr. Henry Guthrie, and he's expected to spend plenty of time on those sermons. He does, and they are well-researched models of what good sermons should be. Unfortunately, not enough people hear them.

Guthrie is assisted by Rev. John Madson, who visits in hospitals and the homes of the elderly. He's called the "visiting minister" and usually reads the scripture on Sunday mornings.

When Guthrie enters the church for Sunday worship, everybody stands up. He wears a black academic gown and a professionally embroidered stole.

The congregation is sparse and mostly quite old, though here and there you can see a younger person in the rows of dark oak pews.

Everything proceeds according to the order in the printed bulletin. The choir sings the *Lord's Prayer*, and an "Amen" after all the spoken prayers. The anthem is a serious and difficult piece, and the choir does it well.

As people leave, many simply shake the minister's hand and say nothing. A few will say, "Good morning, Reverend."

First United would be in serious financial difficulty if it weren't for money left in wills by former members. And the church still has on its rolls some of the old moneyed families of the city who come through whenever there's a financial crunch.

But First United, old and tired as it seems, is a church with a vision. They are well along on plans to tear down their venerable old building. It will be very hard to see it go, because the walls seem to carry the memory – the spirit of all the faith and hard work that has made the church the strong force for good that it has been. But nevertheless, "We've made the hard decisions," says an elder of this fine old church for more than half a century. "We'll carry enough of the symbols – the pulpit and the plaques and the stained-glass windows – into the new structure to keep us in touch with our heritage."

The new structure will be a multi-story, low-cost housing complex, most of it intended for use by seniors. There'll be a smaller, more compact church on the ground floor, and office space for doctors, pharmacists, and other services that seniors might need.

Says Dr. Guthrie: "We have a ministry for and with seniors. That's our calling. We'll minister to the seniors now in our congregation and to the many others – some of them in terrible poverty – who live in this downtown core."

Central United

Central United looks very much like First United. But you sense something very different. There's an ethnic mix here, something we're beginning to see more frequently in our denomination. There are several African Canadians, a few East Indians and various other Asians scattered among the predominantly white congregation. Over on one side is a group of young women and here and there a few young men. There are even a few kids.

The first thing you'll notice, if you go to a service at Central, is that there's an interpreter signing everything that happens for the deaf persons in the congregation. And large print bulletins and hymn texts are available for those with sight problems.

The folks at Central decided they would be inclusive, and they meant it. They became an "Affirming Congregation," which is another way of saying that gay and lesbian people are welcome, and that they can participate in every aspect of the life of the church.

Central United has two ministers. The "senior" minister is George Allison, whom some call "Doctor" but more people call him "George." And with him is Donna Popovsky who is called a "Diaconal Minister." She's in charge of "outreach" for the congregation. They work as a team, even though sometimes there are tensions involved in that.

Both Central and First were built early in the 1900s, and began as neighborhood churches – one Methodist, the other Presbyterian. Many of the worshippers walked to services. It was the center of their community. When those two denominations, and the Congregationalists formed the United Church of Canada in 1925, there was some talk of combining Central and First, but since both were strong and vigorous, the talk never went far.

As the years passed, the original members of the congregation died or moved out of the immediate area. People of other traditions and cultures moved into the neighborhood, replacing the primarily middle-class population who still referred to the British Isles as "the old country."

Then, after World War II, thousands of people moved out into the suburbs. Paved roads, the automobile, and a higher standard of living helped accelerate the trend.

Soon the majority of First and Central members were driving five to 20 miles from home to church.

Then, both congregations suffered the loss of ministers who had been there for several decades: one through death, the other through retirement. Many members, who had a deep loyalty to their ministers but who were beginning to feel the burden of the long trek back and forth, decided to transfer their membership to a suburban congregation closer to home. Some simply dropped out altogether, as church going became less fashionable in the 1960s and 1970s.

Both congregations found themselves hearing the empty echoes of a huge, unused building. Again there were suggestions that First and Central should be combined and one of the buildings sold. The property in the downtown core would have been worth a bundle. Someone in presbytery even made a formal motion to that effect. But they underestimated the tenacity of old but powerful members of both congregations who had huge emotional investments in the buildings.

Those conversations didn't result in the combining of the two churches, but they did get the folks thinking seriously about their mission and their future.

The members of First United are excited about their building plans and their ministry with and for seniors.

Some of the people at Central are excited too. It took planning, convincing, even a bit of arm-twisting, but the board of Central brought in a "consultant" who helped them do some hard-nosed looking at their future. They decided that since they were in the downtown core, they would serve the downtown core.

George Allison was all for it. Donna Popovsky was called to join the ministry because she had a sense of what a downtown congregation could be like and she had the skills to make things happen.

Now, several years later, with the help of some money from the United Church's Mission and Service Fund, Central operates a daycare center for working mothers, a clothing depot and a food bank for people in need. There are various programs for single parents and an active counseling program for people with particular problems, such as domestic violence or AIDS. And Donna often goes to bat for the street people who come into the church looking for help, occasionally going with them to court to help ensure that justice is done.

Attendance is up on Sunday morning. Not by much, but it is up. Many members are developing a sense of mission and involvement. Some are still angry and suspicious. A few have left.

Central has stopped drifting. It has defined a role for itself and its future. If they go under, they'll do so knowing that, while they may not have been successful, they were at least faithful. And the reality is that Central may well go under. Each year they receive less money from the Mission and Service Fund, for the simple reason that United Church people across Canada aren't giving as much.

Korean United

There are actually two churches at Central. Each Sunday morning a small congregation gathers in Central's spacious lounge. A worship center is set up, and a small cluster of people gather.

Many of the congregation are elderly, and for them, the minister speaks in Korean. But there are also a number of young families gathered. In a few instances, one member of the family is not Korean. Some families don't use the Korean language very much in the home. So the service is conducted in English as well, with the minister moving easily between both languages. People don't seem to mind hearing the scriptures read in both Korean and English. "I like it," says Eileen Cho. "I understand the scripture more deeply when I hear it read in both languages."

A frequent subject of the sermons is the situation in Korea. There's concern for a divided country, and for those who suffer because of their faith and their struggle for human rights.

Until recently, there was no Sunday school, but now that some young families have become active, there's a small but thriving class, mostly conducted in English. They use *The Whole People of God* curriculum, and the minister translates the *At Home Leaflets* into Korean so everyone knows what the children are studying.

After the service, the congregation quietly puts everything away and leaves. The others at Central hardly know they are there. Which is sad, because the Korean church has much to share with the rest of the people at Central.

Trinity United

Trinity United technically doesn't exist anymore. It had been located in another part of the downtown area. Like First and Central, the demographics changed, and they found themselves with just a handful of old and faithful people. "You didn't have to be very smart to see the writing on the wall," said Board Chair Francis Robbins. "We had a choice. We could go out with a bang or die with a whimper. And whimpering didn't seem like much fun."

It took a lot of talking through, but in the end the decision was unanimous. The church and the property would be sold. The money would be "invested" as gifts to various United Church institutions. Trinity would live on, in the imaginative programs made possible by the tiny band of elderly folk who were prepared to invest in a future they themselves would not see.

We live in a culture that doesn't want to talk about death. We try to hide from it, to deny it whenever we can – and this applies to the death of organizations as much as to the death of people. Projects, programs, and some congregations are put on life-support systems when they should be allowed to die. But death is a part of life. When we allow something to die, we allow new life to emerge. Trinity faced that reality with open eyes and a kind heart, and found a way for the faith of its people to live on.

Aspen Lake United

If you head down the parkway a dozen kilometers and turn east, you'll find Aspen Lake United Church. It's a small white building with a steeple too tiny for its size. A few years ago, it was one of four churches served by a single minister. A handful of families who remembered "the good old days" were keeping it open. But just barely.

Now, the church is full on Sundays. There's a thriving Sunday school and they have a part-time minister, the Rev. Muriel Clark.

Aspen Lake Church lives in the urban shadow. It used to be "way out of town," and ranchers and farmhands populated its pews. But farms became more mechanized and larger. Fewer people lived in the area until a few farms were subdivided into five- and ten-acre lots and "hobby farmers" began to move in. The city suburbs, meanwhile, crept to within three kilometers of its door.

Few of the city people living in the countryside came to Aspen Lake Church until Clark was asked to come and fill in for a few months. "Just Sunday services, that's all," she was told.

For her, that wasn't enough. She began visiting and phoning and making contacts. Gradually, some of the new families appeared and they brought others. As they did, the character of the church changed. Most of the old families were still there, but the active nucleus was soon made up of urban people who happened to be living in the country.

Aspen Lake Church is at that critical phase. It is getting too big to be a small church. It is still too small to be a big church. Their assets include a prize piece of land, plenty of enthusiasm, and lots of potential.

One thing that bothers them is the possibility of losing the intimate community they have formed. Everybody knows everybody and the minister can call each person by name. When there's a church function it's a family event, with the kids and everybody there.

Even the worship services have that "country family" flavor. There's a small organ with tiny speakers; no choir, though occasionally someone will sing a solo or play an instrument. People enjoy the chatter and gossip before church and over coffee afterwards. Clark greets people at the door as they come in and seems to have something to say to each one of them.

The bulletins, when they have bulletins, aren't typed very neatly. Clark, in spite of her considerable talents, is a terrible typist, and there's no church secretary. Hymns are sung from the words she projects on the wall with an overhead projector.

Unlike many city congregations, people seldom "dress up" for church. As one member said, "Out here, going 'formal' means putting on a clean pair of blue jeans."

Oroville United

An hour's drive beyond the Aspen Lake church, down a winding country road, is the town of Oroville, and right in the middle of town is the old, red brick United Church. It's the largest congregation in what's known as a "three-point charge." "That's because the minister has to 'charge' from one point (church) to another every Sunday morning," jokes Marie Henderson, the Board Chair. Services are held at 9 in the morning at Caustia and at 11 in Oroville. Othello, the other "point," has services on the first Sunday evening of each month.

Every Sunday morning finds the same group of people in Oroville and Caustia. Visitors are rare. The pews are about two-thirds full, which means 30 people in

Oroville and 15 in Caustia. While there's a lively group of children in Oroville, there are seldom any in Caustia.

Small pastoral charges often have financial problems. Some wouldn't be open at all if it were not for help that comes through the Mission and Service Fund of the United Church. Oroville-Caustia received aid from the Mission and Service Fund until a few years ago when, after some hard work and dedication, they became self-sufficient, and now even contribute a little to that fund.

The Oroville-Caustia Pastoral Charge is run by a small group of people who accepted responsibility for it years ago. Sometimes they serve on committees and sometimes not, but everybody knows who makes the decisions.

It seldom happens at meetings. Decisions are made informally and by the time the meetings come around everybody knows what will happen.

Everybody, that is, except the minister. At the moment, it's the Rev. Harry Dexter. This is not only his first church, it's also his first experience in the country. Sometimes he likes it and sometimes he hates it.

Dexter gets along very well, mostly because he's a quiet man who doesn't like to make waves. Perhaps that's why he's never told anyone in the congregation that he is homosexual, and that when he goes away on his day off, it's to visit his partner. It's sad, but Dexter may be right about people's reactions. There are urban congregations served by openly gay and lesbian ministers, but Dexter doesn't trust the folks in his congregation enough to come "out."

Dexter hasn't told anybody, but he's going to look for another church at the end of next year.

That'll come as no surprise to the members. Ministers come and ministers go in this rural church. Some arrive with fire in their eyes to reform the world and rejuvenate the church. Others come in fear and trembling.

Either way, the people of this congregation, more so than in the city churches, know that they are the church, not the minister. When all is said and done, they will do it their way because they were here before the minister and they'll be here long afterward.

As for style of worship, they've had everything from fiery evangelical preaching to contemporary poetry. They've sung everything from hot gospel to cool jazz and lukewarm hymnody. Somehow, it all comes out sounding like Sweet Hour of Prayer.

They're not cynical. It's just that they've been through about one minister every two years or so and they find it hard to be impressed with each new one that comes along.

Meanwhile, young Dexter will continue to serve his apprenticeship with this congregation. Then they will send him on and wonder who is coming next.

"We do the real training of the ministers here," says Henrietta Crammer, who's been a member of the church for 45 years. "They send them out from the theological schools with all kinds of fancy ideas. We show them what the real church is like."

But, always, Henrietta and the others hope that someday a minister will settle down and live with them long enough to learn how decisions really get made in the Oroville-Caustia Pastoral Charge.

Cross Lake United

There's a special flavor to the service at Cross Lake United. The people gather around the fire in the box stove warming themselves against the chill from outside. They talk about the weather and the need for repairs on the church. There is much laughter, and people share their stories as they share themselves. They talk about the fact that many of the local people are not coming out lately and wonder how they could encourage more. But the church is still full for special celebrations of marriage and for baptism, for wakes and for funerals.

Before the service begins, George Derrick, his brother Don, and several other friends are plugging in and tuning up their electric guitars, and they begin to sing choruses they each know by heart, having heard them all their lives – songs such as *I'll Fly Away*, or *Amazing Grace*.

The minister is Aileen Garrioch, an Aboriginal who is studying at a special center for Native ministers. Part of the service is in the language of the First Nations people present and someone translates into English. Part of it is in English and someone translates that into the First Nations language. The Bible is read in both languages.

The small community knows that a special gift is being shared. There is a unique way of worshipping here, a way of viewing the Creator and the Christ. They feel it as they hear the words that are spoken and the songs that are sung.

Near the end of the service, the musicians take charge, and invite various members of the congregation to come forward and offer a personal testimony, make prayer requests of the congregation, or sing a favorite song or hymn. Sometimes, in response, people gather around the person who has spoken, place their hands gently on that person's head or shoulder, and offer prayer. Sometimes people pray from the pews.

The mosaic

There are hundreds of varieties of worship in United Churches across Canada. There is an active French-speaking component, L'Eglise Unie du Canada, which has taken this book and translated it into French. There are many other languages as well, especially in urban areas where the various tongues of Asia, Africa, the Caribbean, and Latin America are spoken. The hope is that each community will find a way to praise God and hear the Word in a style that works for them. All of them are struggling to become the community God calls them to be.

Most of them succeed and make a contribution to the rich, colorful mosaic that is the United Church of Canada.

━━━

Since the third decade of the 20th century, Canadian churches and their leaders have leaned toward either soul care or social care. Instead of embracing both sides of the gospel equation, they have given allegiance to one without full regard for the other. As we turn the corner and head into the 21st century, Canadian Christians and their leaders have the opportunity to begin again. Just as the people of God did almost 100 years ago, we can be anchored on both the solid rock of evangelical conviction and social compassion. We can experience God's love as we inform our social consciences and express our love for people.

Don Posterski and Gary Nelson – from *Future Faith Churches*
(Wood Lake Books, 1997)

Being a minister means waking up every morning knowing that someone, somewhere, is annoyed with you. Upset. Even angry.

Maybe it's something you said in your sermon. You were too political or not political enough. They didn't like the joke you told, or you didn't tell enough jokes. You didn't preach enough of the Bible, or you preached too much Bible. Your theology was too liberal, or too conservative.

Or maybe they simply don't like you as a person. In fact, no matter how brilliant a preacher you are, no matter how compassionate a pastor, or faithful visitor, someone will not like you. I guarantee that every minister reading this book can name at least one person who no longer attends that church because of him or her.

Christopher White – from *Jacob's Blessing* (Wood Lake Books, 1999)

4

All Week Long

So, whether you eat or drink or whatever you do,
do everything for the glory of God.
1 Corinthians 10:31

What happens on Sunday morning in any congregation is the tip of the iceberg. Some people see it as a celebration of what's been happening all week. Others, particularly those in the larger congregations, see it as the gathering of the scattered community. A strong church has both; a dynamic rich Sunday morning worship and small groups where warm fellowship and spiritual growth can be nurtured. One isn't likely to happen without the other.

It's impossible to describe everything that happens in United Churches during the week. Many congregations are really hopping, with things going on practically every night and during the daytime too. Others have very little going on, with Sunday morning being the only important gathering.

Congregational events

Congregations often have several big events during the church year when everybody gets together, pitches in, and has a good time. More and more, these events include people of all ages, from tiny tots to the very elderly. Those of us who no longer have children at home really appreciate the children we encounter in church.

One tradition is the potluck dinner. I've sometimes said that one of the criteria for United Church membership should be a liking for casseroles, because that's what you get (mostly) at potlucks. But then I'm told by friends in other denominations that the same thing applies there.

Every congregation, at some time or other, has a potluck. Each person brings one dish, whether it's salad or lasagna or raisin pie. These are all laid out on a table and then, as the kids say, "Everybody pigs out." Somehow, a reasonable balance of courses always shows up. The food is always delicious and people have a great time afterwards complaining about having eaten too much. Again.

The tradition of the potluck dinner is changing now that both partners are working in many families. Many of them make a quick stop at the deli for something to bring.

Usually, there's an event along with the dinner. It may be the annual meeting of the congregation, or simply a "fellowship time." Sometimes it's a fundraiser. Whatever the purpose, eating together is an ancient and honorable way of building bridges of friendship between people.

It also comes very close to the original idea of "Communion." When the people of the early Christian church gathered in the years just after the resurrection of Jesus, they got together for a meal. The tradition of that meal was handed down to us and is celebrated to this day as the Eucharist or Lord's Supper. But there is an element of Holy Communion in every church supper or picnic.

A highlight of the year for me is the annual *Seder* meal on Maundy Thursday just before Easter. This has become a major event for many, but certainly not all, United Churches. The Seder is the meal Jewish families eat at Passover, and was the meal Jesus (a faithful Jew) ate with his friends a few days before he was crucified. It is the base on which our communion tradition is founded. Usually we move through the various elements of the Seder meal, then into our Christian communion service.

The United Church Women

The most enduring and widespread midweek group is the United Church Women, better known as the UCW. It comes in a variety of styles and sizes.

There's often a deep sense of community among United Church women. They seem to have learned the value of simply being together. Their conversation is not idle gossip, though there may well be some of that. They are simply enjoying being together, sharing their lives and their gifts. When they need someone to lean on, they know each other well enough to do that too.

UCWs will often undertake a specific study program. It may be a book in the Bible or a mission study program. Often, they look at issues affecting women in church and society. Some examine social justice questions and then try to do something about them.

Small groups within the UCW are called "units." They usually meet separately and have specific interests. Once a month or so, the whole gang gets together for programs or a business meeting. Technically, every adult woman in the United Church is a member, though many women who are very active in the United Church may belong to other groups.

Many United Church Women are worried, however, because their membership seems to be aging rapidly, and there are not many young women joining. Some are tired of being asked to cater for yet another dinner, and feel that sort of thing is the responsibility of the whole church – not just the women.

As one that serves

There are groups called United Church Men, or the UCM. Others are called the AOTS. But let's face it; we guys have never managed to get it together as effectively as the women have. And we're poorer for it.

The heyday of the men's movement in the United Church was in the 1950s, when almost every congregation had an AOTS group – those letters being taken from the words of Jesus, quoted in Luke 22:27 RSV: "I am among you **As One That Serves**." There are not nearly as many men's groups now, but the national AOTS organization is still strong and lively.

Men's clubs sometimes get started when one enthusiast gathers several men together to go to a regional gathering, such as the Banff Men's Conference, or to a national event such as the AOTS Annual Conference. Whether or not the conference itself is a success, traveling together provides the first bonds on which the men's club begins to form. The men begin to realize they need this kind of fellowship more than they admit, even to themselves.

Most men's clubs meet once a month over dinner, which they often bring in from a local fast-food outlet. The main agenda is a chance to talk to each other, to share a few laughs and a few pains, and generally to get to know and support each other.

Here and there, small groups of men are getting together to talk about "men's lib." Some of us are beginning to learn that many things about our male culture put us into cages and keep us from being genuinely free and open to the leading of God.

There's little of what one member called "God talk" at most of the men's meetings. In fact, many men find it hard to talk about their faith or about their feelings. They would be tremendously enriched if they learned how.

In many congregations, there's a kind of informal men's group. They get together to paint the walls or fix the furnace or do any of the hundreds of fix-it things that keep the church building in shape. And there's an amazing amount of fellowship and mutual support that happens in these informal gatherings.

Study and support groups

In the last few years, there has been some significant growth in other forms of women's organizations, particularly "Women's Circles." These are primarily about spiritual development, mutual support, and Bible study. They are a very welcome and useful addition to the life of the United Church. In a few places, men's groups are doing the same sort of thing, and sometimes both men and women meet together.

Bev and I are part of two groups, one that's all United Church people, and one that has people from a variety of denominations. Neither group has any official connection with a congregation – someone simply phoned up a few people and said, "Hey, come over to my house." We don't have any particular agenda or program. We talk about whatever is on our minds, but since we are all people of faith, we naturally talk about that quite often. When we've found ourselves in times of deep stress or difficulty, it's these groups that propped us up until we could stand on our own feet again.

Non-church groups

There are many different kinds of groups that meet in or around the church. Some groups simply use the building, such as the hundreds of Alcoholics Anonymous, Al-Anon, and Al-Ateen meetings held in United Churches across the country. So do groups concerned with the handicapped, music, dance, and many other activities.

Often ministers in their counseling refer people to these groups so they can find a bit of friendship and support while they are working through their problems.

Many churches now use their Sunday school facilities for nursery school and daycare programs through the week. Often these are run by a committee of parents under the umbrella of the church organization. In some cases, a private organization rents the facilities.

Some congregations offer space and sometimes leadership to seniors or other special interest groups. And, of course, various community youth groups, such as Cubs, Scouts, Venturers, Brownies, and Guides are often sponsored by congregations. Our own congregation has a group called Making Connections, which is a weekly gathering of young mothers and their children, many of whom have no other involvement in the church. These women gather to learn and to share and to support each other. And the children enjoy the play school.

Church school

The big thing for kids is the Sunday school. Officially, it's called the church school because here and there it meets on a weekday afternoon. Most of the kids and their teachers find it creative, exciting, and really worthwhile. Of course, there are a few places where Sunday school is just plain dull. Much depends on the attitude of the leaders. If they see it as exciting, and if they're willing to put a bit of work into their preparation, things really happen.

Through the Sunday school, many young families become active in the church. Parents realize their children really miss something if they don't have a religious tradition to give meaning and purpose to life. They realize that keeping a child out of church or Sunday school until they can "make up their own mind" doesn't work. To make a choice, children must have something to choose from – some sense of what such a decision would be about.

A few parents try dropping their children off at Sunday school without coming themselves. It doesn't work. There's a powerful message being given the children, a message that says church is really only marginally important. So thinking parents realize that giving children a religious upbringing involves becoming part of the church themselves.

There are generally no requirements or prerequisites for children to become part of the Sunday school. I don't think you'll be asked if your child is baptized, or whether you are members of the church or whether you are married. Like the rest of church, there is no dress code for kids in Sunday school. But it can be quite active sometimes, so casual clothes are probably best. Children are not required to bring an offering, but many congregations provide Sunday school offering envelopes and church school curricula encourage children to give an offering because it helps them sense their own participation in the worldwide healing and outreach ministry of the church.

In most United Churches, Sunday school begins in church where the children are part of the worship service. Children generally sit with a parent or grandparent for this first part, sometimes joining the minister at the front for the theme conversation, after which they go to their Sunday school classes.

One of the big problems in all our Sunday schools is that children no longer attend consistently. They are there one Sunday and not the next, sometimes because of other activities they're involved in, sometimes because they alternate between separated parents. Educational continuity is hard.

A good way to get information about the Sunday school is to phone the church office and get the number of another parent who is active in the Sunday school. They'll be happy to answer questions.

For all the people of God

One of the exciting stories around United Church Sunday schools concerns the *The Whole People of God* church school curriculum and its genesis in Regina a number of years ago.

A group of church school leaders and clergy gathered there to look over the available materials. They were looking for a curriculum that appreciated the gifts children bring to the life of a congregation. They wanted a connection between what adults and children were doing in worship and in study. None of the existing curricula met their needs. So they swallowed hard and determined to write one themselves. After lots of head-scratching, they decided the lectionary was the tool to bring adults and children together. Why not have all age levels work from the same Bible passages each week? If the adults are talking about the prodigal son, the kids would be too.

They did something else. Rather than beginning with educational theories, they began with the realities of the average congregation where there is never enough – never enough space, never enough budget, and never enough leaders and teachers who have training in how to teach children. They even considered the reality of terrified semi-atheists like me teaching eight-year-old boys in the furnace room.

What the Regina folk didn't have in budget or professionalism they made up for in dedication and sheer hard work. It was a heroic effort. The story is told in more detail in *Wood Lake Books: The Story of a Publishing Ministry* by Mike Schwartzentruber, which you can get free for the asking from Wood Lake Books.

After three valiant years, the Regina folk asked Wood Lake Books to help as their publisher. Wood Lake had no idea how big and complicated a project this would be, and the first couple of years almost did it in. Heroic efforts on the part of Wood Lake staff got the job done.

A very United Church curriculum

There's something uniquely "United Church" about that curriculum and how it grew, even though it came to be used internationally and interdenominationally. There are not many denominations where lay people and local clergy would have the courage and confidence to take on such a mammoth project. There are not many denominations where the efforts of a volunteer group and a small-town publisher would be accepted so well by congregations right across the country.

In recent years, *Seasons of the Spirit* has replaced *The Whole People of God* curriculum. Though *Seasons of the Spirit* is now published exclusively by Wood Lake Books, like *The Whole People of God*, it came into being as a result of a massive collaborative effort between many international and denominational partners, including the United Church. Wood Lake Books is also taking the lead in developing online curricula, including *The Best of The Whole People of of Online.*

And I am personally delighted that Wood Lake Books has decided to develop a series of curriculum modules around my book *The Family Story Bible.*

You can keep up-to-date on the latest in the curriculum field (and lots of other things) by checking the Wood Lake Books website (www.woodlakebooks.com). It is interesting that Christian education is becoming much more electronically oriented, with teachers and children finding a wide variety of resources on the Net.

Teen groups

Maybe it's wishful thinking, but I have a hunch there's more activity with youth and young adults at United Churches lately. At least, there is in our area. This is especially true where congregations have cared enough to hire some professional staff to encourage and motivate youth.

It is a very mixed picture, but generally it seems that young people have a higher visibility. They organize themselves under unique names, usually invented by the young people themselves. There's a heavy emphasis on social activities. And music. That's what attracts teenagers and it's also probably what they need. Discovering their own identity seems to be an important part of a young person's growing.

My impression is that youth leaders are becoming more creative. However, it seems the youth groups are getting younger. Older teens often leave the church. We hope they'll come back when children come into their lives.

The choir

My favorite church group is the choir. My travel and speaking schedule doesn't allow me to be part of the choir, but that's the group I'd join first if I could. Choirs don't get together just to make music for the congregation on Sunday morning. They get together because they enjoy each other and they like singing. They welcome anyone, even those of us who can't carry a tune in a bucket.

Larger churches often have big choirs with professional leaders and even paid soloists. Some churches have no choir at all. In between are the churches like ours where we try to make up with enthusiasm what we don't have in musicianship.

In children's choirs, as with adult choirs, the doing is more important than the performing. Friendships develop, skills are learned, and we begin to appreciate the spiritual and musical heritage we have in the United Church. All this is more important than the quality of the singing.

I enjoy it most when the children join the adult choir for a special presentation. I've seen this happening quite often at churches in various parts of the country.

Singles and doubles and in-betweens

Many United Churches used to have a couples' club, a singles' club or solo club, and a variety of other groups centered around a particular need or stage or aspect of life.

Those are still strong and vital in many places, but, more and more, people are getting together along lines of interest. There are Bible study groups and groups looking at ecological concerns, feminist concerns, or social justice issues. Sometimes very small support groups form around very specific concerns.

Many congregations have Amnesty International groups, social justice groups, or groups built around World Vision or The Christian Children's Fund and a host of other international justice organizations. Many churches operate or at least support a food bank, and probably even more have thrift shops. Through these groups, we try to make a difference in the world and in our neighborhood, and at the same time, find a place to belong – a "support group" if you like.

Some groups are built around specific needs. Married couples need to work at their marriage relationship, so in some places there are Marriage Encounter groups. Those who find themselves single, following death or divorce, gather to share their grief and help each other toward a celebration of their singleness. For a while, our congregation had a group called, "Men with wives with cancer."

These special groups are a good place for single people to meet others of their own age and interests. "I did the rounds of the singles' bars," said one woman to me. "I hated it. I felt like I was auctioning myself off to the highest bidder. All I wanted was a few friends my age, and I wanted some of them to be of the opposite sex."

Singles' groups help fill that need. They also provide a place where the pain and bitterness that often comes with divorce or death can be shared and dealt with, a place where God's forgiving grace can be experienced through the love of other people. And it's a place where people can find support to put together a new life.

Many people have come into the United Church as refugees from other denominations where they no longer felt wanted. People who have been divorced; who may be living with someone they are not married to; people who are gay or lesbian; single parents – all have found their way into the United Church. They come because we are known as an inclusive church, even though some of our members are not yet comfortable with them. In spite of our professed inclusiveness, people are sometimes deeply wounded by those attitudes.

We find ourselves in a double-bind. We want to be inclusive of everyone, and that includes folks who still carry the burden of racism, sexism, homophobia, etc. Many folks feel we move far too slowly and others feel we move much too fast. But at whatever speed, bit by bit we're getting there.

Bible study groups

I hear reports of a considerable increase in Bible study groups in the United Church. Part of that is because the secular media, while they don't necessarily treat the organized church very kindly, have given a great deal of space to some of the more radical developments in biblical scholarship.

People have begun to realize that the Bible is an exciting book, and that you don't need to be a scholar to study it and learn from its richness. Nor are you required to believe everything that's in the Bible, and you won't get stomped on if you say, "Hey, I don't believe that!"

Some people are discovering the Bible on the Internet. There are thousands of church organizations of every conceivable variety online. (Again, if you are interested, a good place to start is at www.woodlakebooks.com, the Wood Lake Books website or at www.united-church.ca, The United Church of Canada website.)

Each week, I am astounded at the response I receive to my little "e-zine" called *Rumors*. There's humor and fun and assorted craziness on it, but a major hunk is given over to a reflection on the Bible readings for the coming Sunday from the *Revised Common Lectionary*, which most United Churches use.

Healing the whole person

An exciting new development in the United Church is a renewed interest in spiritual health. More and more groups are gathering to learn and practice the spiritual art of prayer and healing.

Meditative prayer, spiritual retreats, and of course the plain and simple, one-to-one conversation with God we've been using all along, are finding more vital expression in gatherings that happen at various times – often before or after church on Sunday.

And surprise! The medical profession is realizing what Christian people have known all along – that everything is connected. Mind, body, and spirit are all one. In the United Church we've often tended to concentrate on the mind at the expense of the body and the spirit. That seems to be changing. In many congregations, you will find the language of healing more and more a part of the worship service. In a few, but increasing, number of congregations, a portion of the service is used for healing. Sometimes special healing services are held for that specific purpose.

This needs a word of clarification. Don't confuse this spiritual healing with the kind of charade you may have seen some televangelists put on, nor with the sometimes bizarre claims of some New Age practitioners. There's nothing theatrical in what we do. We are talking about healing, which is not the same as curing. When your spirit is healed, your body is more able to fight whatever illness is causing you pain.

I had a very dear friend, Bob Hatfield, who died just before I began the revision that led to this third edition of *This United Church of Ours*. This edition is dedicated to him. Bob was a medical doctor. He had struggled for years against leukemia. He used all that medical science had to offer to overcome his disease, but he worked on his spiritual healing as well, through various forms of meditation, prayer, and humor.

Bob lived considerably longer than most of the patients he had himself diagnosed with that disease. I don't know if that was because of his strong sense of faith – his spiritual work. But I do know that it filled his last years with beauty and grace and meaning. When Bob and his family finally made the decision to let death proceed, he was able to thank God for all that had been, and to have his loving family around him as he began his final journey into the arms of God. Bob was not cured of his leukemia, but he was healed.

There are other kinds of healing. At a special healing service a few years ago, I went forward to ask for healing, because I still carried within me feelings of bitterness and anger over the suicide of my son Lloyd. I came away feeling cleansed and renewed. It's not a one-time thing, of course. I've needed that kind of healing many times, and will continue to need it all my life. I am convinced that my spiritual health and my physical health are fully connected.

Our congregation, and many others, have regular Healing Touch sessions that anyone can attend, and the phone number of a Healing Touch practitioner is listed every Sunday in the bulletin.

An exciting development that began in the Lutheran churches is now spreading across the United Church – the Parish Nurse. The Parish Nurse program takes seriously the concept that Christian healing involves the whole person. The Parish Nurse bridges the gap between theology and medicine, and offers a healing and helpful presence to people of the congregation and community.

Picnics and bazaars

The picnic is another gathering centered around eating. It's often organized by the Sunday school as an end-of-year event, and features all the old standbys that make you realize how old you really are: three-legged race, tug-o-war, and stilts. There's a baseball game where middle-aged men develop sore muscles and sunburns and their kids enjoy out-hitting and out-running them. It may end with a campfire singsong, some prayers, and a meditation.

In some congregations, they have an annual retreat where people of all ages gather for a weekend of fun, study, worship, and just being together. Saturday night may feature a campfire, crazy skits by the kids, lots of songs, and gooey marshmallows. I remember one of those weekends with particular fondness. As we sat there at our lakeside campfire, we were treated to a magnificent lightning storm. All of us, especially the little ones, sat just a little closer to each other as we experienced God's majesty and the closeness of our community.

The Annual Tea and Bazaar is a big event. Most frequently, it's sponsored by the UCW, but one way or another the whole church gets involved. That includes the kids who love the responsibility of running a table or cooking wieners.

People bring crafts, cookies, and pies, all of which are spread on long tables and sold for less than reasonable prices. There's usually a "white elephant" table or a full-blown rummage sale, where one person's junk becomes someone else's treasure.

These teas and bazaars are quite informal and lots of fun. They're a good way to meet some new friends. They're also a good excuse to see people you haven't talked to for a while and to gain a few pounds eating too many date squares and cookies. Because I love pies, and nobody in our house knows how to make them properly, I fill up the freezer with a year's supply.

In the more rural areas, everybody goes to all the teas and bazaars, regardless of whose church they are at. They become, in effect, community events.

They say the teas and bazaars are to raise money. Maybe that's because we still can't justify an event just so people can enjoy being with each other. I think we should have them even if they don't make a dime. They provide some of the cement that holds a community together.

The wider community of faith

We live in a multicultural society. Canadians, I suspect, have never really thought in terms of a "melting pot" when thinking of our rich cultural and religious diversity. "Mosaic" would be a better word.

There are often groups within congregations who reach out and make contact with Buddhists, Muslims, Jews, and other faith groups, and they work to develop understanding with folks from other Christian denominations.

In my congregation, we've had a Seder meal on Maundy Thursday (just before Easter) under the direction of friends from the Jewish Community Centre. In Vancouver, there's an interfaith group that's been publishing a most interesting calendar each year, that shows the special days and celebrations of a wide variety of religions.

Community

God is the god of individual persons, yes. But, even more, God is the god of "a people." I really don't think it's possible to be a Christian without being part of a fellowship. That fellowship needs to worship together. That's central.

But the worship needs to be founded on the caring, growing, studying, working, gossiping, and playing that's been building the community and binding it together throughout the week.

There is much to rejoice about, and the question now is, how much will we risk? The UCW continues to meet the needs of a large number of women in the United Church of Canada and without what it stands for and provides, there would be great feelings of loss. Loss for those who belong to the organization and those who benefit from all that the UCW gives to the church and community.

But as you look to the future and face the realities of an aging and declining membership, how radical are you prepared to be? By radical, I mean, are you willing to return to your roots, to your reason for being. Programs, structures and ways of operating are secondary to the deeply precious reasons why women in the church gather together.

Marion Best – from a speech to the Kamloops-Okanagan
United Church Women, March 1999.

I have seen it many times. The death of someone too young. A disease or a winter highway claims another victim, and the church sanctuary is filled, packed with the stunned and grieving. In the choir, we wait to offer our words, sung like a lullaby that is entirely inadequate and entirely necessary, part of the ritual of mourning and remembering that the church offers.

"Wait," we sing to shattered faces that we dare not look at for fear we may start to sob, "wait, there is more than this. Look," we sing, "God is welcoming your friend. No one is alone. If you do not believe this," we sing, "fear not. We will believe it for you."

I am a wavering and insufficient soprano. But I sometimes sense that this is one of the most important things I do.

Donna Sinclair – from *Jacob's Blessing* (Wood Lake Books, 1999)

5

Hatched, Matched, and Dispatched

—

While they were eating, Jesus took a piece of bread, gave a prayer of thanks, broke it, and gave it to his disciples.

"Take and eat it," he said; "This is my body."

Matthew 26:26

Like every other group, church people have their "in" humor. For instance, those people who show up only for baptisms, weddings, and funerals are called the "hatched, matched, and dispatched" crowd. We don't usually mean it as a put-down. Often, it reflects the pain we feel when people take these events too lightly. Baptisms, weddings, and funerals, plus Holy Communion, are very important to us. To understand the church, you need to know why they are so significant.

If you're reading this chapter because you have a child you'd like to have baptized, and you are wondering what you, and the folks you plan to invite to the service, should be wearing, check back to Chapter 1.

The sacraments

Some things are almost impossible to explain and can really only be understood through experience. That's especially true of the concept of sacrament. A sacrament is something we act out because words simply won't hold all the meaning these events have for us.

It's a matter of personal experience. Like love. If you have ever loved another person, you know love is real, but you may have a hard time explaining why or how. Like love, a sacrament is a mystery. And a mystery can never be explained, though it *can* be experienced. I do hope you'll be open to the experience, and then you'll know why we think they are so important.

There are only two events in the United Church that we call sacraments – baptism and communion. Other denominations see this differently. The Roman Catholic church, for instance, has seven sacraments.

Sacrament and grace

Maybe a few words – words that sound a bit like jargon – will help. We use that "jargon" to describe very powerful realities. These words have a very special significance to Christians and I can only do a half-baked job of telling you what they mean. They are words that become fuller and richer as you grow in your faith. These are emotional words like "love" and "fear." You don't know what love means till you've been loved. You don't know what fear is till you've been afraid.

So let's give it a try. Two words that have a very significant meaning for Christians: sacrament and grace.

A *sacrament* is a sacred act, something we do to mark or point to a holy reality. When I first held my children in my arms, I knew those were sacred moments. When I held the hand of a dying friend, I sensed I was in the presence of something profoundly holy.

Life is full of sacred, holy moments. When we gather together as a church community and together focus our sense of God by reliving a tradition which people have found sacred for many centuries, that is a sacrament.

Grace is easier to explain, but harder to understand and accept. Grace is God's love. It's there. All the time. It washes down over us. God's love is what keeps the universe going. It's the gas in our tank.

Grace is a gift. And God gives us that gift whether or not we know it or want it or deserve it.

Baptism

Because these concepts mean so much to us, we wince a little when people express some of the outdated ideas that go with sacraments such as baptism. For instance, some believe the baby will "go to hell" if it isn't baptized. Others think a baby doesn't have a name or a soul until that "magic" moment.

I've heard people say that God doesn't love an unbaptized person. Others have said that since a baby was "conceived in sin," and therefore "born bad," it needs to be "washed by baptism" before it's "clean."

Some have wondered whether a child can be baptized when there's only one parent around or if the baby is adopted or handicapped or if the parents aren't married or if only one is a Christian.

Throw all those old ideas out. It's all part of the popular fiction about the church and what it teaches. It's what sociologists would call a "folk religion." It reflects the thinking of people who have an idea that religion is somehow a "good thing" – that it somehow protects them from bad things – but they never bother to find out what the church *really* teaches.

No big deal

For instance. A young couple knocked at our door several years ago. "We were wondering if the Reverend could come over and do our baby. Our folks are here, and we're having a party, so we thought it'd be kinda cute to have the kid done now."

"Well," I said, "she's out right now. She'll be back in an hour. But, I don't think she'd just come over this afternoon and baptize your baby."

"Why not?"

"Because baptism is a big deal. It's something the church takes very seriously. You don't just do it on the spur of the moment. You have to think about the promises you make."

"Promises?" Now they were really confused.

I could see this needed more than a doorstep conversation. "Why don't you phone her, make an appointment, and she can explain what it means to have a child baptized."

They never did. And I suspect they went away feeling the church had somehow turned against them.

Or maybe it was no big deal to them after all.

Nothing but love

The power of what we call "grace" struck me one day in church when the minister was baptizing a baby. Talk about undeserved love! That brand new baby couldn't do much besides fuss and cry, smile a little, eat a lot, and wet her pants.

Her mom and dad beamed down at her with nothing but love in their eyes and all of us in the congregation smiled and felt a bit of that love too. As the minister made the sign of the cross on the child's forehead, touched her with the oil of healing, kissed her gently and handed her back to her mom, all of a sudden I knew deep down inside what the minister meant when she talked about "grace."

Inside the parents

When we're talking about the baptism of babies, we're talking, of course, about what happens inside the parents. The baby doesn't know what's going on. But the parents do. Or should. The parents and the church community should feel the holiness – the sacredness of this event.

Baptism isn't like one of the shots the baby gets from the public health nurse. It's plain tap water in the baptismal font and it doesn't protect against anything or cause anything. Baptism symbolizes what we hope is happening in the hearts and minds of the parents and the congregation that's gathered.

If the words and actions don't mean anything to those taking part in the service, they might as well be reciting the alphabet and dancing the rumba for all the good it does. Quite understandably, many ministers and church boards feel it's a bit of a charade if people come to church to say words they don't believe, and participate in a ritual that has no meaning for them.

That's not to say that if you bring a child for baptism you should be able to write a theological paper on the subject. But you should be struggling to understand and to actively live what you believe and you should be willing to try live up to the promises you make in the ceremony. Technically, at least one parent should be a member of the congregation, but it is really up to the board of the church to set the standards and to discuss particular cases.

I was studying in Israel before my first grandchild was born. So I brought back a small bottle of water from the Jordan River for his baptism, and there was enough for his baby sister's baptism a few years later. There's nothing magic about Jordan water. It's the water that comes out of the taps in Jerusalem. It didn't make their baptisms any more or less effective. But for me, it symbolically connected the baptisms of my grandchildren to the powerful story of Jesus and the moment of his baptism.

I was doubly delighted when Bev then developed a book paralleling our grandchildren's baptisms with the baptism of Jesus. It included pictures of the children and of course, pictures of Jesus. Wood Lake Books took the concept and developed it into a fine gift book you can customize for the children in your life. It's called *My Baptism*. If you should buy that book, take a look at the beautiful child on the cover. That's my granddaughter, Zoë!

The promises

So what are those promises we make at a baptism? First of all, the parent or parents are asked whether they really want this child to be a member of the Christian church. Baptism isn't into the United Church of Canada. It's a welcome into the whole church of God. All over the world. All the denominations. Not all denominations agree, but that's how we see it in the United Church. And of course that means that if you've been baptized in another Christian church, the United Church recognizes your baptism.

The parent(s) are asked whether they believe in God. If they don't, the rest of the questions, in fact the whole thing, will be pointless. They are asked whether they'll provide a Christian home for the child and whether they'll encourage the child to be part of the church. They are also asked if they "will join with your brothers and sisters in the mission and ministry of Christ's church."

If the parent(s) say "yes" to that, then the congregation has some promises to make. In our tradition, the whole congregation becomes the sponsor or "godparents" of the child, which is why we're not very enthusiastic about private baptisms in the home. It's the congregation's responsibility to help the parents show the child the love of God.

So the congregation is asked to say "yes," they want that child as part of their community, and they accept their share of the responsibility for that child's growing up. When all those commitments are made, the baptism is performed.

When Bev and I had our kids baptized, we promised to raise them in the church family. It meant being involved with the church ourselves. It also meant a conscious effort to teach them what it means to be Christian. It's far more than saying grace at meals, going to church once in a while, and being nice to each other.

Bev wasn't an ordained minister when we first made those promises with our children. We were just like every other family, trying to figure out how to make sense out of life. Looking back, we realize the commitments we made really enriched our whole family. We and our children have gained far more than we've given.

It seemed to us that we couldn't live up to the promises we made when our children were baptized unless we got involved with the church. It's like being sure your kids are educated. First, you need a school. Sure, there are some who manage to educate their children at home, but they are few and far between. There are also a few parents who have given their children a complete religious education at home, but they're exceptions.

Not that Christianity is all a church affair, any more than education only happens in school. We teach our kids far more at home than the school or the church ever could. But school and church are still important. For most of us they're essential.

Who decides?

More and more United Church boards are taking a tougher stand on the baptism of infants. Parents who have had one baby baptized but who haven't darkened the door of the church since should be asked a few more questions when they come around with baby number two. "You didn't live up to your promises the first time. How can we help you live up to them this time?"

That's why few clergy will baptize children unless at least one parent takes part in a preparation program. Sure, that means some people go off in a snit. It also means that those who take it seriously enough to do some preparation are much more likely to live out their promises. Far more of them become involved in a church community.

Policies

Congregational policies on baptism vary. In some churches, any parent who wants a child baptized gets a child baptized. Others require parents to sign a statement of faith and a promise of church participation.

Many congregational policies simply say that the parents should understand what it is they are doing and promising. The parents should really know what these statements and promises mean now, and in the future. If the church board is satisfied that the parents understand, then it's usually up to those parents and their own conscience to decide what should be done.

Unfortunately, church boards often don't take their responsibility seriously. They heap it all on the minister. The United Church *Manual* says very clearly it's the *board's* responsibility to decide who gets baptized. If the board takes that responsibility lightly, it's no wonder so many parents think of it simply as "a cute thing to do."

The baptismal ceremony

In the United Church, baptism takes place during a regular worship service. Often, an elder or board member introduces the family and the child to the congregation. Then, after the parent or parents have been asked to make some promises about the child's upbringing, the minister takes the child from the parent and with water makes the sign of the cross on the baby's forehead. Some ministers will just sprinkle a bit of water on the child's head, others use the water more liberally. This may be followed by a touch of oil (don't worry – it's ordinary cooking oil) to the baby's forehead as a symbol of healing and peace.

The words spoken at this time are usually, "I baptize you in the name of the Father and of the Son and of the Holy Spirit," and this is followed by a blessing. The minister tells us that the child has been welcomed into the community of faith. Then the child is handed back to the parent. Often a baptismal candle and a certificate are given.

Of course, some children refuse to be held by any stranger, minister or not. Then, the parent simply holds the child while the baptism is performed. Older children stand beside a parent for their baptism. Don't be upset if your baby cries. It's not the first or the last child to find the process a little strange. Perhaps even frightening.

I remember one memorable service when Bev baptized three children from one family. The youngest was about five. Bev had spent time, not only with the parents, but with the children, helping them understand what baptism was about. At the service, the two older ones read very simple statements about what baptism meant: "I like Jesus." "Church people are nice." Not heavy-duty theology, but their own words. The smallest boy held up a picture he had created.

Often, when the child being baptized has older sisters or brothers, they join their parents around the baptismal font, and, as far as they can understand, share in the vows their parents are making. It's also a good occasion for the parents to explain to the older children and to friends what baptism means, and to recall the day when they were baptized.

Sometimes one parent wants a child baptized and the other doesn't. That situation should be discussed with the minister. In most instances, if one parent can't, in good conscience, make the vows, that decision should be respected. But that parent should at least agree to the other parent taking those vows, including the part about raising the child in the Christian faith. Otherwise, baptism may simply drive a wedge between the parents.

Wood Lake Books publishes a small booklet that explains the theology and symbolism of baptism, as well as answers the questions most people ask when they bring a child for baptism.

Adult baptism

Infant baptism is the most common practice in the United Church, but adults are baptized as well. Parents have the right to decide against infant baptism and to wait for the child to make the faith commitment for him- or herself.

I was baptized as an adult, after I was married. It was a deeply moving experience for me, one in which I felt very close to God. I was raised in the Mennonite tradition, which teaches that people should only be baptized when they are adults and can understand what they believe.

I made essentially the same promises at my own baptism as I made at my son's a few months later. I declared myself a Christian and promised to try with all my heart to be faithful to what that meant. I promised to receive the nurture and support of the Christian fellowship, to try to grow in my understanding of my faith, and to work for God's justice and love in this world. When I think about it, that was really a dedication of my whole life.

Membership

A different attitude about "membership" seems to be growing in the United Church. On the one hand, there are many people who hardly ever darken the church door who consider themselves to be "United Church." They expect the church will be there when they need it for a wedding or serious illness or a funeral, but they don't support it, financially or in person.

Perhaps they think it's like some countries in Europe, where the church is supported by taxes. But in Canada, it's the hard work and the cash of those who actively support the church that keep it alive. And it's understandable when these active supporters get a bit ticked off at those who want the church to be there when they need it, but they never support it.

On the other hand, there are increasing numbers of people who are very active in the United Church, but who never join officially. They may have come from another denomination and simply don't want to cut those ties. Others come from no denomination at all. They simply don't see the importance of formal membership, and, for that matter, neither do most others in the congregation. Many people think that if you show up with some regularity and support the church in some way, you are a member.

This can get dicey on occasion because, technically, only members can vote on those things that relate to the faith of a congregation. That rule is often blissfully ignored, but there may be times (such as voting on whether to call a new minister) when a presbytery representative or someone else may insist that only members can vote.

Or at least, that is the way things stand now. The whole issue of what constitutes membership in the United Church is being reviewed, and some changes may well have been made by the time you read this book. So ask your minister to bring you up to date.

Growing up in church

In the traditional United Church pattern, children are baptized as infants and go to Sunday school until they reach their early teens. At that point, they take a class, usually taught by the minister, which runs anywhere from a few weeks to a year. At the end of that time, the young person is expected to decide whether or not to confirm what their parents declared a dozen years earlier.

This Confirmation ceremony has pretty well disappeared. I haven't seen one in years. We used to call that "joining the church," but now a child joins the church at baptism.

However, when children get to be adults, they often realize how much they don't know. For them, and for others of various ages coming into the church for many reasons, congregations often have a series of study sessions each year to look at what it means to join the church. Since the early 1980s, many people in those study sessions have been using this book as the text for introducing people to the United Church of Canada. I wrote the first edition more than 20 years ago, because a minister said to me, "I have ten fine, capable people on my board. But none of them have any background in the church, United or otherwise." This book has been the bestseller (except for hymnbooks and Bibles) in United Church bookstores ever since. This edition contains a study guide, which begins on page 197.

Children and communion

Until recently, teenagers took their first communion after they were confirmed. That's still the situation in some traditional congregations. The idea is that people don't take communion until they are able to make their own statement of faith.

However, in most congregations, people are told their children may take communion if that is the parents' choice. This isn't true in all areas of the country, but the practice is spreading.

The problem with communion in the United Church is not the technicalities of who can and who can't receive it. The problem is that people take it far too lightly. It becomes something many people do without understanding or feeling the deep significance of this sacrament.

Passover

What we call communion or Holy Communion is called the Mass in some denominations, the Eucharist in others. Another term we like to use is the Lord's Supper.

Like baptism, communion is a sacrament that goes back to Bible times. Jesus participated in both. He was baptized by John, a prophet who had come to announce the Messiah. The first Lord's Supper was part of an even older tradition, the Passover meal. As a faithful Jew, Jesus celebrated the Passover every year.

The Passover recalls the time, centuries before Jesus, when the people of Israel were held as slaves. And Moses led them out of Egypt into the "Promised Land."

That experience became the central metaphor for the Hebrew people; the knowledge that God had delivered them out of slavery and into freedom. And that's why the Passover feast is the most important event in the Jewish calendar.

The Passover feast was a full meal. So the one Jesus ate with his disciples just before he was executed, the meal we usually call "The Last Supper," probably included a leg of lamb, bread, and wine. During the meal, Jesus took the bread, thanked God for it, broke it, and passed it around. He said the bread symbolized his body, "broken for you."

Then he took the wine which he called "my blood, shed for you," and asked his disciples to think of that as a symbol of a new kind of relationship with God. He called it "the new covenant."

The covenant

Covenant is a word we don't use too much outside of the church. Lawyers sometimes use it to mean an agreement. In church, it means that and a whole lot more.

When our children became part of our family, through birth and through adoption, Bev and I made a one-way covenant with them, even though we didn't put it into any words. We knew we would love those kids, come hell or high water.

Bev and I haven't always been ideal parents, and our kids haven't always loved us back. In other words, we've been a normal family. But the covenant is there because we can never stop being their mom and dad, no matter what we may do to each other. Or what they might do to us.

God's covenant begins as a one-way promise. Over and over again in the Bible, God says in a variety of ways, "I love you. I promise that I always will. Whether you love me back or not."

We can respond to that love and make it a two-way covenant. That's what we do in the sacraments of baptism and communion.

Communion

When we symbolically reenact that meal in the ritual we call communion, we are saying "yes" to that special covenant relationship God has with the people of the Word, the church.

Sharing the Lord's Supper with our fellow Christians is what we call "a means of Grace." Grace is that special, undeserved love that God lavishes on us. The Lord's Supper is one of the ways we can stay in touch with that love.

It's not that the bread and the wine (often called the "elements") are anything special. In fact, it's usually ordinary bread from the local grocery, though I think communion is nicer when the bread is baked by somebody at home. And the wine is probably not wine at all, but grape juice. Or the wine somebody made in their basement.

That's all part of the symbolism. God can take plain ordinary bread and grape juice and give them a meaning that'll shake us to our roots. In the same way, God can take plain ordinary people, shake us to our roots, and make us part of a special divine plan.

Whether any of that happens or not depends on what we bring to the communion. The circumstances under which the Lord's Supper is celebrated, the music and the surroundings may help. But the essential thing is our faith.

The communion service

There are many ways of celebrating the Lord's Supper. Often congregations use different rituals at different times.

The traditional United Church way of serving communion is for some elders to come forward. The minister gives them trays with the bread, which has been cut into tiny cubes, and the grape juice, which is in little glasses.

The minister is on one side of the communion table and the congregation on the other. That arrangement is an important symbol. We gather around the Lord's table, as a covenant community, and eat together. Sharing the food and drink in this way is an important symbol of our community.

The elders (or board members) serve us and we serve each other. Serving one another symbolizes our caring ministry to the person beside us. When someone serves me the bread and wine during communion in church, that person is being my priest.

Another common practice is for the minister and an elder to stand at the front of the church. The elder (or sometimes another minister) holds a loaf of bread and the minister holds the chalice. People come up to the front of the church. Each one breaks off some bread, dips it in the wine, and "partakes" right there. Sometimes, usually with smaller groups, the chalice and the loaf may be passed or taken around. Some church leaders like to use impressive language, so they call the dipping "intinction."

Some congregations that treasure a strong Methodist heritage, such as the churches in Newfoundland, ask members to come up to the communion rail that runs across the front (chancel) of the church, where they are served communion.

In the United Church tradition, only ordained clergy can preside at communion (except in special circumstances). However, in small study or fellowship groups, people may have something called an "agape meal" or "love feast," without a minister present.

Usually, this is a very informal affair, where food and drink (it may be bread and wine or something else) are passed around as a symbol of the love and affection in that group. This can be very beautiful and meaningful, but, officially, at least, it's not communion.

Generally, in most United Churches, communion is celebrated once a month or, in some cases more frequently. Some only celebrate communion four times a year.

Open communion

The United Church has "open communion." That means we recognize the work and ministry of other denominations and we welcome their members to our communion. There are people who feel you can only come to communion if you are "living a good Christian life," but in the United Church, we come out of our need. I can come to God's table no matter how badly I've messed up my life. In fact, that's when I most need to receive communion.

Communion is not only for those who have their lives all together. It's not a matter of deserving it. It's a gift. Communion is a symbol of God's love for us, especially when we are writhing around in our own muck. And the communion table is God's table, where everyone is welcome!

Weddings

Marriage is considered a sacrament in some denominations, but not in the United Church. Our attitude toward weddings is criticized by some as being too "easy-going" and praised by others as being "open-minded."

The United Church once held some kind of record for sheer numbers of weddings. We still do more than our share of them. That's probably because people who don't have much of a church connection often decide on the United Church. We have lots of folk who think of us as "their" church, which they mostly stay away from. This is the "hatched, matched, and dispatched" crowd I talked about earlier.

That's partly because we're one of the biggest Protestant denominations in Canada. It's also because in many places, especially the west, the United Church is kind of a community church.

Until recently, you couldn't get a decent civil wedding in many parts of Canada. If you went to the "JP," the Justice of the Peace, you got ten minutes in a stuffy room on a weekday. People who wanted a ceremony to give the moment some significance, and a few friends and relatives to stand with them, had to go to the church, whether they believed in God or not.

Fortunately, those days are gone. We have marriage commissioners who often do very fine wedding services. Now, most people who come to the church to be married do so because they genuinely want a church wedding, although there are still a few who don't know that alternatives exist.

Often they want a church wedding for purely sentimental reasons. "My mother was married in a church and she thinks I should be married in one too." Or, "It's such a pretty place with a nice center aisle and we did want a traditional wedding. Besides, the minister is so good-looking."

That kind of thinking raises questions of integrity. When people are married by an ordained minister in a Christian church, it is a religious service – a service of worship. It has to do with entering into a covenant – that special kind of committed relationship – before God and before God's people. The promises are made to each other, to God, and to the community. If the couple has no faith to give the promises some meaning, they are being hypocritical.

Which is not to say that a couple with differing religious traditions should not be married in the church. United Church clergy are usually open and sensitive to the faith of others, whether this be from another Christian denomination or from another faith tradition. They are often very happy to have clergy or other leaders from other religious groups participate in the service, and I have known many

United Church clergy who have participated in weddings held in other churches, temples, and synagogues.

And there are occasions when only one of the couple has a faith that brings them into the church for marriage. This should be thoroughly discussed with the minister, and the non-Christian partner should understand what is going on and agree to it, but should not be asked to say things he or she doesn't believe.

Gay and lesbian couples are now coming forward to be united in a "covenanting service" or a "holy union." It is the decision of each congregation as to whether they will do such services. These services, usually for a couple that is active in the congregation, are becoming more and more common.

Marriage preparation

More and more United Church congregations are insisting that the couple have some preparation for marriage or covenanting. The clergy feel that if they are going to "tie the knot," they have some responsibility to see that it holds.

In some large cities, couples may be asked to go to interdenominational marriage preparation courses. Some congregations simply schedule marriage preparation events at regular intervals and work with several couples at the same time. In smaller churches, the minister is more likely to have two or three private sessions with the couple.

The counseling doesn't lay a "religious trip" on people, at least not as a rule. It's intended to help them face some of the questions that are bound to give them trouble if they don't deal with them creatively. It's amazing how many serious questions about sex, children, relatives, work sharing, money, and other things many couples have never discussed.

Most couples coming to be married are already living together. "We've already worked out all the problems," they say. "We know we can make it." But it doesn't work out that way. Something about being married changes the relationship fundamentally. Even people who are on their second or third marriage need marriage preparation. *Especially* those who are on their second or third marriage because, often, they don't really understand what went wrong the first or even the second go-round.

Even people who have been together for years need to work on their relationship. That's why churches encourage things like Marriage Enrichment and Marriage Encounter. Bev and I have found both those programs very helpful.

Marriage is like a garden. It needs watering, fertilizing, and weeding. If you don't keep working at it, you wind up with an unproductive tangle of emotional weeds. And there comes a time in every relationship when outside, professional help is needed. Bev and I would not be together, thoroughly enjoying our love and friendship after more than 40 years, if we had not struggled through some very tough times with the help of a professional counselor.

The arrangements

Weddings are almost always held on Saturday. I suppose this is because it's the only day of the week when wedding guests aren't working and the church is available. I don't know many clergy who will do a wedding on a Sunday, although I know of one instance where a couple, who had been very involved with the congregation, were married as part of the regular Sunday worship.

If you want to make clergy livid, arrange for the reception hall and everything else and then call the minister at the last moment. It's a great way to get off on the wrong foot. Ministers usually have very busy schedules and need lots of advance warning to arrange marriage preparation and wedding times. Always phone the church first. Ask about the process. In some congregations, couples are asked to fill out a form and agree to certain things before they even begin to discuss a date. It's not as automatic as it used to be.

Enthusiastic friends and relatives sometimes cause problems at weddings. Flashguns popping and cameras that advance and rewind the film very noisily hardly add to the dignity of what is, after all, a service of worship. Most often, wedding guests are allowed to pop and grind happily while the bride is coming down the aisle. Then they are told "no photos" till the signing of the register and the recessional. Some liberties may be granted to a "designated photographer" who has discussed the protocol with the minister before the wedding.

Videotaping enthusiasts can easily turn a sacred service into a circus. Having spent years as a professional TV producer, I can tell you there is no need for the camera person to be popping up and down, shooting from all kinds of angles and using additional lighting. Competent camera operators will set up their camera on a tripod in some inconspicuous place, usually at the back or the side of the church and stay there relying on their zoom lens to vary the shot.

Payment

When Bev and I were married, we slipped the minister a ten-spot in a white envelope and thought that covered things. Looking back, I know it didn't, even then. Bev was a member of that church but up until that point I had made no contribution to that or any other church. Nowadays, many United Churches have a fee schedule that includes something for the use of the church, the caretaker, the organist, and the minister's time. Ask about these charges when you phone the church office.

Most congregations lose money on weddings, but they see it as a mission to the community. As for the ministers, what they receive is often laughable in terms of the time they put in. In fact, photographers get far more for their participation in the wedding than the minister does. Don't make assumptions about these things. Discuss them with the minister well before hand, frankly and openly.

Some congregations have a wedding host, a person who sits down with the couple and discusses the arrangements, what happens when, etc. Such a person can help solve many problems before they happen.

Who can and who can't

There are no hard and fast rules in the United Church about who can get married in the church and who can't. It's up to the church board to make that decision. Often divorced people come because they feel they have been rejected by their own denomination. They want to get married again, but their own church won't do it. Many clergy feel they have a ministry to these people, to help them when they are trying to put their lives back together.

Very young people or couples coming to get married only because the bride is pregnant may run into some tough questions from the clergy. Clergy can and do refuse to perform the ceremony when they feel it would be wrong to do so.

Variations and gimmicks

For a while, the "in" thing was for couples to write their own wedding ceremony, complete with poems by Kahlil Gibran and a friend with a guitar singing *The Wedding Song*. Lately, weddings have become much more traditional and couples are choosing the "standard" service. We haven't gone all the way back to quavering tenors singing *My Hero* and a nervous groom trying to say, "and thereto I plight thee my troth." But few couples today want to write their own ceremony.

Instead, most clergy offer a choice of two or three services and the couple can choose among them. Whether alterations to the wording are allowed depends on the minister.

Another fad which (thankfully) seems to be passing is having the wedding in wild and wonderful circumstances – on mountaintops or floating through the air in parachutes. Bev has turned down requests to do weddings on horseback and in a floating disco. Few clergy have much patience with that sort of thing and many refuse to do weddings outside the church building.

Still, I do know one United Church minister who did a wedding up in a Concorde jet. I don't know if it was before or after it broke the sound barrier.

Funerals

If weddings are a problem for United Church clergy, funerals are even more so. People plan for weddings and there's time to talk about what is going to happen and what it means. But when people find themselves making funeral arrangements for a loved one, there's seldom an opportunity to discuss what these arrangements mean and what the options are. That's why the church has always encouraged people to discuss funeral arrangements with their loved ones while they are still hale and hearty.

While you're at it, make a will. That way, whatever you leave when you die won't all get used up for lawyers' fees. And think about the church when you are making out your will. Many people leave money to the church because they want God's work to carry on even after they are gone.

The gift of life

While you're on the subject, talk with those you love – your parents or your children – about the process of dying. For myself, I don't want to be kept alive by heroic means when there's no longer a reasonable possibility of recovering. I would like my family and my doctor to gently "pull the plug" if that time comes. Also, if there are any used parts still good to anyone, they're welcome. That's why Bev and I have left a "Living Will." It has no legal function, but if the time comes when we can't speak on our own behalf, the Living Will lets our family, our doctor, and others know what our choices would be. And we carry in our wallets a notice that we'd be happy if any organs can be used to help someone else.

I joke with my doctor about that. I tell him I'd like to will my nose to science. Or to an art gallery. Such a magnificent appendage deserves some attention. He tells me I need to do more exercise or there won't be any part of me worth saving.

There's nothing "morbid" or "sick" about discussing your own death. Talking about it won't make it come any faster or delay it any longer. It's simply acknowledging a fact. Life is terminal.

Call your minister

When someone close to you dies, call your minister first. Ministers can help with arrangements, suggest an appropriate funeral director, discuss things like burial or cremation and, most of all, help you through a tough time.

Many congregations run a series of study sessions to talk about these things. I recommend them to everyone, regardless of age. None of us know when we, or someone close to us, will die.

The service

If the one who died was an active church person, then funeral or memorial services should be held in the church, in spite of what some funeral directors may tell you. It's a proper place to say goodbye and to thank God for the life that has been lived.

Although it varies from region to region and from church to church, generally it's not a United Church tradition to have an open casket, at least not in church during the service. In some instances, the coffin may be open during a wake or at the funeral home. Filing past an open casket sometimes becomes a bit morbid, and it can be particularly hard on those closest to the deceased. It takes us away from the real purpose of the funeral, which is to acknowledge our grief and celebrate the continuing life of the person who has died.

More and more people, for some very good reasons, are choosing cremation. Bev and I have told our family that's what we would like. When the body has been cremated and the casket is not present, the service of worship is called a "memorial service," and funeral directors need not be involved in that service. You still need a funeral director however, because they are in the best position to handle many of the legal and other matters relating to a death. Bev and I have joined a memorial society, which ensures that when we die, our funeral expenses will be kept to a minimum.

The service is for the mourners

A memorial service or a funeral should give us an opportunity to acknowledge our grief and our pain. It's a time when we shed our tears openly and we ask God to be with us in our sorrow. But it should also be a service of thanksgiving. We need to thank God for the life that was lived and then say goodbye to a friend or loved one.

It's easy to forget about the children. They also have a need to say goodbye to someone they cared about. I don't think they should be shielded from the grief that surrounds a death, and they certainly shouldn't be told little white lies to make the pain easier. Let the children grieve too.

Bev and I attended a wonderful memorial service for a woman who had been very active in working with children in her church. Not only were several dozen children present, but one of the ministers took the time to sit down with the children during the service, to tell them what had happened to their friend, and to give them a special message which their friend had sent them just before she died.

Some United Churches have had a very significant role to play in funerals and pastoral care for people who have died of HIV/AIDS. Often the persons (most often men), whose partners have died of AIDS, go to the United Church for support after they have been rejected by their own denomination.

I'm always a bit upset when there is no service of any kind to celebrate the life of someone I cared about. I see it often in the newspapers. "No service, at the request of the deceased." But the funeral or memorial service isn't for the person who died. It is for those of us who are left behind. We need a way, for both psychological and faith reasons, to be able to get together and share our sadness and to do the kind of grief work that human beings must do at such times.

Many congregations have a special service a week or so before Christmas. Some call it "Blue Christmas," while others call it, "The Longest Night," and some simply call it a "Service of Remembering." Christmas can be a very difficult time for people who have recently lost someone close to them. It's also for those who are dreading another Christmas alone. This service, if it is sensitive to such needs, provides a way to express some of the grief we feel, anger sometimes too, during a season when everyone is promoting joy, happiness, and family warmth.

The year Bev and I lost our son Lloyd, we found that service deeply moving and helpful. We go every year to remember his life, and often the life of a friend we'll be missing that year. And we go, to stand beside others who bring pain into their Christmas.

Celebrating the pilgrimage

Other events in the journey from birth through death can and should be celebrated in church. Some congregations have ceremonies to celebrate a youngster moving from childhood to adulthood, usually on the 12th or 13th birthday. This is a gift from the Jewish tradition of the bar and bat mitzvah.

Bev and I had a service of rededication on our 25th wedding anniversary. Some congregations have an annual rededication service near February 14, Valentine's Day. Occasionally people even come to mourn the death of a marriage when they face divorce.

The word "celebrate" has a unique meaning in the church. We mean much more than a party. It means to mark an occasion, to make it memorable, and most of all, to see the hand of God in it. So we celebrate birth and death, coming together and going away.

Matchmaking

When the church is really being the church, it becomes a kind of adopted family. Not long ago, I had a conversation with a middle-aged woman who talked of "baby hunger." Her children were all grown, and although there were grandchildren, they lived on the other side of the continent. She needed children to nurture and to love – children who could sit on her lap.

I told her about the time when our children were young, a woman from the church became their "honorary" Aunt Frances. All our relatives lived far away, and the children needed such a relationship, as did Frances. In some churches there's a conscious effort to do some creative "matchmaking." Older persons without children nearby become honorary grandparents to children whose biological grandparents are far away or who are separated by the strains of a divorce.

People going through separation and divorce need emotional support too, and that can happen if the "matchmaker" puts them in touch with someone who's been through it. New people in the community are partnered with people of similar interests. You can easily think of many other creative matches.

It takes effort, but when the church becomes a caring community that works at meeting the social and spiritual needs of its people, the Holy Spirit has a chance to work and lives are enriched.

Like rafts careening down a mountain torrent, those working their way through grief are often swept along by forces much greater than themselves. But though a raft cannot control the stream, it can take occasional corrective actions. Sometimes only a slight course adjustment enables it to avoid foundering on rocks, to evade being crushed against canyon walls.

In surviving the death that has occurred in your life, you can simply allow yourself to be swept along helplessly. Or you can make a few small but crucial choices that affect your direction. And when the torrent does eventually emerge from the canyon, when it slows down into a regular river again, you may find that you are, in fact, a better person.

James Taylor – from *Letters to Stephen:*
A Father's Journey of Grief and Recovery (Northstone, 1996)

6

Telling the New – Old Story

The Spirit of the Lord is upon me, because he has anointed me to bring good news to the poor. He has sent me to proclaim release to the captives and recovery of sight to the blind, to let the oppressed go free, to proclaim the year of the Lord's favor.

Luke 4:18–19

Stuart Daly was one of the busiest doctors in the small city of Trail, BC. I have no idea whether he was the best doctor or whether he saw more patients. But I am willing to bet he spent more time with each patient than almost any other medic.

Dr. Daly cared very deeply about people, even those he had never met before. I'd heard about him, so when Bev and I had the flu, we called him. Dr. Daly loved house calls.

After a couple of needles in our backsides, he sat on the edge of the bed and talked for half an hour.

That wasn't unusual, we soon found out. We heard from others that after bringing news of a loved-one's death, he might stay for hours, sometimes all night, to help them through the pain of grief.

Dr. Daly would never force his faith on anyone. If you asked him a question, you got a straight answer. Otherwise, his faith was expressed more by his actions than by his words.

And he certainly wasn't short of words. Dr. Daly was very articulate about his faith and he enjoyed talking about it. But he felt the life you led communicated far more than the words you spoke, and unless your faith made a big difference to every part of your living, the words were empty.

I'm not saying you go around doing nice things, hoping somebody will notice and be sufficiently impressed so they'll hold still while you bend their ear. Dr. Daly helped people because he liked them and cared about them, whether they ever knew he was a Christian or not.

When I think of what the United Church means by words like "Mission," "Evangelism," and "Ministry," I always think of Dr. Stuart Daly.

Evangelistic styles

When we were living in the Philippines, we got to know missionaries from other denominations. One couple, from a small American group, seemed to live particularly well. They had a lovely house, a big car, and a warehouse full of rich food imported from the U.S. These people spent at least three-quarters of their time writing letters home to raise money for their "work" in the Philippines.

Not far away, another missionary couple lived very poorly. They didn't really have enough and what they did have they kept giving away. They didn't have much time to write those money-raising letters because they were too busy helping people.

Those two styles of mission are evident here in Canada as well. We can see them on a larger scale in the way different organizations and groups reach out to others.

Some religious organizations do a very clever job of selling. They use the same sales techniques as other kinds of advertisers, spending millions to run TV specials. They develop extensive mailing lists and send out glossy brochures. The cost in money and personnel is fantastic.

At the local level, there's a high proportion of time and energy spent in telling themselves what wonderful things they are accomplishing and that they are doing all these things because they are Christian.

The United Church seems to be at the other end of the spectrum. As individuals, you hardly ever hear a peep out of us concerning our faith. We're often too timid to point to the hand of God active in life around us. We're often too embarrassed to raise the subject of faith, so we miss many opportunities to share the good news. United Church people are not good at talking about the things that make them tick.

On the other hand, we're reasonably good at *doing* the Word, at living our faith. The United Church record of working with people nobody else cares about, or going to bat for the underdog, is certainly better than most. For instance, it's no accident that so many food banks and thrift shops are located in, or supported by, United Churches.

Doing and telling

I wish we could learn to tell stories – to talk openly about what we believe and why we believe it. There are some in the United Church who insist it's best to work for God's *Shalom*, to do God's will, and to struggle for truth and justice. Sooner or later people will realize why they are doing these things and will start to ask questions.

It's a good theory, but I don't think it works. I'm not suggesting that we start bragging about what we do, but I think we need to talk about what we believe and why. We can do that with honesty, integrity, and good taste. United Church people often don't know how to talk about their faith, and that is a serious problem. How can our church grow (or even survive) unless we can tell others why we've become involved?

Jesus challenged us not to "hide your light." Our faith stories can be told with gentleness and integrity. We can talk about what we do and why we do it without backing people into a corner or insulting their intelligence. It takes a bit more skill but it can and should be done. Yes, I know some people have sold religion like an underarm deodorant designed to make you acceptable and popular. A genuine faith is not communicated that way.

One to one

The oldest and still the best way to communicate our faith is also the simplest. We talk about our faith the same way and in the same places we talk about everything else. The "front lines" of faith are at home over dinner, driving in the car, over coffee at work, in the aisle at the supermarket, or on the golf course.

There's absolutely nothing more important than telling the story of faith in these everyday places. That's how the gospel spread in the first place and that will always be its most effective communication. No church service, no rally, no television program, no book, no plan or program is as important as this. Yet, in the United Church, that's the kind of communicating we do least well.

Sometimes we use the clergy as a convenient cop-out. We think that, since we "hired" our ministers to talk about religion, all we have to do is pay their salary and the job is done.

In a congregation near us where we sometimes worship, they have a bunch of tiny tots I affectionately call "the rug rats." They worship in that congregation because a few of the parents talked about their church at the local nursery school. They didn't grab other parents by the collar and say, "You gotta come to our church, see!" They were enthusiastic about their church so it came up naturally in their conversation.

One of my favorite parts of the worship service is coffee or tea afterwards. For me, the service isn't over until I follow the smell of coffee and sincerely ask a few people "How are you?" And some of them ask me the same question with the same sincerity. And I like coffee time because I get to exchange a bad joke with John and give Ray a bad time about his ties.

Coffee time after church gives us an opportunity to practice what we preach. It's one of the times we learn how to ask genuinely caring questions. These caring questions open the door to the two-way sharing of faith.

The caring community

Most of us have had the experience of meeting someone and saying "Hi, George. How are things?" You see a moment of hesitation, a flicker of pain behind his eyes, before he says, "Oh fine, fine." You know something is bothering George and you find it a bit embarrassing. So you tell yourself that George doesn't want to talk about whatever is troubling him. It's best to talk about the weather.

But isn't there something we could say or do that would at least let George know we'd be willing to share his pain if that's what he'd like?

There is. Not long ago, I ran into a friend at the airport. I had heard about some really heavy problems in his life. So I gave him an extra long hug. "How about a cup of coffee?" I suggested. After a bit of small talk, he said, "You know, don't you? I could tell by the way you hugged me."

I don't usually know what to say to people when I realize they're hurting. It's taken me many years to free myself up enough to give hugs or take someone's hand, rather than always dishing out unwanted advice. Knowing how to say or do the appropriate thing comes naturally to some. Most of us have to consciously expose ourselves to situations where we can learn. I learned how to hug by being hugged when I was hurting.

Which is not to say we should go around hugging anybody who stands still for a moment. Indiscriminate hugging is offensive, and it can be interpreted as a sexual overture. It never hurts to ask if a hug would be welcome. We learn what's helpful and appropriate in hugging, listening, hand-holding, and helping by being together and learning in small groups. These might be Bible study groups, social issue groups, marriage enrichment or personal growth groups, Christian lifestyle groups, and many other kinds of gatherings.

In these groups, people share their own lives and listen to the stories others tell. They learn how to connect those stories with the story, the story of a loving, creating God who acts in our lives. Some people expect God to speak to them through a lightning bolt, or a loudspeaker in the sky, or a particularly vivid dream. But God most often chooses to speak to us through the life or the voice or the caring of someone we know.

Small groups have helped thousands of us discover how to be more sensitive and open in the hundreds of interactions we have each day at work, at home, and at the shopping center. It's in those conversations that the Word of God is most effectively communicated.

That's evangelism. It's not the only kind, but it's certainly the most effective. Christianity spread around the world, not because we sent out professionals, but because ordinary people like you and me lived and talked about their faith in the ordinary places where they worked and played.

Words and jargon

You are an evangelist when you help another person move closer to God. It may involve holding a hand or listening to a story. It may mean fighting the injustice that holds people down. It may be telling a simple story from our own life's journey.

It doesn't mean using all sorts of religious words or jargon. It doesn't need the high-sounding theological language of traditional liturgy or the equally structured "Jesus talk" of the fundamentalist. It needs the kind of talking Jesus did: simple, everyday, ordinary language, often without any religious words at all. Check the stories Jesus told in the Bible, especially in Matthew, Mark, and Luke, to see what I mean. His stories are simple, short, and beautiful.

God often communicates without the use of any language at all. I've experienced that in the caring hand of someone who reached out and touched my life. That's why it is so desperately important that all of us in our congregations really live out the concept of the caring community. When we express our love and caring for another person, we are (as we say to the children) "being God's helpers." That's evangelism.

A minority group

I'm a member of the United Church because I believe that the people in my denomination hear the call of God clearly and respond with integrity (for the most part). That's not a put-down of anyone else. But if I felt it was happening more often or more faithfully in another faith community, I would join them.

Since I do have those feelings about the United Church, I need to share them with others. But, in order to do that effectively, I've got to realize that I'm swimming upstream.

Christianity is no longer the standard by which society operates. I doubt if it ever really was. Active, involved Christians are now a minority group. And the United Church, even though it's still one of the largest Protestant denominations in Canada, is no longer the "establishment" church. We are a splinter group on the edges of society. We have no built-in credibility. But that's not all bad.

Digging out the answers

If being Christian no longer offers us status, or business connections, or social prestige, then we have some tough questions to ask. Why do I want to be part of this church anyway? There's no social or financial advantage. People will not think less of me if I don't belong. In fact, the reverse is probably true. So why do we have churches and why would I want to belong?

When you start working through those kinds of issues, you're starting to ask questions about what the church's mission really is. Is it to build a more beautiful building than the denomination down the street? Is it to pay off the mortgage? Is it to keep the kids off the street? Is it there to help me get away from the cares and worries of the world? To find comfort and friendship? To help me feel good? To bring me personal salvation? Life after death? Is it a base camp from which to take a run at the world's problems?

Is it all of the above? Or none? What is a church for anyway?

Sometimes, congregations decide to take a serious look at those questions. They organize a series of study sessions, hold a weekend retreat, or bring in a facilitator to help them look at who they are and who they want to become. That can result in something called a "mission statement," an expression of what a congregation is really about. It's a good way to correct the drift that happens when you just go along without ever asking, "Where are we going? And why?"

It doesn't hurt to do this at the personal level as well. For me, the church provides a way of finding meaning in a life that often seems to offer very little of purpose and worth. In the church, I've gradually come to realize that God does love me, that I can see this love lived out in the life of Jesus Christ, and that the caring people of the church can give me a sense of community and strength.

Like most United Church people I came looking for help. But, having received help, I want to return the favor. I want to help others.

Different approaches

Many congregations in the United Church become innovative and develop exciting programs and mission work that makes sense in their area. In hundreds of United Church congregations across Canada, people are involved in the Meals on Wheels program. They take a hot dinner to people, many of them senior citizens, who can't cook for themselves. Some work to support women's shelters, or halfway houses for people who have been in jail. Bev and some friends retrieve polyester pants from the thrift shop. These pants can't be recycled, so they turn them into quilted blankets, which they give to halfway houses.

Hundreds of congregations offer nursery school facilities and many include daycare. A few offer programs where youngsters who might otherwise be "latchkey kids" can go to the church at lunch time and before or after school.

Many people get involved in moral and social issues that our society has never considered before: family violence, sexism, racism, homophobia, ecology, Native issues, militarism, Third-World justice, AIDS, urban development, agricultural land use, and other questions that will determine the kind of life we'll have on this planet.

But the church is not just another advocacy group. We bring a very particular perspective. In the ecological movement, for instance, many groups and individuals talk about saving the ecosystem. The church has a very special answer to the question, "Why should we be doing this?" Some very fine theologians have wondered if, in some mysterious and holy way, the universe is God's body. When we defile this planet with our greed, we defile the body of God!

Christian perspectives get translated into action, and church groups (and Christians as individuals) often get out there to try to solve some of the problems.

Some big city congregations reach out to help people on skid row; the "hookers" and the "winos." Jesus did the same kind of thing.

Some, like my home congregation, run a thrift shop where secondhand clothes are recycled. It's not only good ecology, it provides a place where all of us can find inexpensive clothing for ourselves and our kids. And, in the process, we raise money to help others in our town and overseas. Our United Church Women regularly give money to a variety of causes, both in the church and outside of it.

As I write this, church people of many denominations are deeply involved in helping Kosovo refugees find a place here in Canada, and sending money to help earthquake victims in Turkey.

Many people do their Christian worship and work outside the church. The most respected politician in our city is a man who struggles hard with questions of ethics, morality, and justice. His concerns come directly out of his Christian convictions, though he doesn't say this when sitting around the council table. And he's in church every Sunday because, as he said in the men's group one day, "it gives me a basis on which I can think clearly about what is right and what is wrong."

There's a tendency in some congregations to imply that the only way you can live your faith is to serve on a bunch of committees. That's a good way of doing it for some people. It's not for me, nor for many others. But it's through the church that I find out where God is leading me.

The national church

Many churches work together through their presbyteries or conferences and at the national level on a fantastic variety of mission programs.

There are mission hospitals in remote areas of BC and one in Alberta. There are chaplaincy programs, colleges, and training centers. In Manitoba, there's help for Native people trying to get a fair shake. The Fred Victor Mission in Toronto and First United in Vancouver help people who find themselves on the street. And that's to name just a very few.

Like every other institution, the United Church has been deeply affected by budget cuts. There seems to be a strong trend to see the work of the church as local. "Your mission field is right outside your front door!" some leaders are saying. As we focus our attention on local mission, and as our giving moves more and more to the local congregation, the national or regional church is less and less able to take an active role in social change. More and more, the national and regional offices of the church are focusing on administration rather than on mission. That may be inevitable, but I deeply regret it.

But even with all the cutbacks, the United Church spends a great deal of money helping people in need. Some of the money goes to find out why that need exists so that root causes can be corrected.

The first part is easier and more popular than the second. Nobody can argue with helping a child in trouble. But when we start to ask questions like, "Why is that child in trouble?" we may get some answers that make us squirm.

We may find the child is in trouble because of boozing parents and suggest that part of the problem is liquor advertising. Is that child's father a failed athlete, who watches beer ads during a hockey game on TV, ads that imply he can be a real jock if he drinks enough beer? What happens to the child at the end of the game when daddy is tanked up and frustrated?

Various church leaders, nationally and locally, have had tough things to say about what comes across through the mass media. Some of us are upset at the commercial advertising that is invading the schools. That's when we run into flack from business and government. When it might cut into somebody's profit, people often tell the United Church to back off. It seems that everyone is in favor of social justice as long as somebody else picks up the tab.

Deeper answers

The problems we face on the local scene tend to have their counterparts on the international scene.

When Bev and I were sent to the Philippines in 1961, we worked for the Filipino church. My job was to help develop a radio station that could tell people about new techniques of food production, family health care, and cottage crafts. It didn't take us long to realize the problem was far deeper than a lack of skills. The whole system of international trade was causing the basic problem.

For instance, one of the cottage industries we tried to help was wood carving, something Filipinos are famous for. But it seemed that no matter how hard they worked, or how well they did the job, the woodcarvers always wound up with the same little bit of money in their pockets; just enough to stay barely alive.

When we came back to Canada from the Philippines, I saw one of those carvings in a department store selling for $35. That same carving sold in the markets of Manila for 5 pesos, about $1.25 Canadian, at that time. But the person who put about a week of hard work into the carving got one peso (25 cents). Everyone made a good profit in the system, except the one who did most of the work and needed the money the most.

You don't have to spend much time studying the facts of international development before you come to a couple of very fundamental conclusions. One is that the gap between the rich and the poor is getting wider. We are getting richer. They are getting poorer.

The second is that it really doesn't matter how much aid we send overseas, nothing is really going to change until we rework a system that stacks the whole world's economic deck in our favor. That means we've got to keep ourselves informed through careful and critical reading of the news media, and if possible, through alternative media that are not as closely tied to the commercial system.

TV or not TV

Plenty of United Church people support mission and evangelism projects promoted by other agencies. They respond quickly to TV fund-raising spectaculars and slick promotional techniques, especially when someone shows the pleading eyes of a dying child. When the announcer assures us that all our money goes to the child – hardly any goes to administration – we're hooked.

Who paid for the television program? It costs millions for production and air-time. Why didn't that money go to the child? And why is the child starving in the first place?

Church people think with their hearts. That's good. But we need to think with our heads too, or we're an easy mark for any promoter with a good story.

The United Church is caught between a rock and a hard place. On the one hand, people who try to tell the story of the church's outreach don't want to play on our emotions. On the other hand, few of us really respond to facts. We respond to people. We respond with our emotions, whether we admit that or not.

My personal view is that the United Church leans a bit more to facts and figures than it should, that more "people stories" could be told. But that's a judgment call.

I do think that if more United Church people *really* understood, they'd be willing to invest in the less glamorous but longer lasting attempts at solutions undertaken by our Division of World Outreach and by the Division of Mission in Canada.

Biblical politics

It's hard explaining why church people get involved in things that sound more political or economic than religious. Shouldn't they stick with spiritual matters and leave politics and economics to people who know something about that?

Absolutely. Except that politics and economics are very spiritual matters. Read the Bible. It's full of politics. Jesus is constantly talking about money. "Where your treasure is, there will your heart be also," he says. Where you spend your money indicates what you think is most important. And whatever you think is most important is your religion. If you want to find out what my religion *really* is, look at my cheque book. There is a sense in which everything we do, and everything we *don't* do, is political.

Many of the leaders involved in social justice issues within the United Church haven't explained clearly enough how their work springs from their study of the Bible. It is solidly grounded in their Christian faith, but that connection hasn't been spelled out in a way that the average person can understand. And, unfortunately, many of us in the pews don't make much effort to meet them halfway.

In fact, the United Church has always had a problem communicating with its people about mission and evangelistic outreach programs. Part of that is caused by the structure of the church. We try so hard to include everyone, that it discourages high-profile people from doing a bit of creative drum beating for a particular program or point of view. We're suspicious of statements that aren't checked through several committees, where all the strong ideas are watered down. These committee statements are often dull, bloodless, and hardly ever move people into action. People tend to catch hold of ideas when they are communicated by passionate individuals, even though those with the passion tend to speak from a very personal point of view.

The printed word

One way the story of the church's mission and evangelism effort is told is through *Mandate*, a magazine published at the church offices in Toronto. It's good reading and probably the best way to keep in touch with what's happening in the church's outreach.

Mandate is available by subscription and it's sent to the clergy and other leaders in the congregation. It's a good magazine, but it doesn't get into the hands of church members as much as it should.

The United Church Observer brings us news of what the church is doing and saying in its mission and evangelistic work. And you can order materials about the "Ten Days for Global Justice" that are very helpful in understanding the mission of the United Church of Canada.

One of the most widely read publications in the United Church is the Sunday bulletin. These bulletins, produced by the Stewardship Department, do an excellent job of telling the story, and they often have a direct connection to the Sunday sermon. I almost always find a couple of minutes, after I settle down in the pew, to give it a read. And each Sunday in church, someone reads a "Minute for Mission" focusing on one of the Church's outreach programs.

Many people think Wood Lake Books (the publisher of this book) is a United Church publishing house. It's not. It's an independent business that has no formal connection with any denomination. But Wood Lake Books has a long history of cooperation with all the ecumenical denominations, and especially with the United Church.

What's more, the spiritual roots of the people at Wood Lake Books are very much in the United Church and that shows in what they do. They've published more United Church authors in the last ten years than any other publisher. Check out some of the suggested readings at the end of this book.

The Web

There's great interest among many church people about the possibilities of the Internet. Many congregations have their own home page that gives information about their church. Some conferences and presbyteries are on line, as is the national United Church. The address is: www.united-church.ca. That connection will provide you with all kinds of interesting links to the various parts of the church.

Another link you'll want to explore is the Wood Lake Books site, www.woodlakebooks.com. It will bring you up-to-date on the activities of this lively publishing company.

There are some who feel that the future of the church may be electronic – that we'll eventually stop coming together in congregations and do all of that online. Similar predictions were made when radio first came along, and for television too. It didn't happen then, and I don't think it will happen with the Internet. In fact, "online church" may be an oxymoron – a self-contradicting term. To me, a church is a church only when "two or three are gathered" (to quote Jesus) and when they can look into each other's eyes, and offer hands and hugs when needed.

Which is not to say that some really interesting things won't happen on-line. They are worth checking out. And within the next few years, every congregation (even the really small ones) will have an Internet connection because more and more resources and information are becoming available there.

The spiritual energy crisis

Still, too much of the story is left untold. At the national level, evangelism is way down on the priority list, and that (I'm convinced) is one of the reasons we are a church in trouble.

We can't rely on the secular news media to tell our story. The media rely on hard news – news that almost by definition involves conflict. Somebody must say something that someone else disagrees with. And there must be a strong personality who can be featured in a video clip or a sound bite or quoted in the paper.

Most church news is soft news – about trying for consensus, talking things through until we have agreement, studying issues carefully before we vote on them. So these changes happen over time, and it's hard to say exactly when things changed. But they do. Historians notice, but news reporters don't.

Many more United Church people are living courageous, faith-filled lives in the daily grind of suburban living. These stories lie buried in our lives, waiting to be mined, like gold. It's our greatest natural resource and the answer to our spiritual energy crisis.

My own sudden yearning – it's almost an ache within me – for this contemplative picture makes me believe that there is room for a church more mystical than the one we have now. Such a church would be capable of calling home to it those young people who are carefully mapping and guarding ancient trees, or handing out information about global warming.

Such a church would cherish those times when its members break the artificial boundaries (sometimes created by Christianity itself) between humans and nature. This is a church that could shelter environmentalists and poets, because, as a body, it would cherish the earth and mystery. It would feed the spiritual hunger of the age.

Donna Sinclair – from *Jacob's Blessing* (Wood Lake Books, 1999)

7

Reverend Sir or Madam

—

We have gifts that differ according to the grace given to us.
Romans 12:6

Tom was cutting up a bit as he handed out the bulletins on Sunday morning at our church.

"Programs! Programs!" he started calling in a twangy nasal singsong. "You can't tell who's the preacher without a program. Programs! Get yer programs!" And a few newcomers wondered if they had stumbled into a football game instead of a church service.

Actually, Tom was on to something. In the United Church it can sometimes be hard to tell who is clergy and who isn't. It gets even harder when you try to tell an outsider the differences between an ordained minister, a diaconal minister, a lay pastoral minister, and a layperson. Not to mention staff associates.

So hang on to your hats.

When is a minister a minister?

One of the things we need in this denomination is a lesson in down-to-earth language. We have problems with the words "minister" and "ministry." The average person in the pew knows what the words *do* mean, but our church leaders keep trying to tell us what they *ought* to mean. Any linguist knows that words mean what they mean to a group of people and the only thing you'll get trying to change that is heartburn.

Most of us would say that a "minister" is the person who does the preaching, the baptizing, the burying, the hospital visiting. The work this person does is "ministry." Simple.

But there are many laypeople in the church who have been saying, "Hey! Most of what the ministers do is what we do: caring about people; trying to bring a bit of justice and love into the world; spreading the Good News. Clergy may do that professionally in the church, but many of us are doing it out there in hard-knock country. It's no easier."

Our church doesn't like putting people in order of rank. The "ministry" I have as a layperson is officially considered by the church to be just as important and significant as that of an ordained minister. Officially. There are various things in the structure and rules of the church that show the United Church doesn't really believe this "official" word. Very few people, laypeople or clergy, act as if it were true. But it's a nice thought.

We all feel better when we call what laypeople do "ministry." And it's probably right. But it has only succeeded in fuzzifying things for everybody except the professionals. So I'm going to stick to the popular use of the word. When I say "minister," I mean the people who sometimes wear their collars backward. And I include in that category diaconal ministers, lay ministers, staff associates, and the assorted other categories of folk who work professionally in congregations. Or to use the jargon, "people in paid accountable ministry."

The good, the bad, and the so-so

The United Church doesn't like saying that clergy are better or holier than the rest of us. That's just as well because they aren't. I probably know as many clergy (from many different denominations) as any layperson, to say nothing of being married to one. They come in as many varieties, sizes, degrees of goodness and badness, levels of intelligence, and styles of Christian commitment as do laypeople.

Every minister knows this and many laypeople know it too. But there are some, often those who don't know "The Rev" very well, who expect the clergy to be hovering six inches off the ground. They think clergy should be well above all the problems and temptations that plague those of us who are mere mortals.

I actually had one guy at a service club wonder out loud how it was that a female minister (in this instance, my wife, Bev) could get pregnant!

Few people are that naïve, but we often lay a pretty heavy trip on the clergy. Those who try to live up to this "heavenly calling" either spend most of their life play-acting or wind up in a psych ward.

Most clergy I know try to live decent, moral lives the same way other Christians try. They are bothered by the double standards of folk who think some behavior is okay for others, but not for clergy. If some behavior is "wrong," it's just as wrong for the person who visits the back pew once a year as it is for the minister.

Clergy don't necessarily "succeed" any better at personal morality, family happiness, successful financial management, and all the other things our society tells us are important. What most of the clergy do have is a strong faith. They have roots in the Christian community that help them deal with these problems more creatively. And they have an education that helps them see the ethical and social issues in our society. But you don't have to be ordained to have that.

Zero tolerance

No matter how you slice it, clergy have a lot of influence and sometimes power in the congregation and in the community. They are looked up to and trusted. Which is good, except that there have been a few (very few) who have abused that trust and taken advantage of people. Not too long ago, we swept these situations under the rug. Now we try to bring them out in the open and deal with them, but because we ignored them for so long, there's a backlog of cases. And at this point in our life as a church, we are spending a huge amount of time, energy, and money trying to resolve what we should have dealt with years ago.

Now the United Church has zero tolerance around sexual abuse by church leaders, whether these be clergy or lay. We're encouraged to blow the whistle, quickly and hard. If you have such a concern and don't know where else to go with it, phone the Executive Secretary of your conference. A list of the conference offices, their phone numbers and addresses, is on page 222 of this book.

Ordination and Commissioning

What sets clergy apart in the life of the church is their training for a particular kind of work. No, that's not really the heart of it, because a layperson could have the same training. Some laypeople do.

It's ordination, the laying on of hands by a conference of the United Church, and dedicating the person to a life-time vocation in the ministry. There's also "commissioning," for diaconal ministers, which is very similar.

I don't like that last paragraph because it has too much jargon in it. But I don't think I can unravel it much because for years the United Church has been wrestling with the question of what, specifically, an ordained minister is. And what a diaconal minister really is. And how are they different from laypeople? And the church is still at it, with yet another set of ideas and proposals being circulated. If you want to get a good argument going, just ask that question when you have a batch of clergy together at a party. They'll be at it all night.

While it isn't clear exactly what a minister is, we can at least talk about what a minister *does.* Not that it's easy. Often other professionals working in congregations do the same kinds of things. Aside from being a "professional staff person" in a congregation, there are only a few things that clergy can do which laypeople can't. Except under special license, only *ordained* clergy or licensed Lay Pastoral Ministers can officiate at baptisms, communion, and weddings.

That license is almost routinely given to diaconal ministers. The diaconal ministry was originally intended to focus on social justice work, on education, on pastoral care. It didn't work out that way. Now more and more diaconal ministers are doing exactly what ordained ministers are doing, even though the ordained ministers have more years, and a different kind, of training.

Lay and clergy

Laypeople can lead in worship and preach. They can even conduct funerals. Whether they have the *skills* to do these things is, of course, another question. I'm a layperson. I often lead worship and preach when clergy in our area are sick or away. But I don't have most of the skills and training to do the kind of *pastoral* work a congregation needs. I am not qualified in the ordained ministry.

Many congregations employ laypeople to do Christian education and other kinds of work. They may be full-time and salaried. Some are called staff associates. Many of our overseas missionaries are laypeople. A high proportion of the staff in conference and General Council offices are laypeople. In addition, there are laypeople like myself who are not employed by the church, but who are in full-time Christian work.

To confuse the issue a bit more, there are clergy who don't work in congregations. They work in hospitals, prisons, or university chaplaincies; they teach at theological schools. Some do administrative work in national and conference offices.

So what's the difference? When it's possible for two people to be in identical jobs but one is a "Rev" and the other isn't, it gets so you really can't tell the preachers without a program.

As far as I can tell, the basic difference is that clergy, ordained and commissioned, are "in orders." In theory at least, the presbytery is like a bishop and can "order" ordained and commissioned persons where and how to do their ministry. But, like the power of bishops in other denominations, presbytery's power to give orders to its clergy gets less every year. In actual fact, while the clergy are "in orders," there are few, if any, orders given, except in situations where a real problem has developed.

Lay ministers

There's another group of pastors who are often ignored. These are women and men who have some training, lots of dedication and a willingness to serve small, usually rural congregations. They are called "lay pastoral ministers," and do just about everything regular clergy normally do. Some work for little or no pay. They are not "ordered" clergy. But in a sense they are under a tougher discipline than ordained or commissioned ministers because their license has to be renewed every year or two by presbytery.

I'm not much into predictions, but I think we will see more and more laypeople becoming involved in ministry. Small congregations often can't afford professional ministers, a situation that I think will increase. We may become more and more like the early church, when there was very little church structure and people met in homes to eat together, to pray, and to share their joys and struggles. These groups had leaders, but they were not paid by anyone. They simply did this because they felt called into this kind of ministry.

As the power of the national and regional church decreases, and as the church becomes more and more a minority group within the larger culture, we may see more of these kinds of "house churches" run by lay leaders.

If you're now thoroughly confused about what a minister is, then welcome to the club. You understand the matter about as well as anyone. So let's move on to what it is these church professionals do.

The staff team

There's an important church vocation that's often overlooked – the secretary. A good secretary can be as important to the functioning of the church as the minister. The secretary generally knows who's who, what's what, where's which, and why things are done the way they are. Or aren't.

The minister, by the way, is not supposed to double as church secretary. The congregation is required to provide "adequate secretarial support." Ministers don't generally do that kind of thing very well anyway. Some congregations (especially the larger ones) have an administrator on staff – someone who looks after all the nuts and bolts of running a congregation.

Caretakers are also important members of the staff team. Whether full-time staff or volunteers, they are key people in the operation of the church. Caretakers make a very substantial contribution to the atmosphere of a church, and that is important. They not only need to know how to keep the church clean, but they need people skills. They relate to the many volunteers and folks from outside organizations who use the church.

Some large congregations have full-time musicians who conduct the choir or do the "organizing." Or both. In many congregations, this is a volunteer position, though some get a small honorarium.

The organist or music director (this could be one or two people) is a key person in the planning of the Sunday morning service. If the music leader and the minister are going off in different directions, the service becomes a hodgepodge and the music becomes a performance, rather than a contribution to worship.

A day in the life of the "Rev"

Many of us laypeople have very little idea what goes into a minister's week. We go to church on Sunday morning and often assume that getting the worship service ready is all the minister really does.

Certainly, preparing the service takes hard and creative work. Even though I've had a ringside seat (being married to a minister), I didn't realize how hard it was until I acted as a stand-in for a congregation without a minister for about seven months. It was great for the first couple of weeks. But it wasn't long before I heard the sound of my own fingernails scraping the bottom of the idea barrel. Let me tell you, preparing that service week after week, especially the sermon, is hard, hard work!

How long to write a sermon

As a professional writer, my opinion is that a good sermon takes at least three full days to write. But I've never yet met a minister who could set aside that kind of time. Correction. I know of one very large church where they have a staff of several clergy, one of whom does nothing much except preach. That's a very rare exception.

"So, except for yakking for an hour on Sunday, what else does a minister do?" I heard that comment a few years ago, and came close to being charged with assault.

Many clergy work hard at administration, keeping the organization functioning. They become the chief executive officer of the congregation, particularly if it's a large one. That may involve endless meetings. I've sometimes wondered why more congregations don't hire an administrator and leave clergy to do the work they're trained for.

Many clergy also lead study groups. They can't just come into those groups cold. Preparation usually takes longer than the meeting time.

Pastoral work can and should take up a large slice of the minister's time. That includes visiting people who are in the hospital, calling on people who can't get out, visiting new families, getting in touch with families who are having trouble, and even sitting patiently while someone on the telephone chews their ear over a real or imagined slight.

More often, it means people coming to the minister's office looking for help with a personal problem. Most of us have no idea how often the phone rings in the minister's office or home. People dream up some trivial reason for phoning and wind up unburdening themselves about a problem.

"What took you so long?" I demanded of Bev several years ago when she was still in active ministry. She'd gone to get the mail. That should take five minutes. Then I noticed that she looked rather pale and shaken. She had spent the time with a man who had, quite literally, wiped the remains of his best friend off the floor after a shotgun suicide.

That's not an unusual story.

A kind, informed friend

I have a strong impression that more and more people are going to clergy for help. It may be part of a general recognition that the problems we encounter in life are physical, psychological, social and spiritual, all woven together. Or it may just be that the price is right – usually nothing at all.

But clergy don't have the time, and often not the training, to do in-depth counseling. Wise clergy quickly refer people to medical or counseling pros. I've personally gone to medical doctors, psychiatrists, and clergy for help and advice. Clergy have been most helpful when they've been a kind, informed friend.

Another big item in the clergy time budget relates to the many groups active within the congregation, including the Sunday school, the midweek youth and adult groups, and even some groups only marginally connected with the church.

Many ministers find themselves spending great amounts of time finding leaders, getting groups fixed up with the right kinds of materials, encouraging leaders when they feel discouraged and, hardest of all, figuring out how to ease someone out of a volunteer position without hurting their feelings.

Because the church operates mostly with volunteers, few ministers can demand anything. So they have to rely on tact, diplomacy, people's good will, and the grace of God. Especially the grace of God.

Doing all that involves meetings. Because most church people have daytime jobs, the meetings are in the evening. So the clergy often wind up spending their days at the office and their nights at meetings. It can be a killer.

On top of that are funerals, which seem to come at the most inconvenient times. Clergy usually take their pastoral work seriously, which may mean several visits to the grieving family, plus the funeral service itself. And they often do follow-up visits with those who are grieving. What most of us forget is that often, when the person who dies is a member of the congregation, the minister is also one of the mourners.

And then there are weddings, which involve at least one interview with the couple and probably several more pre-marital counseling sessions. And baptismal interviews, to make sure the parent(s) of the baby know what is involved. And hospital visits. And...

Back in the "good old days" ministers thought nothing of working a 60- to 70-hour week. They sacrificed their family and their health for the church. Most clergy don't want to do that anymore. They want a life the same way you and I do.

"Our former minister used to mow the lawn in summer and shovel snow in winter!" someone complained to the new minister. "I know," said the new minister. "I talked to your former minister on the phone. He doesn't want to do it anymore."

Community ministry

Many clergy feel that to have an effective ministry in a community, they should be involved in community work. So they run for the town council or school board or they become active in the Mental Health Association. It's also a good place to meet new people and to do some grassroots evangelism.

A number of years ago, I met a minister who was sent to a town where the church had died but hadn't been buried. "I join everything in sight and talk to everybody I meet. Maybe that way I'll make enough contacts so that we can breathe a bit of life back into the church." He called it "mouth-to-mouth resuscitation" for a dying church.

It can be very easy to overdo that kind of community involvement. And when you come right down to it, it's not the minister who represents the church in the community. It's you and I. The clergy can help us learn how to do that. But it's *our* job.

Clergy and presbytery

What's a presbytery? What does it eat and how often do you feed it? We'll get into that in Chapter 8, How We Decide.

For now, all you need to know is that the church is organized into congregations, presbyteries, and conferences. Newfoundland Conference has organized itself into two districts, east and west, and eliminated presbyteries. It's a pattern other conferences are looking at with great interest. When representatives of the whole national church get together, it is called the General Council.

Clergy *serve* a congregation, but are not *members* of a congregation. They are members of a presbytery. The presbytery and conference do a number of things on behalf of congregations that they couldn't do individually. In the United Church, the presbytery has the role that a bishop has in other denominations. The presbytery, technically, is the minister's boss, though in reality it doesn't get involved unless there's a serious problem in the minister's relationship with the congregation.

It's a legitimate part of a minister's job to do some work for these other groups in the church. It's not private volunteer work. When a congregation writes a minister's job description, they build in some time for presbytery and conference. Ministers are *required* to attend all meetings of presbytery as well as the annual meeting of conference. Some of them don't, but the rulebook (the *Manual*) says they should. It's part of their job.

Clergy need to get together with other clergy to talk shop, to exchange ideas, and to cry on each other's shoulders. Making sure that your minister has time to be involved with conference and presbytery activities is a good investment in professional health. You may get a different opinion from your minister. Some clergy feel presbytery and conference are a major *cause* of mental distress.

Occupational hazards

Some people expect the minister to know everybody and everything about anything that's going on in the church. Except in a very tiny congregation, that's not possible. Clergy who try to live up to that kind of expectation are probably not very effective. Besides, that's not their job.

It's the people of the congregation who are responsible for the life and work of the church. The minister is their resource person. It's not the other way around.

The minister ought to know, generally, what's going on. At least about the main activities. But it's a healthy thing for clergy to be quite clueless about who is locking up after the meeting or whether the phone bill got paid last month. Clergy should work hard at *not* knowing how to fix anything around the church. They should never know where anybody put anything. And they should make it a point to not know when and where all the meetings and events are taking place. I know what it's like trying to have a family dinner when the phone keeps ringing with folks calling to find out the when and where of events and meetings – information which was all there in the previous Sunday's bulletin.

A clergy friend grins when she tells me she is a "selective feminist. I don't even know where the furnace room is!"

But while wise clergy are very selective about what they admit to knowing, they *do not* enjoy being clueless about things like who is in the hospital or sick at home.

"Why didn't you come to see me when I was in the hospital?"

"I didn't know you were in the hospital. When you filled in the admission form, did you put yourself down as United Church?"

"No, I left that part blank."

"Then how was I supposed to know?"

"Well, I thought you'd just know."

The problem is a whole lot worse in some hospitals where the religion question isn't even asked. Then it becomes doubly important that someone phones the church office and leaves word. I've never met a minister or a church secretary that could read minds.

The care and feeding of clergy

Burnout and rustout are two occupational hazards for clergy. The people of the congregation have some responsibility to help the clergy avoid these problems.

Clergy are often their own worst enemies when it comes to burnout. They have a high sense of vocation. Some are just plain workaholics who think an 80-hour week is normal. Some have job descriptions which not even St. Paul would be able to manage.

Ministry and personnel committees in the congregation can help the minister learn to say "No." Sometimes they can take the message to the congregation that they didn't hire Superman or Wonder Woman. Occasionally, the committee may need to come down hard on clergy who have this kind of suicidal instinct.

Rustout is a more serious problem. It's also more subtle. It's what happens to clergy (and to you and me as well), when they don't pay attention to their own spiritual lives. In the same way that we all become physically run down if we don't pay attention to our diet and exercise, we become spiritually run down if we don't do those things that build spiritual muscles.

Clergy, of course, are specially trained in spiritual development. That's their vocation, and they often do a good job of counseling us laypeople in this necessary art. But they often don't practice what they preach. That's when they need others to minister to them.

Ministry is one of the toughest jobs going. Just dealing with the personalities in any congregation is a full-time job. Every congregation has these people, from the opinionated old-timer to the enthusiastic newcomer, from archconservatives to archliberals, from the very elderly to the very young, from single parents to extended families. Each of them wants the minister to meet their specific needs.

Clergy need to use their built-in safety valves, and we, as members of the congregation, need to make sure they do. A United Church minister is expected to take four weeks paid holiday and three weeks study leave each year. That's not up to the congregation to decide. That's in the rules. The Ministry and Personnel Committee should insist that both be used for their intended purpose.

Do your minister a favor. Ask, "What are you doing on your study leave this year?" Ask that question once a month from February through to June. If you get consistent waffling or some mumble about there not being time, take it up with your Ministry and Personnel Committee. It's their job to insist that holidays and study leave be used fully. Every year. And the congregation should pick up at least some of the cost of that study leave.

It's essential!

Holidays help the burnout. Study leave helps the rustout.

Coming and going

In the United Church, the minister is not "the boss" of a congregation. But neither is a congregation "the boss" of the minister, even though they pay the salary. The two are supposed to work together. But, if push comes to shove, it's important to know that the minister is placed in the congregation by the presbytery. Only the presbytery can hire and fire ministers.

There are special words for hiring and firing in the United Church. A minister is "called." And, when the minister leaves, for whatever reason, the presbytery "declares a vacancy."

Actually, the word "called" is used for a very good reason. When a minister comes to serve a congregation there is far more involved than simply making sure the qualifications match the salary and benefits. God is part of the process. The "call" comes not just from the congregation. It comes from God.

That call, by the way, is no excuse for expecting the minister to work for peanuts. The clergy are also professional people and should be paid as such.

When a congregation needs a minister, the first thing they do is get in touch with presbytery. The presbytery representative will then help the congregation go through a "needs assessment process" to find out what kind of a community they really are, and what kind of minister they really need. When that is complete, the congregation elects a Joint Pastoral Relations Committee, which can only meet when a presbytery representative is present. That's to protect the best interests of all concerned, including the congregation.

The presbytery representative can help the Pastoral Relations Committee find suitable clergy who are interested in a move and help match talents to needs. When the Pastoral Relations Committee has its selection down to one person, his or her name is presented to the whole congregation. Only one name can be presented.

If the vote is favorable, presbytery makes sure everything is in order, checking that both the minister and the congregation are getting a reasonable deal, and other bureaucratic stuff. That includes checking out the pay-scale. There's a minimum salary and housing schedule laid on by the General Council. A congregation can pay more, but not less. The congregation is also required to meet some minimum standards relating to continuing education, book allowances, and other benefits. It's the job of the presbytery representative to make sure the folks in the congregation understand the regulations.

A presbytery can – and sometimes does – say to a congregation, "Sorry folks. That's not a good match. Back to the drawing board!"

Usually, however, both congregation and presbytery agree on a person. The new clergy is then welcomed during a covenanting service in which both clergy and congregation recognize their responsibilities to each other and promise to work *together* in ministry to the congregation and community.

Matchmaking

Most clergy are sensitive enough to know when it's time to move on. There may come a time when pastor and people simply know each other too well and both need a stiff shot of new ideas and experiences. There's no minimum or maximum time a minister stays in a United Church congregation. Some, like former Moderator Walter Farquharson, stayed in the same community with good results for an entire career.

When a move *does* take place, it most often happens in the summertime. It's so much more convenient when all the clergy play "musical pulpits" at the same time of year. The first four weeks on the job are usually vacation time. It feels a bit strange to have a new minister arrive and then go on vacation right away. But that's the way it's done.

It points to a very basic idea. Congregations are not separate units existing in isolation. They are part of the whole United Church, and the clergy are called to serve that whole church. So, for the clergy, it's more like a company transfer.

Occasionally, a minister needs a bit of a nudge to move on, and a good friend in the congregation might be able to help. In fact, most problems of "pastoral relationships," the way clergy and congregation get along, can be dealt with informally. There are formal ways of dealing with problems, but if you get to that point, it usually means somebody's going to get hurt.

Sometimes the presbytery says to a congregation, "Hey, you get your act together before you can call another minister."

In these situations, an "interim minister" may be asked to come in for a while. It might be for a few weeks, but more often for a year – sometimes more.

Sometimes an interim minister is sent in because of the grief over a well-loved minister who has moved or retired or died. Until the congregation gets over that grief, a new minister has no chance of being accepted. An interim may be needed because it takes a little longer than expected to find a good match. It's not a slap on the wrist. An interim minister can be very useful and helpful to a congregation, and can make the transition to a new minister much easier.

Regardless of the reasons for a change in the staff, the presbytery should require a "needs assessment," a time for the congregation to take a serious look at who they are, and what their staff needs might be. Yes, there's a fair bit of work involved. But it's worth it.

All shapes and sizes

The United Church probably has more varieties of clergy than any other Canadian denomination. That's great! The problem is that many congregations, when considering a new minister, go for the "standard brand" and don't realize that a different style of clergy can be a breath of fresh air.

For instance, we have an increasing number of clergy couples in the United Church. Sometimes it gets to be a bit of a chess game to find an arrangement where they can both have congregations. Many opt to serve one church between them. It can be a very exciting arrangement because, often, the strength of one partner complements the weakness of the other.

I know one clergy couple where she is United Church and he is Anglican. I'm sure their life is very interesting.

Some congregations miss a real opportunity by not considering a woman minister. We have more women clergy than any other denomination in Canada. At least half the students training for the ordained ministry are women, which means that the time is coming when half our ordained clergy will be female. That's exactly the way it should be, because women are half the population. And certainly more than half of our active church members are women.

Still, women are discriminated against, often by people who have never experienced a female minister. For instance, there's the idea that men would find it difficult to come and talk to a woman minister. That's just not true. If anything, it's just the opposite. Men generally find it hard to talk to anyone about their deeper problems.

Some of us men find it easier to talk to a woman minister because we're not competing with her. Or perhaps it's because in our growing up we were often able to talk with our own mothers more easily than with our fathers. When we skinned our knees and bruised our noses, it was usually mom who kissed it better.

Besides, some women find it hard to come and talk to a male minister, but they've had to do it for years. Frankly, I think women often make better ministers than men. I think they have a deeper sense of what it means to be a pastor.

Of course, there are lots of other clergy varieties: women and men of various ethnic backgrounds, sexual orientations, ages, handicaps, assets, and interests. A congregation with something outside the ordinary garden variety clergy is often rewarded with new insights and creativity.

Stereotypes

Fortunately, in the United Church, we've eliminated many of our stereotypes. Few of us have an image of the minister as the befuddled old parson drinking tea with the ladies, even though the TV sitcoms love to perpetuate that idea. There are still a few who assume the minister is an authority on everything. That comes from the days when the clergy were among the few educated people in town.

The worst clergy stereotype, one that lives more outside the church than in it, is of the totally out-of-it parson. This parson has never heard a four-letter word, is offended at the mere mention of booze, thinks sex is a number that comes after five, and is some kind of saint who never has to deal with the pressures and temptations the rest of us face.

The clergy I know are down-to-earth worldly people. They are as aware of what happens on the seamy side of life as social workers or bartenders. Often, the counseling they do has them dealing with situations that would curl your hair.

Clergy spouses

I'm a clergy spouse. In the congregations that Bev served during her ministry, the people had never seen a clergy husband before, so they let me do whatever I wanted. I sang in the choir, helped when there were work parties, greeted new people during coffee hour, but refused to be part of any committee or board that made decisions. I refused to take messages for Bev other than to write down phone numbers to call. And I worked hard at being ignorant of all the congregational politics. I didn't even have a key to the church. It was fun being a clergy husband.

Clergy wives often have a harder time of it. They still suffer from a few stereotypes. Those stereotypes are dying fast, but there's enough of them around to cause problems.

Clergy wives are very much like the wives of other professional men. They're intelligent and educated themselves, with their own opinions on matters like religion. And they are likely to have a career of their own.

The same is true for clergy husbands. Fortunately, we've been around for a much shorter time and most congregations simply don't know what to do with us. That's good. We are individuals with our own needs and hang-ups. Clergy husbands and wives are not simply an extension of their spouses.

She can laugh about it now, but one minister I know tells of being interviewed by a Pastoral Relations Committee. "You should have heard them trying to find out what my husband did, without actually coming right out and asking the question. Was he moving with me? Were we getting divorced? Who would look after the children? I didn't tell them. It was none of their business. They wouldn't have been wondering if I'd been a man."

In some instances, clergy and spouse may not share the same religious convictions. Correction. They never share the same convictions. No two people do. They may be close, but they are never identical. In some instances, the spouse is not involved in the church at all. We have as much right to stay away from church as anyone else, or go to a different church if we so choose.

A fire in the belly

The United Church, generally speaking, has well-educated clergy. The standard procedure for a person who wants to become a minister is to take an undergraduate degree at a university, then go on to take another degree at a school of theology.

That's only the educational part of becoming a minister. It is possible to get all the theological degrees in the world and not be ordained. The candidate's home congregation, the presbytery, the conference, and the General Council all have to be satisfied that the person would make a good minister.

It's no shoo-in, even if you're very willing and enthusiastic. Anyone can be considered for ministry, but you've got to go through interviews, psychological tests, and other procedures. You're not finally accepted until you've been through all the training and had a year or so of field testing. At that point, if you have the right stuff, you are ordained or commissioned, usually at a meeting of the conference.

If you are thinking of entering the ordered ministry, explore it carefully. It's not an easy life. Go for it if you've got a "fire in your belly" and you don't want to do anything else. Talk to your minister first, and then if you feel "called," your minister will arrange a meeting with the board or session of your home congregation.

If you haven't been involved in a congregation, the first thing you need to do is become active for at least a year or two. Then think about turning pro.

If you and your church board feel God is calling you into professional ministry, then they will help you find a "discernment committee," a group of people who will meet with you a number of times over the course of several months, to help you ask the right kinds of questions and help you think and pray your way to a sense of certainty about your call. You will meet with various groups asking similar questions all the way along the process of training and preparing for this calling.

That long, involved process doesn't always sit well with passionate converts who have a strong "call" to the ministry. They sometimes feel their sense of being called by God is the only thing that's important and they should be ordained immediately.

The United Church says yes, this personal sense of call is of vital importance. It must be there. If it's genuine, it'll still be there through all the screening and training.

The United Church has a pretty good batting average at selecting clergy. Of course, it's not perfect. People often take great delight in telling you the story they heard about the minister who ran off with the organist. More often, they tell you about a minister who was a bit silly or insensitive in a particular situation.

They seldom say that kind of thing about clergy they know well. I don't think that means the clergy they have known are any better or more capable. It's just that you begin to accept the humanity of someone you've gotten to know. You learn to love them, often more because of than in spite of their human weaknesses.

Homosexual clergy

In the 1980s, the United Church went through a long and painful struggle over whether homosexual persons could be ministers in the church. There's still a lot of pain and misunderstanding, but the issue is clear and settled. Homosexual persons who are in a loving relationship with another, just like heterosexual persons, can be ministers in our church.

From day one, back in 1925, the United Church has said that anyone who considers themselves a Christian can be a member of the United Church and all United Church people are eligible to be *considered* for the ordained or commissioned ministry. If the congregation, the presbytery, the conference and the General Council all think the person is socially, academically, psychologically and morally fit to be a minister, then it's a go. Their sexual orientation should not be an issue.

There are a growing number of congregations where the minister is gay or lesbian, often living in a loving relationship with a partner, and the congregation know this. Most of them are comfortable with it. A few aren't. Usually, once they get used to the idea, they realize it really has no bearing at all on whether the minister is "good" or not. And these clergy are able to minister effectively and well to those members of the congregation who are not yet able to accept the minister's sexual orientation.

There are also a number of congregations where the ministers are gay or lesbian, and the congregations don't know. This is usually because the minister may have deep fears – fears based on real experience – that he or she would not be accepted if the truth were known. I know a number of such ministers. I feel sad and angry that they have to live with their secret. And I pray for these clergy and their congregations. I pray that the time will come soon when the minister finds the courage and the congregation finds the grace to accept each other in Christian love.

Some conservative denominations have torn a pretty wide strip off the United Church for its attitude toward homosexuality. Those denominations are hiding their heads in the sand. Every denomination in Canada has practicing homosexual clergy. They stay well locked in their closets because coming out probably means they'd be kicked out of their church.

I am proud that my church had the courage to face the question head-on and take the flak. We still have a long way to go, and the walk is often painful. We decided, way back in 1925 when we first became a church, that nobody would be excluded from anything because of the way God made them. I think we chose the right path!

A great bunch of people

Altogether, I think the United Church has perhaps the best, most flexible, relevant, and committed ministry of any denomination. They are a great bunch of women and men. And fun too!

United Church clergy follow the grand traditions of the Bible, where God called some of the darndest people to be prophets, leaders, and witnesses. None of them would survive if God's grace didn't help them over some of the rough spots and pickles they get themselves into. Of course, that's true of us laypeople too.

Most clergy find ministry in the local congregation an exciting and challenging vocation. Working with people who are involved because they want to be; learning to live in a community that needs their guidance and help and offers them love in return; doing something their deepest convictions tell them is the most significant job in the world; that has got to be one of the world's finest vocations.

The salary may not be great (though it's getting better), but the fringe benefits are fantastic.

I believe the leader's spirituality is central to the capacity to minister.

I was disturbed to hear a young clergyman say that congregations do not understand the need for time for spiritual discipline. There is an expectation that you will always be busy. It would not be acceptable to ask not to be disturbed because you are in prayer and self-examination, but it would be all right to say you are in a meeting.

Marion Best – from a lecture at Queen's Theological College, Oct. 1995

In spite of our current challenges, there are many wonderful attributes to contemporary ministry. I cannot think of a more exciting and challenging time to be in the church. We do not have to feel defeated; we can make this into a time of opportunity and growth.

One of the keys to a healthy ministry, wherever we are, whatever the size of our congregations, is to realize that we are in a team ministry. We are not lone wolves. We are in a team with the people in our congregations, with colleagues in our own churches, and with colleagues in the other churches and other faiths.

Christopher White – from *Jacob's Blessing* (Wood Lake Books, 1999)

8

How We Decide

The gifts he gave were that some would be apostles, some prophets, some evangelists, some pastors and teachers.

Ephesians 4:11

I worked for the United Church for a while. Part of my job was "media relations." That meant I had to take reporters around to help them get their stories. Often it involved explaining the United Church to them.

One reporter was quite visibly shaken when I introduced her to the Moderator (the highest elected position in the church), who was in the lunch lineup just ahead of us at a conference. "Your Moderator is in the lineup getting his own food like everybody else?"

Often reporters would ask, "Who's in charge here? Who makes the decisions?"

"Well, we don't have any one person in charge," I'd say. "We work through a series of committees so that all those involved can have their say in what we do."

Their response to that was sometimes raised eyebrows followed by a few words I wouldn't want to print.

Nowadays, I often try to explain to my writer friends that the United Church is a "democratic and collegial organization." That's when I see their eyes rolling up into their heads. "Anyway," I say, "it's designed to deal with complicated moral and theological questions, questions about what is right and wrong and what God is saying to the church."

"Does it work?"

"No. Well, sometimes. But nobody's figured out a better way. It's a lot like a democratic government. It doesn't work that well either and we'd scrap it if there was a better alternative."

Of course, our kind of church government carries a price tag. When you have a variety of people with strong convictions, all of them convinced they are being faithful to the call of God, you have a recipe for conflict.

The United Church has had more than its share of conflict in the last two decades. I can't write a chapter about how the church structures work without saying something about that conflict. But, before I do, let's take a broader look at how the United Church tries to operate as an organization.

The Manual and the Year Book

There are two reference books that help you understand this complicated and sometimes crazy organism called the United Church of Canada. Both should be in every church office and available to anyone who wants to see them.

The first is the *Manual* – "the rule book" I was talking about earlier. The other is the *Year Book*. It's two volumes full of statistics, reports, and lists of every congregation and minister and institution in the church. They're both useful and necessary, but they're not the sort of thing you'd take as light reading on vacation. Good for bedtime reading though. Put you to sleep in five minutes flat. Some of that info is available online at www.united-church.ca

To read the *Manual*, you have to be a bit of a legal beagle, which I most certainly am not. The structure and rules it lays out have evolved over many generations and are pretty reliable. They're far from perfect, but they tend to work.

We do *not* use Robert's Rules of Order in the United Church. Our rules of order are laid out in that manual. Although they are similar, they are not the same.

Most congregations don't look at the *Manual* very often. We tend to work by consensus. We talk about it and talk about it till some people are climbing the wall. Finally, when we've all come out more or less at the same place, we make a decision. It's only when we get into a fight that somebody hauls out the *Manual*. When you have to follow strict rules of order, you know you're in trouble.

The board

Most congregations in the United Church have what we call a unified or "official board," sometimes called a "council." It's elected by the congregation at an annual meeting. There may be representatives as well from various groups, such as the United Church Women, the Men's Group, the Christian Education people, the Board of Trustees, and the Youth Organization. Most boards meet once a month. Every committee of the congregation reports to it. More and more congregations are moving toward that kind of structure.

Some congregations have a more traditional form of organization based on two different groups: the *session*, made up of *elders;* and the *Committee of Stewards.* The session looks after spiritual matters, such as baptisms, preaching, worship, etc., and the stewards deal with money, the building, that sort of thing. If you want the jargon, we distinguish between "spiritual matters" and "temporal matters."

The minister, who is a member of presbytery and, therefore, not technically a member of the congregation, can be elected chairperson of the board or session. But most congregations feel it's wiser to have one of the church members serve as chair with the minister as a member. The minister, by the way, is an "ex officio" member of every committee. That means the minister has the right to attend any meeting of any committee in the church, with or without an invitation. Most clergy are far too busy to even think about doing that.

There is quite a variety of ways in which boards organize themselves. Larger churches usually have five basic committees.

The *Finance Committee* or the *Committee of Stewards* raises money for the church, presents a budget to the congregation for approval, supervises spending, payroll, building upkeep, and general office administration. Some congregations put all or part of this responsibility onto the Property Committee.

The *Ministry and Personnel Committee* deals with the many matters that come up in connection with having clergy, secretaries, caretakers, and others employed by a congregation. For more details on that, you might want to go back to Chapter 7, "Reverend Sir or Madam."

The *Sunday School Committee* is now usually called the *Christian Education Committee* or better still, the *Christian Development Committee.* That's more than just a change in name. It represents a broader attitude to what education means in the congregation.

We're beginning to realize that education is a cradle-to-the-grave kind of thing. It's important to have a strong church school for kids. It's also important to have programs for the Christian development of teenagers and adults of every age. Since

The Whole People of God and *Seasons of the Spirit* curricula came along, more and more churches are seeing education as something the whole church does together.

The fifth group is the *Worship and Sacraments* or *Spiritual Life Committee.* Others simply call it the *Worship Committee.* Related to it, and sometimes part of the same committee is a concern for *Congregational Life.* By that we mean things like small group activities, social events, and things that build the sense of community. And sometimes there's an *Evangelism and Communications Committee* somewhere in this mix.

These groups have responsibility for the spiritual life of the congregation, how the Word of God is proclaimed, and how it is lived. This includes taking responsibility for the pastoral care of people.

The Worship Committee also decides on the style and content of the regular worship service. They decide who will be baptized and married and they make many other decisions, which are important to the life of the congregation. Unfortunately, far too many boards simply leave all these decisions up to the minister and go on to things that are less complicated.

Spiritual and temporal

It's these "spiritual" matters which the church considers most important. To be on the Worship Committee, you should, technically at least, be a full member of the church. In fact, you're not supposed to vote on spiritual matters in any meeting, not even a congregational meeting, unless you're a full member.

Adherents, those who may actively support the church but who haven't actually joined, may vote only on "temporal" matters like money and buildings. This is one of those rules that's ignored in many congregations and not a few have found themselves in trouble because of that.

It's one of the reasons why it is important for each of us to make a decision about joining the church. To fully participate, we need to be *members,* not just *adherents.* Another reason is that a congregation is a legal organization under the provincial and federal United Church of Canada Acts. You can attend church every Sunday and be involved in all sorts of church activities without being a member. Being a member means you work with your minister to formally join the congregation.

It's sad but true that the question of membership has become more important, because all too frequently congregations find themselves involved in legal action of one sort or another.

Committees

Evangelism and Communications Committees often have the job of doing things like newsletters, encouraging people to subscribe to *The Observer,* and arranging for audio-visual equipment and supplies. In some places, this is called the *Congregational Life Committee.*

They might also be responsible for analyzing what happens on a Sunday morning: whether people are made to feel welcome, whether the sound system works, and whether the building looks nice. Most importantly, they establish and maintain contact with newcomers. They try to make them feel welcome and get them involved in church life. When these matters are dealt with creatively, the church is strengthened and it's able to do God's work more efficiently.

The gospel calls us, not only to the fellowship of the church, but to reach out in love to others in the community and around the world. To do that, many congregations have two more committees. These committees have a variety of names in different congregations, but the responsibilities shouldn't be neglected. They are *Church in Society* and *World Outreach.*

They are sometimes combined into one group because it's no longer possible to sort out which are international problems and which are strictly Canadian. The concerns are similar – justice, peace, and the integrity of creation. It's the job of this committee, as it's the job of the whole church, to fuss over and do something about the issues I mention in Chapter 10, "Right, Wrong, and Maybe."

Of course, some congregations have far more committees than the ones I've named. And some have far fewer. Many congregations simply don't have enough people for all those committees, so all of the church's business is handled by the whole board.

I don't know if it will become a trend or not, but some congregations have moved to what they call "passion groups." If someone has a passionate interest in something, that person is invited to gather others with similar interests, and this group becomes the "committee." When the passion or the need is no longer there, the passion group dissolves. Yes, of course the passion group folk check with the board before doing anything that would affect others in the congregation.

Presbytery

When the Methodist, Presbyterian, and Congregational Churches got together in 1925, they developed a form of church government they hoped would take the best from their three different styles.

They decided that the presbytery would be one of the key units in United Church organization. It would do some of the things bishops do in other denominations but it wouldn't be just one person. Presbytery would be a group representing the various congregations through their elected representatives as well as their clergy.

All clergy are members of a presbytery. And each pastoral charge sends at least one layperson, sometimes more if it's a large congregation. The idea is to have about the same number of clergy and laypeople.

The presbytery's work is to supervise the local churches. It makes sure that each "pastoral charge" has a minister and that both congregation and minister behave themselves and get on with the work of the church. Every congregation belongs to a presbytery, which is a form of regional self-government.

Conference

Just as a congregation is part of a presbytery, the presbyteries are part of a conference. There are from 2 to 14 presbyteries in each of the 13 conferences. Most conferences cover a geographical area. The exception is the All Native Circle Conference, which is open to Native congregations and presbyteries across the country, though not all First Nations congregations have chosen to be part of that conference.

Conferences have a major role to play in the ordaining of ministers, although all levels of the church are involved to some degree. The conferences also have a major hand in administering money from the Mission and Service fund that is spent on outreach projects within their boundaries. These are called "Mission Support grants." But again, all levels of the church, including those receiving the money, have a hand in the decisions.

There's been much discussion in the church lately about simplifying this structure. Many claim that four levels of government are one too many. And of course a tighter budget always generates such discussion. I think there's a high probability that the role of conferences will be considerably reduced in the next few years. But I've been wrong before.

Newfoundland and Labrador Conference has been experimenting with two districts of the conference in place of the four presbyteries. People in the rest of the church are very interested to see how that works out.

General Council

Every three years, delegates from all across Canada get together for an event called the General Council. The delegates are elected by conferences and are called "commissioners." It's at General Council meetings that national policies are hammered out, and the church as a whole declares itself.

Usually, when General Council is considering an important social issue, it sets up a study group that puts together a paper or document for the whole church to look at. That gets sent around and people are asked to pull it apart, look at it from all sides, and send in their reactions. The findings of the study group are then considered by the following General Council.

If there's a change that involves the Basis of Union, which is the constitution of the United Church, we go through something called a "remit," where all the presbyteries and, in some cases, all the congregations, get to vote.

The way we look in the media

General Council often makes the press, radio, and TV news. Watching this on the TV at home, it's hard not to leap to conclusions about what is being said and done at the General Council. But please don't.

In the first place, our popular media tend to go after the most sensational stories. If something controversial is on the agenda, the media tend to make it sound as if that's all the General Council talked about. Actually, the agenda is full of interesting discussions, and it's too bad they don't get some coverage.

Secondly, so many of the reporters sent to cover church events are Sunday school dropouts. They're cubs. Their ignorance about religion is sometimes amazing. The stories they file reflect that. There are, of course, some outstanding exceptions, religion reporters who do a fine job of reporting. For that I am very grateful.

To find out what is happening in the church, it's best to use reliable channels. Publications like *The Observer* and *Mandate* are helpful. A really good place to find out about the United Church is at its website (www.united-church.ca). Many conferences, presbyteries, and congregations also have websites. A bit of time online will quickly tell you what's available.

The United Church runs an interesting series on the Vision cable network. The program is called *Spirit Connection*. Keep an eye on your local listings. They usually run a special about General Council when it meets, and the information you'll get there is far more reliable than what you'll see or read in the commercial media.

The best way to find out about the General Council is to talk with people who attended. At least two people from your presbytery will have been there.

General Council Divisions

General Council runs the "national office" of the United Church, most of which is located in an office tower at 3250 Bloor St. W. in Etobicoke (Toronto), Ontario.

Actually, we don't often call it the "national office," because it isn't really. It's the General Council office and really has far less power or influence than many people think. Usually, we call it United Church House.

When I described the organization of local congregations, I mentioned a number of committees. These have their counterparts in most presbyteries and conferences. Within the General Council they are called "divisions" and they all have their headquarters at Church House.

People who have been in the United Church a long time often "speak in tongues," but not in the way that's described in the Bible. We use abbreviations. Acronyms. It's an infuriating habit that tends to divide people into the "ins" and the "outs." You'll notice that this is the only place in the book I use those acronyms. (If I ever get to head up anything important in the United Church, I'm going to make a law that anyone who uses an acronym will get their nose painted green.)

Oops! I used the acronym UCW for United Church Women back in Chapter 4. And UCM. And AOTS. Well, paint my nose green! Be sure to order enough paint – it's a good-sized nose!

The functions of the divisions vary a fair bit in the many presbyteries and conferences, and certainly in the congregations. At the national level, they slice the work roughly like this.

The Ethnic Ministries Council serves the various congregations across Canada that attract non-European persons. This includes a broad spectrum of ethnic groups that bring richness and variety into our church.

The Division of World Outreach (DWO) is responsible for the United Church's relationships outside of Canada. These partner organizations include many churches, but also grassroots people's movements, development agencies, and human rights organizations. This division responds when there is a disaster or catastrophe somewhere, but its most important function is sharing in God's mission with partner churches and agencies around the world.

The Division of Mission in Canada (DMC) probably has more involvement with local congregations than any other division. That's because it looks after such things as educational material and social justice issues of every sort, to say nothing of programs on evangelism, worship, the family, poverty, senior citizens, and men's and women's work.

The Division of Ministry Personnel and Education (MP&E) deals with almost everything that affects people in the ordained or diaconal ministry. Some leadership education efforts for laypeople come under their umbrella too. All the work that goes with keeping track of the professional ministry comes under their division. It's a handful.

The Division of Finance (usually just known as "Finance") looks after money, which seems self-evident. That includes keeping track of it and making sure that the pension plan for church workers is in good shape. This division has a number of other functions, such as making sure the United Church is a good corporate citizen, which invests its pension funds wisely and responsibly.

The church works hard to make sure the money is invested in places where it is at least not exploiting people, and hopefully doing some good. When it owns shares in a company, the church will often send someone to the shareholders' meeting to ask questions about the way that company is carrying on its work.

Within "Finance" is the *Department of Stewardship Services* which helps us to be responsible and creative in the way we raise money. The next chapter in this book is called "Money." It's about stewardship in the congregation.

The Division of Communication (Div Com) has a variety of responsibilities. It runs the United Church Publishing House. This includes a publishing program and bookstores in Etobicoke; Dieppe, NB; Montreal; Winnipeg; and Edmonton. And there's a mail order service so you can order anything the United Church publishes or distributes. And the division supports a network of Resource Centres across the country. (All the books I've mentioned, including the ones listed in the back, can be bought through those outlets.) Div Com also supports AVEL, which stands for "Audio Visual Educational Library." AVEL has an excellent collection of video and audio tapes, films and filmstrips for use in church programs.

The division also publishes *Mandate*, a mission and stewardship magazine, and a variety of other resources. Your minister should know what is available, but if not, write to the national Division of Communication, General Council Offices, and ask them. The address is on page 222.

The General Council office

While almost everything the national church does comes under one division or another, there is a kind of umbrella called the General Council Office. It handles personnel, research, archives, and other matters that can't or shouldn't be put in one of the divisions.

This includes *The Observer*, the United Church's official magazine. *The Observer* has editorial independence, which means it can, and regularly does, criticize the church. It's often a kind of "loyal opposition." And it tries to report what is going on as impartially and accurately as possible. *The Observer* is an excellent magazine that's won many awards. And the price is right.

As I write this in late 1999, I have a note from Moderator Bill Phipps that a "major restructuring" may be happening when the General Council meets in the year 2000. Much of the above may have changed by the time you read this. Ask your minister or your presbytery delegate about it.

The Moderator

A new Moderator is elected at each meeting of the General Council, which is usually every three years. The Moderator is not like the Pope or Prime Minister. Perhaps a little like the Governor General, though that's not quite accurate because Moderators *do* take part in the church's decision making. There's no power connected with being Moderator, other than that which goes with being chairperson of the General Council and its Executive. There is a good deal of influence and some prestige. Moderators tend to be highly visible to the church and to the public and they play a major role in interpreting the church to the general public.

Moderators don't speak officially on behalf of the church, though uninformed reporters write as if they do. Moderators represent the church and try to bring their Christian perspective to bear on what they see around them.

By the way, any member of the United Church can hold any elected position. Lay and clergy, women and men, young and old and people of different races have held them all, including the position of Moderator. I fully expect the United Church to be the first major denomination in Canada (perhaps anywhere!) to elect a gay or lesbian person to the top spot.

A denomination

It would be nice not to need an organization. But human beings just don't seem to work together without one. As soon as you get a number of people together to do anything, some kind of organization develops. It may be very loose and informal or it may be very structured. But there will be an organization with some people doing more leading (whether they have titles or not) and some doing more following.

When people get together for worship, work, and mutual encouragement, the organization that inevitably forms is called a denomination (or cult or sect). (The so-called "nondenominational" groups are kidding themselves. They are, in fact, denominations with very predictable characteristics. Anyway, "denomination" is not a four-letter word.)

Who's in charge here?

Every church and every religious group has some kind of organization and it's easy to spend time arguing which is best. To a large extent, the organization reflects the kind of people a church attracts.

Organizations with strong centralized leadership seem to attract people who like to dominate or be dominated. Those that have authority spread up and down throughout the system tend to attract people who like to have a hand in running things.

The United Church seems, for the most part, to be the second kind of organization, though it's easy to find congregations where the leadership is very much "from the top down."

The official position is that the Bible is the "primary source and ultimate standard of Christian faith and life" and that Jesus Christ is the "chief cornerstone." That's where the authority lies. It means that no one person in the church can ever claim to have the last word, which makes it much harder to get anything decided.

The collegial process

In the United Church, we believe that the Holy Spirit communicates both with individuals and with the whole community of God's people that is the gathered church. When we get together, as a church board, as a presbytery, as a conference, or as General Council to make decisions, God is part of that process. What an individual believes must always be tested against what the whole church believes.

It's called the "collegial process." That's different from the democratic process where one person gets one vote. In the collegial process we study, debate, struggle and fuss, and try to be open to God's leading in all that.

I don't know of any better way the church can be faithful. It is important that we do what is right, not simply what is popular. Government by opinion poll is not an option for a church that wants to be guided by God's love.

But that method is full of problems. For one thing, there's a very strong tendency within the United Church to gather only like-minded people into the various groups and committees. In fact, some feel it is not collegial at all. This is especially true of some of the more conservative people in our church who feel they are excluded from many of the church's collegial groups because of their opinions.

It's easy to be critical of the system, and I don't really have any suggestions for improvement. I do know this – most of the people making decisions in the United Church are caring, thinking people even when they find themselves on opposite sides of an issue. No system is perfect, but the United Church has a long history of facing difficult issues with courage. It's hard to lead the pack, because you take most of the criticism. Over the years the United Church has often been in the forefront of many issues of justice and inclusiveness. The media have sometimes made us out to be heavy-handed and uncaring when responding to those who disagree. There's some truth to that charge, but on the whole, I am proud of my church's record.

Difficult trails

A few summers ago, I spent a fine vacation trekking the high Rockies with a group called the Skyline Hikers. From a base camp at the tree line, small groups would set out for each day's hike. The most experienced hiker was the leader who walked at the head of the group. The second most experienced hiker was the last person, the one who always brought up the rear. And there was a firm rule. Never, ever, lose sight of the person ahead of you. If you do, holler like crazy. It was a necessary survival tactic for hiking difficult terrain.

Our church is hiking some pretty tough terrain and the Skyliners' practice might not be a bad metaphor for us. When the leadership and the "followship" are no longer within hailing distance, we have the makings of disaster.

Living with our differences

Somehow, we must learn to be different together. Somehow we absolutely must learn to respect and love each other, even when we disagree deeply. We have to stay within hailing distance. We must want to stay together as a group.

A kind of fundamentalism has crept into our church, and it is there at all points on the theological spectrum. It is the kind of attitude that says, "I have the informed perspective on this issue. I am more faithful to God's word than you are. Therefore, if you do not agree with me, then you are wrong." I am disturbed at how often I have heard that implication, sometimes in my own speaking, sometimes in the words of friends who would consider themselves "liberal" and open, sometimes from friends who are more conservative or evangelical.

That attitude simply doesn't work anymore. My Mennonite forebears moved from central Europe, to Russia, and then to Canada, each time trying to get away from those who disagreed with their faith. Now there's no longer any place left to go. We must learn to live our faith in harmony with our neighbors or we will lose our faith in conflict with our neighbors. This is hardest, and most important, when our neighbor is a Christian who worships and believes differently than we do.

I felt at home in the United Church when I first joined because it allowed me to hold views and opinions that many members would have considered downright "unchristian." I rejoiced in the United Church's broad spectrum of theology, from charismatic spirituality to humanistic social activism.

Now I often feel assaulted by both the right and the left because my theology doesn't include some of the things they feel are essential. That makes me angry because I don't think we can claim to be an inclusive church when we effectively marginalize the folks who don't move with the church leadership.

My church home

But I am still intensely proud to be a member of the United Church of Canada. I am proud because of the quality of the people I find in it. I am proud to be part of a community that has the courage to act on principle, to do what they feel is right, even at great personal and organizational cost.

I am proud to be part of a community that includes people who don't stomp off in a snit when the church decides something with which they deeply and fundamentally disagree. It takes courage and commitment to stay in the family.

I am proud to be part of a church community that grows and changes and listens and struggles, that refuses to get caught in the stagnant waters of yesterday's issues, and that has the courage to swim upstream.

The United Church has a heritage of diversity, of openness, of refusing to be dogmatic about anything. We have been an inclusive church, which means we include the people in our own church family with whom we radically disagree.

We use the word "inclusiveness" quite often. It's more than just a word for us. We really knew it was more than just a word when the United Church of Canada said that gay and lesbian persons must be fully welcome in the church community to the point of being considered for ordained ministry. Now it must become more than words as we find ways of actively including and valuing people and congregations who feel they are trampled on and marginalized by our "inclusive" process.

If we fail – if either the far left or the far right feel left out – we have contradicted our own theology of inclusiveness. We will have denied the vision that created The United Church of Canada.

The struggle

The United Church is a national Canadian church. We're struggling to hear what God is saying through the Bible and through the people in our community of faith. We feel very deeply that we have something to say to a world that seems to be getting more and more complicated and fractured.

It's not a perfect church. Occasionally, I get hopping mad at the things it does and says. But I like the United Church way of doing things better than any alternatives I know. It works because most of the people all the way up and down the ladder are trying to live the gospel as they know it.

Yes, some are clods and some are freeloaders. Some are sound asleep and there are a few rotten apples. There may even be a few who are downright evil. But most United Church people, lay and clergy, women and men, are committed to living and working out their faith as part of the whole church of Jesus Christ.

For that, I thank God!

▃▃▃▃

"If another member of the church sins against you, go and point out the fault when the two of you are alone. If the member listens to you, you have regained that one." Matthew 18:15

Now I have to confess that this is not a text I've ever liked a whole lot. The most shocking aspect of this text is that if you are sinned against, wronged, you have an obligation to the person who has wronged you. The victim has the obligation, not the persecutor.

I know my tendency is to huddle in the corner, nursing my wounded and all too often self-righteous spirit, playing the victim. It presents too great an opportunity to feast on martyr milk, which in turn makes for wonderful conversation with anyone other than the supposed perpetrator. But even when I come to my senses and realize the folly of such self-indulgence, I'm still reluctant.

When I ask myself why is this so, and I'm really honest, I suspect at the root of the problem is fear. To go and talk to someone about how they hurt you takes a lot of courage and love.

David Martyn – from a sermon

[Unlike the American churches] we have not had to deal with a history of black slavery. But we have been forced to acknowledge, and to try to redeem, our triumphalist history with Native people – in court, around meeting tables, in lunch rooms and church halls, climbing on to buses with protesters going to jail. We have learned what it means to have been wrong, and to have done wrong.

Not all of us, in the mainline churches, hear. We have not all come to that realization yet. But by their presence and by their bitter, hard-told stories, Native Christians have touched other delegates at church meetings. Sometimes they have made them cry. And every time that happens, a heart of stone becomes a holy place to encounter God.

We are a healthier Christian church as a result of this long conversation between Native and non-Native members. The consequence of saying, "I'm sorry," could be financial upheaval for a huge institution. But receiving a new heart is never cheap or easy.

Donna Sinclair – from *Jacob's Blessing* (Wood Lake Books, 1999)

9

Money

How does God's love abide in anyone who has the world's goods and
sees a brother or sister in need and yet refuses to help?
1 John 3:17

Money is considered a bad word by some people. At least, it's not a word we say
out loud in church. Instead, we use words like "stewardship."

The definition of stewardship, in the church sense, is "what we do with what
we've got." So stewardship certainly means more than money. It involves the way
we use our time, our talents, our energy, our skills, our earth, and anything else
we have.

Still, our most important symbol of "what we've got" is money. So money is
what I'm talking about in this chapter.

A down-to-earth faith

You can find lots of people who say the church should concentrate on spiritual
things. I agree totally. And since the Bible talks a lot about money, money is one of
those spiritual things we *should* talk about.

Jesus had plenty to say about money. So did other biblical writers. Check
Deuteronomy 8:10–18, Matthew 19:16–29, and 1 Timothy 6:4–11.

Christianity is a very materialistic religion. "Worldly" things like sex, money, and politics are the very things it deals with. Some other major religions try to get you away from all that. "Salvation" becomes so "spiritual" that nasty things like money and sex simply don't affect you anymore. But Christianity doesn't take you away from anything. Christianity takes you right into the middle and helps you use what you have creatively. Our money and our sexuality are gifts of God.

The founder of our church, Jesus Christ, got lots of bad press because he insisted on being involved with "earthy" things. Not that he was particularly concerned with people's wealth (unless it came at somebody else's expense). But he was very concerned about what people did with their wealth and power, with their time and talents, and with their bodies.

Most of all, he was concerned about their attitudes. "Where your treasure is," said Jesus, "there your heart will be also." In other words, when you take out your cheque book or your credit card you are expressing your faith. Or lack of it.

It's important to talk about money. Otherwise, what we do with our dollars might contradict what we claim to believe. We've got to "put our money where our mouth is," as we used to say playing poker. "Put up or shut up!" was also a favorite phrase. Both should be applied to people in the church.

Ten percent off the top

In the Hebrew Scriptures, the rule is that you give the first 10 percent of everything to God. Off the top. Before deductions.

That's the way they did it in Bible times. At harvest time, if you had 100 bushels of grain, the first thing you did was take ten bushels to the temple. It was called a "tithe."

That 10 percent off-the-top figure was used at a time when most people thought they were doing well if they weren't starving.

In many of our third-world sister churches, where the standard of living is far lower than ours, people still take the Bible seriously. They give 10 percent. They tithe.

There are many people in the United Church who set aside their "tithe" just as soon as the paycheque comes in. They find that satisfying and liberating. And, somehow, the rest of the budget problems seem to come into a better perspective when they do that.

Unfortunately, they're a minority. I'm proud of the United Church in many ways, but I'm not a bit proud of the way most of us respond with our money. In Canada, people in our denomination are among the worst in terms of giving to mission – we rank 25th out of 28 denominations. We're 78th out of 86 in North America. That's disgusting!

What's even worse, Canadians as a whole give less to charitable causes (on a per capita basis) than people in the United States.

On the other hand, a friend, a United Church member who does income tax returns for others, tells me that the folks who give significant amounts to the United Church also give far more to other causes.

The church is still suffering from the buck-a-week syndrome. I know people who have been coming to church for years and putting a dollar bill on the plate every Sunday. Their salaries have been going up. All their other expenses have been going up. Their standard of living has been going up.

But the church keeps getting a buck a week. That's changed a bit now that we've got "Loonies" and "Toonies" that go clank when you put them on the plate, so folks may be forced to offer a whole five-dollar bill in its place. Less than half the price of a decent bottle of wine.

Somebody wondered out loud what would happen if everybody in our congregation went on social assistance. Welfare. Then, if one person, just one person in each family would tithe, what would happen? In fact, the church's budget would actually increase.

I personally know United Church people on social assistance who tithe! I also know United Church people who live in homes worth close to a million, who put in five bucks a week.

Pledging

Most congregations in the United Church encourage people to make a pledge at the beginning of the year. They want us to take a look at what we have and how we are doing. Then, they'd like to know how much we plan to give.

It's the only sensible way a congregation can operate. There are regular expenses such as salaries, building repairs, mortgages, and many other things. The board members who draw up the budget need to have a reasonable idea of what kind of income to expect.

It's not that much to ask. We make all sorts of financial commitments. We sign on the dotted line for car payments and mortgages, and those are legally binding.

A church pledge isn't binding. It's a statement of intention. Nobody can predict the future, but we can all take a guess at what it's likely to be. That guess should be the basis of our pledge. If we lose a job or wind up in the hospital or our spouse skips out, nobody would expect us to stick with it.

Making a pledge is simply cooperating with the people we elect to run our congregation. They're trying to run it in a sensible and fiscally sound manner. We wouldn't want them to do any less. So they need our cooperation.

Actually, those people who say, "I'll give what I can," usually mean they'll give what they have left over after they've taken care of everything else. They are telling us what their priorities are, that their faith is a luxury to be indulged only after the "necessities" are looked after. It usually means a severe case of spiritual poverty, and that the church is not one of their priorities. As the old saying goes, "actions speak louder than words."

People who make a pledge take their giving, their commitment, more seriously. The proportion of their income that pledgers give is about three times that offered by people who simply toss their spare cash into the plate on Sunday morning.

Envelopes

In order to keep track of who gives what, so that income tax receipts can be sent out at the end of the year, most congregations use envelopes.

These envelopes also make it possible for you and me to tell our church how much of our offering should be used locally and how much should go to outreach (the Mission and Service Fund) or other special appeals.

Some congregations budget a certain amount for Mission and Service and if not enough comes in designated for that, they'll make up the difference from regular funds. Others just send whatever comes in on the plates.

In our Christian understanding, it's the givers who benefit. We give, first of all, because we need to give. It does us good. It helps us grow. Giving helps us get our perspective straight and our priorities in order. And it becomes a practical statement of what we really believe.

We need to give in the same way that we need to be in a caring relationship with other people. The other day Bev woke up with her arthritis bothering her because it was raining and the clouds were down near our eyebrows. On the way home from an appointment, I bought a large flowering plant. She was delighted and I got a big hug. We give because our love needs to be expressed.

That's why we give our money as a part of our worship. The offering in church is an act of worship, an expression of our love of God, just like communion or prayer. We feel so strongly about money because it is such a powerful symbol of our self-worth. That's why giving our money to God, as an act of worship, is so important. It's a way of giving ourselves to God.

The second reason for giving is that the church needs the money for the work in our own congregation and for the work of the whole church around the world.

Changing attitudes

I was born in the 1930s when we used cash – nickels, dimes, and dollar bills – for everything we bought. If you didn't have the money, you started saving, or you did without. Money was something you could touch and feel and smell.

In the 1960s, most of us had bank accounts, and we began to use cheques more and more. A cheque was as good as cash. Well, almost. Then in the 1970s along came credit cards, and our use of money became even less personal. We didn't pay for things we bought – we paid the credit card company.

Then in the late 1980s and early 1990s, automatic debit cards came along. We began banking by telephone or computer. Now, the cash I carry in my wallet is for small stuff. Incidentals. The important stuff is all done by post-dated cheques, credit or debit cards. If I put cash on the plate on Sunday, I begin to think of the church as just one of those incidentals I pay for with cash. My church becomes a low-priority item.

That's why most churches have available a Pre-Authorized Remittance plan. PAR for short. Bev and I use postdated cheques, but we could also use an authorized monthly withdrawal from our bank account. Most often, the congregation supplies you with a little card you can put on the offering plate when it comes around. It says you've been using PAR.

I find it kind of funny. In our congregation, the folks who give the most to the church, are the ones who don't put any money on the offering plate when it goes by.

The important thing in all this is our attitude. With PAR, our church giving is up there with the other highly important things in our life.

How it all adds up

When you put them all together, the statistics are interesting. In 1998, the people of the United Church gave about $324 million. That sounds like a lot of bucks until you realize that the United Church is a big denomination. Next to the Roman Catholic Church, it's probably the biggest non-profit organization in Canada, with branches in just about every town (though fewer in Quebec). It's bigger than all the service clubs put together.

I don't want to bore you with a bunch of statistics; you can find the latest information at the United Church's website. Our giving in the United Church has been going up, bit by bit, but it hasn't even kept up with inflation. People are giving a smaller percentage of their income to the M&S Fund, and the national church is winding up with less paying power.

Spending the money

The largest slice of the money we send to the national church goes to the Division of Mission in Canada. It's used to support small congregations that wouldn't be able to stand on their feet otherwise, and for various kinds of social service and social action ministries, education, evangelism, and leadership development.

The Division of World Outreach uses its part of the money to work with partner churches and agencies in other countries. Part of that money is set aside for world development and relief. The division supports their partners in long-term sustainable development projects, while at the same time being ready when there are disasters like earthquakes, floods, and wars.

Inflation, coupled with the falling value of the Canadian dollar in international terms, means that the Division of World Outreach has had a hard time fulfilling its promises to partner churches overseas.

Other money goes to help train new ministers, to finance cooperative work with other denominations, and to keep United Church people informed about what is going on in the denomination.

Then, of course, there's administration. So far, the United Church has a good record of spending less than most non-profit organizations to keep the wheels turning. If you want more specific numbers about any of the above, check the Year Book in your church office, or the United Church website.

When you don't agree

A major problem with democracies like the United Church is that there is no way to please everybody. No matter what a church this size does (or doesn't do) somebody is going to be upset. And because the church is doing so many things, all of us can find something that'll tie our shirt into knots.

"How can I give money to something I disagree with?" There are people who have stopped giving to the church because they didn't like what was said about racism or sexuality or something else. If these people were consistent, they'd refuse to pay their taxes if they disagreed with something the government was doing.

Still, it's a good question *if* you've taken a careful look at the subject and studied the facts. It's not a good question if all you know is what you've read in the papers or heard on the radio.

The media feed on controversy. They tend to pick the most radical opinions on opposite extremes of a controversy and present those as representative of the whole church.

If you've checked out the facts and still disagree with the church's actions, then you should be speaking out in your congregation and at presbytery. To simply grumble to yourself and a few friends, then quit, is a cheap cop-out.

On the other hand, maybe you've done all you can to change things. You feel, as a matter of conscience, that you simply can't support a certain thing the church is doing. Then you should send your donation to the United Church office in Toronto with a covering letter that tells the national people how you'd like your money used.

If you disagree with *everything* the United Church does, you're in the wrong denomination.

A lack of connection

One of the hardest things for an organization like the United Church to do, is to keep us all feeling connected with the outreach work that our givings go to. The stewardship people in the national office try valiantly to keep that connection warm. In our congregation, we have a "Minute for Mission" every Sunday, just before the offering, that tells us about a project or venture or a need that our money goes toward. And there's lots of other information available in every congregation, such as *Mandate* magazine.

The reality is that many folks want to be able to be specific about where their money goes. As the national church becomes weaker, more and more money is kept in the congregations. Some congregations choose to support non-United Church agencies and charities. Some of the church growth gurus are saying our mission is "right outside your front door," and the reality of this is reflected in the way congregations keep their money at home. Unfortunately, the money is more likely to go to fix the roof or balance the budget than to mission work.

In the long run, I think it will be the congregations themselves that are going to suffer as the flow of money slows down. That will be especially true of tiny, rural congregations, which can only remain operating if they receive some outside help.

Making our money work for us

The United Church, for the most part, handles its money well. In overseas work and here at home, it generally makes a dollar do more than most other organizations, religious or secular. That's because so much is done by volunteers.

When we start raising funds, we need to be more direct in this United Church of ours. There's nothing wrong with plainly and directly asking people to give to the church. That's the biblical way.

Too often, we pussyfoot around, afraid of offending someone and losing their buck a week. We need to bluntly remind people that what they do with their money is a statement of their faith. If I put two bucks a week on the plate, that would represent about 0.2 percent of my income. I sometimes wonder if God feels offended or hurt by such paltry giving.

Which brings us to that word "stewardship" again. The best definition I've heard so far is, "Stewardship is what you do after you say, 'I believe'."

Or, to quote Jesus again, "Where your treasure is, there your heart will be also."

―――

Mainline churches generally don't expect a high level of commitment. We offer a buffet style: come on in and taste a morsel or two. We offer the sacraments to everyone who professes – by silence – a faith in Jesus. While there was a time when we got sticky about baptizing anyone, most of our churches would rather risk being too open than risk offending someone – even if that person hasn't been in church since their last child was "done." Splash and split is our policy.

Money? We won't talk about money. That might upset you. Volunteer your time? We won't pressure you, except in the vaguest, most unthreatening way possible.

Christopher White – from *Jacob's Blessing* (Wood Lake Books, 1999)

10

This We Believe

You shall love the Lord your God with all your heart, and with all your soul, and with all your strength, and with all your mind; and your neighbor as yourself.

Luke 10:27

Pray then in this way:
Our Father in heaven,
Hallowed be your name.
Your kingdom come.
Your will be done,
on earth as it is in heaven.
Give us this day our daily bread.
And forgive us our debts,
as we also have forgiven our debtors.
And do not bring us to the time of trial,
But rescue us from the evil one.

Matthew 6:7–13

You can't get very far talking about a church unless you talk about what people in that church believe. So let's talk theology.

But first I need to repeat something I said at the beginning of this book. What follows is my own personal perspective. Each person's theology – their system of beliefs – is as unique as a fingerprint. One of the things I believe is that God made each of us unique so that we can experience the holy in our own special way, and share that with others. We learn more from the folk we disagree with, than we do from those who agree with everything we say. So I don't expect you or anyone else to agree with everything that follows. In fact, if you do, you are probably not paying much attention.

So here we go. Theology is simply thinking or talking about God or any question of faith. Most of us do that far more often than we realize. Theology doesn't have to be complicated or academic or dry. It's about everyday life. And it isn't half as mysterious as many people think.

Most of what I know about theology has come from sitting in the pew on Sunday mornings and then trying to apply what I hear and feel to my work and home life. I found some good books that helped me grow in my faith, some of which are listed at the back of this one, on page 219. There have been lots of lively discussions with friends over the years, in study groups and over a cup of coffee. That's the kind of learning I've always liked best. I don't have a university degree in theology and I'm not an ordained minister.

I discovered along the way that, as long as I relax, I can take the subject seriously without taking myself and my own opinions too seriously. When I do that, talking and studying theology is fun!

Building a personal faith

Back in 1925, when the Presbyterian, Methodist, Congregational, and community churches got together to form the United Church of Canada, they set out 20 *Articles of Faith*. They were a statement of what those churches, at that time, could agree on. I think they saw those Articles of Faith as bare-bones Christianity.

Working out your own faith is a bit like building a house. You need a good solid foundation and structure. You need a roof that doesn't leak. If you've got that, you can redecorate, even move walls around, without having the house tumble down around your ears.

I remember seeing a house in rural Ontario a few years ago. There was a rickety center section to which one lean-to after another had been added over the years. Some people's faith (their theology) is like that house – a series of lean-tos. One afterthought leaning against another and a few isolated ideas not attached to anything. Not a good place to live, and not a faith that's going to work for you.

A personal faith has to be more than an idea from here, a scripture verse or two from there, and a few wise old sayings. What we say about one part of our faith should make sense in terms of the other parts.

Our personal faith, our spirituality, needs to work for us in good times and in bad. A few of my friends have put together a personal spirituality that seems to be very thin. It didn't seem to help them much when pain and tragedy came along. A personal faith needs to stand the test of tragedy, as Bev and I found ours did when our son died a few years ago.

The Articles of Faith give us an outline. If you look beyond the musty language, you can find a useful description of what the United Church believed about 75 years ago when it was formed. We're no longer at that place in our denominational journey, so those Articles of Faith are probably not a good place to start if you're new at talking or thinking about religion.

A personal statement

What follows is my *personal* statement of faith (just as this whole book is my *personal* description of the United Church). Many people in the United Church would agree with what I'm about to say and many would not. That really doesn't matter. I'm offering an outline of what I believe, because I hope it will help to get you thinking about what you believe.

My statement doesn't cover the waterfront. There's plenty more I could say about any one of these subjects. After the first edition of this book was published, people kept asking me to expand on this chapter. So I did. The book is called *God for Beginners* and is published by Northstone Publishing, an imprint of Wood Lake Books. In the U.S., the book is called *Christianity for Beginners* and is published by Abingdon Press.

God

The best way to learn what God is like is to study the life of Jesus. By what Jesus was, by what he said and did and in the way he died and overcame death, we see a clear picture of God.

But people were thinking and learning about God long before the time of Jesus. Thousands of years earlier, a couple named Abraham and Sarah set out on a pilgrimage. They were led by a God who seemed to have chosen them to get something important started.

The children of Abraham and Sarah became the Hebrew nation. They seemed like such an unimportant little band of people, always being set upon by more powerful nations. But these people had a God who seemed to stick with them, a God who heard their cry and brought them out of slavery in Egypt and into a Promised Land.

They called this God "Yahweh." (Jehovah is an English version of "Yahweh.") Through Moses, they were given a series of commandments and, through the prophets that followed, the Hebrew people repeatedly heard Yahweh say, "I will be your God and you shall be my people."

For the Hebrews, this was a covenant – permanent and binding on both sides. (You might want to go back and reread what I said about covenant in Chapter 5.) Over the centuries, they came to four very important conclusions about God.

First, the Hebrews realized that there was only one God and that was Yahweh.

Second, they learned that Yahweh was just. This God wasn't like some of the kings and despots they saw around them, who would play favorites and bend rules. What God said, God meant.

Third, they learned that God was good. God wanted the best for them as a nation. They even began to suspect that God actually loved them, though they weren't sure what that meant.

Fourth, they discovered that the covenant was not with individuals, but with the whole people. They were all in it together. What one of them did affected all of them. Furthermore, God's love and God's punishment came to them as a people, not as individuals.

That's the basic story told in the Hebrew Scriptures, or to use the more traditional term, the Old Testament. Now we get to the part traditionally called the New Testament, but which I prefer to call the Christian Scriptures.

Jesus

All this time, the prophets had been hinting, sometimes even predicting, the coming of a Messiah. This would be someone who could save the Hebrew people and offer them new hope.

Many people expected a Messiah who would look like Brad Pitt and who would sweep across the nation on a fancy chariot and kick out the hated Romans who occupied their country.

Well, the Messiah *did* come. As promised, but not as expected. Mary was a young country girl. Joseph was the village carpenter. When Mary was gloriously pregnant, they took a trip to Bethlehem to be counted in the census. We all know the rest of the story. Or, we think we do.

A number of years ago, I visited a cave-like stable in a Lebanese village. The professor who showed it to me said it probably was very similar to the stable in which Jesus was born.

It was stinking dirty. Rats and cockroaches scurried away as we walked in. The animals were scrawny and mangy. It didn't look a bit like our Christmas card pictures.

Then I thought about Mary, really just a girl, giving birth to her first child in that stinking stable, probably without a midwife and certainly without modern medical help. I thought about that and the image of Jesus on the cross came to mind. I realized that Jesus came into the world the same way he left – in misery and pain.

When God became human in Jesus of Nazareth, there was no holding back. Jesus wasn't half-God, half-human. Jesus was completely both. On the human side, Jesus had every potential weakness, every problem, every passion that we have. God didn't fake it. Jesus was not walking around pretending to be human.

If God lived with a body like mine, lived with fears and fantasies the way I do, knew the joy of one moment and the horror of the next, ran into trouble with the authorities, was teased and taunted and made to look like a fool and was finally hung up like a common crook, then God knows what it's like to be human. To be one of us. That's very important to me.

Jesus also knew what it was like to be God. He was able to say, "The Father and I are one," which meant he was both completely human and completely God at the same time. It's one of those things we puzzle over. A paradox. Our experience tells us it's true, even though our minds complain that it doesn't make sense.

When Jesus was about 30, he began a ministry that was to change the world. He gathered a small group of disciples (or followers or pupils) around him and spent hours and days teaching them. When crowds gathered, he told stories. We call them parables.

These parables were far more than cute stories to illustrate a point. Jesus used them to push people to the edge of their understanding. They always felt they understood, but never completely. And each time they heard or read the parable again, they found new truth there.

A complex person

The crowds often gathered around Jesus because of reports about what he did: healing cripples, curing the blind, feeding thousands with just a little food. But they stayed to listen because he spoke with authority, using words they could understand. They didn't understand everything. But they got enough to make them want more – to make them want to grow.

Jesus was a complex person. He was different things to different people. That's why there are four different accounts of his life, death, and resurrection, each one seeing Jesus from a different perspective. Those are the four gospels – Matthew, Mark, Luke, and John – that you find in the Bible.

When Jesus died, he showed us what sin really is, what it means to be totally alone, totally separated from God. When he hung there on that cross, the agony shuddered through his body. Abandoned by his best friends and feeling abandoned by God, he yelled, "My God, my God, why have you forsaken me?" He was yelling for all of us who are caught in the hell of separation from God. Caught in living death.

It was real pain. Real fear. Real anger. Jesus was abandoned by his friends. And he certainly felt forsaken by God. He died in screaming bloody pain.

Jesus didn't die as some sort of prepayment. I can't go out and be as rotten as I want because my sins are paid for in advance. Jesus died so that all of us could experience with him the full impact of human sin.

On the surface, it sounds as if the story of Jesus comes to a very tragic end. He was executed out on the edge of town where thousands of people had been crucified before him. Not what you'd call a great finish for a Messiah.

Except that it wasn't the finish. It was only the beginning. Soon there were whispers going around, people claiming he was alive. Others yelled, "Hogwash!" But the stories kept right on. So did the arguments.

He had been put in a borrowed tomb. A huge stone was rolled in front so nobody could steal the body.

But, somehow, the stone was rolled away and the body was gone.

People still argue about what really happened. In the end, it's not something you can prove. You see, it's not the absence of his corpse from an empty tomb that convinces us. It's his presence in our empty lives!

The resurrection

The opposite of death is life. The opposite of sin is love. The opposite of despair is hope. Often, the pain on one side may be the beginning of joy on the other.

That's why we call the Friday Jesus gasped out his life, Good Friday. We call it "good" because it made Easter possible, and because it was God's Friday.

Jesus not only died for us. Jesus rose for us. Separation, death, and despair are never the final answer in God's way of doing things. God's love is the ultimate power. It is the power that overcomes the sin of alienation, the sin that crucified Jesus on the cross. At Easter, we celebrate the triumph of life over death.

One of the pictures you often see in our churches was drawn by United Church artist Willis Wheatley. It's a drawing of Jesus laughing, which he called "Jesus Christ – Liberator." It's the laughter of togetherness. Jesus laughs with us in the love that liberates us from the icy power of alienation.

That's why we sometimes call ourselves an "Easter People." We're a people of the resurrection. We can celebrate a deep-down joy, even when we're so low it's hard to know which way is up.

The birthday of our church

Before Jesus died, he told the disciples he wouldn't leave them. After he died there was, for a short while, the joy of the resurrection. But then he was gone again. The disciples wandered around, not sure what to do, disorganized and confused.

They gathered for the annual harvest feast, though it almost seemed more like a meeting of a memorial society.

Suddenly, something happened. They described it later as the sound of rushing wind. Tongues of fire danced among them. They began to speak in strange languages, yet the people who gathered around understood every word.

Some said they were drunk, but one of the disciples, a wiry fisherman named Peter, gave what turned out to be the first sermon of the Christian Church. Looking back on it later, they knew it was the day the Church was born. We have celebrated that birthday ever since as Pentecost.

The tiny band of disciples, hurt and confused because their leader was gone, became filled with power and possibilities. They called it the Holy Spirit. From that beginning, the Christian faith spread literally all over the whole world. Now there probably isn't a single country anywhere that hasn't got a Christian church of some kind.

Why a church?

Many people wonder if we really need a church in which to express our faith. Do we need all that organization, all that tradition, all the stuff that goes with a church?

I can only speak for myself. I tried to take a "distance education" course once. "I don't need classes and cranky instructors and all that stuff. I can work on my own!" Except I didn't. After an enthusiastic start, it dropped off. The plain truth is that I need others to help me get where I want to go. I can't make it on my own.

I also need a way of thinking about my faith, a way to talk about it, a way to express it. A few years ago I heard some lectures by Rabbi Wosk of Vancouver. I asked him why Jews need all the stuff that is called the Torah – all the structure and background and rules and traditions. The Rabbi took the glass of water from his speaker's stand. He poured some of it on the floor. "The water on the floor is the same stuff as the water in the glass. But to drink it, I need it in the glass."

In other words, the church and its traditions provide the container – the structure – through which we can experience our faith. And yes, of course there are many different kinds of "containers."

The Holy Spirit

The Holy Spirit isn't something different from God. It's simply a term we use to help understand that God is everywhere. In a sense, God is far away and beyond anything we can understand or describe. At the same time, God is right here with us and in us. That's another contradiction, but it's also true to our experience.

God, as the Holy Spirit, is around us and in us, in every part of every fiber of our body, and in every cell and atom of creation. The Holy Spirit is God leading us and comforting us.

The Holy Spirit is also God clearing the way for us to do and be things we never thought possible. People have found courage in their faith to accomplish everything from small, day-to-day tasks to heroic deeds. And they've found courage to endure problems that otherwise would have crushed them.

When we are aware of God as, somehow, part of every fiber and nerve in our body, something bigger than we can describe or even know, something that gives us a sense of peace or better still, *shalom*, then we know the presence of the Holy Spirit.

We're not as aware of the Holy Spirit in the United Church as they are in some other faith traditions. And we're beginning to realize we can't leave this essential source of power out of our Christian faith. Thinking and analyzing and working for

God's justice is exactly what we should be doing. But if we don't have God's spirit providing the strength to do all that, we're going to run dry. Burnout time.

That's why United Church people are borrowing from some other faith traditions – drinking from other cups, if you like. The idea of "spiritual directors" – people trained to help us walk and grow in our faith journey – came to us from our Roman Catholic friends. Now it is a growing movement in the United Church.

We've also tried to pick out the useful parts of some of the New Age spirituality, and looked back into our ancient roots to discover gifts like Christian meditation, healing touch, prayer groups, and contemplative prayer. We need to be much more open to non-Christian forms of spirituality, while also digging deep into our Christian traditions to find the treasure hidden there.

Some of us have grown in spirituality through gifts from our First Nations community. They often have a strong tradition of meditation and spirituality. Perhaps they'll teach us.

United Church retreat centers (there are several across the country) are beginning to offer more courses in spirituality and meditation. So are various other schools and institutions. Your church office should have information about these.

Let's be clear what we're talking about. Spirituality is a very quiet thing. You don't know it's there until you stand close to someone who has allowed their spirituality to grow. Some express it by holding their hands up and by the way they speak. For most, it's a very quiet, subtle thing. One church leader described the spirituality of a person he had met in an inner-city congregation: "Somehow, when you were with her, you just wanted to be a better person."

A deep spirituality is the greatest gift we can receive as we live and grow in the church. It's not something foreign that we import. It is there, inside each one of us, waiting like a seed in springtime to grow and blossom. Those seeds grow in a garden called the church. A garden is successful only when the plants within it are vigorous and strong.

I'm convinced that the United Church of Canada will survive only to the extent that its people (you and me) develop a strong, lively, spirituality.

Three in one

Christians have three ways of describing God. We call that the Holy Trinity. The word Trinity isn't mentioned in the Bible, but the three ways of understanding God certainly are. The concept of the Trinity evolved later as a way of describing what people found as they read their Bibles and experienced God's presence.

We think of Yahweh, the God of our ancestors, as all-powerful, everlasting, all-holy, all-loving. God as Creator! Eventually we simply run out of superlatives because there's nothing we can ever say about God that would do justice to the reality.

That's why it's helpful to think of God as a parent, a strong, just, and loving mother or father. Of course, if you have not had a happy family life, that may not be a very helpful metaphor at all. You may then need to think of God as your very best aunt, or uncle, or friend or teacher or social worker you can imagine.

When we think of God who knows what it's like to be us, we think of Jesus: God the Son. One of the names for Jesus was "Emmanuel," which means, "God with us." So, if we want a flesh-and-blood example of what God is like, we think of Jesus the Christ.

And sometimes we're aware that God is right around us and inside us. That's when we speak of God as the Holy Spirit.

There aren't three Gods, just three different ways of knowing one God. Think of it as a braid of hair. All the hair begins on the same head, but you can separate it into three strands that make up a braid. Every strand is dependent on the other two, and at the tip, they all come together again. Our joyful, lifelong journey is getting to know the love of that God who is known to us in so many ways, but most particularly through these three strands of spirituality we call the Holy Trinity.

Of course there are far more than three ways of thinking about God. A Jewish friend recently gave me a list of 100 names for God. And I'm told that many years ago a monk published a booklet called *1,000 Names for God.*

It doesn't matter much what you *call* God, but it does matter that you have an awareness of a God of love and justice active in your life.

Some people feel the traditional formula, "Father, Son, and Holy Spirit," should be replaced, and it often is in songs, prayers, and sermons. We've kept it in the baptism service to keep our connection with other, more traditional denominations, for whom this formula is fundamental.

Revelation

God communicates with us in many ways. We call that communication "revelation." Some kinds of revelation are dramatic. Others are very ordinary. Slow, careful study is revelation. Day-by-day living is revelation.

God's most important communication came in the form of a human being, when God said, "Look, I'll show you what I'm like." In Jesus, I see more clearly than anywhere else what God wants me to be and do.

God speaks to us through scriptures. The Bible tells a story of people struggling to know the will of God and of God struggling to get through to them. By reading that story, we can come to know God's will for us too.

Revelation may also come in a sudden insight, a gift of the Holy Spirit. It may follow months of wondering and puzzling, or it may come suddenly, as a surprise.

We can read and hear the story of "saints," people who have been open to what God is trying to tell them. Saints are simply ordinary people who have taken the time to listen.

God speaks to us through our traditions. That includes our family traditions such as how we celebrate a birthday. And it includes our church traditions. How we honor and mark the seasons of our lives leads us to an understanding of what they mean. God is quite capable of communicating through a wide variety of traditions, of which the United Church tradition is only one.

God speaks to us through science and logic. There is no contradiction between science and religion, even though scientists and religious people have often argued. But something cannot be scientifically true if it is not also religiously true. Much of the argument between scientists and religious people has been pretty silly. There is, for instance, the old chestnut about whether the story of creation in the Bible (there are actually two stories of creation) is right or whether it is the scientific explanation that's correct. Both scientists and religious people make the mistake of thinking of the Bible as primarily a historical or scientific document. It's neither. It's the stories, songs, and sayings of a people struggling to understand the work of God in their lives.

Very often at church meetings, there's a prayer that God will be part of the deliberations and decisions of that meeting. I believe that when people do the very best they can with their decision-making, God is part of that.

Certainly, God communicates through nature. When Noah saw the rainbow, he understood it to be a message from God. When I work in my garden, God speaks to me through the wonder of growing plants.

It's easy to mistake the beauty of nature for the voice of God. I've heard people say, "I can worship God just as well on the golf course as I can in church." That may be true. But I've never met anyone who did.

Of course, God isn't limited to any of the things I've mentioned. God may thump you or me on the head with a particular experience or speak to us through a moment of grief or pain or joy. God communicates in a billion and one different ways.

There is a book in the Bible called *Revelation*. It's a book written in a kind of code to a group of Christians caught in a particularly dangerous situation. Some people have used that book, quite irresponsibly, to predict things like the second coming of Christ and the end of the world. That's pure fantasy and a convenient cop-out for people who are trying to run away from the realities of life. Some people find it easier to dream about "pie in the sky" than to respond creatively to a hurting world.

Prayer

One of God's favorite ways of communicating with individuals is through prayer. But prayer, like so many other things in the Christian faith, is hard to describe. It's something you understand only when you've experienced it.

When Bev was away at school before we were married, I wrote her letters almost every day. Now that we've been married for more than 40 years, we still need to keep communicating. It's easier now that we are both more-or-less retired, and we don't go to the office most days. But for a while, we got so busy that we didn't have time to really talk. So we had a little ritual. Saturday mornings, before we got dressed or did anything else, we sat down for a long cup of coffee and just talked. We might talk about how to get a spot out of the rug, or about our kids, or about a problem in our marriage.

For love to be born and for love to grow, there must be communication. In our relationship with God, prayer is that communication. Bev and I would lose our marriage if we didn't make a conscious effort to spend time with each other. In the same way, we can lose our faith if we don't make a conscious effort to spend time with God.

God is easy to talk with. God understands any language spoken by anybody – the simple words of a two-year-old, the complicated language of a professional theologian, or the coarse language of a street person. In fact, prayer doesn't really need words at all.

Some people "can't think of anything to say," when they pray. They spend time in silence, just listening for whatever God has to tell or show them. Prayer should never be forced. It is a natural thing to do, but it needs learning, like a child learning to walk or talk. It needs constant practice, like learning to play a musical instrument. But even if you haven't prayed for a long time and you feel awkward and uncomfortable, your prayer is heard.

The Bible

The Bible is the world's most amazing book. There are three parts to it: Hebrew Scriptures, the Apocrypha, and the Christian Scriptures. The Apocrypha is usually included in Bibles used by the Roman Catholic Church. The rest of us, including the United Church, use the other two portions, although occassionally, here and there, a few of us are beginning to discover treasures in the Apocrypha.

The Hebrew Scriptures began as stories told around the campfires by straggly shepherds, as songs sung on lonely hillsides, and as rules and records and regulations written down by a few scribes.

Gradually, some of the stories, writings, and songs began to have more authority than others as people agreed, "God speaks to us through this."

The Christian Scriptures had similar beginnings but came together during a much shorter time. After that first Easter, the disciples expected Jesus to return very soon. So they didn't bother to write things down. They simply told and retold the stories of what Jesus had said and done.

As time went by and some of the original witnesses died off, the first Christians started to write things down so that more people might know the story of Jesus and the early church.

There were many stories about Jesus written down, and various letters and papers by early church leaders were collected. Not all the stories agreed with each other. It didn't matter. Each of those writings had something important in them. But it wasn't until about 300 years after Jesus that the Bible, as we know it today, was decided upon.

The Bible is often abused. People go to it for a phrase here or a sentence there to support a favorite idea. The Bible is such a rich mine of experiences, you can find material there that, when used the wrong way, will support just about anything.

That's one of the reasons we have such a variety of denominations and religious groups. Each claims to have founded its faith on the Bible. Each group (including the United Church) can easily find things in scripture that seem to support what it's preaching.

Then how does anyone know which interpretation is right? There's no easy answer to that, but there are a few clues.

If you went into the forest near my home and walked up to one of the trees, you might say, "Aha! This is a birch tree. Therefore, this is a birch forest."

You would be wrong. It's a pine forest with a few birch trees in it. To see what the forest is like, you need to back away and take a broad look at the whole thing.

Similarly, when you want to know what the Bible says, you've got to look at the whole book. Only by understanding the Bible's whole context can you decide how to interpret any part of it.

Here's another clue. One of the significant differences between Christianity and Islam is the way we regard our scriptures. According to the Islamic view, the prophet Mohammed was sent to bring a book, the Qur'an. With Christians, the central thing is Jesus, the Messiah. In Islam, the prophet points to the book. In Christianity, the book points to the Messiah.

If the whole purpose of the Bible is to point to the Messiah, then everything in it should be understood in terms of that Messiah. So whenever we read something in the Bible, we need to ask, "How does this tally with who Jesus Christ was, with what he said and did?"

A final clue. The church is there to help us. We can check our understanding against what the church internationally and through the ages has understood. We're not in this by ourselves.

Every Christian should undertake a systematic Bible study and they should do it with trained, responsible help. A good way is to join or organize a group in your church that studies the scripture readings before each Sunday. It makes the Bible come alive and adds depth and meaning to Sunday worship. This is one of those times when the special training of our clergy can be of tremendous help.

Most United Churches use the *Revised Common Lectionary.* That's a series of readings, four for each Sunday, that covers all the important themes and ideas in the Bible during the course of a three-year cycle. I spend some time reading and reflecting on those lections each week, so that when I go to church I hear those readings more deeply, and the whole service speaks to me more completely.

The Bible is the most powerful and the most dangerous of all books. Picking out a bit here and there can lead to spiritual and personal disaster.

It is important to remember that the Bible is not primarily a book of history or a book of rules or a book of preaching, though you'll find all of those in the Bible. People in biblical times often told stories to communicate their faith. Some of those stories were historical and some were not.

It's important not to get caught up in arguments about how much of the Bible is historically accurate, and how much is not. That's an interesting discussion, but it's not the main show. First, let the stories speak to you. They can do that whether they are historically accurate or not. When you've fallen in love with this marvelous book – when you have learned how it can feed your soul – then you might want to listen to what the scholars are saying about how much of the Bible is historical.

It's a bit like a good meal. The food is delicious, so you enjoy it and you let it provide strength and nourishment for your body. That's the main thing. Later you may ask the host for the recipe, but that comes after you've enjoyed the food. You can starve to death if all you do is collect and analyze recipes.

Born again

We hear the phrase "born again" used all over, even in ways that have nothing to do with religion. The phrase comes from the Gospel of John where Jesus is talking to Nicodemus. It's the only place Jesus uses those words. I think he was trying to tell Nicodemus that believing meant more than changing the surface of things. It meant turning your personal world upside down and inside out. It meant changing your whole outlook on life, your reasons for doing things and, most of all, your relationship to God. It meant starting all over.

It's possible to be "born again" in many ways. It may come as a flash of love and joy so powerful you never forget the moment. It can also happen slowly, over a long period of painful searching. Either way, it changes your life. Dramatically.

Some people say they have been "born again," but their emotional high doesn't change the way they handle money, how they vote, or how they relate to the poor and underprivileged here and in other countries. It's a little like my old VW. The odometer went all the way up to 99,999, then back to zero. "I have a born-again car," I told my friends. But it was still the same car with all the same squeaks, rattles, and problems. Nothing had really changed.

The danger is that such a born-again experience may simply inoculate us against the real thing. One strong emotional experience doesn't make a life. Christian faith is like being in love with another person. You can say, "I love you," and have a deep experience of love and commitment. But that love and commitment must be lived every single day. As soon as we stop living our love, it begins to die.

Another word we often use for being born again, a better one actually, is "conversion." People change from one way of seeing life to another. The way we think, act, and live, changes. Our values are converted. Many of us find that conversion is an ongoing process, as we discover new areas of our living that need God's love.

The rules

One of God's gifts to the Hebrew people was the "Law." Much of the Hebrew Scriptures is about God's law and our response to it. The law was both an overall principle by which to live and a series of "rules and regulations." Those laws were continually refined and simplified.

One great summary was the Ten Commandments. Another was quoted by Jesus as two commandments only – to love God and to love your neighbor as yourself. In the end, Jesus condensed all laws into one. "Love one another as I have loved you."

Laws are important. We need them to set the boundaries of behavior when some people aren't willing to live by love. But laws also tend to be rigid. They don't take into account all the unusual circumstances in which people find themselves. It's easy to use the law, or "moral absolutes" as some are calling them now, to control people and to make them over according to your own biases.

Still, the laws are useful and important. In our family, we always had rules about things like bedtime, behavior, meals, and so on. But there were also times when we set aside those rules because there was a more important consideration.

Jesus tells us that rules are there to be used and obeyed, but love is a more important consideration. It's so easy to become lawyers when God wants us to be lovers.

Sin

There's a popular concept of sin. It's reflected in a wall plaque that reads, "Everything I like is indecent, immoral, or fattening." Under that concept, sin is a collection of nasties like smoking, drinking, gambling, sleeping around, or using naughty four-letter words. When those things are destructive to people, they are sinful. So are things like greed, pettiness, back-biting, pride, envy, and refusing to see our part in the sin of other people.

These sins are all symptoms of a more basic disease called "sinfulness." It is the disease of separation from God's love. We are always "living in sin" because, one way or another, we are always running away from God.

When Bev and I have a battle over something, one of us eventually has to swallow our pride and say, "Hey, I'm sorry." Until that happens, we both feel rotten. We both hurt because we are separated from each other. It's far worse when we're separated from God.

The problem is that our separateness from God is built-in. Our basic selfishness seems to be there the moment we're born. That's what theologians have sometimes called "original sin." Bridging that gap is what the journey of faith is all about. It does not mean that we are "born bad."

A concept I like much better is called "original blessing." We are created, as the Bible says, "in the image of God." In some essential, fundamental ways, we are God-like. Or as someone once said, "God don't make trash."

The hardest thing to do is to see your own sin. It's far more fun to spot it in other people. That's especially true of the sin of arrogance. We assume we know better than others "who are not as far along on their journey," or "who are not as liberated," or "who have not yet come to know Jesus." We Christians have a particular fondness for this sin. We tend to see the arrogance in everyone except ourselves.

Confession

"The harder I tries the behinder I gets." I saw that as a bumper sticker once and liked it. Sometimes I feel as if that applies to my moral life too. I really would like to have my life all together, to do all the right things at the right time, etc., etc. But, as some other wag said, "After I got it all together, I forgot where I put it."

Paul, in the Bible, had the same problem. "I want to do good, but I don't. I don't want to do bad, but I do. There's no help for me."

We keep screwing up. We are people. People screw up. That's why there are erasers on pencils. We keep having to say, "I'm sorry," especially to the people we love. Especially to the God we love. In the church, we call that "confession."

Over and over we need to tell God we're sorry. And it helps us to grow if we tell God very specifically what we're sorry about.

In the United Church, we confess our sins directly to God. We do that in prayer at home, at church, or anywhere. Sometimes we should also talk things over with another person. It really helps to tell another person what's bothering us. Often that other person can help us forgive ourselves and accept God's forgiveness.

Grace

Over my desk I have a quote from Martin Luther, the German reformer who kick-started the Protestant Reformation in the 16th century. "You are a sinner. Therefore, sin boldly."

Luther isn't telling me to go and do all sorts of rotten things. He's telling me to recognize the fact that I am going to mess up. That's a given. So I shouldn't go walking on eggshells, trying desperately to stay out of trouble. "Live your life creatively and boldly," he seems to be saying, "and when you find you've done stupid things or even been profoundly cruel and unjust, know that God's grace is there for you."

Grace is a key Christian concept. Grace is God's love for us, regardless of what we might do. God's grace is there for us whether we want it or not – whether we know it or not. So we're called to love God and love our neighbor, and work for truth and justice. When we fall flat on our faces, God's love is there to help us to our feet again.

Forgiveness

When we say to someone, "Please forgive me!" they usually want to do that. But human patience wears thin if we keep screwing up over and over.

Not God's. God seems ready to forgive over and over and over, long past anything we humans can imagine.

Sometimes it seems as if God doesn't have any standards. No pride. God can get angry, but doesn't seem to stay angry. We do our worst, but as soon as we make the first tiny step back toward God's love, there it is.

The amazing thing about this love, this grace, is that we can never earn it. We can do things that will damage the love we have for each other. And we can do things that will violate our love for God. But we can never earn that love in the first place. That's part of that whole idea of "covenant." God has decided to love us, whether we deserve it or not, whether we love back or not.

When we are loved by another person, that love is the most precious gift they can give. When we are loved by God, it is the ultimate gift. And that love gives us our worth, our "justification" as the theologians call it. That love means we're precious to God. What more do we need?

Growing in faith

In a darkened basement, a single match can mean hope until, with that match, we find a candle to light. With the light from that candle, we find the fuse box and, with the electric light, we find the door leading to the sunlight. Each light dazzled our eyes until we found a greater light that made the previous one seem so small by comparison.

Our growth in faith is like that. Each new experience, each new learning, makes earlier ones seem insignificant. The important thing, of course, isn't which light we're using now, but whether we keep on searching for a greater one.

The Christian faith is not something you arrive at. It's something you grow in. It's a process. A pathway. A journey. We often call ourselves pilgrims. We're on our way together, and we know we're headed in the right direction, even though we may take a few detours.

We know we're on the right road because it's been marked by others who have gone before us. And we have the sure light of the whole Bible to see the pathway, the company of fellow pilgrims called the church who help us see the way. One of my favorite hymns, and one we sing quite often in our church, is an African song from *Voices United – We Are Marching in the Light of God!* Singing that song, standing beside my friends in the church, gives me strength to keep on my journey of faith.

But when all is said and done and you've fried your brains trying to understand the Christian faith, there is always more mystery. A mystery is not a puzzle you are trying to solve. Mystery is a well from which you draw life-giving water. Wonderfully and mysteriously, the level of the water never goes down – the well of faith never runs dry.

Sin matters. But in this time of transition, when so many of the old values come under question, and so many of the old questions are treated as irrelevant, even those who know that sin matters have grown wary of pointing fingers and saying, That's a sin!

We need to name the sins we see. By refraining from identifying sin as sin, we do no favor to ourselves or to the sinners. And remember, those sinners may be ourselves as well as others. By refraining from naming the sin as sin – from fear, from embarrassment, from a desire not to offend – we progressively train ourselves to accept the unacceptable. We allow people to persuade themselves that they really haven't done anything wrong, after all.

James Taylor – from *Sin: A New Understanding of*
Virtue and Vice (Northstone, 1997)

In light of the hunger for the transcendent, the heart's craving for "spirituality," the mood and style of Christian worship will be increasingly charismatic. While it is impossible to be over-cerebral, it is certainly possible to be one-sidedly cerebral. This latter imbalance, rendering the church lopsided for too long, will be redressed as community-life and personal devotion, social righteousness and intellectual rigor are restored to proper proportion. Head and heart, understanding and effusiveness, doctrine and dancing, ardor and affection will be accorded their rightful place.

Victor Shepherd – from *Fellowship*, March 1999

11

Right, Wrong, and Maybe

In the beginning, God created the heaven and the earth... So God created human beings in the divine image...and God blessed them and said to them, "Be fruitful and multiply, fill the earth and subdue it." So it was, and God saw all creation, and it was very good.

Excerpts from Genesis 1 (paraphrased)

When you sing in the choir, you get to see things others miss. When Bev was the minister at Westbank United, I sang in the bass section. I got a good view of everything.

One Sunday, just as Bev was finishing her sermon, the door at the back opened tentatively. A man entered. I could see he was a bit unsteady on his feet. Iris, who always sat at the back of the church for just such situations, quickly found him a chair and invited him to sit. She whispered something into his ear, and he nodded.

Now it was time for communion. Along with a number of others chosen to serve the communion that Sunday, Iris came up to the front. After the prayers and the invitation to everyone to "take and eat," Iris served the bread to the back rows, including our late visitor.

As she offered the plate of bread to him, he looked startled and in a loud voice said, "What the hell is this?" I couldn't hear her words, but Iris evidently explained it to his satisfaction. "Oh!" he said loudly.

Then the sacramental wine was served. (As in most United Churches, it was actually grape juice.) When Iris took the tray of glasses to the man in the back, he said, "Good! I could use a drink." And so the service proceeded to its conclusion.

I saw the man again downstairs in the hall where we have coffee. My guess is that Iris invited him down for coffee and a sandwich. Around him, in quiet conversation, were several men who I knew were members of AA, Alcoholics Anonymous. I went over to him to offer him my greetings. "You wouldn't want a drunk in this church," he said, when I invited him to come back again. "Why not," said one of the men. "You wouldn't be the only one."

I wish I could tell you a happy ending about the man finding a new direction for his life. He apparently came to an AA meeting at the church during the week, and he was back in church the following Sunday. Several of those AA men had tried to find out where he lived so they could keep in contact with him. He wouldn't tell them, and after the second Sunday he just disappeared.

The reason I'm telling you this story is because Iris and those men welcomed this person, even though he was quite clearly a little drunk and was badly in need of clean clothes and a bath.

It was one of those moments when I found myself genuinely proud of my United Church. It's a story like that which illustrates in a fundamental way how social justice concerns are at the very heart of my denomination.

The two sides of morality

The story illustrates what some would call a weakness, but which others see as a strength.

The United Church has been called "morally spineless" and "a church without standards." But others say it's simply taking Jesus seriously when he said, "The one of you who is faultless shall throw the first stone." Both sides have a point.

To talk about morals and ethics, let's divide Christians into two groups: those who worry about personal sin, and those who have a concern for corporate sin.

People concerned about personal sin take a hard line on things like sleeping around, abortion, divorce, and shoplifting. These people sometimes forget that they are part of a society that is guilty of corporate sin as well.

When governments, businesses, and other institutions (large and small) do things that hurt people, that's sin, just as surely as rape and murder are sins. When we pollute our rivers or oppress people economically or socially, it is sin. It's corporate sin and we all share the guilt.

People in the second group sometimes put such a heavy emphasis on corporate sin, they forget about personal sin. They may become very accommodating to whatever social changes are taking place in our society. Changing sexual standards, for example. They oppose government-run lotteries, but rarely say anything about the individuals who buy the tickets.

United Church leaders tend to be more the second kind of Christian than the first, at least judging by public statements made by conferences and General Council. However, the majority in the pews are more concerned with personal morality, and often don't understand what conferences and General Councils are talking about. Both groups could listen harder, because there's wisdom in both perspectives.

The only question left

Most Christian churches believe that questions of right and wrong are central questions. As a society, we put maximum energy into questions like, "Does it work? Is it profitable? Is it legal?" But the church maintains that the central question must be, "Is it right? Does it serve the best interests of all of God's creation?"

When you think of it, that's about the only question left for humanity. With our technology developing so rapidly, the "Will it work?" or "Is it possible?" questions can almost always be answered "Yes."

It certainly is possible for the nations of the world to spend hundreds of millions of dollars a day (I'm not exaggerating!) on armaments while millions of people don't have adequate housing, education, or medical help. But is it right?

It is possible to perform abortions early in the pregnancy without much discomfort to the woman. But is it right?

Responses

There are at least three ways a church or an individual can respond to those kinds of questions. Two ways are easy. One is hard.

The "Who cares?" way of decision-making is the easiest of all. You simply say, "Well, there's no way you can know what's right and wrong, so never mind. Do whatever feels good. And smile!" You turn your decision-making over to the crowd you run with.

The "Right's right!" method is a bit harder. You have to stand up for something. You say, "There's an absolute right and an absolute wrong to everything. For instance, divorce is wrong. Therefore, nobody gets a divorce. Period."

You turn your decision-making over to some "authority," who tells you exactly what those absolute rights and wrongs are. These "authorities" usually claim to know exactly how to interpret "scripture," whether it's the Qur'an, the Communist Manifesto, capitalist economics, or the Bible.

Then there's the "Jesus way" and it is tough. It makes us think and choose. There's no United Church statement on how to make moral choices, but I think this third method would be endorsed by many in our denomination.

To understand this method, you have to look at the way Jesus decided what was right and wrong. Jesus had great respect for the Law, the rules by which the people of Israel tried to live. There's a story in the Gospel of Luke (18:18–27) about a wealthy man who came to Jesus and asked what he needed to do to have "eternal life." The first thing Jesus told him was to pay attention to the rules. He also told the man that there was much more to life than rules, but that was a good place to start.

On the other hand, when the lawyers of Jesus' time started getting picky about his friends eating corn on the Sabbath, Jesus didn't deny that they had broken Jewish law. He said, "The Sabbath is made for people. People were not made for the Sabbath" (Mark 2:23–28). In other words, rules are there for your sake and mine. We're not here for the sake of the rules.

The gospels are peppered with stories of Jesus encountering people who had broken the law. He approached them all with love and understanding. Jesus' first concern always seemed to be for the people involved.

In the Gospel of John (8:1–11, RSV) there's a story about a woman caught in adultery. In those days, sex with someone outside of marriage was a capital crime, though it was only the women who got punished for it. The woman in this story should have been executed by stoning, according to the law. And a crowd of people standing around her had rocks in their hands.

Jesus was quick to see the sin of the folks with the rocks in their hands – the sin of pride and self-righteousness. So he said, "The one of you who is faultless shall throw the first stone." One by one they went sneaking off, knowing they were in no position to condemn the woman.

Jesus didn't say that what she had done was okay. But he didn't condemn her either. He said, "Go, and sin no more."

What he did was the right thing for that woman in that situation at that time. The person was more important than the rules. But it is important to note that Jesus' concern was not only for the woman. It was also for the guys with the rocks in their hands.

Facing the hard questions

One of the hard moral questions is always, "What is the loving thing to do?" When my kids were small and ran out on the street without looking, I scolded them. Sometimes I punished them. They didn't like it, but it was the loving thing to do.

Another central question is, "What will result in the greatest good for the greatest number of people involved?" In other words, justice with love. It can be a real dandy to sort out, because sometimes the loving thing to do for the individual perpetuates injustice for others.

The Bible indicates quite clearly that whenever somebody does something wrong, all of us are involved. As members of a society, we are part of the climate in which sin grows. So we need to ask God's forgiveness, while we do whatever we can to change the climate.

As a church, we need to consider all these things when we work through various moral and ethical issues which are almost never clear-cut. Then, as a church and as Christian individuals, we need to be a force for morality and justice in all aspects of society.

Choosing your battles

I find it really difficult sometimes. There are so many causes that need help, so many wrongs that need struggling against, so much justice to be struggled toward. I don't know where to begin. I'd like to work towards a cleaner environment. I believe we need to do something about poverty, especially among women and the elderly. I am keenly interested in international justice issues. On and on it goes. I feel burned out just thinking about it.

A few years ago, Clarke MacDonald, a former Moderator of the United Church, shared some wisdom with me. "Ralph," he said, "choose one or two causes that you can really give yourself to. Work as hard as you can for those. As for the other causes and issues, know enough so you don't get in the way and so you can be supportive where possible."

A few samples

Here are a few samples of things people have in mind when they ask, "What does the United Church have to say about the ills and struggles of our world?" Quite a lot, as it turns out. You could fill a library on any one of these issues, so don't consider what follows any more than a quick run-through.

Drugs

Smoking is harmful to health, both for those who smoke and for others around them. Many folks are allergic to tobacco smoke, and smokers usually have an "aura" about them. Other than saying that it's a Christian responsibility to take care of the body, and to be concerned about the welfare of others, the United Church hasn't said much about smoking.

There was a time when many people (myself included) smoked at church meetings. Not anymore. In my home congregation, there's no smoking anywhere in the building.

Booze is certainly the big one. Most United Church members probably take a drink or two. I do myself. But we also realize that alcohol abuse is one of our most serious social problems in Canada. It causes untold misery and costs us millions. Many congregations have Alcoholics Anonymous, Al-Anon, or Alateen groups that use their facilities regularly.

The official United Church position is that, while you can take a drink and still be a Christian, the smartest thing is to stay clear of the stuff.

We probably panicked a bit when marijuana first hit us in the 1960s. Now we know that it creates many of the same problems as booze. On the other hand, some experts say it's less harmful than alcohol or tobacco.

Hard drugs are a major social hazard causing all kinds of personal consequences for the user, and a variety of social problems. It's a very complex problem that's getting worse every year. Education and law enforcement don't seem to be working. The United Church has been saying to governments, look at the underlying causes and work on those. Don't just treat the symptoms.

Prescription drugs are legal and respectable. But these drugs, along with booze and grass, are also part of the problem, the desire for a quick, easy way out of life's problems. And there are social addictions such as workaholism, gambling, and shopping which are part of the same picture. Workaholism is the one I have the most trouble with.

Real answers come in straightening out the problems in our lives that make us turn to these drugs. That's a lot more difficult than popping a pill or pouring a shot of Scotch.

Hard answers, which point to long-term changes, force us to turn to our faith. Not for an instant "miracle," but for the courage our faith provides, and the support and counsel the church community can give.

Gambling

We were caught napping on this one. When casinos and lotteries were legalized in the 1960s and 1970s, only a few of our people yelled.

The church has always said that gambling is wrong. Most United Church people couldn't see a problem spending a few dollars on a lottery ticket or on a Saturday night bingo, especially when the proceeds went to a good cause. Now, as casinos are opening all over, more and more people in the United Church are pointing out that the folks who do the most gambling are the ones who can least afford it. For many, gambling is an addiction that's harder to handle than booze or dope.

The United Church has said that no congregation or any other part of the church should take money raised from gambling. Some people think that's silly. Others agree that it's wrong to raise money, even for worthy causes, by using other people's weaknesses and addictions.

Sex

It would be so easy for the church to use the "Who Cares?" method of decision-making on this one. Or even the "Right's Right!" way. There are plenty of people who want the church to say only one word on the subject: "No!"

That kind of response never worked and it isn't appropriate today. It's foolish to ignore the fact that teenagers become sexually active very early, that living together has become common, even respectable, and that the "no sex before marriage" ideal is no longer honored in Canadian society. Most couples coming to be married in the church are already living together.

You'll find many responses to all this in the church. I still believe that lifelong commitment in marriage, and the sexual fidelity that goes with it, is still the way God calls us to be. Others say that it's the commitment, the caring, the life-giving relationship that's important, not the legality of marriage.

I believe most United Church people would say that sex is not "bad." It isn't dirty. It is beautiful and fulfilling. But it can also be dangerous, destructive, and exploitative.

Homosexuality

The United Church has struggled mightily over the homosexuality issue for many years, but I think the matter is finally settled. That's not to say that we have universal agreement. Some are still fighting angrily against it.

But I think it is now clear from official statements and, more importantly, from the attitude expressed by the majority of United Church people, that sexual orientation really has no bearing on full participation in our community. That includes the ordained ministry. We're gradually learning that homosexual people can also live in caring, loving, committed relationships.

Which is not to say that gay and lesbian people don't get hassled in church, sometimes. But it is happening less and less, and more and more they are being accepted as individuals who, like all the rest of us, are created in the image of God.

Abortion

Here the United Church has made a statement, though it hasn't always been accurately reported.

We're not "in favor of abortion." I don't know anyone in the United Church who has ever made that kind of statement, even though the Church has been quoted as having said that.

What we have said is that there are some situations in which abortion is the lesser of two evils. When all the available solutions to a problem are bad, you pick the one that is least bad.

The United Church position is, basically, that there are times when abortion is necessary and that it's up to the woman and her doctor to decide when that is.

Abortion is not a substitute for birth control. On that everyone agrees, I think. But a vocal minority in the church says "no" to abortion under any circumstances. To them, abortion is killing, plain and simple.

Divorce

The United Church is not in favor of divorce either. But, again, it is the least bad thing in many instances. It's true that many couples simply pack it in when the going gets a bit rough, instead of working at their commitment, getting help with their problems, and struggling to build a better relationship. Many people are far too casual about marriage commitments.

But to say "No divorce, ever!" would be condemning some people to a living hell. To rule that if you've been divorced you can never marry again is equally harsh.

That's why so many refugees from other denominations come to the United Church to be married, and why we have so many "blended families." Our clergy often spend long hours counseling people who come from other denominations with a great burden of guilt and hurt. Some ministers feel quite angry when they see the shattered faith of people who have had rule books thrown at them.

Divorce always causes pain, especially when there are children involved. And something that causes pain is wrong. But sometimes it's the only thing that can be done when a marriage has died or when a relationship is destroying someone. Divorce is sometimes less wrong than staying married.

Abuse

We're only now becoming somewhat dimly aware of the extent to which sexual, psychological, and physical abuse happens in families, often in families that seem to present a picture of respectability. It also happens in various clubs, athletic organizations, and other helping organizations. And in churches of every denomination. Women, children, and the elderly are the most frequent victims.

The traditional response of the United Church (and pretty well every other church and organization) had been to sweep such problems under the carpet. Now we are just beginning to recognize that we have a moral responsibility to name it, to work to prevent it, and to deal firmly with the aggressors. To look the other way is to be a party to the crime.

It's my personal opinion that male adults (like me) have a particular responsibility for working on this problem, because most often it's male adults who have been the abusers.

Many churches, along with other groups such as the Scouts, sports organizations and others, now insist that volunteers who work with others who may be at risk (mostly children) must have a criminal record check before they begin this work. That includes the clergy and other church professionals.

I find it very sad that this is necessary. But it is. There certainly is no watertight solution. There is help from conferences and national church offices to help congregations protect themselves and the weaker ones in their care.

It's not just the weaker ones who need protecting, of course. Leaders need to be protected against false accusations. And there needs to be a way of offering forgiveness and second chances to those who have made mistakes in the past.

I have a friend who spent time in jail because he had embezzled money from his company. When he came out of jail, he was invited to church. He knew he needed a church to help him get his life together. He made no secret of the fact that he had been in jail for embezzling money. The congregation, in a great act of Christian faith, asked him to be the church treasurer.

Crime and punishment

The United Church has an official position against taking human life as a means of punishment. Its reasons are simple. We humans don't have the right to make that kind of irrevocable judgment. Killing is wrong, for whatever reason. Furthermore, it doesn't do any good. There is no evidence anywhere that capital punishment prevents others from killing.

That official position is quite clear but considerably different from that of the average church member. Like the average Canadian, most United Church people would feel that at least in the case of the killing of law officers, the penalty should be death.

Our official stand on capital punishment springs out of our general attitude toward the way we handle those people who violate our laws. After looking at the way Jesus related to people who were in trouble with the law, the church has come to say that the purpose of our justice system should be to turn people around to a better way of life. It should never be used to get even.

The church also points to a fact that is easily documented by studying trial records. Those who have money and connections are treated much better by the law than those who don't.

Censorship

All of us are realizing that television, particularly, and mass media in general, affect the way we think and act, far more than we dare to admit. Those who claim it doesn't affect them at all should consider that advertisers wouldn't spend billions of dollars if that didn't translate into sales. The question really is, do we want to be affected that way?

Saskatchewan Conference came out strongly against "the present proliferation of advertising." They claimed "the values propagated by some advertising and the gospel preached by the church are in direct conflict."

It's not just advertisements that influence us. The programs do, too. Many of us are worried about the increasing violence and exploitative sex that occupies so much TV time. For others, the concerns go deeper and include role-stereotyping, superficial news reporting, manipulation of children and, most of all, the advertisers who use our fears to sell us products.

What we've not figured out is how to do something about these problems, without violating the fundamental freedom of expression. As a culture, the pendulum has swung hard in the direction of personal freedom, and it needs to move back a bit toward the concept of personal and social responsibility.

Caring for creation

"Everybody is in favor of ecology," a young enthusiast once told me, as if that was like being in favor of motherhood. Actually, ecology is a very fundamental issue for Christians. It's about our relationship to the world God created and gave us to care for. It's as much an attitude as a science. It's a way of seeing ourselves as deeply connected to everything on this whole planet.

Sometimes we think of the world as God's body, and polluting the air is the fouling of God's breath, God's spirit. It means that ecological concerns are part of the same fabric as personal morality, social concerns, and international justice issues.

All of us share a common, human tendency. We love to get riled up about mistakes other people are making. It's way more fun getting into a sweat over Brazilian rain forests than about Canadian forests. After all, if we stop cutting trees here in Canada, that'll cost us jobs. Saving the rain forest costs jobs in Brazil, too, jobs of people who have no unemployment insurance or welfare.

One of these days the penny will drop. Ecology costs. Jobs, money, standard of living. It's good not to use Styrofoam cups in church and to recycle our newspapers. But those are two-bit responses to multi-billion dollar problems. We are not going to do anything significant about the ecology of our planet until we take a radical drop in our standard of living. Us, here in Canada. Not the people in the Third World. Their standard of living is already ecologically responsible. They have no choice.

If we want air to breathe, water to drink, and healthy food to eat, it's going to cost us.

Christians have a good word to use here. Stewardship. A steward is someone who takes loving care of something that belongs to someone else. We are stewards of God's creation. Even more, we are invited to be participants in that creation because God loves us and trusts us to deal kindly with it.

Because of our growing concern, and because we were asked to do this by our First Nations members, a new line "to live with respect in Creation" was added to our Creed.

Politics

There has never been a time when the church wasn't involved in politics. The Bible is often more political than religious, although in biblical days people didn't really distinguish between the two. Jesus was very political.

It wasn't until the Reformation, when people were reacting against the strong political power of the Holy Roman Empire, that the idea of separating church and state came along.

The United Church has never had political power, but it has always had political influence. It has never been able to deliver a block of votes to any candidate. Nor has it ever tried or even wanted to. But it can and does speak out on issues that involve ethics and morals, especially the ethics and morals of governments and corporations.

For many years, there has been a disagreement between the evangelical and the liberal elements in our church. The liberal group feels that the church not only has a right, it has an obligation to speak out. We have to change the systems that put people down, and that involves politics. The evangelical group feels you must begin by changing people. The people then go out and change oppressive systems. There is truth in both positions.

Often the church speaks out through petitions and resolutions from presbyteries, conferences, and other church bodies. I don't really think that does any good, although it does make us feel as if we've done something. And the church simply doesn't have the political influence it had, even a few years ago. We've got to find other ways to speak to the social and political process.

Militarism

Everybody is against war. The only question is: how do you prevent it?

People sitting in United Church pews represent a variety of viewpoints. Many of them side with the military establishment and say the only way to prevent war is to be so strong nobody will attack you. Therefore, you must have superior weapons.

The United Church position is that this results in an insane escalation of armaments all over the world, which could easily end in the total destruction of our planet. Nobody would win. Everybody would lose.

Besides, if the money and energy put into building bigger and better weapons were put into solving problems, we could head off potential wars. If we took the money now going into armaments and spent it on a better lifestyle for the Third World, and to address the huge ecological concerns facing our planet, we could do those jobs and have money left over. Everybody would win!

International relations

We've always been a strong missionary church. Sometimes we've tried to "convert" people in other parts of the world to our way of thinking. More often, we've tried to work beside them in their struggles to grow and develop.

The question is much larger than simply giving money. The United Church believes we should act politically and economically here in Canada to support our fellow humans in other parts of the world. It isn't just a matter of giving aid. It's a matter of changing some of the systems of trade, economic control, and industrial power that keep us rich and them poor.

As long as the world's economy is structured in such a way that we maintain our privileges at their expense, we can't expect them to be grateful for the bit of aid we offer – or to expect our aid to do much good.

Minority rights

Through the years, the church has had a history of supporting people who had somebody else's foot on their necks. Some of these groups are overseas. Some are right here in Canada.

One minority asking for their rights are Canada's first citizens, Canada's First Nations people. Many within the church have felt a strong call to support our Native sisters and brothers in their struggle for what they see as basic "human rights." And the United Church has taken strong official and unofficial action in this regard.

As I write this, the United Church is starting down a long, pain-filled road. For many years, the United Church and several other denominations worked with the federal government to operate a number of residential schools, where First Nations children were sent. The intent was to give these young people the skills to take their place in our white culture. But the result was that we stripped them of their culture and identity, and often of their pride.

The United Church has issued formal apologies to First Nations people, in 1986 and 1998, because we became aware that even with our best intentions, we were part of what some have called "cultural genocide."

Most of the teachers and administrators in the residential schools were good and kind people, and genuinely wanted the best for their students. I don't think we have a right to be critical of them. They walked by the light they had. They were part of a society that was convinced that the best way to help First Nations people and other cultural minorities was to educate them into the dominant society. It was this conviction that drove much of the world mission movement until a few decades ago. We now recognize the destructiveness of that attitude, but the blame (if there must be blame) must be borne by our whole society.

But that's not the most painful part of the story. There were a few who physically and sexually abused the children in their charge. That was wrong then, as it is wrong now. It has resulted in a number of lawsuits that will take years to resolve and will involve huge sums of money. It is entirely possible that all the national assets of the United Church will be gone when these suits are eventually resolved.

It is a traumatic time for the United Church. We genuinely want for justice to be done and for reconciliation to happen. As I write this, it is very hard to know how this tragic drama will end.

Sexism

Another group that has been denied fair treatment, even though it's not a minority, is women. Most United Church people would agree with the principle that men and women should be treated equally. There should be equal opportunity and equal pay for equal work. They don't agree on what needs rearranging in order to make this happen.

For instance, many see the concern for inclusive language as rather silly. "They're making a mountain out of a molehill," I heard one woman complain.

Within the United Church, a vocal minority of men and women say the issue is very close to the heart of our faith. Sexism restricts us to playing a role. We are pushed into thinking and behaving in ways that society prescribes, rather than developing individually as free children of God.

Others see male domination as the essence of what is wrong with our society and our world. The world is run by people with power over others. That's a masculine way of doing things. Jesus said, "Love one another!" That's the nurturing or feminine way of seeing life. (The people expressing this view would hasten to add that many men are very nurturing and many women are power hungry.)

Concerns around sexism amount to far more than simply changing "chairman" to "chairperson," though that's important, too. It's a question of who we truly are as people made in the "image of God" – a God who is neither male nor female.

Depending on your point of view, the United Church is either "capitulating to strident feminists" or "making progress toward human liberation" more quickly than most other groups, certainly more quickly than any other denomination in Canada.

Churchgoer values

A study done by Reginald Bibby of the University of Lethbridge showed that the values of church people generally (and United Church members in particular) didn't differ much from the rest of the Canadian population. I found that a very sad commentary on the Christian Church.

Bibby is partly right. A very large segment of the church population come Sunday by Sunday for a kind of "verbal massage." It feels good to be in church. It's comforting to hear the old hymns and to listen to the Bible being read. And, if you don't listen too closely, even the sermon is comforting.

On either side of this majority we have an enthusiastic minority – some on the "evangelical right" and others on the "social action left." If Bibby had measured those two groups, the most committed 20 percent, rather than the majority at the center, he would have found some differences.

That's not just hopeful conjecture. Unless Canadians are very different from Americans in this regard, significant church involvement does make a difference. The Gallup research organization found that people deeply involved in churches and synagogues are three times more active than others in social, charitable, and civic activities, such as feeding the hungry, housing the homeless, and caring for the sick. These people dug into their pockets too. Members of churches and synagogues spent more than twice as much on these initiatives as all the corporations and foundations combined.

To soar like an eagle

It seems that it's the intensity of the involvement, not whether you're "conservative" or "liberal," that counts. And that's consistent with what Jesus taught. He didn't care a whole lot about the kind of theology we espoused. He was more concerned about what kind of life we lived. "You'll know them by the fruit they produce," he said.

There's a lot of vitality in the church, and we see it often in those who are most liberal and those who are most conservative. These two extremes in our church have the stuff that could get a lot of jaded pew-sitters off dead center. But they'll never do that until they learn to listen to each other and to recognize that each has a valuable element of the gospel which the other has missed.

I think we may have forgotten how to see the value in our differences. But I see some signs that we're beginning to relearn it. I hope I'm right. If I'm wrong, then the United Church of Canada may have lost its sense of inclusiveness and, perhaps, its reason for being.

Alone, the right and left wings of the United Church flop around on the ground, unable to fly. And the rest of the world doesn't hear our statements and resolutions and sermons. They just see us flailing away at each other. "What a bunch of turkeys!" they think.

If we could love and respect each other through our differences, we could, as the prophet Isaiah said, "renew our strength," and "mount up with wings like eagles."

We could do miracles!

The greatest gift the mainline Protestant churches – including the United Church of Canada – can presently offer to the worldwide Christian movement may well lie in our ability to maintain a thriving center. Such an option will differ dramatically from the strident sectarianisms of the left and the right, but will also resist the middle-of-the-road wishy-washiness. More to the point, a desire to find the vibrant center will leave us well poised to embrace our rich congregational diversity without feeling threatened by that diversity, as well as the multi-hued heritage that is available to us from the wider church, if we have the discipline to acquaint ourselves with it. I am certain that it was the availability of that vital, vibrant center within the United Church, that made it possible for me, a lost and lonely former semi-hippie wayfarer, to hear and to embrace the gospel of Jesus Christ some 20 years ago. And I am equally certain that a denomination that is willing to reclaim that vital center will be well poised to welcome many other wayfarers, ex-hippie or otherwise!

Foster Freed – from a sermon preached at the annual meeting of
BC Conference, 1999

12

The Impossible Dream

—

For where two or three are gathered in my name,
I am there among them.
Matthew 18:20

Just a very few years ago, I was at a service of worship in Vernon, an hour's drive from my home. It was a meeting of the BC Conference of the United Church. At the end of that service, I was to be inducted as the President of the Conference.

We were receiving communion. With me in the worship were my son-in-law, Don, and my first grandchild, Jake, who was just a year old. "May I give Jake his first communion?" I asked Don. "Sure, Grandpa!" he said cheerfully.

As I held Jake in my arms, I broke off a piece of the bread, dipped it in the wine, and put it in Jake's mouth. At that moment I was overwhelmed by a prayer I found deep inside myself.

"God, when Jake grows to be a young man, let there be a strong and vigorous and faith-filled church that he can be part of. If he chooses too.

"But God, if that isn't possible, let the church move into the future with vigor and enthusiasm and power, so that if it goes down in flames, I can say to Jake, 'You should have been there. That was my church, Jake, and it bet everything on the future. It went down in flames, but it was a glorious struggle.'

"But God, please don't make me have to tell Jake that the church just slowly faded away, and the last we heard of it was a weak little whimper. Please God, I don't want to tell that story to Jake."

Depth, diversity, and despair

A few minutes later, I was inducted as President of the BC Conference of the United Church. It's the highest position in any Conference, though like the Moderator, there isn't any power attached to it. I explained to non-church friends and to my children that it's as close as the United Church gets to having bishops.

"You, Dad? A bishop?" said Mark, my eldest son.

"Yes," I said. "And don't forget that makes you a son of a bishop."

I'm not sure what I gave to the church in BC as I traveled around during my one-year term, but I received a much deeper sense of its depth, its diversity, and of the fine, dedicated people who are its leaders. But I also sensed it was a church in deep trouble. From the heydays of the 1950s, when churches sprouting in all the suburbs were almost instantly filled, the United Church is now a very much smaller, and a very chastened image of its former self.

We've had trouble adjusting. Clergy and other leaders will tell you it's not numbers that matter, but the quality of the church's life and mission. But they worry anyway when participation drops off, year after year. And they feel guilty and sometimes angry when people my age pointedly tell them how the church was bursting at the seams in the 1950s, how the Sunday school was always full, and how the minister always preached inspiring sermons. There's more than a slight rosy tint in our glasses when we look backwards.

"What are we doing wrong?" is the question implied in our hand-wringing reflections. Well, there is a clear answer. We are not doing anything wrong! There has been a huge shift in public attitude in all of North America, but especially Canada. It has affected every single organization – political parties, service clubs, churches, everything.

A number of social scientists have written on this. One of them pin-points the watershed – the symbolic moment. It was when a young woman put a flower in the muzzle of one of the state trooper's guns during the Kent State University riots. I vividly remember seeing that moment on TV. Most social scientists agree that from the 1960s onward, there has been a steady erosion of commitment to organizations and respect for authority. Less and less do we see ourselves as part of a group or country or church. More and more we see ourselves as individuals. And we have far less faith and trust in our leaders. Leaders of any kind – political, medical, community, sports, religious.

I often do what's called "the rubber chicken circuit." I talk at service clubs and other organizations. At every one of them I see the confirmation of the social scientists' theories. The heads are gray, the numbers are down, and the organization lives mostly on memories and on the commitment of a shrinking group of gray-haired people. In every one of them – Rotary, Kiwanis, Canadian Club – I see the same problems as I see in the mainline church.

It's not hard to find critics who point out all the flaws in the United Church and who claim to know exactly why the church is no longer what it used to be. But the same thing is true in every major denomination – the mainline churches and many of the evangelical churches. Yes, there are mega congregations in the evangelical denominations that are growing rapidly. But they are growing at the expense of many small congregations. And the overall denominational numbers are down.

So it's not something we are doing wrong. It is the society in which we live. It is the times in which we live. Let's stop beating ourselves for social changes beyond our control.

Closet Christians

At the same time, there are all kinds of indicators that most people in Canada consider themselves Christians. An even higher percentage will say "Yes" when the pollster asks them if they believe in God. Genuine atheists are really hard to find. There's also a deep interest in things religious. The media often give prime coverage to a story about religion, especially if there is an element of controversy around it.

A CBC reporter told me not long ago, "I don't know anybody who goes to church." That says more about the narrowness of that reporter's experience than about the church. Because while church attendance in Canada is down, there are still far more people involved in the church than there are involved in organized sport. There is of course, far more money in sports, which is no doubt why it gets so much more attention.

So while interest in things religious or spiritual is high, church attendance is down. Confidence and trust in religious leadership is down. For those who do attend, the church is one among many activities of equal priority – hockey for the kids, the movies, TV specials.

Scientific leapfrogs

I don't do predictions. I'm not going to try to tell you what the church will be like as we move through this new millennium. But I am convinced that the human animal is incurably religious. In the years since the development of the scientific method, and the huge leaps in technological innovation, some pundits have been predicting the total demise of religion. But it hasn't happened. Far from it.

In fact, as scientific developments have leapfrogged over each other, and as science has become in itself a kind of religion, humans are hungering for deeper answers than science can provide.

Science can see facts. The human spirit can see truth. It works something like this. If I, a storyteller and a dreamer, point to a rainbow, I say, "Wow! Look at that. It is beautiful! Glorious! For me, that rainbow is a symbol that a loving, creator God is at work."

Now if I were a scientist, I would say, "A rainbow is the result of refraction of light through particles of water." And I'd be right, of course. The scientist and the storyteller in me see the truth of the rainbow in different ways, and both are necessary and right.

I am writing this book on a computer, which is a marvel of technology. I find it a wonderfully useful tool, even though I have no idea how it works. I want the gifts of technology. I want to be able to fly to many parts of the world in airplanes that are comfortable and safe. When I am ill, I want the best of medical science to help me.

A mystery

Science offers us almost unimaginable opportunities for genuine progress, as well as the possibility of cataclysmic self-destruction. But even at its best, science isn't enough to live on. All the science in the world can do nothing more than fill my brain with data, some of which may become useful information. But when, within all that information, we can see wisdom, then we can make science work for us, rather than against us.

Only when I am wise enough to know that, as a human being, I am more than the sum of my parts, that I am a miracle of creation, can I use science wisely. Only when I see all creation as a miracle – not a scientific wonder, but a miracle – can I use science to green the world, rather than turn it into ashes.

Such wisdom is not learned in schools. It is God given, and very near the heart of what we call religion or spirituality. It is at the heart of mystery.

"Mystery" is a very powerful, very spiritual idea. It's not a puzzle to be solved. It is a reality that we reflect on, dream about, discuss, experience, and proclaim. Part of that mystery is the hunger, the yearning we humans have for something more than food, water, and shelter. We long for deeper relationships with others. We long for people to love, and we long to be loved ourselves.

And we long for a reality beyond that – we yearn for, we search for the holy, the numinous, the spiritual. Why we do that is part of the mystery, although I know a very old story that tells how humans are made in the image and likeness of God. Perhaps, when we find God, we will also find ourselves. The story comes from a very old and precious book that tells of other people, in other troubled times, who have searched for and sometimes experienced God. You can read that story yourself – in the Bible.

In that quest for the holy, every human society has generated a religion of some sort. That yearning for God has not gone away, even though many no longer go searching for God in the churches. The society you and I will experience in Canada in the first decades of the new millennium will be searching too. We can't help it. And so we will grow a church, a community of searchers who will gather sometimes to tell each other where they have found spiritual food for their journey – where they have encountered God in their lives.

A new church will be generated out of the past, out of the stories and songs and teachings that have come to us from the Bible. And the new church will be generated out of our life experiences as we struggle to stay human in a consumer society.

There will be a church of some kind for me in the last third of my life, for Jake in the first third of his, and for you. Whether it will resemble the United Church of Canada – whether it will be a continuation of today's church or something totally new – I don't know. But there will be a church, if we approach the future with courage and generosity and an openness to the mystery.

The changing church

I was astounded when Wood Lake Books editor Mike Schwartzentruber asked me to do a third edition of *This United Church of Ours*. It seemed like such a short time since I'd done the second edition, and I remembered how many changes there had been in our denomination in one decade, from 1980 to 1990.

Then, when I sat down to read that second edition, I realized the changes in the last decade had been even more profound. The biggest change, and the hardest one, was in my sense of the future. When I wrote the first two editions, I had a good sense of where the church was going. I could write with reasonable confidence about the future. Now I can't do that.

I remember the ancient oriental curse, "May you live in interesting times." I have no doubt that the first years of the new millennium will be "interesting" for all of us, and certainly interesting for the church. Since you have read this far in this book, I assume that you have some interest in a church that became 75 years old in the year 2000. What kind of a church will we create? We can mine the past for ideas and inspiration, but we will create the new church out of the future, and we never know what that future is until it is upon us.

Is it worth it?

What it all boils down to in the end is: why bother? Certainly, we could use a sleep-in on Sunday morning. We have enough to do without running off to church events all week. Expenses are plenty high without somebody holding an offering plate under our noses. There are plenty of questions to bug us without adding "What does God want?" to the list.

Most of us don't gain much social status from being part of a church. We don't get brownie points for being Christian. There may be a few business contacts, but it's hardly worth it. Church going Christians are very much a minority group. And, according to the values of the marketplace, we're losers.

I began going to church in the first place while I was a "jock" at a local radio station, doing an open-line show. "Ralph's Party Line," they called it. One of the first open-line shows in Canada. We advertised used cars, soap, deodorant, and breakfast cereal – everything I needed to clean me up, make me smell nice, fill my belly, and take me somewhere. But I didn't have anything important to go to. Like every young male struggling to get ahead in the world, I was "all stressed up with no place to go."

I didn't have any great, flashing-lights conversion. I'm not saying those "born again" experiences don't happen to people or that they are not valid. I'm just saying it hasn't happened to me. As I've been nurtured in the church, I find myself really appreciating the gift of faith given me by the church. So I genuinely believe that in our tired and sometimes hurting tradition – in the heritage of faith we've received – we can find some (though not all) of the building blocks for a new church that will evolve.

Our various life experiences are among those building blocks. The only life experiences I can share are my own, so I'll offer some of those, in the hope that they'll help you reflect on yours.

Why doesn't somebody do something?

It's a lonely world out there in "the jungle." Almost everybody, it seems, is on the make and there are very few genuine friendships. But I find, when I'm with my friends in church, I'm not trying to prove as much.

I see the young families in church, struggling to build a future for their children, and I remember when my kids were small. I worry about the children. All of them. Every parent does.

I remember how I wanted my kids to be part of something where there were other adults and other kids willing to talk about significant things. I knew that just dropping my kids off at Sunday school would give them a double message about how important I thought my faith really was, so for the sake of my kids (among many other reasons), I became involved in the church.

Did it pay off for me? That's probably the wrong question, because parenting is not something you do for the "payoff." But I'm delighted when I see in my kids (they're all middle-aged now!) a strong sense of values, of what is right and wrong.

Every night, I read the paper and I watch the TV news and I get angry and wonder, "Why doesn't somebody do something?" Then I realize, once again, that the "somebody" has to include me.

Living in relationship

Bev and I have a pretty stable relationship right now, but it hasn't always been that way, and we'll probably hit some rocky times again. One of the things that's really helped is being part of a number of study groups in the church. None of them were about marriage, but it's surprising how much of what we talked about related to home and family life. And, aside from some good ideas, it was good to know that other people have the same kinds of problems.

These groups were also an excellent place to get to know people in other situations: people who were divorced or widowed, who were single parents, who had remarried or who had never married. I learned from the lives they've lived. Bev and I learned how to make a marriage work during the Friday afternoon hassle when everybody is going in a different direction. Or at three in the morning when somebody's barfing their guts out.

Most important of all, we found friends we could call when the whole world seems to be falling apart. Friends who will come and listen to our anger and our fear.

It is through the church that I first found friends who were comfortable telling me they were gay or lesbian. They had patience with me while I worked through my inherited, ingrained prejudice – until I could see them as strong, creative individuals with a deep sense of morality.

To dream the impossible dream

There's another reason I'm in the church, that's bigger than all of them though it's connected somehow. When my writing is going well, and Bev and I are getting along fine, there's still a hole in there – kind of a hunger. And when things are not going well, that hunger becomes a sharp pain.

Sometimes, when I'm out on a walk or lying in bed waiting for sleep, I dream an impossible dream. I have a dream, a sense of God calling again and again, asking me to do something with my life. In the dream my life is deeply important to God.

At first my ego tells me that means God is calling me to do something that'll attract worldwide attention. To be a hero. To be famous. But that turns out to be my dream, not God's.

If I stay with God's impossible dream, I feel a simple call to live creatively and caringly. To do the best I can with my writing and speaking. To take time to talk with the neighbors and to actually listen to what they say. To think less selfishly when I decide how to vote. To live in a more caring relationship with God's creation.

When I have that dream, for a while I believe the improbable teaching that God loves me – that I am important to God. Specifically me. Ralph. With a splitting headache, sweaty palms, and a zit on the end of my nose. When the dream fades, I know I need more time in prayer and meditation or, sometimes, long conversations with friends in the church.

So much of the time it seems impossible that God considers me, and those insignificant relationships, to be part of a holy and creative purpose. It is so much easier to see all of life as petty and pointless, a pitiful bunch of humans thrashing around till we destroy ourselves and the planet with us.

And yet, sometimes when I share that dream with friends, they tell me they also dream God's impossible dream. They tell me what I already know – that the dream is shared by people of faith, by people of many kinds of faith, all over the world. And that if the dream is delusion, then it is a wonderful, creative, hopeful delusion. If the dream is truth, then it is the only truth worth struggling for.

They tell me what I already know, that the dream is nurtured, given life and purpose and focus, in the community of faith we call the church, where we gather to dream as God's people.

They tell me that to dream God's impossible dream means life! And for now at least, I know of no better place to dream the impossible dream, than in this United Church of ours.

Not long ago, I was at an event where we did one of those typical kinds of exercise where you complete a sentence with ten words, then cut back and back until you're left with the two words that are most important to you. The sentence we were to finish was, "The United Church is...

I came up with my ten words, but do you know what was one of the last words left on my page? I was left with "The United Church is... fun." And I meant it!

Despite all the litigation, despite the questions about our future, despite all those things which can bring us down, I was struck that for me, the United Church is a fun place to be, full of people who know and love one another, who attempt in our fumbling, bumbling ways to be faithful to the call of Christ, and who, in the end, can laugh at ourselves and what's going on around us, even as we take those events very seriously.

It's a great church which I love deeply and will always be thankful that God has provided.

David Allen – Executive Secretary, Toronto Conference

The tough decades are far from over. But we confidently declare that the church will be reborn, and that the new birth will start with local congregations. Sometimes the church that is arriving will look a lot like the old one, and at other times will be unrecognizable. If it survives the trauma of its birth (and we believe it will), it will be more whole. It will know its weaknesses, and will not be frightened by them.

Above all, in a society that often seems devoted to the pursuit of individual gain, it will recognize its own value as the carrier of memory and compassion, mystery and love, song and prayer.

Donna Sinclair and Christopher White –
from *Jacob's Blessing* (Wood Lake Books, 1999)

Study Guide

About This Guide

Since it was first released in 1981 (with a second edition in 1991) no book (except for Bible and hymnbooks) has been more used by United Church people as a study resource than *This United Church of Ours*. That's because they found it informative and fun.

The study groups during the first ten years used a guide prepared by Rev. Beverley Milton, who is married to author Ralph Milton. During the second ten years, Norma Goughnour wrote a new guide based on the work of Bev Milton.

This guide is based on the work of both those writers, but is designed for use with this third edition. Because the church has changed so much, the book has changed significantly. This guide can't be used with the earlier editions without a great deal of confusion and misinformation.

Permissions

You are free to copy short portions (a paragraph or three) of this text in your church bulletin or newsletter. And you can copy short portions for study group purposes. You are not free to copy whole chapters without permission from Wood Lake Books.

Variety

No two study groups are alike. What works with one might not work at all with another. So this resource guide offers you maximum flexibility to tailor the materials to fit your specific needs.

In designing this guide, we assumed that you, the leader, have some knowledge and background about the United Church in particular and the Christian faith in general. That does not mean you need to be an expert. But you should know where to go for answers.

We also assume that you, the leader, have read the whole book *This United Church of Ours*, 3rd edition. But don't feel you'll be required to know everything. Feel free to bring in other leaders from your congregation who might help out with any particular session.

Who can participate

A study of *This United Church of Ours* is not just for people new to the church. Hundreds of study groups across Canada have used the book to revitalize their church. Here are a few of the many kinds of groups that have enjoyed this study:

• teen-age communicants class

• adults new to the United Church

• seasoned members wanting to know more about their church.

• boards, sessions, worship committees – groups of clergy

• groups doing a needs assessment in order to call a new minister

For those who would like to study the Christian faith at an introductory level, we recommend *God for Beginners*, also by Ralph Milton (see the Additional Reading list on page 219).

A special note to clergy

During the past 20 years, as study groups across Canada have used *This United Church of Ours* as a resource, many have shared with us their successes and disappointments. We've been delighted that hundreds of church boards, worship, stewardship, and other committees, have used this resource to help them become more familiar with their church, and to enrich their faith. In fact, the first edition of this book was written specifically for church board members.

We've come to the conclusion that the most successful studies have happened where the clergy have run a series of worship services related to the themes in this study session.

So we suggest you suspend the use of the lectionary for a few weeks, or change just one of the readings for each of the weeks while you are focusing on the United Church and your own congregation. If you are using *The Best of Whole People of God Online* or *Seasons of the Spirit* lectionary-based curriculum, make the church school aware that you will be on different themes during that period.

While a small group (or several groups) are doing the actual study, the entire congregation is invited to participate. A few weeks before the sessions, someone reviews *This United Church of Ours* for the congregation and a joint order is placed for anyone wishing to read the book, even if they are not part of the study group.

Congregational involvement can be quite extensive. This study guide suggests that various congregational leaders be invited to talk about their work in the church. It means those leaders are encouraged to think about what they are doing. The life of the entire congregation can become more intentional in the process.

We suggest that you preach a sermon on the upcoming theme in the study group. The sermon becomes an introduction to the week's topic for those in the study group, and is a useful commentary to those simply reading the book. Everyone will learn a little about your congregation and the denomination as a whole. You'll find some homiletical ideas in the study guide. Each chapter has a scriptural citation that may be helpful.

Why not introduce the participants in the study to the congregation during the first worship service in the series, perhaps with a special prayer or commissioning during the Sunday morning service. Among other things, this will lend importance to the group and generate creative discussion about the topics. If you list their names in the bulletin each week, other church members would be encouraged to talk with them about the study sessions.

At the end of the series, a celebrative service of baptism, membership and/or renewal of covenant might be held. Sometimes that's followed with a potluck lunch or supper.

The whole thing becomes a fine way to build congregational identity and purpose, a way to build esprit de corps, and a way to celebrate our United Church community. Some congregations have used a study session based on *This United Church of Ours* to launch very successful stewardship campaigns, or before launching a new congregational initiative.

A final word – this from author Ralph Milton. Don't be afraid to disagree openly with the text of this book. It's a personal description by one person. He claims nothing more.

Leading A Successful Study Group

Fellowship

Study groups serve many purposes. One of them is fellowship. This is particularly true in larger congregations where folk may not know each other.

There will be many kinds of people in your group and it is important for them to find some common ground and to feel comfortable with each other. Name tags can be very helpful even if the group is not large. And it's always nice to have coffee or tea and perhaps cookies or muffins during the first session.

Encourage the friendly "gossip" as people arrive, and after the study session itself is concluded.

Number of Sessions

We suggest 12 sessions. Experienced leaders can easily develop this material into more sessions or fewer sessions. But this guide is based on the 12 chapters in the book.

Storytelling

It's important to get people telling personal stories as soon as they are comfortable doing so. That means you, the leader, must be prepared to do some storytelling too.

For instance, if you ask your group to recall some early church experiences, it's helpful if you begin by telling something from your childhood or by sharing another early experience. The more personal stories you share, the more likely people in your group will share their own experiences.

Try to help people understand that when they tell personal stories or share feelings, there is no "right" and "wrong." Don't ever allow anyone in your group to criticize or deny someone else's story or feeling. The appropriate response is a story or emotion of our own. Cultivate warmth and acceptance, rather than judgment.

Language

People often know less about their faith and about the church than we assume. Words and ideas we take very much for granted may need to be explained, preferably with a personal story or anecdote to give them meaning.

One of our problems in the United Church is that we don't use a religious vocabulary as easily as people in some churches do. Please be sensitive to this, and help people to find ways to express themselves without resorting to slogans and catch-phrases.

Group Size

You will have your own views on what sizes are best for a study such as this. We feel that most of the questions should be discussed in small subgroups of two, three, or four. But we have not put those instructions in each study session. You decide for yourself what size of group works best.

Preparation

Please review the materials in this resource guide before each session. Select and adapt it to your own needs. Use only what you think is useful. Don't try to cover all the discussions suggested. There's far more in each one than you can possibly cover in a session.

Patterns

Encourage people to express a variety of opinions. Be sure they feel free to disagree with what Ralph says in the book. He has described his own faith journey and experience, but that's all it is. It is important that you encourage openness to differing ideas and concepts.

Develop an informal pattern for your sessions. Begin and end on time. Allow a few moments of informal conversation. If you feel comfortable, begin and end each meeting with a short prayer.

Most importantly, enjoy yourself! If you are relaxed, your participants will be too. To help that happen, prepare well, but then don't take yourself too seriously. Be flexible and sensitive to the needs of the people in your group.

Assumptions

Every one of these sessions assumes that the participants have read the relevant chapter in the third edition of *This United Church of Ours*. It would be wise to make this quite clear as you begin. This implies that each person has their own copy of the book. They should be encouraged to underline, to write questions and comments in the margins, and to generally make the book their own.

Involving the congregation

I hope you read the "special note to clergy," even if you are not a clergy person. If you are a layperson, take the time to discuss the entire program with your minister. Invite your minister to at least browse through this edition of This United Church of Ours, and through this Study Guide. Draw your minister's attention to that note to clergy about sermons paralleling the study sessions. Discuss the possibilities for involving congregational leaders, and perhaps the whole congregation.

Resources

There's an excellent selection of books recommended on page 219. If you don't already have them in your library, they would make an excellent addition to it. Then you could have them on display for some of the sessions so that participants could borrow them for additional reading.

Attitude

As much as possible, discuss things in terms of the way they happen in your congregation. If someone asks a question and you don't know the answer, make a note of it and promise to find out from the appropriate person.

Try not to have this group turn into a complaining session. Church people sometimes tend to play a destructive little game called, "Ain't it Awful," in which everyone takes a turn bellyaching. But if there is a legitimate concern, ask, "What can *we* do about that?" Who knows, you might have something really valuable to suggest.

Chapter 1
Nuts and Bolts

Since this is the opening session, more time should be spent getting to know each other. So put on some coffee and cookies, introduce yourself, and try to get folks to introduce themselves. Even if they spend most of the time talking about themselves, that's just fine. Don't push them or ask them any tough questions at this point.

If they seem in the mood to talk about things, ask them to skim through the various topics in that first chapter to find things they were surprised at, disagreed with, or had a different experience of. (After all, things may be different in your particular church.)

As the name of the chapter implies, this is where we deal with miscellaneous questions people sometimes worry about when they first come to church. There may well be other questions of this nature. Let them know that most of these things are dealt with in more detail later, but make a note of concerns raised so you can bring them up at the appropriate time.

Suggestions for the minister

If you've had new people come into your church, it might be possible to invite some of them to speak for a few minutes each about why they came to the church, and what they found when they got there. Or others who have been part of the church for some time might reflect on what it would be like to come into your congregation as a stranger.

It might be good to reflect on some of the hospitality issues faced in your congregation, and to compare those with biblical passages on hospitality. Hospitality, in biblical times, was the process of receiving outsiders and changing them from strangers to guests. Check out Matthew 10:14–23, which is rather severe; or 1 Thessalonians 1:9; Philippians 5:16; or Mark 9:37. Both the *Oxford* and *Harper's* Bible commentaries have helpful passages on hospitality.

This could lead to a fine sermon on your congregation's hospitality.

Chapter 2
I'm Not Religious, But...

1. One way to get to know each other and to develop community is to build on some common experiences. In *This United Church of Ours,* Ralph Milton writes about his early experiences in the church. Briefly share your own early church memories, then ask others if they have memories they'd like to share. Where/when/how did you first come into contact with the church? What is your most vivid memory? Any funny or embarrassing moments that you can share?

2. When someone says "I'm not religious," what do you think they mean? Why do you think "being religious" seems to have a negative association to so many people?

3. What is an atheist? How is an atheist different from an agnostic? What is a cult? What cults are you aware of? How do these function? What does the book say is the difference between a religion and a cult?

4. What happens at your church that keeps you coming back? That challenges you? Strengthens you? Gives you stability? Helps you care for other hurting people? How could things be changed if this feeling is not present for all?

5. In 1925, the Union Churches, the Methodists, most of the Presbyterians, and the Congregational Churches formed the United Church of Canada. A United Church crest was developed to symbolize this union. (Bring a copy of the crest from church bulletin covers, *The Observer,* or other church publications.) Look at the crest together and talk about the meaning of the shape, the words, and each of the symbols and their roots in our tradition.

   Note that there is no symbol representing the Evangelical United Brethren who became part of the United Church in 1968, nor is there a symbol for the hundreds of community churches in western Canada that joined the union.

   Ask each person to think about which symbol best speaks to them right now. Talk about your own congregation. When did the congregation begin? What year was the building constructed? If your congregation was established before 1925, out of which tradition did it come?

6. *Shalom!* This is a word you will hear a lot in the United Church. It is a Hebrew word for "peace" and is used both as a greeting and as a farewell by Hebrew people. Our English word "peace" does not do full justice to the word *shalom,* as it means much more than the absence of war. It means harmony, wholeness,

and justice for all. It's easy to focus on the bad news; that's what newspapers and TV mostly cover. But why not think of good things that have happened in your world, in your community, in your church.

Suggestions for the minister

This would be a very good occasion to share your own story with the congregation. What was your religious upbringing? What does being a Christian mean to you personally? What are your struggles? This kind of sermon is often hard to do, but it is usually very deeply appreciated by the congregation. It might be good not to include the story of how you were called into ministry, because that would fit better in connection with Chapter 7. And comments on why you remain a Christian and in the United Church might be more useful when you preach in connection with Chapter 12.

Chapter 3
Sunday Morning

You may wish to invite one or more members of your congregational worship committee to join you for this session. Or perhaps your minister might be available. Whichever it is, that person should see the questions you plan to discuss far enough in advance to fill in any blanks in their knowledge.

1. You might open this session by spending a few moments in the total group remembering Sunday morning worship: the good, the bad, and the hilarious experiences in the United Church and in other churches you've attended. (You might want to read a story from Ralph's book, *Angels in Red Suspenders*. Some suggestions: "When God Laughs," p. 76; "Now that's class," p. 78; or "Dangerous Goods," p. 79.)

2. What is a lectionary? Does your congregation use the *Revised Common Lectionary*? Why?

3. Are there parts of the worship service you don't enjoy? Is it necessary that everyone enjoys everything? Share the idea of worship as a smorgasbord, where there is always something for everyone, but not everything is for everyone. How could the worship service be used to meet the needs of a broad spectrum of ages and needs? Were you familiar with other forms of worship at other points in your faith journey? If so, what were they?

4. Look back at the different churches described in the book. Each has its own style and way of doing things. In which church would you feel most comfortable? Why? Which of the worship styles would be most meaningful to you? Why? Which of the churches described is most like yours? How is it similar? How does it differ?

5. Take a guided tour of your church sanctuary or place of worship. (If this isn't possible, perhaps the group could draw a large scale diagram of the sanctuary floor plan.) What is the first thing you notice when you enter? The design and condition of a worship space says something about the people who worship there. What does your place of worship say about you?

6. If your church was burning and you could rescue only one thing out of the building, what would it be?

Suggestions for the minister

This would be a good time to preach on the theology and perhaps a little on the history of worship. In many congregations, people have very little sense of why the worship follows a certain format or style. What do we do here and why do we do it? If the worship service is a kind of theatrical performance, who are the actors? Who is the coach? Who is the audience? Is the sermon the main thing? How do you go about preparing a service of worship? How do we know if we are worshippers or merely an audience?

Chapter 4
All Week Long

1. Begin by asking people what the word "family" means to them. Has society's concept of family changed over the last few years? In what way? Make a list of all the midweek activities and congregational events at your church. Is there a place for you in one of these groups? What other needs do you have that the church might help you meet? How could that happen?

2. Invite a number of people in your congregation to talk with your group about what goes on at your church during the week. You might include a member of the UCW and a member of a men's group. What is their purpose? What do they do? How often do they meet?

3. Talk with the church school superintendent. How is the church school set up? What curriculum is being used and why? What are the joys and problems of being involved in the church school? What do the children share with us?
4. Interview the choir leader. How do people in the choir see their role? How is the music chosen?
5. There are no doubt many other groups or activities in your church. There probably isn't time enough to talk about all of them. Be ready with a list of names and phone numbers of various leaders, in case someone in your group would like to make contact with one of them.

Suggestions for the minister

This might be a good opportunity to hold up the work of the whole church during the Sunday worship. Leaders of various groups within the church might offer very short presentations of who they are, why they exist, and what they do. That might be followed by a meditation on community, interdependence, sharing, and the growth of faith in community.

Chapter 5
Hatched, Matched, and Dispatched

Again, you may wish to invite your worship committee to be part of this discussion. Obtain copies of the baptism, communion, marriage, and funeral services from your minister and give them to participants at the beginning of the session. It's okay to photocopy for this purpose. (Note: You may well choose to divide this chapter into two or three sessions.)

1. Show a series of drawn or real symbols (e.g. maple leaf, a stop sign, a copyright symbol, a poison symbol, a handshake, two people hugging etc.). What meanings are these symbols conveying? What are some other examples of symbols? Sometimes it is difficult to express our deepest feelings in words, so we use an action or symbol to express those feelings. We think of the sacraments in that way. These acts are symbols of spiritual truth and power. They are the "visible" Word.

2. Ask people if they have been baptized, and if so, where and how. What does baptism mean to them now? Do they feel the United Church is being too strict about baptism? Not strict enough?

3. Look at the baptismal service. Ask someone to read it aloud. What words do you find interesting? Bothersome? Does any part of it inspire you? Make you angry? In what circumstances should the church refuse to baptize a baby? Why?

4. Ask people if they've been to a communion service lately. Did it have any meaning for them? Have they ever participated in a communion service in another church or another denomination?

5. Hand out copies of the communion service. Like baptism, communion is a ritual that goes back to biblical times. Jesus participated in both. When we symbolically reenact the Last Supper in communion, what are we saying? In most United Churches, the elements are ordinary bread and grape juice. How is this part of the symbolism?

   There are different ways of celebrating the Lord's Supper. Invite the participants to share different ways that they have experienced. Which way does your congregation most often use? Why? Which way or ways were most meaningful to you? Why?

6. Communion speaks of a "new covenant." What is a covenant? What is "new" about this ancient symbol?

7. What covenants have you entered into in your life? Was there a token or symbol associated with them?

8. Marriage. Try to have some knowledge of where people in the group are in relation to marriage, and be aware of any sensitivities they may have. Do not assume that all couples living together are married. It might be wise to begin this discussion with a storytelling opportunity, where people are invited to say where they are and where they've been. Look together at the wedding service(s) used in your congregation. What commitments or covenant are the two people asked to make?

9. What is your congregation's policy on marriages and marriage preparation? What type and amount of marriage preparation is available? Does your church provide any help to those now married to enrich or strengthen their married life? Some participants may have been to a Marriage Enrichment or Marriage Encounter event. You might invite them to share some of that experience.

10. Funerals. This may be a difficult session because some members may be actively grieving or experiencing a loss and you will need to be sensitive to this.

Start the session by inviting people to share a personal experience they have had with death, or with the loss of someone or something very important in their lives. First, you may wish to share a personal experience that will help others to share theirs. The story you offer does not need to be about death; it could be about any loss that involves grief, such as divorce, a friend or family member moving away, the loss of a job, etc.

11. Together, look at the funeral service. Remember that some people, especially the younger ones, may never have been to a funeral service. Read some of the most significant portions out loud.

12. What is the difference between a funeral service and a memorial service? What makes a funeral or memorial service meaningful for you? Why?

Suggestions to the minister

If you are developing a sermon about the topics in this chapter, you'll have a problem deciding what to leave out. Concentrating on communion as the central sacrament might solve that. Tracing its Hebrew roots in the Exodus story, and its Christian roots in the early church, might lead us to the question of what the sacrament is about now. Why do we bother? What are some of the symbols imbedded in the communion: the gathering around the table, the serving of each other, the significance of the bread and the wine or grape juice.

Again, if there is a layperson who could, in a few words, describe what one or more of these celebrations meant to her or him, it would add a personal witness to the strength of the homily. And if communion can be served, that would be most fitting.

Chapter 6
Telling the New – Old Story

If your congregation has an Outreach Committee or Evangelism Committee, ask someone from that committee to come and participate in your discussion.

1. As the leader, why not begin with a few simple personal stories. Speak candidly and openly about how you are living your Christian convictions, and about how you communicate those to others. Ask if the participants know someone in your church or community who is communicating their faith. Gently, without pushing, ask the participants how they communicate the Christian good news.

2.   Part of *telling* the story is *hearing* others' stories – really "hearing" what they are saying – and living out the concept of the caring community. Spend some time together discussing how to be a good listener. Here are some hints or tips: Try to get the other person to feel your support. Don't interrupt. Hear the whole story. Don't laugh unless you laugh with the other person.

3.   Pass around a variety of resource materials about the United Church's mission work: various issues of *Mandate, The Observer,* material about local UCW projects, and a copy of your own congregation's annual report. Invite people to spend a bit of time looking at the material. Ask each person to choose a project that interests them and ask them to tell the rest of the group about it. How does it tell the Christian story?

4.   In what way does your congregation do its outreach? Thrift Shop? Food Bank? Other projects?

5.   Are there people within your congregation who live their Christian convictions outside of the church – in politics, in the community, in their workplace?

6.   How well does your congregation tell its story?

7.   How well do I communicate my Christian faith? At work? At home? With friends? Why is this so difficult?

8.   What does our congregational annual report, especially the budget, say about how we spread the Good News?

Suggestions for the minister

Again, a layperson who can speak about their own outreach, or the outreach of a group within the church, would add considerably to any sermon on this subject. A sermon about why we need to do this, why it is that Christian faith doesn't really "take" until we consciously try to live it, would seem to be a valuable reflection on our mission. Again, if you can share some of your own struggles in this regard, that would be helpful.

Chapter 7
Reverend Sir or Madam

1. You might begin this session by inviting your clergy to share with you why they chose to become ministers. What do we mean when we say someone is a "minister"? What do we mean by someone's "ministry"?

2. List some desirable characteristics of a minister. After you have a long list, cross out all those that are not absolutely essential. Discuss what you have left. Is it possible for one person to have all those qualities?

3. Discuss stereotypes of ministers – e.g. the perfect, omnicompetent, tranquil, scholarly, strait-laced, spiritual paragon of parental virtue. Do people in your congregation have any of the stereotypes in their heads?

4. What do you do when you discover that your minister is a human being with bad points and good points? How do members of a congregation cope with a minister's weaknesses? How do you support the minister then?

5. How does a congregation express its appreciation to its minister? How does a minister express appreciation to the congregation? How do we encourage each other in our Christian work?

6. What style of leadership do you find most effective? Could more than one style work equally well? Would this depend on circumstances? Encourage the group to give examples with their answers.

Suggestions for the minister

This is the Sunday when the story of your call to ministry would be very helpful. Be sure to include the struggles and the setbacks and the difficulties. If you have other ordained or diaconal people on staff or in your congregation, they might be asked to share their stories as well. The sermon could end with a call to everyone to live the gospel.

Chapter 8
How We Decide

1. Invite the chairperson of your church board, or another experienced board member, plus your presbytery representative to join you in this session. If possible, draw an organizational diagram of your congregation and display it on the wall of your meeting room.

2. Who is on your board? How do they get on the board? What committees are represented on the board? What are the functions of these committees?

3. How does an individual within the congregation express concerns? Are you heard when you have something to say about what happens in your local church? Why? Why not? What is the difference between "being heard" and "being agreed with"?

4. Who are your delegates to presbytery? How can an ordinary church member have a concern heard by the presbytery?

5. The United Church follows not only the democratic process, but also the collegial process. What does "collegial" mean in your congregation? What are the dangers of collegialism?

6. Much healing needs to take place in our church. What issues need healing in your local church? In our national church? Discuss how this might be accomplished without getting into debates on the issues themselves.

Suggestions for the minister

The theology of decision making could be the stuff of an excellent sermon. Some reflection on the legacy of the early church might be useful. Is there a "Christian" way of decision making? Does this apply to secular politics? If secular politics is "the art of the possible" as some have observed, what is church politics? What happens when one person in a congregation has a strong sense of conviction that others do not share?

Chapter 9
Money

You may wish to invite the chairperson or an active member of the Committee of Stewards to join you for this session.

1. One way to get people to express their feelings on a touchy subject is to have them tell what others are saying. List some comments people have overheard about money and the church. An obvious one to start the ball rolling is, "Why is the church always asking for money?" Discuss these responses. Why is the question of money so touchy for so many of us?

2. Discuss what Jesus meant when he said, "Where your treasure is, there your heart will be also." How does this relate to our giving to the church?

3. Look at your own local church budget. How is it doing at this point in the year? Why are the givings up (or down) right now? Does our congregation spend its money wisely? What would you like to see happen?

4. What does our church budget say about what our church believes? How much do we spend on ourselves and how much do we spend on others? How important are children? Young people? Hurting people in our community?

5. Some people make a connection between their givings and their agreement with the local and national church policies. What is your view on this?

6. Look at the words you sing when the offering is brought forward in your weekly worship service. What do these words say? Do we mean them? Are you giving as much as you can? Do you see any need to? What do you receive from your giving?

7. Challenge people to go home and to quietly and prayerfully look at their cheque book and credit card statements, to see what those say about themselves, their values, and their faith. Be sure to tell them nobody is going to ask them to report on this.

Suggestions for the minister

It's often really hard to preach about stewardship in your own congregation. We'd suggest that instead, a sermon about money might be in order. What does money symbolize? What does it mean to us? It has been said that the game we play is called "Power," and money is the way we keep score. Why is it that we can discuss our sex life more easily than we can discuss the money we make and how we spend it?

It might be helpful to ask someone, such as the chair of the Stewardship Committee, to talk for a few minutes about the congregation's stewardship.

Chapter 10
This We Believe

As you lead this session, encourage people to share differing views and beliefs. Avoid setting Ralph up as an "authority" with the "right" answer. Like all of us, Ralph is on a journey of faith and is learning as he moves. All we can do is share the bit of light we have at this moment. Have a copy of Ralph's book *God for Beginners* on hand. It was developed specifically as a response to those who read this chapter and wanted more.

1.   Think back to your early childhood. What did you think God was like? Did you have a picture in your mind? (Leader should share first.) Have your ideas changed much over the years?

2.   In his book *God for Beginners* (p.60), Ralph describes some of the ways people think of God: as a general, a coach, a computer hack, a cop, a rock star, a kindergarten teacher, a social worker, a parent, a lover, an artist. What is your reaction to those descriptions? How would you describe God? List all the words people have heard or used, to describe God. Do these do an adequate job? Can we describe God?

3.   What does the United Church believe about Jesus? Look again at the *New Creed* (VU918) to start this discussion. Read it out loud together. Why is this so important to our understanding of Jesus?

4.   We believe Jesus was also uniquely God in human form. Why is this equally important to our understanding? What does the *New Creed* say Jesus' purpose on earth was? How did he achieve this? What did Jesus show us? Why do we sometimes call ourselves an "Easter People"?

5.   We talk about God as the Creator, God as the Son, and God as the Holy Spirit. How would you describe the Holy Spirit? Have you ever been aware of the Spirit of God in your life? How?

6.   How do you feel about prayer? Many people never consciously stop and specifically pray. Are there other ways of praying? What is the purpose of prayer?

Suggestions for the minister

There's so much in this chapter, it's hard to know where to begin. We suggest beginning at the center, with a sermon on Christology. However, we recommend that it not be a sermon on what you know of Christology, but as much as possible an account of your personal experience of Christ. If there are people in your congregation who have had experiences of the presence of Christ, you might ask them to tell their story.

Chapter 11
Right, Wrong, and Maybe

It may be helpful to point out that this chapter, and Chapter 10, are very closely tied together. In that last chapter we looked at our beliefs. In this chapter we talk about how we *live* those beliefs.

1. In the *New Creed* (VU918) it says: "We are called...to seek justice and resist evil." But who decides? How do we know what is just and what is evil? As a group, try to come up with a definition of justice and evil.

2. Many in the church feel the central questions must be, "Is it right? Does it serve the best interests of all of God's creation?" Ralph describes three kinds of moral decision-making in our society: "Right's right!" "Who cares?" and "The Jesus way." Can you think of examples of the "right's right" way? The "who cares" way? What is the "Jesus" way?

3. Think of an experience in your life when you learned that something you said or did was hurtful or harmful or even destructive. It might be helpful if you gave an example from your own experience. This might be an environmental action, a situation where a prejudice you weren't even aware of surfaced, a justice issue to do with Native rights, etc. What made you realize this? How did you feel? What did you do? Did you change? What helped you change? What did it feel like to be different?

4. What were the consequences of this change in attitude or behavior? Where you teased, ostracized, or even punished?

5. Ralph has touched on a lot of moral issues facing us today. Have the group choose one issue they'd like to think about. Apply the three methods of decision-making to the problem. Try to help people understand each other and the positions they come from. Try to get a sense of the complexity of these issues. It is *not* necessary that everyone agree.

6. What are a few of the most important moral issues you feel will confront us in this new millennium? Should the church as a whole be speaking out on these issues? What about your own congregation? What about you, personally? When the question "Does it serve the best interests of all creation?" is applied, does it change the perspective at all? How does "to love and serve others" come into it?

7. Where do we find strength for our own moral growth? How does the Holy Spirit come into this? Where does the Bible come into the process? How does the church help us in personal decisions?

Suggestions for the minister

Again, there are any number of "handles" in this chapter that could work into a strong sermon. However, it might be most helpful to tell some stories, not of how social and justice problems are "solved," but how people are creatively involved with being part of the solution. If these examples can spring from your own congregation, that would be best. But examples from the national scene can be found in *Mandate* or *The Observer*. And of course, stories out of your own experience are always strong. Again, there may be people in your congregation who could speak for a few minutes on this question.

Chapter 12
The Impossible Dream

During this last session, it is important for the group to gather up the threads of what they have been studying for the past weeks. This would be a good time for them to share the faith stories that hopefully have been growing over this time. The key question then becomes intensely personal. Why am I a Christian? Why do I bother? Why am I in this church? Everything else that follows in this session is designed to get at those primary questions.

Of course, it would also be nice to make this a kind of celebration. Food and laughter always go with celebration. Perhaps somewhere in this session, you could ask the participants to talk about what they have received from others in the group. And, as a leader, you might reflect on what each of the participants (be sure to include all of them) has given you.

1. What is it about this congregation that keeps you here?
2. What is your own personal "faith hunger"? What is God calling you toward?
3. We looked at the *New Creed* as one description of faith. What kinds of things would we put into a personal creed? Invite people to spend a few moments individually writing something of a personal statement of faith. If they feel comfortable doing so, people may share these with the group.
4. Now that we know more about what the United Church is and what makes it tick, how are we going to share our faith journey and our feeling of belonging

with others? Spend some time dreaming together about the future of your church.

Suggestions for the minister

If some of the people in the study group are going to be baptized, confirmed, or transferred into your congregation, you might invite them to share the personal statements of faith developed in the last session, as part of the liturgy. You may invite others in the congregation to reflect on the personal question. And of course, it would be important that you, as the pastor of the congregation, share some more of your own faith journey, and your answer to the question, "Why bother?"

Additional Reading

Barnett, Thomas and composer Donald Patriquin. *Songs for the Holy One: Psalms and Refrains for Worship.* Kelowna: Wood Lake Books, 2004. A passionate rendition of the 150 psalms using inclusive language and paired with original refrains.

Douglas, Scott. *Strange Angels: And Other Plays.* Kelowna: Wood Lake Books, 2004. A remarkable collection of ten contemporary and thought-provoking plays covering a wide range of topics and themes.

Edmison, Kathy. *Growing a Healing Ministry: A Resource for Congregations and Communities.* Kelowna: Wood Lake Books, 2004. Guides readers through the process of establishing this type of ministry as well as revealing its biblical roots.

Graham, Rochelle, Flora Litt, and Wayne Irwin. *Healing from the Heart. A Guide to Christian Healing for Individuals and Groups.* Kelowna: Wood Lake Books, 1998. Meditation resources, healing services, and well-tested and practical hands-on healing methods.

Harpur, Tom. *Prayer: The Hidden Fire.* Kelowna: Northstone Publishing, 1998. Reveals the power and universality of prayer. It is invaluable for anyone wishing to learn more about prayer, or wanting to deepen their spiritual roots.

— *Prayer: The Hidden Fire. Journal and Companion Guide.* Kelowna: Northstone Publishing, 1999. A way to deepen your self-understanding and open creative communion with God.

— *Finding the Still Point: The Spirituality of Balance.* Kelowna: Northstone Publishing, 2002. Focuses on a spiritual approach to coping with stress.

Mangan, Louise and Nancy Wyse. *Living the Christ Life: Rediscovering the Seasons of the Christian Year.* Kelowna: Wood Lake Books, 2001. Activities to help build community and bring Christian practice into daily life.

Meyer, Chuck. *Dying Church – Living God: A Call to Begin Again.* Kelowna: Northstone Publishing, 2000. A provocative and challenging manifesto on the current state and future hopes of the church.

Milton, Beverley, and Margaret Kyle. *My Baptism: The Story of Jesus' Baptism and My Baptism Memories.* Kelowna: Wood Lake Books, 1998. Tells the story of Jesus' baptism, with space to tell the story of a child's baptism next to it.

Milton, Ralph. *Angels in Red Suspenders: An Unconventional and Humorous Approach to Spirituality.* Kelowna: Northstone Publishing, 1997. A collection of stories about the life of faith and joy – joy found not only in happiness and celebration, but in the midst of pain and sorrow as well.

— *Essence of Julian.* Kelowna: Northstone Publishing, 2002. A condensed and paraphrased version of Julian of Norwich's writings.

— *God for Beginners.* Kelowna: Northstone Publishing, 1996. A lively, fun description of what most Christians believe, in the easy-going and readily understandable language Ralph Milton is known for.

— *Is This Your Idea of a Good Time, God? Discovering Yourself in Biblical Stories.* Kelowna: Wood Lake Books, 1995. You'll be caught up in the web of life and loss, faith and failure, that connects your life to these great stories.

— *Julian's Cell.* Kelowna: Northstone Publishing, 2002. A unique work of historical fiction, this book imagines Julian's life as it could have been.

— *Man to Man: Recovering the Best of the Male Tradition.* Kelowna: Wood Lake Books, 1993. A look into the roots of men's common experiences to find what's valuable there.

— *Sermon Seasonings: Collected Stories to Spice Up Your Sermons.* Kelowna: Wood Lake Books, 1997. Wendy Smallman, Ed. Humorous, moving, and memorable stories to spice up any sermon or devotional.

Milton, Ralph, and Margaret Kyle. *The Family Story Bible.* Kelowna: Northstone Publishing, 1996. A fresh, contemporary perspective on the Bible.

Parent, Mark. *SpiritScapes: Mapping the Spiritual & Scientific Terrain at the Dawn of the New Millennium.* Kelowna: Northstone Publishing, 1998. An overview and analysis of nine of the most significant spiritual movements of our time.

Posterski, Don, and Gary Nelson. *Future Faith Churches: Reconnecting with the Power of the Gospel for the 21st Century.* Kelowna: Wood Lake Books, 1997. The good news that some churches have found ways to embrace faith that is both personal and social.

Reeves, Nancy. *I'd Say Yes, God, If I Knew What You Wanted: Spiritual Discernment.* Kelowna: Northstone Publishing, 2002. Stories from 75 men and women of 11 different faith traditions illustrating 27 decision-making methods.

Scorer, Tim. *Experiencing the Heart of Christianity: A 12 Session Program for Groups.* Kelowna: Wood Lake Books, 2005. A companion to the bestselling book by Marcus Borg, this 12 session experiential program enables leaders to engage with issues that lie at the heart of Christianity today.

Sinclair, Donna, and Christopher White. *Jacob's Blessing: Dreams, Hopes, & Visions for the Church.* Kelowna: Wood Lake Books, 1999. An excellent book for those wishing to explore the dreams and visions of a future church.

Sinclair, Donna and Christopher White. *Emmaus Road: Churches Making Their Way Forward.* Kelowna: Wood Lake Books, 2003. Offers to readers what those first disciples experienced on the road to Emmaus – an encounter with hope.

Taylor, James. *Everyday Parables: Rediscovering God in Common Things.* Kelowna: Wood Lake Books, 1995, 2005. A thought-provoking book that will take you on a journey of reflection as you connect your everyday life to a deeper reality.

— *Everyday Psalms: The Power of the Psalms in Language for Today.* Kelowna: Wood Lake Books, 1994, 2005. The Psalms live again through translation into images and language from contemporary experience.

— *John for Beginners: a Bible Study for Individuals and Groups.* Kelowna: Wood Lake Books, 2001. This Bible study invites both new and longtime learners into an intimate and personal exploration of the Gospel of John.

— *Precious Days & Practical Love: Caring for Your Aging Parent.* Kelowna: Northstone Publishing, 1999. Practical information on the emotional upheaval of caring for an aging parent.

— *Sin: A New Understanding of Virtue and Vice.* Kelowna: Northstone Publishing, 1997. A level-headed discussion of virtue in the modern world.

Wilson, Lois Miriam. *Miriam, Mary & Me: Women in the Bible.* Northstone Publishing, 1996. A marvelous storybook for children and an inspirational resource for adults.

— *Your Child's Baptism.* A handy booklet that answers lots of questions about, and explains the theology and symbolism of, baptism.

Wylie, Betty Jane. *Family: An Exploration.* Kelowna: Northstone Publishing, 1997. For those who care about the Canadian family, what it is and how it operates, what makes it special and what will help it survive, this book will be helpful.

Addresses &
Phone Numbers

General Council Offices
3250 Bloor St. West, Suite 300, Etobicoke, ON M8X 2Y4
Tel: 416-231-5931 or 416-231-7680 (voice mail)
Fax: 416-231-3103 E-mail: info@united-church.ca
Website: www.united-church.ca

Newfoundland and Labrador Conference
320 Elizabeth Avenue, St. John's, NL A1B 1T9
Tel: 709-754-0386 Fax: 709-754-8336 E-mail: unitedchurch@nfld.net

Maritime Conference
32 York Street, Sackville, NB E4L 4R4
Tel: 506-536-1334 Fax: 506-536-2900 E-mail: info@marconf.ca

Synode Montréal and Ottawa Conference
225-50th Avenue, Lachine, QC H8T 2T7
Tel: 514-634-7015 Fax: 514-634-2489
E-mail: synode.mo@istar.ca (Montréal)
moconferenceucc@bellnet.ca (Ottawa)

Bay of Quinte Conference
PO Box 700, 67 Mill Street, Frankford, ON K0K 2C0
Tel: 613-398-1051, 1-888-759-2444 Fax: 613-398-8894
E-mail: bayq.conference@sympatico.ca

Toronto Conference
65 Mayall Avenue, Downsview, ON M3L 1E7
Tel: 416-241-2677, 1-800-446-4729 Fax: 416-241-2689
E-mail: torontoconference@bellnet.ca

Hamilton Conference

PO Box 100, Carlisle, ON L0R 1H0

Tel: 905-659-3343 Fax: 905-659-7766 E-mail: office@hamconf.org

London Conference

759 Hyde Park Road, Suite 252, London, ON N6H 3S2

Tel: 519-672-1930 Fax: 519-439-2800 E-mail: lonconf@execulink.com

Manitou Conference

319 McKenzie Ave. North Bay, ON P1B 7E3

Tel: 705-474-3350 Fax: 705-497-3597 E-mail: office@manitouconference.ca

Manitoba and Northwestern Ontario Conference

170 St. Mary's Road, Winnipeg, MB R2H 1H9

Tel: 204-233-8911 Fax: 204-233-3289

E-mail: office@confmnwo.ca

Saskatchewan Conference

418A MacDonald Street, Regina, SK S4N 6E1

Tel: 306-721-3311 Fax: 306-721-3171 E-mail: ucskco@sasktel.net

Alberta and Northwest Conference

9911-48 Avenue NW, Edmonton, AB T6E 5V6

Tel: 403-435-3995 Fax: 403-438-3317 E-mail: coffice@anwconf.com

British Columbia Conference

4383 Rumble Street, Burnaby, BC V5J 2A2

Tel: 604-431-0434 Fax: 604-431-0439 E-mail: bcconf@bc.united-church.ca

All Native Circle Conference

367 Selkirk Avenue, Winnipeg, MB R2W 2M3

Tel: 204-582-5518 Fax: 204-582-6649 E-mail: allnative@mts.net

RALPH MILTON is one of Canada's best-known religious communicators. Broadcaster, publisher, engaging speaker, and bestselling author, he has lived everywhere from rural Grass River, Manitoba, to urban New York, to exotic locales in the Philippines. His humorous, easy style makes him one of the most popular writers of our time. A founder of Wood Lake Books, Ralph recently received an Honorary Doctorate of Sacred Letters from St. Stephen's College in Edmonton, Alberta. Ralph and his wife Beverley, a retired United Church minister, live in Kelowna, British Columbia.

What readers are saying about CareerXroads

CareerXroads is the best of the best....I can't do without it. Neither should you.
Joyce Lain Kennedy, Syndicated Career Columnist

From 1996–2003 *CareerXroads* has sat next to my computer. I cannot image looking for a job or doing recruiting without it.
Richard Stone, The Princeton HR Networking Group

I am a career management consultant. The first two suggestions I give all new job seekers at any level is to get a copy of *CareerXroads* and get some business cards printed.
M. Moore

For anyone looking for a job, *CareerXroads* is a gold mine of valuable information — with pointers to almost limitless information about all aspects of job search. One section alone, about career advice and management, is worth the price — and that's just nine of the 486 pages.
Peter Zollman, Classifieds Intelligence Book Review

Given the myriad of job sites on the web today, it's a good thing someone's keeping tabs on them.
J. Getman, Purple Squirrel

Love your book, wouldn't recruit without it.
Mike Williams

No HR library is complete without a copy of *CareerXroads*, it is considered the "bible" for Internet recruiting.
Bill Gaul, Destiny Group

I

What attendees are saying about Gerry Crispin and Mark Mehler

We had a record attendance for the tech talk series the night you spoke. The presentation that you gave was highly informative and very polished. I was positively thrilled with your talk and so were those job seekers in the audience.

Janie L. Hermann, Information Services Librarian, Princeton Public Library

You guys were fantastic! I am so glad that I was able to meet you. The conference was overwhelming with the amount of information!

Julianne Wolk, Manager Strategic Staffing, footstar

You two were great — even at 7 AM in the morning. Congrats.

Mary Claire Ryan, Director of Sourcing, Abbott Laboratories

Out of all of the seminars and HR trainings, the information you provide is top-notch, and I appreciate your sharing your personal experiences with me. *CareerXroads* is EXCELLENT and I continue to impress friends and colleagues with what I have learned from it.

Marc Bowman

You guys were THE BEST session at the SHRM conference, in my book. Interesting, informative, timely and funny.

Kathy Dorsey

Why you need this book.

You'll immediately benefit from the straightforward, experienced reviews that lead you to the best results the web has to offer for employment. This unique, objective format has made CareerXroads the world's leading reference guide to job and resume sites for 7 straight years. Since the beginning of the industry Crispin & Mehler have been monitoring, cataloging and following the trends of the Internet recruiting marketplace. They are:

- Recognized Experts – Included in the Top 100 Influential people in the Recruiting Industry.
- Seasoned speakers around the world on Best Recruiting Practices.
- Frequently quoted in the *Wall Street Journal, Fortune Magazine,* and the *Washington Post.*
- Trends oriented: What's Hot and What's Not… where to go and what you can ignore.
- Experienced with over 50 years combined experience in HR and recruiting.

"Gerry Crispin and Mark Mehler continue to impress us with their ability to corral and make sense of thousands of electronic job boards and recruiting resources, published in their annual *CareerXroads* book."
Kevin Wheeler, ERExchange

career (cross) roads

Gerry Crispin & Mark Mehler

"CareerXroads is the best of the best...
I can't do without it. Neither should you."
Joyce Lain Kennedy, Syndicated Career Columnist

MMC Group
Kendall Park, NJ
mmc@careerxroads.com

CAREERXROADS
©2003 by **Gerry Crispin & Mark Mehler**
Published by MMC Group

Crispin, Gerry.
    CareerXroads : the 2003 directory to job,
resume, and career management sites on the Web /
Gerry Crispin & Mark Mehler. – 8th ed.
    p. cm.
    Career crossroads
    Career X roads
    Includes index.
    ISBN 0-9652239-8-1   ISSN 1088-4629

1. Job hunting–Computer network resources–Directories.
2. Web sites–Directories. 3. Electronic mail systems–Directories.
I. Mehler, Mark. II. Title. III. Title: Career crossroads IV. Title: Career X roads

HF5382.7.C368 2002   025.06/331702/02573
                                              QBI02-842

TRADEMARKS

A number of words in which we have reason to believe trademark, servicemark, or other proprietary rights may exist have been designated as such by use of initial capitalization. However, no attempt has been made to designate as trademarks or service marks all personal computer words or terms in which proprietary rights might exist. The inclusion, exclusion, or definition of a word or term is not intended to affect, or to express any judgement on the validity or legal status of any proprietary right which may be claimed in that word or term.

Every effort has been made to obtain up-to-date and reliable information.

We assume no responsibility, however, for errors or omissions and reserve the right to include or eliminate listings as well as edit and comment on the sites reviewed based on our judgement as to what is useful for job-seekers and recruiters. We will post corrections as part of our updates.

With the Internet's World Wide Web growing at a rate unlike any phenomenon known before, we have offered the purchasers of CareerXroads an option of registering with our site and receiving updates via email.

We offer new job-related sites the opportunity to be included in these updates at no cost based on our determination of their value to our audience. A form for new site reviews is available at www.careerxroads.com. Please send new information, comments, corrections or any other correspondence to: mmc@careerxroads.com.

MMC Group
P.O. Box 253
Kendall Park, NJ 08824
732-821-6652
mmc@careerxroads.com
www.careerxroads.com

CareerXroads 2003

The World's Leading Reference Guide to
Job and Resumé Websites.

How to use this Directory

There are no standards that dictate what a job, resume or career management website should look like — what information it should contain, how it should be organized, how the quality of that information might be measured, what means should be used to search it, deliver it, or even what services might be provided.

Our organization of this Directory and our comments throughout *CareerXroads* are framed from the job seeker's point of view:

CareerXroads				WEB SITE NAME
www.careerxroads.com				SITE ADDRESS (URL) SITE NAME
Mark Mehler/Gerry Crispin MMC Group, P.O. Box 253, , Kendall Park, NJ 08824 Ph: 732-821-6652 Fax: 732-821-1343 E-mail: mmc@careerxroads.com				CONTACT INFORMATION
JOBS: N/A		RESUMES: N/A		NUMBER OF RESUMÉS POSTED NUMBER OF JOBS POSTED
Cost to post	Cost to see	Cost to post	Cost to see	
N/A	N/A	N/A	N/A	
DISCIPLINE		LOCATION		SITE INFORMATION
N/A		N/A		
SPECIALTY		FEATURE		
N/A		N/A		AGENT
AGENT: None				
CareerXroads is in its eighth print edition and is now live on the web. The authors conduct over 100 speaking engagements a year. If you've read this far and haven't registered at our site for updates — DO IT NOW. We won't be sending you anything other than our updates — no spamming, no strange e-mail challenges or opportunities and no advertising. "Where Talent and Opportunity Connect on the Internet."				SITE REVIEW

- How can I reach this website (**URL**)? How can I reach the owners (**CONTACT INFORMATION**)?
- Is this site committed to providing opportunities (**JOBS**), the approximate number of (**JOBS**) posted and the number of (**RESUMÉS**) posted, or the means to communicate my skills and interests (**RESUMÉS**)?
- Can a job seeker post their (**RESUMÉS**) and see (**JOBS**) for free or for a fee? Can recruiters see (**JOBS**) or post (**RESUMÉS**) for free or for a fee?
- Are most of the jobs posted at this site organized with any critical emphasis such as the educational degree or specialty requirements (**SPECIALTY**), discipline (**DISCIPLINE**) or geographic emphasis (**LOCATION**)? Does the site have an (**AGENT**) that will push jobs or resumes to a PC?
- Is the site easy to use? Is the information limited or extensive? How much does it cost? What else can job seekers, or employers, do to connect here (**REVIEW**)?

The 2003 CareerXroads Directory is organized into two distinct sections:

- An alphabetical listing of 500 reviews of the best sites with the top 50 high-lighted, and
- A cross reference index of sites by a common feature or area of empha-sis. The cross reference listings include (See Table of Contents for page numbers.):

  - **A Master List:** 2,585 sites in alphabetical order with the 500 best sites highlighted.
  - **Associations:** 283 professional societies and trade organizations with job boards.
  - **Best of the Best:** The top 50 sites for 2003.
  - **Career Management:** 35 sites whose main focus is information about careers, job search and counseling. These sites are also described in the *Resources* section.
  - **College:** 762 job and resumé sites for entry level, college, internships and high school students.
  - **Corporation Staffing Pages:** 500 companies' web addresses — all the firms listed on *Fortune* magazine's list of the largest publicly traded firms. We highlighted the sites that offer the best job seeker experience.
  - **Diversity:** 97 job and resumé sites that focus their attention on gender, ethnicity, sexual orientation, veteran status, etc.
  - **Jobs and Resumés–FEE or FREE:** 2,585 sites in the 2003 directory contain jobs or resumés. We differentiated between those sites that are free for recruiters to post open positions (458) or see candidate resumés (352) as well as those that cost a fee. We also list sites that charge a fee to job seekers (112).
  - **Location:** 1,047 sites that focus exclusively on a specific US (city, coun-ty, state or region) or International (country) location. 330 of these sites are international.
  - . **Specialty:** 1,958 niche sites emphasize an academic discipline, indus-try focus or professional specialty. The categories in this listing include: business–162, communications–70, contract/project–46 customer serv-ice and technical support–8, education–94, engineering–196, enter-tainment and media–47, executive–52, health care–126, hospitality and food services–71, human resources–59, information technology–409, law and order–46, military transition and security clearance–32, non-profit–89, public sector–59, sales (retail sales and services)–51, sales (prof. sales and marketing)–43 science–152, trades, non-exempt and hourly–85, miscellaneous–60.

Rating System

We selected what we considered to be the best job and resume sites for 2003 based on several criteria: We looked at the ease of access, value of the content, navigation, business model, real world marketing strategy and technology.

For 2003 we reviewed over 4,000 sites, included over 3,000 in the indexes, 500 reviews in this directory and designated 50 as the "Best of the Best." We also indexed sites that did not make the 500 best list for 2003, and listed the URLs to Fortune 500 corporations. Everyone must judge their own best sites by the results they achieve. We have designated this icon as our symbol for these sites.

THIS BOOK IS NEVER OUTDATED

Most printed Internet directories are outdated before they even hit the bookstore but *CareerXroads* is designed to always be current. This book is completely researched and updated for each edition.

Register for FREE monthly updates at www.careerxroads.com/registration.

CareerXroads DISCLOSURE STATEMENT

Not one of the 500 + sites we have selected for review, nor any of the more then 3,000 sites we have chosen to catalogue and cross reference in this the 8th edition of *CareerXroads* have paid for the privilege. We chose them from the 4,000 + we considered strictly on the basis of our observations and opinions about the future direction of online recruiting.

We both have backgrounds in human resources that biased our thinking to which sites we would use if we were recruiters or job seekers. We left the contingency and retained agency employment world to others who can do it more justice then we can.

Our experience also includes long standing connections with recruitment print advertising. Newspapers and trade publications are well represented here (by their online components) and have the ability to compete in the electronic recruiting medium.

We have contributed significantly to the look and feel of the Career infoFinder, Resume infoFinder and HR Jobs infoFinder products described in the Resources section of this edition. We believe these products are at the cutting edge of a new generation of productivity tools that will be integrated into the desktop "command center" used by recruiters and jobseekers alike. *CareerXroads* database can also be accessed via the web through our website at: www.careerxroads.com.

We both have strong opinions about disclosure, metrics and the ability for a job seeker or recruiter to view what they need in seconds via a website. This opinion created long hours of research as many job sites do not understand the significance of what they have created. Our opinions in *CareerXroads* reflect this point of view.

During 2003 we will be working full time to educate and consult on aspects of the employment industry that increase recruiter and job seeker productivity. We can be contacted to assist you with corporate job page design, reviewing recruiting technologies, Internet recruiter training and selection of applicant tracking systems. Contact us at: (732) 821-6652 or mmc@careerxroads.com.

Register for Free updates at www.careerxroads.com and we promise that your email will not be sold, traded or leased.

We wish you all Good Hunting!

Gerry and Mark

About the Authors

Gerry Crispin and Mark Mehler are human resource professionals who have spent their entire careers (50+ years) in just about every facet of the employment industry. Between the two of them, they have worked in career planning and placement, contract recruiting, executive search, recruitment advertising and human resource management. They began their collaboration in the early 1990s, after meeting in a group that supports human resource professionals in transition. The Princeton Human Resource Network Group meets every third Saturday at 8 a.m. and boasts over 500 alumni throughout the country.

Response to the first edition was overwhelming and the next year demand depleted the first printing within weeks. Since 1998 Joyce Lain Kennedy, a nationally syndicated career columnist, has ranked *CareerXroads* among the top 10 best books in career management.

Committed to educating and sharing their expertise with companies, professionals, colleagues, journalists and just folks looking for a job, Gerry and Mark, still enjoy the challenge of the employment marketplace. They respond to more than 100 recruiter e-mails a day, speak to dozens of journalists a month, teach thousands of recruiters each year, advise start-ups and investment analysts on the future possibilities, and still have time to respond to e-mails from job seekers regarding which sites they should use in their job searches.

Both Gerry and Mark fervently believe that if you follow the job seeker, you'll never lose sight of what is next.

Interested in having Gerry & Mark work with your organization? Their partnership is known for its real-time consulting, geared to improve employment processes in some of the world's most competitive firms.

Gerry and Mark conduct nearly 100 presentations about the Internet each year for employers, professional associations and job seekers. Their presentations include everything from national and international associations to regularly scheduled one-day workshops on strategic staffing and selection/evaluation of applicant tracking systems (using an Internet-ready computer lab) with Cornell University and other organizations.

Education & Training

We conduct training courses for recruiters. We emphasize strategies that are geared toward improving their employment processes. Our focus is the application of emerging technology. These programs are conducted through Cornell University and other sponsoring organizations. All programs are conducted in computer labs with participants wired to the web. Customized presentations and seminars for corporations based on their unique needs and circumstances are provided.

Consulting

We are currently assisting more than a dozen corporate staffing organizations, independent employment websites, universities and other organizations with one or more of the following:

- Identifying gaps in current processes
- Facilitating the development of employment technology priorities
- Assessing the best technologies in applicant tracking systems

The CareerXroads Colloquium Conference

CareerXroads Colloquium Best Recruiting Practices conferences bring together corporate staffing professionals in the space who get it. This invitation-only event allows corporate staffing strategists to freely discuss their staffing issues and best results

We hold four major conferences a year and bi-monthly luncheon meetings on the east coast and across the USA. We limit the conferences to 40 participants (no more then 2 from any company) and the lunches to 20. We ask the participants prior to the meetings what topics they would like to discuss, take a census of the group and then volunteers present their best practice. Discussion follows and we also go through issues that people need help in resolving. The format has worked well and sharing is a pre-requisite for this handpicked audience. What is discussed in the room stays there, and we do not allow any press to attend the day meetings.

The purpose of this invitation only event is to facilitate a network forum for employment strategists free of vendor and supplier restraints. If you would like additional information on potentially becoming a member please either call 732-821-6652 or e-mail mmc@careerxroads.com

Acknowledgements

For the 2003 — 8th edition of *CareerXroads* there are many individuals who have helped us along the way.

Our spouses, Diane and Beth, who know what it is like to not see your husbands for days as they closet themselves behind computers to research job and resume sites. Without their support we would not have any reason to continue or anything else for the last twenty odd years.

Our children, Jamie Beth, Gerry, Lauren and Dara. They are our cheerleaders. To Gerry's first grandchild, Brendon who keeps him on track with conversations that only grandparents would love.

Lauren Mehler and Bonnie Marko, our researchers who found hundreds of new sites this year.

Barb Ruess, our PR consultant who helps *CareerXroads* stay ahead of the pack.

Janet Gallo, the graphic designer who each year gives us our new look.

Grandpa Nat Liebeskind (Mark's father in-law) who can stuff a copy of *CareerXroads* into a jiffy bag faster then a speeding bullet.

Sal Madalone of Premier Graphics who continues to support a fledgling business-grown beyond our wildest dreams.

The members of the Princeton Human Resource Network Group, both old and new who share a commitment to one another's success. Dick Stone (Stoney) the Princeton Group's founder and one of our biggest cheerleaders who has kept the Princeton Group going for over 12 years. This group's alumni directory would make the Fortune 500 blush with envy.

Our HR colleagues, recruiters and cyberfriends. We have spoken or emailed to thousands of web owners about what they are doing or trying to do. We thank them all for sharing. We are particularly indebted to the insights of the authors who are participating in this edition:

Michelle Dumas, Jeremy Eskenazi, Glenn Gutmacher, Tony Lee, Yves Lermusiaux, Karen Osofsky, David Sears, John Sullivan, John Vlastelica and Wendell Williams.

Thank you,
Gerry and Mark
mmc@careerxroads.com

Table of Contents

FOREWARD

Designing Corporate Staffing Sites that Address Customer Experience: It's the Customer's Context not the Employer's Content that Makes the Difference.

By Gerry Crispin & Mark Mehler

E-mail: mmc@careerxroads.com

After examining the Web site staffing pages for each company in the Fortune 500, we concluded that the promise of Internet recruiting for the job seeker is still more smoke and mirrors than reality. The jobseeker's experience of the recruiting process on the digital plane is far from satisfying.

Claims that companies are well on their way to applying customer relations management (CRM) techniques to the employment process are a myth. Simply stated, 460 (92 percent) of firms show some evidence of offering opportunity via their Web site. However, 105 (22.5 percent) cannot meet the simple expectation of an active job seeker wanting to find a job and apply for it. The majority 360 (72 percent) meets only rudimentary informational needs and even struggle to collect data efficiently. Only three (one percent) of the companies we visited online could satisfy a prospect's (very reasonable) expectation to be informed of the status of their application. Our picks for the **"Top 25 Corporate Staffing Sites"** (www.careerxroads.com/top25) still have miles to go before they can claim to meet their customer's needs. However, as benchmarks they do offer good measure of how much has been achieved in moving employment to the Internet. They are the Best of the Best.

This white paper attempts to describe a set of basic principles and standards for the design of corporate Web site staffing pages based on customer expectations. The good news is that all the sites are works in progress and (hopefully) improving constantly.

Setting the Stage

It's so easy to see when you sell a house. You have an enormous range of choices to consider. There is the market, the housing stock and the location. There are recent, similar sales in the area (are they ever really similar?). There is the functional condition of the house, the agent (if you choose one) and the agent's experience and

1

connections to the market. The list is endless but, when all is said and done, you'll likely end up focusing serious attention on one single checklist. This is the list where you will spend your time, invest your money and constantly obsess over each and every detail before a prospect's visit. Why? Simply stated, you know from personal experience that the potential (and more importantly qualified) buyers will be distracted if they stumble over a loose doorsill, see a cluttered room that hides the salient features, are put off because the rug is dirty, etc., etc. All the supply chain rhetoric, marketing gimmicks and special techniques will walk out the door if you aren't attending to – what? The customer's experience.

There are two hidden lessons for recruiters in this housing analogy (without extending it too far.) First and most important to ask who the buyer is, who the seller is, and whether the market favors the buyer or the seller. Everything flows from the answer to this question. This locus of control may shift back and forth in the next few years but employers who automatically assume and behave as if they are buying a talent commodity will be making a fatal mistake. Without debating the merits of these trends here, we believe the evidence is overwhelming – candidates will develop enormous control over their job choices and, this shift in context fundamentally rewards them to exhibit behaviors of an informed consumer. The employer process that assesses and qualifies candidates will take place. And yes, it will be automated and monitored but (and this is a critical but) the timing and pacing of selection will be completely under the control of the buyer – the candidate.

The second lesson is that few buyers are ready to purchase when they first walk through the door. They are not prepared to put down a binder, submit a mortgage application, or answer simple questions about their qualifications or interest. People show up intending to compare prices, get ideas about how to improve their own home or consider whether they need to upgrade. They may have quality of life issues regarding a local school system or places of worship. First time buyers have an entirely different agenda. You get the picture. Only you aren't selling a single house. You are selling an opportunity for today and tomorrow and the day after that… Your candidates may want to know details about how they will be led.

Your worst-case scenario isn't that a qualified candidate will go to your site and see the rough details of your firm's management capability, career opportunity, and challenge and then not pursue the opportunity. No, the worst-case scenario is that every visitor will have exactly the same experience and either they will all leave or, worse yet, all apply.

Expectations for the next 10 years and beyond are clear. Hiring systems that shift to customizing the experience of candidates as customers will be successful.

What is a Customer Experience?

There is no single accepted operational definition for customer experience in the hiring process. No standard of measure, no metric rule we can debate, no yardstick

2

we can apply to a visitor encountering a company's Web site for the first time. What we are attempting to formulate here is the means to develop a common set of principles that influence – positively and negatively – that visitor's experience. What dimensions does the customer experience depend on?

It might be something as simple as the placement of the Careers button on a home page. As one of four tabs on the navigation bar of the company's home page, clearly printed in 18-point type, your customer doesn't even have to think about it, just link to it. As a 4-point afterthought buried next to the privacy link on the bottom of a page cluttered with other choices, it might never be found. Quickly getting where they want to go is a big part of a customer's experience.

It might be as complex as the unintended consequence of a Job Requisition approval process. Consider what it means when every opening requires an approved requisition-even core positions at the firm, before initiating any hiring action? Would a qualified candidate touring your firm today (yesterday, last week, last month, last year) see the position you will post tomorrow? No? Then, is there a generic description available and searchable in a Careers section? Or, is there any indication offered about the frequency that this job is filled – internally, from the outside? Is the career content area linked to the search engine for open positions or agents? Is there a link to someone performing this job? Is there a means for visitors to determine whether they have the qualifications necessary to compete for the position, succeed in the job? At what point are visitors invited to be informed when the position is approved? What experience have you designed?

We propose five general principles that influence a customer's experience.

Five Design Principles

Each year since 1999, we have examined the Web sites of the Fortune 500. We approach each site intent not only on establishing trends from year to year, but also to determine if these trends make any sense – can they satisfy the reason I may have come here in the first place.

Instead of itemizing the cool features or conducting superficial polling questions of non-random samples of job seekers like, "Would you spend 30 minutes completing this application?" we constructed five general factors we believe influence the quality of a visitor's experience.

Each of these five principles was operationally defined and measured at each site during the summer of 2002. We plan to build on these efforts, develop an assessment checklist and collect data to refine it.

The five principles are Readiness, Navigation, Image, Relevance and Feedback

1) Readiness
All visitors aren't active job seekers, chomping at the bit to apply. On the other hand, employers aren't so ready themselves when it comes to positions they will need

to fill but haven't yet announced (maybe they want to ensure a priority for current employees, maintain secrecy about business plans or, simply don't engage in workforce planning activities). In any case, Readiness is the range of career-related expectations a visitor enters the site with. It is a paramount consideration in designing a satisfying customer experience. These expectations set the stage for whether their experience is positive or negative. For example, a recently laid off job seeker looking for a similar position, confident about their skills and competencies and willing to fully share their personal profile will react differently to the same site than a college graduate exploring entry-level positions and wondering if his training is sufficient to compete for an opening. We wanted to systematically construct different scenarios representing an employer's targeted audience. We believe there are four Readiness variables:

- A visitor's **Motivation** is likely to be: active – seeking a new job right now; comparing – intent or, just curious, about how their current position or skills, company, etc. stack-up to what they might find if they were to seek another opportunity, or; exploring – seeking new career options, future positions and what will be necessary to learn in order progress, get promoted, etc. The only truly passive candidates aren't looking for a position, don't exhibit curiosity and have little interest in taking any action. They will find themselves at your site by accident. Other staffing strategies must be employed before your site will be effective.

- Visitors enter a corporate site with a **Self-Image**, beliefs about themselves that they are already qualified, can be qualified with training or are unqualified. Their experience can contradict, confirm or possibly change this self-perception.

- Visitors have expectations about the **Availability** of a position. The employer is expected to have a related open position if available. If not, the visitor wants to know if it is planned and, if not planned is it likely to come open. Otherwise, the position/career isn't available at all. What would a highly motivated, qualified person experience if the position they seek is absent and no content is available to emphasize its importance to the corporation? We believe the experience will be negative. On the other hand, would large numbers of poorly qualified candidates whose search produced no result still apply if they could? Then what happens?

- Visitors are **Willing to Act** (or not) by the experience they gain at your site. They may be willing to declare their interest for a job or career option without offering any personal information in return (search engine usage, interest agents). They may be willing to learn what it will take to successfully compete or succeed in a given job or career (interest inventories, job description, testimonials, career progression, etc.). They may comply with instructions to answer questions about themselves (screening, profiling,

4

application) or simply to submit their résumé. They might refer others, be willing to accept future E-mails about the company or respond or some other action. They also might simply abandon the staffing pages having taken absolutely no action. How high is your abandonment rate? Was it likely that the visitor's expectation was initially to leave without taking some action or, was it more likely the expectation changed due to one of the other five principles?

Table 1: Readiness Matrix

Candidate Self-Image	Candidate Motivation	Position Availability	Candidate Willingness to Act
Qualified	Active-Current	Open	Declaring Interest
Training Expected	Comparing	Planned	Learning
Unqualified	Exploring	Likely	Complying
	Passive	Not Likely	Referring
			Remaining in Touch

Take a minute to consider the combination of variables that make up the expectations of your audience. Which combination(s) represent the ones you want to target? The ones you need to dissuade from applying? You only have to go to a site like Exxon Mobil (www.exxonmobil.com/career/index.html) to see an example where the site's orientation ("I Wonder.") has been carefully designed to manage some expectations and not others. Are qualified active candidates seeking open positions and willing to immediately forward their position satisfied here? (The answer is no). On the other hand, consider what other expectations are met and why this is one of the best company Web sites.

Table 2: Fortune 500

40 Companies (8%) - No Web site (2) or no staffing pages at all

65 Companies (13%) - Static, qualified active job seekers expectations not met

282 Companies (56%) - Adequate, offers pos. exp. to qualified active job seekers only

113 Companies (23%) - Interactive, pos. exp. to customers with different expectations

Table 2 represents just how few sites actually offer something to visitors who are not active, qualified job seekers.

2) Navigation

On the face of it, getting around a site should be a simple process. How hard is it really to search for and find a job? Answer a few questions? Ask a few questions? Evidence of just how easy can be found in something as simple as the number of layers it takes to get to the text of the job. Every click a visitor must make linking them from one page to the next might be experienced as heightening their anticipation or, more likely, increasing their frustration. We've long held that three clicks is a reasonable standard for a visitor whose active expectations are to find and review jobs and then apply. What we mean by this is that from the company's home page, the visitor will need to travel no more than three more pages to find a description of a specific job. What we actually found among sites we studied is that their job descriptions lay from 1 to 7 links away form the home page. Half of all sites were four links away from the home page.

Table 2: Distance to jobs from the home page

.6% - Required 1 click to see the job description

5.9% - Required 2 clicks

25.8% - Required 3 clicks

50.9% - Required 4 clicks

13.6% - Required 5 clicks

3% - Required 6 clicks

.2% - Required 7 clicks

Just getting to the jobs represented only a fraction of the problems that we encountered. Contributing to our overall experience were broken links on 45 sites. A sample of other elements contributing to navigation included:

- Where the Careers button is placed on the company home page. You might think this a trivial problem but contrast an Abbott (www.abbott.com) or Tricon Global (now Yum Brands www.yum.com) with Delta (www.delta.com), Pathmark (www.pathmark.com) or Quantum (www.quantum.com).
- A consistent navigation bar for all staffing pages.
- Logical placement of options for searching jobs.
- Practical display of the search results.
- Ability to combine (shopping cart) search results for viewing and application.
- Null sets: Searches that produce no jobs with little option but to return to the search page.

- Number of options to apply. Reasons for limiting. Benefits to using digital methods.
- Cross-linking to relevant content.

3) Image

Much has been said about branding and a company's staffing image is readily apparent the moment you link from the home page to the staffing pages. Building a consistent theme throughout the site is a difficult task few companies have mastered. A few will engage the visitor and then not follow through. Nowhere is the image better represented and carried through than Kodak - "Picture Yourself At Kodak" (www.kodak.com - note: Their Careers button is hidden at the bottom of the home page). Other sites that create and follow through with an engaging and consistent image include:

- Anheuser-Busch Companies, Inc. *"We Tap Talent"*: www.anheuser-busch.com
- Arrow Electronics *"BEST Company You've Never Heard Of"*: www.arrow.com
- Cinergy Corp. *"Cinergy is the Power of Change"*: www.cinergy.com
- Duke Energy Corporation *"We Generate Energy...Momentum...Futures"*: www.dukenergy.com
- Goldman Sachs Group, Inc. *"Minds. Wide Open"*: www.gs.com
- Johnson & Johnson *"Small Company Big Company Impact"*: www.jnj.com
- Minnesota Mining and Manufacturing Company *"Catch Our Spirit at 3M"*: www.3m.com
- Navistar International Corporation *"One Professional. One Tremendous Challenge"*: www.navistar.com
- NCR Corporation *"We're passionate about making a difference. Are You?"*: www.ncr.com
- Schering-Plough Corporation *"We're driven by innovation. What drives you?"*: www.schering-plough.com

4) Relevance

Assuming a company knows their target audience you would think they would simultaneously inform visitors about their people, policies, benefits, and the communities in which they live and work, and do it in a way that engages them with interest and interactive capabilities. Fully 20 percent of the firms studied offer little or no content. Of the remainder, the majority offers content in three areas:

- A list of benefits with descriptions.
- College specific content, seldom including the colleges targeted.
- General description of the company culture/diversity.
- Standard links to company Mission/Values.

Significant "agent" capability and "refer a friend" opportunities are found on about 30 percent of the Web sites — typically hosted by third party applications that tend not to be as seamless as they first appear. Most agents are cumbersome, poorly placed and typically require full disclosure by the visitor. Few are user-friendly interest agents that can quickly be engaged (see below for examples).

Less frequently encountered content but clearly of significant interest in building a positive experience are content areas like:

- Career Support: development programs, career progression/career support programs, success competencies, leadership competencies, career navigators/career matrices/career paths, training required.
- Work Life Balance.
- Specialty Areas: alumni, high school to work, union, craft, internships.
- Company Functional Area Descriptions.
- Employee Profiles, Testimonials, Day-in-the-Life.
- Virtual Tours of Facilities, Maps.
- Employment Process Flow Charts.
- Frequently Asked Questions.
- Community Links.
- Career Events.
- Interest Inventories.
- Awards.

Examples of the best practices below are not all there are. However, we were continuously amazed at how, for example, "A Day-in-the-Life" can exist on a major corporation's site and still be so poorly presented that it would totally turn off even the most intrepid candidate. The contrast between concept and application on top sites like Federated Department Stores' College site, www.Retailology.com that continues to break new ground, serves to highlight the vast difference in what it takes to create a quality experience.

Agents based on Interest
- Dana Corporation: www.dana.com
- Computer Sciences Corporation: www.csc.com
- Intel: www.intel.com
- Williams: www.williams.com

Career Path
- Deere & Company: www.deere.com

Community Links
- Corning Inc.: www.corning.com
- CDW Computer Centers, Inc.: www.cdw.com

Community Involvement
- McKesson Corporation: www.mckesson.com

Day-in-the-Life
- Bear Stearns: www.bearstearns.com
- Eli Lilly: www.lilly.com
- Progressive – Test Drive an Insurance Agent: www.progressive.com

Degree Matrix
- Occidental Petroleum Corporation: www.oxy.com

Diversity Statistics
- Aetna: www.aetna.com

Job Descriptions
- Coca-Cola: www.cocacola.com
- Hewlett-Packard: www.hp.com

Product Focus
- Boeing: www.boeing.com

Recruiter Profile
- Parker Hannifin Corporation: www.parker.com

Salary
- Lyondell Chemical Company: www.lyondell.com

Specialty
- Agilent Technologies – Alumni: www.agilent.com
- EMC Corporation – College: www.emc.com
- Sears, Roebuck and Co – College: www.sears.com
- Xerox Corporation – Sales: www.xerox.com

Testimonials
- Conoco: www.conoco.com
- Aid Association for Lutherans: www.aal.org
- Ford Motor Company – Meet Our People: www.ford.com
- Intel Corporation: www.intel.com

Values
- Anixter International Inc.: www.anixter.com
- Mars Inc.: www.mars.com

Work Perks
- Advanced Micro Devices: www.amd.com

Worklife Programs
- Du Pont De Memours (E.I.): www.dupont.com

5) Feedback

This was the easiest principle to assess. It is (almost) always missing. Feedback is not thanking a candidate for submitting a résumé and then saying "we will keep your résumé on file, match it against openings and maybe, just maybe, if you are a

really lucky and a great fit, and we get around to it, we'll let you know we are interested but, meanwhile, don't bother us." Feedback is doing what Apple
(www.apple.com) does in explaining that if you register, you will always be able to
enter the site and obtain the status of your application. Feedback is doing what State
Farm (www.statefarm.com) does by displaying an "Ask the Recruiter" option prominently on their site – and then answering the questions every day. Feedback is providing self-assessment tools that let you better understand whether your values are
shared, where you will best fit in, how you will best compete, and what you can do
through training, etc. to improve your competitive chances. Companies like General
Motors Corporation (www.gm.com), Texas Instruments (www.ti.com), Guardian Life
Insurance Co. of America (www.glic.com) accomplish this but these exceptions stick
out in a significant way. The reasons for a general lack of feedback are legion but all
are unacceptable if the customer experience is to become a priority.

It wouldn't be fair to complete this paper without mentioning our personal
favorites. Among the 25 best sites on the Fortune 500 list, Apple, Microsoft, Xerox,
TI, Federated (www.Retailology.com) and, most unusual, Robinson (CH)
(www.chrobinson.com) are able to engage visitors with the broadest range of expectations and still create a powerful customer experience.

Final Comment

Nothing that we've written here is either rocket science or set in stone. We have
however, attempted to add to the debate on how we might systematically examine the
creation of customer experiences in the employment process rather than simply
repeating the mantra that it (whatever "it" is) is important. We focused on the critical
area of the company Web site because it is the most visible recruiting aspect and available to all. These principles apply however to every aspect of employment.

Gerry Crispin and Mark Mehler *consult internationally on employment staffing strategies. They are the co-authors of CareerXroads (1996-2003), the world's leading job site reference guide. The can be reached at mmc@careerxroads.com or 732-821-6652.*

RESOURCES

Tools, Toys and Tips to Succeed

This year we've dedicated space to the places we've discovered that aren't covered by CareerXroads. If you are looking for a resource and don't find it between the covers of our directory, send us an email and we'll track it down for you.

AGENCIES

Third party placement agencies come in many flavors. Some offer job site services on the side but, most are devoted to building resume databases to serve paying clients. Here are a few of the most likely suspects.

PEOs

The letters stand for "Professional Employer Outsourcing." The concept of a PEO is quite simple. A company literally "shifts" its employees (hopefully those that aren't critical to its mission) to a PEO allowing the company to focus on its core business. The "moved" employees are now managed and paid by the PEO and, essentially leased back to their old employer. Variations on this theme are allowed and although PEOs must meet strict legal requirements, considerable debate over abuses continues. Bottom line: a job seeker might go to work at one company but be the employee of another.

According to Staffing Industry Analysts, Inc. (www.sireport.com), the "Top Ten U.S. PEOs" (prior to their newest listings after close of 2002) were:

1. Administaff Inc (www.administaff.com)
2. Gevity HR (www.gevityhr.com)
3. ADP TotalSource (www.adptotalsource.com)
4. Epix Holdings Corp. (www.epixweb.com)
5. TriNet Inc. (www.trinet.com)
6. Paychex Business Solutions (www.paychex.com)
7. Oasis Outsourcing (www.oasisadvantage.com)
8. Strategic Outsourcing Inc. (www.soi.com)
9. Presidion Solutions Inc (www.presidionsolutions.com)
10. TeamStaff Inc. (www.teamstaff.com)

Temporary/Personnel Supply Agencies.

Unlike an employee at a PEO that might work for one specific firm, employees that are supplied by temporary and contingent/contract firms will work one place one day and another the next week. According to Staffing Industry Analysts, Inc. (www.sirepot.com), the "Top Ten U.S. Personnel Supply are:

1. Adecco Staffing Services (www.adecco.com)
2. Manpower Inc (www.manpower.com)
3. Kelly Services Inc. (www.kellyservices.com)
4. Spherion Inc. (www.spherion.com)
5. Robert Half Interational Inc. (www.roberthalf.com)
6. TEKsystems Inc. (www.teksystems.com)
7. Volt Information Sciences Inc. (www.volt.com)
8. Randstad North America (www.randstad.com)
9. CDI Corp. (www.cdicorp.com)
10. On Site Engineering & Management, Inc. (no web address)

Retained Executive Search

At the top end of placement are the retained executive search firms which are contracted for a specific assignment to find individuals for key roles in companies worldwide. The Executive Recruiter Newsletter, Published by KennedyInfo (www.kennedyinfo.com), a division of BNA, calls lists the following firms as the world's largest:

1. Korn/Ferry International (www.kornferry.com)
2. Heidrick & Struggles (www.heidrick.com)
3. Egon Zehnder International (www.zehnder.com)
4. Spencer Stuart (www.spencerstuart.com)
5. Russell Reynolds Associates (www.russrey.com)
6. Ray and Berndtson (www. RayBerndtson.com)
7. The Amrop Hever Group (www.amrophever.com)
8. TMP Worldwide Executive Search (www.tmpsearch.com)
9. Whitehead Mann Group (wmann.com)
10. Intersearch (www.intersearch.org)

Job seekers should be aware of these and similar firms because their collective efforts represent a significant part of the staffing industry. You can also search out individual agencies at Oya's Directory of Recruiters (www.i-recruit.com), Kennedy Info's Executive Agent (www.executiveagent.com), the Directory of Canadian Recruiters (www.directoryofrecruiters.com), and Searchfirm (www.searchfirm.com).

3rd Party Online Exchanges

If you are really intent on finding a job via headhunters, they can be found networking online at sites like:

Bridge Path (www.bridgepath.com), CareerKey (www.careerkey.com), Christian Recruiters Affiliated (www.christianrecruiters.com), Corp2Corp (www.corp2corp.com), DegreeHunter (www.degreehunter.com), ExecGlobalNet (www.execglobalnet.com), IT-Temp (www.it-temp.com), Net-temps (www.net-temps.com), Recruiter Connection (www.recruiterconnection.com), Recruiter Networks (www.recruiternetworks.com), Recruiters Alliance (www.recruitersalliance.com), Recruiters Café (www.recruiterscafe.com), Recruiters Online Network (www.recruitersonline.com), Recruitment JOBZ.com (www.recruitmentjobz.com), Splitit.com (www.splitit.com), Subcontract.com (subcontract.com) and Top Echelon (www.topechelon.com), and US-Recruiters.com (www.usrecruiters.com). You can even find work in a placement agency through Branch Staff Online (www.branchstaffonline.com).

Third Party Staffing Associations

Finally (whew), agencies belong to organizations and associations to support legislation or get additional visibility and credibility with employers. Here are a few of these (not including the state associations):

Alliance of Medical recruiters (www.physicianrecruiters.com)
American Staffing Association (www.staffingtoday.net)
Association of Executive Search Consultants (www.aesc.org)
Association of Financial Search consultants (www.afsc-jobs.com)
International Association of Corporate and Professional Recruitment (www.iacpr.org)
National Association for Alternative Staffing ((www.naas-net.org)
National Association of Computer Consulting Businesses (www.naccb.org)
National Association of Executive Recruiters (www.naer.org)
National Association of Health Care Recruitment (www.nahcr.com)
National Association of Legal Search Consultants (www.nalsc.org)
National Association of Personnel Services (www.napsweb.org)
National Association of Physician Recruiters (www.napr.org)
National Association of Professional Employer Organizations (www.napeo.org)
National Banking & Financial Services Network www.nbn-jobs.com
National Insurance Recruiters Association (www.nirassn.com)
National Technical Services Association (www.ntsa.com)
Physicians Employment (www.physemp.com)

APPLICANT TRACKING
(See Hiring Management)

ASSESSMENT, SCREENING & TESTING
The hot term this year is "pre-screening". An oxymoron if there ever was one. Just remember- a test is a test is test. In a frustrating quest to reduce unqualified responses, employers are lining up to force jobseekers to respond to qualifying questions through automated online questions. The screening tools appear as stand-alone services or integrated through company websites and hiring management systems. This would be a good thing- if the jobseekers could only get some feedback to use as guidance for what they need to learn or the experiences they need to accumulate. Employers should read Wendell Williams article in this year's edition (or reread last year's article) and visit his website at www.scientificselection.com for what it takes to validate a test. Jobseekers should research a company web site carefully before applying. An interesting new site, still limited, is the Interview Exchange (www.interviewexchange.com) where jobseekers can actually browse the profiles of other applicants for a job before applying.

ASSOCIATIONS
We've been predicting the growth of career services through professional associations and specialized alumni associations for several years. This is their time. The 2003 directory includes hundreds of association and we have even created a separate index for the best association job sites. Use the search engine at the American Society of Association Executives' site (http://info.asaenet.org/gateway/OnlineAssocSlist. html) to find which of the 6589 associations cover your specialty.

CAREER FAIRS — ONLINE
We're not fans of "Virtual Career Fairs". Too often these events are masquerading as time dependent postings of openings and company profiles. Most services that offer virtual career fairs charge participating companies a premium to drive traffic to job site and offers little added value for the employer. Things are changing however and HotU (www.hotu.com) is representative of a new type of interactive application employers can customize to "meet and greet" online. Services like these actually create a real-time connection between groups of potential applicants and recruiters.

CAREER ADVICE/CAREER MANAGEMENT
Here's a potpourri of sites that can enhance your career management strategies. Try to avoid fee-based sites wherever possible. Risking more than a few dollars just isn't something we would recommend (see our comments under resume distribution services). If you really need a "coach" and can afford it, go to the major outplacement services or check out the members of the International Association of Career

Management Professionals (www.iacmp.org). If you can't afford the price, stick with your college placement office or get services through your alumni or professional association.

The sites below can help you find people or job leads, research companies, write resumes and much more.

10 Minute Resume
www.10minuteresume.com

Site provides job seekers with a free step by step process to have a formatted resume and cover letter (www.10minutecoverletter.com). Job seekers can also have their resume on their own web page for free. Owners sell tracking capabilities for job seekers to monitor what sites they have posted their resume to for $9.95 a month. Resumes that are completed via the site may be held in private or they can be distributed to a recruiters network (not recommended).

Be an Actuary
www.beanactuary.com

Great career information on how to become an actuary. There were only 5 jobs posted on our last visit and several were for internships. It only takes one ! CXR was very impressed by the stats page on which industries hire actuaries, the number by industry and even individual company. If number crunching is your thing this is your career site of choice.

Ask the Employer
www.asktheemployer.com

Ask the Employer is a career management site that specializes in forming networking connections between online mentors and mentees. Job seekers can sign up for a free bi-weekly email newsletter on tips and tricks to land your next opportunity.

Business Week Online Career Center
www.businessweek.com

Career Insider Newsletter, Discussion Forums, Career Questions can be asked via emails and responses given with numerous career articles from the website and publication.

Canadian Careers.com
www.canadiancareers.com

CC provides career information for those north of the border. Interesting articles on exploring career options, marketing yourself and finding work are available.

CareerBabe
www.careerbabe.com
Fran Quittel provides interesting job tips from her prior columns. Job seekers need to check out the resume writing tutorial for great suggestions on staying ahead of the curve.

Career Consulting Corner
www.careercc.com
CCC provides profiles on over 350 career products from interviewing skills assessment to videos on skills identification. The site also allows job seekers to post their resume and recruiters to post jobs and view resumes for free.

CareerPlus
www.career-plus.com/life/links/locale.html
This is (literally) a world class resource worth noting if immigration/emigration is a possibility. The site offers a blow by blow description for every country.

Career Services Kiva
www.careerserviceskiva.com
Career Services Kiva is dedicated to college career counselors. The site contains career articles, research briefs and much more. Links to college career services job sites are also available.

Career Talk
www.careertalk.com
Career Talk offers career management tips for job seekers and recruiting tips for hiring managers. Articles on interviewing and recruiting tips are also available. The owner will respond to all emails regarding career questions.

Careers-Internet.org
www.careers-internet.org
The Institute For Career Research provides vocational guidance information for many generations of young people and is utilized by thousands of teachers, librarians, and counselors. The service is used in over 20,000 schools and public libraries throughout the US and Canada . Sample tests and results are available on the site. Interesting write-ups on career occupations with required traits, education (a listing of colleges who provide degree programs in the field of choice), what you will do, pluses and minuses of the job, where you will work, earning potential and an introduction to the occupation. Well done and geared to the high school and college student market.

Disabilityinfo.gov
www.disability.gov

Links and information to everything job seekers and employers may want to know about about hiring individuals with disabilities.

Eliyon
www.eliyon.com

A tool designed for employers to research individuals in competitive firms, Eliyon has a organizes information about people found randomly on billions of internet pages into tight informative profiles on 10 million people. A fee-based service (approximately $1500 per month) that is geared for the proactive recruiter, jobseekers might try a demo to see if what they can find out about a prospective hiring manager.

fuc*ed company.com (replace the * with another letter)
www.fuc*edcompany.com

Gossip, rumors and more can be found about what employers are doing to their employees. Check out the "Super Happy Fun and Slander column for best results. Fuc*ed also has tens of jobs and resumes posted but many were quite stale.

Go Army
www.goarmy.com

A brilliant effort by the US army to turn a "day-in-the-life" into an engaging game for 16 year olds. If critical disciplines like nursing and engineering could invest in tools like these, it might help stem the decline of students choosing these majors.

GradSchools.com
www.gradschools.com

A lengthy list of links to graduate school programs in almost any discipline one could imagine. Chat rooms and discussion boards allows prospective students to learn from their peers what it really is like in a grad school. At the "Information Center" prospective students are given step by step free assistance in writing application essays.

Hard@Work
www.hardatwork.com

Hard@work is one of our favorite water coolers on the web. Day-to-day employer/employee problems are discussed, and readers can send in their comments. Check out any of the sections, from Sisyphus & Us and the Rockpile to Stump the Mentor. This site will make you laugh and is worth signing up for their monthly emailed newsletter.

InfoGist Career infoFinder and Resume infoFinder.
www.infogist.com

The site offers resume and job searching tools that simultaneously searches, ranks and delivers job leads or resumes from 100 fee and free job sites. The features and capabilities (yes, we are biased) are among the best on the market. Jobseekers can download a free trial

International Career Development Library (ICDL)
icdl.uncg.edu

The International Career Development Library (ICDL is a free, comprehensive collection of full-text resources for counselors, educators, workforce development personnel and others providing career development services. The database runs the gamut from career counseling to youth activities. This site is definitely worth a visit.

iResign
www.i-resign.com

If you need advice on how to get through an awkward resignation this is the place to gain an edge. Numerous templates of resignation letters and articles on career advice abound here. The site appears to be selling job leads of resigning employees. Could be the freshest leads of all. This could be the job analog of ambulance chasing.

Job Bus (Canada jobs)
www.jobbus.com

The site provides links to hundreds of links by job category to Canadian corporations that it says are hiring. Owners also own the job board www.canadian-jobs.com.

Job Hunters Bible
www.jobhuntersbible.com

JobHuntersBible.com is provided as a career resource by Dick Bolles, author of What Color is your Parachute, a best selling career guide. The site offers the author's insight into why the web is another tool for the job seeker's kit bag.

JobStar: the California Job Search Guide
www.jobstar.org

JobStar originated with a local library system in the Bay Area and has expanded to cover several additional regions (including NJ). One of the best career information sites on the web JobStar offers original content, over 300 free salary surveys and "Ask Electra", a local librarian (Mary-Ellen Mort, who delivers job search information to anyone who email her a question.

JobWeb
www.jobweb.org

JobWeb is the creation of the National Association of Colleges and Employers (NACE). This site has excellent career management content for college students including links to hundreds of additional resources. Positions for Career Planning and Placement professionals and corporate college employment positions can be viewed through "jobwire". The association is beginning to develop its own job site for college students, NACElink, that is in its early stages of development.

Jobs and Moms.com
www.jobsandmoms.com

Interesting Q & A on the balancing act of being a mother and holding down a full or part-time job. Mothers should check out the site's "work from home" section as numerous links to associations and other resources are provided. The site owner offers a telephone consulting service for a fee.

Military Career Guide Online
www.militarycareers.com

The Military Career Guide Online is a compendium of military occupations, training, and career information, and is designed for use by students wishing to explore the armed forces. Detailed information on 152 enlisted and officer occupations can be found here.

My Future
www.myfuture.com

My Future is geared to high school graduates who are not sure what they want to do when they grow up. The site includes a work interest quiz, resume assistance and practical information for those not sure if they are going to college. Information on joining the military can also be found.

My Road
www.myroad.com

MyRoad.com is a partnership with Peterson's, WetFeet.com and Renewal Associates to build an education and career planning resource website. For $19.95 information is provided on choosing colleges, majors and careers. Online tools are designed to facilitate a career planning process.

Nevada JobConnect
www.nevadajobconnect.com

Nevada JobConnect is charged with overseeing and providing workforce development services to employers and job seekers in Nevada. For employers, Nevada

JobConnect offers recruiting, retention, training and retraining, as well as valuable information on labor law and labor market statistics. For job seekers, Nevada JobConnect offers career development information, job search resources and training programs. One of the better state sites.

Operation ABLE of Michigan
www.operationable.org

Since 1986, Operation ABLE of Michigan has been helping mid-career and older workers obtain work and remain employable throughout their lifetime while also helping businesses develop a competent and dependable workforce. There is also a national ABLE network composed of agencies across the United States that includes offices in: Boston, Chicago, Los Angeles, Michigan, Nebraska, Vermont, Washington, D.C.. All are not for profit run agencies.

Quintessential Careers
www.quintcareers.com

Quintessential Careers has over 1,500 free pages of content to assist jobseekers. Randall S. Hansen the site's owner writes a "Career Doctor column" that is syndicated in newspapers. Job seekers should consider his resume critique for $15 before spending big bucks. Links to the owners career articles and other vendor products are also available.

Red Guide to Temp Agencies
ww.panix.com/~grvsmth/redguide/intro.html

If only this guide were available everywhere. The Red Guide offers refreshingly open and detailed reviews of temp agencies in New York City by the temps that used them. A labor of love run by a career temporary worker.

Researching Companies Online
home.sprintmail.com/~debflanagan/index.html

Researching Companies Online is an interactive tutorial that provides a step-by-step process for researching companies and industries using a wide variety of free resources on the net. The tutorial provides explanations on how to use numerous online tools. The site is simple, easy to use and well worth the effort.

Resume Tutor
www.umn.edu/ohr/ecep/resume

At Resume Tutor, job seekers will find excellent advice on how to prepare a resume. Check out the six steps to the perfect resume. Each step is easy to follow and very focused. A valuable check list is provided to critique your work.

The Riley Guide
www.rileyguide.com

Margaret F. Dikel (formerly Riley), the mother of all job link lists offers comments on hundreds of sites. Links to career articles and advice abound on this free site.

Retailology
www.retailogy.com.

College students looking to work in retail should to click on the goldfish icon to access this company's college site which is chock full of retail industry information. Federated Stores has created a walk through via the sites "think tank" to discussion questions on life in the retail world.

Salary.com
www.salary.com

Salary.com provides free basic intelligence on job market data for positions in every conceivable function. For $49.95 job seekers can obtain a premium report with multiple location information. Corporations can purchase industry specific studies for $795. Corporations and job seekers should clearly understand that this site does not disclose where it gets its data. This makes their fee-based services a bit less inviting.

Telecommuting, Telework and Alternative Officing
www.gilgordon.com

Telecommuting, Telework and Alternative Officing is managed by Gil Gordon, one of the world's leading experts. Updated every two weeks, this site offers great insight into what it takes to work from home or develop a telecommuting effort. Great articles and links to industry information and products. Gil has a new telecommuting training program for company's in-house use.

Troops to Teachers
www.jobs2teach.doded.mil

Troops to Teachers assists military personnel who wish to transition their skills to the public or private teaching profession. Jobs are posted for all to see for free. Jobseekers can participate in mentoring sessions hosted by volunteers or via bulletin boards peer discussion groups.

Vault
www.vault.com

The job seekers gossip column for what's hot and what's not in corporate America. Job seekers can now purchase Vault career guides for opportunities in numerous industries for $29.95. Access to the message (824,000) boards remains free. For those who wish to see the archived boards the cost is $2.50 per month per user.

WetFeet
www.wetfeet.com

WetFeet serves up excellent jobseeker and company research on career-related issues. Guides to occupations cost $27.95. Corporate industry reports can cost hundreds to thousands of dollars depending on the subject but are designed to help employers compete more effectively for top talent. Interesting career articles, city reports, discussion boards and Q&A's are available for free.

HIRING MANAGEMENT SYSTEMS

Few jobseekers really know what goes on behind the online façade of a company's staffing pages. Technology allows prospects information to be weighed and graded, broken down and reassembled, ranked and responded to before a pair of eyes ever sees it. Chances are no eyes ever will. Hundreds of vendors are vying for the right to sell their version of "THE end-to-end, global, integrated, customer-relations enhanced Employment Process ". Our best advice to jobseekers is to use technology to find companies with openings but then find a real person in that target company to deliver you as a referral. Employers should see Mark Mehler and Ed Struzik's checklist before purchasing or attend one of our classes through Cornell (links are on our website).

JOB DISTRIBUTION SERVICES

Employers are looking for better, cheaper and more convenient ways to send their open positions to multiple web sites. Services like eQuest, GoJobs, Recruit-USA, HodesIQ, Viper and many more have made some headway in 2002 (although they may actually limit choices in some ways despite their claims to distribute to thousands of sites).

Job posting aids are extremely valuable and an essential part of a recruiter's "toolkit". They offer real convenience, labor savings and, increasingly, improved metric capabilities. Once installed however it is a lot of extra work for a recruiter to experiment with a site outside the choices presented by the service. The vendors have a tendency to load up on niche job boards that are little more than collections of mirror sites- multiple Urls with a common job or resume data base. Employers are then lulled into a false sense of security that all their bases are covered when in actuality they are missing important opportunities.

Eventually, these services will evolve in two directions: The first will be to send a posting to a cluster of affiliated sites at a lower cost or single price - see careercast.com or jobfest.com for examples. The second will be a comprehensive search to find and post to several extremely targeted micro-niche specialty job sites (typically associations) with a demonstrated capability to reach their audience.

METRICS

Employers are getting better at measuring their hiring process and its impact on their company but there is still much work to be done. According to a survey by The Society for Human Resource Management (SHRM) in 2001, there are a significant number of companies that don't even know how many employees they have!

Excellent resources can be found at the SHRM site (www.shrm.org) and Staffing.org (www.staffing.org).

NEWSLETTERS

(Jobseekers see Career Advice in this section). The list below is a short list of daily, weekly and monthly information sources we track specific to Employment and Staffing world. These are by no means the only informative and interesting news sources available but, it's a start.

>   CareerXroads.com (www.careerxroads.com)
>   ERExchange.com (www.erexchange.com)
>   Interbiznet.com (www.interbiznet.com
>   Kennedyinfo.com (www.keenedyinfo.com)
>   Online Recruitment www.onrec.com
>   Recruiter.com (www.recruiter.com)
>   Recruiters Network (www.recruitersnetwork.com)
>   Riley Guide (www.rileyguide.com)
>   Sorcerer's Apprentice (www.netrecruiter.net/resource.html)
>   Staffing Industry Analyst (www.sireport.com)
>   Staffing.org www.staffing.org
>   The Tiburon Group (tiburongroup.com)
>   Weddle's (www.weddles.com)

NEWSPAPERS

Newspapers are finally energized. A few are developing models that balance their individual strengths within a collective network. Accepting their location niche status was critical. They are recognizing that their print component powerfully supports online urgency and convenience rather than the other way around. We've recognized several newspapers in this edition and listed hundreds in the location index. Search for any newspaper by going to the Newspaper Association of America's newspaperlinks (www.newspaperlinks.com).

RESUME DISTRIBUTION

Note to job seekers: We can't say it more strongly than this- Don't pay anyone to distribute your resume to recruiters. They really don't look at them. Typical services charge $25 to $50 along with the most preposterous claims and promises.

TRAFFIC

Recruiters and the job sites that they use to reach jobseekers are constantly looking for the "golden rule", the one best measure of a site's worth. Traffic, variously defined as the number of visitors to a site in some predetermined time (a month for example) is often touted to support these claims. ALEXA (www.alexa.com) is a service offering site traffic rankings. Go to Alexa and type Monster.com (or any of your favorite sites) into the search window. Monster's traffic rating (Nov 2002) is 95 meaning that of all the sites Alexa tracks Monster.com is the 95th most frequently visited site. Do the same for the IEEE (7660) or SHRM (8118). Which site is the obvious choice if you are seeking electrical engineers or human resource professionals active in their respective professional associations? You'll need more than traffic comparisons.

For jobseekers the real value of Alexa is the section listing the answer to "people who visit this site also visit..." Look for other sites that professionals visiting association and other niche sites go.

VMS - Vendor Management Systems

According to a report offered for sale by Staffing Industry Analysts, Inc. (www.sireport.com, VMS Decision Guide, 2002, $745), Vendor Management Systems are internet-based applications that enable companies (both staffing firms and their customers) to capture the information about the hiring and management of temporary and/or permanent staff. The report lists 58 applications including many reviews along with detailed analyses about how to match company needs with the appropriate system. For employers it is important to understand that these systems may be standalone websites such a eWork.com, eLance.com or Subcontract.com. They might be a feature of broad-based applicant tracking systems like Deploy.com and Peopleclick.com or a module of an even broader enterprise wide system like PeopleSoft. The majority however are independent systems like White Amber (www.whireamber.com) or part of the new service offerings of traditional temporary and contract staffing firms like Ultrasource owned by Manpower (www.manpower.com), Enthusian owned by Spherion and, WorkCard owned by Adecco.

What all this means for the jobseeker is that if you can't get into the company you've targeted through the front door for a permanent position, their might be an opening for contract, freelance or temporary positions available through their VMS vendor's portal.

JOB SEEKERS

Creating Byte-Able Resumés For Electronic Job Searching

By Michelle Dumas

E-mail: resumes@distinctiveweb.com

Over the last several years, the most common questions about resumés asked by job hunters have progressively shifted to a new line of inquiry. The majority of queries are no longer about functional versus chronological resumé styles, whether to keep or remove experience from 25 years ago, or whether to include dates of education. With the advent and subsequent explosion of the role of the Internet in the job search process, questions have turned overwhelmingly to issues of electronic resumé creation and transmission.

- What are the different types of electronic resumés?
- What are the differences between an e-mail resumé, a scannable resumé, and a web resumé?
- How do I know which resumé format to use?
- How do I format my electronic resumé to ensure that the recipient can read it?

No wonder there is so much confusion! In just a few short years, there has been a complete revolution in the rules and techniques of job hunting. As applicant tracking technologies have come into common use among headhunter firms, large corporations, and even mid-size and small businesses, recommended resumé formats and methods of transmission have rapidly evolved and changed with the advancing technologies. Further complicating things, have been the increasing availability of personal web space for online resumé portfolios and the accelerated growth and popularity of independent resumé database services such as Monster.com.

What does this mean for today's job hunter? While the Internet has opened unprecedented doors of opportunity in the job search process, for those who have not taken the time to learn and apply the rules it can mean disaster!

While few job hunters have time to spend months studying the most recent technologies and recommendations for the creation of electronic resumés, before venturing into cyberspace with your resumé it is critical that you take the time to learn and understand a few simple concepts. Knowing your audience and the formats most acceptable by those audiences are essential pieces of knowledge for the Internet job hunter.

The human reader. The traditional, printed, hardcopy resumé (yes, it does still have a place in job hunting!) is created to attract the human eye and attention. With the advantages of word processing applications, sophisticated formatting is possible and applied strategically to create eye-appeal and draw the readers' attention to key qualifications.

The computer reader. The electronic or computer-optimized resumé is designed, first and foremost, to be readable by the computer. There are several types of electronic resumés, but the common element of all is the ability to be searched by keyword. Of course, once your resumé has been tagged as matching a keyword search it will be reviewed by a human, so compelling, easy-to-read content is just as important in the electronic, byte-able resumé as in the traditional resumé.

Miss these points and the effects could be severe. You might send out hundreds of resumés only to sit at home and wonder why nobody, not even one company or headhunter, has called you for an interview. There are fundamental formatting differences between traditional and electronic resumés. If you do not understand these differences, your resumé will make it into very few — if any — resumé databases.

Resumé Formats

What are the differences between keyword, scannable, web, traditional and text resumés?

Traditional resumés are designed to compel the human reader, through persuasive language and design, to take further action and call you for an interview. Layout and page design are critical and should be planned strategically to draw the eye to areas of emphasis. The most effective traditional resumés are focused on achievements and written in powerful, active language that captures and holds the attention of the reader.

Also a printed, hardcopy format, a scannable resumé is designed primarily for accurate scanning into a computer. Captured as an image, scannable resumés are fed through OCR (optical character recognition) software that reads and extracts the text. The extracted text is stored in a database and later recalled by keyword from an applicant tracking system.

Text resumés are just what the name implies, an ASCII-formatted version of either your traditional or scannable resumé. You will need two versions of your text resumé. The first, created without line breaks, will be used for uploading to online resumé databanks. The second, created with line breaks, will be used for e-mailing directly to employers.

The phrase *keyword resumé,* as it was first used, referred most often to either a scannable or text resumé that incorporated a focus on nouns and phrases that employers were likely to use when searching for an applicant. Sometimes the keyword resumé had a section at the beginning or end that listed the keywords separated by commas or periods. Today, there is no need to maintain both a keyword and a non-keyword resumé. Keywords have become such an essential element in resumés that you should insure that every version of your resumé, whether meant for the human or the computer reader, incorporates the keywords most important in your field or industry.

Still confused? Our recommendation is to simply maintain several separate versions of your resumé.

Traditional resumé. If you wish to send a hardcopy, paper version of your resumé and are certain that the recipient does not utilize an applicant tracking system, you should send your traditional resumé. It is worth a call to the HR department to learn how they handle resumés, but if you still cannot find out, you have two choices:

- Send both a traditional resumé and a scannable resumé (cover all bases).
- Send the scannable resumé and bring a copy of your traditional resumé to the interview.

While we do not necessarily recommend e-mailing your traditional resumé as an attachment to a message, increasingly, employers and recruiters are actually requesting this. The most frequently requested formats for attached resumés are Microsoft Word and Adobe PDF. If you choose to send the MS Word version of your traditional resumé, be aware that your formatting may be incompatible with the recipient's system. While usually still readable, font and bullet sizes and styles may be different from what you intended. These problems can be minimized, although not always eliminated, by embedding the fonts into the document. This is a simple process, and the MS Word help files will guide you through it. If the recipient has the free Adobe Reader installed, Adobe PDF files will appear on the recipient's system precisely the way they appear on your system. If given the choice between sending an MS Word file and Adobe PDF file, always opt for Adobe PDF.

Scannable resumé. Employers rarely request scannable resumés anymore. If they utilize an applicant tracking system, they will likely request that your resumé be e-mailed, either as ASCII text or as an attachment. E-mail allows the recipient to enter your resumé directly into the database, eliminating the extra steps of scanning and OCR. However, there are still occasional calls for scannable resumés, and you need to be ready when you receive a request for one. As described above, if you are sending a hardcopy, paper version of your resumé and know or suspect that an employer makes use of applicant tracking, you should send a scannable resumé. You may also decide to send a traditional resumé as a supplement. Whatever you choose, *always* be certain that your scannable resumé incorporates the critical keywords for your industry and field.

ASCII text resumé. If you conduct any of your job search on the Internet, ASCII-formatted resumés are critically important tools. Always have two up-to-date text versions of your resumé on disk. This is the fastest way to contact potential employers and to apply for jobs advertised online. You must also have a text version of your resumé if you wish to post in online resumé databanks. Because the text versions of your resumé will nearly always end up in a searchable database, you should *always* incorporate industry-critical keywords in the text.

A final type of electronic resumé is the web resumé, also known as the online resumé. Created using HTML, your web resumé may be uploaded to space provided by a web-hosting provider. Eliminating the compatibility problems associated with word-processed resumés sent as e-mail attachments, web resumés offer the advantage of maintaining layout and design on the systems of anyone with a web browser. Available for viewing around the clock, conveying a technology-savvy image, and allowing the ability to add supporting content to your resumé (effectively creating an online portfolio promoting your qualifications), web resumés are becoming a progressively important tool in the job search. The creation of a web resumé or resumé portfolio is far beyond the scope of this article, but if web resumés are an electronic format that interest you, be aware that many professional resumé services have begun offering web resumé design and hosting at affordable prices.

Preparing Byte-Able Resumés

What do I need to know about incorporating keywords into my resumés?

Keywords are generally defined as nouns or phrases that an employer will use when searching for an applicant with your skill set. To maximize the recall of your resumé in a search, you will want to use as many keywords in your resumé as possible.

1. Keywords should focus on technical and professional areas of expertise, industry-related jargon, and your work history. Also, include the names of associations and organizations of which you are a member.
2. Whenever possible, use synonyms of keywords in different parts of your resumé and if you use initials for a term in one section, spell the term out in another. This is where the keyword summary becomes useful.
3. Always be specific. For example, while it may be fine to include the phrase "computer literate," you will also want to list the specific software that you are proficient in using.

With careful attention to rhythm and flow, it is possible to prepare a resumé that is keyword optimized, but that also includes the powerful, compelling, active language of a traditional resumé. Not only will this simplify your resumé preparation, but it will also insure that the content of all versions of your resumé will be optimized for both the computer and the human reader. Furthermore, if you incorporate a professional summary and bulleted list of qualifications in the text of your resumé, there is little if any need to prepare a separate keyword summary.

Unfortunately, it is impossible to recommend a specific list of the best keywords to use in your resumé, as the *best* keywords are different for every individual and depend mainly on your unique career objective and background.

How do I maximize the scannability of my resumé?

Early projections regarding the growing popularity of scanning resumés have not matched forecasts. The main reason for this variance has been the increased use of e-mail as a transmission mode. Although an e-mailed resumé will still be entered into a tracking system, it can be done so automatically, with no need for scanning. However, some corporate websites and employment ads still recommend scannable resumés, so you will need to be prepared.

Keep in mind the reason that your resumé will be scanned (to store it in an applicant tracking system) and how it will be searched (by keywords), and then write your resumé content appropriately. Confusing the issue, many modern OCR systems are able to accurately translate even fairly complex formatting. In many cases, even your traditional resumé could be scanned, run through an OCR program, and accurately translated and stored. However, if the recipient does not have the most up-to-date software and system, your scanned traditional resumé may become a jumble of indistinguishable words when run through the OCR program. For this reason, it will be best if you prepare your scannable resumé using a simple design and format. Here are some tips for creating a resumé that can be accurately scanned and stored in all systems:

1. Always print your resumé on white or very light-colored paper. Never use colored or patterned paper for your scannable resumé.
2. Use 8½" x 11" paper. Never use formats that are printed in a folder style or on 11" x 17" paper.
3. Send your resumé flat in a large envelope. Do not fold or staple it.
4. Use a standard sans serif typeface such as Helvetica or Arial.
5. Use a font that is 10 to 14 points in size.
6. Your name should be the very first line. Do not have any other information on this line.
7. Each phone number and e-mail address should be placed on a separate line

and your address should be typed in standard format.

8. Don't ever condense spacing between letters to try to save space. Each letter should be separate and not touch.
9. It is okay to use boldface and capitals to highlight certain sections of your resumé, however, make sure the letters do not touch.
10. Never use underlines.
11. Don't use vertical lines, boxes, or graphics. Horizontal lines are generally okay, but make certain that they do not touch the text.
12. Most OCR software can handle bullets, but use them sparingly.
13. Always send crisp originals of your resumé. Photocopies and faxes do not scan well.
14. If the employer gives specific instructions for formatting your resumé, follow them!

How do I prepare an ASCII text version of my resumé?

Preparing the two required versions of your text resumé is not difficult. Once converted to ASCII format, you will be able to e-mail your resumé in response to an ad or paste it directly into web-based forms and submit it to Internet resumé databanks. To prepare your ASCII resumés properly, follow these simple steps:

1. Using your word processing program, open your word-processed resumé and use the "Save As" function to save a copy as a "Text Only" or "ASCII (DOS)" document. Title your document with an easily distinguishable name; perhaps "resume_internet.txt"
2. Close your word processing program and re-open the ASCII file. You will not be able to see your changes until you have done this. Note that it has been stripped of virtually all original formatting.
3. Go through your new ASCII document line by line. Align all text flush to the left-hand margin.
4. Remove all centering, right hand margin, and justification alignments.
5. Although you should no longer see them, if visible, remove all graphics, artwork, and special character formatting.
6. Remove all tab characters.
7. Remove all columns.
8. Replace bullets with a simple ASCII asterisk (*).
9. Carefully check the spelling and the accuracy of your data.
10. If you wish, use ASCII characters to enhance the appearance of your resumé. Asterisks, plus signs, or other keyboard characters can be used to create visual lines that separate sections of your resumé and make it easier to read.

The above steps convert your resumé to ASCII without line breaks. When pasted into a web-based form, your resumé will automatically wrap to the size of the window.

If you intend to transmit your resumé by e-mail, you must take several final steps:

1. Save the changes to your "resume_internet.txt" file.
2. Once you have saved it, use "Page Setup" to change your page margins to 1" Top and Bottom; 1" Left, and 2" Right.
3. Use "Save As" again, this time saving your resumé as "Text Only with Line Breaks." Give your file a unique name, such as "resume_email.txt"

These additional steps insert line breaks at approximately 65 characters per line to prevent line wraps in unintended places. While some e-mail systems automatically insert line breaks in outgoing messages, many do not, so this extra file insures that the recipient will receive your e-mailed resumé in a readable format rather than as several long lines of unbroken text. Your e-mail resumé is now ready to be copied and pasted into the body of e-mail messages.

Your two new ASCII resumés will be universally readable, no matter what computer system the recipient uses. They are also easily manipulated for entry into applicant tracking databases and eliminate the inherent difficulties of scanning and converting your paper resumé with OCR systems.

There is no denying that the Internet has caused what was once a straightforward process to become complex and confusing to many job hunters. Yet, the benefits far outweigh the negatives. Like never before, job searchers have immediate access to announcements and advertisements of openings around the globe. They have the ability to conduct detailed research on companies of interest. And they have unprecedented opportunity to cost effectively promote their qualifications to hundreds or even thousands of hiring authorities at just a tiny fraction of the cost of doing so through traditional methods. While the new skills you must learn may seem daunting at first, by understanding the concepts and creating your byte-able, electronic resumés, you are well on your way to an efficient, effective Internet job search.

Michelle Dumas is a nationally certified professional resumé writer and career coach specializing in resumé preparation and career marketing for the global job market. As founder and executive director of Distinctive Documents, she provides comprehensive resumé services in all 50 states and internationally. For more information visit her web site www.distinctiveweb.com or call 800-644-9694

Virtual Networking

By Glenn Gutmacher

E-mail: glenn@recruiting-online.com

Nowadays, the job application process is simple thanks to fax, in-store application kiosks, and e-mail and Web submission; as a result, it is not uncommon for recruiters to receive hundreds of candidates for a single position. Assuming your skill set and background are comparable to the other applicants and presented well (keyword-optimized resumé, thoughtful cover letter, etc.), then what is it that helps you stand out?

One of the techniques used by successful recruiters to find the right candidate that's also invaluable for job hunters is *networking*. Find people who are decision-makers at companies hiring in your industry/location/function, or are one or two steps removed because they may know the right person(s) or are a friend of a friend who is. Let them make an introductory call for you (or just mention the referrer's name when you do) and you're a giant step closer to an interview!

Why Networking Works

For the purposes of this article, I'll assume you've tapped everyone you know for who they know (perhaps to the point of being annoying!) and even after following those networking leads to their natural end, you are still not having much luck.

Don't get frustrated! First realize that people have a conscious and/or subconscious psychological preference toward responding to people with whom they have a *connection*. When it comes to most job applicants, where the employer doesn't know them personally, any connection is better than none. At the very least, being able to name-drop someone in the first paragraph of your cover letter that the recipient will recognize usually elevates your resumé toward the top of the pile.

I know this from my own testing: I periodically apply to companies for positions for which I'm qualified and have a name-drop. Then I will submit a second application for the same positions using alias contact information that also routes back to me, a mirror image of the first resumé and cover letter, referencing an exact parallel work history (same job titles, work dates, locations, etc., but substituting other company names)—but without a name-drop. Guess which version garners responses over 100 percent more often?

Networking's Exponential Boost via the Internet

While face-to-face networking is ideal, your circumstances may not allow enough of it: Limitations on your time or your location prevent you from going to industry meetings, conventions and other events where networking with people traditionally occurs. But if you have Internet access, a whole other world is opened to you and you can start leveling the playing field by making connections virtually.

You have numerous *free* online channels to tap. Here are some of my favorite categories: 1) company websites; 2) trade association sites; 3) user group sites; and 4) listservs.

Company Websites

Start with a search on one of the job boards listed in *CareerXroads* by your industry and location (most good boards have those fields as distinct search criteria). Some boards let you determine which firms are hiring heavily (*e.g.,* Monster.com has a link from the bottom of each job posting showing all other postings by that company).

Once you have found some promising companies, visit their websites. Most job postings indicate the host company's site. If it's not obvious, it may be implied. For example, if the e-mail address to submit resumés ends in @company.com, then the site is likely www.company.com. Otherwise, try typing the company name at your favorite general search engine or directory site. When we searched for "Country Insurance & Financial Services" (in Bloomington, IL) on Yahoo.com, the right one was the first result.

Once on the right site, don't just jump to the careers section. See who works there, especially in the department(s) to which you'd apply. Ideally, look for an "employee directory" or "staff list" link, often found under the "company" link.

If you can't find names there, you may find them under other sections (e.g., sales management under the "Products" section) and at least you can find senior-level staff names by perusing the "news" or "press releases" section of the site (often under the "about [us/our company]" section). After all, company news quotes about product releases, earnings reports, etc., are attributed to executive staff—as well as names in releases about recent hiring announcements!

If you want to make your approach by phone, you can call the company main number and ask for that person's extension. If you prefer e-mail (phone is nice, but you may be able to convey a fuller pitch by e-mail), you obviously need an exact e-mail address. The good news is that most all companies have a standard format: firstname.lastname@company.com, first initial then last name, or something similar. So if you can find just one person's e-mail address on the site, you can figure out the e-mail for your target!

If that doesn't yield enough contact names, you can find senior personnel at most companies with a websites by doing a search for their annual report. For example, to find the latest annual report for Cisco and companies that work with it, on Google.com, try: "2001 annual report" cisco filetype:pdf (searches for 2002 reports won't yield much until mid-2003). To narrow results to a specific company, replace the company name with its domain (i.e., site:www.cisco.com rather than cisco). For public companies, you'll find that and more with a service like www.secinfo.com (registration is free), which has all their federally required report filings.

Another trick to finding e-mail addresses of people is Yahoo's Advanced People Search http://email.people.yahoo.com/py/psAdvSearch.py. It doesn't have everyone but you're sure to find people, especially at larger organizations. Just input what you know on the search form: it works even if you want to find people at a particular company but don't know anyone's name there. For example, to tap mutual fund giant Fidelity Investments, just type Fidelity Investments in the "Organization Name" field, and under "Organization Type", select "Company". Note that many of the results are home addresses! Nifty, eh?

Trade Associations

When job postings are hard to find, that doesn't mean opportunities don't exist. Many times, you can create your own job description if you fill a need. The issue is how to match your background, skills and interests to the companies that could profit from your involvement. Don't assume human resources personnel know how to do that! In fact, because recruiters aren't involved day-to-day in the departments they hire for, they may not have a clue as to how you might meet a possible need, or even what future needs may be. And your skills may translate to different areas than the keywords in your resumé indicate. What to do?

You need to get in front of the hiring managers, ideally as senior in the organization as possible—they should be the folks who have the vision to see how someone could fit into the company puzzle in non-obvious ways. You can get to know them virtually through the online components of professional associations.

A few of my favorite Internet tools are:

- ASAE (basically, the association for the people who run associations), with over 6,500 groups indexed http://info.asaenet.org/gateway/OnlineAssocSlist. html. Find your industry in the Category pull down menus (typically works better than the keyword box). You might be tempted to select a state as well, but I recommend leaving that menu alone: this database typically stores only the main headquarters location for a group. Realize that many associations' networks operate strongest on a geographic level, and will have local chapters. A very active chapter with tons of members might be in your area, but that won't appear in the search results.

- Association Central www.associationcentral.com — perhaps the largest database
- Yahoo! Organizations search http://dir.yahoo.com/business_and_economy/organizations/professional

Once you've found some associations' sites, there's often quite a bit you can tap into for free. (Though some premium features may require you be a dues-paying member, my unemployed clients have found in many cases that if they mention their status, they can get access fees waived.)

For example, in the insurance industry, the Risk & Insurance Management Society www.rims.org has links to their local affiliates, which includes the San Diego chapter www.sandiegorims.org. In turn, that includes a list of board members with contact information, an employment page with jobs, and a list of other related sites, including a free RISK listserv you can subscribe to, along with a searchable archive (more about listservs later). Or at the American Risk and Insurance Association www.aria.org, you see their conference program, which includes presenters' names, titles, institutions and e-mail addresses.

User Groups

I think of user groups as the poor, grassroots cousin of trade associations. They focus on one particular subject niche and usually one locality; typically have a websites, a listserv (covered in next section) and meet once a month. Because they're typically smaller, lesser known and vendors in the industry aren't all over them, requests for job (and other) aid tend to be better supported.

While user groups are predominately in the computing arena, a growing number are in finance, medical and other fields where altruistic sharing of specialized information is helpful. You can find user groups in your area through any of the following directories:

- http://directory.google.com/Top/Computers/Organizations/User_Groups/
- http://dmoz.org/Computers/Organizations/User_Groups/
- http://dir.yahoo.com/Computers_and_Internet/Organizations/User_Groups/
- http://msdn.microsoft.com/usergroups/find.asp (has convenient search capability tied in)

You should also search for your city. For example, Boston's technical community has done a great job categorizing user groups www.bostonusergroups.com as has the greater New York City area www.objdev.org/metro. To find others, type "user group" along with keywords for your nearest city and industry name on your favorite search engine.

Listservs

I saved the best for last. Listservs are where committed professionals share information, typically via e-mail based subscription lists on very specific topics. Though it's usually free to register, the fact that people must take the step to subscribe already separates them from the pack. Some are run by associations and are meant to be networking tools for their members. All of them have a list owner or moderator who controls which messages are posted and who is subscribed.

If you violate their rules, you're out, so be careful. But if you use them properly, they become a key tool in your virtual networking effort. Upon joining, you get the e-mail address to which you can send messages. If accepted, the message is redistributed to every member's e-mail box. Likewise, you will receive every message sent by any other member. The idea is that you share information (give as well as get) and everyone benefits. The good news is, if the list doesn't prove useful, you can always unsubscribe.

The biggest searchable directory of lists is Catalist www.lsoft.com/catalist.html. They've cataloged about a quarter of the 200,000-plus public listservs in existence (many more private listservs exist). You can search by a generic keyword (e.g., finance), by member size, etc. All lists found here are free. Click the list you want for simple subscription instructions. Ditto for private companies that allow you to create listservs free or join existing ones. Two of the biggest in this arena are Topica www.topica.com/dir/ and Yahoo! Groups www.yahoogroups.com.

Larger lists tend to have more information sharing than smaller ones, but the latter can be just as good if they're well targeted and the participants are active. If a list is locally focused, it may hold in-person networking events as well (e.g., I joined a career networking list run by a Massachusetts synagogue found on Topica that is a great service on- and off-line).

On most listservs I subscribe to, I never post a message. However, I do note the contact information for posters who appear *in the know* or are connected in a way that may be useful. I send them a direct, personalized message (not via the listserv) and see what develops. The results are usually quite worthwhile.

How to Approach e-Contacts

Finally, a common question is how do you approach people you find through the above methods. I recommend a low-key, short message along the lines of "I found your [name of listserv] list posting about [whatever topic] interesting and it appears you're savvy about the [your target industry] field. I'm looking for a position in that arena and have good skills to offer. Could you recommend any resources, upcoming events or people in [your geographic area] that I should contact who might have useful information?"

This combines initial flattery with your attempt to build credibility and a low-key request for names of contacts, employers, events, etc., that should trigger many suggestions they can rattle off in a quick reply. What's important is you didn't ask that person directly for a job. That's a turnoff. Never ask anything that can result in a "no" answer; keep the questions open-ended to foster more dialogue. Ideally, you'll trade a few e-mails with lots of people and you'll end up with a bunch of mini-mentors who keep their eyeballs open on your behalf.

Also, never include your resumé in the initial e-communication: Many people are reluctant to open messages containing file attachments, especially from people they don't know, for fear of downloading a virus. Alternatively, a resumé pasted in the message body makes the e-mail too long a read, which is also a turnoff. However, simply including the Web address of your resumé online is fine. (Web space comes free with most every Internet access account—learn how to upload your resumé and take advantage of that.) If they're curious about you, you've provided an easy option to learn more.

Glenn Gutmacher has taught Internet sourcing techniques to small placement agencies up through Fortune 500 employers since 1997 as well as teaching online search methods to job seekers. He was named official Internet recruiting certification instructor for NEHRA members in 2000, for the Boston Herald's *Jobfind.com in 2001 and for the* Boston Globe's *BostonWorks.com in 2002.*

Flight Simulators in Business?

By R. Wendell Williams, Ph.D.

E-mail: rww@ScientificSelection.com

You know about them — airlines use simulators to hire and train pilots; NASA uses simulators to hire and train astronauts; motor vehicle departments use simulators to examine drivers; and, the military uses simulators to select and train equipment operators. In virtually every critical job, simulators provide real-time, real-life environments that allow organizations to make training and placement decisions. Why? Simulators expose every applicant to highly controlled conditions, evaluate skills objectively and provide detailed feedback about performance. Simulations reinforce what participants do well and help them improve areas where they do poorly.

Question: What do simulators have to do with business? Answer: they are a growing response to how to get the most out of employees, give them specific feedback about personal development needs and make fair and objective hiring and placement decisions.

Two Minute History

Simulations are not new. The earliest recorded application occurred about 4,000 years ago. In 2200 B. C., the Chinese began using simulations for selecting government workers. A few years later, in 1115 BC, potential government officials had to complete simulations in music, archery, horsemanship, writing, and arithmetic.

The earliest recorded application of simulations in the United States was in 1814, when the federal government began to systematically test surgeons and military academy cadets. Just before the civil war, the Treasury Department required applicants for some accounting positions to write a business letter, demonstrate ability with arithmetic and to show some knowledge of accounting principles. Around the turn of the century, simulations were used to hire and train motorcar operators, ship captains and salesmen.

During WWI, soldiers completed simulations that included mental alertness tests, motivation, morale, psychological problems and discipline. In WWII, simulations were used to measure such things as emotional and interpersonal reactions to stress, ability to solve problems, memory and physical ability. Business' latest interest in simulations has been spurred by an increase in job complexity, competitiveness and the risk of making a bad hiring or placement decision.

ATT was one of the first business organizations to adopt simulations in the 1950s. Aspiring jobholders were required to complete a series of exercises that resembled tasks required for successful job performance as a manager. These exercises included things like analyzing typical business situations and making recommendations, deciding how to process stacks of papers in a hypothetical in-basket and engaging in discussions with subordinates, peers and managers. The ATT simulations helped employees experience what the future job would be like and created a level playing field to place qualified candidates in jobs regardless of race, color or age.

False Beliefs Lead to False Expectations

Some people seem to think that anyone can become anything they choose. These same folks seldom realize that equal opportunity and equal skills are not the same thing. Everyone deserves a chance to try out for a job for which they are qualified, but not everyone has the right amount of analytical ability, planning skills, motivation or interpersonal skills to be a manager, salesperson or high involvement team member, for example. High performance only happens when job requirements and employee skills are matched.

Research shows that unequal job skills can have serious consequences for employers; i.e., the top 50 percent of workers are at least twice as productive as the bottom; about 20 percent of salespeople produce 80 percent of the sales; and, about 70 percent of managers don't have the skills to manage people. When organizations do not use simulations to hire or promote employees, productivity differences are the norm, not the exception. On the other hand, when job simulations are used, personal bias is significantly reduced and job skills are fairly evaluated. In fact, job-valid simulations are universally recommended (and sometimes required) by the EEOC for making hiring and placement decisions.

Simulation Types

There are about 15 different job families in most organizations, but to simplify things, we'll use three generic job families as examples:

- Executive Family – long range thinking, conceptualization, strategic planning, public presentation, etc.
- Mid-Manager Family – coordinating departments, acquiring resources, clearing obstacles, communicating vision and values, developing subordinates' career skills, etc.
- First-Line Manager Family – coaching, counseling, developing jobholder

skills, tactical problem solving skills, project planning, etc.

Job simulations for these families often use what psychologists call "multi-trait, multi-method" designs. That is, they measure a whole compliment of job skills and do it several times using different methods. These methods include exercises that resemble critical job activities faced by either Executive, Mid or First-Line Managers. They may require analyzing numbers and developing recommendations; working with subordinates, managers, public officials; or developing short or long-range plans. Executive simulations, for example, require a considerable amount of abstract thinking and analysis while First-Line Manager simulations would be more related to getting certain tasks accomplished. The actual level of difficulty and complexity of each simulation always depends on skills the job requires for success.

External Applications

Organizations that use simulations to hire external job applicants significantly reduce their hiring and legal risk. Only about one in six applicants are able to pass job simulations; but the ones who do become natural high performers who require minimum training and coaching. Organizations using simulations enjoy unusually high employee performance, less turnover and significantly less training expense. These benefits occur because the simulations help ensure that only fully qualified external applicants receive job offers.

Internal Applications

There is nothing quite as frustrating as promoting a successful jobholder into a position for which he or she is unqualified. Usually, the employee becomes discouraged while the organization risks losing a valuable asset. Internal simulations are often used to either identify employees for promotion or provide feedback about skills and development opportunities.

In a promotion or reorganization application, the exercises are usually generic and designed to measure broad job-skill areas. Simulations used for diagnosing skill deficiencies are usually more job specific. A 727 pilot candidate, for example, would be asked to fly a 727 simulator, not a 707 simulator. A business professional would be asked to complete a series of detailed simulations that measured specific job knowledge or career experience. Simulations designed to diagnose skills are always highly detailed and job specific while simulations designed to assess promotion potential are less specific and measure core skills.

Preparing for a Simulation

Simulations normally measure four job-related areas:

1. Cognitive ability (learning, technical knowledge, problem solving)
2. Planning ability (organizing, project planning, time management, prioritiz-

ing)
3. Interpersonal ability (coaching, teamwork, presentations, persuasion, customer service, fact finding, negotiation)
4. Attitudes, Interests and Motivations (likes, dislikes, preferences, attitudes)

Exercises can be presented in any order and format. They may include pencil and paper tests, resolving problems in role-plays with trained assessors, processing in-basket paperwork, taking phone calls, making presentations, gathering information, analyzing business problems, and making recommendations. All the while, the candidate will be observed and performance evaluated by trained observers. Sometimes, performance will be given at the end of each section, but usually, it takes time to gather the data, look for trends and prepare feedback. Simulations are not always enjoyable, but they are among the most valuable and accurate methods for delivering honest, no-nonsense feedback about job skills.

Dr. Wendell Williams is managing director of ScientificSelection.com. Dr. Williams is a widely recognized consultant in personality, performance management, performance appraisal, job competencies, selection testing, and web-enabled recruiting tools. Wendell can be reached at 770-792-6857, his web site is www.ScientificSelection.com.

RECRUITERS

Workforce Planning: The Key To True Strategic Staffing And Recruiting

By Jeremy Eskenazi

E-mail: Jeskenazi@RivieraAdvisors.com

If professionals in the recruiting and staffing profession could predict what positions, roles, functions and skills would be needed by organizations in the future, could they be more successful? The answer is absolutely. Why then do many recruiting and staffing professionals feel as if they are always operating in a reactive mode? The reason is often that true *workforce planning* is not being accomplished inside the organization. What is workforce planning? Workforce planning is a process to assess workforce content and composition to respond to future business needs. Simplified, workforce planning is a systematic process to analyze the gap between what a business has in the way of organizational talent and what it needs in the future. Often workforce planning adds an additional important component, an assessment and plan for addressing the gaps that were identified.

Instead of starting over each time we get a requisition or a request to fill a job, a recruiting and staffing professional who uses workforce planning will have already developed plans and sourcing for the needs previously identified. To most recruiting and staffing professionals, this whole idea sounds great, but the reality is that many will question why spend time and energy on developing plans when the view of recruiting itself is reactive – change is constant in our world. So why bother?

Benefits of Workforce Planning

The *why* of workforce planning is grounded in the benefits to managers. Workforce planning provides managers with a strategic basis for making human resource decisions. It allows managers to anticipate change rather than being surprised by events, as well as providing strategic methods for addressing present and anticipated workforce issues.

Some components of workforce planning, such as workforce demographics, retirement projections and succession planning, are familiar to managers. Workforce planning provides focus to these components, providing more refined information on changes to be anticipated, the competencies that retirements and other uncontrollable actions will take from the workforce, and key positions that may need to be filled. This in turn allows managers to plan replacements and changes in workforce competencies.

Organizational success depends on having the right employees with the right competencies at the right time. Workforce planning provides managers the means of identifying the competencies needed in the workforce not only in the present but also in the future and then selecting and developing that workforce.

Here are a few other real reasons to do workforce planning:

- Due to shifts in the labor market, planning for workforce needs is a critical concern for businesses across all industries.
- The labor pool does not dynamically expand in direct correlation to most company's talent needs (for example: yes, there may be a large number of workers that have been affected by layoffs but organizations may be seeking workers with specific skills that are not readily available).
- Companies in a growth mode are increasingly challenged to acquire critical talent required to achieve business objectives over the long term, but with specific milestones in the short term.
- Workforce planning enables *relationship* rather than *incident* recruitment. That is—you can understand what specific types of people, competencies, and skills you will need in the future and develop relationships with sources of that talent well before you have a need to fill a role.

As a recruiting and staffing professional, if you lead or participate in a workforce planning initiative, you will be placed squarely into the strategic business planning process for your organization. You can align your daily recruiting tasks to the outcomes you learned by doing workforce planning. For recruiting and staffing professionals, as well as generalist Human Resource professionals who have responsibilities for recruiting, here are a few other great reasons to do workforce planning:

- HR and Recruiting professionals are viewed more as strategic business partners by the businesses they support.
- Provides HR and Recruiting professionals a blueprint to "stay the course."
- Shifts from a transactional mode.
- New business developments and changes are easily incorporated, priorities shift on the basis of collaboration with the business.

How to *Do* Workforce Planning
Many recruiting and staffing professionals like the idea of workforce planning,

but often it gets pushed aside in favor of more reactive work (like filling requisitions). But few really understand how to get a grasp on how to do workforce planning. In reality, the workforce planning process is really a *coordination* process. Getting the data necessary to analyze the workforce is often the most daunting task. To gather the data, you simply need to interview managers of individual workgroups inside your organization and then you will consolidate and analyze that data. You'll create a set of standard questions to ask each manager Overall, here are a few steps in how to *do* workforce planning:

- Review the current workforce supply. Take a look at the competencies or the employees presently available inside the organization to achieve business objectives.
- Review the future workforce supply. Review your current supply and add in any known variables (prior demand, known openings, attrition, perform- ance review data), add in unknown variables (transfers, terminations, com- petitive factors).
- Develop a demand forecast. Assess what competencies or employees will be required to achieve business objectives for a specified time in the future.
- Review the gaps. The gap is the sum of comparing current and future sup- ply to demand forecasts. Gaps can be filled by transfers, acquiring talent externally, outsourcing, contracting, etc.

If you are going to lead a workforce planning effort, here are some specific actions you can take:

1. **Planning.** Take a look at your organization, and break it into chunks. Take a look at your organizational structure and go down to the most basic work- group level (such as Division, Department, Team, etc.), and determine who are the workgroup leaders. You'll then need to create a list of standard ques- tions you'll want to ask them about their business and their workgroup. Here are some examples of questions to ask:

   - What are the key business goals and objectives for the next year? Two years?
   - What is our competitive environment like, how will it impact your abil- ity to meet these goals and objectives?
   - What are the critical processes that are needed to meet those goals? What are the key success factors for achieving future outcomes?
   - What are the key work activities associated with these success factors?
   - What are the barriers to optimally performing the work activities?
   - What talent pools can affect those barriers?
   - What does your current talent pool look like today that may impact

your ability to achieve success in the future?
- What people capabilities are needed to deliver on those critical processes?
- What are the most critical people issues you currently face?
- What do you think the most critical people issues will be in one to two years?
- Which positions, capabilities are most critical to your business?

2. **Prepare Workgroup Leaders.** Make sure you prepare the managers you'll be interviewing. You may want to call, visit or send an e-mail and let them know the purpose of the interview you'll be having with them. Perhaps you can even send them some of the sample questions you'll be asking them about in your interview. You will also want to gather a list of all the employees in each workgroup and bring that with you to your interview with each workgroup manager.

3. **Conduct Workgroup Leader Interviews.** During your interview, you'll want to clearly identify the future business state for the workgroup...what will need to be done in the workgroup in the next 1-2 years (or longer)? What are the goals and objectives of the workgroup, and more importantly, what skills and competencies will be required of the team? You will then review each of the current employees and assess them based on the skills and competencies needed in the future. This should be a quick and fast assessment, not a lengthy review of each employee. You should then discuss the perceived gaps in the business needs and the competencies of the current workgroup.

4. **Analyze Outcomes and Develop the Demand Analysis.** After you gather all of the information from the interviews you'll want to track what you learned on a simple spreadsheet that will identify what your workgroups told you about what they have, what they will need in the future, and what their future demand requirements will be for talent.

5. **Gap Analysis.** You can then review the information you have learned from the exercise and create your assumptions. You can make a good guesstimate of what types of positions, people and competencies will be needed in the future.

6. **Building Plans.** Now you will be able to plan on how gaps will be addressed (Will you "build or buy": will your develop talent internally or go out and attract new talent with the right skills and competencies you need?) You'll want to now plan your execution of the staffing plans and align the resources you will need.

Conclusion

47

With the information that you have gathered, not only will you have developed a sense of the people needs of the organization today and in the future, you have now built a relationship with the business that makes you much more of a strategic business partner rather than a recruiting and staffing executor. The information in a workforce plan can then lead you to build broad sourcing programs that focus on the future needs of the organization while at the same time you can focus on the execution of individual searches. Overall, you cannot build a building without a blueprint—so why build a company without one as well?

Jeremy M. Eskenazi, SPHR is managing principal of Riviera Advisors, Inc. (www.RivieraAdvisors.com), a leading human resources consulting firm. Jeremy has more than 17 years of experience running global staffing functions for companies like Universal Studios, idealab!, and Amazon.com and regularly speaks and writes about recruiting and staffing issues.

Candidate's Bill of Rights: The Ten Pet Peeves
(Based on real questions from real job candidates)

By Tony Lee

E-mail: Tony.Lee@wsj.com

#1: Is there anybody out there?

"How do I know you got my application? Are you interested in me?"

#2: I can't find you.

"I've searched your site, but your jobs aren't anywhere," or "I can't find your URL."

#3: Are your positions dated?

"Are these jobs fresh? How can I tell?"

#4: Do you really want me?

"I see lots of young, smiling faces on the company's site, but I'm 56 will you even consider hiring me?"

#5: Are you misleading me?

"The description you wrote makes the job sound a lot better than it really is."

#6: You're not thorough.

"I can't make an informed decision about applying based on the little bit of information you've given."

#7: No hassles please.

"Please weigh your needs against my level of inconvenience."

#8: What's your level of confidentiality?

"How do I know you won't call my boss and colleagues and start checking up on me?"

#9: How much information do you really need?

"Some companies say be creative without any direction and others act like they'll penalize me for not drawing within the lines."

#10: Allow for feedback.

"I need to ask a question before I'm willing to apply, but I don't know how."

Bottom Line

Treat all candidates like customers.

Make the job-search process as easy as possible.

Keep graphics simple.

Test-drive your site every few weeks.

Remember the Golden Rule.

Tony Lee *is editor in chief/general manager of CareerJournal.com, CollegeJournal.com CareerJournalEurope.com, and CareerJournalAsia.com.*

Insights on Jobseeker Behavior Online

By Yves Lermusiaux

E-mail: yves@ilogos.com

The activities of corporate staffing departments are, at the core, comparable to those of e-commerce in that the staffing department is in the business of *selling* jobs. Just like good sales people, staffing professionals need to know and understand their customers. This article will help you to understand more about your primary external customers—the jobseekers—their behavior online and how you can leverage that knowledge to your advantage.

The corporate website is a vital projection of the corporate image and a key communication and transaction platform for customers, investors, suppliers and business partners, and the general public. The corporate website is also a valuable point of contact with jobseekers, through the use of a dedicated careers subsection of the site

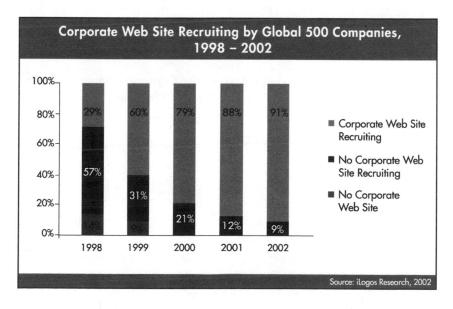

Corporate Web Site Recruiting by Global 500 Companies, 1998 – 2002

Source: iLogos Research, 2002

devoted to attracting and acquiring talent.

Large corporations have increasingly recognized and responded to the power and potential of using the corporate website in the recruiting strategy. Corporate website recruiting has steadily increased in the Global 500, from 29 percent having a careers section in 1998, to 91 percent in 2002.[1]

Visitors to the corporate website represent a ripe pool from which to recruit. The traffic—customers, shareholders, competitors, and jobseekers—represents a large, desirable group of potential candidates. To gain the most benefit from these potential candidates, it is imperative to understand the behavior and attitudes of the total stream of corporate career website visitors.

There are three aspects to successful recruiting on the corporate career website:

- How to attract jobseekers to the corporate career website?
- What expectations do jobseekers have of the corporate career website?
- How can recruiters best capture information from jobseekers?

How to Attract Jobseekers to the Corporate Career Website?

Website traffic is the most critical resource to a corporation's careers section. Without it, job positions do not get the necessary exposure to candidates. Corporations, encouraged by the consumer branding campaigns from the major job boards, have been lead to believe that they need the job boards' help in driving traffic to their careers sections. Quite to the contrary, survey results show that the corporate website is the best source of candidate traffic. Three times as many candidates come to the corporate website careers section from word of mouth (34 percent), and from a homepage/within-the-site link (38 percent), than from job boards (12 percent). In light of this, corporate resource allotment and spending should be directed accordingly.

What Expectations Do Jobseekers Have of the Corporate Career Website?

Keyword search has been considered to be a user-friendly way to pinpoint specific information with few clicks. However, career website visitors much prefer searching job listings by job category and/or by location. Almost three times as many career website visitors would choose to search job listings by job category and/or location over searching by keyword.

Although this would seem to be a relatively easy practice to implement, more than half of Fortune 500 companies have no searchable jobs database options by any criteria available to jobseekers on the corporate career site[2]. Once visitors are attracted to the career section of the corporate website, the right tools and functionality need to be offered to encourage the next step towards applying to open job positions. Providing search tools for visitors to filter listings reduces the scope of a job search to just those positions that fit the candidate's interests. That smoother process for the

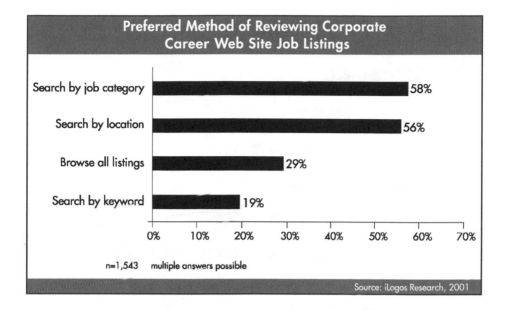

Preferred Method of Reviewing Corporate Career Web Site Job Listings

Method	Percentage
Search by job category	58%
Search by location	56%
Browse all listings	29%
Search by keyword	19%

n=1,543   multiple answers possible

Source: iLogos Research, 2001

jobseeker translates into a higher candidate capture rate.

How Can Recruiters Best Capture Information from Jobseekers?

There is a growing realization among corporate recruiters that the resumé needs better formatting in order to align supply and demand, and develop a more automated process. The content of the resumé is wholly determined by the candidate (candidate-driven), and often lacks the key pieces of information that the recruiter needs for efficient and automated screening. What is required is a transformation in the way information flows from candidates to recruiters, such that information is pulled by the recruiter's needs (recruiter-driven), rather than pushed by the candidate's perception of relevancy.

Today, online candidates welcome the opportunity to divulge much more specific information to speed up the process and facilitate a better fit. A significant majority of survey respondents indicate a willingness to provide details on their personality, work-style preferences and references. Candidates are willing to provide information they deem relevant or material to their matching to the requirements of a job position.

A high percentage (95 percent) of online candidates are willing to communicate details of their past work experience. In addition, jobseekers are willing to provide information if it improves the match to a job position. For example, 77 percent of online jobseekers are prepared to indicate their preference for business travel—information not easily nor often found on resumés.

Recruiters can use the interactivity of the Web to pull the information that they need from candidates in order to make a proper and faster hiring decision. This

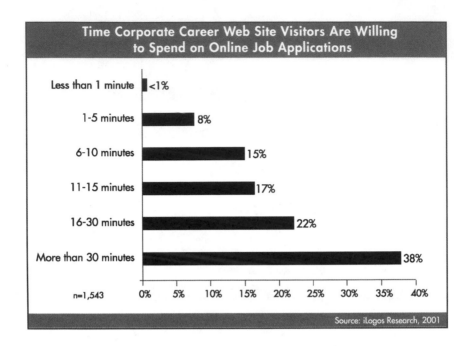

Time Corporate Career Web Site Visitors Are Willing to Spend on Online Job Applications

Less than 1 minute	<1%
1-5 minutes	8%
6-10 minutes	15%
11-15 minutes	17%
16-30 minutes	22%
More than 30 minutes	38%

n=1,543   0% 5% 10% 15% 20% 25% 30% 35% 40%

Source: iLogos Research, 2001

includes asking direct questions about the match between candidates' skills and the requirements of the position. Skills-based questions can be asked of career website visitors 24/7 and, with the right back-end processing, can effectively be used to pre-screen candidates and automatically generate a short list. There has been concern however, over whether the candidate is willing to take the time and trouble to provide the answers the recruiter is looking for. Survey data and experience are clear; candidates do respond to skills-based questions.

A large majority of candidates, 88 percent, are willing to answer questions about their skills. The survey respondents indicate that career website visitors are nearly as willing to provide answers to skills-based questions as they are willing to provide more conventional resumé information such as their phone number, and work experience. The percentage even exceeds the percentage of those willing to provide other types of information (including personal references, and salary range).

How Much Time Will Jobseekers Spend?

Web users are often characterized as impatient, liable to abandon a website if it takes too long to fulfill the purpose of the site visit. Those characteristics have resulted in corporations limiting their expectations of what they can request from an online jobseeker's brief visit. In direct contradiction, corporate career website visitors indicate a very high tolerance for longer online application methods. 92 percent of candidates are willing to spend more than six minutes applying online to a job of high interest. 60 percent of candidates are willing to spend more than 15 minutes applying online to a job of high interest.

More significantly, those who are willing to take more time applying online are also more disposed to use that time to communicate in-depth information about their skills and competencies. Willingness to spend considerable time applying is not limited to those who are actively looking for jobs.

Optimize Your Process

Corporate recruiters can leverage candidates' time to the fullest by using automated skills-based questionnaires and self-service candidate profiles to gather the information on skills and competencies that recruiters need to make a well-informed decision.

- Incorporate skills-based questions individualized to the particular requirements of each job position into the online job application process.
- Don't make the resumé the only way to apply.
- Have automated processing systems in place to take advantage of skills-based questions for prescreening, and short-listing qualified candidates.
- Create company-specific templates of skills to help corporate recruiters best query online jobseekers.
- Make best use of information gathered online by placing it in a centralized skills database available to recruiters and hiring managers.

The corporate career website is both a leading corporate ambassador, and a significant candidate sourcing and prescreening tool. Survey data makes clear the need to accommodate a visitor stream rich in its diversity, comfortable with web-based information exchanges, and demanding in its expectations. These online jobseekers want to utilize self-service Internet information resources to educate and prescreen themselves for corporate career choices. In response, they will commit their time; share information on their skills, experience and credentials; and communicate their goals and preferences.

Yves Lermusiaux is president and founder of iLogos Research (www.ilogos.com). iLogos Research is the independent research and consulting division of Recruitsoft. Recruitsoft (www.recruitsoft.com) powers enterprise-wide staffing management for Global 1000 companies.

References
1. Global 500 Web Site Recruiting, 2002 Survey available at www.ilogos.com
2. Trends in Fortune 500 Careers Web Site Recruiting available at www.ilogos.com

Outsourcing the Recruiting Function: Is it Right For You?

By Karen Osofsky

E-mail: kareno@tiburongroup.com

Over the last ten years there has been a growing emphasis on outsourcing non-core functions of business operations. Companies are outsourcing such operations as the computer help desk, mail room/reproduction services, call centers, benefits administration, payroll and other operations that generate high overhead and low contribution to the bottom line.

Recently there has been an increased focus on the opportunity to outsource the recruiting function. You may be asking: "Why would a company even consider outsourcing recruiting? Recruiting is the role that helps attract the future leaders of the company, the first step towards building a company's most important asset — its people. Who could possibly do this better than an insider? Is recruiting really a viable candidate for outsourcing?"

Absolutely! While we don't advocate outsourcing the entire function, there are aspects of the process that are ideal for outsourcing. If approached strategically and methodically, this can be a tremendous asset to an organization. The direct results will be improved cycle time, decreased cost, and stronger relationship management between the internal recruiters and both their internal clients and active candidates. When the process is not well defined, the results can lead to miscommunication, a backlog of qualified candidates, and lots of finger pointing.

The purpose of this article is to provide a framework by which companies can determine if outsourcing is right for their needs and how to maximize the benefit. It will review the following:

- What to Outsource
- Determining When Outsourcing Is Right For You
- Tips on Selecting a Vendor
- Keys to a Successful Outsourced Relationship
- Measuring results

While some companies do outsource the entire recruiting function, from the point where the requisition is approved to offer acceptance, the most typical outsource relationships center around the front-end of the recruiting process. We define the front-end as all the steps in the process that take place prior to an onsite interview. They include:

- Determination of sourcing strategy
- Ad development
- Job posting management
- Ad response management
- Database mining
- Advanced Internet research
- Direct research
- Direct sourcing
- Initial candidate telephone screen

Depending on an organization's structure and resource availability any or all of the above process steps are great candidates for outsourcing.

Why the front-end? The front-end process steps tend to be those that are time consuming, require significant attention to detail and are somewhat repetitive. These are the steps that are critical to managing effective candidate flow and significantly impact cycle time and cost per hire. Because of the nature of this type of work, internal recruiters either spend too much time on this detail and not enough time in building relationships with the hot candidates or with the hiring managers. Or, recruiters do not spend enough time on these tasks and end up relying too heavily on using search firms as their primary candidate source, dramatically (and unnecessarily) driving up costs.

With the exception of the initial telephone screen and some direct sourcing, the front-end of the process includes those steps that require the least amount of direct candidate contact, leaving the majority of the relationship building to the internal recruiters. Outsourcing this time consuming, yet very necessary, detail work allows the recruiters to use their time most effectively by freeing them up to focus on maintaining contact with the most qualified and interested candidates.

Determining when Outsourcing is Right for You

How do you determine whether your company can gain efficiencies by outsourcing? How do you decide what to outsource and what to keep inside?

In order to determine if outsourcing is right for you, you first need to have a very thorough understanding of your current workflow. It's time to dig into the detail. Do you know the amount of time your recruiters are spending on each task? Are they efficient? Do you have a strong understanding of where there are bottlenecks? Do you have a breakdown of your highest cost activities? Specifically:

- Are your recruiters full life cycle recruiters or do you have a sourcing team in place?
- Who is responsible for determining your sourcing strategy? Do you feel that you are posting your jobs to the most effective complement of sites? Are your postings updated regularly?
- Who is responsible for writing the postings? Are your ads compelling? Are they motivating? How do they compare with the competition?
- What percent of your current hires do you make through search firms? Are your recruiters reliant on them to fill many positions below the executive level?
- When candidates respond to job ads how long does it take to review the responses? Longer than 48 hours from time of receipt? How long does it take for the recruiter to make initial contact with the high potential candidates? Longer than 48 hours from the time the résumé was reviewed?
- Is there ever a time when the recruiters are too busy to review all of the responses and only focus on the first few qualified candidates?
- Are you maximizing the benefit of the candidate databases to which your recruiters have access, both internal and external? Do your recruiters have enough time to search them effectively? Do they know how to use them most efficiently?
- Is candidate flow sufficient with the tools you currently have in place? Are you taking advantage of advanced Internet mining techniques to uncover résumés that are not in databases or names of potential candidates to contact?
- Do your hiring managers feel as though they are getting the appropriate amount of attention from the recruiting department?
- Do candidates feel that their recruiting experience has been positive, even if they did not receive an offer? Do you ever get feedback that the recruiter was not available to them to assist them through the process?

If the answers to any of the above questions were less than optimal, then your company can probably benefit from outsourcing some or all of the front-end process steps.

Tips on Selecting a Vendor

Vendor selection is always challenging and often it is difficult to make a clear apples-to-apples comparison between vendors. While cost is always an important consideration, the lowest cost alternative may not always provide the most optimal results. Before embarking on any vendor selection be sure that your goals are clearly outlined. If you cover the topics outlined below, you should be able to develop a detailed review of how each vendor may be able to support your needs.

- **Methodology:** Does the vendor have a structured methodology that they follow to insure timeliness, follow-up, clear communication and accuracy?
- **Project Management Skills:** What is the vendor's track record with project management? What is their structure for managing large outsourced projects?
- **Sourcing Experience:** What is the skill level of the individuals doing the Internet and direct sourcing? What kind of training have they had?
- **Resource Dedication:** What resources will they dedicate to your specific needs? How are the resources allocated?
- **Scalability of Resources:** Do they have the ability to quickly ramp up or ramp down resources as your hiring needs fluctuate?
- **Creative Resources:** Review samples of job ads that they have written for other clients. Are they creative, compelling and well written?
- **Technology Experience:** What is their experience using candidate databases and applicant tracking systems? If you do not have a database for them to access, do they have access to a system that they can use for your project?
- **Screening Skills:** What is the skill level of the recruiters that will be conducting the telephone screens? Are they seasoned at screening candidates over the phone? Do they have the skills to probe for additional information or are they call center individuals that will need to follow a very specific interview script with little variation?
- **Flexibility:** As the relationship grows are they flexible enough to adapt to new needs and process improvements?
- **Reporting Mechanisms:** What types of status meetings/reporting do they provide?
- **Success Measurements:** How do they typically measure success? Is that reasonable?
- **Openness to Learn your Business:** Does their model include spending time learning more about your business and how to best market the company to candidates?
- **Cost containment:** Does their fee structure allow for capping of costs?
- **References:** Always get a minimum of three references

Keys to a Successful Outsourced Relationship

Outsourcing part of the recruiting function is very significant and much is at stake. The biggest factor influencing success is the relationship between the vendor and the client company at all levels. There needs to be an upfront commitment from senior management and the front-line teams to work together as a single unit. From the start of the relationship all references to "vendor/client" should be dropped and everyone involved needs to be referred to as the recruiting team regardless of whose payroll they are on.

Once there is a commitment to the relationship, the following will help result in a productive, successful, ongoing outsourcing arrangement:

- **Unified Strategic Vision:** Principals at the top of both organizations need to share the same vision for the goals of the relationships. These should be outlined in writing in the contract and statement of work. The principals need to ensure that the vision is passed down to all the members of the team so there is complete agreement on the direction of the project.

- **Measurable Results:** Clearly define the deliverables and the measurements for success. Make sure that they are realistic and attainable and do not pin a vendor into a corner that will either make it difficult for them to achieve success or that will create a situation where meeting the success criteria results in a less than break-even situation.

- **Regular Status Meetings:** Timing is essential in recruiting so weekly status meetings with the various individuals involved in the day to day process is a critical success factor. The meetings should have a structured agenda focused on reviewing key deliverables. They should offer the opportunity for an open forum for problem resolution.

- **Access to Hiring Managers:** The individuals responsible for sourcing need to have access to the hiring managers to be able to listen to the way they define their needs and how they describe the attributes of the types of individuals that will be most successful in their organization. Too often the vendor is shielded from the hiring manager and only receives information second or third hand. This is very unproductive and leads to increased lead times and costs.

Often the client fears the vendor will bother the busy hiring manager too much or will undermine the role as the internal recruiter. In a good outsourced relationship these fears cannot be farther from the truth. Allowing the vendor to participate in a meeting with hiring manager to better understand their needs leads to more accurate candidate development and quicker turn around. It only serves to allow everyone to succeed faster. Most often the hiring manager appreciates that the vendor wants to understand the detail and idiosyncrasies of their positions and helps strengthen the partnership between the vendor and the client.

- Shared Accountability: Now that the vendor and company are the recruiting team there needs to be shared accountability for deliverables. The responsibilities of each party need to be clearly defined and adhered to. The vendor cannot be successful if the client does not deliver on their end and vice versa.

- Regular Reporting: Monthly metrics reports should be produced to evaluate where the project is to plan and to identify opportunities for improvement.
- Senior level involvement: Principal level meetings should take place on a monthly or quarterly basis to renew the shared vision and confirm that both parties have a consistent viewpoint on the status of the relationship.
- Willingness to make changes: Any long-term relationship is evolutionary and both parties need to be flexible enough to make changes in process, resources, and personnel to ensure project success and fluid day-to-day operations.

Measuring Success

Vendors should be measured on deliverables that they can control. If their role is complete once the candidates are screened and deemed qualified for the position then their deliverables should not be tied to hires.

Measure deliverables against an improvement over the metrics that were in place prior to the outsourced relationship and not against an arbitrary number that sounds good. Success should be defined as the ability to answer affirmatively to these questions: By outsourcing are processes improved? Have you resolved some of the issues that led you to outsourcing? Consider the following success measurements:

- Decrease in cycle time to generate a qualified candidate
- Decrease in cost per hire
- Improved candidate experience
- Improved hiring manager experience
- Increased number of qualified candidates being forwarded to hiring managers
- Improved candidate communication and hiring process experience

Summary

Outsourcing is a great way to streamline processes, improve relationships, reduce costs, and improve cycle times. It isn't right for every organization and requires a willingness to change thinking and significant dedication to be successful.

Before jumping on the outsource bandwagon do the appropriate due diligence to determine if outsourcing will address internal challenges and specifically how they will be addressed. Also determine if your organization is ready for the dramatic change in division of responsibility.

When selecting a vendor dig into specifics about their processes, skills, tools, and flexibility. Can they deliver specifically to your needs? Always speak to references.

Successful outsourced relationships are those where there is consistent and open communication, shared accountability, regular metrics and status reporting, and enough breathing room to make changes as needed.

Measure success on deliverables that the vendor can control. Don't choose arbitrary measures. Set specific standards based on improving what was broken in the first place.

Karen Osofsky is a principal and co-founder of Tiburon Group Inc, a recruitment optimization consulting firm that helps companies leverage technology, the Internet and process to improve recruiting effectiveness and reduce costs. www.tiburongroup.com phone: 773-907-8330 ext. 502

Recruiter Competencies: Back to the Future

By David Sears

E-mail: dlsears@iteamtalent.com

The Internet has become the most visible and most trafficked venue of today's employment marketplace. And e-recruiting has transformed the recruitment industry, moving towards eventual dominance as the primary channel for talent sourcing. But e-recruiting is also proving to be a little bit like the sorcerer's apprentice: Once conjured and set in motion, e-recruitment intake is proving hard to stop. Ease of delivery (34 percent of Fortune 500 companies now require that job seekers respond online, up from 27 percent in 2000) enables the volume of inbound resumés to continue regardless of demand. In fact, e-recruiting at times seems best at overproducing resumes in proportion to the actual number of opportunities.

The ease and anonymity of e-recruiting activities also make it a deceptive process for both job seeker and job buyer. It lulls participants into thinking that talent sourcing, screening and placement are passive activities—that it's about *minding* a stream of information instead of *finding* key players or engaging work opportunities.

In the midst of a dizzying array of technology-based recruiting options, we often lose track of the reality that recruiting continues to be, above all, a social phenomenon. All hiring, much like all politics is local: hiring ultimately results from social connection among new employee, hiring manager, recruiter and others involved in attracting, recruiting and selecting. In a business world where recruiting technology alone no longer provides strategic advantage, it's time to rethink the matter recruiting competencies.

Pipelines and Networks

The operative image for the recruitment *minding* model is the pipeline—with e-recruitment and related employment technologies being the valves, conduits, pumps and joints. Recruiters, by extension, are responsible for balancing flow against demand. That's by no means a negative image, especially when looked at from the perspective of talent strategy in a dynamic, market-driven talent economy.

But when you look at it from the vantage of the recruiting professional, the image for the talent *finding* model—and the recruiter competencies that go with it—is more appropriately the network. And three *back to the future* core recruiter competencies are network related:

- People connectedness
- Information connectedness
- The ability to close

A recent book—one that is about neither recruiting nor technology—revives and highlights some crucial and timeless points about how people actually find and connect with people whether it's to find a job, get the best price on a new gadget, or even transmit a deadly disease. *The Tipping Point* considers how phenomena as varied as clothing fads, crime trends, disease epidemics, urban legends and runaway bestsellers actually happen. What turns a non-starter idea, process or product into a sensation? According to *Tipping Point* author Malcolm Gladwell, it's often because of small things that happen at the margin: the impact of a few people; mundane but persistent messages; seemingly minor changes in context and environment. And so it is with successful recruiting.

Competency #1: People Connectedness

Know the game "Six Degrees of Kevin Bacon"? Its premise is that if you name any movie personality (of any era) and identify the other movie personalities they've worked with, you'll soon enough find a film in which one of these other movie personalities has shared the screen with actor Kevin Bacon. There are usually about five connections in between.

The more generic six degrees of separation notion isn't just for film stars. It originated in a 1950s psychological experiment where a random sample of 160 residents in Omaha, Nebraska was asked to send a package addressed to a Massachusetts-based stockbroker. The idea was to forward the package to a friend, relative or acquaintance—a connection—that would get it closer to its ultimate destination. When the packages ultimately arrived, a tally was made of the number of stops along the way—most reached in five or six steps. Six degrees of separation is one measure of our human connectedness, that is, the proximity and reach of our people networks. It turns out that Connectors, those with extensive, varied and constantly evolving networks of acquaintances, are disproportionately crucial to the spread of social phenomena—in fashion, travel, political beliefs and music, as just a few examples. In my experience as practitioner and consultant, this connectedness also has huge payoffs for recruiting.

Do you hate headhunters? Do you wonder where the value is in those substantial fees, especially with all those resumés free for the taking on the Internet? The value, at least for the good search professionals, is their connectedness—not just that they *know of* people (the Internet is the perfect medium for finding names, roles and locations), but that they *know* people and know both talent seller and talent buyer deeply enough to complete the employment exchange. The competency is connectedness.

Connectedness is about human networks. In the deep dark pre-Internet job board days of 1974, a classic sociology study, *Getting a Job,* reported results that most of us know intuitively and routinely pass on as advice to job seekers all the time. Researcher Mark Ganovetter studied the activities of several hundred suburban Boston job seekers His findings. the majority, 56 percent, found jobs through personal connections. That proportion probably stands up pretty well even today.

Just as interesting as the job-finding power of these connections is their weakness: Job making connections didn't typically follow from close friends or relatives. Rather, they came through casual acquaintances—people who spend most of their time in different worlds, where they hear of opportunities that the job seeker—occupying his or her own world –otherwise might not hear about.

And just as interesting for our purposes is our failure to understand that this networking impact for job finding is not a one-way street. It works for talent finding as well. The math is simple· If 50 percent or more jobs are found through networking then 50 percent or more jobs must be filled through networking as well. Truly valuable recruiting connectors play an essential part in the job networking process. They have connections in a wide range of settings—their connectedness is eclectic and inclusive. This doesn't mean that they have to be linked to all the talent networks upon which their organizations depend. It does mean, however, that their connectedness should extend to connectors in other essential networks. Some of these connectors will inevitably be professional, search firms for example. But successful recruiting connectors will seek out and cultivate the networks that will produce key talent.

One other point about connectors: they may well be, but don't have to be technologically savvy. If you're a staffing leader do you lose patience with recruiters who just don't seem to get—and never will—the time, reach and effort-saving benefits of recruiting technologies? Who carry their searches around on little scraps of paper? Who are always on the phone or always seem to be buttonholing someone in the hallway instead of getting power sourcing? Next time your frustration wells up, consider this about people connectedness: Human society with its six billion network nodes (a.k.a. people) has been shown to have a separation of six. Research shows that the best the Internet can so far do—with hundreds of thousands of servers and routers—is a separation of 10. Like John Henry, human connectors are still a recruiting phenomenon to be reckoned with.

Competency # 2: Information Connectedness

One thing that technology-based recruiting solutions excel at is storage and rec-ollection: Given adequate human-supplied cues (key words for example, or coded attributes), applicant tracking systems (ATS) can store, retrieve, sort and filter vast amounts of prospect data into meaningful bites. Of course talent sellers and their agents can and do anticipate this. Résumés often involve considerable reverse engi-neering—i.e. plugging in the words that will pull them into the net of keyword search. The end result: the search for talent nuggets can still be a dig through a mas-sive mountain of ore. It happens, though, that there are some people who are stars at information mining.

Just as there are people specialists—connectors who can be relied upon to net-work us to other people, there are also connectors who can be relied upon to link us to essential information. Whether you term them subject matter experts, authorities or mavens (derived from Yiddish, meaning accumulator of knowledge), Information Connectors play an especially important role in a society and business culture awash in information.

Consider the information abundance that both makes and breaks e-recruiting. Even with industry and vendor consolidation, job posting and career sites number in the tens of thousands. And even these formal, commercial channels represent only the surface of the recruiting information/misinformation universe. Ironically, it's more important than ever to have human guides to this vast marketplace. But the role of these mavens—though it begins with the accumulation of knowledge—is really more about filtering, reducing and synthesizing recruiting information.

Mavens for the career- and job-finding side of the equation have been around for some time. For example, Richard Bolles' *What Color Is Your Parachute?* was first pub-lished nearly 36 years ago. Yet, despite an army of mavens and would-be mavens for employment selection, there are remarkably few for talent sourcing. *CareerXroads,* of course, is just such a maven. Gerry's and Mark's collaborative researching and filter-ing are good means for both job- and talent-seekers to evaluate, select and create exchanges through the best e-recruiting resources.

At the same time, *CareerXroads* can't be all things to all job seekers, recruiters or employers. There is just too much geography and too many emerging professional and industrial niches for that. This means that recruiters must, at some point, be their own mavens: seeking out and mastering the (increasingly electronic) resources they need to unearth talent. Of course, there's a left-brain and right-brain aspect to this. Some recruiters are and will be better as connectors of people, while some are and will be better as information builders, filterers and synthesizers. The very best recruiters will cultivate and appropriately mobilize both competencies.

Competency # 3: Closing

The last mile phenomenon has always bedeviled technology. For example, the Internet potential of e-commerce and media content delivery has often been plagued and sometimes undone by bandwidth problems—the reality that information transmission highways at some point have to connect with millions of homes and businesses served by the electronic equivalent of back roads and cow paths.

And so it is with e-recruitment. For example, as much time and efficiency as employers may gain through electronic job posting and online resumé intake, they quickly lose through the slowness and inefficiencies that too often take over once the resumés reach their destination—whether physical desk or virtual desktop. Traditional resumé screening, interviewing, employment offer and hiring processes— the last but indispensable mile of recruiting— have often been left untouched by recruitment technologies. In some cases their importance has been neglected or under-resourced because of the fascination, potential and novelty of e-recruiting.

Hiring managers are—or should be—the ultimate employment closers. But recruiters (either as recruiting specialists or as HR business partners) also play an essential role—no less essential than before the advent of e-recruitment, and probably more so because of it. E-recruitment risks being a particularly anonymous and disengaged process. But employment decisions continue, at least for now, to be uniquely human processes involving aspects of advocacy, negotiation, financial planning, psychology and sales. Thus, it's more important than ever that recruiters be proactively involved in the last mile: to balance e-recruitment speed with human responsiveness; to complement e-recruitment neutrality with emotion and advocacy; above all, to work through the human issues, conditions and details that ultimately make employment successes or employment failures.

David Sears *is a principal of McDermott-Sears Associates, LLC (www.mcdermottsears. com), a New Jersey-based consulting firm specializing in talent management, compensation and business benchmarking services. His book* Successful Talent Strategies, *published by AMACOM, was released Fall 2002.*

Top Five Things You Can Do To Get Your Employees To Own Recruiting

By John Vlastelica

E-mail: john@recruitingtoolbox.com

It's a Team Effort

I don't care how good you are recruiting is a team effort, and our success as an in-house recruiter or recruiting manager is wholly dependent on our ability to turn our hiring managers, interviewers and (most) employees into strong recruiting owners.

Creating recruiting ownership in our organizations requires risk taking and experimentation, a willingness to share information we may not be used to sharing, and leadership. We might even have to admit we need help. That's hard for some folks. But, the reality is, great recruiting leaders — at any level — know that they aren't the (hiring) decision makers most of the time and have the skills to help people help themselves.

Create Ownership with Internal Metrics. Create peer pressure and tap into a manager's need to solve problems.

This is where you might need to share info you're not used to sharing, and be willing to take a few arrows. You must capture and openly share metrics at your client managers' staff meetings. For internal metrics, show at least these three basic metrics:

- Aged open jobs (open 30 days, 60 days, 90 days)
- Hires-by-source (especially highlight employee referrals generated from within each group)
- Offer-to-hire ratio (total offers made, plus percent accepted offers)
- And maybe one or two other key metrics (however, cost per hire, for example, usually doesn't motivate an individual manager)

Break out each of these metrics — for an entire business group — by department manager. Pass out a one page spreadsheet that's updated bi-weekly. Ask for 10 minutes at the staff meeting to review the progress, talk about big wins and losses, and — assuming your group wants stuff better, faster, and cheaper — ask, "What are we going to do to get these numbers up?" Better yet, ask the VP of the group to participate, and have him/her ask each hiring manager to share what he or she is doing that's working, and not working. Then, let the problem solving — and peer pressure — begin. Leverage the best practices in the room, and get your most successful hiring managers talking about the personal investment they make in recruiting and how their peers might experience similar success by doing X, Y, and Z. You facilitate, you expose the problem areas and successes, and let them do a lot of the work. Be open, not defensive, and you might gain some real insight into — and help managers take ownership for — the recruiting issues needing the most attention.

(By the way, you don't need any sort of high-end applicant tracking system to capture info in the three primary data categories listed above — you can track it all via job posting dates, offer letter generation dates, new hire start dates, and new hire orientation "how'd we find you?" questionnaires).

Create Ownership with External Metrics. Tap into natural company competitiveness.

This requires access to a little benchmarking data, and a little data gathering when offers are declined. The goal here is to talk about the successes of other companies — again, at department staff meetings –and diagnose why your company's results are better and worse in some areas. How do you get this external data? First, understand that it's unlikely you'll get really specific information from your competition. Instead, you'll end up with qualitative, anecdotal data. I suggest you start with the data easiest to gather: your declined offers. Track decline reasons, what companies your best candidates are declining you for, and — ideally — get feedback through a candidate satisfaction survey. Try and find out why you're losing people. Is it:

- Money or benefits?
- Something that happened in the interview?
- A slower response time?
- Uninteresting work or company?
- Poor expectation setting early on, so that the offer was disappointing?
- A bad "word on the street" about your company's future?
- A bad experience with the hiring manager?

Next, try and find out what your people-competition is up to. Bring in ads from the trade journals, print out pages from their career site (including dates of recruiting activities, like open houses or on-campus interviews), and ask your employees who used to work there (or recent hires who declined the competition's offer to come work for you) about the way they find, interview and close/hire people. If you have more resources to research this, you can get sneaky and send one of your trusted employees over to do some secret shopping, and report back on what the competition does differently. You can also get great info from networking at SHRM/EMA events. And, if you have big bucks, you can even buy some data — by industry and geography — from places like Saratoga or Staffing.org. Either way, it's more about the conversation with your department managers than the data itself. Your goal is to uncover any cause-effect data that might explain the differences in your recruiting success relative to other companies. Once you have the information, you need to get managers thinking about your:

- Company reputation
- Candidate sourcing channels and their effectiveness
- Interviewing style
- Candidate response time and candidate expectation setting
- Offer packages and process

Help your management team see how the recruiting pain they experience (quality, cost, speed) is connected to these areas. Compare your processes, your techniques, and your abilities to the competition. Then ask:

- How does your effectiveness in these areas (above) likely affect your ability to attract, select, and recruit the people we need?
- What's the low-hanging fruit, the high ROI things we can more easily change in the way we recruit to improve our ability to get great people?
- What sorts of changes are realistic, given our culture, budget, and headcount?
- What might happen if we experiment, and try doing a few things differently for three months in department X, and then compare before-and-after results to see what worked?

If you — as the recruiter or recruiting leader — aren't asking these questions and driving constructive conversations around recruiting, who is? It's possible — and probable — that these conversations are happening without you in the room, without proper context, without data. Get involved, start running recruiting like a product marketing effort, where competitive data helps drive strategy, process, and behavior changes within your company.

Involve Them (If they build it, they will do it). Involve your client managers and your best existing recruiting owners in (re)building your recruiting programs and processes.

Recruiting is a means to an end: better business results. Tap into the people who depend on the business results — and experience the real pain of not hiring the right people to get those results — to develop and improve the way you acquire great talent. Take a look at some of the following programs and processes:

- Interviewer Training
- Interview and Decision Making Process
- College Recruiting (college selection, on-campus process, candidate placement within the organization, closing process)
- Closing Process and Key Company Selling Points
- Recruiting Vendor Selection (advertising, headhunting, key systems)

What would happen if your employees with the best track record around hiring agreed to meet with your ad agency and recruiters to share their best techniques for selling candidates on the company and job? What would happen if your best interviewers heavily participated in designing and delivering interviewer training? What would happen if you brought a star operations/logistics employee in to look at your recruiting supply chain/process?

Ownership 101 teaches us that employee involvement — in diagnosing, defining and fixing the problems that impact us — drives better ideas, more commitment and faster implementation.

How do you pick the people who are most likely to contribute to these programs? Select people from a list who:

- Have significant recruiting pain, so the motivation and incentive is there
- Have a track record of great candidate sourcing, selection and closing
- Already like you, and have some confidence in both your abilities and intentions
- Have strong influencing skills, so that others will follow their lead once new programs and processes are ready for roll-out

Too many of us — whether it's due to insecurity, lack of experience or belief that involving the clients in the process will slow us down — don't involve our clients in the creation and implementation of recruiting programs. The reality is that employee-involvement is a requirement for great recruiting success.

Make Ownership Easier. Removing barriers to referrals. Gain a deep understanding as to why employees don't do more to help the company recruit great people, then fix what's broken.

Too often, we set ourselves up to fail. We make it too hard for our employees to contribute to our company's — and our own — success. What can you do to make it easier for your employees to help recruit great talent? First, fix your employee referral program.

- Focus almost all of your recruiter-to-employee candidate sourcing communication on the top 25 percent most critical positions, prioritized by your client group's managers and VP

- Stop sending out useless HR-speak job postings, loaded with core competencies and generic skill requirements. These might be fine — and even required — for job ads on your website, but they don't help employees make targeted referrals.

- Start sending out profiles of the ideal candidates for your most critical openings, including the ideal candidate's current job title, the five companies they probably work at now, the type of college degree they should have, and the specific accomplishments they should have made in the past two years. Get this info from your best performing job incumbents, and the managers who depend on these people.

- Don't wait for the referrals to come to you. Actively solicit the referrals.
  - Go to staff meetings in other departments, asking engineering about the best finance people they worked with, and asking operations about the best engineering people they worked with. Pass around a sheet of paper to capture names and job titles, right then and there. Make it simple.
  - Review a list of the year's past hires, and see if there are people — in any part of your company — from your target companies. Also, see if you hired people who have worked for the vendors who sold to your target candidates. Then, call these employees, and ask for their help as you try to identify great people from these target companies.
  - Attend new hire orientation with a single sheet of paper for each new hire. Request the name, company name, and contact info for the very best people they worked with at their past companies (whether these leads are looking for work or not, whether they knew them well or just know them by reputation).

- Stop requiring resumés. Start accepting sticky notes. You want leads, names of great people. Request e-mail addresses and phone numbers, and send every person submitted a note that includes what they might learn, do, and contribute if they joined your company. If it's OK to use the employee's name, cc: the employee on the e-mail to his/her lead.

- Always follow up on every referral that comes in for these critical jobs, especially when you solicit them. The surest way to stop referrals from coming in is to ignore them. If you don't follow up with employee referrals, your employee looks stupid to his/her friends, and will stop helping you. Don't embarrass your employees by dropping the ball.
- Track referrals generated by employee and department, and share this information at department meetings to reinforce this ownership behavior.

Reward Recruiting Ownership. Effective rewards will reinforce good recruiting behavior, and set the standard around employee recruiting ownership.

What can you do to reward the employees who make time for recruiting?

- Build recruiting capabilities — and results — into your performance management criteria, even for non-managers. Make recruiting a core competency, that HR includes on the performance management forms, and incorporate it into what's evaluated in any 360-degree feedback tool.
- Take recruiting metrics into staff meetings, and publicly acknowledge individual and team successes in front of managers and execs.
- Give cash rewards or vacation days to employees who refer great new hires, and always follow up with the employee to thank him for referring any candidate who made it to the interview stage (whether hired or not).
- Get credit in company newsletters or at company meetings to employees who drive recruiting for their group, whether that manifests as volunteering for campus recruiting trips, generating a ton of referrals, helping to close a great new candidate, or problem solving a broken recruiting process within their team.

Increase Recruiting Success

The recruiting and HR functions tend to be under-resourced. Not surprisingly, the best recruiting functions — across industries — have a highly leveraged employee base. Getting your hiring teams involved and motivated to acquire great talent requires some experimentation, patience, and a little letting go. Remember, sharing responsibility with your hiring teams is not a sign of recruiting-department weakness; instead, it's the smart thing to do. Exposing recruiting challenges to some of the best problem solvers in the company and reinforcing ownership with the hiring teams will certainly improve your ability to recruit better, faster, and cheaper than before.

The benefits are clear. Quality and speed go up, costs go down. Candidate satisfaction and hiring team satisfaction goes up, which drives your credibility up as well. The bottom line is that a recruiting culture of ownership breeds phenomenal behaviors and results.

John Vlastelica has spent most of his HR and recruiting career working in wireless telecom and e-commerce. He recently ended his four-year career at Amazon.com to start Recruiting Toolbox, a specialized consulting firm that partners with HR, recruiting and management teams to improve their ability to recruit, manage and retain people. For more information visit www.recruitingtoolbox.com.

How Recruiters Can WOW Managers And Become Corporate Heroes

By Dr John Sullivan

E-mail: johns@sfsu.edu

During tight economic times it's always hard for recruiters to justify their existence. One way to avoid having to continually walk on eggshells is to build up some political capital with managers. Even if you are lucky enough to work for a company where results alone are rewarded, it never hurts to have a few senior managers singing your praises. This article is designed to give you some aggressive tips on how you can impress your hiring managers and move your recruiting tactics up to the level of WOW.

What is a WOW?

I work in Silicon Valley where almost everyone knows the meaning of the term WOW. Just in case you don't. A WOW is something you do that is so unique, powerful or clever that the managers involved literally vocalize their positive reaction with the word WOW when they hear about what you did. Unfortunately, many recruiters are conservative. They aim for the mundane and as a result, they usually hit it. If you want to truly stand out, instead of doing many ordinary things, do a few extraordinary things that really get noticed:

- Report extraordinary results
- Utilize unique or creative candidate finding tools
- Be innovative in convincing them to apply
- Market and build your brand
- Apply unique uses of technology
- Be innovative in candidate assessment
- Engage in extraordinary approaches on selling the finalists on the job
- Have recruiters help move/redeploy employees internally
- Start workforce planning and forecasting

Steps In WOWing A Manager

WOWing managers takes an aggressive state of mind as well as a list of best practices. Think of it as a continuous process of developing new approaches. Below are some examples of different tools and strategies that you can use to WOW your manager.

1) Report Extraordinary Results

After you communicate your WOW results, everything else you do just becomes "icing on the cake."

- **Report your results.** At least twice a year send a report to your hiring managers outlining your major successes in recruiting. Be sure to highlight each of the top performing people in the business unit that were recruited by you. Report your speed (time to fill) and the quality of your hires (their performance level on the job vs. the average worker in that job). Provide comparisons that show how each (of your) manager's recruiting results exceed the average for the company.
- **Quantify the business impact.** Demonstrate the performance differential (in the dollar value of their increased output) between top performers and average performers. Show managers the economic value they received by spending the extra time and resources that it takes to hire top performers.
- **Report what works.** Periodically report back to each key manager which recruiting sources and tools are producing the highest (and lowest) quality applicants and hires within their business unit. Use this information to convince your managers that you know what works and what doesn't in recruiting. Next educate them with a list highlighting which recruiting tools are being used by the most successful hiring managers, in order to motivate them to try some of those successful recruiting approaches.
- **Manager satisfaction.** Periodically survey your hiring managers to assess their degree of satisfaction with your recruiting services. Be sure and ask them what they want more of and less of in recruiting. On a later date, report back to them the actions you have taken to modify your recruiting approach to better fit their unique needs.

2) Candidate Finding Tools

Few things excite managers more than having people they know and respect (but that they thought were out of reach) apply for one of their jobs.

- **Dream candidates.** Identify your hiring manager's and top performers' dream candidates by asking them directly to name names. Examples include mentors or mentees, their best previous manager, their best previous co-worker, the competitor's best performers etc. Over time build a relationship with each one. Your goal is to identify each of the dream candidate's specific criteria for changing jobs. Next, show each candidate how you will meet most or all of their decision criteria. When they formally apply, hand carry the application to the manager... and wait for the WOW!

- **Offer turndowns.** Track the must have finalists that rejected your offers in the past two years. After six months (or whenever their new company undergoes a downturn) contact them to see if they would consider a new offer

- **First day hire referrals.** When you hire an employee from a major competitor, ask them on their first day who else is good at their former firm. Also let them know that they will get a referral bonus if they help bring the targeted candidate on board.

- **Utilize unusual sources.** Try nontraditional recruiting sources. For example, rather than recruiting at job fairs, instead recruit at trade fairs. If the hiring manager wants "risk takers", recruit at organizations that attract risk takers (skydiving and adventure travel clubs). If you want creative thinkers and innovators don't expect to find them using traditional recruiting sources.

3) Convincing Potential Candidates to Apply

Top performers are probably already employed, and as a result, most are not actively seeking a new job. If you want to coerce employed top professionals into applying for a job at your firm you must use recruiting tools designed exclusively for employed people.

- **Top performer referrals.** Rather than wait for the top performers in the hiring manager's department, you should proactively seek them out and demonstrate to them the vital role they need to play in recruiting. Build a relationship with these employees in order to get them to identify their top referrals. In addition, ask them to do the initial contacts and later to help you sell the candidate. The likelihood of them applying for and later accepting a job with your firm is the highest of all types of candidates.

4) Building Your Brand

Nothing gets you noticed faster than being written up and recognized by external sources.

- **Get written up externally.** Identify the publications that influential managers read on a regular basis. Study the articles these publications run on recruiting and related topics in order to determine the criteria they use for selecting recruiting best practices to write up. Build relationships with their writers and editors. Submit articles to them, which highlight your best-in-class hiring practices. Whenever possible, mention the hiring manager's

77

name or include a quote by them in the article. At the end of each recruiting season publish a report that cites your WOW's. Don't be subtle...brag when you can.

5) Unique Uses of Technology
The best candidates are well versed in the use of technology. In fact, in many cases, unless you also utilize technology in recruiting, candidates will tune you out.

- **E-mail newsletter.** Send a monthly e-mail newsletter to each of the top candidates on your targeted list. Include in the newsletter information about the company, its new products and innovations that might excite external candidates. Profile key team members and the hiring manager in the newsletter. Offer these friends of the company subscribers' product discounts and opportunities to participate in company training or events where they can meet key people.
- **Push jobs.** You might supplement the e-newsletter occasionally with a personal "how are you doing" e-mail. When you identify a job that's appropriate, e-mail it directly to people it fits on your candidate mailing list.

6) Candidate Assessment
Anything you can do to improve the accuracy and decrease the monotony of application screening and interviewing will be greatly appreciated by hiring managers and candidates alike.

- **Remote interviews.** Set up interviews with potential candidates at well attended industry events. Also set up videoconference interviews to bring in candidates whom otherwise would not be available for face-to-face interviews.
- **Five great no uglies.** Managers get frustrated with large piles of resumés, and even more frustrated when that pile also contains resumés from obviously unqualified candidates. Get a member of their team to help you refine your screening technique until you can (without error) select five great resumés to present to the hiring manager. Few things will WOW a manager quicker than receiving a small number of great resumés, without a single "ugly" resumé in the bunch.

7) Selling the Finalists on the Job
Finding great candidates is only half the job. You also have to develop a sales strategy in order to get the very best to select your offer from the many offers that top candidates are likely to receive.

- **Offer sheet comparisons.** Provide managers with side-by-side offer comparison sheets. This single sheet shows managers how your offer stacks up against each of your major competitor's (likely) offers. Your firm's strong points are listed on the sheet along with arguments that a manager could use to better explain your weak points. The competitor's strong and weak points are also listed in order to educate the manager and also to help strengthen their arguments.
- **Use market research.** Ask every new hire what they liked and disliked in your offer letter. Use that information to refine your future offers. Also capture new hires' offer letters from other firms in order to see how your offer compared. Use surveys and focus groups at tradeshows to identify the expectations and the offer acceptance criteria of top performers.

8) Internal Employee Placement

For most firms, external hiring fills only half of the open professional and management positions. The other half is filled through internal placement. Fortunately the skills that external recruiters have can also be used for internal recruiting and placement.

- **Utilize employee referrals for internal placements.** Employee referrals are the best sources for external hiring and they are equally as effective in internal redeployment. Ask your firm's top performers who else is good within the organization. Identify these internal candidate's dream jobs and attempt to find them that position internally (before some external recruiters find it for them at another firm).
- **Identify who is at risk of leaving.** When top employees quit, not only does it hurt the firm but it also increases your workload. Prevent turnover by keeping your ear open about who's actively looking for a job. If you find your employees on job boards, at job fairs etc. notify their manager and provide them with a plan to motivate and excite that employee. Act as a talent scout and identify the internal people that could make a significant contribution to the business unit of your hiring managers. Of course always solicit internal talent within your company's accepted norms.

9) Workforce Planning

Managers are concerned about keeping their pipeline filled with talent to meet future needs. Recruiters can help managers develop short-term local workforce plans. Some things they can do include:

- **Baby boom replacements.** Develop a pool of mid-level manager candidates that can be hired and developed to replace the legions of soon-to-be-retiring baby boomers within your firm.

- **Bench strength.** A bench strength plan identifies and develops individuals that can fill in short term or take over if an employee suddenly leaves. Such a plan is increasingly essential because organizations are now so lean as a result of layoffs that the impact of losing a middle manager is now greater than ever. A bench strength plan differs from traditional succession planning in that it only covers key jobs within a single department. Individual managers are held responsible for developing and cross training at least one individual to fill a temporary or permanent vacancy in every key job.

10) Miscellaneous Things You Can Do

In addition to the ideas listed above, here are some others that, while powerful, don't fit into any single category.

- Forecast the future. Absolutely nothing impresses hiring managers more than predicting the future or giving them a heads-up before a major event. Warn hiring managers when you know that someone on their team is currently actively looking for a job. Or, forecast an upcoming layoff at a competitor and show how it can be an opportunity to poach their top talent. In addition, if you were to warn them about an upcoming internal hiring freeze (or an upcoming unfreeze), so that they have time to take the appropriate action, you are likely to be considered a hero.
    - **Promise service levels.** Spell out, in writing, your minimum and maximum guaranteed service levels in such areas as:
        - Your response time to questions from hiring managers
        - The maximum elapsed time from requisition approval to seeing resumés
        - The maximum time to produce candidate offer letters, etc.
    - **Prioritize your customers.** You don't have the time or the resources to do it all well so you need to realize that great recruiting in business impact or mission critical positions will make you a hero much faster than filling high volume hourly positions. Prioritize your positions, business units and hiring managers according to their business impact.
    - **Reward great recruiting.** Convince your performance management and incentive compensation managers to measure and reward managers for great recruiting and retention. If hiring managers receive a substantial performance bonus for great recruiting and retention, managers will invariably begin to demand more innovation from you, as their recruiter. Incentives for recruiters can also spur greatness and innovation

Conclusion

Recruiting these days isn't much different from that TV series, *Survivor*. It is a "dog eat dog world" where only the very best can survive. Recruiters who want job security need to know that it takes much more than hard work and effort in order to stand out (hard work and maximum effort are minimums these days, just to maintain your job). What is needed in recruiting is a shift in approach. Rather than doing many things well, it is also important that you do a few things in an extraordinary manner.

It might initially seem difficult to stand out in recruiting but actually it's not that hard because most recruiting is relatively mundane. The standard approach (search the job boards, let the ATS sort resumés and then a behavioral interview) excites few managers or candidates. In my opinion, if you want to guarantee your job security, the conservative route is not the way go. Instead, market yourself and build your brand as an innovator and an expert in recruiting. Get people to talk about you and the way you approach your work. In short, do things that are memorable. Try to develop at least one new WOW recruiting practice each quarter as part of your continuous improvement effort and to help to keep your mind fresh.

Dr. John Sullivan is professor of management and human resources at San Francisco State University.

REVIEWS

CareerXroads 500 Best
The world's leading reference guide
to job and resumé websites.

123 USA hire.com

www.123USAhire.com

Todd Stancombe
11620 N. Community House Rd., Suite 200, Charlotte, NC 28277
Ph: 800-224-1381   E-mail: contactus@123hire.com

JOBS	100s		RESUMES	1,000s
Cost to post	Cost to see		Cost to post	Cost to see
Fee	Free		Free	Fee
DISCIPLINE			LOCATION	
ALL			USA/SOE	
SPECIALTY			FEATURE	
ALL			Gateway	
AGENT: N/A				

123usahire.com is the gateway to a network of location specific sites with reasonable disclosure and a focus on Charlotte (www.123charlotte.com), Jacksonville (www.123jacksonville.com), Raleigh (www.123raleigh.com), and Norfolk (www.123norfolk.com). Sold in November 2001 this site has obvious intentions to expand nationally. One job posting costs $195. Vendor alliances with assessment tools, reference checking, drug screening and an audio-enhanced company profile make this a site to watch. Site provides a decent search engine for an easy ride.

3D Site

wwww.3dsite.com/#jobs

Daniele Colajacomo
1738 1/2 Topanga Skyline Drive, Topanga, CA 90290
Ph: 310-455-9848   E-mail: dani@3dsite.com

JOBS	10s		RESUMES	N/A
Cost to post	Cost to see		Cost to post	Cost to see
Free	Free		N/A	N/A
DISCIPLINE			LOCATION	
IT/Communications			USA	
SPECIALTY			FEATURE	
New Media/Computer Graphics/Graphic Arts			N/A	
AGENT: Jobseeker				

3DSite is a community-based effort focused on the computer graphics industry (3-D, artists, modeling and special effects) on a freelance or full-time basis. The site is one of the web's pioneers. 3DSite's job seekers can view posted jobs on the site for free, or for $4 per month, can enlist the site to scour the web for graphics openings and forward them via email (site searches 50+ job boards and newsgroups/mailing lists). 3DSite has been doing this since 1997, and it still seems like a heck of a deal. Jobs can be posted for free by employers. The site offers limited disclosure regarding ownership or privacy issue. Long list of industry links for 3D professionals.

4Work

www.4work.com

5650 Greenwood Plaza Blvd., Suite 250, Greenwood Village, CO 80111
Ph: 303-741-9701   Fax: 303-741-9702   E-mail: sales@4work.com

JOBS	1,000s		RESUMES	N/A
Cost to post	Cost to see		Cost to post	Cost to see
Fee	Free		N/A	N/A
DISCIPLINE			LOCATION	
ALL			USA	
SPECIALTY			FEATURE	
ALL			N/A	
AGENT: Jobseeker				

4Work.com is still relatively low key in advertising its services. The owner claims 304,000 registered job seekers are receiving job alert notices. Employers pay $.15 for each job email sent out, but have the ability to control the number sent. The minimum employer fee is $25 and the maximum charge is $75. Jobs are date posted for freshness. Job postings are also obtained from careerexchange.com. Check out "Your Career" which has interesting articles onwork-related issues. Owners also sponsor www.4labor-soflove.org which helps volunteers and non-profit organizations find each other.

6FigureJobs

www.sixfigurejobs.com

Ryan Price
Workstream Inc., 40 Richards Avenue, 3rd Floor, Norwalk, CT 06854
Ph: 800-605-5154   Fax: 203-855-5349   E-mail: sales@6figurejobs.com

JOBS	1,000s		RESUMES	100,000s
Cost to post	Cost to see		Cost to post	Cost to see
Fee	Free		Free	Fee
DISCIPLINE			LOCATION	
ALL			USA	
SPECIALTY			FEATURE	
ALL			Executive	
AGENT: Jobseeker				

6FigureJobs is a "go to" resource for executives searching for their next opportunity. The site claims the average salary of its clients (posted resumes) is $147,000. Profiles are kept indefinitely. Recruiters pay either $225 for a job posting or $575, which includes access to the resume database for one month (owners claim 250,000 resumes ijn their database). Most of the openings can be viewed on the site with detailed descriptions and direct contact information. Job seekers register and receive all matching openings via email. We were impressed with the site's level of disclosure and clarity. Job seekers can even search for a headhunter in their profession. At www.6figureselect.com, recruiters are offered search services for $3,000 - $15,000. Site guarantees to provide five interested candidates in 10 business days. www.6figuremba.com is another site in 6Figures' network. Ownership has changed to workstream in 2002.

A2Zmoonlighter

www.a2zmoonlighter.com

5001 Baum Blvd., Suite 696, Pittsburgh, PA 15213
Ph: 888-678-0136

JOBS	10,000s	RESUMES	100,000s
Cost to post	Cost to see	Cost to post	Cost to see
Free	Free	Free (See Notes)	Free (See Notes)
DISCIPLINE		LOCATION	
ALL		USA	
SPECIALTY		FEATURE	
ALL		Contingent	
AGENT: N/A			

A2Zmoonlighter.com was launched for night owls looking for a second job. Recruiters can post their projects for free. Job seekers must agree to pay 10% of the total project value once they land the job. Employers pay the site directly, they take their 10% cut and the balance is paid to your night owl. The site caters to information technology, office, creative and businessconsulting opportunities. The site claims over 235,000 registrants and 13,000 clients. Job seekers must register to see where the night action is.

AboutJobs.com

www.aboutjobs.com

Jeff Allen
180 State Road, Suite 2U, Sagamore Beach, MA 02562
Ph: 508-888-6889   Fax: 508-888-3151   E-mail: jobs@aboutjobs.com

JOBS	1,000s	RESUMES	N/A
Cost to post	Cost to see	Cost to post	Cost to see
Fee	Free	N/A	N/A
DISCIPLINE		LOCATION	
ALL		USA	
SPECIALTY		FEATURE	
ALL		COLLEGE	
AGENT: Jobseeker			

AboutJobs.com is the gateway to its network of sites: InternJobs.com, OverseasJobs.com, Resortjobs.com, and SummerJobs.com.These sites provide entry-level, college and some experienced opportunities in the U.S. and internationally. AboutJobs.com charges $42 to post an opening for a four-week period or $295 for a 1 year run. All jobs are posted with direct contact information and date of posting. Recruiters can have their openings emailed to the site's members for $300 per job. The site's keyword search engine gets you where you need to go. Job seekers can sign up for periodic updates for career news and job hunting tips.

Abracat

www.abracat.com

David Teitler
361 Broadway, Suite 100, New York, NY 10013
Ph: 212-965-2900   Fax: 212-334-3307   E-mail: advertising@adone.com

JOBS	100,000s	RESUMES	100,000s
Cost to post	Cost to see	Cost to post	Cost to see
Fee	Free	Free	Fee
DISCIPLINE		LOCATION	
ALL		USA	
SPECIALTY		FEATURE	
ALL		Gateway	
AGENT: Jobseeker			

Abracat serves as the classified site for 1,200 small market newspapers throughout the U.S. and Canada (formerly adone). Most of the publications are small daily and weekly newspapers that have help wanted advertising. Job postings come directly to this site from the individual papers that are members. Job seekers can use an agent (Ad Hound) to identify job categories and regions for their next opportunity. After registering, applicants will receive emails listing opportunities that match their requirements. For the job seeker whose desired location can be narrowed to an area covered by several of these small markets this site offers access to over200,000 jobs.

Absolutely Health Care

www.healthjobsusa.com

Ken Levinson
CJ Ventures, 6542 Hypoluxo Road, Suite 294, Lake Worth, FL 33467
Ph: 800-863-8314   Fax: 800-357-8684   E-mail: ahc@medoptions.com

JOBS	10,000s	RESUMES	10,000s
Cost to post	Cost to see	Cost to post	Cost to see
Fee	Free	Free	Fee
DISCIPLINE		LOCATION	
Health Care		USA	
SPECIALTY		FEATURE	
Nursing/MD		Gateway	
AGENT: Jobseeker			

Absolutely Health Care is one of four sites in this family that offers opportunities in over 100 healthcare categories organized into three areas:www.nurse optionsusa.com (RNs and nursing management), medoptionsusa.com (pharmacists, medical imaging, respiratory therapists, physician assistants and nurse practitioners) and rehaboptionsusa.com (physical, occupational and speech therapists and assistants). Recruiters pay $150 to post a position for90 days which includes resume database access for the category and state they are recruiting. Unlimited access for 90 days costs $1,440. Recruiters openings are pushed out to 2,000 additional sites for no extra charge. Job seekers can click on a map of the U.S. and search by job category.

Academic Employment Network

www.academploy.com

Christopher J. Gaudet
266 Gray Road, Windham, ME 04062
Ph: 888-254-0987   Fax: 888-254-0987   E-mail: info@academploy.com

JOBS	100s	RESUMES	100s
Cost to post	Cost to see	Cost to post	Cost to see
Fee	Free	Fee	Fee
DISCIPLINE		LOCATION	
Education		USA	
SPECIALTY		FEATURE	
Teaching, K-12, University		College	
AGENT: N/A			

The Academic Employment Network (AEN) lists available positions at colleges, primary and secondary educational institutions for faculty, staff, and administrative professionals. Educational districts can advertise their openings for $95 per position for a 30-day run. The site's search engine will allow the job seeker to access openings by state and gives the number of openings (Great touch). Positions include elementary and secondary teaching openings as well as administrative jobs. Bus driver and janitor positions were also listed. Position descriptions are very basic, but get the job done. Cost to post a resume to the site is $9.95 for six months. Schools must have an annual subscription to access the resume database.

Academic Physician & Scientist

www.acphysci.com/aps.htm

Martha McGarity
345 Hudson Street, 16th Floor, New York, NY 10014
Ph: 212-886-1261   Fax: 212-627-4801   E-mail: mmcgarit@lww.com

JOBS	100s	RESUMES	N/A
Cost to post	Cost to see	Cost to post	Cost to see
Fee	Free	N/A	N/A
DISCIPLINE		LOCATION	
Health Care/Education		USA	
SPECIALTY		FEATURE	
MD/Research		N/A	
AGENT: N/A			

The Academic Physician and Scientist site includes openings from a bi-monthly print publicationthat is mailed free to every faculty physician, scientist, senior resident and fellow at 125 U.S. medical schools, 400 major teaching hospitals, 16 Canadian medical schools, and academic and professional societies. Employers who pay for the print get the web for a 60 day run. Positions can be viewed by subject (administration, basic science, clinical science) or by the site's search engine.

Academic Position Network
www.apnjobs.com

1655 124th Lane NE, Blaine, MN 55449
Ph: 612-767-5949   Fax: 612-767-5852   E-mail: info@apnjobs.com

JOBS	10s	RESUMES	N/A
Cost to post	Cost to see	Cost to post	Cost to see
Fee	Free	N/A	N/A
DISCIPLINE		LOCATION	
Education		USA	
SPECIALTY		FEATURE	
Teaching K-12, University		N/A	
AGENT: N/A			

The Academic Position Network, launched in 1992, offers mail, email, phone and even a self-service web template to post teaching as well as senior-level openings at universities across the U.S. Recruiters pay $95 per posting for a 90-day run, and positions are posted within 24 hours of receipt. Institutions can obtain quantity discounts for volume job advertisements (10 or more run $50-$70 each depending how they are sent to the site).

Access: Networking in the Public Interest
www.accessjobs. org

Noreen Banks
1001 Connecticut Ave., NW Suite 838, Washington, DC 20036
Ph: 800-417-6351   Fax: 202-785-4212   E-mail: accesscntr@aol.com

JOBS	10s	RESUMES	1,000s
Cost to post	Cost to see	Cost to post	Cost to see
Fee	Free	Free	Fee
DISCIPLINE		LOCATION	
Non-Profit		USA	
SPECIALTY		FEATURE	
ALL		N/A	
AGENT: N/A			

Access, launched in 1996, is trying to be the nonprofit employment clearinghouse for recruiters and job seekers. This site has over 700 openings posted on an average day, with about 50 in the International zone. The cost to post a job is $95 for 30 days. A resume database is included in the job posting price. The site provides career fairs across the U.S. andcounseling for job seekers. Job seekers are charged $10-$15 to attend the career fairs. Owners also provide career counseling for a fee.

Accessalesjobs.com
www.accesssalesjobs.com

Max Brammer
1160 Sherwood Ct. S., Salem, OR 97302
Ph: 503-871-1355   E-mail: info@accessalesjobs.com

JOBS	100s		RESUMES	1,000s
Cost to post	Cost to see		Cost to post	Cost to see
Fee	Free		Free	Fee
DISCIPLINE			LOCATION	
Prof. Sales & Marketing			USA	
SPECIALTY			FEATURE	
Sales			N/A	
AGENT: N/A				

Accessalesjobs.com specializes in sales and marketing jobs. An easy to navigate, simple design offers employers a quick posting feature and pricing that is reasonable ($75 for one posting or $149 for unlimited posting for a month and access to the resume database). Jobs can be searched through the site's search engine or by region. Jobs are date-posted with location, title and company name.

Accounting.com
www.accounting.com

Ryan Cahill
701 Colorado Avenue, Stuart, FL 34994
Ph: 781-329-3660   E-mail: info@accounting.com

JOBS	100s		RESUMES	1,000s
Cost to post	Cost to see		Cost to post	Cost to see
Fee	Free		Free	Fee
DISCIPLINE			LOCATION	
Business			USA	
SPECIALTY			FEATURE	
Finance/Accounting			N/A	
AGENT: N/A				

Accounting.com is a great URL. For $75 employers can post a job for one month. For $250 fiveads can be placed and recruiters are given access to the site's resumes database for two months. The site's search engine makes looking for a job an easy task. The positions have direct contact information and most have lengthy descriptions. A discussion forum and links forprofessional development, including state organizations and industry resources are an added value. CPA and accounting firms get their first job listing for free. Job seekers take note.

Actor's Worldlink

members.aol.com/aworldlink

aworldlink@aol.com

JOBS	N/A	RESUMES	100s
Cost to post	Cost to see	Cost to post	Cost to see
N/A	N/A	Fee	Free
DISCIPLINE		LOCATION	
Entertainment & Media		USA	
SPECIALTY		FEATURE	
Actors		N/A	
AGENT: N/A			

So you want to be in showbiz? Actor's Worldlink allows actors to place their headshot and resume on the site for about $6 a month. Directors can view the information for free and hopefully make someone a star. No disclosure. Still moving a year later.

Ad Age

www.adage.com

Donna fields
Crain Communications, 711 Third Ave, New York, NY 10017
Ph: 212-210-0156   Fax: 212-210-0111   E-mail: dfields@crain.com

JOBS	100s	RESUMES	N/A
Cost to post	Cost to see	Cost to post	Cost to see
Fee	Free	N/A	N/A
DISCIPLINE		LOCATION	
Communications/Prof. Sales & Marketing		USA	
SPECIALTY		FEATURE	
Advertising/Public Relations/Sales		Network	
AGENT: N/A			

Advertising Age was powered by Monster so don't get confused by the link to them- its a vestige of their relationship. All Ad Age print ads are posted online and an online only ad will cost $250. This is an important industry publication and should be considered for advertising and PR.

Advance Careers

www.advancecareers.com/

Randy Schmidt
30 Journal Square, Jersey City, NJ 07306
Ph: 201-459-2832   Fax: 201-653-1189   E-mail: rschmidt@advance.net

JOBS	10,000s	RESUMES	100,000s
Cost to post	Cost to see	Cost to post	Cost to see
Fee	Free	Free	Fee

DISCIPLINE	LOCATION
ALL	USA

SPECIALTY	FEATURE
ALL	Gateway

AGENT: Both Recruiters & Jobseekers

Advance Careers a subsdiary of Newhouse publications and is the gateway to a powerful local network of career sites in 52 markets across the U.S. The site is allied with local newspapers that feature local and national news, sports, entertainment and lifestyle information, as well as classifieds. A single job posting costs $150. Each position becomes part of a candidate/employer search and matching service for 30 days. This enables the employer to match each job posted with a candidate database and invite employer-selected candidates to apply for the posted position. Local does matter, and these folks have a successful approach which will only get better. The network's sites include:New Jersey Online (nj.com ó The Star-Ledger, The Times, The Jersey Journal), Michigan Live (mlive.com ó Ann Arbor News and six other papers), Cleveland Live (cleveland.com ó The Plain Dealer)Oregon Live (oregonlive.com ó The Oregonian), Alabama Live (al.com ó Birmingham News, Mobile Register, The Huntsville Times), NOLA Live (nola.com ó The Times-Picayune), MassLive (masslive.com ó Union News, Sunday Republican), Syracuse Online (syracuse.com ó Syracuse Newspapers) Staten Island Live (silive.com ó Staten Island Advance) and PennLive (pennlive.com). Another 37 sites with the URL format hire[city].com can be found for Atlanta, Austin, Baltimore, Bellevue/Redmond [Eastside], Boston [Mass], Charlotte, Cincinnati, Columbus, Dallas, Denver, Houston, Kansas City, Louisville, Memphis, Milwaukee, TwinCities, Philadelphia, Phoenix, Pittsburgh, San Antonio, San Francisco, San Jose,Seattle,St. Louis, and Tampa Bay. FirstJobs.com is Advance Career's site for folks just entering the job market, part-timers, and seasonal employees. For job seekers this is a one stop shop that they should not pass up.

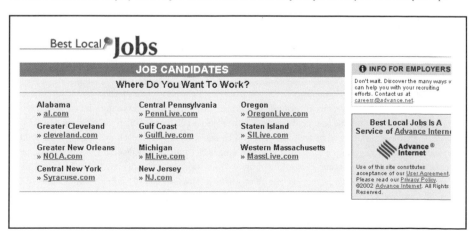

ADVANCE for Careers
www.advanceforcareers.com

Jennifer Montone
Merion Publications, Inc., 2900 Horizon Drive, King of Prussia, PA 19406
Ph: 800-355-5627   E-mail: advance@merion.com

JOBS	1,000s	RESUMES	N/A
Cost to post	Cost to see	Cost to post	Cost to see
Fee	Free	N/A	N/A
DISCIPLINE		LOCATION	
Health Care		USA/	
SPECIALTY		FEATURE	
Nursing/Allied Health		N/A	
AGENT: Jobseeker			

Launched in March of 2002, ADVANCE for Careers stores resumes but they are not accessible to employers- simply available for job seekers to send off. Openings are posted for 2 weeks and pricing varies. The site is the online arm of the ADVANCE family of print publications for Nursing and Allied Health Professionals. Their current job posting packages incorporate both print and online advertising and differ based on the print publication rates.

Adventures in Hospitality Careers
www.hospitalityadventures.com

Lisa Welch
PO Box 1743, San Marco, TX 78667-1743
Ph: 512-396-9707   Fax: 512-396-9708   E-mail: Info@hospitalityadventure

JOBS	100s	RESUMES	10,000s
Cost to post	Cost to see	Cost to post	Cost to see
Fee	Free	Free	Fee
DISCIPLINE		LOCATION	
Hospitality & Food Services		USA	
SPECIALTY		FEATURE	
ALL		N/A	
AGENT: Both Recruiters & Jobseekers			

Adventures in Hospitality Careers was re-launched in April 2001. Recruiters can order a one-week free trial to post jobs and search the resume database. The charge is $100 for unlimited job postings and resume access for one month. For an additional $25 jobs will be listed at the top of each posting page. Recruiters can input their desired criteria and the site willsend emails as candidates register at the site. Search templates make storing and searching easier. Jobs ranging from waiter to executive chefs can be found here. Job seekers can up the ante by paying $10 per month to be a "Hot Candidate" as their resume will be posted on the Employer Homepage.

AEC JobBank

www.aecjobbank.com

Frederick Hornblower
3740 East Orchard Road, Littleton, CO 80121
Ph: 877-645-7730   Fax: 720-489-0556   E-mail: sales@aecjobbank.com

JOBS	100s	RESUMES	1,000s
Cost to post	Cost to see	Cost to post	Cost to see
Fee	Free	Free	Fee
DISCIPLINE		LOCATION	
Engineering/Trades, Non-exempt & Hourly		USA	
SPECIALTY		FEATURE	
Civil/Construction		N/A	
AGENT: Jobseeker			

AEC JobBank is an online database and search engine for jobs and resumes for the architecture, engineering, real estate and construction industries. Recruiters pay $75 to post a job and $125 for 30-day access to the site's resume database. The site claims 8,000 resumes with 1,000 new candidates being added per week. The AEC JobBank also offers free trials. A tool box with a resume builder, personal message center, job agent and user profile is provided for job seekers. Openings can be searched by keyword or by industry for speedy access. Job seekers are emailed when a recruiter requests their resume. CXR loves it when niche sites go out of there way for job candidates.

JOB SEEKER TIP

Most job seekers will work in corporations that have between 500–1,000 employees.

Contact your local chamber of commerce to obtain a list and monitor their websites for openings.

AfterCollege
www.aftercollege.com

Roberto Angulo
330 Townsend Street, Suite 202, San Francisco, CA 94107
Ph: 877-725-7721   Fax: 415-495-7535   E-mail: info@aftercollege.com

JOBS	1,000s		RESUMES	10,000s
Cost to post	Cost to see		Cost to post	Cost to see
Fee	Free		Free	Fee
DISCIPLINE			LOCATION	
ALL			USA	
SPECIALTY			FEATURE	
All			College	
AGENT: Jobseeker				

AfterCollege (formerly The Jobresource.com) was launched October 1996. Recruiters pay $35 to post a position and $15 per campus department they would like the job sent to. Access to the resume database for a 24 hr. period costs $159. The site states it collects over 1,000 postings a month and 4,500 resumes. It presently has over 63,000 resumes in its database, but like all college sites, the numbers fluctuate dramatically. A link to yahoo maps makes for an easy relocation ride. Jobs are nicely displayed with links to the corporate site. Employers can be searched by function, and links to the company home pages are displayed. The site's business model has them actively contacting departments and student organizations to providefree web-hosting services in return for the use of the site as a channel to the students. Owners claim access to 915 departments and groups on 301 universities. Very smart. CXR appreciates players when they stretch their business model to compete in an ever chaning recruiting world. We wish AC well.

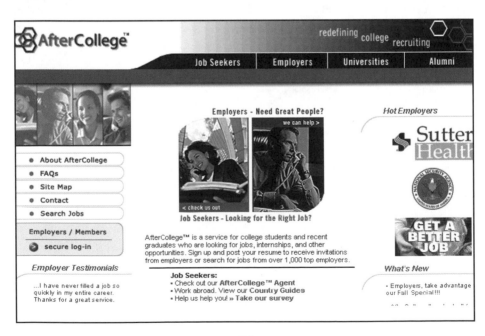

AIRS - Advanced Internet Recruitment Strategies

www.airsdirectory.com

White River Junction, VT
Ph: 800-466-4010   Fax: 888-997-5559   E-mail: sales@airsmail.com

JOBS	10s	RESUMES	1,000,000s
Cost to post	Cost to see	Cost to post	Cost to see
Free	Free	Free	Free
DISCIPLINE		LOCATION	
Human Resources		USA	
SPECIALTY		FEATURE	
Employment		Netwroks/Newsletters/Training	
AGENT: Both Recruiters & Jobseekers			

AIRS offers links to job sites, career sites, intranet-Internet software templates, applicant tracking tools, web-based private resume database services, website hosting services, multiple-site posting tools, resume robots, resume builders, resume distribution tools and more. Recruiters can post jobs and search the sites resume database for free. This is one web center we would use to connect to a new position.

AJCJobs.com (Atlanta Journal Constitution)

www.ajcjobs.com

Christy Davidson
Cox Newspapers, PO Box 4689, Atlanta, GA
Ph: 800-846-6672   E-mail: cdavison@ajc.com

JOBS	1,000s	RESUMES	10,000s
Cost to post	Cost to see	Cost to post	Cost to see
Fee	Free	Free	Fee
DISCIPLINE		LOCATION	
ALL		USA/SOE/GA/Atlanta	
SPECIALTY		FEATURE	
ALL		N/A	
AGENT: N/A			

Slow to get it but, years of incremental improvements deserve recognition. AJCjobs, the online version of the Atlanta Journal Consititution is a smoothly integrated and easy to navigate site with a reasonable resume database, employer feature options, virtual career fair capability and connections to AJCJobs.com. Solid content rounds out an excellent site. This Cox publications flagship is building local alliances in the community through radio etc. that might yet take back the high ground.

AllCountyJobs.com

www.allcountyjobs.com

Chris Russel
AllCountyJobs.com, LLC, 674 Orchard Street, Trumbull, CT 06611
Ph: 203.767.7393   Fax: 203-268-1464   E-mail: info@allcountyjobs.com

JOBS	100s		RESUMES	N/A
Cost to post	Cost to see		Cost to post	Cost to see
Fee	Free		N/A	N/A
DISCIPLINE			LOCATION	
ALL			USA/NOE/CT	
SPECIALTY			FEATURE	
ALL			Gateway	
AGENT: N/A				

AllCountyJobs is a gateway to a network of sites in Fairfield county, New Haven, and Hartford County as well as two skill niches- CTHighTech.com and CTHealthCareers.com Each has 100+openings. Employers pay $99 for 8 week postings.

AllRetailjobs.com

www.allretailjobs.com

Don Firth
Jobs in loggistics, PO Box 611297, North Miami, FL 33261
Ph: 305-940-9234   Fax: 305-940-9235   E-mail: Don@allretailjobs.com

JOBS	1,000s		RESUMES	1,000s
Cost to post	Cost to see		Cost to post	Cost to see
Fee	Free		Free	Fee
DISCIPLINE			LOCATION	
Retail Sales & Services			USA/	
SPECIALTY			FEATURE	
ALL			N/A	
AGENT: Jobseeker				

Launched in March 2001, AllRetailJobs.com covers 22 retail industry categories:apparel, auto, banking, catalog, convenience, department, discount, drug, electronics, hardware, home, hotel,Internet, jewelry, music, office, pharmacy, restaurant, specialty, sporting goods, supermarkets and toys. Recruiters pay $150 to post a job for 60 days and $150 to access the resume database. AllRetailJobs.com was designed and is marketed by the creators of jobsinlogistics.com. Unlike the specialty niche, the retail marketplace may not be as easy to segment. The assumption that either job seekers or employers care about retail-specific experience might make sense for the auto or hotel industry, but we would expect experience in toys, for example, to translate easily enough to discount.

Allied Health Opportunities
www.gvpub.com

Jerry Paldino
Great Valley Publishing Company, 3801 Schuylkill Road, Spring City, PA 19475
Ph: 800-278-4400   Fax: 610-948-4202   E-mail: sales@gvpub.com

JOBS	100s	RESUMES	N/A
Cost to post	Cost to see	Cost to post	Cost to see
Fee	Free	N/A	N/A
DISCIPLINE		LOCATION	
Health Care		USA	
SPECIALTY		FEATURE	
Allied Health/PT/OT/Pharmacy/Speech/Nuclear		N/A	
AGENT: N/A			

Allied Health Opportunities charges $25 to post positions that are listed in this publisher's magazines ('PA Today', 'For the Record' and 'Today's Dietitian' as well as their newest 'Social Work Today') in addition to print costs. Multiple packages are available. Health Care fields covered include:Cardiovascular Technologists, Cyto-technologists, Dietitian, Emergency Medical Technologists, Health Information, Medical Assistants, Nuclear Medicine Technologists,Occupational Therapy, Pharmacy, Physical Therapy, Radiation Therapy, Respiratory Therapy and Speech Pathology. Simple search engine.

AMFMJobs
www.amfmjobs.com

Mark Holloway
Broadcast Employment Services, PO Box 4116, Oceanside, CA 92052
Ph: 760-754-8177   Fax: 760-754-2115   E-mail: admin@amfmjobs.com

JOBS	10s	RESUMES	10s
Cost to post	Cost to see	Cost to post	Cost to see
Free	Free	Fee	Free
DISCIPLINE		LOCATION	
Entertainment & Media/Prof. Sales		USA	
SPECIALTY		FEATURE	
Radio		N/A	
AGENT: Jobseeker			

AMFMJobs may produce the next shock jock. Site is also coupled with TVJobs.com and DigitalTalent.tv Recruiters can post jobs for free, and they are listed in the order they are received. Openings will remain online for 30 days or longer if necessary. Recruiters can view resumes for free, and job seekers pay $15 (after a 30 day free trial) to have their resumes posted and view open jobs for one year. The site allows recruiters to save their favorite resumes for later use. Guests can view many of the features of the site prior to joining. The site offers good design, coupled with excellent added features for the job seeker and recruiter.

America's Job Bank

www.ajb.dni.us

E-mail: info@ajb.dni.us

JOBS	1,000,000s		RESUMES	100,000s
Cost to post	Cost to see		Cost to post	Cost to see
Free	Free		Free	Free
DISCIPLINE			LOCATION	
ALL			USA	
SPECIALTY			FEATURE	
ALL			Major Hub	
AGENT: Both Recruiters & Jobseekers				

With over 940,000 jobs and 400,000 resumes America's Job Bank (AJB) is like the orient express - always on the go. We have been critical of this site for not keeping up with the times, and although AJB does push far too many job seekers to contact state employmemt centers for employer contact information the plusses far outweigh any negatives on this site. Job searches can be narrowed to within five miles (or expanded to 100 miles) of a zip code for better targeting. Job seekers can prepare their resumes online via a resume builder, but they must register with the site to do so. The links to the U.S. government resources for careers, including the development of *OneNet", are world class, but not as user friendly as they may become with outside alliances with private job sites. Job seekers can access local company information by industry sector with a few clicks of the mouse. On the employer side, resumes can be viewed with an agent. This is a free site linked through to every employment office, outplacement office and college in the country. Any employer who doesn't post here automatically, or have a service cross-post for them, is missing the boat. Cleaning the site of outdated jobs and resumes would surely enhance the speed of access. AJB continues to be awork in progress. Maybe if they spoke to more employers....

America's Preferred Jobs

www.preferredjobs.com

Mark Hudson
133 Johnson Ferry Road, Marietta, GA 30068
Ph: 800-488-1902   Fax: 770-541-0507   E-mail: preferredjobs@mindspring.

JOBS	100,000s		RESUMES	100,000s
Cost to post	Cost to see		Cost to post	Cost to see
Free	Free		Free	Fee
DISCIPLINE			LOCATION	
ALL			USA	
SPECIALTY			FEATURE	
ALL			Gateway	
AGENT: Both Recruiters & Jobseekers				

America's Preferred Jobs (APJ) is a multi-site career hub gateway to greater then 100,000 posted positions and resumes. The site shows daily statistics on the most active job categories. Job seekers use the site search engine to view openings across the U.S. and register for a monthly email newsletter. APJ will push positions to job seekers who register their skill sets and resumes for employers. Employers can post jobs for free under the basic plan or pay a one-time $15 fee for links to the company website. The resume database, blind ads, unlimited postings, pre-screening, online job fairs and company profiles and button bannerads start at $75 per month. "Net Interview" allows employers to set up custom interviews that are delivered to the recruiter. Links to salary surveys, career guides, and a separate internship program section have added much to this site's value. A partnership with CareerBuilder.com and CareerShop.com have greatly enhanced their traffic numbers, but the marketing of this siteneeds work as it is unknown.

American Accounting Assoc.

accounting.rutgers.edu/raw/aaa/index.html

AAA, 5717 Bessie Drive, Sarasota, FL 34233
Ph: 941-921-7747   Fax: 941-923-4093   E-mail: aahq@packet.net

JOBS	100s		RESUMES	10s
Cost to post	Cost to see		Cost to post	Cost to see
Fee	Free		Fee	Free
DISCIPLINE			LOCATION	
Business/Education			USA	
SPECIALTY			FEATURE	
Teaching, University/Finance/Accounting			N/A	
AGENT: Jobseeker				

American Accounting Association is a new site to CXR. Recruiters pay $250 for posting in TheAccounting Review publication it online component. The ad will run on the web for 6 months. Openings are called "placement listings" and are all are from universities looking for professors in business or accounting. Only association members can post their resumes.

American Advertising Federation
www.aaf.org

Peter Shih
1101 Vermont Avenue, Suite 500, Washington, DC 20005
Ph: 800-999-2231   Fax: 202-898-0159   E-mail: aaf@aaf.org

JOBS	1,000s	RESUMES	N/A
Cost to post	Cost to see	Cost to post	Cost to see
Fee	Free	N/A	N/A
DISCIPLINE		LOCATION	
Communications		USA	
SPECIALTY		FEATURE	
Design/Writing		College/Intern	
AGENT: Jobseeker			

The American Advertising Federation (AAF) has joined the Community Career Network, an Internet network of job sites for industry-specific professional and trade associations, publications and educational institutions. Recruiters pay $150 for one posting or $500 per month for unlimited postings. Job seekers who apply to individual positions are asked if they want their resumes to be public or kept confidential. Many openings have salary ranges listed. Job seekers are advised that it is their responsibility to remove personal information. There were over 1,500 openings listed with a vast range of opportunities. Jobs ranged from a housekeeper to a Dir. of Community Insight. One valuable asset is their annual listing of more than 1,500 college internships. Links to internships are provided.

American Assoc. of Clinical Chemistry
www.aacc.org

AACC, 2101 L Street NW - Suite 202, Washington, DC 20037-1558
Ph: 800-892-1400   Fax: 202-887-5093   E-mail: info@aacc.org

JOBS	100s	RESUMES	100s
Cost to post	Cost to see	Cost to post	Cost to see
Fee	Free	Free	Fee
DISCIPLINE		LOCATION	
Science		USA/	
SPECIALTY		FEATURE	
Chem., Chemistry/Clinical		N/A	
AGENT: N/A			

The American Assoc. of Clinical Chemistry offers access to professionals with clinical chemistry background at a cost of $120 per posting. A subscription of $1300 for 10 postings includes access to the resume database. Solid service.

American Assoc. of Critical-Care Nurses
www.aacn.org

Kathy Huntley
101 Columbia, Aliso Viejo, CA 92656
Ph: 800-899-2226   Fax: 949-362-2020   E-mail: info@aacn.org

JOBS	100s	RESUMES	N/A
Cost to post	Cost to see	Cost to post	Cost to see
Fee	Free	N/A	N/A
DISCIPLINE		LOCATION	
Health Care		USA	
SPECIALTY		FEATURE	
Nursing/Critical Care		N/A	
AGENT: N/A			

The American Association of Critical-Care Nurses launched AACN Career Opportunities in April 1998. Employers seeking critical care nurses can post their openings online for $225 for 60 days (over the cost of their journal's print ad). Positions are listed here by title, then easily scanned by location, posting date, full-time, part-time or contract. Even a link to Yahoo Maps is available for driving instructions. The association publishes several journals and offers print and online options. Job seekers who are members of this association have access to the freshest job openings ahead of the general public. Recruiters can place ads through Kathy Huntley at Slack, Inc. 800-257-8290 x 249.

American Astronomical Society
www.aas.org

Dawn-Marie Craig
AAS, Suite 400, Washington, DC 20009
Ph: 202-328-2010   Fax: 202-234-2560   E-mail: jobs@aas.org

JOBS	10s	RESUMES	N/A
Cost to post	Cost to see	Cost to post	Cost to see
Fee	Free	N/A	N/A
DISCIPLINE		LOCATION	
Education/Science		USA	
SPECIALTY		FEATURE	
Teaching, University/Astonomy		N/A	
AGENT: N/A			

The American Astronomical Society posts openings for stars, or at least star-gazers in a very competent career services section. You just have to click on their "Job Register Statistics" and examine their "supporting data" for a detailed plot that suggests an alien intelligence must be the cause. Cost to post is $100 per job and that includes both a print publication and the web. Most of he openings are for Post Doctoral research and teaching positions. Employers who think creatively about the kinds of mathematical, instrumentation and other technical skills they require in more mundane positions might discover a great match. After all, the number of candidates visiting will far exceed the jobs available in this discipline. Reach beyond the sky.

American Chemical Society - JobSpectrum.org
www.acs.org

Mary Funke
1155 16th Street, NW, Washington, DC 20036
Ph: 888-667-7988   Fax: 202-872-4615   E-mail: sales@jobspectrum.org

JOBS	1,000s	RESUMES	1,000s
Cost to post	Cost to see	Cost to post	Cost to see
Fee	Free	Fee (See Notes)	Fee
DISCIPLINE		LOCATION	
Science/Engineering		USA	
SPECIALTY		FEATURE	
Chemical/Chemistry		N/A	
AGENT: Both Recruiters & Jobseekers			

The American Chemical Society JobSpectrum offers excellent career services for its 160,000 members. Ads from C&E News are listed for members only for an initial two weeks. After that they are open for all to see. Recruiters pay $250 to post a job on the site and can search the resume database for $450 per month. Members of ACS can ask a career consultant for adviceand do a salary comparison. Over 60 volunteer consultants, all ACS members, are available. Resumes can be submitted for feedback as well. Employers and job seekers are also invited to participate in national or regional "employment clearing houses", where job interviews are arranged at various conferences. The cost is a few hundred dollars. Links to employment trends are worth a visit for anyone thinking of going into the chemistry field.

American College of Healthcare Executives
www.ache.org

One North Franklin, Suite 1700, Chicago, IL 60606
Ph: 312-424-2800   Fax: 312-424-0023   E-mail: employmentservice@ache.org

JOBS	100s	RESUMES	1,000s
Cost to post	Cost to see	Cost to post	Cost to see
Free	Fee	Fee (See Notes)	Free
DISCIPLINE		LOCATION	
Health Care		USA	
SPECIALTY		FEATURE	
Administrative		EXECUTIVE	
AGENT: N/A			

American College of Healthcare Executives has over 30,000 members and great services. This organization has no idea of the value of its database. All resumes are easily accessible and free. Excellent design allows recruiters to view a summary and drill for details. Jobs can be accessed only by members and can be posted free by recruiters. Members can register for job and career workshops for under $200 per person. If you are an executive seeking employment or an organization seeking talent in this field, this site is a must.

American Corporate Counsel Assoc.

www.acca.com

Wanda Briscoe
1025 Connecticut Avenue, Suite 200, Washington, DC 20036
Ph: 202-293-4103   Fax: 202-293-4701   E-mail: webmistress@acca.com

JOBS	100s	RESUMES	100s
Cost to post	Cost to see	Cost to post	Cost to see
Free	Free	Fee (See Notes)	Free
DISCIPLINE		LOCATION	
Law & Order		USA	
SPECIALTY		FEATURE	
Attorney		N/A	
AGENT: N/A			

The American Corporate Counsel Association, with over 10,000 members has a searchable database of openings and resumes for in-house corporate counsel. Positions are easily searched by keyword, date, location, legal specialty or title. Several hundred new positions are listed every two weeks and deleted after two months. Recruiters can post their openings and search the resume database for free. Job seekers have to be members of the association to post their resume which can be listed open or confidentially. A lengthy list of career links rounds out this association site.

American Institute of Architects Career Center

www.aia.org

1735 New York Avenue, NW, Washington, DC 20006
Ph: 800-242-3837   Fax: 202-626-7547   E-mail: infocentral@aia.org

JOBS	100s	RESUMES	100s
Cost to post	Cost to see	Cost to post	Cost to see
Fee	Free	Free	Free
DISCIPLINE		LOCATION	
Engineering		USA	
SPECIALTY		FEATURE	
Civil/Architecture/Construction		N/A	
AGENT: Both Recruiters & Jobseekers			

AIA Career Center (formerly EArchitect) is the website of the American Institute of Architects. Members can post a position for $120 (non-members $175) for 30 days. Access to the resume database is included in the price. Positions are listed by title, employer and location. Job seekers do not have to be members of the association to post their resumes for free. Links to local AIA chapter career centers is also available for MA, DC, KS and PA. A salary survey of 27 positions at architectural firms is also available for $200. The organization has over 66,500 members. Recent graduates can join AIA for free for their first year.

AmericanJobs.com
www.americanjobs.com

Kevin Romney
PO Box 7544, Bloomfield Hills, MI 48302
Ph: 248-481-2005   E-mail: americanjobs@mailroom.com

JOBS	1,000s	RESUMES	100,000s
Cost to post	Cost to see	Cost to post	Cost to see
Fee	Free	Free	Fee
DISCIPLINE		LOCATION	
ALL		USA	
SPECIALTY		FEATURE	
ALL		Gateway	
AGENT: N/A			

AmericanJobs.com was launched in 1994 and is still a general hub for job seekers and recruiters. Recruiters pay $49 to post unlimited positions and view the sites resume database for a 90-day run. Other packages are available. The site's job database is easily viewed. Openings can be searched by keyword, state, or job category. All replies are date posted. Themarket for "Career Hubs" has gotten much tougher. Yet, with several hundred thousand jobs and resumes this site might be worth exploring.

American Marketing Assoc.
www.ama.org

Bob Wallach
American Marketing Association, Suite 5800, South Wacker Drive, Chicago, IL 60606
Ph: 800-262-1150   Fax: 312-542-9001   E-mail: info@ama.org

JOBS	100s	RESUMES	10,000s
Cost to post	Cost to see	Cost to post	Cost to see
Fee	Free	Free	Fee
DISCIPLINE		LOCATION	
Prof. Sales & Marketing		USA	
SPECIALTY		FEATURE	
Sales		N/A	
AGENT: Jobseeker			

The American Marketing Association (AMA) consists of more than 41,000 worldwide members in 92 countries and 500 chapters throughout North America. A job posting costs $150 and the resume database (36,000) access is $300 (both posting and access is 30 days). Job seekers must register to view openings. If you are looking for marketing talent the AMA may be a valuable addition to your efforts.

American Physical Therapy Assoc.

www.apta.org

1111 North Fairfax Street, Alexandria, VA 22314
Ph: 800/999-2782   Fax: 703/684-7343   E-mail: ptbadvertising@apta.org

JOBS	100s	RESUMES	N/A
Cost to post	Cost to see	Cost to post	Cost to see
Fee	Free	N/A	N/A
DISCIPLINE		LOCATION	
Health Care		USA/	
SPECIALTY		FEATURE	
Allied Health/Physical Therapy		N/A	
AGENT: N/A			

The APTA's PTBulletin Online has more than 100 positions that can be easily viewed by job category, location, practice setting and practice area. Employers pay $25 if members and $50 otherwise. Definitely an adjustment worth exploring.

American Soc. for Quality

www.asq.org/net/career

Cynthia Nazario
600 N. Plankinton Ave., P.O. Box 3005, Milwaukee, WI 53201
Ph: 800-248-1946   Fax: 414-272-1734   E-mail: cnazario@asq.org

JOBS	100s	RESUMES	1,000s
Cost to post	Cost to see	Cost to post	Cost to see
Fee	Fee	Fee	Fee
DISCIPLINE		LOCATION	
Business		USA	
SPECIALTY		FEATURE	
Operations/Manufacturing/QA		N/A	
AGENT: N/A			

The American Society of Quality, (ASQ) has more than 117,000 individual and 1,100 corporate members worldwide. ASQ has formed an alliance with Job and ResumeMatch to provide job posting and resume viewing services. Individual job postings cost $125. Unlimited posting packages ($695/quarter) are also available however recruiting discounts are only offered to corporate members. Resumes can be viewed for $595 a month. Only ASQ members may view job postings or post their resume. This site is very hard to navigate, so remember the job center URL above or you will have trouble finding the correct pages.

American Soc. for Training & Development

www.astd.org

ASTD, 1640 King Street, Box 1443, Alexandria, VA 22313
Ph: 888-491-8833   Fax: 703-683-1523   E-mail: jobbank@astd.org

JOBS	100s	RESUMES	100s
Cost to post	Cost to see	Cost to post	Cost to see
Fee	Free	Free	Fee
DISCIPLINE		LOCATION	
Human Resources		USA	
SPECIALTY		FEATURE	
Training		N/A	
AGENT: Jobseeker			

American Soc. of Training & Development was founded in 1944. ASTD has over 70,000 members in 100 countries representing 15,000 multinational corporations. Recruiters pay $350 for 100 words or less for 30 days. Jobs are date posted and easy to view either through the site's search engine or by scrolling the entire listing. An e-learning community, this is the place to be go if training is key. Resume access comes with the cost of posting. Job seekers can chat online for help.

American Soc. of Agricultural Engineering

www.asae.org

Pamela Bakken
ASA, 2950 Niles Road, St. Joseph, MI 49085
Ph: 616-428-6337   Fax: 616-429-3852   E-mail: bakken@asae.org

JOBS	10s	RESUMES	10s
Cost to post	Cost to see	Cost to post	Cost to see
Fee	Free	Free	Free
DISCIPLINE		LOCATION	
Engineering/Science		USA	
SPECIALTY		FEATURE	
Bio/Agriculture/Food Science		College	
AGENT: N/A			

This resource rich site is the monthly membership publication of the American Society of Agricultural Engineering — the society for engineering in agricultural, food, and biological systems. Jobs can be posted for $110 and includes publication in both "Resource" magazine and on the web site. Members can post their resume for free (non-members pay $55). Posted positions are in industry as well as the academic community. One great feature- "Organizations who have hired agricultural and biosystems engineering graduates in the recent past." Fabulous idea and a new potential best practice opportunity for other sites.

American Soc. of Assoc. Executives

www.asaenet.org/careers

Tammy Cussimanio
1575 I Street, NW, Washington, DC 20005
Ph: 202-626-2723   Fax: 202-371-8825   E-mail: mbrsvccen@asaenet.org

JOBS	100s	RESUMES	100s
Cost to post	Cost to see	Cost to post	Cost to see
Fee	Free	Free	Fee

DISCIPLINE	LOCATION
Non-Profit/Communications	USA

SPECIALTY	FEATURE
Public Relations	Executive

AGENT: Jobseeker

The American Society of Association Executives (ASAE) has 25,000 members who manage over 10,000 leading trade and philanthropic associations. ASAE members can post positions for $200, while non-members pay $300. Each additional job posting is $100 per posting. The fee includes searching the site's resume database. The job listings may be searched by keyword or scrolling. Recruiters can access a blind profile of job candidates and send them an email to determine their interest. ASAE career headquarters acquires about 100 new positions a month. Job seekers can have a resume review and mock interview sessions for a fee ($65-$100). Many of the jobs posted provide salary levels. ASAE has done an outstanding job for their members.

109

American Soc. of Civil Engineers

www.asce.org

Heather Duvall
1801 Alexander Bell Drive, Reston, VA 20191
Ph: 800-548-2723   Fax: 703-295-6222   E-mail: hduvall@asce.org

JOBS	100s	RESUMES	N/A
Cost to post	Cost to see	Cost to post	Cost to see
Fee	Free	N/A	N/A
DISCIPLINE		LOCATION	
Engineering		USA	
SPECIALTY		FEATURE	
Civil		N/A	
AGENT: N/A			

The ASCE publishes the ASCE News and Civil Engineering magazines. If employers advertise in either print publication they will be posted to the website for free during the month their material runs in the print. Posting to the website alone costs $1.00 per word (with a minimum of 50 words) for 30 days. Openings are listed under civil engineering and university classifieds. Despite this society's inability to construct a logical online pricing scheme, the organizations professionals in this field still join.

Apartment Careers

www.apartmentcareers.com

Jason Brown
14900 Landmark Blvd, Suite #300, Dallas, TX 75240
Ph: 877-856-6668   Fax: 972-774-9334   E-mail: info@apartmentcareers.com

JOBS	100s	RESUMES	10,000s
Cost to post	Cost to see	Cost to post	Cost to see
Fee	Free	Free	Fee
DISCIPLINE		LOCATION	
Retail Sales & Services/Trades		USA	
SPECIALTY		FEATURE	
Real Estate		N/A	
AGENT: Both Recruiters & Jobseekers			

Apartment Careers (AC), was launched in 1999. This site provides staffing services for multi-family property owners. Over 374 jobs were posted with recruiters paying $50 to post a position. For $250 recruiters can post two openings and have access to the resume database for 30 days. AC will match incoming resumes to the posted job specifications and email notification to the employer. Job seekers are provided with career resource links for job hunting and resume preparation assistance. Up to 3 resume formats along with video files, photos or other scanned documents can reside on this site. Openings range from housekeepers, maintenance supervisors and leasing agents to information technology professionals. A lengthy list of industry association lists rounds out the site.

Archaeological Fieldwork Opportunites
www.cincpac.com/afos/testpit.html

Ken Stuart
E-mail: kps1@cornell.edu

JOBS	100s	RESUMES	N/A
Cost to post	Cost to see	Cost to post	Cost to see
Fee	Free	N/A	N/A
DISCIPLINE		LOCATION	
Non-profit/Miscellaneous/Education		USA/	
SPECIALTY		FEATURE	
Archeology		N/A	
AGENT: N/A			

There still are fabulous volunteer efforts worth digging up. This site's home page informs you that "Donations of $2.00 to help defray the cost of this service are welcome via PayPal". The site maintains hundreds of listings, each is well documented and easy to navigate. OK, so many of these jobs are seeking students and free volunteers. Well heeled sites should consider adopting these "orphan" labor of love sites like this one. Take a trip here if only to donate.

Army Career & Alumni Program
www.acap.army.mil

200 Stovall Street, Alexandria, VA 22332
Ph: 800-445-2049   Fax: 703-356-7183   E-mail: hoffmanJ@hoffman.army.mil

JOBS	10,000s	RESUMES	N/A
Cost to post	Cost to see	Cost to post	Cost to see
Free	Free	N/A	N/A
DISCIPLINE		LOCATION	
ALL		USA	
SPECIALTY		FEATURE	
ALL		Military Transition	
AGENT: N/A			

The ACAP mission is to "provide timely and effective transition assistance to all Department of Defense personnel and their family members." ACAP operates centers at major military installations around the world and provides mobile or remote services to other Army installations. Anyyone can now access this site to view job opportunities with direct contact information. An updated list of military-sponsored job fairs can be found by going to ACAP Centers and Events.

ArtHire

www.arthire.com

Jarir Maani
1841 Spruce Street, Berkeley, CA 94709
Fax: 509-472-5467   E-mail: info@arthire.com

JOBS	10s		RESUMES	10s
Cost to post	Cost to see		Cost to post	Cost to see
Fee (See Notes)	Free		Free	Free
DISCIPLINE			LOCATION	
Entertainment & Media/Communications			USA	
SPECIALTY			FEATURE	
Graphic Arts/Writing			Contingent	
AGENT: N/A				

ArtHire, launched in August 1998 is geared for visual/music/sound/voice artists, and creative writers. Job seekers can leave their portfolios for recruiters to view. This is a pay-for-performance site, where employers shell out $299 only when they hire an artist. Part-time, contract, projects and regular jobs are featured here. Artists can apply online, via email or send the opening to a friend. Recruiters and job seekers can sign up for an agent and have openings/notices of new artists that match their requirements pushed to their desktops. Positions listed are from across the USA and not just CA and NY. Several are also from international countries. Well designed, a great pricing model, and the owners have the right attitude to make this a successful site.

Asia-Links

www.asia-links.com

Mei-Ling Leong
1270 Oakmead Pkwy.,, Suite, Sunnydale, CA 94085
Ph: 408-245-9264   Fax: 408-245-9284   E-mail: sales@asia-links.com

JOBS	10s		RESUMES	10,000s
Cost to post	Cost to see		Cost to post	Cost to see
Fee	Free		Free	Fee
DISCIPLINE			LOCATION	
ALL			INTL/Pacific Rim	
SPECIALTY			FEATURE	
ALL			Executive	
AGENT: Employer				

Asia-Links (A-L) was launched in 1997 for technology professionals (engineers, sales, marketing and executives) in the U.S. and Asia. Recruiters pay $150 to post a position or $500to access the resume database with unlimited job posting for 30 days. A-L will also advertise job postings in their newsletter and send them to candidates with matching interests. "Ask Sean" provides helpful information on immigration and visas.

Asia-Net

www.asia-net.com

Mike Nishi
1-F, Unosawa Tokyu Bldg,,, 1-19-15 Ebisu, Shibuya-ku, Tokyo, 153-0013 Japan
Ph: 810-357-953080   Fax: 810-357-953070   E-mail: help@asia-net.com

JOBS	100s	RESUMES	1,000s
Cost to post	Cost to see	Cost to post	Cost to see
Fee	Free	Free	Fee
DISCIPLINE		LOCATION	
ALL		INTL/Pacific Rim	
SPECIALTY		FEATURE	
ALL		Diversity	
AGENT: Jobseeker			

Asia-Net, an active site since 1994, was reviewed in one of the early editions of CareerXroads. Ownership has changed hands, but this continues to be a high perfomance sitewith an excellent ability to deliver the goods. Their premise continues to be that "whoever has the most emails wins." Recruiters post jobs, and the site sends emails (over 140,00 in the database) to skill-matched potential job seekers and promises that candidates are replying in 72 hours. The site builds community and works to connect bilingual talent with opportunities in the U.S., Singapore, Japan and Hong Kong. Demographics of the Asia-Net community can easily be viewed. The last price we saw was $2,000 per email push of a job to their members.

Assoc. for Financial Professionals

www.afponline.org

Shannon Hatfield
7315 Wisconsin Avenue, Suite 600 West, Bethesda, MD 20814
Ph: 301-907-2862   Fax: 301-907-2864   E-mail: agreen@afponline.org

JOBS	100s	RESUMES	1,000s
Cost to post	Cost to see	Cost to post	Cost to see
Fee	Fee (See Notes)	Fee	Fee
DISCIPLINE		LOCATION	
Business		USA	
SPECIALTY		FEATURE	
Finance		EXECUTIVE	
AGENT: Jobseeker			

The Association for Financial Professionals was launched in February 1999 with over 14,000 individual members. This 20-year-old association understands the financial marketplace. Only members can access the entire job database, but non-members can get a pretty good peek for free. Openings at all levels, from clerks to vice presidents are posted. Recruiters pay $250 to post an opening for 60 days and to access the resume database. Career fairs sponsored by the association are also available. Managed by Boxwood technology.

Assoc. for Women in Mathematics

www.awm-math.org

Aileen Gormley
4114 Computer & Space Sci. Bld, University of Maryland, College Park, MD 20742
Ph: 301-405-7892   Fax: 301-314-9363   E-mail: awm-ads@awm-math.org

JOBS	10s	RESUMES	N/A
Cost to post	Cost to see	Cost to post	Cost to see
Fee	Free	N/A	N/A
DISCIPLINE		LOCATION	
Education		USA	
SPECIALTY		FEATURE	
Teaching, University/Mathematics		DIVERSITY	
AGENT: N/A			

The Association for Women in Mathematics emphasizes teaching positions at the university level (although we did see a few private corporations looking for statisticians here). With over 4,100 members, this group encourages women to consider careers in the mathematical sciences. Recruiters pay $1.50 per word with a $150 minimum fee. Openings are posted in date order with links to the poster's site. Their numbers (jobs) may be small but they do add up. Site has helpful links to other sites with jobs and career content.

Assoc. of Clinical Research Professionals

www.acrpnet.org

Brian Lonergan
1012 14th Street, NW, Suite 80, Washington, DC 20005
Ph: 202-737-8100   Fax: 202-737-8101   E-mail: acrp@jobmark.com

JOBS	100s	RESUMES	N/A
Cost to post	Cost to see	Cost to post	Cost to see
Fee	Free	N/A	N/A
DISCIPLINE		LOCATION	
Science		USA/	
SPECIALTY		FEATURE	
Bio/Clinical Research		N/A	
AGENT: N/A			

Just launched during the summer of 2002, the ACRP Career Center has more than 100 posted positions including 50 for CRAs. The association has 17,000 members. Current price to post is $200. Can't get more targeted than this.

Assoc. of eX-Lotus Employees

www.axle.org

6 Dexter Road, Lexington, MA
Ph: 781-862-4058   E-mail: advertising@corporatealumni.com

JOBS	10s	RESUMES	1,000s
Cost to post	Cost to see	Cost to post	Cost to see
Free	Free	Free	Free
DISCIPLINE		LOCATION	
IT		USA	
SPECIALTY		FEATURE	
Lotus Notes		N/A	
AGENT: N/A			

The Association of eX-Lotus Employees has 2,300+ members participating in this site. New to CXR, this is site has little money involved. Employers can email job listings for free. The people in the navigation bar's picture deserve to be hired for being willing to show themselves. Site is powered by Corporate Alumni and is developng a culture that deserves recognition. Examine the directory of where employees are now.

Atlanta Smart City

www.atlantasmartcity.com

Rosita Smith
Metro Atlanta Chamber of Commerce, 235 A. Young Blvd. NW, Atlanta, GA 30303
Ph: 404-880-9000   E-mail: rsmith@macoc.com

JOBS	100s	RESUMES	N/A
Cost to post	Cost to see	Cost to post	Cost to see
Free	Free	N/A	N/A
DISCIPLINE		LOCATION	
ALL		USA/SOE/GA/Atlanta	
SPECIALTY		FEATURE	
ALL		N/A	
AGENT: N/A			

Designed to attract high-tech workers to Atlanta, GA, this chamber of commerce-sponsored site has glitz. The introduction would definitely get a Silicon Valley techie to think about a move.Try "work" for the job pot of gold. Job seekers can search via company name, industry, job category or title to links of area corporations. Employers can post a company profile to the site and have a link to their site for free. Job seekers can utilize a lengthy list of local professional associations links.

AttorneyJobsOnline
www.attorneyjobs.com

1010 Vermont Avenue NW, Suite 408, Washington, DC 20005
Ph: 800-296-9611   Fax: 202-393-1553   E-mail: job@attorneyjobs.com

JOBS	1,000s	RESUMES	1,000s
Cost to post	Cost to see	Cost to post	Cost to see
Free	Fee	Free	Fee
DISCIPLINE		LOCATION	
Law & Order		USA	
SPECIALTY		FEATURE	
Attorney		N/A	
AGENT: N/A			

AttorneyJobsOnline was launched in April 1999 and is the successor to AttorneyJobs, The National and Federal Legal Employment Report, which was published monthly since 1979. The last hard-copy edition of AttorneyJobs was printed in June 1999. Members pay $15 for a 30-day subscription. A selected section titled, "Hot jobs," can be browsed for free, but is a subscription teaser for employers who are willing to pay $200 for one-week exposure. The standard job database costs $100 for a 30-day run. Government openings can be posted for free. The site claims thousands of attorney and law-related openings, clerkships, fellowships and legal search positions in the public and private sectors. Headhunters can submit coded candidate resumes for employers to view. Site claims opportunities around the world but we could only view USA openings. Career questions can be emailed to a legal career counselor and are selectively answered.

JOB SEEKER TIP

Find a map of where you live.

Draw a commutable circle. Call your local library to obtain a list of the corporations within your circle and find their URL. Of the Fortune 500, 498 have websites and most post job openings.

AuntMinnie.com
www.auntminnie.com

Phillip Berman
1350 North Kolb Road, Tucson, AZ 85715
Ph: 619-522-0880   Fax: 707-276-2492   E-mail: berman@auntminnie.com

JOBS	1,000s	RESUMES	N/A
Cost to post	Cost to see	Cost to post	Cost to see
Fee	Free	N/A	N/A
DISCIPLINE		LOCATION	
Health Care		USA	
SPECIALTY		FEATURE	
MD/Radiology		N/A	
AGENT: N/A			

AuntMinnie.com is a community site for radiologists and related professionals in the medical imaging field. Recruiters and job seekers who wish to utilize this site must register. We did and, fortunately, they allowed us to use our standard passwords. Openings are searched by profession, location or keyword. Job seekers will appreciate when searches are done. AM provides the number of open listings by state and by profession. Registration also assures that matching job seeker profiles can be sent to employers with one click. Recruiters pay $225 to post a job for one month. AM is well designed with the customer in mind.

117

Australian Job Search
jobsearch.gov.au

JOBS	10,000s		RESUMES	N/A
Cost to post	Cost to see		Cost to post	Cost to see
Fee	Free		N/A	N/A
DISCIPLINE			LOCATION	
ALL			USA	
SPECIALTY			FEATURE	
ALL			N/A	
AGENT: N/A				

Australian Job Search offers the most intuitive search process we've yet seen. Pick an occupation an you'll immediately be shown several sub areas. Each area has the number of current openings next to it to eliminate chasing imaginary openings. Choose one, two or all with a single click and, next, you'll see a map of the country showing the number of jobs of the type selected that are currently available by state. Click a state and you'll see the state broken into regions. This works all the way down to neighborhoods- always with the number of available positions clearly presented. When you start with 50,000 fresh jobs, you get where you are going. Kudos to the Aussies for this excellent model.

Autojobs.com
www.autodealerjobs.com

Steve Brown
Steve Brown & Associates, Montrose, CO 81401
Ph: 888-915-1112   Fax: 970-240-1986   E-mail: sales@autojobs.com

JOBS	100s		RESUMES	1,000s
Cost to post	Cost to see		Cost to post	Cost to see
Fee	Fee		Fee	Free
DISCIPLINE			LOCATION	
Retail Sales & Services			USA & Canada	
SPECIALTY			FEATURE	
Automotive			N/A	
AGENT: N/A				

AUTOjobs.com offers both "help-wanted" and "position-wanted" services. Recruiters can post openings for $150 (2 weeks). Jobs can include a logo, e-mail link and hyper link back to the company web site. Job seekers can post their "position wanted" ad for $75 for 3 months. The site breaks out openings by dealership departments and then by region of the USA and Canada. Easy to use positions are listed here for Franchise Dealers, OEM, Aftermarket, Manufacturers, Suppliers, Independent Retailers, Repair Facilities, Rental, & Collision Repair Facilities

Autobody Online
www.autobodyonline.com

Bob Richards
Box 599, 1050 Dale Drive, Hudson, IA
Ph: 800-367-6575   Fax: 319-988-5538   E-mail: sales@csiauto.com

JOBS	10s	RESUMES	10s
Cost to post	Cost to see	Cost to post	Cost to see
Free	Free	Free	Free
DISCIPLINE		LOCATION	
Cust. Service & Tech. Support/Trades		USA	
SPECIALTY		FEATURE	
Automotive		N/A	
AGENT: N/A			

Autobody Online, provides opportunities for automotive body technicians thoughout the USA. Collision Services offers a free service for recruiters to post positions and view resume profiles, which expire after 60 days. Jobs and resumes can be searched by state or title (i.e. body technician, management, paint technician, estimator or other). All openings have links to the recruiters site for additional information. A discussion forum adds to the tremendous industry content to entice a return visit. Job seekers and employers can easily find what they need and get back to work.

AV Jobs
www.avjobs.com

Amanda Lahey
Airline Employment Ass't. Corp., PO Box 260830, Littleton, CO 80163
Ph: 303-683-2322   Fax: 888-624-8691   E-mail: info@avjobs

JOBS	100s	RESUMES	100s
Cost to post	Cost to see	Cost to post	Cost to see
Free	Fee	Fee	Free
DISCIPLINE		LOCATION	
Miscellaneous/Engineering		USA	
SPECIALTY		FEATURE	
Aviation/Pilots/Aerospace		N/A	
AGENT: Jobseeker			

Airline Employment Ass't Corp. & AV Jobs WorldWide requires all pilots, mechanics and engineers to pay $19.95 for a basic membership. Only the job of the week can be viewed for free. Recruiters can search the resume database for free and receive contact detailed pilot background data (i.e. types of planes flown and dates of navigation). Chat rooms, industry salary data make this a site to visit if you wan to fly the friendly skies. Best practice disclosure of jobs posted by function and recency makes this site a top notch choice despite its cost to the jobseeker.

John Ellis
Unit 1, Lyes Farm, Cuckfield Road, Burgess Hill, West Sussex, Sussex RH15 8RG United Kingdom
Ph: 440-144-4241177 Fax: 440-144-4253388 E-mail: accounts@aviationjobsearch.com

JOBS	1,000s	RESUMES	1,000s
Cost to post	Cost to see	Cost to post	Cost to see
Fee	Free	Free	Fee
DISCIPLINE		LOCATION	
Miscellaneous		INTL/Europe/UK	
SPECIALTY		FEATURE	
Aviation/Pilots		N/A	
AGENT: Jobseeker			

The aviationjobsearch.com home page invites visitors to register and promises to notify them when new jobs are posted. The site also discloses that 3,905 jobs are in the database. Openings are broken into "in the air" and "on the ground" positions. Most positions that we saw listed here were in Europe, and ranged from check-in attendants and baggage handlers to flight crew and catering staff. Access to the resume database is for a fee but no information was available on the site. Posted openings by agencies are separate from corporate postings,and the price was 95 pounds for four weeks. Job seekers can register their resumes at the site, but are not advised what happens with it. Some added disclosure would be worthwhile.

JOB SEEKER TIP

Each month, you need to obtain 100 new job leads...

and make 10 telephone calls a day to new contacts. This will yield 4–6 interviews a month.

No fair calling Mom more than once a week.

BA Jobs

www.bajobs.com

Conrad V. Lopez
855 El Camino Real, Suite 401, Palo Alto, CA 94301
Ph: 650-833-8018   Fax: 650-833-8001   E-mail: helpdesk@bajobs.com

JOBS	1,000s	RESUMES	1,000s
Cost to post	Cost to see	Cost to post	Cost to see
Fee	Free	Free	Fee

DISCIPLINE	LOCATION
ALL	USA/WEST/CA/San Francisco

SPECIALTY	FEATURE
ALL	N/A

AGENT: Job Seeker & Recruiter

BAJobs (Bay Area) is simplicity in motion, with an elegant design for the San Francisco area. Lots of improvement has been made since the site's launching in 1997. Employers post positions for $125 (access to the resume bank is $1,000 per quarter). Job seekers can either use the search engine, occupation listing, or index of companies to find openings, as well as receive information on how many times their resumes have been viewed. Of the 1,282 jobs posted, only 66 were in information technology. Last time we paid a visit both numbers were double. Corporate information can be linked to each opening. A salary wizard, local career events, links to other Bay Area resources and good disclosure make this a local site worth a visit.

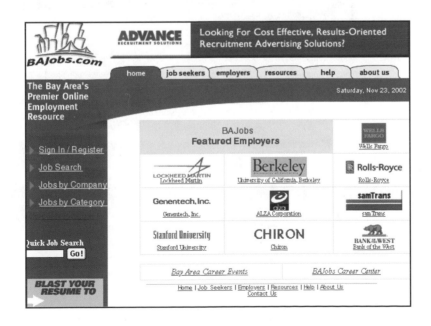

Backdoorjobs

www.backdoorjobs.com

Michael Landes
14 Main St., Goldens Bridge, NY 10526
Ph: 914-232-9366   E-mail: listings@backdoorjobs.com

JOBS	100s	RESUMES	N/A
Cost to post	Cost to see	Cost to post	Cost to see
Fee	Free	N/A	N/A
DISCIPLINE		LOCATION	
Miscellaneous		USA	
SPECIALTY		FEATURE	
Ourdoors/Adventure		N/A	
AGENT: N/A			

Launched in 1997, Backdoorjobs.com is an adventure site for unique internships, summer jobs and other part-time opportunities to explore different and strange careers like an Alaskan river guide. An informative and enjoyable site to peruse. Site owner is the author of The Back Door Guide to Short-Term Job Adventures. The programs profiled offer their jobs season after season, summer after summer, or year after year. A small fee is charged ($75 for six months; $150 for one year) and many nonprofit programs are listed for free. The content changes at least once a week and during peak hiring seasons it can change on a daily basis.

Backstagejobs.com

www.backstagejobs.com

Patrick Hudson
4517 N Central Park Ave. #3 W, Chicago, IL 60625
Ph: 773-509-9424   E-mail: ads@backstagejobs.com

JOBS	100s	RESUMES	100s
Cost to post	Cost to see	Cost to post	Cost to see
Free	Free	Free (Contact info)	Free
DISCIPLINE		LOCATION	
Entertainment & Media/Trades		USA	
SPECIALTY		FEATURE	
Stage craft		N/A	
AGENT: N/A			

Backstagejobs is what it says it is- behind the scenes. Job listings are sorted by job type. Internships are kept separate. Employee profiles (The Contact Sheets) are short paragraphs that list the applicants' skills (depth of knowlege and desire),and contact information. They are sorted by city/geographic area.The site provides links to other theatre job sites, and some links to acting/audition sites,in order to help jobs seekers find work ("if you don't find one here, try one of these other job sites"). These are non-sponsored links. The site also boasts an exhaustive links page to theatre and live entertainment related web sites and internet resources.

Bakery-Net
www.bakery-net.com

Brenda Sizemore
Donohue-Meehan Publishing Co., 2700 River Road, Suite 303, Des Plaines, IL
Ph: 847-299-4430   E-mail: bsizemore@penton.com

JOBS	10s		RESUMES	10s
Cost to post	Cost to see		Cost to post	Cost to see
Fee	Free		Free	Free
DISCIPLINE			LOCATION	
Hospitality & Food Services/Retail			USA	
SPECIALTY			FEATURE	
ALL			N/A	
AGENT: N/A				

With over 22,000 registered users and Penton Publishing as its new owner Bakery-Net continues to get a rise out of us. Employers post positions for $25-$40 per job for 30 days after registering. Resumes can be posted and viewed for free. Resumes are listed by date and the title of the position wanted is highlighted for ease of reading. There are some great recipies listed if you are baking for large parties (chocolate rugalach for 265 mmm!). Be prepared to answer questions regarding your affiliation with the industry if you register.

BankJobSearch (BAI)
www.bankjobsearch.com

Lori Dicker
Bank Administration Institute, One North Franklin, Suite 1000, Chicago, IL 60606
Ph: 800-224-9889   Fax: 800-375-5543   E-mail: mkennedy@bai.org

JOBS	100s		RESUMES	N/A
Cost to post	Cost to see		Cost to post	Cost to see
Free	Free		N/A	N/A
DISCIPLINE			LOCATION	
Business			USA	
SPECIALTY			FEATURE	
Finance/Banking			N/A	
AGENT: N/A				

BankJobSearch.com offers forums, information about events, an online publication and a free job posting service. The Bank Administration Institute (BAI) is a professional organization devoted to improving the financial services field. Jobs can be searched by location, job category, company or keyword. Openings are viewed by date of posting, job title, company and location. There were over 260 openings listed here on our visit. To our surprise, it is all free. The site provides industry salary surveys for a fee.

bankjobs.com
www.bankjobs.com

Charles Bentley
Careers Inc., 104 Woodmont Blvd., Nashville, TN 37205
Ph: 800-999-6497   Fax: 615-242-2785   E-mail: info@bankjobs.com

JOBS	100s		RESUMES	1,000s
Cost to post	Cost to see		Cost to post	Cost to see
Fee	Free(See Notes)		Free	Fee
DISCIPLINE			LOCATION	
Business			USA	
SPECIALTY			FEATURE	
Finance/Banking			N/A	
AGENT: Jobseeker				

Bankjobs.com tries to keep visitors up-to-date on industry happenings while providing job services. Recruiters pay $45 to post a position. The resume database costs $895 per year for unlimited searches, but the resumes can be searched for free without the contact information so you can check the database for free to determine if it is worth purchasing. Owners claim to receive 200+ new resumes per week. Job seekers are asked to submit a resume to obtain a password to search for openings. A job preview is available without registration. Several major national banking institutions individually post hundreds of jobs to this site.

Bay Recruiter.com
www.bayrecruiter.com

John Brennan
Bay Recruiter Alliance,
Ph: 415-865-9453   E-mail: jbrennan@sfchronicle.com

JOBS	1,000s		RESUMES	1,000s
Cost to post	Cost to see		Cost to post	Cost to see
Fee	Free (See Notes)		N/A	N/A
DISCIPLINE			LOCATION	
ALL			USA/WEST/CA/San Francisco	
SPECIALTY			FEATURE	
ALL			N/A	
AGENT: N/A				

The Bay Recruiter Alliance is a community consortium that includes the San Francisco Chronicle. This site works a little differently then most. Employers pay $149 per job posting for a 30 day run. The site automatically searches its candidate profile database for matches. Candidates are informed by email that an opening has matched their posted profile and are then encouraged to return to the site to answer the qualifying questions the employer has posted. If the candidate achieves the score required by the employer's screened in response they receive an e-mail and are advised to contact the candidate directly. Job seekers must register to view posted positions.

Benefit News Online

www.benefitnews.com

Michelle Yosslowitz
Thomson Financial, 1455 Research Blvd., Mclean, VA 20850
Ph: 770-988-9558   E-mail: info@benefitnews.com

JOBS	10s	RESUMES	10s
Cost to post	Cost to see	Cost to post	Cost to see
Free	Free	Free	Free
DISCIPLINE		LOCATION	
Human Resources		USA	
SPECIALTY		FEATURE	
Benefits		N/A	
AGENT: N/A			

Benefit News Online is brought to you by the publishers of Employee Benefit News, a specialty-magazine serving human resource benefits professionals. Excellent articles on every conceivable benefit area can be accessed from this site. Visitors must register, but then can view or post openings and search listed resumes for free. Jobs and resumes are posted for 60 days, then deleted. Speaking as a human resources professional, their newsletter is by far one of the best. Register to have the newsletter pushed to your desktop. Unfortunately, the newsletter doesn't include jobs.

JOB SEEKER TIP

Do not rely 100 percent on the Internet to obtain your next job.

You still need to network, use employee referrals and obtain as many contacts as possible.

Do not get "webitis."

BenefitsLink
www.benefitslink.com

Mary Hall
1298 Minnesota Avenue, Suite H, Winter Park, FL 32789
Ph: 407-644-4146   Fax: 407-644-2151   E-mail: maryhall@benefitslink.com

JOBS	100s	RESUMES	1,000s
Cost to post	Cost to see	Cost to post	Cost to see
Fee	Free	Free	Fee

DISCIPLINE	LOCATION
Human Resources	USA

SPECIALTY	FEATURE
Benefits	N/A

AGENT: Job Seeker

Arriving at BenefitsLink job seekers can easily find opportunities by state, title, location or employer. For a niche site the design is perfectly tailored to provide job seekers and recruiters with exactly what they want. Instructions to post an opening are easy to follow and flexible enough for anyone. The cost is $200 for a 60-day listing which includes access to the resume database. Resume database access alone is $200 per month. Ads are also emailed to the sites 2,985 registered job seekers. Recruiters know exactly the number of hits their job ad receives because it is recorded at the top of each posting. There is no charge for job seekers to subscribe to the mailing list. Tremendous industry information is available, which makes the job seeker return again and again. BenefitsLink has been building a community connection since 1995, and hasn't given up ground to its competitors. What few other sites understand as well as this one is the importance of up-front disclosure. Simplicity is a virtue, and this site is stillone of the best in its class.

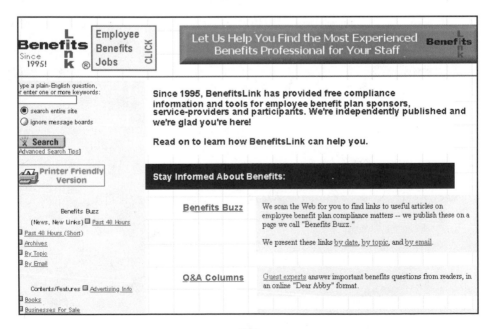

BigFiveTalent.com
www.bigfivetalent.com

David B. Hunegnaw
691 North High Street, Suite 301, Columbus, OH 43215
Ph: 866-238-2536   Fax: 614-228-2866   E-mail: info@bigfivetalent.com

JOBS	1,000s	RESUMES	1,000s
Cost to post	Cost to see	Cost to post	Cost to see
Fee	Free	Free	Fee
DISCIPLINE		LOCATION	
Business		USA	
SPECIALTY		FEATURE	
Finance/Accounting/MBA		EXECUTIVE	
AGENT: Jobseeker			

BigFiveTalent.com, launched in March 2001 and allows recruiters to post a position and have access to the resume database for one month for $120. The site obviously focuses on current and former employees of the major bean counting/consulting firms, type A personalities who for whatever reason have gotten off the "I have to be a partner by 30 train." Job-seeker contact information can be public or private as they need to have worked for one of these firms to gain access to the site. Openings are date-posted and many offered salary information. Job seekers must submit a resume before gaining access to openings. It is ironic to note that the Big Five (no four, no three) firms also advertise here.

BioExchange.com
www.bioexchange.com

Eric Stone
758 Clementina Street, San Francisco, CA 94103
Ph: 888-835-6276   Fax: 888-835-6276   E-mail: career@bioexchange.com

JOBS	100s	RESUMES	10,000s
Cost to post	Cost to see	Cost to post	Cost to see
Fee	Free	Free	Fee
DISCIPLINE		LOCATION	
Science		USA	
SPECIALTY		FEATURE	
Bio/Biotech/Pharm/Life Science		N/A	
AGENT: Both Recruiters & Jobseekers			

BioExchange.com started in July 2000 and offers opportunities in the life sciences (molecular biology, biotechnology and bioinformatics). Statistics regarding openings are prominently displayed on the home page and next to each job category. Recruiters pay $150 to post a position for 90 days and can have access to the resume database for $1,000. Recruiters can create a resume search agent and prospects with matching skill sets will be sent as they are posted. Job openings can be viewed by keyword, category, location, company, all jobs or international. Job seekers can view employer profiles, maintain a perpetual listing of all openings they have applied to but must repond to all interested openings through BE. What would stop a job seeker from going direct ? CXR applauds sites that provide metrics to job seekers and employers.

Biofind

www.biofind.com

Regent House, Heaton La, Stockport, Cheshire United Kingdom
E-mail: advertising@biofind.com

JOBS	10s	RESUMES	1,000s
Cost to post	Cost to see	Cost to post	Cost to see
Fee	Free	Free	Free
DISCIPLINE		LOCATION	
Science		INTL & USA	
SPECIALTY		FEATURE	
Bio/Biotech/Pharm/Life Science		N/A	
AGENT: Both Recruiters & Jobseekers			

Biofind promises a "one-stop-shop for world wide Biotechnology industry information, gossip and news. The site does have an excellent variety of content and job tools. The "Cartoon of the day" is a fun addition. The "Rumor-Mill" and "chat" room are great features for building community. Site specializes in diagnostics, pharmaceutical, medical device and biotechnology. Biofind pushes resumes (2,567) to recruiters and positions to job seekers. Stats are posted on the jobs page and include the % breakdown of jobs in the database by category. Recruiters pay $250 to post a position (55 were listed). Higher rates add "rumor mill" references to your job. Resumes are free to see. A European site with (mostly) USA jobs. All previous openings are archived and should be studied by job seekers to target companies.

BioSpace.com

www.biospace.com

Timothy Fredel
245 11th Street, San Francisco, CA 94203
Ph: 415-355-6500   Fax: 415-977-1070   E-mail: employersupport@biospace.com

JOBS	100s	RESUMES	1,000s
Cost to post	Cost to see	Cost to post	Cost to see
Fee	Free	N/A	N/A
DISCIPLINE		LOCATION	
Science		USA	
SPECIALTY		FEATURE	
Bio/Pharm/Life Science		N/A	
AGENT: N/A			

Jobs at BioSpace.com will be posted within 24 hours of receipt. Each job runs for 4 weeks at a cost of $175. Current BioSpace clients who have a company profile will pay $120. Two days before the job expires, employers receive a traffic report via email that indicates the number of times each job was accessed (great feature) and, of course, you can request to run the job ad again for another four weeks. Postings are checked by the site every Friday to verify they are still open. BioSpace.com's home page provides a daily update of industry news. The site career center lists links to jobs by company and hundreds are listed in alpha order. Career Fairs are run across the USA costing $2-6,000.

BioView (Monster)

www.bioview.com

Mike Pauletich
807 Broadway, Oakland, CA 94607
Ph: 510-208-5744   Fax: 510-268-0408   E-mail: info@bioview.com

JOBS	1,000s		RESUMES	10,000s
Cost to post	Cost to see		Cost to post	Cost to see
Fee	Free		Free	Fee
DISCIPLINE			LOCATION	
Science			USA	
SPECIALTY			FEATURE	
Bio/Pharm/Life Sciences			N/A	
AGENT: Jobseeker				

BioView is now owned by Monster and we hope that it is not folded in with their other acquisitions and allowed its own identity. This site continues to provide job seekers with the number of openings by job function. A separate category for contract (66) positions has also been created. A single job posting is $225 for 60 days. Access to resumes costs $1,000 per month or $4,000 per year. The site also offers job agents to passive job seekers. BioView publishes an opt-in daily email newsletter that includes listings of new jobs posted to the site. Listings of industry layoffs, conferences and corporate profiles gives job seekers and recruiters added reason to visit. Posted openings can be "wrapped" from a corporate site to BV or other sites of the recruiters choosing. This is a major time saver. Biolinks offers hyperlinks to associations, research tools, journals and much more.

Bio.com

www.bio.com

Julie Chang
Bio Online, 2855 Telegraph Ave., Berkeley, CA 94705
Ph: 510-548-1171   Fax: 510-548-1173   E-mail: sales@bio.com

JOBS	1,000s		RESUMES	N/A
Cost to post	Cost to see		Cost to post	Cost to see
Fee	Free		Free	N/A (See Notes)
DISCIPLINE			LOCATION	
Science			USA	
SPECIALTY			FEATURE	
Bio/Pharm			N/A	
AGENT: Jobseeker				

Launched as a bulletin board in 1992, bio.com continues to provide services for the life science and pharmaceutical research community. Over 1,700 jobs are listed. Recruiters pay $185 to post a position for 30 days. The site requests that job seekers post their resume so they can apply for online positions. Job seekers can register for up to 5 agents to push positions to them via email, as well as an opt-in feature to have life science recruiters contact them. Employers can add interview questions to their job postings. No resume database is available for recruiters to view. A moderated career forum includes interesting questions and relevant answers. Job seekers should check out the career guide section for added advice. CXR particularly enjoyed the article "Burn Your Resume; Build a Resume Portfolio" by Don Straits. The site provides volumes of industry content to attract the job seeker.

129

The Black Collegian Online

www.blackcollegian.com

Pres Edwards
IMDiversity, 909 Polydras Street, 36th Floor, New Orleans, LA 70112
Ph: 504-523-0154   E-mail: info@black-collegiate.com

JOBS	1,000s		RESUMES	10,000s
Cost to post	Cost to see		Cost to post	Cost to see
Fee	Free		Free	Fee
DISCIPLINE			LOCATION	
ALL			USA	
SPECIALTY			FEATURE	
ALL			College/Diversity	
AGENT: N/A				

This is the electronic version of the 30+ year-old Black Collegian magazine, a well known national career opportunities publication that targets the college market. Employers post jobs directly for $175 for a 60-day run, or they can obtain an annual membership for unlimited postings. Only with a site membership can recruiters gain access to the resume database. CareerCast technology has recently been installed to make job seeker and recruiters journey's a smooth ride. Opportunites can be searched by keyword, location or job function. All keyword matches are highlighted for ease of reading. Job seekers can view all posted openings by the same employer with one click. The resume database allows students and young professionals to post their backgrounds (in confidence if they wish). Black Collegian also owns IMDiversity. Interesting career articles for the recent college graduate are well written and on target. Check out the articles on studying abroad.

Black Voices.com (CareerBuilder)

www.blackvoices.com

Barry Cooper
Tribune Company, 435 N. Michigan Avenue, Chicago, IL 60611
Ph: 312-222-4474   E-mail: careers@blackvoices.com

JOBS	100s		RESUMES	10,000s
Cost to post	Cost to see		Cost to post	Cost to see
Fee	Free		Free	Fee
DISCIPLINE			LOCATION	
ALL			USA	
SPECIALTY			FEATURE	
ALL			DIVERSITY	
AGENT: Jobseeker				

Black Voices.com (BV), started in 1997 is a wholly owned subsidiary of the Tribune Companies and claims 800,000 members have registered here. Job seekers will only be seeing opportunities that recruiters have targeted for BV. Powered by CareerCast's technology all keyword searches are highlighted for ease of viewing. Job seekers can keep their resume private or open to all employers, obtain an agent who will ask for their email/skills and send matching jobs to their desktop. We especially like the Q & A columns from the Chicago Tribune that are posted here. Job seekers should check out George Fraser's "Getting Your Foot in the Door". BV charges $175 per job posting per month and $500 for access to the resume database. BV also publishes a quarterly magazine targeted to alumni from historically black colleges and universities.

The Blue Line

www.theblueline.com

Kevin Woodside
872 S. Milwaukee Ave., Suite 270, Libertyville, IL 60048
Ph: 800-475-6183   Fax: 847-548-0333   E-mail: kevin@theblueline.com

JOBS	100s	RESUMES	N/A
Cost to post	Cost to see	Cost to post	Cost to see
Free	Fee	N/A	N/A
DISCIPLINE		LOCATION	
Law & Order		USA/MDW	
SPECIALTY		FEATURE	
Police		N/A	
AGENT: Jobseeker			

The Blue Line has partnered with militaryhire.com to provide opportunites for those men and women who wear the badge. Job seekers pay $59.95 for a one year subscription to view all openings. Jobs can be posted for free. Featured department job ads can be seen for free and posted at a cost that ranges from $199-$268 for one or both sites. The owner's monthly publication is for those in police, fire, EMS, dispatch and corrections. Job seekers are pushed a bi-weekly update on posted positions via email or sent a print version. The owners state that 50% of their job seeker/openings come from the midwest with the balance distributed over the USA. The site concentrates its efforts in IL, WI, MI and MO and has several hundred fresh openings per month. A teaser edition of the publication is on the site so visitors can see the opportunities they missed out on. For the top brass, thepoliceexecutive.com has been created.

Boston Job Bank

www.bostonjobs.com

Charles Jukiewicz, Jr.
2 Watson Street, Somerville, MA 02144
Ph: 617-625-1969   E-mail: info@bostonjobs.com

JOBS	1,000s	RESUMES	1,000s
Cost to post	Cost to see	Cost to post	Cost to see
Fee	Free	Free	Free
DISCIPLINE		LOCATION	
ALL		USA/NOE/MA/Boston	
SPECIALTY		FEATURE	
ALL		N/A	
AGENT: Both Recruiters & Jobseekers			

Boston Job Bank original shareware presence, is still in evidence on the site. Recruiters are invited to post their openings at $50 for two months, and the site promises the job will be up in 24 hours. Recruiters can then send the check. A long list of links to Boston-based employment agencies is available. Resumes are presently free for recruiters to view. Jobs are date-posted (over 2,000 on our last visit) and daily skill-matched positions will be emailed to all registered job seekers. Boston Job Bank is designed so that the sliders go down easy. Well done.

Boston Works- Boston Globe

bostonworks.com

Paige Montgomery
320 Congress Street, Boston, MA 02125
Ph: 888-566-4562   Fax: 617-929-7026   E-mail: advertise@boston.com

JOBS	10,000s	RESUMES	100,000s
Cost to post	Cost to see	Cost to post	Cost to see
Fee	Free	Free	Fee

DISCIPLINE	LOCATION
ALL	USA/NOE/MA/Boston

SPECIALTY	FEATURE
ALL	N/A

AGENT: Both Recruiters & Jobseekers

Boston.com (a great URL) in partnership with The Boston Globe, has created BostonWorks as the ultimate source for job listings and career management information in the greater Boston area. Recruiters have access to 15,000 jobs and 300,000 resumes. Owners advise they receive 20,000 new resumes a month. The site has great content, online chat, salary calculator and everything else you would expect from a major publisher. The basic price is $195 for one listing for 28 days, and access to the resume database is $150 for one user per month. Recruiters can "wrap" their website openings so no manual posting is necessary. Job seekers can search the help-wanted classifieds from The Boston Globe. Especially helpful is the globe 100 listing of the top performing Massachusetts companies. Niche sections include healthcare, biotechnology, finance, technology, education, sales and legal. The site is also building networks both local and national.

Brainbench
www.brainbench.com

Ian Strain
14901 Bogle Drive, Chantilly, VA 20151
Ph: 703-437-4800   Fax: 703-437-8003   E-mail: ian.strain@brainbench.com

JOBS	N/A	RESUMES	1,000,000s
Cost to post	Cost to see	Cost to post	Cost to see
N/A	N/A	Free	Fee

DISCIPLINE		LOCATION	
IT		USA	

SPECIALTY		FEATURE	
ALL		Testing	

AGENT: N/A

Brainbench continues to expand as it offers pre-employment testing with a twist. The site is attempting to set standards for information technology, finance, human resources, sales and administration by certifying that individuals have passed their testing requirements. Recruiters have access to an opt-in candidate database that includes test results on over 1 million pre-screened candidates. Owners claim over 3.7 million participants have taken their tests. Over 80 percent are information technology professionals. Recruiters pay $8,000 for access to one regional resume database in the U.S. and $6,800 for two to four additional regions. Examples of certifications include Java, Oracle, Linux, Flash 5, Cisco Network Design, Perl, Internet Security, Financial Auditing, Pharmaceuticals Clinical Trials and Fireworks 4. They even have a test for childcare fundamentals.

Brainhunter.com
www.brainhunter.com

99 Atlantic Avenue, Suite 200, Toronto, M6K3J8 Canada
Ph: 416.588.7111   Fax: 416.588.9239   E-mail: sales@brainhunter.com

JOBS	100s	RESUMES	100s
Cost to post	Cost to see	Cost to post	Cost to see
Fee	Free	Free	Fee

DISCIPLINE		LOCATION	
ALL		INTL/Canada	

SPECIALTY		FEATURE	
ALL		N/A	

AGENT: N/A

Originally a 3rd party site, Brainhunter.com has evolved to a job site hosting service for dozens of associations. What is clearly evident from their home page are the links to the associations they power and a simple means to post on them (Insurance, HealthCare, Human Resources, Engineering, Legal, etc.) Check out the mix and see if any are on your target list. Positions are $350 to post and resume access (with one posting) is $850 for a month. A good model with a decidedly Canadian emphasis and quite a few US client associations.

BrassRing.com
www.brassring.com

4701 Patrick Henry Drive, Suite 1901, Santa Clara, CA 95054
Ph: 888-999-6505   Fax: 408-970-4938   E-mail: info@brassring.com

JOBS	10,000s	RESUMES	100,000s
Cost to post	Cost to see	Cost to post	Cost to see
Fee	Free	Free	Fee
DISCIPLINE		LOCATION	
IT		USA	
SPECIALTY		FEATURE	
ALL		Gateway	
AGENT: Both Recruiters & Jobseekers			

BrassRing.com is a venture of The Washington Post Company, Tribune Company, Gannett Co., and venture capital firm Accel Partners. Other components include job fairs (once part of Lendman, Westech, etc.), career services, testing, web hosting, resume management and applicant tracking systems (formerly Hiresystems). This juggernaut that has not been able to put it all together and develop synergy between the properties. The Brass Ring site is, in effect, a portal to the various services. The site claims that it has partnered with over 5,000 companies. Recruiters pay $200+ to post one job depending on the location of the opening. Plenty of packages abound like a $3500 package for a 3 month access to the resume database. The search engine works well and asks the job seeker for keyword, state, country and jobs within 10, 25 or 50 miles from home. Job seekers must provide a resume to BR to apply online as contact information is not shown but a link to the hiring companies site is available. Job searches can also be saved for future reference. Interesting articles on resume preparation and career management. A shopping cart feature gives the job seeker a smooth ride. Headhunters and placement agencies are not welcome.

134

BroadbandCareers.Com
www.broadbandcareers.com

949-488-8858
Broadband Media Communications, Inc., 31892 Via de Linda, Suite 100, San Juan Capistrano, CA 92675
Ph: 877-329-6600   Fax: 949-488-8858   E-mail: sales@broadbandcareers.com

JOBS	1,000s	RESUMES	1,000s
Cost to post	Cost to see	Cost to post	Cost to see
Fee	Free	Free	Fee
DISCIPLINE		LOCATION	
IT		USA/	
SPECIALTY		FEATURE	
Telecommunications		N/A	
AGENT: N/A			

BroadbandCareers.Com claims to be the official career site for several professional associations including the Society of Cable Telecommunications Engineers (SCTE), Women in Cable & Telecommunications (WICT) and the Society of Satellite Professionals (SSPI). Site has thousands of positions and resumes and charges $250 to post a position which includes reviewing resumes. Site uses IIRC and Data Frenzy distribute positions from client companies here.

CallCenterCareers
www.callcentercareers.com

Mauri Kingdon
Boulder Valley Partners, 6325 Gunpark Drive, Suite 102, Boulder, CO 80301
Ph: 877-562-8588   Fax: 303-530-0154   E-mail: info@callcentercareers.com

JOBS	100s	RESUMES	10,000s
Cost to post	Cost to see	Cost to post	Cost to see
Fee	Free	Free	Fee
DISCIPLINE		LOCATION	
Cust. Service & Tech. Support		USA	
SPECIALTY		FEATURE	
Call Center/Customer Support		N/A	
AGENT: Both Recruiters & Jobseekers			

CallCenterCareers.com offers interesting resources for employers that range from posting jobs($99 for unlimited postings for 30 days) to tracking stats and access to the resume database (unlimited search and job postings for 30 days is $199). Job seekers can register their email and skill sets and new openings will be pushed to their PC twice a day. Openings are posted with direct contact information or job seekers can apply online. A resource page and industry resource link will lead you to several call center and help desk associations. Job seekers must register to view open positions but do not have to leave their resume. All pricing is disclosed. Small issue- site's sister business is executive search. Be careful out there.

CallCenterJobs.com

www.callcenterjobs.com

Jim Moylan
CallCenterJobs.com, Inc., 2700 Glades Circle Suite 104, Weston, FL 33327
Ph: 953-855-888   Fax: 954-385-6444   E-mail: Jim@callcenterjobs.com

JOBS	1,000s	RESUMES	1,000s
Cost to post	Cost to see	Cost to post	Cost to see
Fee	Free	Free	Fee
DISCIPLINE		LOCATION	
Cust. Service & Tech. Support		USA	
SPECIALTY		FEATURE	
Call Center/Customer Support		N/A	
AGENT: Jobseeker			

CallCenterJobs.com charges $95 to post an opening for 60 days and $190 per month to review resumes (with one job posting). It is part of a network of sites whose gateway is teleplaza.com. CallCenterJobs.com claims 150 new postings and 750 new resumes are acquired each month. Site is designed so that job seekers can search for companies with call centers in their Metro Area. From there they can link to an employer's site and view openings as well as apply for open positions. Teleplaza organizes and categorizes extensive call center industry information on on the Internet.

CallCenterOps

www.callcenterops.com

Beth Hankinson
500 - 1225 East Sunset Drive, Bellingham, WA 98226
Ph: 604-434-4623   Fax: 604-434-4613   E-mail: info@callcenterops.com

JOBS	10s	RESUMES	10s
Cost to post	Cost to see	Cost to post	Cost to see
Free (See Notes)	Free	Free	Free
DISCIPLINE		LOCATION	
Cust. Service & Tech. Support		USA	
SPECIALTY		FEATURE	
ALL		N/A	
AGENT: Jobseeker			

CallCenterOps offers complimentary call center job listings and a resume database to connect employers and job seekers. CXR loves metrics and next to each job and resume category are the number of postings for each group. All openings remain active for 60 days and are date-posted. The site provides information to those who are involved in real-time customer service via a call center or help desk. A free email newsletter is also available. Costs are covered by advertisers through the sale of books and other gear via affiliate programs with Amazon.com, Staples, 3M, Franklin Covey, etc. Extensive resources include links to other job sites and a discussion forum.

CampusCareerCenter.com

www.campuscareercenter.com

Matthew Casey
2464 Massachusetts Ave., Suite 210, Cambridge, MA 02140
Ph: 617-661-2613   Fax: 617-661-2620   E-mail: info@campuscareercenter.com

JOBS	100s	RESUMES	1,000s
Cost to post	Cost to see	Cost to post	Cost to see
Fee	Free	Free	Fee
DISCIPLINE		LOCATION	
ALL		USA	
SPECIALTY		FEATURE	
ALL		COLLEGE	
AGENT: N/A			

CampusCareerCenter.com (CCC) is stepping to the plate to assist companies in hiring entry-level college graduates. Site metrics show 11,000 jobs and tens of thousands of resumes. All job seekers register their candidate profile to access the site. Site's search engine is easy to use and numerous career resources are available. Recruiters can post a position for $150 for 90 days (prices start at $2,500 per year to search the resume database). Site states it has agreements with 1,500 colleges in the US and abroad. What that means is that they have hired student reps to display flyers and convince their friends to send a resume to the site. A chatroom is available for students to share information. Site's international section is not ready for primetime- we found limited openings posted.

CanadaIT.com

www.canadait.com

Peter Standeven
CanadaIT Ventures Inc., 13065 - 19th Avenue, Surrey, British Columbia V4A 7S5 Canada
Ph: 604-538-6015   Fax: 604-538-6790   E-mail: peter@canadait.com

JOBS	100s	RESUMES	N/A
Cost to post	Cost to see	Cost to post	Cost to see
Free	Free	N/A	N/A
DISCIPLINE		LOCATION	
IT		INTL/Canada	
SPECIALTY		FEATURE	
ALL		N/A	
AGENT: N/A			

One of the more interesting resources in Canada for information technology people and organizations, CanadaIT.com includes current news and employment information. More than 1,700 Canadian information technology companies have become CanadaIT.com members. Job postings remain free and no change is in sight. CanadaIT.com was first launched in 1996 as a place where organizations from around the world could find out what was going on in the Canadian IT industry. Positions are searched by job type, location, title or company name. All are date posted. Recruiters can also post company profiles. Job descriptions are easy to read with direct contact information.

Canada Jobs.com
www.canadajobs.com

Sara Parent
Ph: 800-258-6852   E-mail: sales@canadajobs.com

JOBS	10s	RESUMES	N/A
Cost to post	Cost to see	Cost to post	Cost to see
Fee (See Notes)	Free	N/A	N/A
DISCIPLINE		LOCATION	
ALL		INTL/Canada	
SPECIALTY		FEATURE	
ALL		N/A	
AGENT: N/A			

JobBus.com and its affiliate site, Canadajobs.com, charges recruiters $100 (US) to post a job for a 60 day run. Job Bus has hundreds of links to corporate job pages, and highlights openings posted to Canadajobs. These two sites are general in nature, with openings that range from advertising to transportation. Job seekers will appreciate that the categories with current openings are highlighted as links. Resumes can be posted to the site but there is no resume database for recruiters to search. Interesting career articles and extensive links to other job sites in Canada are worth a visit. Unfortunately, only a few dozen openings are listed here.

Canjobs.com
www.canjobs.com

Laurian Soper
Canjobs.com, 512 Woolwidch Street, Suite 2, Guelph, Ontario N1H 3X7 Canada
Ph: 519-763-9660   Fax: 519-837-3408   E-mail: info@canjobs.com

JOBS	1,000s	RESUMES	N/A
Cost to post	Cost to see	Cost to post	Cost to see
Fee	Free	N/A	N/A
DISCIPLINE		LOCATION	
ALL		INTL/Canada	
SPECIALTY		FEATURE	
ALL		Gateway	
AGENT: Jobseeker			

Canjobs.com (formerly Canadajobsearch.com) was launched in March 1999 and is a gateway for provincial (8) and city sites (15) throughout Canada. Recruiters pay $89 to post a job and view the site's resume database for a 60 day run. Jobs can be searched by keyword, province or career type. If job searches come up empty the site offers the most recent posted opportunities as an alternative. Positions contain complete job descriptions, contact data and date of posting. Examples of url's job seekers can search are: www.ontariojobs.com (provinces) www.halifaxjobs.com (cities). Recruiters and job seekers can access a discussion area by registering at the site.

CareerBank

www.careerbank.com

2106-D Gallows Road, Vienna, VA 22182
Ph: 703-448-5044   Fax: 703-902-0290   E-mail: sales@careerbank.com

JOBS	100s	RESUMES	10,000s
Cost to post	Cost to see	Cost to post	Cost to see
Fee (See Notes)	Free	Free	Fee
DISCIPLINE		LOCATION	
Business		USA	
SPECIALTY		FEATURE	
finance/Accounting		N/A	
AGENT: Recruiter			

CareerBank.com provides opportunities in accounting and finance for banking professionals. The site's owners have set a pay for position job posting feature. Jobs can be posted for free, but if you want job seekers to view them at the beginning of the search results page, you have to pay a fee. To hit the top of the list recruiters are charged $270 (resume database access is $899 per month). The site will also search its resume database on a daily basis and if there are candidates with matching skills, the top ten matches will be forwarded. A job sweeper feature claims to automatically pull jobs from a company's website into the database for $499 per month. CareerBank.com also provides online tools for tracking applicants who use CareerBank.com facilities to apply for jobs. For job seekers, candidates search jobs by keyword, location or company, and job seekers can opt-in for an email newsletter. Interesting career articles and an industry salary survey are worth a visit.

CareerBoard

www.careerboard.com

Peter Tuttle
CareerBoard, 27600 Chagrin Blvd, Suite 300, Cleveland, Ohio
Ph: 877-619-5627   E-mail: webmaster@careerboard.com

JOBS	1,000s	RESUMES	1,000s
Cost to post	Cost to see	Cost to post	Cost to see
Fee	Free	Free	Fee
DISCIPLINE		LOCATION	
ALL		USA/MDW	
SPECIALTY		FEATURE	
ALL		Gateway	
AGENT: Jobseeker			

CareerBoard is a gateway to a regional niche network of job sites showcasing opportunities in several Ohio locations. Employers pay $150 to post a single opening. Unlimited job postings and access to the resume database costs $500 per month, (with a three-month minimum). Employers receive email reports on activity. Date of posting is also listed. Jobs can be searched by type of job or keyword. Job seekers (60,000 registered) can elect to have openings pushed to their email address and have a Personal CB to store multiple resumes and job notifiers. CareerBoard's locations include Northeast Ohio (cleveland.careerboard.com), Northwest Ohio (toledo.careerboard.com), Cincinnati (cincinatti.careerboard.com), Columbus (columbus.careerboard.com), and Southeast Wisconsin (milwaukee. careerboard.com).

Careerbuilder

www.careerbuilder.com

Bob Montgomery
333 Research Court, Suite 200, Norcross, GA 30092
Ph: 888-670-8326   Fax: 703-259-5790   E-mail: info@careerbuilder.com

JOBS	1,000s		RESUMES	1,000s
Cost to post	Cost to see		Cost to post	Cost to see
Fee	Free		Free	Fee

DISCIPLINE		LOCATION	
ALL		USA	

SPECIALTY		FEATURE	
ALL		Major Career Hub	

AGENT: Jobseeker

What a change a year makes. Careerbuilder (CB) owned by Gannett, Tribune, Knight Ridder has merged with Headhunter.net to now be one of the largest job site networks on the web. Funny thing happened with this acquisition- the Headhunter.net folks are now running the company and almost all of the CB people have moved on. Behind the scenes CB searches 130 online classifieds including the USA Today newspaper empire (once they figure out how). Recruiters can post a job to CB for $200 a month and have access to the resume database for $900 for a single user. Job seekers can register to have openings "pushed" to their desktop. Openings are easy to view with direct contact information and the ability to apply online. Coverletters, selected opportunities, and multiple resumes can be saved to the site for future use. CB claims 3.9 million resumes and 400,000 jobs posted. CB has gone back to basics and it will be interesting to see how they attack the hourly market through their newspaper network.

140

Career Buzz

www.careerbuzz.com

Kurt Schwartz
3 Regent Street, Suite 304, Livingston, NJ
Ph: 888-784-6487   Fax: 973-992-7543   E-mail: ads@careerbuzz.com

JOBS	100s		RESUMES	N/A
Cost to post	Cost to see		Cost to post	Cost to see
Fee	Free		N/A	N/A
DISCIPLINE			LOCATION	
ALL			USA	
SPECIALTY			FEATURE	
ALL			N/A	
AGENT: Jobseeker				

Career Buzz offers solid content with a stinging attitude. Job seekers register their email and up to 5 search categories so matching positions will be pushed to their PC on a daily basis. A keyword search offers views of positions by date of posting, location, title and company name. Openings can also be viewed by a featured employers alpha listing. Jobs are posted for $25 for 30 days, after which they are automatically deleted. Buzz Words gives good career advice with a little humor thrown in. Street Buzz has a chatroom, but it does not get much action. We especially liked "Chillin", where you can win prizes playing numerous trivia games. Recent site upgrades have given CB more buzz then in prior years' reviews.

Career Connector

www.careerconnector.com

Sandra L. Wearne
UNETY Systems, Inc., 184 Shuman Blvd., Suite 100, Naperville, IL 65063
Ph: 630-961-2100   Fax: 630-305-3277   E-mail: career@carerconnector.com

JOBS	10,000s		RESUMES	1,000s
Cost to post	Cost to see		Cost to post	Cost to see
Free (See Notes)	Free		Free	Fee
DISCIPLINE			LOCATION	
Trades, Non-Exempt & Hourly			USA/MDW/IL/Chicago	
SPECIALTY			FEATURE	
ALL			College/Intern/Co-op	
AGENT: Both Recruiters & Jobseekers				

Career Connector concentrates on job opportunities in Chicago, IL. The site posts job stats on the home page of total openings (and new postings for the previous week). Each job search shows the total jobs found, date of posting and the categories that are matched from the search criterion. Jobs, internships, co-ops, apprenticeships and job shadowing are separate search options. This is the first time we have seen a site where a job seeker can go to a company and preview a job. Over 3 dozen corporations were listed in this category. Recruiters can view the resume database for $125 per month or see content for free but pay $25 each for contact information. Recruiters can post jobs for free, but to be at the top of the job seeker's keyword list it costs $50 per job posting. Openings can be featured on the home page of this site for $500 per month. Larger job boards should take notice of the disclosure and technolgogy on this site as CC has hit almost all of CXR's hot buttons.

141

CareerCross Japan

www.careercross.com

Richard Bysouth
Wako Shibuya Bldg. 4F, 1-22-12 Dogenzaka Shibuya,, Tokyo, 150-0043 Japan
Ph: 813-532-53033   Fax: 813-532-53131   E-mail: info@careercross.com

JOBS	1,000s	RESUMES	1,000s
Cost to post	Cost to see	Cost to post	Cost to see
Fee	Free	Free	Fee
DISCIPLINE		LOCATION	
ALL		INTL/Pacific Rim/Japan	
SPECIALTY		FEATURE	
ALL		N/A	
AGENT: Jobseeker			

CareerCross (CC) Japan was launched September 2000. CC concentrates on Japan and looks to expand to other countries. Jobs can be searched by education, location, job titles, and languages spoken and separated by employer or recruiter (headhunter). As is typical of this part of the world most of the opportunities posted were through third-party recruiters. Recruiters pay about $400 to view the resumes and various packages start at about $675 for two postings and resume access.. Community news on living in Japan and other local information rounds out the site. There were over 963 employer/recruiter direct positions posted to this site on our visit which is a high number with the present economy of Japan.

CareerEngine Network

www.careerengine.com

Career Engine Network, 200 West 57th Street, Suite 1103, New York, NY 10019
Ph: 212-775-0400   Fax: 212-775-0901   E-mail: info@careerengine.com

JOBS	1,000s	RESUMES	1,000s
Cost to post	Cost to see	Cost to post	Cost to see
Fee	Free	Free	Fee
DISCIPLINE		LOCATION	
ALL		USA	
SPECIALTY		FEATURE	
ALL		Diversity/Gateway	
AGENT: N/A			

CareerEngine is the power (and gateway) behind 6 category-specific and diversity career sites. Most offer postings for $125-$175 for two months. CareerEngine matches job applicants to employers through confidential resume hosting and public online job posting features. Job seekers scroll a map of the US to view the number of openings posted by state. Searches can be done by keyword or location. CE does not have a resume database but the 6 category sitesprovide recruiters access for $200 per month. Several recruitment advertising firms have made alliances here to post to these sites. Individually, no marketing is apparent, although CE's success in developing a distribution network via agencies is applauded. The network includes publications and pure plays.

Career Espresso/Emory University

www.sph.emory.edu/studentservice/Career.html

John Youngblood Jr.
Rollins School of Public Health, 1518 Clifton Road, Atlanta, GA 30322
Ph: 404-727-8323   Fax: 404-727-3996   E-mail: jyoungb@sph.emory.edu

JOBS	100s	RESUMES	N/A
Cost to post	Cost to see	Cost to post	Cost to see
Free	Free	N/A	N/A
DISCIPLINE		LOCATION	
Government/Helath Care		US	
SPECIALTY		FEATURE	
Public Health		College	
AGENT: N/A			

Career Espresso, developed by John Young Blood, has been percolating since December 1996, and stands out from other job libations geared toward college graduates. Affiliated with ASPH - Association of Schools of Public Health makes this one of the best sites to click and find a job. The owner has hundreds of jobs posted for public sector healthcare graduates and experienced professionals by date of posting. Jobs can be searched by title, type, date, organization, state, city, classification, industry or country. Rollins School of Public Health has a restricted area for internships Job seekers should check out the career action tip sheets for "how-to" advice.

CareerExchange.com

www.careerexchange.com/

Jason Moreau
CareerExchange Interactive Corp., 6425 Christie Ave., Suite 300A, Emeryville, CA 94608
Ph: 510-845-3591   Fax: 510-845-3608   E-mail: jobs@careerexchange.com

JOBS	1,000s	RESUMES	100,000s
Cost to post	Cost to see	Cost to post	Cost to see
Fee	Free	Free	Fee
DISCIPLINE		LOCATION	
ALL		USA	
SPECIALTY		FEATURE	
ALL		N/A	
AGENT: Jobseeker			

CareerExchange.com has been posting jobs and resumes to its site since 1996. One reason we really like this site is that the owners are always trying new ways to enhance it. Job seekers can register their skills and matching jobs will be sent to their PCs. The site lists thousands of positions in Canada and the U.S. and also has an international component. The search engine can be used by keyword, title, state, province, full-time, contract or part-time. CXR especially appreciates that job seekers can view openings by newest to oldest which eleviates stale postings. Employers can post a job for $90 for 60 days. The resume database can be searched for free but contact information costs $9.95 each.

CareerExposure

www.careerexposure.com

Mike Pullman
805 SW Broadway, Suite 2250, Portland, OR 97205
Ph: 503-221-7779   Fax: 503-221-7780   E-mail: sales@careerexposure.com

JOBS	1,000s	RESUMES	10,000s
Cost to post	Cost to see	Cost to post	Cost to see
Fee	Free	Free	Fee
DISCIPLINE		LOCATION	
ALL		USA	
SPECIALTY		FEATURE	
ALL		DIVERSITY	
AGENT: N/A			

CareerExposure is the gateway for a network of four sites that can be searched by keyword, job type, location, industry or company. Once you find an interesting job, it is easy to apply online. Selected openings can be saved to be applied for at a later time. Corporate profiles are an added touch for job seekers to gain an edge. Unfortunately, many are not live links. Recruiters pay $149 to post to CE for 60 days. DiversitySearch.com, MBACareers.com and CareerWomen.com cost an extra $49 each as a package. Recruiters who purchase a package for $6,500 for unlimited job postings with access to the resume database for 1 year. Job seekers should check out "Up Close & Virtual for interesting interviews with business professionals.

CareerFables.com

www.careerfables.com

Susan Magrino
Workforce OS, 1799 Old Bayshore Hwy.,, Suite 219, Burlingame, CA 94010
Ph: 650-777-4350   Fax: 650-777-4318   E-mail: smagrino@careerfables.com

JOBS	1,000s	RESUMES	1,000s
Cost to post	Cost to see	Cost to post	Cost to see
Free	Free	Free	Fee
DISCIPLINE		LOCATION	
ALL		USA	
SPECIALTY		FEATURE	
ALL		Diversity	
AGENT: N/A			

CareerFables.com, launched in 2001, offers to match opportunity (jobs) and talent (candidates) and email the resulting matches to job seekers and employers. The site emphasis is support for mid-career change,(those of us who are up there in years) a major difference from just finding a job. CareerFables is still ahead of its time, but it will be a hard sell to hiring managers. Corporate memberships are $1,200 for one user while headhunters pay $1,500. This price provides access to the resume database and unlimited job postings. Owners also provide TheSkillsMatch technology tool that allows employers to monitor internal employees skills inventory.

CareerFile

www.careerfile.com

Cynthia Welch
Adams Tech Center, 39 Park Avenue, Adams, MA 01220
Ph: 413-528-4769   Fax: 413-528-4735   E-mail: admin@careerfile.com

JOBS	10,000s	RESUMES	10,000s
Cost to post	Cost to see	Cost to post	Cost to see
Free(See Notes)	Free	Free	Fee
DISCIPLINE		LOCATION	
ALL		USA	
SPECIALTY		FEATURE	
ALL		Gateway	
AGENT: Both Recruiters & Jobseekers			

CareerFile was founded in 1995 and is a gateway to nearly 350 local area job sites (sites are not independent urls). Employers can post openings in one geographic niche and search the resume database for free. A regional/national posting and resume search cost $45 per month. Job seekers must register with the site to view posted openings. The site's search engine leads job seekers to match their skills with location and job category or keyword options. CareerFile also functions as an applications solutions provider for employers, offering site licensing for technology use and hosting.

JOB SEEKER TIP

Plain vanilla resumes will not work in the year 2003.

Tailor each one to the position you are going after. Remember, most resumes are placed in an automated system, and unless the "key buzz words" match an opening, your resume will never be seen.

Tony Lee
Dow Jones & Co., Route 1 at Ridge Road, South Brunswick, NJ 08852
Ph: 609-520-4305   E-mail: cwc-news@interactive.wsj.com

JOBS	10,000s	RESUMES	10,000s
Cost to post	Cost to see	Cost to post	Cost to see
Fee	Free	Free	Fee
DISCIPLINE		LOCATION	
Business/Sales		USA & INTL	
SPECIALTY		FEATURE	
Finance/		Executive/Gateway	
AGENT: Jobseeker			

CareerJournal.com (CJ), a separate but connected part of the Wall Street Journal, is an obvious choice to seek out executive opportunities or drive top candidates to a corporate site. Job seekers need to focus their search by extensively refining the criteria by keyword, location, commute distance, job category or explore the site's corporate partners. The keywords used in a job search are highlighted in the results for easier viewing. Exclusive news coverage, monthly profiles of top executive recruiters, salary data and more will attract executives. The site has excellent career content and effective email job alerts. Using CareerCast's technology the site seamlessly transfers corporate website openings onto this heavy traffic site and facilitates "combo" buys with other papers in the CareerCast network. These positions, however, can be at all levels, not just executive positions. Job seekers can utilize the "calendar of career events" to find organizations for assistance in their search. The resume database costs recruiters $1,000 a month, with a three-month minimum. Other services include a Kennedy publication listing of executive recruiters. Content alliances with the Society for Human Resource Management and the American Society for Training & Development have added white papers on important employee issues. Recruiters pay $275 to post a job directly into CareerJournal.com's JobSeek database using an online form or a credit card. CollegeJournal.com is the college side of the site. CJ also has sites for careerjournaleurope.com and careerjournalasia.com.

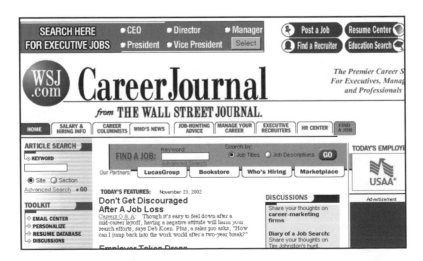

146

CareerLink- Applied Info. Mgm't Institute

www.careerlink.org

Dee Studt
AIM Institute, 118 S. 19th St., Suite 1A, Omaha, NE 68102
Ph: 877-345-5025   Fax: 402-345-5028   E-mail: cindyg@nebraska.org

JOBS	1,000s	RESUMES	10,00s
Cost to post	Cost to see	Cost to post	Cost to see
Fee	Free	Free	Fee
DISCIPLINE		LOCATION	
IT		USA/MDW/NE	
SPECIALTY		FEATURE	
ALL		Executive	
AGENT: N/A			

CareerLink provides a user-friendly way for companies to recruit talent within a specific region. There are applicant tracking tools, easy to understand metrics, multiple-site posting tools (www.whohasjobs.com), resume builders,and other services to help simplify the business of recruiting management talent. Employers are charged $150 to post for 30 days and $2500 per year for resume access.

CareerMarketplace

www.careermarketplace.com

Richard Posey
Critical Mass Systems, 1400 N. Park Blvd., #1103, Grapevine, TX 76051
Ph: 817-996-3500   E-mail: rp@careermarketplace.com

JOBS	1,000s	RESUMES	10,000s
Cost to post	Cost to see	Cost to post	Cost to see
Fee	Free	Free	Fee
DISCIPLINE		LOCATION	
ALL		USA	
SPECIALTY		FEATURE	
ALL		Gateway	
AGENT: Both Recruiters & Jobseekers			

CareerMarketplace.com is the gateway site to Critical Mass's network. Richard Posey, the owner, was one of the first to create a network of niche sites and owns some great urls. CareerMarketplace links to more than 40 of these sites with the format "jobtitle.com." Recruiters pay $40 for 60 day postings for up to 3 sites and additional packages are available. Some of these sites offer resume access with job postings. Sites are in IT, engineering, accounting, marketing and sales. See the master index for other sites available. Metrics are displayed on the number of open jobs by industry. Job seekers must register to apply as all jobs are coded. Company profiles are available for viewing but few had open positions listed. Recruiters can have resumes and job seekers can have openings pushed to their pc by registering their email address. CM has added many new features to gain a higher plateau in CXR's eyes.

Career Mart

www.careermart.com

Darren Grant
19495 Biscayne Blvd., 7th Floor, N. Miami, FL 33180
Ph: 800-272-4237   Fax: 212-599-6645   E-mail: darren@careermart.com

JOBS	100s	RESUMES	10,000s
Cost to post	Cost to see	Cost to post	Cost to see
Fee	Free	Free	Fee
DISCIPLINE		LOCATION	
ALL		USA	
SPECIALTY		FEATURE	
ALL		N/A	
AGENT: Both Recruiters & Jobseekers			

Career Mart revs up its image through its affiliation with the Ferrari Racing Team. The site, established in 1995, continues to be a visible presence at conferences, often paired with its owner, BSA advertising. Career Mart pushes job openings to applicants whose skills match the openings for free, includes a search engine that offers viewing by job category, state, region, country or keyword search. Recruiters can have resumes pushed to their desktop. Employers pay $225 per state or $500 per region to post a job opportunity for two weeks. Searching the resume database costs $500 per month per category. Nick Corcodilos alias, "Ask the Headhunter", articles are featured for job seekers.

CareerMidEast.com

www.careermideast.com

CareerMidEast
Ph: 202-525-9259   Fax: 202-526-9393   E-mail: sales@careermideast.com

JOBS	1,000s	RESUMES	100,000s
Cost to post	Cost to see	Cost to post	Cost to see
Fee	Free	Free	Fee
DISCIPLINE		LOCATION	
ALL		INTL/Middle East	
SPECIALTY		FEATURE	
ALL		Gateway	
AGENT: Jobseeker			

CareerMidEast.com is the gateway to a network of 12 Middle Eastern country sites. (Bahrain, Egypt, Emirates, Jordan, Kuwait, Lebanon, Morocco, Oman, Qatar, Saudi, Tunis and Yemen). The site claims over 160,000 resumes and 3,653 job postings. All positions are posted by date with detailed information. Position requirements may include gender. Recruiters pay $750 to post unlimited openings and view the resume database for three months. As an alternative, recruiters can purchase credits (20 credits for $79). Each credit entitles recruiters to access one resume. Career related questions can be posted to "Inji" the site's expert who promises to respond. Simple FAQs answer most recruiter questions. Job seekers must register to use the site.

CareerMVP.com

www.CareersMVP.com

Chris Sparks
The Sparks Group, PO Box 7918, Greensboro, NC 27417
Ph: 336-854-9852   Fax: 336-292-4065   E-mail: advertising@CareerMVP.com

JOBS	100s	RESUMES	N/A
Cost to post	Cost to see	Cost to post	Cost to see
Fee	Free	N/A	N/A
DISCIPLINE		LOCATION	
ALL		USA	
SPECIALTY		FEATURE	
ALL		N/A	
AGENT: Jobseeker			

CareerMVP.com is the gateway to a large network of location and industry sites from the owners of BusinessMVP.com. There is a career site for every state, 57 cities(www.citymvp.com) and one for 11 industries. Employers are charged $195 a year for 3 job postings for the state and industry and $95 per posting to the city site. Each collects emails to push openings to job seekers . CareerMVP offers a free affinity email address to protect confidentiality. Each industry category lists the number of openings. . Specialty sites include:MarketingMVP (advertising), Technology MVP (IT, ERP, telecom), Finance MVP (banking, finance, risk), MedicalMVP (healthcare, biotech), ManufacturingMVP (chemicals, engineering, furniture, plastics, textiles), HVACCareers.com (heating, refrigeration), AgricultureMVP (farming), AminMVP (call center), HospitalityMVP (travel), HollywoodMVP (entertainment) and InternationalMVP (languages). This site goes where the jobs are hot as the functional groups change all the time. The citymvp was launched in August, 2002.

Career One (HotJobs)

www.careerone.com.au

Level 2, Wharf 12, Plymouth, NSW, Australia Australia
Ph: 800-555-010   E-mail: advertiser-inquiry@careerone.com.au.

JOBS	1,000s	RESUMES	100,000s
Cost to post	Cost to see	Cost to post	Cost to see
Fee	Free	Fee	Free
DISCIPLINE		LOCATION	
ALL		INTL/Pacific Rim/Australia	
SPECIALTY		FEATURE	
ALL		Site hosting	
AGENT: Both Recruiters & Jobseekers			

Careerone is an Australian site that partnered with HotJobs several years ago. The site represents the hopes of the newspaper industry in Australia. This is arguably the number one site. Launched in 1998, recruiters pay $150 Australian plus 10% GST to post a job. Access to the site's resume database costs an additional fee. Job seekers search by keyword, location, job type, newspaper, and position level (we especially like the "level index"). All jobs are date posted. Site has all the features expected of the best of class.

CareerOwl

www.careerowl.com

CareerOwl Institute, #22 - 3552 West 41st Avenue, Vancouver,, British Columbia V6N4J9 Canada
Ph: 877-695-7678   Fax: 877-329-7678   E-mail: sales@careerowl.net

JOBS	1,000s		RESUMES	1,000s
Cost to post	Cost to see		Cost to post	Cost to see
Fee	Free		Free	Fee
DISCIPLINE			LOCATION	
ALL			INTL/Canada	
SPECIALTY			FEATURE	
ALL			College	
AGENT: N/A				

Started by professors, CareerOwl has signed up students and alumni of major universities, colleges and technical schools across Canada. Employers can post job ads for jobseekers to view and e-mail candidates, or they can search among the thousands of students, grads, and experienced workers to create a short list of candidates. Cost is just $25 to post ($100 for foreign jobs). Confidentiality is high.

CareerShop.com

www.careershop.com

Jim McArdle
CareerShop, Inc., 1701 Park Center Drive, Orlando, FL 32835
Ph: 407.532.1982   Fax: 407.532.1876   E-mail: sales@careershop.com

JOBS	10,000s		RESUMES	100,000s
Cost to post	Cost to see		Cost to post	Cost to see
Fee	Free		Free	Fee
DISCIPLINE			LOCATION	
ALL			USA	
SPECIALTY			FEATURE	
ALL			N/A	
AGENT: Jobseeker				

CareerShop.com offers customized web-based capabilities for employers that include applicant tracking tools, multiple site posting tools, private resume database capabilities, resume robots, resume builders, and just about any other tool an employer might need in order to build a private label career site. Career Shop also has streaming video capabilities. The site's agent will email positions matching a job seeker's registered skills each week. Recruiters pay $195 per month to post a position. Resume database access is $585 per quarter which includes unlimited job postings and cross postings to 3,000 individual sites. Recruiters should ask for a listing of the cross posting sites to be sure they are relevant. Dr Randall Hansen, aka the "Career Doctor" will respond to questions. This site consistently upgrades its products and services each year.

CareerSite.com
www.careersite.com

Ed Farrell
130 South First Street, 3rd Floor, Ann Arbor, MI 48104
Ph: 734-213-9500   Fax: 734-213-9011   E-mail: sales@careersite.com

JOBS	10,000s		RESUMES	100,000s
Cost to post	Cost to see		Cost to post	Cost to see
Free	Free		Free	Fee
DISCIPLINE			LOCATION	
ALL			USA	
SPECIALTY			FEATURE	
ALL			Job Distribution Services	
AGENT: Jobseeker				

CareerSite.com offers applicant tracking functionality and a gateway to networks of newspaper classi-fied sites (advance/employment wizard). CareerSite will push matching openings to job seekers who reg-ister their skills. After a three-month free trial, recruiters pay $25 per month (3 month min.) to post 6 jobs for a 30 day run. Additional postings cost $50 each. Access to the site's 200,000+ resume/profile database costs $395 for six months. Jobs can be automatically scraped (copied) weekly from an employer's site and posted here. Cross-posting jobs to other websites such as altavista.com and America's Job Bank are also available. Job seekers search openings by listing their skills, industry desired and location for ease of view-ing. The number of matches is shown and a shopping cart is provided for later viewing. A career resource area provides links to salary surveys, relocation information and the resume assistance

Careers2000.net
www.careers2000.net

Sam Shah
1223 S. Hurstbourne Parkway, Louisville, KY 40222
Ph: 800-898-0969   Fax: 502-214-4003   E-mail: support@careers2000.net

JOBS	1,000s		RESUMES	10,000s
Cost to post	Cost to see		Cost to post	Cost to see
Fee	Free		Free	Fee
DISCIPLINE			LOCATION	
ALL			USA	
SPECIALTY			FEATURE	
ALL			N/A	
AGENT: Both Recruiters & Jobseekers				

At the outset we want to state that we do not like sites like Careers2000.net. We feel that they emphasize career strategies that are bankrupt (we absolutely don't believe spamming employers with jobseeker resumes has any value whatsoever). On the other hand, sites like this are attractive. Job seekers are promised that their resume will be sent to thousands of employers (even in specific industries). For a fee, job seekers are guaranteed results. Amazingly the site subscribes to the BBB (Better Business Bureau Online) implying that they independently will handle any complaints.The basic service is free. Recruiters pay $145 to post unlimited jobs to Careers2000.net. Agents will send matching resumes for free. All jobs are date posted with direct contact information and many have salaries listed. Professional resume writing services are available for $125. Links to state employment offices across the USA are also available.

Careers in Construction

www.careersinconstruction.com

Simon Lodge
151Rosebery Avenue, London, UK United Kingdom
Ph: 440-207-5056840 Fax: 440-207-5056755 E-mail: simon.lodge@construct.ema

JOBS	1,000s	RESUMES	10,000s
Cost to post	Cost to see	Cost to post	Cost to see
Fee	Free	Free	Fee
DISCIPLINE		LOCATION	
Trades, Non-Exempt & Hourly/Engineering		INTL/Europe/UK	
SPECIALTY		FEATURE	
Architecture/Construction/Civil		N/A	
AGENT: Jobseeker			

Careers in Construction is a UK based site that may be among the best niche sites in combining the power of several magazines with the internet. Recruiters post positions for 350 pounds for 1 month or advertise on one of three key print journals. Recruiters can view resume profiles and receive contact information for 49 pounds per profile. Job seekers can view openings by function (architects, building services, infrastructure etc.). When the job seeker clicks on the company logo, full details of the job are provided. Some opportunities in other countries are maintained. Freelance openings are in a separate section. Site is well designed and easy to view. Company profiles are especially well done.

CareersinFood.com

www.careersinfood.com

3830 Pioneer Road, Rogersville, MO 65742
Ph: 877-329-1693   E-mail: adv@careersinfood.com

JOBS	1,000s	RESUMES	1,000s
Cost to post	Cost to see	Cost to post	Cost to see
Fee	Free	Fee	Free
DISCIPLINE		LOCATION	
Hospitality & Food Services/Science		USA	
SPECIALTY		FEATURE	
Quality Control/Research		N/A	
AGENT: N/A			

Careersinfood.com serves up opportunities in the food and beverage manufacturing industries.The site claims to have over 7,000+ confidential profiles of job seekers. Corporate recruiters pay $250 to post jobs and access the resume database for a 30 day run; headhunters pay $150. Job seekers must complete a candidate profile (brief resume builder) before being given access to openings. Several major players in the beverage/food industry and numerous headhunters have jobs posted. Job seekers who opt for confidentiality are provided with a reference code. A monthly newsletter is pushed to the PC's of 20,000 subscribers. Links to industry resources is an added plus.

Careers in Government

www.careersingovernment.com

Inge Weinberg
29485 Fountainwood Street, Agoura Hills, CA 91301
Ph: 818-991-9653   Fax: 707-202-2037   E-mail: info@careersingovernment.com

JOBS	100s		RESUMES	1,000s
Cost to post	Cost to see		Cost to post	Cost to see
Fee	Free		Free	Free
DISCIPLINE			LOCATION	
Government			USA	
SPECIALTY			FEATURE	
ALL			N/A	
AGENT: Jobseeker				

Careers in Government (formerly Jobs in Government) was launched in 1996. Recruiters pay $90 to post an opening. The annual fee is either $750 annually (paid up front based on size of workforce) or is a $65 monthly access fee for unlimited job postings and access to the resume database. The resumes are automatically deposited in the employer's bank sorted according to the job being advertised. Job titles range from administrative assistant to water treatment specialist. The format for job descriptions is well designed (the large type is appreciated by the older folks). As is the rule in the public sector, all jobs have salary ranges posted. A directory to executive recruiters is also available.

JOB SEEKER TIP

With each email that you send...

...your salutation should have your name, address, email and telephone number where you can be contacted. Do not take for granted the person receiving your email has this information.

Casino Careers Online
www.casinocareers.com

Beth Deighan
506 West Patcong Avenue, Linwood, NJ 08221
Ph: 609-653-2242   Fax: 609-653-2212   E-mail: info@casinocareers.com

JOBS	100s	RESUMES	10,000s
Cost to post	Cost to see	Cost to post	Cost to see
Fee	Free	Free	Fee

DISCIPLINE	LOCATION
Hospitality & Food Services/Retail/Miscellaneous	USA

SPECIALTY	FEATURE
Hotels/Resorts	N/A

AGENT: Both Recruiters & Jobseekers

Casino Careers Online, launched in 1998, seeks to improve the chances for job seekers and more than 100 casino properties worldwide that are using the site. Corporations create job profiles for their openings, the site searches its resume database for matches and the recruiter can view candidate information. Passive job seekers looking to protect their contact data can set up a blind email box with modified profile information. Job seekers can view jobs around the world, apply online or link directly to the company website. Recruiters pay $400 for a three-month posting which includes access to a resume grabber. An annual membership that includes access to the resume database runs from $5,000-$10,000. Postings can be changed anytime. Owners client list includes most of the players in this industry. 7 come 11.

Centerwatch

www.centerwatch.com

Sally Memmolo
22 Thomson Place 36T1, Boston, MA 02210
Ph: 617-856-5900   Fax: 617-856-5901   E-mail: jobwatch@centerwatch.com

JOBS	100s		RESUMES	1,000s
Cost to post	Cost to see		Cost to post	Cost to see
Fee	Free		Free	Fee
DISCIPLINE			LOCATION	
Science			USA	
SPECIALTY			FEATURE	
Bio/Pharm/Clinical Research/Clinical Trials			N/A	
AGENT: Jobseeker				

Centerwatch.com is dedicated to clinical research personnel. This is a publishing company covering the clinical trials industry. JobWatch is a print publication that reaches 30,000+ clinical research professionals each month. Job listings cost $1.50 per word or $200 for 150 words for 30 days. This cost covers both the print publication and the website. Jobs are posted by category, from biostatisticians to scientific affairs and have direct contact information. The resume database can be viewed for $350 per month. Subscribers can receive the publication via email. A listserve provides what it is like to work in this industry.

Charity Village.com

www.charityvillage.com

Reesa Rosen
CharityVillage Ltd., 160 Main Street South, P.O. Box 92536, Brampton, Ontario L6W 4R1 Canada
Ph: 800-610-8134   Fax: 416-352-6055   E-mail: careers@charityvillage.com

JOBS	100s		RESUMES	N/A
Cost to post	Cost to see		Cost to post	Cost to see
Fee	Free		N/A	N/A
DISCIPLINE			LOCATION	
Non-Profit			INTL/Canada	
SPECIALTY			FEATURE	
ALL			N/A	
AGENT: Jobseeker				

Charity Village.com was launched July, 1995. This is a portal with an extensive directory of non-profits, hundreds of openings and a best practice FAQ for the job seeker- "Job seeker help". Recruiters pay $110/US or $CDM 157 to post an opening for 60 days. Jobs are date posted and can be searched by "newest jobs posted", title or keyword. Content including non-profit news, organizations, suppliers and much more.

Christian Jobs Online
www.christianjobs.com

Jose Gomez
ChurchForce, Inc., 10029 N. Aster Avenue, Tampa, FL 33612
Ph: 800-711-9796   Fax: 530-509-8968   E-mail: sales@christianjobs.com

JOBS	1,000s	RESUMES	1,000s
Cost to post	Cost to see	Cost to post	Cost to see
Fee	Free	Free	Free
DISCIPLINE		LOCATION	
Non-Profit		USA	
SPECIALTY		FEATURE	
ALL		Telecommuting	
AGENT: Both Recruiters & Jobseekers			

Christian Jobs Online (CJO) was launched October 1996 and has recently been acquired by ChurchForce. CXR appreciated the homepage stats of CJO which is already changing under new management. Instead of metrics advising the number of openings by category the site now posts the number of visitors currently online- we're not sure why. Recruiters pay $75 to post a position and can view the site's resume database with contact information for free. Contract and project positions can also be posted. The site's privacy policies are easy to view and in plain English. Job seekers can apply for openings but there is a fee. Job seeker pay $17-$97 for additional services. For the dollars job seekers receive emailed job matches, can upload a photo and resume in word to the site and have access to online career coaching. We have heard of passing the plate to support one's church but to charge job seekers to apply to openings that employers have paid to post goes a little too far.

Chronicle of Higher Education
www.chronicle.com

1255 23rd Street NW, Washington, DC 20037
Ph: 202-466-1050   Fax: 202-296-2691   E-mail: help@chronicle.com

JOBS	1,000s	RESUMES	N/A
Cost to post	Cost to see	Cost to post	Cost to see
Fee	Free	N/A	N/A
DISCIPLINE		LOCATION	
Education		USA	
SPECIALTY		FEATURE	
Admininistration/Teaching, University		N/A	
AGENT: Jobseeker			

The Chronicle of Higher Education reaches over 150,000 visitors a week online and 500,000 readers in print. The site posts over 1,000+ jobs each week from the publication of the same name. Every type of faculty, research, administration and executive position is listed with the number of openings posted next to each category. Job seekers can view openings by job function or by keyword search. The cost to post is $195 for a 30-day run (web only). Interesting career articles are also available. The Chronicle continues to upgrade their site's capabilities.

Chronicle of Philanthropy

philanthropy.com

1255 Twenty-Third Street N.W., Washington, DC 20037
Ph: 202-466-1230   Fax: 202-223-6292

JOBS	1,000s	RESUMES	N/A
Cost to post	Cost to see	Cost to post	Cost to see
Fee	Fee (See Notes)	N/A	N/A
DISCIPLINE		LOCATION	
Non-Profit		USA	
SPECIALTY		FEATURE	
ALL		EXECUTIVE	
AGENT: Jobseeker			

The Chronicle of Philanthropy has 100,000 print and 60,000 web viewers per month. Openings are posted from their publication and recruiters can now post to the website without the print. Jobs posted to the web cost $195 for a 45 day run. Openings can be viewed by job type, field of endeavor or keyword search. Executive positions have been separated from the pack. Openings are listed in alpha order by state with date of posting on each. The magazine is a bi-weekly publication. Interesting news and advice columns abound here.

Classified Employment Web Site (CLEWS)

www.yourinfosource.com/clews

Ken Cunningham
Your Info Source, PO Box 1804, New Port Richey, FL 34656
Ph: 727-360-8728   Fax: 727-360-4544   E-mail: info@yourinfosource.com

JOBS	10s	RESUMES	100s
Cost to post	Cost to see	Cost to post	Cost to see
Fee	Free	Free	Fee
DISCIPLINE		LOCATION	
IT/Engineering		USA	
SPECIALTY		FEATURE	
ALL		Security clearance/Military Transition	
AGENT: Recruiter			

Classified Employment (CLEWS) is strictly for U.S. employers who need professionals with top-secret clearance. Employers can access the site for $20 a month after a $40 registration fee. Resume contact information will cost recruiters either $10 per resume or $195 per month for unlimited access. Job postings are either $5 per response for the first 20 and $2.50 per response for all thereafter (or $95 per month for unlimited usage). Employers will receive up to 50 responses and then no more. Everything about this site is coded and there is even a tour to get a peek at their security. Job seekers who become members are advised on the number of times their resumes is viewed. A list of over 400 employers who hire classified individuals is available by email for $12.95. Job seekers must respond to openings via the site. After 9/11 these people are in high demand.

COACH's Job Board
www.coachhelp.com

Warren Swann
Comprehensive On-Line Access to Coaching Help, 1025 North Central Expressway, #300-343, Plano, TX 75075
Ph: 800-339-9652   E-mail: coach@coachhelp.com

JOBS	10s		RESUMES	100s
Cost to post	Cost to see		Cost to post	Cost to see
Free	Free		Free	Free
DISCIPLINE			LOCATION	
Education			USA	
SPECIALTY			FEATURE	
Teaching/Sports Coaching, K-12			N/A	
AGENT: N/A				

The owners of Coach's Nationwide Job Board are always scoring points for job seekers and recruiters. Openings are free to post and resumes free to view. Resumes can be viewed by sport and are posted in alpha order with years of experience, and state. Jobs can be searched by sport and viewed by title, school and location. Complete detailed job descriptions and contact information is available. For individuals who are really into sports, check out the "coaching library". An online coaches' association operates this site to provide the latest information on the profession.

Cold Fusion Advisor (CF Advisor)
www.cfadvisor.com

Alpha Forum, Inc., 276 Fair Street, Kingston, NY
Ph: 800-217-2723   E-mail: editor@cfadvisor.com

JOBS	1,000s		RESUMES	100s
Cost to post	Cost to see		Cost to post	Cost to see
Free	Free		Free	Free
DISCIPLINE			LOCATION	
IT			USA	
SPECIALTY			FEATURE	
Cold fusion			N/A	
AGENT: N/A				

CF Advisor, alias Cold Fusion Advisor, lists hundreds of jobs that can be viewed for free. Jobs can be searched by country, state, area code, permanent or contract, on-site or telecommute (this is unique), languages, experience level, salary and benefits required. That is quite a list and may bring matching problems. Recruiters can post their information for free and view the resume database at no charge. Options to purchase banners may be of interest to recruiters. The site had over 732 resumes and 1,933 jobs posted, and the last posted makes the top of the page. A CF discussion area is another way for recruiters to potentially find prospects.

College & University Personnel Assoc.
www.cupahr.org

CUPA-HR, 1233 20th Street, NW, Suite 30, Washington, DC 20036
Ph: 202-429-0311   Fax: 202-429-0149   E-mail: ksutherland@cupahr.org

JOBS	10s	RESUMES	N/A
Cost to post	Cost to see	Cost to post	Cost to see
Fee	Free	N/A	N/A
DISCIPLINE		LOCATION	
Human Resources/Education		USA/	
SPECIALTY		FEATURE	
ALL		N/A	
AGENT: N/A			

The College & University Personnel Association (CUPA) offers job postings for $2.50 per word. Best buy if you are looking for Human Resource professionals in a University setting. Cost for a 200 word ad in their monthly print publication + online is $750 total.

JOB SEEKER TIP

Look smart when responding to a job opportunity.

If you have the job contact's name use it.
Take the extra effort and either go online to find
this information or call the corporation direct.

Stuart Nachbar
141 West 28th Street, 9th Fl, New York, NY 10001
Ph: 800-442-3614   Fax: 212-714-1688   E-mail: stuart@collegecentral.com

JOBS	10,000s	RESUMES	N/A
Cost to post	Cost to see	Cost to post	Cost to see
Fee	Free	N/A	N/A

DISCIPLINE	LOCATION
ALL	USA

SPECIALTY	FEATURE
ALL	COLLEGE

AGENT: Jobseeker

College Central Network (CCN) was founded in May 1997 and focuses on community colleges and small to midsize schools nationwide. CCN started as a major play with schools in the Northeast and has expanded its territory and also has made inroads with alumni services. The site offers ASP management tools to 160 school career centers and through them expects to reach 1 million students by the end of 2002. Rates to post to the Network will be $100/job/month paid by credit, $150/job/month by invoice. There is an additional $50 to "push"—e-mail a posting to students or alumni who are a match with the employer's degree, job target, job type and job location Government agencies, branches of the U.S. armed services, and schools can post jobs for free. College Central's additional services include a resume builder that students can modify and export to other sites.The site continues to have linkages to virtual job fairs in partnership with colleges and universities, economic development agencies and professional associations. Over the last five years, these virtual events have involved more than 600 schools. CCN looks to provide added value and is much more than a job board for college students.

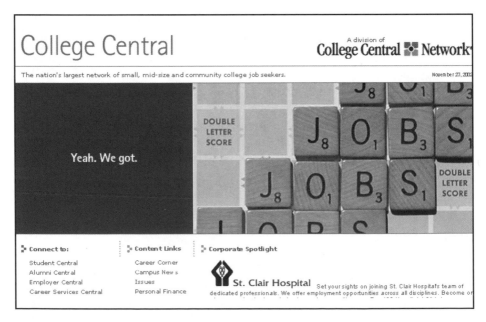

College Grad Job Hunter

www.collegegrad.com

Brian Kreuger
1629 Summit, Suite 200, Cedarburg, WI
Ph: 262-376-1000   Fax: 262-376-1030   E-mail: webmaster@collegegrad.com

JOBS	10,000s	RESUMES	10,000s
Cost to post	Cost to see	Cost to post	Cost to see
Fee	Free	Free	Fee
DISCIPLINE		LOCATION	
ALL		USA	
SPECIALTY		FEATURE	
ALL		COLLEGE	
AGENT: Both Recruiters & Jobseekers			

College Grad Job Hunter launched January 1995, strives to bring together entry-level job seekers with corporate America. Internship and regular positions are easily found. Job searches are done by keyword, location, job category, full or part-time, experience level or date of posting. Recruiters pay $125 per job or $695 per month for unlimited postings. The site's resume database access is included in all job posting packages. The site will email matching posted jobs with student's skills for everyone who registers. An online career forum allows students to submit employment questions that "Brian" will answer. The site owner's book has tremendous career content and can be read on the site. College Grad Job Hunter is simple, well done and always looking for a new marketing edge.

College Job Board

www.collegejobboard.com

Paul Dooley
70 Walnut Street, Wellesley, MA 02481
Ph: 781-239-8106   Fax: 708-575-4825   E-mail: contactus@collegejobboard.zzn.com

JOBS	1,000s	RESUMES	10,000s
Cost to post	Cost to see	Cost to post	Cost to see
Fee (See Notes)	Free	Free	Fee (See Notes)
DISCIPLINE		LOCATION	
ALL		USA	
SPECIALTY		FEATURE	
ALL		COLLEGE	
AGENT: Jobseeker			

College Job Board allows recruiters to post positions and try the resume database for a 14 day free trial. Jobs can be posted for $18 per school or $295 for all 6,570 colleges. Posted openings will also be sent to over 60,000 other url's for no additional cost (check the list as there are some unique addresses). The site also has access to 30,658 high schools and vocational schools where jobs can be posted. Openings are listed for one week if they are temporary and two to four weeks if they are full-time or internship posts. Access to the resume database costs $500 per month. Recruiters can design pre-employment screening questions and keep all of their data on the site's applicant tracking system. Students and alumni must register before they can view job openings. (We appreciated the short form here, which is a better version than many other sites.) Links to college scholarship programs are also available.

College of Healthcare Infor. Mgmt. Exec.
www.cio-chime.org/default.html

CHIME, 3300 Washtenaw Avenue, Suite 225, Ann Arbor, MI 48104
Ph: 734-665-0000   Fax: 734-665-4922   E-mail: tkamara@cio-chime.org

JOBS	10s	RESUMES	10s
Cost to post	Cost to see	Cost to post	Cost to see
Free	Free	Fee	Free
DISCIPLINE		LOCATION	
IT/Health Care		USA	
SPECIALTY		FEATURE	
Management		Executive	
AGENT: Jobseeker			

The College of Healthcare Information Management Executives (CHIME) supports its 700 members with job listings. Jobs are posted on the website for free and recruiters can have them mailed to the healthcare CIO membership though the monthly newsletter for $500. The site pushes new openings out to 150 members a week. Contact information on the resumes posted is coded. Recruiters email the college staff to get the contact information at awizauer@cio-chime.org. Recruiters will love this site for its directory of members that can still be viewed for free.

College Recruiter
www.collegerecruiter.com

Steven Rothberg
3722 W. 50 St., Suite 121, Minneapolis, MN 55410
Ph: 800-835-4989   Fax: 952-915-1102   E-mail: Steven@collegerecruiter.com

JOBS	10,000s	RESUMES	10,000s
Cost to post	Cost to see	Cost to post	Cost to see
Fee	Free	Free	Fee
DISCIPLINE		LOCATION	
ALL		USA/MDW/MN	
SPECIALTY		FEATURE	
ALL		COLLEGE	
AGENT: Both Recruiters & Jobseekers			

College Recruiter.com started November 1996 and concentrates on part-time, internship and entry-level positions for the college crowd. Recruiters pay $125 to post an opening for one month ($695 for unlimited postings in a month) and obtain access to the resume database. Jobs can be scrapped off a corporate site and posted in bulk for $1.995 per year. The site claims over 160,000+ resumes in their database, with none over 90 days old. There are over 1,000 colleges linked to this site. Jobs can be viewed by keyword, state or province (Canada), job category, or experience level. Job seekers can see openings without a registration process. A total of 64,000 students subscribe to a semi-weekly email newsletter. Over 500 career related articles are featured.

Colorado Online Job Connection

www.coloradojobs.com

Charlie Milliet
100 Mesa Avenue, Durango, CO
Ph: 877-919-5627   Fax: 970-259-7904   E-mail: sales@coloradojobs.com

JOBS	100s		RESUMES	100s
Cost to post	Cost to see		Cost to post	Cost to see
Fee	Free		Free	Fee
DISCIPLINE			LOCATION	
ALL			USA/WEST/CO	
SPECIALTY			FEATURE	
ALL			N/A	
AGENT: Jobseeker				

Colorado Online Job Connection has brought Coloradojobs.com and Channel 7 - KMGH (TV) together. Many different disciplines can be found for jobs and resumes. Employers pay $100 to post a 30-day listing. Resume database access is $195 for 30 days. Job seekers are invited to post their resume to the database but it is not mandatory to gain access to the posted positions. Mountain Jobs has been created for those who wish to work and live on high. Site is also affiliated with www.denverjobs.com and www.jobsincolorado.com

Community Career Center

www.nonprofitjobs.org/

Gino Maini
2160 W. Charleston,, Suite L345, Las Vegas, NV
Ph: 702-259-9580   Fax: 702-259-0244   E-mail: info@nonprofitjobs.org

JOBS	100s		RESUMES	100s
Cost to post	Cost to see		Cost to post	Cost to see
Fee	Free		Fee	Fee
DISCIPLINE			LOCATION	
Non-Profit			USA	
SPECIALTY			FEATURE	
ALL			N/A	
AGENT: N/A				

Community Career Center (non-profit jobs) claims AARP, The American Cancer Society, and several other well-known charities are members. Site charges $25 to post resumes. Recruiters pay $125 per job for a 60-day posting (or to become members). Many jobs have salary data listed for each opening. Resumes posted to the site can only be seen by member companies. There were 200 jobs listed by title, employer, location and date on our visit. This "for profit" site with its emphasis on non-profit work is worth the visit for the list of non-profits alone.

computerjobs.com
www.computerjobs.com

Mary McAuley
280 Interstate N. Pky., SE, Suite 300, Atlanta, GA 30339
Ph: 800-850-0045   Fax: 800-850-0369   E-mail: sales@computerjobs.com

JOBS	1,000s		RESUMES	100,000s
Cost to post	Cost to see		Cost to post	Cost to see
Fee	Free		Free	Fee

DISCIPLINE		LOCATION	
IT		USA	
SPECIALTY		FEATURE	
ALL		N/A	

AGENT: Jobseeker

CAREER X ROADS

2003

TOP SITE

The first thing you notice when entering computerjobs.com is their extensive disclosure regarding the number of jobs in each location and skillset (6,542) 875 in ERP, 751 in Atlanta, etc.). Aggressive disclosure of their goals, privacy statement, marketing and services is as good as it gets. A total of 20 location sites and 18 skill sites and several others (H-1B, entry level) make this a true niche network. Employers can post a position for $200 for a 4 week run. Resumes (260,000) can be viewed for free but contact information comes with a monthly subscription package. Cost varies by region of the USA from $250-$695. Extensive services for job seekers include salary surveys for contract and regular positions. Email notification of job matches is available for anyone who registers. The sites include locations such as: alabama, atlanta, boston, carolinas, chicago, dc, denver, detroit, florida, la, new york, ohio, philadelphia, phoenix, portland, seattle, silicon valley, st. louis, texas, twincities, and skill sets such as:as/400, data warehousing, database systems, e-commerce, erp, executive, hardware, help desk, legacy systems, networking, new media/graphics, project management, quality assurance, technical recruiting, technical sales, technical writer, unix and windows developer. Job seekers can save their search criteria and selected jobs to return another time. Job seekers must register to utilize the site's powersearch for jobs. User groups can also be found for additional job leads. The owners of CJ continue to enhance this leading information technology employment site.

Computerwork.com
www.computerwork.com

Jim Ingham
4500 Salisbury Road, Ste. 350, Jacksonville, FL 32216
Ph: 800-691-8413   Fax: 904-296-3292   E-mail: sales@computerwork.com

JOBS	10,000s		RESUMES	100,000s
Cost to post	Cost to see		Cost to post	Cost to see
Fee	Free		Free	Fee
DISCIPLINE			LOCATION	
IT			USA	
SPECIALTY			FEATURE	
ALL			Gateway	
AGENT: Jobseeker				

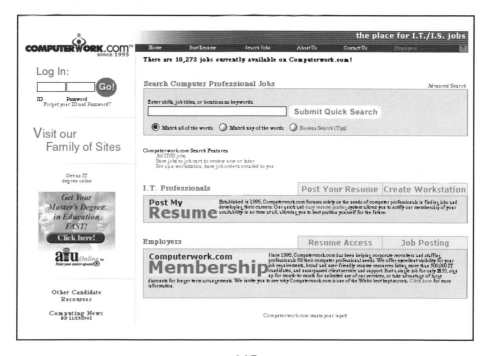

Computerwork.com was launched in 1995 as the gateway to a niche network of information technology specialty and regional sites. Job seekers can place their skills online and have positions pushed to them via the site's agent. Recruiters pay $75 for one job posting and can search the resume database for matches for $295 per month. Job seekers apply through the site, which forwards resumes to the employer or emails employers directly. Each search returns the number of matches with date of postings. The 66 sites in the network provide the number of openings on each Sites include:C++, Oracle, Java, Unix and Cobol, as well as sites across the U.S. such as www.computerwork.com/cfm-bin/other_sites.cfm. This is one of the few sites that advises recruiters the cost to post a job and number of resumes in the database on the homepage. We like full disclosure, and this site continues to be an open book.

165

Construction Gigs

www.constructiongigs.com/

Ph: 781-383-0054   E-mail: bob@constructiongigs.com

JOBS	100s		RESUMES	100s
Cost to post	Cost to see		Cost to post	Cost to see
Free (See Notes)	Free		Fee	Free
DISCIPLINE			LOCATION	
Trades/Engineering			USA	
SPECIALTY			FEATURE	
Construction/Civil			N/A	
AGENT: N/A				

Construction Gigs was established August 1997 for all trades and professionals in construction. Recruiters can post links to their corporate job pages for free. Resumes can be viewed by recruiters with contact information for free. Job seekers pay $30 to post their resume for one-year. This simple site has great value.

ConstructionJobs.com

www.constructionjobs.com

Todd Scholl
G. Peterson Consulting Group, Inc., 227 N. El Camino Real, Suite 2, Encinitas, CA 92024
Ph: 877-767-7747   Fax: 760-944-6550   E-mail: info@constructionjobs.com

JOBS	100s		RESUMES	1,000s
Cost to post	Cost to see		Cost to post	Cost to see
Fee	Free		Free	Fee
DISCIPLINE			LOCATION	
Engineering/Trades			USA	
SPECIALTY			FEATURE	
Construction			N/A	
AGENT: N/A				

ConstructionJobs advertises in more than 10 industry publications. The job board also participates in industry trade shows and several job distribution services including GO Jobs and RecruitmentBox. Owner has also been busy forging alliances with 6 construction industry associations. Construction Jobs.com was started as a secondary business by a niche headhunting firm. Now the headhunting business is going away and this site is their main source of income. Recruiters can post jobs for $125 for 60 days or view resumes and post unlimited jobs for $795 per month. It is interesting that a former headhunter will not allow third party recruiters on this site. Owners have made positive changes to the site design- when w first took a look, job seekers could only access the jobs if they placed their resume in the database. Design of the search demonstrates that the site understands the skills and competencies required. If CXR were seeking a position in the field, we would be comfortable here.

Construction.com

www.construction.com/CareerCenter

Janet Kennedy
McGraw-Hill, Two Penn Plaza, 9th Floor, New York, NY 10121
Ph: 212-904-6433   Fax: 212-904-2074   E-mail: construction_careers@construction.com

JOBS	100s	RESUMES	1,000s
Cost to post	Cost to see	Cost to post	Cost to see
Fee	Free	Free	Fee
DISCIPLINE		LOCATION	
Trade/Engineering		USA	
SPECIALTY		FEATURE	
Civil/Construction		N/A	
AGENT: Jobseeker			

The newly enhanced Construction.com Career Center is brought to you by well-known brands in the Construction industry; Engineering News-Record, Architectural Record, Design-Build and the Dodge Regional Publications, divisions of the McGraw-Hill Construction Information Group. Employers pay $250 to post a position and $350 to access the resume database. Specialized search engine focuses on the industry at all levels. Use the state map and immediately see how many positions are listed in every location. Content is significant and includes an opt-in newsletter for industry trends and more.

Contract Job Hunter

www.cjhunter.com

Jerry Erickson
P.O. Box 3006, Bothell, WA 98041
Ph: 425-806-5200   Fax: 425-806-5585   E-mail: staff@cjhunter.com

JOBS	1,000s	RESUMES	10,000s
Cost to post	Cost to see	Cost to post	Cost to see
Fee	Fee	Free	Fee (See Notes)
DISCIPLINE		LOCATION	
IT		USA	
SPECIALTY		FEATURE	
ALL		Contract	
AGENT: Recruiter			

Contract Job Hunter belongs to Contract Employment Weekly which has been in business for over 32 years serving computer contract service firms. The website charges $300 per month (additional offices are charged $100 per month) for unlimited job postings, access to the site's resume database and 10 joblines per week in C.E. Weekly. Resumes that are submitted to the site are emailed to recruiters who advertise jobs on the site. Job seekers can have a link to their online resume posted to the site under their name. For recruiters this is a pot of gold. For job seekers the site charges $20 for 52-week access to jobs on the website. A chatroom for contractors has been created for additional sources.

Cool Works - Jobs in Great Places
www.coolworks.com

Bill Berg
PO Box 272, Gardiner, MT 59030
Ph: 406-848-2380   Fax: 406-848-2320   E-mail: greatjobs@coolworks.com

JOBS	10,000s	RESUMES	1,000s
Cost to post	Cost to see	Cost to post	Cost to see
Fee	Free	Free	Fee
DISCIPLINE		LOCATION	
Hospitality/Entertainment/Retail/Miscellaneous		USA	
SPECIALTY		FEATURE	
Sports/Outdoors/Adventure/Resorts		COLLEGE	
AGENT: Jobseeker			

Cool Works provides cool jobs that most of us only dream about. Started in 1995 Bill Berg - Mr. Cool himself provides 75,000 openings at camps, national parks, ski resorts, cruise lines and every other outdoor facility you can imagine. Quite a few jobs link directly to employer sites. Employers pay $85 per month to post a job and multiple packages gain access to the resume database. Most postings are seasonal, so job seekers need to keep timing in mind. A free newsletter that provides skill matched openings is emailed to job seekers on a weekly basis. . Openings are now posted by: national parks, camp, resort jobs, internships, and location so job seekers always get a positive response. For us old geezers, "older & bolder" provides jobs geared for those with RV's or where housing is provided. Clients are trying out the site's new online applicant tracking system geared for seasonal positions. These folks have always understood what it takes to build a niche.

coroflot
www.coroflot.com

Greg Moore
Core 77, Inc., 561 Broadway, 6th Floor, New York, NY 10012
Ph: 212-965-1998   Fax: 212-965-1838   E-mail: copilot@coroflot.com

JOBS	100s	RESUMES	1,000s
Cost to post	Cost to see	Cost to post	Cost to see
Fee	Free	Free	Free
DISCIPLINE		LOCATION	
Communications		USA	
SPECIALTY		FEATURE	
Graphic Design		N/A	
AGENT: Jobseeker			

At Coroflot, job seekers can view postings for management level, exhibit, graphic, industrial, interior, interactive, pop/retail or 3-D design. Openings can be viewed by date, title, company and location. All jobs are date posted. Recruiters can view resumes for free or post a job for $150 for a 90-day run. Job seekers can post their portfolio along with a resume. Job seekers can have posted openings sent to their pc via email. Well designed and easy to view, Coroflot is a keeper for the creative crowd. Owners day jobs are in media design.

Corporate Gray

www.bluetogray.com

Carl Savino
Competitive Edge Services, PO Box 342, Fairfax Station, VA 22039
Ph: 703-690-6381   Fax: 703-690-1687   E-mail: carl@corporate-gray.com

JOBS	10,000s	RESUMES	10,000s
Cost to post	Cost to see	Cost to post	Cost to see
Free	Free	Free	Fee
DISCIPLINE		LOCATION	
ALL		USA	
SPECIALTY		FEATURE	
ALL		Military Transition/security clearnace	
AGENT: Both Recruiters & Jobseekers			

Corporate Gray was created in June 1998 to provide services for those individuals returning to private industry from the military. Recruiters can post their first 5 jobs for free or unlimited openings for $100 per month. Access to the resume database, company profiles and unlimited job posting is $300 per month. Up to 5 resume search agents are included that forward candidates matching openings via email. The site runs military job fairs across the USA. Job seekers must register before they can search for jobs. Openings can be viewed by simple keyword or occupation and via an advanced engine by keyword, security clearance, occupation, country, state, city, salary range, percentage of travel, education, relocation or specific employ ers Jobs are date posted and can be saved for future viewing. Corporate profiles of hundreds of defense contractors are available.

Corrections Connection

www.corrections.com

159 Burgin Parkway, Quincy, MA 02169
Ph: 617-471-4445   Fax: 617-770-3339   E-mail: advertising@corrections.com

JOBS	100s	RESUMES	1,000s
Cost to post	Cost to see	Cost to post	Cost to see
Free	Free	Free	Free
DISCIPLINE		LOCATION	
Law & Order		USA/	
SPECIALTY		FEATURE	
Corrections		N/A	
AGENT: N/A			

Launched in 1996, the Corrections Connection has this niche locked up pretty tightly. Employers get everything for free - no cost to post or view resumes. Nearly 100 jobs are posted and more than 1000 resumes are available. No, we don't know how they are making money and we're not going to ask.

Craigslist
www.craigslist.org

915 Cole, San Francisco, CA
Ph: 415-566-6394   E-mail: questions@craigslist.org

JOBS	1,000s	RESUMES	10,000s
Cost to post	Cost to see	Cost to post	Cost to see
Fee	Free	Free	Free
DISCIPLINE		LOCATION	
IT		USA/WEST/San Francisco	
SPECIALTY		FEATURE	
ALL		Gateway	
AGENT: N/A			

Craigslist remains an urban legend. The site was discovered in 2001 by the mainstream press after an article in the Wall Street Journal quoted Forrester Research's ranking of Craigslist as "the most effective site for recruiting." Craigslist is an old-fashioned, community-based, bulletin board style site that has what everyone else wants, a personality you remember and the complete trust of its users. The owner, Craig Newmark, is a self-described "hardcore Java and web programmer who grew up wearing a plastic pocket protector and thick black glasses." He started Craigslist in early 1995 to connect to people and let them know about cool events in and around San Francisco. Job categories range from accounting to writing. Jobs are easy to view with the number of openings posted next to each job category. Openings cost $75 to post for a 30 day run per region. Craigslist also allows posting and browsing of resumes by location for free. All are deleted after 30 days. What cannot be denied is that Craigslist has the right touch in this locale and has expanded to major cities throughout the U.S.(Atlanta, Austin, Boston, Chicago, DC, Denver, Los Angeles, New York, Portland, Sacramento, San Diego, Seattle, Vancouver) in addition to the four Bay area sites. It has yet to be seen if Craig can take this business model across the country.

JOB SEEKER TIP

Good job hunting should be inclusive not exclusive.

Look at opportunities with the thought of "how does this fit me." Find a way to say "yes", this has possibilities rather than no, it's too far to travel.

Creative Hotlist

www.creativehotlist.com

Mike Krigel
Communication Arts, 110 Constitution Drive, Menlo Park, CA 94025
Ph: 650-815-4226   Fax: 650-326-1648   E-mail: advertising@creativehotlist.com

JOBS	100s	RESUMES	10,000s
Cost to post	Cost to see	Cost to post	Cost to see
Free (See Notes)	Free	Free	Free
DISCIPLINE		LOCATION	
Communications		USA	
SPECIALTY		FEATURE	
Arts/Graphic		N/A	
AGENT: N/A			

Creative Hotlist is owned by Coyne & Blanchard who publish Communication Arts magazine. The magazine has a paid circulation of 72,000 subscribers. Recruiters who wish to post jobs must register to receive a password via email they will never remember. The first two job postings are free as recruiters are then asked to buy credits for $100 each or $375 to post 4 jobs. Job seekers can view openings by zip code or region/state, job category, experience, new listings to the site, or type of company. An initial search then brings select categories and industries. Searching by zip code shows how many miles the opportunity is from their location. Individual search options work really well, and all matches were on target. Resumes can be viewed for free as they are searched the same way. Copywriters, creative directors and graphic designers are plentiful here.

Dave's ESL Cafe (English as a Second Language)

www.eslcafe.com

Dan Sperling
22287 Mulholland Hwy., #381, Calabasas, CA 91302
Ph: 800-309-0290   Fax: 818-713-9113   E-mail: sperling@escafe.com

JOBS	100s	RESUMES	100s
Cost to post	Cost to see	Cost to post	Cost to see
Fee	Free	Free	Free
DISCIPLINE		LOCATION	
Education		INTL/Pacific Rim/Korea	
SPECIALTY		FEATURE	
Teaching, K-12, ESL		N/A	
AGENT: N/A			

Dave's ESL Cafe (English as a Second Language), started in 1995, posts teaching positions from around the world. Recruiters pay $75 per posting or $200 for four postings for 30 days. Dave has also created a site for teaching jobs in Korea (escafe.com/jobs/korea). Openings are posted by date of receipt. Just under 400 resumes can be viewed for free. Job discussion forums and a job information journal where teachers who have taught in foreign countries posttheir experiences make this site worth a visit.

DaVinciTimes

www.davincitimes.org

Tom Mushow
PO Box 223, Dewitt, NY 13214
Ph: 315-445-5845   Fax: 315-445-9401   E-mail: davinciads@davincitimes.org

JOBS	100s	RESUMES	1,000s
Cost to post	Cost to see	Cost to post	Cost to see
Fee	Free	Free	Fee
DISCIPLINE		LOCATION	
IT/Engineering		USA/NOE/NY/Syracuse	
SPECIALTY		FEATURE	
ALL		N/A	
AGENT: Both Recruiters & Jobseekers			

DaVinciTimes has taken on a new look as the site was originally written from the point of view of Leonardo DaVinci whose stories are no longer available. Created in January 1998, the site is a collaboration of upstate New York businesses (with primarily engineering/information technology jobs) who felt that working together to draw more technical talent to the area was a constructive alternative to simply competing for scarce resources. Now, with 47 corporate members, this model proves corporations can collaborate to effectively recruit talent. Job seekers can search by specialty, tech positions, location, intern/co-ops or even non USA citizen listings. Visitors can peruse local informatiion including time to commute. Member corporations can join for $2,000 a year to post unlimited jobs and receive resumes matched against openings via email. Full membership is $4,000 a year which includes access to the resume database. Third party recruiters are not welcome. An applicant tracking system may be in the works for the future.as an added member benefit. DaVinciTimes is always trying new ideas and is always willing to listen to recommendations. They've worked hard to build a community model.

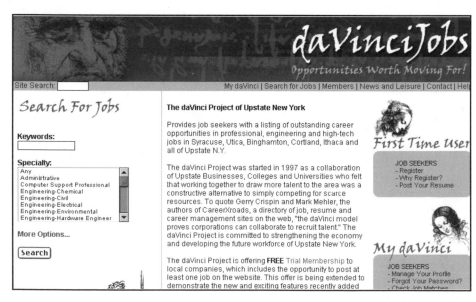

DegreeHunter.com
www.degreehunter.com

Jason Hill
15105 D John J Delaney Drive, Suite 171, Charlotte, NC 28277
Ph: 704-608-0518   E-mail: administrator@degreehunter.com

JOBS	100s	RESUMES	1,000s
Cost to post	Cost to see	Cost to post	Cost to see
Fee (See Notes)	Free	Free	Fee
DISCIPLINE		LOCATION	
ALL		USA	
SPECIALTY		FEATURE	
ALL		N/A	
AGENT: Both Recruiters & Jobseekers			

DegreeHunter.com caters to advanced degreed professionals in nursing, medical, health care, legal, engineering physician or MBA opportunities. Recruiters can post openings for free but pay $44.93 to view contact data from an appliicant. Job seekers can apply for posted openings but then it is up to the recruiter if the contact is worth paying for. Job seekers can view career assessment profiles on each area this site specializes in. All job seekers must register to gain access to contact information. Site advises that they review every job and resume before it is placed in their system which is a step in the right direction.

DesignerMax.com
www.designermax.com

Larry Holly
PO Box 230094, Fair Haven, MI 48023
Ph: 810-725-6323   E-mail: lholly@aiis.net

JOBS	100s	RESUMES	1,000s
Cost to post	Cost to see	Cost to post	Cost to see
Fee	Free	Free	Fee
DISCIPLINE		LOCATION	
Engineering		USA	
SPECIALTY		FEATURE	
Design		N/A	
AGENT: Jobseeker			

DesignerMax.com (DM) is special in that it offers recruiters statistics by job category (i.e. how many members match the company's requirements). DM even goes so far as to advise about years of experience and average hourly salary. Searching for work is easy by completing a required skills checkbox. Short job descriptions with direct contact information is available. Recruiters pay $25 to post 10 positions per month and search the site's resume database. An easy to understand privacy policy and a service that pushes openings to job seekers so they can respond themselves stands out. Resumes can be kept confidential from employers. Job seekers and recruiters who need a life should check out the daily cartoon.

Destiny Group-Military Transition Center
www.destinygroup.com

Bill Gaul
The Destiny Group, 750 B Street, Suite 1840, San Diego, CA 98101
Ph: 619-696-8700   Fax: 619-696-8795   E-mail: info@destinygrp.com

JOBS	100s		RESUMES	10,000s
Cost to post	Cost to see		Cost to post	Cost to see
Fee	Free		Free	Fee
DISCIPLINE			LOCATION	
ALL			USA	
SPECIALTY			FEATURE	
ALL			Military Transition/Gateway	
AGENT: Both Recruiters & Jobseekers				

The Destiny Group founded in 1997 is the gateway to a network of military transition sites such as academy-grads.com, davjobs.com, mil2civ.com, miltaryspouses.com, troopstoteachers.com, and vets4hire.com. The owners claim to work with the Alumni Associations of U.S. military service academies to provide career transition services to their alumni and to corporations seeking to hire them. They have expanded their network of 18 sites they cross post to. These include reserve officer associations and other groups providing military transition assistance- as well as partnerships with portals like military.com The site's search engine guides jobseekers by profession, location, company name. A map of the U.S. makes drilling to location a snap. Corporate recruiters pay $150 to post one position and headhunters need to contact the site for pricing information. Cost to gain access to the site's partner databases range from $2,500 - $13,500 per year (includes access to an ATS system). Site also holds national monthly military recruiting conferences. Staffers who have never recruited in this arena should consider attending "The Secrets of Military Recruiting Revealed" seminar. For many corporations, the military are too often an overlooked source of quality candidates.We're especially interested in Destiny's experiment with a VIP database that will give the jobseekers access to a mentor networking tool to reach other veterans already positioned in business. It's a blind system and 100% opt in, with about 20,000 "mentors" already signed up.

Developers.net (Tapestry.net)

www.tapestry.net

Dayle Bowen
Tapestry.net, 3040 Valencia Avenue, Suite 5, Rio Del Mar, CA 95003
Ph: 831-440-5700   Fax: 831-440-5701   E-mail: dbowen@tapestry.net

JOBS	100s	RESUMES	100,000s
Cost to post	Cost to see	Cost to post	Cost to see
Free	Free	Free (See Notes)	Fee (See Notes)

DISCIPLINE	LOCATION
IT	USA

SPECIALTY	FEATURE
Software Developer	DIVERSITY

AGENT: Job Seeker

Developers.net and its owner, Tapestry.net, continue to impress us with their understanding of community and the power of email. Having sold a majority stake in Asia-Net (where their initial concept of collecting emails began) to Softbank in 2000, Tapestry.net continues to stretch the web envelope by extending their model in two directions. A pay-for-location model in cities like Washington DC, Seattle, Boston and San Francisco is one approach. The site claims to have collected over 125,000 emails of software, hardware and systems professionals. Members' profiles are matched with posted openings and emailed to candidates. Openings can also be searched by keyword at the site. Recruiters pay $200 for a 30-day run. Tapestry.net's other approach is to focus on a flat fee pay-for-performance model by pre-screening candidates for technical and Asian-language bilingual positions.

JOB SEEKER TIP

No job is filled until the person starts.

On more than one opening we have found that the initial offer was rejected and the person never started.

DICE High Tech Jobs Online
www.dice.com

Pete Steiner
4101 NW Urbandale Drive, Urbandale, IA 50322
Ph: 877-386-3323   Fax: 515-280-1452   E-mail: sales@dice.com

JOBS	10,000s		RESUMES	10,000s
Cost to post	Cost to see		Cost to post	Cost to see
Fee	Free		Free	Fee

DISCIPLINE		LOCATION
IT		USA

SPECIALTY		FEATURE
ALL		Contingent

AGENT: Both Recruiters & Jobseekers

DICE was once upon a time (pre-web) a major bulletin board and today it continues as a top site for information technology- contract, consulting and permanent jobs. DICE is a frequent advertiser on national radio, visible on billboards and easily found in many specialty publications(look for the pair of fuzzy dice). Numerous alliances with technology sites drive information technology professionals to this site in droves. Dice claims over 28,000 jobs. Tens of thousands of people have registered their email to view job postings. The industry may be down, but scarce skills will always be in demand. Job seekers can register their skills for a site agent. The site search engine can sort jobs by keyword, state, type of job or area code. Recruiters can post opportunities but they are limited to the state in which the position is listed. Job seekers can post their profile for 30 days, and then they need to re-enter the site to keep it active. Profiles are sent to member employers on a daily basis. (DICE will also forward 10 candidates each day from their hot list files.) Employers can search the profile database by keywords. However, there are two types of searchable databases. The newest are "announced candidates" for job seekers looking within the next 30 days. Cost for 1 job is $275.This niche site built a solid reputation, expanded beyond its contract beginnings and, more importantly, knows how to promote its service. Special site pages have been added and include 28 major cities across the U.S. and Canada. The site will also crosspost open positions to Black World Today Careers, Women In Technology International, and Webgrrls International.

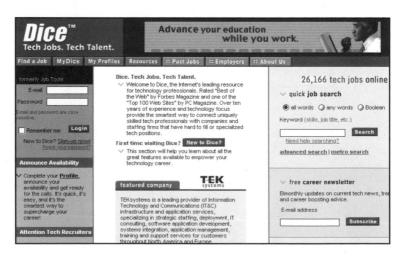

176

DirectEmployers
www.DirectEmployers.com

E-Recruiting Association, Inc., 4040 Vincennes Circle, 4th Floor, Indianapolis, IN 46268
Ph: 317-874-9000   Fax: 317-874-9100   E-mail: info@directemployers.com

JOBS	10,000s	RESUMES	N/A
Cost to post	Cost to see	Cost to post	Cost to see
Fee	Free	N/A	N/A
DISCIPLINE		LOCATION	
All		USA/	
SPECIALTY		FEATURE	
ALL		N/A	
AGENT: N/A			

DirectEmployers is the E-Recruiting Association's main asset and is listed as a 501 (c) (6) non-profit. In actuality the association was created as an employer trade organization whose main purpose is a common goal to aggregate all their openings through a single portal. Member prices vary from thousands to tens of thousands of dollars but, when it comes down to the bottom line, this site effectively drives its visitors directly to a company's job pages and can provide the metrics to justify its cost. For job seekers, this site allows you to examine ALL the jobs for all of the members. Lots of buzz was generated when the site launched in 2002. Sustaining its effort year after year will be a challenge but we acknowledge it has become a player. Employers are consistently positive about DirectEmployers although we don't know why this model would include third party recruiters. An alliance with NACE (National Association of Colleges and Employers) scheduled to launch in 2002-2003 will be closely watched.

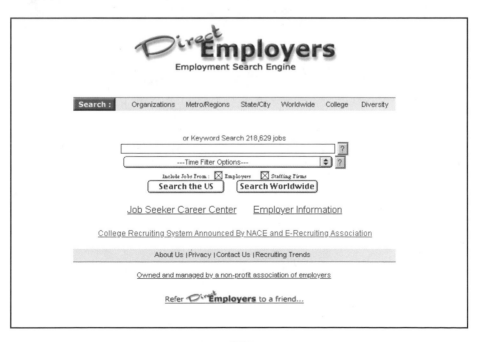

DiversityInc.com

www.diversityinc.com

Carl Braun
317 George Street, Suite 420, New Brunswick, NJ 08901
Ph: 732-509-5205   E-mail: cbraun@diversityinc.com

JOBS	1,000s		RESUMES	1,000s
Cost to post	Cost to see		Cost to post	Cost to see
Fee	Free		Free	Fee
DISCIPLINE			LOCATION	
ALL			USA	
SPECIALTY			FEATURE	
ALL			DIVERSITY	
AGENT: Jobseeker				

DiversityInc.com was launched in 1998 and has gained quite a following by offering news briefs and subscriber options for its original articles and repackaged news feeds to corporate employees. Options are fee based but some limited content is free. At the core of this model is a great marketing idea to offer client companies content they can pass along to their employees. Site plans to launch its first print publication before the end of 2002. All openings are date posted with large block type. Various pricing packages are offered. Subscriptions to the news feeds are $25,000 per year with unlimited corporate access to their articles. Another approach to pricing is $30 for one user per year for access to the articles. Recruiters pay $195 to post a job for 60 days.

DiversityLink.com

www.diversitylink.com

Milton Spain
PMB 157, 11338 Kenyon Way, Suite B, Rancho Cucamonga, CA 91701
Ph: 909-989-8416   Fax: 909-945-4896   E-mail: diversity@diversitylink.com

JOBS	100s		RESUMES	100s
Cost to post	Cost to see		Cost to post	Cost to see
Fee	Free		Free	Fee
DISCIPLINE			LOCATION	
ALL			USA	
SPECIALTY			FEATURE	
ALL			DIVERSITY	
AGENT: N/A				

DiversityLink.com emphasizes opportunities for women, ethnic minorities, people with physical challenges, seniors, and others. DiversityLink.com is among a growing group of sites that can "scrape" a company's job openings directly from the company's web site. Recruiters pay $150to post a position for 60 days. Cost to access the resume database depends on the site package purchased. Openings can be viewed by job category or keyword search and all are date posted. Resumes are deleted after 120 days in the database.

Drug Information Association
www.diahome.org

800 Enterprise Road, Suite 200, Horsham, PA 19044
Ph: 215-442-6100   Fax: 214-442-6199   E-mail: dia@diahome.org

JOBS	1,000s	RESUMES	N/A
Cost to post	Cost to see	Cost to post	Cost to see
Free	Free	N/A	N/A
DISCIPLINE		LOCATION	
Science		USA	
SPECIALTY		FEATURE	
Pharmaceutical		College	
AGENT: N/A			

The Drug Information Association (DIA), a nonprofit scientific association, has over 27,000 members working for regulatory agencies and academia as well as the pharmaceutical, biological and medical device industries. Positions are posted from all over the world. USA positions are easy to view and search with date of posting clearly identified. Positions will be posted for 60 days and are primarily from the USA and Canada. There were over 2,000 jobs listed on our last visit. Internships are in a separate field and are listed with some of the largest pharmaceutical firms. In prior years this site had a resume database which is no longer available.

Dubuque- AccessSuccess
www.accessdubuque.com/jobs

Dick Landis
Telegraph Herald, P.O. Box 688, Dubuque, IA 52004
Ph: 563-588-5778   Fax: 563-588-5782   E-mail: dlandis@wcinet.com

JOBS	100s	RESUMES	1,000s
Cost to post	Cost to see	Cost to post	Cost to see
Fee	Free	Free	Fee
DISCIPLINE		LOCATION	
ALL		USA/MDW/IA/	
SPECIALTY		FEATURE	
ALL		N/A	
AGENT: N/A			

What makes this small town newspaper, Dubuque- AccessSuccess, atypical is that all the jobs posted here are automatically cross-posted to the State of Iowa job-recruitment site at www.smartcareermove.com. This regional site orginally focused on high tech and professional positions. Today, jobs in all 24 categories can be seen - agricultural, manufacturing, hospitality, etc. Resumes in this database are about 30% local and 70% national. The out-of-area resumes appear to come from people who want to work in the Dubuque area - i.e. their spouse has accepted a new job nearby. Launched in 1997, the site charges employers $50 for a 30 day posting and access to the resume database for 10 days for $75. Clients with contracts for print get a discount.

e-itwizards.com
e-itwizards.com

Barbara Kellogg
974 Breckenridge Lane, Suite 204, Louisville, KY 40207
Ph: 800-576-6573   Fax: 720-294-0596   E-mail: louisville_office@e-itwizards.com

JOBS	1,000s	RESUMES	100,000s
Cost to post	Cost to see	Cost to post	Cost to see
Fee	Free	Free	Fee
DISCIPLINE		LOCATION	
IT		USA	
SPECIALTY		FEATURE	
ALL		N/A	
AGENT: Both Recruiters & Jobseekers			

E-itwizards.com claims to haves access to over 4+ million jobs from 2,000 job boards and 100 search engines. Owners are using spidering technology and the results are emailed to the recruiter and job seeker. Recruiters pay either $25 per day or $300 for 3 months unlimited job postings. Resume spider technology access is $25 per day or $175 per month for unlimited users. WizTest has 41 different skill sets that an applicant can be quizzed in. WizPoster will cross post jobs to over 2,000 boards. Site owners claim to have 5,500 openings posted and 225,000 resumes on this site. Interesting use of technology but it all boils down to results.

ecampusrecruiter

www.ecampusrecruiter.com

Jason Weingarten
Simpedia Networks, 2336 SE Ocean Blvd., Suite 324, Stuart, FL 34996
Ph: 773-975-7882   Fax: 773-975-7884   E-mail: advertise@simpedia.com

JOBS	1,000s		RESUMES	1,000s
Cost to post	Cost to see		Cost to post	Cost to see
Fee	Free		Free	Fee
DISCIPLINE			LOCATION	
ALL			USA	
SPECIALTY			FEATURE	
ALL			COLLEGE	
AGENT: Jobseeker				

ECampusRecruiter.com was launched February 2000 and caters to the college and internship crowd. Recruiters can post one opening for $175 for 60 days. Unlimited job posting and access to the resume database is $325 per quarter. The site seeks representatives on college campuses to reach students. Online job fairs are also available. Job seekers must register to access the site. Openings are broken out by entry level, internship, graduate school jobs and part-time/local and all are date posted. Site has introduced online software services - campus management systems for college career centers and has 40 campuses using it.

Editor & Publisher

www.mediainfo.com

Hazel Preuss
770 Broadway, New York, NY 10003
Ph: 646-654-5302   E-mail: hpreuss@editorandpublisher.com

JOBS	100s		RESUMES	10s
Cost to post	Cost to see		Cost to post	Cost to see
Fee	Free		Fee	Free
DISCIPLINE			LOCATION	
Communications/Entertainment & Media			USA	
SPECIALTY			FEATURE	
Writing			N/A	
AGENT: N/A				

Editor & Publisher magazine posts its job openings via this website for it's 150,000 readers. Only subscribers can access the latest and greatest postings. All jobs are posted for free access 5-7 days from the actual posting date. Openings here run the gamut from academic to editorial to production/tech. Recruiters pay $13.25 per line per week to advertise. Job seekers can view openings by topic, and all are date posted. Job seekers can post positions wanted for $6.75 per line per week. All rates include publication in the print magazine.

eFinancialCareers

www.efinancialcareers.com

George Ball
29-33 Scrutton Street, Stapleton House, London, UK United Kingdom
Ph: 440-207-3097712 Fax: 440-207-4263329 E-mail: clientservices@efinancialcareers

JOBS	1,000s	RESUMES	10,000s
Cost to post	Cost to see	Cost to post	Cost to see
Fee	Free	N/A	N/A
DISCIPLINE		LOCATION	
Business		INTL/Europe	
SPECIALTY		FEATURE	
Finance/Accounting		College	
AGENT: Jobseeker			

EFinancialCareers, launched in September 2000, specializes in the securities, investment banking and asset management industries. Job seekers can view openings by investment sectors (accounting to risk management), salary, location or keyword. Opportunities are from around the world but primarily Europe (London, Frankfurt, Paris) and the US. A sprinkling of Pacific Rim (Hong Kong, Singapore and Tokyo) jobs can be found. Employers pay £75-£110 pounds to post an opportunity. Access to the resume database is a separate fee. An Ask the Expert section assists college graduates with interesting articles and supports a separate internship and jobs database.

eJobStores

www.eJobStores.com

Fran Grossman
10130 Northlake Blvd, Suite 214-319, West Palm Beach, FL 33412
Ph: 561-775-3584   Fax: 561-625-3122   E-mail: jobs@eJobStores.com

JOBS	1,000s	RESUMES	1,000s
Cost to post	Cost to see	Cost to post	Cost to see
Fee	Free	Free	Fee
DISCIPLINE		LOCATION	
ALL		USA	
SPECIALTY		FEATURE	
ALL		Gateway	
AGENT: Jobseeker			

EJobStores.com was launched in 1995 (under Real Estate Job Stores, Inc.) and today has a network of more than 200 non-health care sites feeding into this gateway. (A second network of health care sites can be found under HealthCareJobStores.com). A long list of geographic sites is also available. Fran, the site's owner, was one of the original folks to build a network of urls. Everything from "Administrativeassitantjobs" to "Webjobs" and "Alabamajobstore to Wyomingjobstore (and just about every specialty in between) is here. Fran wants to prove that if you have the right url the job seekers will come. A job opening for a single industry can be posted for $175 for 60 days ($25 for each additional jobtitle/industry site). Geographical job postings are $125. Unlimited job postings to all the sites, plus resume access is $699 per month. An industry salary survey is powered by the people who visit the site. Recruiters need to check the metrics on each site they are considering purchasing as some have limited postings.

Electric job.com
www.electricjob.com

Marc Sampson
6200 Aurora Ave., Suite 410W, Des Moines, IA 50322
Ph: 888-482-2562   Fax: 515-278-6025   E-mail: info@electricjob.com

JOBS	100s	RESUMES	1,000s
Cost to post	Cost to see	Cost to post	Cost to see
Fee	Free	Free	Fee
DISCIPLINE		LOCATION	
Trades, Non-Exempt & Hourly		USA	
SPECIALTY		FEATURE	
Electrical/Electronic		Gateway	
AGENT: Both Recruiters & Jobseekers			

Electricjob.com, hvac.com, plumbjob.com and havjob.com are a network of sites where recruiters are invited to pay $495 to post unlimited jobs and gain access to the site's resume database for 3 months ($195 to post a position for 90 days, resume access for 1 year is $1,145). Other packages are available. Job seekers can register to receive positions matching their interests. Resumes can be posted anonymously or with open contact information. The site posts the current count of resumes for sales, construction superintendents, electricians, technicians, engineers, managers and estimators, and contains neat niches. CXR loves metrics and any niche site that provides what the customer wants is a winner.

Electrical Employment
www.cossin.com

Dr. Chuck Cossin
P.O.Box 21, Farmington, MI 48332
Ph: 734-591-6650   E-mail: chuck@cossin.com

JOBS	100s	RESUMES	100s
Cost to post	Cost to see	Cost to post	Cost to see
Free	Free	Free	Free
DISCIPLINE		LOCATION	
Trades, Non-Exempt & Hourly		USA	
SPECIALTY		FEATURE	
Electrical/Electronic		N/A	
AGENT: N/A			

Electrical Employment is a simple, free self-service site for electrician jobs for the electrical trade. Profiles and positions include email contact only. Ideal model for a local community trade association.

Emplawyernet

Chet Olsen
Legal Recruitment Network, 1990 Westwood Boulevard, Los Angeles, CA 90025
Ph: 800-270-2685   Fax: 310-234-6635   E-mail: roz@emplawyernet.com

JOBS	1,000s		RESUMES	1,000s
Cost to post	Cost to see		Cost to post	Cost to see
Free (See Notes)	Fee		Free	Fee
DISCIPLINE			LOCATION	
Law & Order			USA	
SPECIALTY			FEATURE	
Attorney			COLLEGE	
AGENT: Jobseeker				

Emplawyernet's premier members pay $14.95 per month to have access to over 4,411 job listings. Openings are obtained from other sites and newspapers as well as those posted to this site. Law students can have 6 months of free membership. Members can also have matched positions emailed to their PC. Basic membership is free and includes access to a sampling of legal jobs and the opportunity to list a resume to the site's database. Job seekers can post their resumes confidentially. Employers can post a starter job for free, but it will only be seen by the site's paid members. A standard listing costs $150, and is emailed to 140,000 potential candidates. Firms can list biographies and candidates can send anonymous inquiries which are held by the site for 90 days. A new resume database is free to direct legal employers only. Headhunter pay a fee. A monthly newsletter is also available. All the F. Lee Bailey's in the crowd should check out "legal trvia" to test their knowledge.

employMAX

Al DiPalo
1704 Clearwater - Largo Road, Suite F2, Clearwater, FL 33756
Ph: 727-499-4500   Fax: 727-499-9414   E-mail: info@employmax.com

JOBS	100s		RESUMES	1,000s
Cost to post	Cost to see		Cost to post	Cost to see
Fee	Free		Free	Fee
DISCIPLINE			LOCATION	
ALL			USA	
SPECIALTY			FEATURE	
ALL			N/A	
AGENT: Jobseeker				

EmployMAX is owned by a third-party staffing company. Employers pay to get access to the site's resume warehouse. Resumes are acquired via a "spider" -resumes are found and not necessarily delivered by job seekers. But, the site then asks job seekers to update their profiles. If job seekers do not respond, the resumes still remain in the EmployMAX system for up to 24 months. Employers can post a job for $99 and gain access to the site's resume database for $895 a quarter. Job seekers can obtain "EXPERTease" that uses multimedia and special effects to present their background to employers for free. The catch is that they must place their resume on the site. EmployMax offers just about every service to employers, including site hosting, resume evaluation, an interview questionnaire builder, personality testing, multiple site postings and broadcast emails. Search firms can post jobs and resumes for potential splits with other firms. A low cost 1 month trial for $295 renewable for $100 each month was introduced in the Fall of 2002.

184

EmploymentGuide.com

www.employmentguide.com

Trader Publishing Company, 295 Bendix Rd., Virginia Beach, VA 23452
Ph: 877-876-4039   Fax: 757-321-8328   E-mail: sales@empguide.com

JOBS	10,000s	RESUMES	100,000s
Cost to post	Cost to see	Cost to post	Cost to see
Fee	Free	Free	Fee
DISCIPLINE		LOCATION	
ALL		USA/	
SPECIALTY		FEATURE	
ALL		Gateway/Home	
AGENT: Both Recruiters & Jobseekers			

EmploymentGuide.com has been through several iterations as it merged and then absorbed CareerWeb. This gateway to HealthCareerWeb.com gets its message out in numerous cities with a print product right next to those real estate and used car ad publications. Site also offers ResumeTrader - a fee based resume distribution tool (we don't approve of these in general). Jobseekers answer position-specific questions to help match postings and assist in screening. Site also claims to have a successful work-at-home center at which business owners can post their work-at-home opportunities; an Education Resource center in which schools can advertise their educational program; and, a seperate Heathcare site - HealthCareerWeb.com - with matching applicant system. Costs start at $120 to post a position for 30 days and the same cost allows access to the resume database.

EmploymentPartner

www.employmentpartner.com

Joe Stanley
PO Box 278, Greenberg, IN 47240
Ph: 800-840-3545   E-mail: patsy@employmentpartner.com

JOBS	100,000s	RESUMES	100,000s
Cost to post	Cost to see	Cost to post	Cost to see
Fee	Free	Free	Fee
DISCIPLINE		LOCATION	
ALL		USA	
SPECIALTY		FEATURE	
ALL		Gateway	
AGENT: Jobseeker			

EmploymentPartner.com is a gateway to a network of nearly 53 locally sponsored city sites. Job seekers must register and a password will be emailed to them. Jobs can be searched by discipline, level (manager, director, etc.), city, and keyword. Job descriptions are easy to view and can be sent to a friend. The site has an agent that will send matching jobs via email to job seekers if they post a resume on the site. First-time recruiters can have a 30 day free trial. The cost to post a position is $95 to 195 depending on the location selected. Access to the resume database runs from $375-$595 per month. The number of openings listed is posted with each job search. A sample of sites include: Chicago Careers Online, Colorado Springs Careers Online, Nashville Careers Online, Orlando Careers Online, South Jersey Careers Online, Spokane Careers Online and Tucson Careers Online.

Employment Wizard

www.employmentwizard.com

Ed Farrell
130 South First Street, 3rd Floor, Ann Arbor, MI 48104
Ph: 888-314-5873   Fax: 734-213-9011   E-mail: ebf@careersite.com

JOBS	10,000s		RESUMES	100,000s
Cost to post	Cost to see		Cost to post	Cost to see
Fee	Free		Free	Fee

DISCIPLINE	LOCATION
ALL	USA

SPECIALTY	FEATURE
ALL	N/A

AGENT: N/A

The Employment Wizard is powered by Careersite.com. EW offers a gateway to the classified sections of more than 100 newspapers from different parts of the country, including the Anchorage Daily News (AK) and the Charleston Daily Mail & Gazette (WV) . Rates for job posting depend on the paper that is selected. This is a great site for job seekers looking for leads in cities off the beaten track, and boasts an excellent search engine. Once a recruiter registers they can access the resume database. Site charges $40 for contact information but candidate profiles can be viewed for free. Site claims over 250,000 resumes which is the combined total from all of the newspapers.

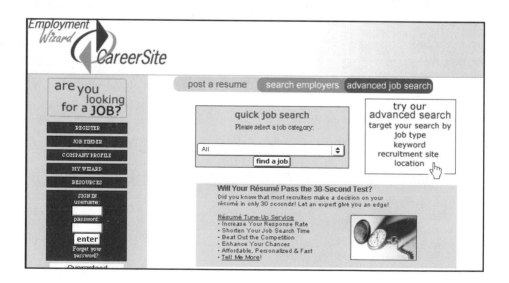

Energy Jobs Network

www.energyjobsnetwork.com

Matt Richards
428 E. 2nd, Edmund, OK 73024
Ph: 866-356-2638   Fax: 405-844-5444   E-mail: sales@energyjobsnetwork.com

JOBS	100s		RESUMES	1,000s
Cost to post	Cost to see		Cost to post	Cost to see
Fee	Free		Free	Fee
DISCIPLINE			LOCATION	
Engineering/Science			USA/	
SPECIALTY			FEATURE	
Energy			N/A	
AGENT: N/A				

Energy Jobs Network is the ASP that hosts the job board for 18 different energy associations and media companies. Launched in April of 2001, the site will post employer positions for $150 for 30 days and provide access to the resume database for $495. Energy companies are able to post their jobs one time, pay one rate and receive multiple site (18-sites) exposure for their postings. Sites include:National Energy Marketers (NEM), Electricity Forum:, National Energy Services Assoc.(NESA), Independent Petroleum Association of the Mountain States (IPAMS), Natural Gas & Energy Association of Oklahoma (NGEAO), Independent Petroleum Association of America (IPAA), European Energy Jobs, Canadian Electricity Association (CEA), Power & Gas Marketing Magazine and more.

Energyjobs.com

www.energyjobs.com

Andrew Powell
1511 Valley Run, Durham, NC 27707
Ph: 678-784-6139   E-mail: info@energyjobs.com

JOBS	1,000s		RESUMES	1,000s
Cost to post	Cost to see		Cost to post	Cost to see
Fee	Free		Free	Fee
DISCIPLINE			LOCATION	
Engineering			USA	
SPECIALTY			FEATURE	
Electrical/Electronic/Energy/Utilities/Power			N/A	
AGENT: Jobseeker				

Energyjobs.com sole focus is the energy industry. Recruiters pay $195 to post a position. Access to the resume database is $300. Job seekers can have openings that match their skills pushed to their PCs by registering their email addresses. Jobs have a quick and advanced search feature and all responses must go through the site. All jobs are date posted, and can be viewed by date, job title, company and location. Job seekers should check out the "top 10 things employers dislike seeing in a resume".

EngineerJobs.com
www.engineerjobs.com

Jean Eggertsen
Engineering Job Source, 2016 Manchester #24, Ann Arbor, MI 48104
Ph: 734-971-6995   Fax: 734-677-4386   E-mail: advertise@engineerjobs.com

JOBS	100s	RESUMES	1,000s
Cost to post	Cost to see	Cost to post	Cost to see
Fee	Free	Free	Fee
DISCIPLINE		LOCATION	
Engineering		USA	
SPECIALTY		FEATURE	
ALL		N/A	
AGENT: Jobseeker			

EngineerJobs.com has been around for nearly six years and has openings from across the USA. EJ targets engineering and IT professionals. New advertisers may post up to 15 positions at no cost for 60 days. Normally, employers pay $30 to post a position. Resume access and up to 200 postings is $250 for a 60 day run. Job seekers who register receive positions via email on a weekly basis. All states are listed on the home page for easy viewing. A simple search engine (keyword) allows candidates to search by state for exact matches.

Engineering Central
www.engcen.com

Bill Denham
10920 Springmont Dr., Unit 11, Richmond, British Columbia V7E 3S5 Canada
Ph: 866-576-3466   Fax: 510-217-9286   E-mail: admin@engcen.com

JOBS	100s	RESUMES	1,000s
Cost to post	Cost to see	Cost to post	Cost to see
Fee	Free	Free	Fee
DISCIPLINE		LOCATION	
Engineering		USA	
SPECIALTY		FEATURE	
ALL		COLLEGE	
AGENT: N/A			

Engineering Central offers openings that range from entry level to director levels. Recruiters can post a position for $30 for a two-month run which includes access to the resume database. Job seekers can search the site using keywords, job categories or the featured openings. Entry level positions are kept on a separate page for easy access. EC has two search engines for job seekers to utilize. Excellent detail is offered about how to use the site to its fullest potential. Openings have direct contact information. Recruiters should check out the sites posting stats as it gives a clear picture of EC's traffic.

EntertainmentCareers.Net

www.entertainmentcareers.net

Brad Hall
10622 Kinnard Avenue - A, Los Angeles, CA 90024
Ph: 310-441-9963   Fax: 310-475-8985   E-mail: sales@entertainmentcareer.net

JOBS	100s		RESUMES	1,000s
Cost to post	Cost to see		Cost to post	Cost to see
Free	Free		Free	Fee
DISCIPLINE			LOCATION	
Entertainment			USA/WEST/CA	
SPECIALTY			FEATURE	
Acting			N/A	
AGENT: Jobseeker				

EntertainmentCareers.Net was launched March 1999 and and provides openings from accounting to writing. Jobs can be posted for free for 60 days and the cost to view the resume database is $100. All jobs are date posted with contact information. Industry job line telephone numbers are available. Internships and experienced openings are in separate groups for ease of viewing. For job seekers entering the acting profession reading "How do I become an Extra" gave us an incentive to keep our day jobs. Openings are in every facet of the entertainment community.

Entry Level Job Seeker Assistant

www.dnaco.net/~dantassi/jobhome.html

Joseph E. Schmalhofer
E-mail: dantassi@dnaco.net

JOBS	N/A		RESUMES	10s
Cost to post	Cost to see		Cost to post	Cost to see
N/A	N/A		Free	Free
DISCIPLINE			LOCATION	
ALL			USA	
SPECIALTY			FEATURE	
ALL			College	
AGENT: N/A				

Entry Level Job Seeker Assistant links to corporate job sites and job boards. The best feature is that graduating students can post their resumes for free and they can be viewed by any visitor. Resumes can be searched by field of interest from accounting to world wide web development.

EnviroNetwork.com
www.environetwork.com

Dan Krebs
322 7th Avenue, New York, NY 10001
Ph: 212-279-4350   Fax: 212-279-4290   E-mail: dan@naturalist.com

JOBS	10s	RESUMES	1,000s
Cost to post	Cost to see	Cost to post	Cost to see
Fee	Free	Free	Free
DISCIPLINE		LOCATION	
Engineering		USA	
SPECIALTY		FEATURE	
Environmental		N/A	
AGENT: Jobseeker			

EnviroNetwork gives job seekers and recruiters stats on the homepage regarding number of openings (40) and resumes (2,652). EN claims it was launched in 1994. Recruiters pay $195 to post an opening. Non-profits are charged $75 Openings can be searched by U.S., international, state or job category. Jobs are date posted and the site's search engine is easy to use. Scrolling access to the resume database is free as contact information is at the bottom of each listing. Searching by country, state, or job category comes with the purchase of a job posting. The site is part of the www.naturalist.com network.

Environmental Career Opportunities
www.ecojobs.com

PO Box 678, Stanardsville, VA 22973
Ph: 800-315-9777   Fax: 804-985-2331   E-mail: ecosub scription@mindspring.com

JOBS	100s	RESUMES	N/A
Cost to post	Cost to see	Cost to post	Cost to see
Fee	Free	N/A	N/A
DISCIPLINE		LOCATION	
Engineering		USA	
SPECIALTY		FEATURE	
Environmental		N/A	
AGENT: Jobseeker			

Environmental Career Opportunities (ECO) is a print newsletter for job seekers as well as an online job board. ECO reaches over 30,000 readers every two weeks. Recruiters pay $89 to post a position for one week. For $158, ads can be placed on the site for two weeks and in the print journal for four weeks. For an extra $90 openings can be pushed to environmental professionals' (5,000) desktops via email. Print publication costs the job seeker $29 for two months. Openings are date posted and in conservation and environmental areas of the public, private and educational sectors. Lengthy job descriptions are listed by category and include direct contact information. There is no search engine. Site is simply designed and could use an upgrade.

Environmental Career.com
www.environmental-jobs.com

100 Bridge Street, Building C, Hampton, VA 23669
Ph: 757-727-7895   Fax: 757-727-7904   E-mail: eccinfo@environmentalcareer.com

JOBS	1,000s		RESUMES	100s
Cost to post	Cost to see		Cost to post	Cost to see
Fee	Free		Free	Free
DISCIPLINE			LOCATION	
Non-Profit/Science			USA	
SPECIALTY			FEATURE	
Environmental			N/A	
AGENT: N/A				

Environmental Career.com is a recruitment consulting firm in the environmental (conservation) field. Recruiters pay $79 for a 30-day run, and if you are a nonprofit organization, you can post at a 50 percent discount. Access to the resume database is $100 per month. Positions are included in the organization's National Environmental Employment Report newspaper (subscription costs $19 for three months). Jobs can be searched by title or the site's search engine. Job seekers must register to the site to apply for openings. Interesting list of links for college environmental programs and distance learning is available.

Environmental Jobs and Careers
www.ejobs.org

David Brierley
37 Shattuck Street, Lawrence, MA 01843
Ph: 978-682-5237   E-mail: info@ecoemploy.com

JOBS	100s		RESUMES	N/A
Cost to post	Cost to see		Cost to post	Cost to see
Fee	Free		N/A	N/A
DISCIPLINE			LOCATION	
Non-Profit/Science/Engineering			USA	
SPECIALTY			FEATURE	
Environmental			N/A	
AGENT: N/A				

Environmental Jobs and Careers was launched February 1998, and offers extensive links to environmental job pages from USA and Canadian public and private organizations. Recruiters pay $1.30 per 1,200 words per day ($1.10 for most nonprofit organizations with an $15 minimum) to post a job for 30 days. Jobs ranging from a bicycle field program coordinator to a wildlife biologist can be found. Links to industry salary surveys and an alpha listing to employer environmental job pages (see the map of the USA) keeps this site on our 500 list.

ER Exchange

www.erexchange.com/

David Monaster
251 West 81st, Suite 4G, Brooklyn, NY 10024
Ph: 646-505-0412   Fax: 646-349-3421   E-mail: david@erexchange.com

JOBS	10s	RESUMES	N/A
Cost to post	Cost to see	Cost to post	Cost to see
Fee	Free	N/A	N/A

DISCIPLINE	LOCATION
Human Resources	USA

SPECIALTY	FEATURE
Employment	Recruiter Network

AGENT: N/A

ER Exchange has been one of our favorite bulletin boards for human resources recruiting professionals since it's inception in 1998. David Manaster, the site's owner, has branched out into recruiting conferences where many of the article writers speak on various recruiting topics. Recruiters can view and post jobs for $100 for a 30-day run. Jobs are listed by title, company, location and date of posting with direct contact information included. The archive of articles for recruiters is the best content in the industry. Corporate recruiters need to be advised that many of the "lurkers" to the site/s board are headhunters.

Erp-Jobs.com

www.erp-jobs.com

Michael Levesque
14845 Yonge St., Unit 6, Suite 146, Aurora, Ontario L4G 5M4 Canada
Ph: 905-726-3133   Fax: 905-726-3854   E-mail: sales@erp-jobs.com

JOBS	100s	RESUMES	1,000s
Cost to post	Cost to see	Cost to post	Cost to see
Fee	Free	Free	Fee

DISCIPLINE	LOCATION
IT	INTL/Canada

SPECIALTY	FEATURE
ERP	N/A

AGENT: N/A

Erp-Jobs.com was launched in 1998 and has useful links for job seekers as well as newsletters, connections with industry specialists and much more. Employers pay $125 to post positions for skill sets such a ERP, SCM, CRM, EDI, EAI, E-Commerce and Linux NETWORK. Recruiters who pay $200 receive one job posting and access to the resume database for 30 days. Recruiters should check out the site's home and job posting page as extensive statistics on the job seekers who view this site can be found. An international site, Erp-jobs has opportunities posted for Canada and the U.S., (85 percent of the site traffic is in North America), Europe (eight percent in the UK and France) South America (three percent) and the Pacific Rim (four percent). Job seekers would benefit if the site posted the number of openings in each category as several were empty.

EscapeArtist.com
www.escapeartist.com

832-1245 World Trade Center, Panama City, Republic of Panama
Ph: 011-507-3170139 E-mail: info@escapeartist.com

JOBS	N/A	RESUMES	N/A
Cost to post	Cost to see	Cost to post	Cost to see
Free	Free	N/A	N/A
DISCIPLINE		LOCATION	
Miscellaneous		INTL/	
SPECIALTY		FEATURE	
Adventure Overseas		N/A	
AGENT: N/A			

EscapeArtist.com is a Panamanian based job site that offers employers an unusual platform for jobs in exotic climes. Job seekers can search recent postings or by category and location. Positions range from a Hair Stylist in New Zealand to a Security Specialist in Afghanistan. If you are looking to escape the corporate rat race for far away places EscapeArtist might have the key. Great content accompanies these fascinating jobs.

JOB SEEKER TIP

Check emails and voice messages every two hours.

Always stay in touch with contacts and do not let time go by. Best response is by email as telephone tag is a loser's game.

193

Escoffier On Line - Employment Resources

www.escoffier.com

George Cook
The Escoffier On Line Network, PO Box 483, Point Lookout, NY 11569
Ph: 516-897-5153   E-mail: comments@chefjobsnetwork.com

JOBS	100s		RESUMES	10s
Cost to post	Cost to see		Cost to post	Cost to see
Fee	Fee		Free	Fee
DISCIPLINE			LOCATION	
Hospitality & Food Services			USA	
SPECIALTY			FEATURE	
Restaurant/Chefs			Gateway	
AGENT: Jobseeker				

Like the best restaurants in NYC, Escoffier On Line (EOL), is the gateway behind the Chefs Food Network and continues to add interesting flavors to its menu. The site posts positions from all over the world for chefs, bakers, food and beverage managers and other food service employees. The site offers content that keeps food professionals returning. Employers have access to a pool of top talent by posting an ad here (as well as on affiliate sites such as www.chefjobsnetwork.com, and webfoodpros.com which share the same database). Recruiters who post ads for management positions pay $99 with line/food prep job openings added for free. Access to the resume database is $100 per month. Volunteer organizations can post openings for free. An opt-in, biweekly newsletter features interesting job opportunities, highlights employers and keeps regular visitors up to date through forums. CXR admires sites that gives a money back guarantee. Fine websites are like fine wine, they grow on you.

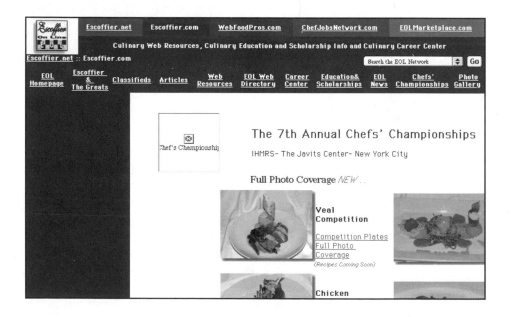

ESLworldwide.com

www.eslworldwide.com

E-mail: eslworldwide@eslworldwide.com

JOBS	100s		RESUMES	100s
Cost to post	Cost to see		Cost to post	Cost to see
Free	Free		Free	Free
DISCIPLINE			LOCATION	
Education			USA	
SPECIALTY			FEATURE	
Teaching, k-12, ESL			N/A	
AGENT: N/A				

Since 1999 ESLworldwide.com (English as a second language) has been providing job postings and teacher resumes for free. Recruiters need to register to post jobs and view the sites resume database. Job seekers can view openings without registering but must do so to submit a resume to the site. (An ID and password will be emailed back to those who register.) Interesting information and statistics on teaching opportunities overseas that include salaries and requirements by country can be found here. ESL had 745 USA openings alone which advises of the strong market for teachers. We highly recommend that anyone thinking of teaching abroad read the FAQs on this site and ask questions in the site's forum section.

eWorkExchange

www.ework.com

Jay Brandeis
717 Market Street, 5th Floor, San Francisco, CA 94103
Ph: 888-743-9675   Fax: 415-546-3889   E-mail: jbrandeis@ework.com

JOBS	100s		RESUMES	1,000s
Cost to post	Cost to see		Cost to post	Cost to see
Fee	Free		Free	Fee
DISCIPLINE			LOCATION	
IT			USA	
SPECIALTY			FEATURE	
ALL			Contingent	
AGENT: Jobseeker				

EWork Exchange claims to offer over $26.6 million in services related to employers that are advertising projects for independent professionals. EW claims 300,000 registered independent professionals. The site lets both employer and contractor build free mini websites, "web-sumes and project pages, to present details that will speed their mutual understanding of each other's offerings and facilitate the connection/hiring process." Recruiters pay $100 to post a job profile for 30 days. The system sends qualified candidates to the recruiter. If the job is filled before your time expires, you can post another opening for the balance. The owners are provided a template for contract business and complete sourcing. Payroll, benefits, invoicing and other services are all online. All disciplines are represented, but the site is heavily focused on contract information technology.

exBigFive.com
www.exbigfive.com

222 North LaSalle, Suite 1500, Chicago, IL 60601
Ph: 626-578-1980   Fax: 626-578-0660   E-mail: customer-support@exbigfive.com

JOBS	100s		RESUMES	100s
Cost to post	Cost to see		Cost to post	Cost to see
Fee	Free		Free	Fee
DISCIPLINE			LOCATION	
Business			USA	
SPECIALTY			FEATURE	
ALL			Executive	
AGENT: N/A				

exBigFive.com offers access to current and former employees of the major consulting/accounting firms. Recruiters pay $150 to post a job and $300 to access the resume database for a month. These funds are "returned" when someone is hired since the site charges $6,500 for a placement. Job seekers must apply through the site and can see limited company information. Job seekers can register their information and employers can only see their resume if they release the data. Owners are in the third party staffing business. Like the name says, site is geared for individuals who work/worked for the big five who want to broaden their horizons.

ExecSearches.com
www.execsearches.com

Laura Gassner Otting
Suite 15N, Hollywood, FL 33019
Ph: 888-238-6611   Fax: 954-252-3743   E-mail: info@execsearches.com

JOBS	10s		RESUMES	N/A
Cost to post	Cost to see		Cost to post	Cost to see
Fee	Free		N/A	N/A
DISCIPLINE			LOCATION	
Non-Profit			USA	
SPECIALTY			FEATURE	
ALL			EXECUTIVE	
AGENT: Jobseeker				

ExecSearches.com, launched in 1997, is geared for senior level players ($100,000+) in the nonprofit arena. Recruiters pay $95 to post a position for 30 days. Openings can be searched by job function, keyword, industry or region of the USA (job seekers are advised to "select all" as there are less then 100 openings posted on most days). Jobs are displayed in large type (for us older folk) with detailed job descriptions and direct contact information. Executives who wish to have their resumes reviewed pay $95 for a 50-minute telephone interview. Job seekers (24,000) who register their email addresses will receive weekly job postings and career articles.

ExecuNet

www.execunet.com

Dave Opton
295 Westport Avenue, Norwalk, CT 06851
Ph: 800-637-3126   Fax: 203-840-8320   E-mail: execunet@execunet.com

JOBS	1,000s	RESUMES	N/A
Cost to post	Cost to see	Cost to post	Cost to see
Free	Fee	N/A	N/A
DISCIPLINE		LOCATION	
ALL		USA	
SPECIALTY		FEATURE	
ALL		EXECUTIVE	
AGENT: N/A			

ExecuNet is one of the premier sources for executive job leads over $100,000. Last year more than 10,000 different search firms and corporations posted over 30,000 jobs on this site for free. Over 70% of their members are employed and 67% have advanced degrees. The site is an executive life insurance policy. Job seekers pay $150 a quarter to access leads via the web or receive hard copy. Included in the price is a resume review which all job seekers should take advantage of. Job leads cover all fields and specialties and are updated daily Recruiters can post jobs for free, and each posting lasts 45 days. More than a website, ExecuNet operates both on and off the Internet. Monthly networking events are held at 70 local chapters in 48 cities (11 added in the Fall of 2002) and members receive several hardcopy job search and career management newsletters to help members in advancing their careers. The site has interesting security features. Subscribing members, for example, are not allowed to share job leads. Career tips and resources are extensive. Salary survey data is gathered from members and represents an interesting market price perspective.

ExecutiveRegistry.com
www.executiveregistry.com

Kennedy Information, One Phoenix Mill Lane, 5th Fl., Peterborough, NH 03458
Ph: 800-531-0007   E-mail: support@executiveregistry.com,

JOBS	100s		RESUMES	100s
Cost to post	Cost to see		Cost to post	Cost to see
Free	Free		Free	Free
DISCIPLINE			LOCATION	
ALL			USA/	
SPECIALTY			FEATURE	
ALL			Executive	
AGENT: N/A				

ExecutiveRegistry.com is a new service from Kennedy Information, the "Red Book" directory of Executive recruiters. The site is for executive-level job seekers who exceed salary levels of $100K. All postings on the site are from Exec Search agencies that agree to abide by strict disclosure obligations. This is used as a feature to convince jobseekers that their data is safe with the headhunters since their corporate counterparts can't access it. What a novel idea (tongue-in-cheek). Still, the site is connected to the industry and represents an excellent source for execs.

experience.com
www.experience.com

Allyson O'Hara
One Faneuil Hall Marketplace, Third Floor, Boston, MA 02109
Ph: 800-489-7611   Fax: 617-536-0499   E-mail: employerinfo@experience.com

JOBS	10,000s		RESUMES	100,000s
Cost to post	Cost to see		Cost to post	Cost to see
Free	Free		Free	Fee (Free Notes)
DISCIPLINE			LOCATION	
ALL			USA	
SPECIALTY			FEATURE	
ALL			COLLEGE	
AGENT: N/A				

Experience.com focuses on serving the job search needs of college students. This site claims it reaches 3 million students through its magazine and has partnered with 600 colleges and universities including several ivy league schools. The site sells technology that allows recruiters to post their jobs to multiple college career centers via one-stop shopping. The site automates the career offices of college campuses. Employers pay to post jobs and search the resume database across multiple schools. In speaking with site management, experience.com describes themselves as the "glue between the school and the corporation hiring management systems." Experience.com services are geared to employers who do large volume college recruiting. Pricing is on a tiered basis based on size of school or company.

Farms.com
www.farms.com/careers

Chris Lanteigne
148 Fullarton Street, Suite 1400, London, Ontario N6A 5P3 Canada
Ph: 877-438-5729   Fax: 519-438-3152   E-mail: chris.lantgeigne@farms.com

JOBS	10s		RESUMES	100s
Cost to post	Cost to see		Cost to post	Cost to see
Fee	Free		Free	Fee
DISCIPLINE			LOCATION	
Miscellaneous			USA	
SPECIALTY			FEATURE	
Agriculture			N/A	
AGENT: Jobseeker				

Farms.com careers section (also found via agricareers.com and eharvest.com) is a niche that reminds us of an early morning TV show entitled "the modern farmer". Their latest job postings include a swine area manager and a top farm assistant, just in case you are thinking of making a change to a more rural setting. Job postings cost recruiters $199 US/$249 CDN for 30 days, and the site's online resume database will email new resumes to recruiters for $500 US/$700 CDN for a three-month period. Openings can be viewed by industry, years of experience, career type, city, state, country or keyword. All jobs are date posted. Job seekers who register their email can receive the site's weekly newsletter which includes the latest job postings.

Fashion Career Center.com
www.fashioncareercenter.com

Martin Weitzman
275 Madison Avenue, New York, NY 10016
Ph: 800-967-3846   E-mail: fashioncc@aol.com

JOBS	100s		RESUMES	1,000s
Cost to post	Cost to see		Cost to post	Cost to see
Fee	Free		Free	Fee
DISCIPLINE			LOCATION	
Miscellaneous			USA/MDA/NY	
SPECIALTY			FEATURE	
Merchandising, Apparel, Textiles, Fashion			N/A	
AGENT: Both Recruiters & Jobseekers				

The Fashion Career Center was launched in 1998 and is a great fit for the New York niche marketplace. Membership costs $845 for unlimited job posting and resume database access for six months. Resume database access alone is $595 per year. Additional jobs can be posted for $60 for a 60-day run. Search agents will push openings to job seekers and matching resumes to recruiters. Openings are date posted with direct contact information. A long list of links to the fashion schools and colleges across the U.S. can also be found. For those who truly want to be in the "rag" business this is the place.

FatJob.com

www.fatjob.com

Ray Chang
1755 E. Bayshore Road, Suite 17D, Redwood City, CA 94063
Ph: 650-366-9500   E-mail: sales@fatjob.com

JOBS	10,000s	RESUMES	10,000s
Cost to post	Cost to see	Cost to post	Cost to see
Free	Free	Free	Free
DISCIPLINE		LOCATION	
ALL		USA/WEST/CA/San Francisco	
SPECIALTY		FEATURE	
ALL		Start-Ups	
AGENT: N/A			

FatJob.com is concentrating its effort on start-up companies in the Silicon Valley/bay area of California. The site lists information technology jobs and resumes (as well as engineering, sales, marketing, operations and management) for over 4,000 corporations. Recruiters can post positions for 30 days and view the site's resume database for free. Resumes and jobs are all date posted. Job seekers will need to bring their "scrolling fingers" as openings are listed by topic and the site has no search engine. The site claims 36,154 jobs are posted. CXR loves the owners entrepreneurial spirit but wonders where the dollars will come from?

FedWorld.gov Federal Jobs

www.fedworld.gov

National Technical Information Service, 5285 Port Royal Road, Springfield, VA 22161
Ph: 703-605-6000   E-mail: webmaster@fedworld.gov

JOBS	1,000s	RESUMES	N/A
Cost to post	Cost to see	Cost to post	Cost to see
N/A	Free	N/A	N/A
DISCIPLINE		LOCATION	
Government		USA	
SPECIALTY		FEATURE	
ALL		N/A	
AGENT: N/A			

FedWorld.gov Federal Jobs allows job seekers to browse for government openings. The site's search engine offers keyword and state searches. The database is updated twice a week. This is one of the few sites that post the salary range for all positions. The openings are gathered from hundreds of human resource offices in the government. The site advises that many federal job announcements are not posted here because even in the government there are competing sites. Employment forms can be downloaded right from the site.

Federal Jobs Digest

www.jobsfed.com

Ph: 800-824-5000   Fax: 914-362-0059   E-mail: webmaster@jobsfed.com

JOBS	100s	RESUMES	N/A
Cost to post	Cost to see	Cost to post	Cost to see
Free (See Note)	Free	N/A	N/A
DISCIPLINE		LOCATION	
Government		USA	
SPECIALTY		FEATURE	
ALL		N/A	
AGENT: N/A			

Federal Jobs Digest claims more federal vacancies than any other source. Indications are that over 14,000 vacancies are listed at the site. Agencies can post 1 opening per month for free. Site provides a fee service where (for $25) it will advise job seekers which federal jobs will match their qualifications. Resumes are sent via the web and the site does a search of the federal job database to match the job seekers skills with current openings. Site continues to claim they have 800,000 high quality job candidates. Really? We still do not understand the claims made by this site (which are not new).

Federation of American Soc. for Exp. Biology

www.faseb.org

Carol Bieschke
9650 Rockville Pike, Bethesda, MD 20814
Ph: 301-530-7020   Fax: 301-571-0699   E-mail: careers@faseb.org

JOBS	10s	RESUMES	1,000s
Cost to post	Cost to see	Cost to post	Cost to see
Fee	Free	Free	Fee
DISCIPLINE		LOCATION	
Science		USA	
SPECIALTY		FEATURE	
Bio/Biomedical/Life Sciences		N/A	
AGENT: N/A			

FASEB's CAREERS OnLine allows employers the flexibility of searching its applicant database and browsing the credentials of qualified applicants identified in the keyword search results. Applicants are identified by an assigned identification number. For employers wishing to obtain total access to the applicants listed in the Applicant DataNet, a subscription is available for an annual fee of $300-$1000. Representing a dozen scientific and technical journals and publications, this developing site reaches 50,000 to 100,000 life (biomedical) scientists and technicians. The costs for a job posting ranges from $200 to $900. Research scientists, internships and post doctorates are the focus.

Feminist Career Center
www.feminist.org

1600 Wilson Blvd, Suite 801, Arlington, VA 22209
Ph: 703-522-2214   Fax: 703-522-2219   E-mail: femmaj@feminist.org

JOBS	100s	RESUMES	10s
Cost to post	Cost to see	Cost to post	Cost to see
Free	Free	Free	Free
DISCIPLINE		LOCATION	
ALL		USA	
SPECIALTY		FEATURE	
ALL		DIVERSITY	
AGENT: Jobseeker			

The Feminist Career Center has partnered with Ms. Magazine to allow recruiters to post positions and review resumes for free. Job seekers have access to over 100 positions listed by region and title. All jobs are date posted with direct contact information. The site's resume bank can be searched by title, city or state. Job seekers can register their email and have the latest openings pushed to their pc. An extensive list of internship links makes this site worth a visit.

Film TV Production Jobs (Mandy.com)
www.mandy.com

John Hoare
89 Mayfield Road, London, N8 9LN United Kingdom
Ph: 440-208-3746847 Fax: 440-208-3746924 E-mail: john@mandy.com

JOBS	100s	RESUMES	10s
Cost to post	Cost to see	Cost to post	Cost to see
Free	Free	Free	Fee
DISCIPLINE		LOCATION	
Entertainment & Media		USA	
SPECIALTY		FEATURE	
ALL		N/A	
AGENT: Jobseeker			

Film TV Production Jobs (Mandy.com) offers recruiters job postings for free. Job seekers can search openings by skill, art department, crew, pre- and post production, location or fully paid. Openings are date posted with contact information. Mandy has added a weekly email to over 82,000 subscribers who receive posted openings. A small resume database can also be posted and accessed for free. Many of the resumes have amazing graphics. The owners sell a directory to international film and TV production called -who would have guessed- "Mandy's".

Financial Executives Institute

www.fei.org

FEI, 10 Madison Avenue, PO Box 1938, Morristown, NJ
Ph: 973-898-4626   E-mail: careerservices@fei.org

JOBS	10s	RESUMES	100s
Cost to post	Cost to see	Cost to post	Cost to see
Fee	Free	Fee	Fee
DISCIPLINE		LOCATION	
Business		USA	
SPECIALTY		FEATURE	
Finance/Accounting		EXECUTIVE	
AGENT: N/A			

Financial Executives Institute (FEI) is an organization for senior finance and accounting professionals (CFO's, CEO's, Presidents). Claiming 15,000 members from over 8,000 companies this may be where the head bean counters meet. Recruiters post positions for $269 for 60 days. Members of FEI can post jobs for free. The site's resume database can be accessed for $600 per month. Member corporations receive a 50 percent discount. FEI members get initial dibs for 10 days on all job postings. Anyone can view them after this period. Openings can be searched by date, title or state Even with only 16 jobs posted this is where the elite meet.

Financial Job Network

www.fjn.com

Linda Brooks
15030 Ventura Blvd., #378, Sherman Oaks, CA 91403
Ph: 818-905-5272   E-mail: info@fjn.com

JOBS	100s	RESUMES	1,000s
Cost to post	Cost to see	Cost to post	Cost to see
Fee	Free	Free	Fee
DISCIPLINE		LOCATION	
Business		USA	
SPECIALTY		FEATURE	
Finance/Accounting		EXECUTIVE	
AGENT: N/A			

The Financial Job Network, launched in November 1996, hosts openings for companies seeking global finance and accounting professionals in all industries. Positions and resumes can be searched by keyword and multiple options such as location, job title, industry and category. Positions range from entry level and internships to corporate presidents. Recruiters pay $225 to post a position for 90 days or $750 for 15 job postings and access to the resume database for five months. FJN clients are Fortune 1000, multi-national and global executive recruiting companies. Job seekers must apply through the site for all opportunities.

Financial Times Career Point

www.ftcareerpoint.com

Peter Highland
No1 Southwark Bridge, London, UK United Kingdom
Ph: 800-628-8088   Fax: 845-566-8220   E-mail: peter.highland@ft.com

JOBS	1,000s		RESUMES	10,000s
Cost to post	Cost to see		Cost to post	Cost to see
Fee	Free		Free	Fee
DISCIPLINE			LOCATION	
Business			INTL/Europe	
SPECIALTY			FEATURE	
Finance/Accounting			N/A	
AGENT: Jobseeker				

Financial Times Career Point charges recruiters 225 pounds to post a job for three weeks. Viewing the site's resume database costs £500. Resumes are deleted after six months. Openings can be searched by keyword, job type, level, salary, location or date of posting. All jobs are date posted with contact information. Excellent career articles can be accessed. The Works section has interesting news, views and statistics on the world of work. Recruiters should check out "The future of HR:beyond operations to partnership". The print edition of the Financial Times is a highly regarded publication published in 14 cities around the world. For recruiters who travel in international finance this is a definite publication to post openings.

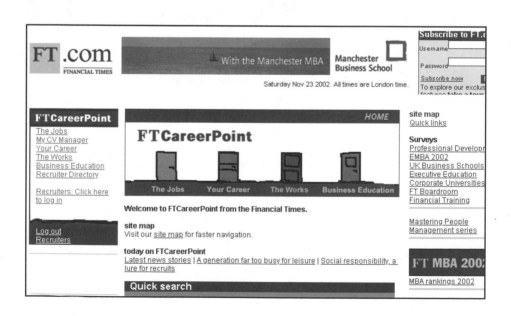

Financial Women International

www.fwi.org/

Angela Elder
200 N. Glebe Road, Suite 820, Arlington, VA 22203
Ph: 703-807-2007   Fax: 703-807-0111   E-mail: info@fwi.org

JOBS	100s	RESUMES	1,000s
Cost to post	Cost to see	Cost to post	Cost to see
Fee	Free	Free	Fee

DISCIPLINE	LOCATION
Business	USA

SPECIALTY	FEATURE
Finance/Accounting	DIVERSITY

AGENT: Both Recruiters & Jobseekers

Financial Women International (formerly National Assoc. of Bank Women) was founded in 1921 and is dedicated to furthering the cause of women in the financial services industry. Membership costs $159-$199 as the lesser fee is for individuals who will receive all information online only (you gotta luv it!). The cost to post a job is $270 for a 60-day run, which includes skill matching resumes that will send up to 10 resumes per day to the recruiters desktop. Resume datasbase access is $699-$899 per month. Job seekers need to register and create a profile before they can access career opportunities. Jobs that match their profile are immediately emailed to job seekers. Registration is by accounting, corporate finance, investment management and banking. Numerous industry articles are available.

Finishing.com

www.finishing.com

Ted Mooney
503 Brick Blvd., Suite 106, Brick, NJ 08723
Ph: 732-477-1447   Fax: 732-477-1974   E-mail: mooney@finishing.com

JOBS	10s	RESUMES	10s
Cost to post	Cost to see	Cost to post	Cost to see
Fee	Free	Free	Free

DISCIPLINE	LOCATION
Business/Trades	USA

SPECIALTY	FEATURE
Operations/Manufacturing/metal finishing	N/A

AGENT: N/A

Finishing.com was launched April 1995 and continues to provide services for its niche in metal finishing (plating, anodizing, powder coating, etc.). Job seekers can post their resume/profile with date of posting and include their contact information. Positions can be posted via the site's online form for $144 for a three-month run. Recruiters can view resumes for free, and the last one in is the first one listed. Job seekers need to join the site's chatroom discussions to find their next employer. An up to date calendar of industry events is also a good job searching tool.

Fish4Jobs

www.jobhunter.co.uk/

3rd Floor Broadway Chambers, 14-26 Hammersmith Broadway, London, W6 7AF United Kingdom
Ph: 020-860-07000   Fax: 020-874-17505   E-mail: jobsales@fish4.co.uk

JOBS	10,000s	RESUMES	N/A
Cost to post	Cost to see	Cost to post	Cost to see
Fee	Free	N/A	N/A
DISCIPLINE		LOCATION	
ALL		INTL/Europe/UK	
SPECIALTY		FEATURE	
ALL		N/A	
AGENT: Jobseeker			

Fish4Jobs.com, is a UK site where recruiters pay £250 per week to post openings for a 4 week run. The site claims 44,407 jobs online (white and blue collar openings). The site agent pushes positions matching skills and interests to job seekers who register. Career channels can be searched for openings in secretarial, sales, marketing, IT, engineering, construction or accounting. Fish has been developed by Newsquest Media Group, Northcliffe Newspapers, Trinity Mirror, Guardian Media Newspapers and the Regional Independent Media Group. Interesting career articles from hobsons.com are also available.

Fish jobs

www.fishjobs.com

PO Box 688, Jacksonville, OR 97530
Ph: 541-899-4975   Fax: 541-899-4976   E-mail: howard@hmj.com

JOBS	100s	RESUMES	100s
Cost to post	Cost to see	Cost to post	Cost to see
Fee	Free	Free	Fee
DISCIPLINE		LOCATION	
Miscellaneous		USA	
SPECIALTY		FEATURE	
Fishing Industry		N/A	
AGENT: N/A			

Definitely not as fishy as it might look, fishjobs is owned by a headhunter and the site appeals to seafood, fisheries or aquaculture companies seeking to fill sales, marketing, management, operations or quality control positions. Recruiters can post jobs for $250 for a 6-month run and then resumes (shown without contact info) can be requested. Jobs are listed by region with brief descriptions and direct contact data. Opportunities here ranged from managers of fish farms to government jobs related to the industry.

FlipDog (Monster)

www.flipdog.com

Kevin Mullins
5 Clock Tower Place, Maynard, MA 01754
Ph: 877-887-3547

JOBS	100,000s	RESUMES	100,000s
Cost to post	Cost to see	Cost to post	Cost to see
Fee	Free	Free	Fee
DISCIPLINE		LOCATION	
ALL		USA	
SPECIALTY		FEATURE	
ALL		Multi-site Search	
AGENT: Jobseeker			

FlipDog.com (FD) owned by Monster claims to give job seekers access to 304,913 US jobs and 49,942 international openings. FD aggregates jobs from company websites. The site is also accepting resumes that employers can search. Job seekers can register their skills along with their email addresses, and the site will push matched openings to their PCs. The problem we have with FlipDog is that when we do a search for a specific company, the result is only a partial listing of the jobs on their site. If the technology improves, this could be part of an end game, although adding staffing firms to this mix just confuses the core value proposition. Recruiters can post a position for $145 to get to the top of the site's list, otherwise posting a job is $95 for a 30 day run. The resume database costs $3,000 for recruiter access.

Food Industry Jobs.com

www.foodindustryjobs.com

HRsmart.com, 1200 Commerce Drive, Suite 102, Plano, TX 75093
Ph: 888-471-9675   Fax: 561-470-9677   E-mail: fijsales@hrsmart.com

JOBS	100s	RESUMES	1,000s
Cost to post	Cost to see	Cost to post	Cost to see
Fee	Free	Free	Fee
DISCIPLINE		LOCATION	
Hospitality & Food Services/Retail		USA	
SPECIALTY		FEATURE	
ALL		N/A	
AGENT: Both Recruiters & Jobseekers			

Food Industry Jobs.com was launched in 1997 and serves recruiters that pay $50 for 60 days for job postings. Employers can purchase unlimited job postings and access to the resume database for $200 for 90 days. Recruiters can cross post openings to hundreds of other employment sites. "Candidate Scout" looks for resumes that match job specifications and emails recruiters when that person is available. "Career Scout" provides job matches via email to job seekers. The site posts the number of openings next to each job category for ease of use. A list of headhunters and corporations in the food industry is also available.

foodservice.com
www.foodservice.com

David Samia
1000 Mansell Exchange West, Suite 300, Alpharetta, GA 30022
Ph: 800-200-8143   Fax: 678-424-2200   E-mail: marketing@foodservice.com

JOBS	1,000s	RESUMES	1,000s
Cost to post	Cost to see	Cost to post	Cost to see
Fee	Free	Free	Fee
DISCIPLINE		LOCATION	
Hospitality & Food Services/Retail		USA	
SPECIALTY		FEATURE	
ALL		N/A	
AGENT: Jobseeker			

Foodservice.com brings an employment center style to the food industry. Recruiters pay $75 to post a position for 30 days and gain access to the resume database. Jobs can be searched bykeyword, location or profession. Openings range from administrative to bus person to warehouse. Job seekers who register their email, location, profession or keywords can have position matches pushed to their PCs. Site's weekly newsletter has over 34,000 subscribers. For job seekers interested in the high volume restaurant world this may be a kitchen with a place for you. Forums and chatrooms discussing industry issues and gossip round out the site.

FortBendJobs
www.fortbendjobs.com

Kelley Smith
P.O. Box 391, Sugar Land, TX 77487
Ph: 281-494-3632   Fax: 281-494-0173   E-mail: info@fortbendjobs.com

JOBS	100s	RESUMES	100s
Cost to post	Cost to see	Cost to post	Cost to see
Fee	Free	Free	Fee
DISCIPLINE		LOCATION	
ALL		USA/SOW/TX/Houston	
SPECIALTY		FEATURE	
ALL		N/A	
AGENT: N/A			

Launched in September, 2000, FortBendJobs.com caters to a local niche in Ft Bend County, West/Southwest Houston. Recruiters can post positions for $29 for a 2-6 week run. Access to the few resumes here is $149/month with unlimited job postings. An agent matches jobs that match a job seekers interests and notifies them via email. Other features include a "Schools and Training" page which has links to colleges in the Fort Bend area; an e-list where Fort Bend area job seekers can meet, network and ask career related questions; and, links and information about the Fort Bend area for people interested in relocating. Free trials are available.

Funeral Net
www.funeralnet.com

Carrie Fenelon
516 SE Morrison, Suite 700, Portland, OR 97214
Ph: 800-721-8166   Fax: 800-943-5552   E-mail: turk@funeralnet.com

JOBS	10s		RESUMES	10s
Cost to post	Cost to see		Cost to post	Cost to see
Free	Free		Free	Free
DISCIPLINE			LOCATION	
Miscellaneous			USA	
SPECIALTY			FEATURE	
ALL			N/A	
AGENT: N/A				

Funeral Net is one of those niche sites that CXR will never bury. The owner provides free job and employment wanted notices (79) as a service to the industry. Jobs are listed by title, region and date of posting, and there were 65 on our last visit. Short job descriptions and direct contact information are easy to view. Apprenticeship postings are also available. Links to college mortuary science programs are listed under funeral career information.

funjobs.com
www.funjobs.com

Lesley Vossler
TagMar, Inc., 410 W. Fallbrook, Suite 204, Fresno, CA 93711
Ph: 559-490-2800   E-mail: info@funjobs.com

JOBS	100s		RESUMES	1000s
Cost to post	Cost to see		Cost to post	Cost to see
Fee	Free		Free	Fee
DISCIPLINE			LOCATION	
Hospitality & Food Services/Retail/Miscellaneous			USA	
SPECIALTY			FEATURE	
Sports/Outdoors/Resorts			College/Summer	
AGENT: Jobseeker				

Launched in the Fall of 2001, funjobs emphasizes Hospitality, Food & Beverage, Adventure & Active Travel Operators (ski areas, national parks, dude ranches, whitewater rafting etc.), and Recreation industries. Recruiters can post positions for $87 for a 60 day run. For $400, employers will get a 3 month subscription to services that include resume access and 20% job posting discounts. Site is well designed to show off unique positions- typically outdoors- parks and ski lodges, youth camps and cruise ships. Openings can be searched by category, location, education, job type, duration of opportunity or keyword search. CXR did not see any circus clowns or high wire walkers. Job seekers can create and store up to 5 resumes and 5 cover letters that can be used to respond to any job. However, only one resume can be active at a time.

Future Access Employment Guide
www.futureaccess.com

Bill Havlice
PO Box 2187, Granite Bay, CA 95746
Ph: 916-797-1868   E-mail: webmaster@futureaccess.com

JOBS	100s	RESUMES	100s
Cost to post	Cost to see	Cost to post	Cost to see
Fee	Free	Free	Free
DISCIPLINE		LOCATION	
ALL		USA	
SPECIALTY		FEATURE	
ALL		N/A	
AGENT: N/A			

The Future Access Employment Guide's database was launched January 1994, and is available to any and all WAP-enabled hand held wireless devices. The site's search engine allows jobs to be viewed by keyword, city, state, zip code or country. A brief synopsis of openings is first viewed and, if interested, job seekers can drill to complete descriptions with direct contact information. Recruiters should check out the sites metrics page as it is very impressive. Resumes in the database are made up of 21% IT, 17% sales and marketing, 3% hardware engineers, 2% biotech and the balance misc. Recruiters pay $5 per month to post positions.

GasJobs.com
www.gasjobs.com

Robert Cosgrove
Mikich Company, PO Box 701, Carrboro, NC 27510
Ph: 800-733-6808   Fax: 919-933-3771   E-mail: info@gasjobs.com

JOBS	10s	RESUMES	10s
Cost to post	Cost to see	Cost to post	Cost to see
Free	Free	Free	Free
DISCIPLINE		LOCATION	
Health Care		USA	
SPECIALTY		FEATURE	
MD/Anesthesiology/Nuses		Gateway	
AGENT: Both Recruiters & Jobseekers			

GasJobs (GJ) was launched in November 1998. GJ is a free site for anesthesiologists, certified registered nurses (CRNA) and recruiters. Openings can be viewed by state or keyword search (many of the openings are posted by third-party staffers). Both the resumes and jobs include date of posting. Many of the posted resumes were over a year old but great for sources. All who register can receive jobs or resumes via email. The owners also own med2020.com, which is a multi-specialty physician site, and mdjobs.org.

GasWork.com
www.gaswork.com

PO Box 368, Sulphur Springs, TX 75483
Ph: 800-828-2203   Fax: 903-885-6958   E-mail: support@gaswork.com

JOBS	10s		RESUMES	10s
Cost to post	Cost to see		Cost to post	Cost to see
Free (See Notes)	Free		Free	Free
DISCIPLINE			LOCATION	
Health Care			USA	
SPECIALTY			FEATURE	
MD/Anesthesiologist/Nursing			N/A	
AGENT: Both Recruiters & Jobseekers				

GasWork.com is for anesthesiologists and certified registered nurses with this specialty (CRNA). Hospitals and corporate recruiters can post jobs for 15 days for free- headhunters pay $250. Recruiters can search openings/resumes by state, specialty or all jobs. Resumes and jobs are posted by date of receipt. Recruiters and job seekers that register will have openings or resumes sent to their desktop via email. Hospital recruiters must still be under the influence since most jobs were posted by third party recruiters. The site search capability and the display of information is all first rate.

GayWork.com
www.gaywork.com

Tom Longobardo
955 North Vista Street, Los Angeles, CA 90046
Ph: 323-512-2922   Fax: 323-512-2924   E-mail: info@gaywork.com

JOBS	100s		RESUMES	1,000s
Cost to post	Cost to see		Cost to post	Cost to see
Free	Free		Free	Free
DISCIPLINE			LOCATION	
ALL			USA	
SPECIALTY			FEATURE	
ALL			Diversity	
AGENT: Jobseeker				

GayWork.com is a free site created in March, 1999 targeting the gay and lesbian community. Recruiters can obtain resumes and post jobs for free. Owners have formed a partnership with Monster.com although all jobs and resumes viewed here are independent of Monster (recruiters and job seekers are encouraged to use Monster.com's services). Site demographics show members in healthcare, education, etc. Salary and location information is also available. Excellent gay and lesbian resources are presented along with helpful articles. This site has made significant progress in the last year.

GeoCommunity Career Center

careers.geocomm.com

Glenn Letham
4588 East Highway 20, Suite A, Niceville, FL 32578
Ph: 850-897-0110   Fax: 850-897-1001   E-mail: editor@geocomm.com

JOBS	100s	RESUMES	1,000s
Cost to post	Cost to see	Cost to post	Cost to see
Fee	Free	Free (See Notes)	Free
DISCIPLINE		LOCATION	
IT		USA	
SPECIALTY		FEATURE	
GIS/Cad		N/A	
AGENT: Both Recruiters & Jobseekers			

GeoCommunity Career Center was launched in June 1999 and claims to be the place for geospatial technology professionals. Recruiters can post a job for $60 for 30 days. Employers pay $85 to place their openings at the top of the list and have it emailed to the sites 27,000 daily newsletter subscribers. The site's resume database can be viewed for free. Resumes are organized into one of three groupings:experienced, students/grads or consultants. Job seekers can have their resumes rise to the top of the listings for $25 (for 30 days) and have it sent to recruiters via email. Openings are date posted. Discussion boards in GIS, MapPoint, Metadata, MapInfo, ArcView, INGR,MobileLBS, and GIS jobs are available. We especially appreciated the K-12 GIS list for educators to share experiences with their students.

GeoWeb Interactive

www.ggrweb.com

Geo Web Services Inc., Suite 208, Houston, TX 77036
Ph: 713-995-7370   E-mail: gsi@geowebinteractive.com

JOBS	1,000s	RESUMES	1,000s
Cost to post	Cost to see	Cost to post	Cost to see
Fee	Free	Free (See Note)	Fee (See Note)
DISCIPLINE		LOCATION	
IT/Engineering		USA	
SPECIALTY		FEATURE	
GIS/Cad		N/A	
AGENT: Both Recruiters & Jobseekers			

GeoWeb Interactive emphasizes openings for information technology, science and engineering professionals, and claims more than 1,000 hiring clients. Employers who post a job for $195 for 40 days will have it automatically emailed to thousands of registered visitors. Jobs will also be posted to newsgroups. The resume database and unlimited job postings cost $1,490 per quarter (a sampling of the resume database can be viewed for free). News subscribers can post their resumes for free (or become site members for $49 for six months and have their resumes sent to 1,000 agencies and potential employers). CXR has never been a fan of job seekers paying for resume blasting services. Additional resources for JAVA professionals is found in the GeoJava Corner.

GetJobs.com
www.getjobs.com

PO Box 35621, Briarwood, NY 11435
Ph: 718-657-8391   Fax: 718-526-0291   E-mail: sales@getjobs.com

JOBS	1,000,000s		RESUMES	1,000s
Cost to post	Cost to see		Cost to post	Cost to see
Fee	Free		Free	Fee
DISCIPLINE			LOCATION	
ALL			USA	
SPECIALTY			FEATURE	
ALL			N/A	
AGENT: Jobseeker				

GetJobs.com, has changed from a free job posting and resume site to a fee site. Jobs can be searched by category, location, job type or keyword. Openings are in many disciplines. Recruiters pay $99 to post a job and gain access to the resume database. Jobs are easy to view and are date posted with title, location and name of organization. The owners provide an email newsletter that is sent to 40,000 subscribers which has a ad cost of $40 per weekly issue. A long list of newsgroups can also be searched. An article on "how to hire a headhunter" makes for interesting reading.

GIScareers.com
www.giscareers.com

Jacob Bunt
Suite M PMB 471, Redmond, WA 98552
E-mail: info@giscareers.com

JOBS	10s		RESUMES	10s
Cost to post	Cost to see		Cost to post	Cost to see
Free	Free		Free	Free
DISCIPLINE			LOCATION	
IT			USA	
SPECIALTY			FEATURE	
GIS			N/A	
AGENT: N/A				

GIScareers.com was launched July 2001. The owner caters to all aspects of GIS from remote sensing to mapping to geographic analysis. Recruiters can post a position and see resumes for free. Information is well presented. Resumes and jobs are date and the country is indicated with little flags to designate them. Site's search engine allows viewing by country, state or type of job. Job seekers can elect to keep their resume off line or limit contact information. Nice design.

GIS Jobs Clearinghouse

www.gjc.org

Stephen Lime
6224 Glen Circle, Lino Lakes, MN 55014
Ph: 651-765-8964   E-mail: gjc-info@gjc.org

JOBS	100s	RESUMES	100s
Cost to post	Cost to see	Cost to post	Cost to see
Fee	Free	Free	Free
DISCIPLINE		LOCATION	
IT		USA	
SPECIALTY		FEATURE	
GIS/CAD		N/A	
AGENT: N/A			

The GIS Jobs Clearinghouse (Geographical Information Systems) is highly unusual in that the site recommends links to additional GIS job sites. Find-GIS, Geo Job Source, GeoSearch, GeoComm Classifieds, Gis Careers, Geo Web, GISJobs.com, EcoEmploy and GIS Connection can be found under other internet resources. Operating as a free job service since 1992, recruiters are now asked to pay $25 to post a position for 60 days. Resumes can be posted and viewed for free. The site has hundreds of resumes online, with hundreds more coming in each month. Resumes can be browsed by date, which also shows their position and location.

GISjobs.com

www.gisjobs.com

Christopher D. Lading
GISjobs.com, LLC, P.O. Box 331, Appleton, WI 54912
Ph: 920-733-7164   E-mail: info@gisjobs.com

JOBS	100s	RESUMES	100s
Cost to post	Cost to see	Cost to post	Cost to see
Fee	Free	Fee	Free
DISCIPLINE		LOCATION	
IT/Engineering		USA	
SPECIALTY		FEATURE	
Civil/Construction/GIS		Gateway	
AGENT: Jobseeker			

GISjobs.com, CIVILjobs.com and CADDjobs.com invite recruiters to post positions for the geographic information systems, construction and computer aided design specialities respectively. Recruiters pay $50 to post a position for 30 days. Volunteer or unpaid positions may be posted for free. Job seekers pay $10 to post their resume for 90 days. Site will "push" skill matched positions to all who register their e-mail. A salary survey adds value. However, when the site reports that their 60 openings and 60 resumes were each searched 500,000 times in a month, we would encourage asking a few questions.

GoFerretGo

Ephren W. Taylor, Jr
9875 Widmer Road, Lenexa, KS 66215
Ph: 877-504-0808   E-mail: sales@goferretgo.com

JOBS	10,000s	RESUMES	10,000s
Cost to post	Cost to see	Cost to post	Cost to see
Fee	Free	Free	Fee
DISCIPLINE		LOCATION	
Retail Sales & Services/Trades		USA/MDW/MO/Kansas City	
SPECIALTY		FEATURE	
ALL		College/High School	
AGENT: N/A			

GoFerretGo was launched August 1999 by two Kansas City teenagers who came up with the idea to tap 15-21 year olds who want part-time work with local employers. The site charges $99 to post a position for one week for high school and college students. For $214.13 (?) jobs go to the top of the recruiting page. Job seekers can receive the site's newsletter. Employers pay $95 for ad placement. Resume access and unlimited job postings costs $295 per month. The site claims 25,500 registered users as well as 14,000 resumes in the database. Job seekers must register at the site to view open positions. What CXR loves about this site is that job seekers who put in their zip code can search openings within 5, 10, 25 (up to 150) miles from home. These kids "get it".

GOJobs

www.gojobs.com

Jonathon Duarte
2102 Business Center Drive, Irvine, CA 92612
Ph: 949-838-0055   Fax: 949-756-1756   E-mail: sales@gojobs.com

JOBS	1,000s	RESUMES	N/A
Cost to post	Cost to see	Cost to post	Cost to see
Fee	Free	N/A	N/A
DISCIPLINE		LOCATION	
ALL		USA	
SPECIALTY		FEATURE	
ALL		Job Distribution	
AGENT: N/A			

GoJobs.com's search engine allows job seekers to view openings by keywords, job category, area code or state. Openings are listed by location, title, company, category and date of posting. Job postings are all date posted and many were stale (over 90 days old). More than a Job Site, gojobs will distribute employers openings to any combination of over 2000 Internet job boards and newsgroups. Various packages are available and services include tracking results.

GoJobsite UK

www.gojobsite.co.uk

Langstone Technology Park, Langstone Road, Havant, Hampshire, P09 1SA United Kingdom
Ph: 440-870-7748500 Fax: 440-870-7748501 E-mail: jobsite@jobsite.co.uk

JOBS	10,000s		RESUMES	N/A
Cost to post	Cost to see		Cost to post	Cost to see
Fee	Free		N/A	N/A
DISCIPLINE			LOCATION	
ALL			INTL/Europe/UK/Ireland/Italy/Spain	
SPECIALTY			FEATURE	
ALL			Gateway	
AGENT: Jobseeker				

GoJobsite UK was launched in 1995 and rebranded in November 2000. The site is the gateway to a niche network of European sites (France, Germany, Ireland, Italy Spain and the UK) with claims to more than 67,000 jobs posted in the last month from 35 industries. Job seekers who search the database are immediately shown the number of open jobs by category and the date of each posting. Positions posted here range from accounting to travel. Job seekers can search for openings posted in the last 24 hours or the previous seven days to minimize duplication. Recruiters pay 100 pounds to post a job for two weeks. Job seekers (900,000) can register their email and have targeted openings sent to them directly. Connections to Manpower as a major investor are important in more ways than one.

Governmentjobs.com

www.governmentjobs.com/

Ward Komers
222 North Sepulveda Blvd., Suite 2000, El Segundo, CA 90245
Ph: 310-662-4700   Fax: 310-778-9937   E-mail: info@governmentjobs.com

JOBS	1,000s		RESUMES	N/A
Cost to post	Cost to see		Cost to post	Cost to see
Fee	Free		N/A	N/A
DISCIPLINE			LOCATION	
Government			USA	
SPECIALTY			FEATURE	
ALL			N/A	
AGENT: N/A				

Governmentjobs.com was launched March, 2000. Recruiters can post positions for $90 for a 60-day run. Jobs can be searched by location, keyword, job category or salary. A long list of links to public agenciesand cities that are hiring is also available. We love public sector openings as they post exact salary ranges for all positions. Owners have ability to host sites and provide applicant tracking services ($2K per year). Excellent content.

Graduating Engineer & Computer Careers Online

www.graduatingengineer.com

Todd Eckle
CASS Communications, 1800 Sherman Avenue, Suite 300, Evanston, IL 60201
Ph: 847-733-3178   Fax: 847-424-8075   E-mail: todd.eckle@graduatingengineer.com

JOBS	100s	RESUMES	N/A
Cost to post	Cost to see	Cost to post	Cost to see
Fee	Free	N/A	N/A
DISCIPLINE		LOCATION	
IT/Engineering		USA	
SPECIALTY		FEATURE	
ALL		COLLEGE	
AGENT: N/A			

Graduating Engineer & Computer Careers Online has openings that range from accoustical to textile engineering and computer related disciplines. A major supplier of college information, Cass Communications launched this site in mid-1999 and geared it to college graduates who have been out of school for three years or less. Students can create up to three separate resumes and cover letters, and apply for openings using any combination. The site does not have a resume database although one is being considered for the future. The site also tracks which jobs a student has responded to and records when a hiring manager views their resume. Employers pay $100 to post positions for 30 days under as many majors as they choose. "DoctorJob" responds to job seeker career questions.

Graphic Arts Information Network

www.gain.org

Graphic Arts Technical Foundation, 200 Deer Run Road, Sewickley, PA 15143
Ph: 412-741-6860   Fax: 412-741-2311   E-mail: info@gatf.org

JOBS	10s	RESUMES	10s
Cost to post	Cost to see	Cost to post	Cost to see
Fee	Free	Free	Fee
DISCIPLINE		LOCATION	
IT/Communications		USA/	
SPECIALTY		FEATURE	
Graphic Arts		N/A	
AGENT: N/A			

The Graphic Arts Information Network is portal supported through a graphic arts technical foundation and offers extensive content including lists of hundreds of related associations, links to schools, careers and much more. Cost to post jobs is $95/members; $245/non-members.

GrassIsGreener.com (Employon.com)
www.grassisgreener.com

Matt Rolfe
EmployOn, 22700 Shore Center Drive, Cleveland, OH 44123
Ph: 800-448-3735   Fax: 216-502-0073   E-mail: support@employon.com

JOBS	1,000,000s	RESUMES	1,000,000s
Cost to post	Cost to see	Cost to post	Cost to see
Free (See Notes)	Fee (See Notes)	Free	Fee
DISCIPLINE		LOCATION	
ALL		USA	
SPECIALTY		FEATURE	
ALL		Multiple Site Search	
AGENT: N/A			

GrassIsGreener.com is a multi-site search engine. The site claims to have 4,153,000 jobs that it has acquired from job boads, corporate sites and community sites. Job seekers will be paying for access in 2003. At CXR presstime the cost data was not available. Openings can be searched by title, location, distance to a desired city, job description or keyword. Job seekers have no idea which sites this tool can search. The site does not search sites that are "sensitive" to being searched (typically fee sites such as monster.com). The sources of the jobs listed are shown, but narrowing the search from tens of thousands isn't trivial. EmployOn,the sites owner, has acquired 1.5 million resumes. Recruiters can access the database for $1,500 per year. The tool brings back a short brief of the resume, and recruiters can collect candidate emails to send out a blast notice (leads) to all who meet the specifications. For headhunters "ClientMatch" matches jobs with resumes.

Great Insurance Jobs
www.GreatInsuranceJobs.com

Scott Kotroba
1235 North Orange Ave, Orlando, FL 32804
Ph: 800-818-4898   Fax: 407-898-0444   E-mail: sales@greatinsurancejobs.com

JOBS	100s	RESUMES	1,000s
Cost to post	Cost to see	Cost to post	Cost to see
Fee	Free	Free	Fee
DISCIPLINE		LOCATION	
Business		USA/	
SPECIALTY		FEATURE	
Insurance		N/A	
AGENT: N/A			

Launched in 2001, Great Insurance Jobs costs $175 to post for 60 days and $250 to access the resumes. Job seekers can post publicly or confidentially. Connected to eQuest's job distribution, it has gotten a bit of play. It is easy to manuever at the site. Not much risk. No staffing agencies allowed.

Great Summer Jobs

www.greatsummerjobs.com

Virginia Armstrong-Whyte
Peterson's A div. of Thomson Learning, 2000 Lenox Drive, Lawrenceville, NJ 08648
Ph: 800-338-3282   Fax: 609-243-9150   E-mail: reachout@petersons.com

JOBS	1,000s	RESUMES	1,000s
Cost to post	Cost to see	Cost to post	Cost to see
Fee	Free	Free	Fee
DISCIPLINE		LOCATION	
Trades, Non-Exempt & Hourly		USA	
SPECIALTY		FEATURE	
Sports/Outdoors/Adventure		COLLEGE	
AGENT: N/A			

> **Gone out of recruiting business.**

Great Summer Jobs has been created by the American Camping Association and Peterson's, which is known for its college guides. The site lists summer camp openings across the USA. Recruiters must post on this site early (before October) in the season, as jobs are filled quickly. The cost for employers to post is $349 to post up to 100 jobs for the 10-month season which includes access to the resume database. Jobs can be searched by type of position and location. Job seekers can apply directly, or they can complete an online application and send it to as many employers as they wish. Also listed is information on the typical types of jobs; what you can expect in salary, and a well-written piece on "winning resumes that get you the interview".

Green Dream Jobs

www.sustainablebusiness.com/jobs

Rona Fried
SustainableBusiness.com, 231 W. Pulaski Road, Huntington Station, NY 11746
Ph: 631-423-3277   E-mail: rona@sustainablebusiness.com

JOBS	1,000s	RESUMES	N/A
Cost to post	Cost to see	Cost to post	Cost to see
Fee	Free	N/A	N/A
DISCIPLINE		LOCATION	
Engineering/Science		USA	
SPECIALTY		FEATURE	
Environmental		N/A	
AGENT: N/A			

Green Dream Jobs was launched in September 1996 to promote openings in companies that are environmentally responsible. Recruiters pay $50-$125 to post an opening in 2 job categories for a 60 day run. Each additional category costs $50. The site's search engine allows job seekers to view positions by location, job type, skill level or keyword. Job postings are date listed with brief descriptions and contact information. All job types are here, from communications to travel & leisure. A lengthy list of other environmentally friendly job sites can also be found.

Green Energy Jobs

www.greenenergyjobs.com

Latitude 56 Ltd, Lunga Estate, Argyll, Scottland PA318QR United Kingdom
E-mail: info@greenenergyjobs.com

JOBS	100s		RESUMES	N/A
Cost to post	Cost to see		Cost to post	Cost to see
Fee	Free		N/A	N/A
DISCIPLINE			LOCATION	
Engineering/Science			INTL/	
SPECIALTY			FEATURE	
Energy/Renewable			N/A	
AGENT: N/A				

Giving new meaning to the phrase "walking the talk", Green Energy Jobs offers postings for employers of professionals in renewable energy and operates totally "off grid" on wind energy itself. The site charges $149 per month for a posting. This international site has a fabulous "latest vacancies" button on its home page, which allows you to instantly scroll recent listings by country. The site is a gateway to a network of renewable energy sites including:www.solarpowerjobs.com, www.hydrogenjobs.com, www.windpower-jobs.com, www.hydropowerjobs.com, www.tidalpowerjobs.com, and www.wavepowerjobs.com

Hcareers

www.hcareers.com

Katie Assar
300-38 Fell Avenue, North Vancouver, British Columbia V7P 3S2 Canada
Ph: 604-904-8991   Fax: 604-904-8992   E-mail: info@hcareers.com

JOBS	1,000s		RESUMES	10,000s
Cost to post	Cost to see		Cost to post	Cost to see
Fee	Free		Free	Fee
DISCIPLINE			LOCATION	
Hospitality & Food Services			INTL	
SPECIALTY			FEATURE	
ALL			Gateway	
AGENT: Both Recruiters & Jobseekers				

Hcareers was launched in December 1998, and is competing for the hospitality industry employers and job seekers. The owners have created a network with hcareers.ca and hcareers.co.uk (Canada and UK). Recruiters can post a job for $199 for 45 days and review the resume database for one year for $1,635 (includes 15 job postings). Recruiters who purchase 15 or more jobs will get access to resume detective, an agent that will send emails when resumes matching requirements are received by the site. The USA site has 6,052 jobs posted; the UK site has 1,326 postings and Canada has 638. The site claims jobs are cleaned out every 45 days. Jobs are listed in date-posted order, and many have salary ranges. Many national chains have openings posted. A careers newsletter is pushed to 200,000 job seekers.The site posts its traffic numbers for all to view.

HMonster.com (Monster.com)

www.hmonster.com

5 Clocktower Place, Suite 500, Maynard, MA 01754
Ph: 800-666-7837   E-mail: sales@monster.com

JOBS	10,000s		RESUMES	10,000s
Cost to post	Cost to see		Cost to post	Cost to see
Fee	Free		Free	Fee
DISCIPLINE			LOCATION	
Health Care			USA	
SPECIALTY			FEATURE	
MD/Nursing/Allied Health			N/A	
AGENT: Jobseeker				

HMonster (formerlyHealthcare.monster.com) was MedSearch and has for several years been totally integrated into Monster.com. The resume database and job search areas are part of the hundreds of thousands of jobs and resumes in the main site. Monster claims 77 healthcare categories for job seekers from IV therapy to oncology. The site also provides an emailed newsletter. Several interesting articles on the healthcare field can be found here. A job can be posted for 60 days for $305. Access to the resume is sold locally, regionally or nationally from $400 for 2 weeks to $8,500 per year for 1 user.

H1B Sponsors

www.h1bsponsors.com

57 Mullai Nagar 3rd Street, P.N. Pudur, Coimbatore, Tamilnadu, 61041 India
Ph: 914-224-38609   E-mail: admin@h1bsponsors.com

JOBS	100s		RESUMES	10,000s
Cost to post	Cost to see		Cost to post	Cost to see
Free	Free		Free	Fee
DISCIPLINE			LOCATION	
IT/Miscellaneous			INTL	
SPECIALTY			FEATURE	
ALL			Immigration	
AGENT: Recruiter				

H1B sponsors.com is a potential matchmaker between the 195,000 new foreign-born workers allowed in the U.S. each year and their sponsors. Recruiters can search the resume database for $100 for 3 months and post jobs for free. The site has also created another facility for non-information technology professionals looking for sponsorship. Job seekers must submit their resume to the site to view openings. Resumes run the gamut from admin (2,855), java (10,857) to technical recruiters (27). Resumes are purged from the site after 3 months. Extensive immigration information is also available.

Health Care Job Store

www.healthcarejobstore.com

Fran Grossman
10130 Northlake Blvd, Suite 214-319, West Palm Beach, FL 33412
Ph: 561-775-3584   E-mail: jobs@healthcarejobstore.com

JOBS	1,000s		RESUMES	10,000s	
Cost to post	Cost to see		Cost to post	Cost to see	
Fee	Free		Free	Fee	
DISCIPLINE			LOCATION		
Health Care			USA		
SPECIALTY			FEATURE		
MD/Nursing/Health Care			Gateway		
AGENT: Jobseeker					

Health Care Job Store was launched in 1995 and today has a network of 325 healthcare sites feeding into the gateway. (A second network of non-healthcare sites can be found under eJobStores.com). Fran, the site's owner, was one of the original folks to build a network of urls. Everything from admission jobs to wellness jobs (and just about every medical specialty inbetween) can be found here. Fran wants to prove that if you have the right URL the job seekers will come. Single openings can be posted at $175 for 60 days with additional sites usually costing an additional $25. Unlimited job postings to all the sites, plus resume access, is $650 per month. Many other packages are available. An industry salary survey is powered by the people who visit the site.

Health Care Recruitment Online

www.healthcareers-online.com

Rich Sierra
9000 W. Sheridan St1. $1, Pembroke Pines, FL 33024
Ph: 800-322-1463   E-mail: info@healthcarerecruitment.com

JOBS	100s		RESUMES	10,000s	
Cost to post	Cost to see		Cost to post	Cost to see	
Fee	Free		Free	Fee	
DISCIPLINE			LOCATION		
Health Care			USA		
SPECIALTY			FEATURE		
MD/Nursing/Allied Health			Gateway		
AGENT: N/A					

Health Care Recruitment Online is the gateway to a network of sites launched in 1996. The owner's objective is to connect nurses and allied health professionals. Jobs can be searched by category and location. Recruiters pay $125 for a 30-day job posting. Appmatch.com has 20,000 resumes that recruiters can view for $995+ depending on the specialty and regions. The site network includes pharmacyjobs online.com, mdrecruitmentonline.com, radiologyjobs.com, rnjobs.com and rrtjobs.com, prtjobs.com, rehabonline.com and labjobsonline.com. HCRO has been in CXR since the early days as the site's ownership is in this business for the long haul and stands behind their work.

Health Care Source

www.healthcaresource.com

A. Russell Smith
Call24, Inc, 196 Boston Ave, Suite 3000, Medford, MA 09876
Ph: 800-869-5200   Fax: 800-829-6600   E-mail: info@healthcaresource.com

JOBS	1,000s	RESUMES	10,000s
Cost to post	Cost to see	Cost to post	Cost to see
Fee	Free	Free	Fee
DISCIPLINE		LOCATION	
Health Care		USA/	
SPECIALTY		FEATURE	
ALL		N/A	
AGENT: N/A			

HealthCareSource works with 250 hospitals in 30 states. It enables hospitals to post jobs on their own web site and simultaneously on America's HealthCareSource and on America's Job Bank. Since it is used by hospital HR people on a daily basis to update jobs, mark jobs as filled, and track applicants, all jobs on America's HealthCareSource are current. Like similar portals that serve to drive candidates directly to the employer, this model has great legs if they can get the word out. Employers can pay for single postings ($95 for 80 days) and to access the resume database ($125). Searching jobs is made easier by clicking location, then hospital and type of job.

JOB SEEKER TIP

When responding to a telephone message...

...always speak slowly, leave your telephone number twice. Once at the beginning of the conversation and again at the end.

HEALTHeCareers

www.healthecareers.com

Carol Moore
Applied Recruitment Technologies, 9200 E. Panorama Circle, Suite 120, Englewood, CO 80112
Ph: 303-414-1060   Fax: 800-423-1229   E-mail: employers@healthecareers.com

JOBS	100s	RESUMES	1,000s
Cost to post	Cost to see	Cost to post	Cost to see
Fee	Free	Free	Fee
DISCIPLINE		LOCATION	
Health Care		USA	
SPECIALTY		FEATURE	
MD/Nursing Practitioner/Phsician Assistant/Social Work		N/A	
AGENT: Jobseeker			

HealtheCareers was launched in June 1997, and is tying together a network of healthcare professional societies and associations that will drive their members to HEALTHeCareers. The site is growing one segment at a time, and currently has 19 associations in the network. The owners claim to reach hundreds of thousands of members of these associations who are potential advertisers, candidates, etc. Employers pay $195 to post a position for 30 days for non-physician openings ($700 for a physician/surgeon posting). The price includes access to the resume database. Employers access this database through the discipline(s) of their active job posting(s). In other words, if you have a cardiology opportunity online, you can search cardiologist resumes. The network includes:the American Academy of Physician Assistants, the American Assoc. of Medical Assistants, the American Academy of Nurse Practitioners, theAmerican Assoc. of Oral surgeons, the American College of Cardiology, the American College of Physician Executives, the American College of Preventive Medicine, the American Dietetic Assoc., the American Gastroenterological Assoc., the American Psychiatric Assoc., the American Psychiatric Nurses Assoc., the American Society of Clinical Pathologists, the American Society of General Surgeons, the American Society of Radiologic Therapists, the Healthcare Information and Management Systems Society, the Medical Group Managament Assoc. American Assoc. of Cardiovascular & Pulmonary Rehabilitation, American College of Chest Physicians, American College of Occupational & Env. Medicine, American College of Physician Execs. and the Nat'l.l Assoc. of SocialWorkers.

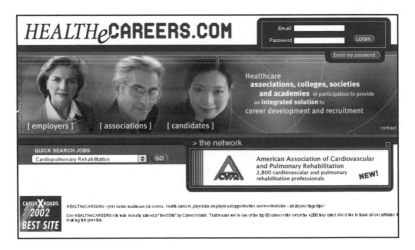

HigherEdJobs.com
www.higheredjobs.com

John Ikenberry
Internet Employment Linkage, Inc., 200 Innovation Bldv., Suite 205, State College, PA 16803
Ph: 814-861-3080   Fax: 814-861-3082   E-mail: advertising@HigherEdJobs.com

JOBS	1,000s	RESUMES	1,000s
Cost to post	Cost to see	Cost to post	Cost to see
Fee	Free	Free	Fee
DISCIPLINE		LOCATION	
Education		USA	
SPECIALTY		FEATURE	
Teaching, University		N/A	
AGENT: Jobseeker			

HigherEdJobs.com founded in 1996 is geared for university, college or administrative staff openings. Home page statistics advised that there were 4,108 faculty and staff positions available at 658 colleges and universities (over a 10% increase from the prior year). Positions ranged from academic advising to volunteer programs. Jobs can be viewed by administrative, executive, faculty, part-time/adjunct, state or institution. Recruiters pay $135 to post a position for 60 days. For employers who purchase the unlimited job posting package ($1,895) this includes access to the resume database for one year. The site gives the number of openings by category, date of posting, application deadline and a detailed description of each opening. Universities can also provide profiles of their schools with detailed information.

HireAbility.com
www.hireability.com

Amy Renz
HireAbility.com, LLC, 13A Red Roof Lane, Salem, NH 03079
Ph: 603-627-0008   Fax: 603-890-9075   E-mail: arenz@hireability.com

JOBS	100s	RESUMES	1,000s
Cost to post	Cost to see	Cost to post	Cost to see
Fee	Free	Free	Fee
DISCIPLINE		LOCATION	
IT		USA	
SPECIALTY		FEATURE	
ALL		Contingent/3rd party staffing exchange	
AGENT: Jobseeker			

Launched in 1998 HireAbility.com provides jobs for IT contract employment. Site directs all job seekers to obtain a password before they can search the site' openings. Recruiters pay for job postings depending on their annual volume. Prices range from $16 per month to $160 per month to access the resumes. Owners have geared this site to provide services for third party recruiters. Corporations can utilize these services to streamline their IT temporary recruiting efforts.

Hire Deaf.com
www.hiredeaf.com
E-mail: cs@hiredeaf.com

JOBS	100s	RESUMES	N/A
Cost to post	Cost to see	Cost to post	Cost to see
Fee	Free	N/A	N/A
DISCIPLINE		LOCATION	
ALL		USA/	
SPECIALTY		FEATURE	
ALL		Diversity	
AGENT: Jobseeker			

Hire Deaf.com is a niche site serving the deaf community. Employers pay $50 to post a job for 30-days. A weekly bulletin with jobs gets pushed out to those who opt in. Resumes are not accessible. Nearly 1000 jobs are posted and 10,000 job seekers are registered here.

HireDiversity.com
www.hirediversity.com

Kirsten McGregor
Hispanic Business Inc., 425 Pine Ave, Santa Barbara, CA 93117
Ph: 800-810-7521   Fax: 805-964-7239   E-mail: hd@hirediversity.com

JOBS	1,000s	RESUMES	100,000s
Cost to post	Cost to see	Cost to post	Cost to see
Fee	Free	Free	Fee
DISCIPLINE		LOCATION	
ALL		USA	
SPECIALTY		FEATURE	
ALL		Diversity	
AGENT: Jobseeker			

HireDiversity.com was launched in 1998 and offers both job postings and resume searches for minorities, women, disabled, veterans, bilingual and mature workers. Postings are up for 60days and cost $275, and resumes are searchable for 90 days for $1,500. With an advanced search engine that allows job seekers to view openings by state, city, occupation, date or keyword phrase, and an area for sophisticated boolean searches, this site is ahead of the pack. Job seekers are given a resume ID number to log onto the site which they will shortly forget. Solid diversity articles are posted. Diversity forums are open for job seekers to join anddiscuss their interests. Numerous government agencies and a handful of non-profit organizations have openings posted. Job seekers should check out "Who's Hiring" as displays of corporate logos and job postings make for easy viewing. A calendar listing of job fairs is available.

hirehealth.com

www.hirehealth.com

Rick Fulton
Career Innovations, 407 Richmond Avenue, Point Pleasant, NJ 08742
Ph: 888-750-4473   Fax: 888-350-4473   E-mail: sales@hirehealth.com

JOBS	1,000s	RESUMES	100,000s
Cost to post	Cost to see	Cost to post	Cost to see
Fee	Free	Free	Fee
DISCIPLINE		LOCATION	
Science/Health Care		USA/MDA/NJ	
SPECIALTY		FEATURE	
Bio/Pharm/Nursing/MD		Gateway	
AGENT: Both Recruiters & Jobseekers			

Hirehealth.com targets the pharmaceutical, biotechnology and healthcare industries in a big way Job seekers who register their email can have skill-matched positions sent to their desktops. The cost to post a job is $275 for 60 days. The cost to access the resume database is $6,000 per year. Jobs are date posted and show a "score" that job seekers will have no idea what it means. The site claims to have 119,672 resumes that are deleted after six months. The owners sponsor live job fairs across the USA. The site needs more disclosure and a privacy statement. Hiremed.com is another HH site that focuses on the healthcare side of business. Recruit Minds is an associate employment agency also owned by this company.

HireinaClick

www.hireinaclick.com

Suresh Raghavan
Sastha.com Inc., 131 Hall Place, Grosse Pointe Farms, MI 48236
Ph: 248-355-9621   E-mail: sasthacom@comcast.net

JOBS	100s	RESUMES	N/A
Cost to post	Cost to see	Cost to post	Cost to see
Fee	Free	N/A	N/A
DISCIPLINE		LOCATION	
ALL		USA	
SPECIALTY		FEATURE	
ALL		Gateway	
AGENT: Jobseeker			

JobinaClick.com and HireinaClick.com are gateways to a niche network of 400 specialty sites launched in 1998. Postings are maintained for 120 days and cost $125. Recruiters visit nichejobs.com to review the url listings and select 3 that pertain to their opening. The site offers specialty jobs mailing lists (14,500 subscribers) for job seekers to join. Free discussion boards by job function are available with designated areas for college interns. Additional sites include HRMJobs.com, BuyingJobs.com, SupplyJobs.com, MaterialsJobs.com, ChemistryJobs.com, WeldingJobs.com, EconomicsJobs.com, SellingJobs.com, E2Ejobs.com, MedicoJobs.com, DataWarehouseJobs.com and others.

Hireskills.com

www.hireskills.com

Tony Gilmore
82 Palomino Lane, Suite 503, Bedford, NH 03110
Ph: 603-625-0541   Fax: 603-625-4172   E-mail: customerservice@hireskills.com

JOBS	10s	RESUMES	N/A
Cost to post	Cost to see	Cost to post	Cost to see
Free	Free	N/A	N/A
DISCIPLINE		LOCATION	
Trade, Non-Exempt, Hourly		USA	
SPECIALTY		FEATURE	
Graphic Arts/Packaging/Printing		Contingent	
AGENT: Both Recruiters & Jobseekers			

Hireskills.com, launched May 2000, focuses on sales and skilled non-exempt employees in the printing, publishing and packaging trades. This site is a division of a search firm (Sprouts & Standish) specializing in the hiring of graphic arts people with experience in the printing and packaging industries. Recruiters can post an opening for $240 for a 60 day run. Unlimited resume and job posting access costs $6,000 per year.. Folks here would likely work in printing plants, but increasingly the graphic arts professionals themselves will be working independently and remotely. Job seekers must register to view openings. A lengthy list of linksfor printing or publishing employers is available. Job seekers can register to be emailed matching openings. Problem is that they have to return to the site to view them.

Historically Black Colleges and Universities

HBCUCareerCenter.com

William R. Moss III
HBCUCareerCenter.com LLC, 7846 Grandlin park Ct, Blacklick, OH 43004
Ph: 614.284.3007   Fax: 215.438.1975   E-mail: Staff@HBCUCareerCenter.com

JOBS	100s	RESUMES	1,000s
Cost to post	Cost to see	Cost to post	Cost to see
Fee	Free	Free	Fee
DISCIPLINE		LOCATION	
ALL		N/A	
SPECIALTY		FEATURE	
ALL		Diversity	
AGENT: Jobseeker			

Launched in February 2002, this Alumni network of Historically Black Colleges and Universities is an interesting site for its focus and commitment. Employers pay $45 to post a job for 30 daysand $1200 to access resumes for a year. Percentagewise they might not have a significant portion of the alumni but, we do like the way they feature alumni throughout the site. Worth a look.

HollywoodWeb

www.hollywoodweb.com

Brett Crosby
926 Second Street, Suite 402, Santa Monica, CA
Ph: 310-899-4434   E-mail: admin@hollywoodweb.com

JOBS	100s	RESUMES	100s
Cost to post	Cost to see	Cost to post	Cost to see
Free	Free	Free	Fee
DISCIPLINE		LOCATION	
Entertainment & Media/Commun ications		USA	
SPECIALTY		FEATURE	
Actors/Directors/Crew/Writing		N/A	
AGENT: N/A			

HollywoodWeb is a virtual "cattle casting call" for all the entertainment projects. Directors, actors, actresses, writers, technicians, models and extras can also be part of this cyber audition. All union members can register their area of interest, scan in a "headshot" and send it to the site via e-mail for free (snail mail will cost you $15). Resume profiles can be viewed for free but contact information comes with a fee. Site is run by a talent agent. Site is extremely simple to use and offers members clearly defined services.

Horticultural Jobs

www.horticulturaljobs.com

J.M. Eason
6407 Market Street, Charlotte, NC 28215
Ph: 309-279-1942   Fax: 208-694-3910   E-mail: sales@horticulturaljobs.com

JOBS	10s	RESUMES	10s
Cost to post	Cost to see	Cost to post	Cost to see
Fee	Free	Free	Free
DISCIPLINE		LOCATION	
Science		USA	
SPECIALTY		FEATURE	
Horticulture/Life Sciences		N/A	
AGENT: Jobseeker			

Horticultural jobs is evidence of just how fertile the recruitment landscape is, and just how quickly sites like this one can sprout up. Employers pay $50 to post a position for 60 days ($150 for unlimited postings for one year) and resumes can be viewed for free (look carefully for the link as it is the last category under the job titles). Job postings note the number of openings next to each job category. Resumes and jobs are date posted and have direct contact information. Landscape management, nursery positions and many similar openings flourish here.

Hospital Jobs Online
www.hospitaljobsonline.com

LJ Burrows
3043 N. Mt. Baker Circle, Oak Harbor, WA 98335
Ph: 360-675-5600   E-mail: admin@hospitaljobsonline.com

JOBS	10,000s	RESUMES	10,000s
Cost to post	Cost to see	Cost to post	Cost to see
Fee	Free	Free	Fee
DISCIPLINE		LOCATION	
Health Care		USA	
SPECIALTY		FEATURE	
Nursing/Allied/MD		Gateway	
AGENT: Jobseeker			

Hospital Jobs Online was launched in April 1997 and is the gateway to a network of healthcare sites including 4nursingjobs.com, 4alliedhealthjobs.com and 4mdjobs.com. Recruiters pay $150 to post a job. Resume access is $1,500 per quarter or can be included in posting packages. Resume access alone is $500 per month. Jobs can be searched by category or location. Job seekers must register their email before being allowed to apply for openings. Jobs are date posted and job seekers can add a cover letter to each opening they wish to apply for. Links to the posting company's site are also available to provide more information. A lengthy alpha list (by state) of hospital websites is also available for job seekers to view.

HospitalityJobsOnline
www.hospitalityonline.com

Tom Ferree
PO Box 677, Gig Harbor, WA 98335
Ph: 253-941-4950   Fax: 253-946-6818   E-mail: sales@hospitalityonline.com

JOBS	100s	RESUMES	N/A
Cost to post	Cost to see	Cost to post	Cost to see
Fee	Free	N/A	N/A
DISCIPLINE		LOCATION	
Hospitality & Food Services		USA	
SPECIALTY		FEATURE	
ALL		N/A	
AGENT: Jobseeker			

HospitalityJobsOnline advised on our visit that 333 jobs had been posted in the last 15 days and 100 in the last 6 hours. The site caters to hotels, resorts and restaurants. Recruiters can post a position for $200 ($170 if pre-paid). Job seekers can browse openings for management jobs or hourly positions by title, company or location. Job seekers can apply directly to the company or through HospitalityJobsOnline. Job categories advise the number of openings in each. Recruiters can link a company profile to each opening to give insight into benefits, size of organization, etc. Job seekers who register their email addresses and skills can have "hospitality hound" email matching opportunities to their desktops. Direct contact information is available even though the owners of the site are in the headhunting business.

Hospitality Link

866 S.E. 14th Terrace, Suite 128, DeerField Beach, FL 33441
Ph: 954-579-1802   Fax: 954-421-1046   E-mail: info@hospitalitylink.com

JOBS	100s		RESUMES	100s
Cost to post	Cost to see		Cost to post	Cost to see
Fee	Free		Free	Free
DISCIPLINE			LOCATION	
Hospitality & Food Services			USA	
SPECIALTY			FEATURE	
ALL			N/A	
AGENT: N/A				

Hospitality Link offers opportunities in management, culinary, food & beverage, marketing and finance. Openings are displayed with detailed job specs and direct contact information. Recruiters can post unlimited jobs for 3 months for $100. Candidate information is easily searched and free with contact data. Great design and worth exploring.

JOB SEEKER TIP

Audit your job search.

The job search is in three steps: leads, good paper (resume) and good interviews. If you are not getting any interviews that means your resume needs to be redone. If you are not getting any call backs for second interviews that means your communications skills need work.

HotJobs.com
www.hotjobs.com

406 West 31st Street, New York, NY 10001
Ph: 877-468-5627   Fax: 212-944-8962   E-mail: sales@hotjobs.com

JOBS	100,000s		RESUMES	1,000,000s
Cost to post	Cost to see		Cost to post	Cost to see
Fee	Free		Free	Fee

DISCIPLINE		LOCATION	
ALL		USA	

SPECIALTY		FEATURE	
ALL		Major Career Hub	

AGENT: Jobseeker

HotJobs was acquired by Yahoo in 2002 and continues to be one of the leading job boards on the web. A new president has recently come on board and we look for interesting changes. HotJobs.com has several career channels, allowing users to easily find and apply for a position in various industry-specific areas. Job seekers can surf targeted fields like sales and marketing, retail, technology, human resources. Each channel links job seekers directly from the HotJobs.com home page to profiles of featured employers and a searchable job database. Industry articles on each job channel are also available. Hotjobs.com also connects job seekers to employers who use its web-enabled products SoftShoe, and Resumix- staffing resume management and applicant tracking solutions. Employers post a job for $220 for a 30-day run and access the resume database for $2,445 per quarter. Will continued Super Bowl advertising in 2003 take this site to another level? Job seekers can select opportunities by direct employers or staffing firms, keyword, job interest, location or level. Jobs are date posted with the initial title of opening, company name and location shown. More information can then be viewed. A job seeker's agent and the ability to block a corporation from viewing one's resume give added security. Openings are clearly labeled if they are posted by an employer or staffing firm. With a new owner and a new president, 2003 will be an interesting year for this major career hub.

Hot Nurse Jobs

www.hotnursejobs.com

Canada
Ph: 800-889-8555   Fax: 858-509-4118   E-mail: info@hotnursejobs.com

JOBS	100s		RESUMES	100s
Cost to post	Cost to see		Cost to post	Cost to see
Fee	Free		Free	Fee
DISCIPLINE			LOCATION	
Health Care			INTL/Canada/USA	
SPECIALTY			FEATURE	
Nursing			Gateway	
AGENT: N/A				

Hot Nurse Jobs really is a legitimate health care job site (despite the name) where employers can post an opening for $98 per month (includes access to the resume database). Recruiters can access the resume database alone for $78 per month. Site claims to have hundreds of resumes that are less then 3 months old. Jobs are for RN's, traveling nurses, mgmt., nurse educators, CRN's, LPN/LVN, CNA/nurse aids, NP, paramedic, EMT, Canadian, camp, and nurse analysts. Openings are viewed by state or function with contact information. A link to Canadiannurse.com is where the positions north of the border are listed. Other sites include campnursejobs.com and medicaljobsonline.com

HoustonEmployment.com (Employocity)

www.employocity.com

Kristi Power
550 Westcott, Suite 460, Houston, TX 77007
Ph: 713-807-75050   Fax: 713-807-7555   E-mail: info@houstonemployment.com

JOBS	1,000s		RESUMES	100s
Cost to post	Cost to see		Cost to post	Cost to see
Fee	Free		Free	Fee
DISCIPLINE			LOCATION	
ALL			USA	
SPECIALTY			FEATURE	
ALL			Gateway	
AGENT: N/A				

A simple site launched in 1997, HoustonEmployment.com is the main site in this niche location network (formerly Employocity). Employers can post jobs for $175 for 30 days (other packages are available) and for $350 can access the resume database. Job seekers can maintain their confidentiality and resume on site for one year. About 2,000 jobs are here, and the site claims as many as 2,000 new resumes are added for all 10 cities. The cities include:AustinEmployment.com, BirminghamEmployment.com, ChicagoEmployment.com, DFWEmployment.com, DetroitEmployment.com, HoustonEmployment.com, LAEmployment.com, NYCEmployment.com,PhoenixEmployment.com, SFBayEmployment.com

HRJunction

Nancy Peterson
NHC Group, Inc., P.O. Box 508, Marlborough, MA 01752
Ph: 508-624-9641   Fax: 508-624-9991   E-mail: info@hrjunction.com

JOBS	100s	RESUMES	N/A
Cost to post	Cost to see	Cost to post	Cost to see
Fee	Free	N/A	N/A
DISCIPLINE		LOCATION	
Human Resources		USA/	
SPECIALTY		FEATURE	
ALL		N/A	
AGENT: N/A			

HRJunction is a nicely designed free site from JobMark, a site hosting company. Site was inspired by Bret Hollander of Netrecruiter fame. More than 100 positions are free to see and were free to post. Resume database is in the works.

HR.com

www.hr.com

Silvi Verder
124 Wellington Street E, Aurora, Ontario L4G 1J1 Canada
Ph: 877-472-6648   E-mail: sales@hr.com

JOBS	1,000s	RESUMES	1,000s
Cost to post	Cost to see	Cost to post	Cost to see
Free	Free	Free	Fee
DISCIPLINE		LOCATION	
Human Resources		USA	
SPECIALTY		FEATURE	
ALL		N/A	
AGENT: Both Recruiters & Jobseekers			

HR.com was launched in August 1999 as a portal for human resource information. Job seekers must register to access the 1,743 openings posted to the career center which many arrive here from a partnership with another site. Recruiters can post positions for free but, if they want their job to rise to the top of the listing the cost is $150. There are 28,000 job seekers registered of the 130,000 site members. The resume database can be accessed for free. For those who post jobs, the site's agent will send candidates who match the skill requirements to the recruiter's desktop via email. Job seekers can have matching jobs sent to their PC. All openings are date posted with direct contact information. A weekly emailed human resources newsletter and online discussion forums add value. Basic membership is free but, access to the 6,000 articles, product reviews and other features costs $150 per year. Great content, fabulous alliances, solid leadership from a savvy owner and a url to die for make this site one to watch.

234

HRIM Mall

www.hrimmall.com

Jim Morrone
5603-B W. Friendly Ave, No. 269, Greensboro, NC 27410
Ph: 336-643-8241   Fax: 336-643-9519   E-mail: sales@hrimmall.com

JOBS	10s	RESUMES	N/A
Cost to post	Cost to see	Cost to post	Cost to see
Free	Free	N/A	N/A
DISCIPLINE		LOCATION	
Human Resources		USA	
SPECIALTY		FEATURE	
HRIS/Employment		N/A	
AGENT: N/A			

A new look for the HRIM Mall offers free job postings and contains links to hundreds of other resources on the web. While the site doesn't provide a job matching service, it does send notification of newly posted openings to a large opt-in list. Corporate recruiters can post unlimited opportunity listings for free. About 75 positions are posted each month. A long listing of human resource job sites is also available. More companies and job seekers should be taking advantage of this site.

hs people (Human Services)

www.hspeople.com

Andrea Goode
Vary Goode Services, Inc., PO Box 73, Centerville, MA 02632
Ph: 888-912-1114   E-mail: info@hspeople.com

JOBS	10s	RESUMES	100s
Cost to post	Cost to see	Cost to post	Cost to see
Fee	Free	Free	Fee
DISCIPLINE		LOCATION	
Non-Profit		USA/NOE/CT/ME/MA/NH/RI/VT	
SPECIALTY		FEATURE	
Case Workers/Psychologists		N/A	
AGENT: Jobseeker			

hs people.com offers a list of leads to mental health, non profit, and human services professionals (case management, program directors and substance abuse counselors). Recruiters pay $100 to post 1-5 jobs. Access to the resume database is $300 for 3 months which includes 5 job postings. Jobs can be found by function or state, and job seekers will appreciate that only those with openings are shown. All jobs have contact information. Job seekers must register to view openings, and the registration process asks very specific questions about background and interests. The site records the positions that the job seekers applied to via a "careercart". A long list of career assistance articles is also available.

HTML Writers Guild Job List
www.hwg.org

110 E. Wilshire Avenue, Suite G-10, Fullerton, CA 92832
Ph: 714-526-4963   E-mail: membership@iwanet.org

JOBS	100s		RESUMES	100s
Cost to post	Cost to see		Cost to post	Cost to see
Free	Fee (See Notes)		Fee	Fee
DISCIPLINE			LOCATION	
IT			USA	
SPECIALTY			FEATURE	
New Media			N/A	
AGENT: N/A				

The HTML Writers Guild (HWG) boasts 150,000 members in more than 160 countries. In 2001 the Guild joined with the International Webmasters Assoc. The HWG-Jobs discussion list is for members to receive help wanted postings. Just send your opening to hwg-jobs-request@hwg.org. Membership in the guild costs $49 per year. The IWA has a career center that charges recruiters $150 to post an opening for a 60 day run. Resume content can be viewed for free but contact information has a cost. Jobtarget manages the job pages of this site and a lot more disclosure and better navigation is needed.

i-resign.com
www.i-resign.com

Tim Snaith
Portland Intelligence Ltd, 5 Clipstone Street, London, W1W6BB
Ph: 020-790-70258   Fax: 020-790-70251   E-mail: info@i-resign.com

JOBS	100s		RESUMES	N/A
Cost to post	Cost to see		Cost to post	Cost to see
Fee	Fee		N/A	N/A
DISCIPLINE			LOCATION	
ALL			INTL/Europe & USA	
SPECIALTY			FEATURE	
ALL			N/A	
AGENT: N/A				

Launched in 1999, i-resign.com offers unique perspectives for jobseekers since all the postings are from people leaving their jobs. Membership is $45. Check out the i-resign guide to boredom or how to survive the first week in a new job. The services include excellent suggestions on how to get out of a bad situation, an automatic resignation letter generator, resignation advice, a database of imminent and current job openings. We can almost believe this claim as having the internets freshest jobs.

idealist.org
www.idealist.org

Ami Dar
Action Without Borders, Inc., 79 Fifth Avenue, 17th Floor, New York, NY 10003
Ph: 212-843-3973   Fax: 212-564-3377   E-mail: lea@idealist.org

JOBS	1,000s		RESUMES	N/A
Cost to post	Cost to see		Cost to post	Cost to see
Fee	Free		N/A	N/A
DISCIPLINE			LOCATION	
Non-Profit			USA	
SPECIALTY			FEATURE	
ALL			N/A	
AGENT: Jobseeker				

Idealist.org has 29,000 clients in 153 countries involved in this nonprofit community organization site. If you are a non-profit, community based group, volunteer center, school or museum whether public or private this may be the place for recruiting or seeking an opening. Founded in 1995 to build a network of neighborhood contact centers in communities around the world this site has ease of navigation that the big $$ sites would drool over. Recruiters in the USA pay $50 to post a position. Internships and volunteer opportunities from other countries can be posted for free. The site will email daily openings to their 70,000 electronic newsletter subscribers. Openings can be viewed by using the site's search engine or by country. Jobs are posted from all over the world in every occupation but it is primarily US based (1,577 of the1,700 + are USA based). Other sites take note, as total stats on openings and by job function are easily accessible

iHire Job Network
www.ihirejobnetwork.com

Lori Bryan
110 N. Public Square, Suite 2-2, Angola, IN 46703
Ph: 877-798-4854   Fax: 219-624-2442   E-mail: info@ihireinc.comom

JOBS	100s		RESUMES	10,000s
Cost to post	Cost to see		Cost to post	Cost to see
Fee	Free		Free	Fee (See Notes)
DISCIPLINE			LOCATION	
ALL			USA	
SPECIALTY			FEATURE	
ALL			Gateway	
AGENT: Recruiter				

IHire Job Network wants to have its hands in numerous job niches. The owners have 31 sites in accounting, law, secretarial, HR, construction, buiilding trades, real estate, insurance, nursing, nutrition medical secretaries, mental health, pharmacy, physicians, mid-level practitioners, therapy, network administrators, programmers, qc, mfg. engineers, teachers (elem/secondary), school administrators, retail, social services, hospitality, chefs, law enforcement and security, Recruiters pay $95-$250 to post a job for 60 days. The site will send unlimited matching resumes to recruiters via email- there is no database to be searched. All sites have the number of job openings posted on the home page. The owners advise that resume databases are not co-mingled. Recruiters and job seekers should view the process flow chart for ease of access. Job seekers should select "all states for ease of navigation. Pre-employment questions are asked on openings.

ihispano.com
www.ihispano.com

Joaquin Amador
20 N. Clark Street, Suite 2900, Chicago, IL 60601
Ph: 312-279-2000   Fax: 312-346-1438   E-mail: support@ihispano.com

JOBS	100s		RESUMES	100s
Cost to post	Cost to see		Cost to post	Cost to see
Fee	Free		Free	Fee
DISCIPLINE			LOCATION	
ALL			USA	
SPECIALTY			FEATURE	
ALL			DIVERSITY	
AGENT: Jobseeker				

ihispano.com was launched in November 1999 and is owned by an executive search firm. Jobs can be searched by keyword, location, category or min. salary. Several major corporations have openings posted. Recruiters pay $150 to post a job for 60 days. For $3,500(6 month membership) recruiters can post up to 500 openings and have access to the resume database. Solid advice on writing cover letters and resumes is available. Site has improved during the last year.

IMdiversity.com
www.imdiversitycom

Preston Edwards
909 Poydras Street, 36th Floor, New Orleans, LA 70112
Ph: 504-523-0154   Fax: 504-523-0271   E-mail: sales@imdiversity.com

JOBS	10,000s	RESUMES	10,000s
Cost to post	Cost to see	Cost to post	Cost to see
Fee	Free	Free	Fee
DISCIPLINE		LOCATION	
ALL		USA	
SPECIALTY		FEATURE	
ALL		College/Diversity	
AGENT: Jobseeker			

Created by the owners of Black Collegian magazine, IMdiversity.com reaches out to underrepresented minority professionals. The site is organized into villages representing the African, Asian, Hispanic, Native-American, Women and International communities. Specific to each village are content areas with solid articles on career management and other topics. The site search criteria includes:job category, city, state or keyword with the number of openings listed by job title. Job seekers appreciate being able to quickly screen the postings. Job seekers can register to have matching openings sent to their PCs. Recruiters pay $175 per job posting for 60 days. They can view the resume database and post unlimited jobs for an annua lcost of $9,000. Job seekers can keep their contact information confidential if they choose. Many Fortune 500 corporations have entry level as well as experienced openings posted. A perenial top site pick by CXR, the owners have been in the diversity and publishing business for more than 30 years and understand what it takes to create relationships.

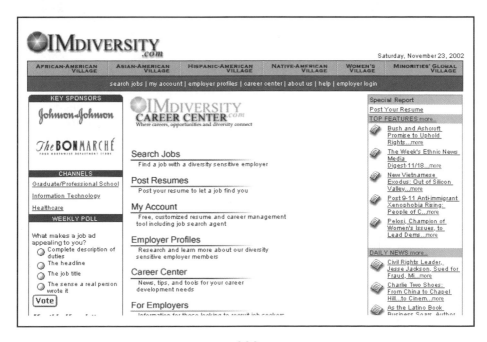

Independent School Management (ISM)

www.isminc.com/pubs/mart/mm.html

Weldon Burge
1316 N. Union Street, Wilmington, DE 19806
Ph: 302-656-4944   Fax: 302-656-0647   E-mail: ism@isminc.com

JOBS	100s	RESUMES	N/A
Cost to post	Cost to see	Cost to post	Cost to see
Fee	Free	N/A	N/A
DISCIPLINE		LOCATION	
Education		USA	
SPECIALTY		FEATURE	
Teaching/Administration, K-12		N/A	
AGENT: N/A			

The Independent School Management's Career Corner (ISM) reaches 12,000 private school administrators, faculty and staff. Management Mart, the site's print publication, costs $64 for a 3 line header, $89 per 0.5 inch copy and $64 for a 6 line footer. If recruiters buy the print they get the website for free (backwards). Faculty ads are not posted in the site's print publication but can be added to the site for $21 per opening. Jobs are searched by administrator or teaching categories. Site's owners are involved in publishing information for school administrators and consulting in this arena.

Infectious Disease Soc. of America

www.idsociety.org

66 Canal Center Plaza, Suite 600, Alexandria, VA 22314
Ph: 703-299-0200   Fax: 703-299-0204   E-mail: info@idsociety.org

JOBS	10s	RESUMES	100s
Cost to post	Cost to see	Cost to post	Cost to see
Free	Fee (See Notes)	Free	Free
DISCIPLINE		LOCATION	
Health Care		USA	
SPECIALTY		FEATURE	
MD/Infectious Diseases		N/A	
AGENT: N/A			

IDSA is the Infectious Diseases Society of America, a 40 year old organization that includes over 6,000 physicians, scientists and other health care professionals. Jobs can be posted for free for a 3 month run, but can only be seen by members of the association. The site's resume database (155) can be viewed for free with contact information included. Posted resumes were for internists and pediatricians in private or academic clinical practices, research, pharmaceutical or public health. Membership dues cost $215 per year.

InfoMine

www.infomine.com

Renee Robertson
640-580 Hornby Street, Vancouver, British Columbia Canada
Ph: 604-683-2037   Fax: 604-681-4166   E-mail: renee@infomine.com

JOBS	100s	RESUMES	100s
Cost to post	Cost to see	Cost to post	Cost to see
Fee	Fee	Fee	Free
DISCIPLINE		LOCATION	
Engineering/Trades		INTL/Canada	
SPECIALTY		FEATURE	
Mining		N/A	
AGENT: N/A			

InfoMine's "Careers" section was launched in 1994 and, according to the portal's owners, digs deep to serve folks in the mining industry. Recruiters can post jobs for $200 for a 60-day run (these positions are given a priority "hot jobs" icon. All other jobs are gathered from various sources which allows the site to charge job seekers $19.95 per month). Job seekers are also charged $100 to post a resume. Jobs are listed by date of posting, position or location. It has no search engine, bare bones and simplistic. Resumes can be viewed for free. Charging both employers and those they seek is a tough balancing act but hey, they've been at this niche for 8 years now and show about 500 current jobs and 1000 resumes.

Inside Careers

www.insidecareers.co.uk

Nick Murteira
The Quandrangle, Unit 3, 49 Atalanta Street, London, SW6 6TR United Kingdom
Ph: 020-756-57900   Fax: 020-756-57938   E-mail: sales@cmi.co.uk

JOBS	10,000s	RESUMES	10,000s
Cost to post	Cost to see	Cost to post	Cost to see
Fee	Free	N/A	N/A
DISCIPLINE		LOCATION	
Finance/Engineering/Legal		INTL/Europe/UK	
SPECIALTY		FEATURE	
Accounting		College	
AGENT: N/A			

Inside Careers is a partnership with several UK associations:the Institute of Management Consultancy, the Chartered Institute of Patent Agents, the Institute of Logistics and Transport, the Institute of Chartered Accountants, the Institute of Actuaries, the British Computer Society, the Institute of Taxation and the Engineering Council. Recruiters pay to post jobs in the sites print edition and the web is an added service. Jobs can be searched under key recruiters. Each association has individual content with detailed information on each profession. Job seekers must register with the site to apply for openings. Numerous career articles are available on each profession. Many graduate trainee positions are posted. A lot of thought went into the design of this site.

Institute for Supply Management

`www.ism.ws`

Cheryl Chadwick
PO Box 22160, Tempe, AZ 85285
Ph: 800-888-6276   Fax: 480-752-7890   E-mail: cchadwick@ism.ws

JOBS	100s	RESUMES	1,000s
Cost to post	Cost to see	Cost to post	Cost to see
Free	Fee (See Notes)	Fee (See Notes)	Free
DISCIPLINE		LOCATION	
Business		USA	
SPECIALTY		FEATURE	
Operations/Manufacturing/Purchasing		N/A	
AGENT: N/A			

Institute for Supply Management (ISM), formerly the National Association of Purchasing Professionals, allows recruiters to post positions for 30 days and view resumes for free. Membership is required for job seekers to post their resumes or apply to positions. Membership costs $170 per year. Searching can be done by keyword, location, years of purchasing experience, or certification. During our visit, over 1,300 resumes were visible with date of listing and direct contact information. The site is well designed and a great service for members. We still recommend they open the jobs up to all.

Institute of Electrical and Electronics Engineers

`www.ieee.org`

Debra Grant
445 Hoes Lane, PO Box 459, Piscataway, NJ 08855
Ph: 800-701-4333   E-mail: jobsite@ieee.org

JOBS	100s	RESUMES	1,000s
Cost to post	Cost to see	Cost to post	Cost to see
Fee	Free	Fee	Fee
DISCIPLINE		LOCATION	
IT/Engineering		USA	
SPECIALTY		FEATURE	
Electrical/Electronic/Computer/Hardware		N/A	
AGENT: Jobseeker			

The Institute of Electrical and Electronics Engineers (IEEE) has over 365,000 members and continues to try to get their career site to a playable level. Recruiters pay $150 to post a position online for a 30 day run. Up to 25 pre-employment questions can be customized to qualify job seekers. The resume database can be accessed for $1,795 when a recruiter pays to post four jobs at a cost of $540. Openings can be searched by keyword, company name, category, education, years of experience, expertise, location, percent travel or salary. Only IEEE members can apply to jobs online but job seekers should not dispair - the name of the listing company is prominently displayed so go direct. IEEE has partnered with hire.com to host their site, but it seems they have forgotten that helping, not teasing, potential members may increase their desire to join. The association we hoped would "get it" when it comes to providing services for the profession is still searching for the right lightning bolt.

Instrumentation Soc. of America

www.isajobs.org/

67 Alexander Drive, Research Triangle Park, NC 20187
Ph: 919-549-8411   Fax: 919-549-8288   E-mail: isajobs@isa.org

JOBS	100s	RESUMES	10s
Cost to post	Cost to see	Cost to post	Cost to see
Fee	Free	Fee	Free
DISCIPLINE		LOCATION	
Engineering		USA	
SPECIALTY		FEATURE	
Electrical/Electronic/Instrumentation & Control		N/A	
AGENT: Jobseeker			

The Instrumention Society of America (ISA) job board was launched in July 2000, and serves more than 39,000 members worldwide. There are presently over 400 openings listed. Positions are posted for 60 days, and cost $295. Resumes are available for free, and there were over 74 on our last visit. Members post their resumes for free, non-members pay $50. This site is well designed and very easy to view.

Int'l Customer Service Assoc.

www.icsa.com

Robin Goldstein
401 N. Michigan Avenue, Chicago, IL 60611
Ph: 800-360-4272   Fax: 312-245-1084   E-mail: icsa@sbs.com

JOBS	100s	RESUMES	100s
Cost to post	Cost to see	Cost to post	Cost to see
Free	Free	Free	Free
DISCIPLINE		LOCATION	
Cust. Service & Tech. Support		USA	
SPECIALTY		FEATURE	
Customer Service		N/A	
AGENT: N/A			

The International Customer Service Association now allows anyone to post and search their jobs databank for free. Last year you had to be a member. Openings are posted for 90 days and are all date posted. Recruiters can register for free access to the resume databank. A listing of headhunters in this field is also available.

Int'l. Foundation of Employee Benefit Plans

www.ifebp.org/jobs

Barbara Pamperin
Job Posting Service, PO Box 69, Brookfield, WI 53008
Ph: 888-334-3327   Fax: 262-786-8670   E-mail: jobposting@ifebp.org

JOBS	10s	RESUMES	10s
Cost to post	Cost to see	Cost to post	Cost to see
Fee	Free	Fee	Free
DISCIPLINE		LOCATION	
Human Resources		USA	
SPECIALTY		FEATURE	
Benefits		N/A	
AGENT: Jobseeker			

The International Foundation of Employee Benefit Plans is a 50 year old organization that has 35,000 members and posts jobs and resumes for all to see. Recruiters pay $185 ($160 for members) for a 60-day job posting. Links to recruiters' email addresses and websites are also included. All are emailed to members who have subscribed to the site's JobsDirect email list. Several hundred benefits and compensation positions are listed with direct contact information and date of posting. Job seekers can post their resumes for 180 days for $30 (free for members). Recruiters can view the text of the resumes which now also have contact information. Internships are listed separately and only those states where openings exist can be searched. A long list of links to benefits information sites is also available.

Int'l. Seafarers Exchange

www.jobxchange.com

Jonathan Mednick
BlueSeas International, 214 SE 3rd Place, Dania Beach, FL 33004
Ph: 954-986-5488   E-mail: info@jobxchange.com

JOBS	10s	RESUMES	10s
Cost to post	Cost to see	Cost to post	Cost to see
Free	Fee	Fee	Free
DISCIPLINE		LOCATION	
Trades/Miscelaneous		USA	
SPECIALTY		FEATURE	
Maritime		N/A	
AGENT: Jobseeker			

The International Seafarers Exchange just keeps sailing along. According to the site's owner, cruise and maritime jobs are so highly desirable that the site only allows job seekers to see a preview of the job, not the contact information. Employers can post jobs directly (140,261 on 2,635 vessels available). The site has over 3,000 crew members registered each paying $30-$69 to be listed for six months to one year. Job seekers receive a skills evaluation and their resume is converted to a career profile. The site will push job information to all members. The site claims it screens the resumes and does not accept everyone. Recruiters can access the crew database for free. For broadcasting openings via email the cost is $75 per job. Site isn't deep but it does cover a lot of surface area.

Intelligence & Defense Careers

www.intelligencecareers.com

Bill Golden
PO Box 6506, Prince William, VA 22195
Ph: 800-919-8284   E-mail: customerservice@intelligencecareers.com

JOBS	100s	RESUMES	1,000s
Cost to post	Cost to see	Cost to post	Cost to see
Fee	Free	Free	Fee
DISCIPLINE		LOCATION	
Government/Engineering/Science/Business		USA/	
SPECIALTY		FEATURE	
ALL		Security Clearance	
AGENT: N/A			

Intelligence & Defense Careers, launched in 1999, offers 1000s of opportunities for the slightly skewed and sometimes strange jobs for analysts, linguists, engineers and security professionals. Are you interested in being a Serb-Croation translator? How about a counter Terrorism expert. You can apply although we expect the screening process goes beyond what you may have experienced elsewhere so be prepared. Not all the jobs require security clearance. In fact, that is one of the many search parameters. Various subscription packages offer a range of fees and include the "harvesting" of (for example) 10 specific jobs from your corporate website. Site also describes where they advertise to reach the job seekers.

InterEC.NET

www.interec.net

Amrish Lal
San Jose, CA
Ph: 408-268-5295   E-mail: interec@interec.net

JOBS	10s	RESUMES	10s
Cost to post	Cost to see	Cost to post	Cost to see
Free	Free	Free (See Notes)	Free (See Notes)
DISCIPLINE		LOCATION	
Engineering		USA	
SPECIALTY		FEATURE	
ALL		N/A	
AGENT: N/A			

InterEC.NET, launched in 1998, concentrates on chemical, electrical and mechanical engineering. The site's owners only take direct job postings (no headhunters) and openings are posted for free for a 60-day run. The site invites corporations to post banners for a fee of $200 per month to cover their costs. Resumes are viewed for free and contact information (email) is available. Recruiters only need to fill in the area of specialization, education, and years of experience to view the resume database. Recruiters should check out the website statistics, as this site gets over 60,000 visitors a month. Job seekers will appreciate the list of links for engineering salary surveys.

InteriorDesignJobs.com

www.interiordesignjobs.com

Patricia Kaestner
3047 Flat Rock Place, Suite 4, Land O Lakes, FL 34639
Ph: 813-494-5926   Fax: 813-996-5934   E-mail: idjobs@mindspring.com

JOBS	10s		RESUMES	10s
Cost to post	Cost to see		Cost to post	Cost to see
Fee	Free		Free	Free
DISCIPLINE			LOCATION	
Trades/Miscellaneous			USA	
SPECIALTY			FEATURE	
Interior Design			N/A	
AGENT: N/A				

InteriorDesignJobs.com was created for professional decorators in June 1999. Recruiters pay $120 to post a position for a 60-day run. Job seekers can post their resumes confidentially for 60 days. Recruiters view them for free. Resumes and jobs are date posted and can be searched by functional categories or location. A long list of industry association and education links is also available.

Internet Career Connection

www.iccweb.com

James Gonyea
1151 Maravista Drive, New Port Richey, FL 34655
Ph: 727-372-1333   Fax: 727-372-0394   E-mail: gonyea@iccweb.com

JOBS	100s		RESUMES	1,000s
Cost to post	Cost to see		Cost to post	Cost to see
Free	Free		Free	Free
DISCIPLINE			LOCATION	
ALL			USA	
SPECIALTY			FEATURE	
ALL			N/A	
AGENT: N/A				

The owners of Internet Career Connection launched their business in 1989 on AOL, and were pioneers in this industry. The site acts as a portal to various help wanted databases such as HW-U.S., HW-Government Jobs, HW-International Jobs and the Worldwide Resume and Talent Bank. The database is built through a network of independent sites in cities throughout the country. Jobs (116) can be posted for free for a four-week period. Internships and volunteer openings (24) are listed in a separate database for ease of access. Each job category gives the total number of openings. Jim describes his site as his payback to job seekers and recruiters as all aspects of the site are free.

The Internet Job Source

www.statejobs.com

Joseph Shieh
PO Box 45, Guilderland, NY 12084
Ph: 518-869-9279   E-mail: jobsource@aol.com

JOBS	100s	RESUMES	1,000s
Cost to post	Cost to see	Cost to post	Cost to see
Fee	Fee	Fee	Free

DISCIPLINE	LOCATION
Government	USA

SPECIALTY	FEATURE
ALL	Gateway

AGENT: N/A

The Internet Job Source, launched in 1997, is the gateway to a niche location network of several cities and states. Statejobs.com, NYJobSource.com, BostonJobSource.com, DCJobSource.com, CaliforniaJobSource.com and ValleyJobs.com are in this fold. The site claims to serve up opportunities for USA companies as well as local, state and federal government agencies in 30 states. Extensive links to government opportunities can indeed be found here. The current cost to post jobs is $395 per year (unlimited postings) and this includes access to the resume database. Jobs can be searched by location, category, keyword or date of activity. Job seekers must register and submit a resume with the site to apply for openings.

TIP FOR RECRUITERS

Make it a point to treat job seekers like you would want to be treated.

You cannot return every telephone call but you can respond to emails.

IrishJobs.ie
www.irishjobs.ie

Ken Fitzpatrick
12 Clanwilliam Square, Grand Canal Quay, Dublin, Ireland
Ph: 353-167-09900   Fax: 353-917-96647   E-mail: info@irishjobs.ie

JOBS	1,000s	RESUMES	1,000s
Cost to post	Cost to see	Cost to post	Cost to see
Fee	Free	Free	Fee
DISCIPLINE		LOCATION	
ALL		INTL/Europe/Ireland	
SPECIALTY		FEATURE	
ALL		College/Executive	
AGENT: Jobseeker			

IrishJobs.ie, launched in 1995, is one of our favorite international sites. With almost 30 categories of vacancies, IrishJobs accommodates and represents all areas of industry and business, and invests heavily in a variety of media to drive candidates. Job seekers post their resumes to any one of the site's resume databases - graduates, executives or international. Job seekers set up their own private template of skill terms and the site searches for exact job matches. "Rooms" for executives and graduates are easily navigated. Annual contracts for job postings and access to one of their 14 CV databases range from 3000 Euro to 8000 Euro depending on whether it is a general, executive or graduate vacancy. Resumes can be searched under four databases:IT, engineers, non-IT, graduates and IT international (profiles viewed only). The site will email information for £3,000 for six months. Jobs can be viewed with direct contact information. My Career Manager allows job seekers to create their own personalized recruitment website with agents, etc.. Well designed and a positive job seeker experience is what makes Irish Jobs a top site.

ITCareers.com

www.itcareers.com

Deanne Holzer
155 Bovet Road, San Mateo, CA 94402
Ph: 800-227-8365   E-mail: onlineservices@itcareers.net

JOBS	1,000s	RESUMES	N/A
Cost to post	Cost to see	Cost to post	Cost to see
Fee	Free	N/A	N/A
DISCIPLINE		LOCATION	
IT		USA	
SPECIALTY		FEATURE	
ALL		Gateway	
AGENT: Jobseeker			

IDG's ITCareers is the gateway for ITworld.com, a site geared to IDG's publications (InfoWorld, ComputerWorld, CIO, JavaWorld, LinuxWorld, Sun World and NetworkWorld). Internationally, IDG's JobUniverse.com offers additional exposure in Europe. Add to the print pricing or post direct for $200 for a 60-day run. Jobs can be searched on one page for the USA and on jobuniverse.com for international openings. Great content, surveys, white papers, webcasts and connections to the real world. ITCareers allows companies to wrap all the jobs on their corporate site, which essentially means that job seekers can search a much more complete database of each company's openings. Corporations can feature their logo which links to all of their posted openings. Job seekers have the ability to "find similar openings" - a great feature.

IT Toolbox Forums

www.ittoolbox.com

Jason Pierce
9201 E. Mountain View Road, Suite 124, Scottsdale, AZ 85258
Ph: 610-280-9961   Fax: 610-280-9963   E-mail: advertising@ittoolbox.com

JOBS	10s	RESUMES	N/A
Cost to post	Cost to see	Cost to post	Cost to see
Free	Free	N/A	N/A
DISCIPLINE		LOCATION	
IT		USA	
SPECIALTY		FEATURE	
ALL		N/A	
AGENT: Jobseeker			

IT Toolbox's OpenIT is a series of forums for specialized information technology skills that allow employers to post on message boards for free. The box was launched in July 1998 and continues to provide real value to the IT world. Jobs can be posted for 45 days. Rich content and discussion lists are available. The sites include BAAN, BI, CPP, CRM, Database, DW, EAI, EBIZ, ERP, JAVA, KM, Linux, Networking, Oracle, PeopleSoft, SAP, SCM, Security, Siebel, Storage, Unix, VP, WD and Wireless. Job seekers need to apply through the site as no contact information is given.

ITonlinejobs

www.ITonlinejobs.com

Raymond Brown
7672 Shuler Dr., Memphis, TN 38119
Ph: 901-674-1536   E-mail: sales@itonlinejobs.com

JOBS	100s		RESUMES	1,000s	
Cost to post	Cost to see		Cost to post	Cost to see	
Fee	Free		Free	Fee	
DISCIPLINE			LOCATION		
IT			USA		
SPECIALTY			FEATURE		
ALL			N/A		
AGENT: Employer					

Relaunched in 2002, ITonlinejobs offers employers 6 month postings (way too long) for $75.00. The resume database is only searchable by the site's employees. A Job Seeker Agent matches jobs to individual interest and forwards openings (or notification) via email. Employers can place ads, edit/review these ads at any time during its activation period. Additional features include:applicant tracking tools for recruiters, private chat sessions with recruiters and perspective employees, resume re-write, resume critique and resume distribution. Site also delivers news daily to recruiter's desktops.

JobAds

www.jobads.com

Jayne Shaddock
133 Johnson Ferry Road, Marietta, GA
Ph: 888-881-5627   Fax: 770-951-0566   E-mail: sales@jobads.com

JOBS	10,000s		RESUMES	10,000s	
Cost to post	Cost to see		Cost to post	Cost to see	
Fee	Free		Free	Fee	
DISCIPLINE			LOCATION		
ALL			USA		
SPECIALTY			FEATURE		
ALL			N/A		
AGENT: N/A					

JobAds advises job seekers about the number of openings in each category right on their homepage. The first 15 job postings are free at JobAds. An additional four months of unlimited job postings and resume database access costs $75. One year unlimited access is $150. The site's focus is on accounting, health, admin., IT and sales but 45 total job categories are covered. Job seekers search by keyword, job title, company name, location, educational requirements and percent of travel required. Resumes remain active for 90 days. Each position description includes website links to the posting company's site, email links, date of posting and contact information. Banners are CPM priced and positioned according to the employer's desired location. The site also features a career book store, monthly newsletter and discussion groups.

JobAsia

Lippo Sun Plaza 12th Fl., Ste., 28 Canton Road Tsim Sha Tsui, Kowloon, Hong Kong China
Ph: 852-239-63003   E-mail: sales@jobasia.com

JOBS	1,000s		RESUMES	N/A
Cost to post	Cost to see		Cost to post	Cost to see
DISCIPLINE			LOCATION	
SPECIALTY			FEATURE	
AGENT: Jobseeker				

JobAsia was launched in 1997, and is a general recruiting site for the Pacific Rim listing over 400,000 registered job seekers. Positions can be viewed by specialty, title, industry, location, years of experience, education, keyword or date of posting. Many corporations have job postings on this site. Vistors must register to become members and have full use of the site. Openings are displayed with a company profile, logo and fully detailed description and contact information. Metrics on visitors are shown for all to see. Job seekers can take a test dirve before registering. Like most international sites pricing is hard to come by.

JobBank USA

Melinda Robinson
1417 S. 14th Street, Box 331, Fernandina Beach, FL 32034
Ph: 904-491-1771   Fax: 253-295-8010   E-mail: sales@jobbankusa.com

JOBS	1,000s		RESUMES	1,000,000s
Cost to post	Cost to see		Cost to post	Cost to see
Fee	Free		Free	Fee
DISCIPLINE			LOCATION	
ALL			USA	
SPECIALTY			FEATURE	
ALL			N/A	
AGENT: Both Recruiters & Jobseekers				

JobBank USA is an online recruiting and employment site with a metasearch tool to view links to newspapers and regional, national, international or industry-specific job sites. On the main site, recruiters can post a position for $195 for 60 days and it will push jobs to all job seekers who register. A one year site membership provides unlimited job postings and access to the resume database for $1,495. Recruiters place candidate specifications into the database, and any new resumes that match are automatically forwarded. The site claims to add an average of 100,000 resumes each month. JB USA has partnered with several sites to sell a CD-Rom archive of 1.3 million resumes. Recruiters can split job orders by paying a membership fee of $59 for 3 months services. Recruiters can also purchase access to corporate directories. CXRwonders if the legal departments of those firms listed know their telephone books are being bought and sold here.

JobBoards.com
www.jobboards.com

Nathan Heerdt
3938 North Hampton Road, Powell, OH 43064
Ph: 800-241-4649   Fax: 614-792-7622   E-mail: info@jobboards.com

JOBS	1,000s	RESUMES	100,000s
Cost to post	Cost to see	Cost to post	Cost to see
Fee	Free	Free	Fee
DISCIPLINE		LOCATION	
ALL		USA/MDW/OH/IN/KY	
SPECIALTY		FEATURE	
ALL		N/A	
AGENT: Both Recruiters & Jobseekers			

JobBoards.com was launched in June 1998, and wants to be a local provider for jobs in Ohio, Indiana, Kentucky, MI and other regions. Jobboards.com cost is a one time $75 set up fee and $149 per month to post unlimited jobs and review the resume database. Site has 100,000 resumes in the database. Free trials may be available. Jobs can be searched by city or category (technical, professional,hourly or medical). Openings are date posted with links to corporate site. A long list of company profiles can be viewed for additional job searches. Career tools are provided by a link to careerlab.com. Recruiters can register for a monthly newsletter and have access to a resume database for a fee. Links to local information in each of the communities served is well described, from arts and entertainment and restaurants to shopping.

JobCentro
www.jobcentro.com

Eddie Batiz
952 Postal Way, Suite 7, Vista, CA
Ph: 877-547-6122   Fax: 760-732-1213   E-mail: info@jobcentro.com

JOBS	1,000s	RESUMES	10,000s
Cost to post	Cost to see	Cost to post	Cost to see
Fee	Free	Free	Fee
DISCIPLINE		LOCATION	
ALL		USA	
SPECIALTY		FEATURE	
ALL		Diversity	
AGENT: Employer			

JobCentro.com is an employment resource designed to connect Hispanic job seekers with employers looking for qualified personnel in all fields. Recruiters pay $195 to post a position fora 30-day run. Access to the resume database is $1,500 per quarter. Other packages are available. The site is sponsored by the U.S. Hispanic Chamber of Commerce. An advanced search feature allows jobs to be searched by industry, title, location, salary, keyword or date of posting. Jobs (2,982) are listed by date of posting, title and location. Job seekers should check out the tips and tools for help with their search.

JobCircle.com
www.jobcircle.com

Joe Stubblebine
4 West Prescott, West Chester, PA 19380
Ph: 877-966-0050   Fax: 610-431-2003   E-mail: sales@jobcircle.com

JOBS	1,000s	RESUMES	10,000s
Cost to post	Cost to see	Cost to post	Cost to see
Fee	Free	Fee	Free

DISCIPLINE	LOCATION
IT/Engineering	USA/MDA

SPECIALTY	FEATURE
ALL	Security Clearance

AGENT: Both Recruiters & Jobseekers

BAM! Job seekers entering JobCircle.com are immediately asked their zip code. Launched in 1999, JC provides excellent online employment features for information technology professionals in the Delaware Valley and beyond (CT, DC, DE, OH, MD, NY, NJ, PA, VA and WV). Recruiters can view the resume database and post unlimited jobs for $3,500 per year. Individual postings cost $100 for 30 days. Jobs are also sent to 21 news groups. Statistics on jobs (3,933), company profiles (1,698) and job seekers (64,130) are posted. Resumes that match a recruiter's criteria are pushed to the employer, and jobs are pushed to the job seeker. A keyword search engine displays results with direct contact information. Openings have direct contact information and links to the posting organization's site. you can't miss their billboards on the New Jersey Turnpike. The site conducts pink slip parties to gain job seeker resumes for its database. Several forums are run for technical and employment/recruiter discussions. Recruiters can have free 7 day site trials. Jamie Fabian is the site's exclusive career coach offering helpful articles to visitors in transition. Check out "Dealing with a Bad Boss".

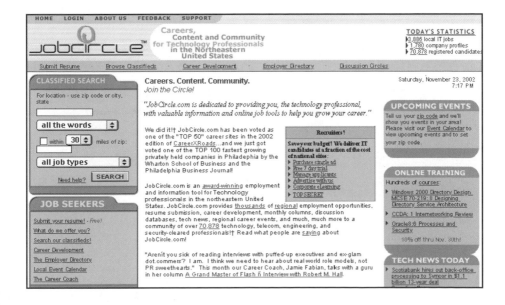

253

JobFactory

www.jobfactory.com

Jack Davis
123 NE 3rd Ave, Suite 448, Portland, OR 97232
Ph: 503-238-2491   Fax: 503-238-4698   E-mail: jobfact@jobfactory.com

JOBS	100,000s	RESUMES	N/A
Cost to post	Cost to see	Cost to post	Cost to see
Fee	Free	N/A	N/A
DISCIPLINE		LOCATION	
ALL		USA	
SPECIALTY		FEATURE	
ALL		Diversity	
AGENT: Jobseeker			

The JobFactory website was launched in 1996, and offers access to 40,000 corporate employment sites as well as links to 3,787 telephone job lines, 1,067 newspapers, 5,056 recruiters, etc. There is a big problem in overload, and without a ranking system, a job seeker could be here forever. The owners charge $75 per month to post one opening ($200 to post unlimited jobs) with a $10 discount for recruiters who advise about bona fide physical limitations in their openings. "JobSpider" claims to search 3.1 million jobs, which is more hype than reality. The owners started their business by placing disabled individuals in jobs, and the site has a great list of disability links. Even better is its ability to link to the classified pages of nearly every newspaper in the world within three clicks.

jobfind.com

www.jobfind.com

Erin Purcell
Herald Interactive, 254 Second Avenue, Boston, MA 02494
Ph: 781-433-7800   Fax: 781-433-7889   E-mail: jobfind@jobfind.com

JOBS	10,000s	RESUMES	10,000s
Cost to post	Cost to see	Cost to post	Cost to see
Fee	Free	Free	Fee
DISCIPLINE		LOCATION	
ALL		USA/NOE/MA/Boston	
SPECIALTY		FEATURE	
ALL		N/A	
AGENT: Both Recruiters & Jobseekers			

Jobfind.com offers an excellent alternative resource for New England-based job seekers. While you can't easily find the information on this site, the owner is still the Boston Herald. Positions can be searched across the USA, but the Northeast is the site's homebase. The owner also runs conventional job fairs. Recruiters pay $100 to post a position for 30 days. The site's resume database can be accessed for $400 per month. This site is a model for providing clearly understandable pricing for all services. Other sites would be well advised to study the layout. An agent will email matching resumes to employers daily from the database for $175 for 60 days. Job seekers can search corporate sites by alpha and the number of openings is clearly posted. An agent is provided so job seekers can register their email addresses and skills and have jobs pushed to their desktops. Job seekers need to read "The Five P's of Job Hunting" to keep their search in perspective.

Job Index.co.za

www.thejobindex.co.za

Stiaan Pretorius
36A Biesie Road, George, South Africa
Ph: 274-487-41027   Fax: 274-487-44137   E-mail: stiaan@thejobindex.co.za

JOBS	100s	RESUMES	1,000s
Cost to post	Cost to see	Cost to post	Cost to see
Fee	Free	Free	Fee
DISCIPLINE		LOCATION	
ALL		INTL/Africa/South Africa	
SPECIALTY		FEATURE	
ALL		N/A	
AGENT: Both Recruiters & Jobseekers			

Job Index.co.za was launched in August 2000, and concentrates on South Africa. Job postings are general in nature with a concentration in information technology and sales. Unlimited job postings cost 300 rand per month, which includes access to the resume database. Openings can be searched by job category and country. Next to each job category the site indicates the number of openings in the database. Many jobs have salary ranges listed with direct contact information. Resumes stay on the site for eight weeks. Job seekers are advised via email after six weeks to return to the site to update their resumes, or they will be deleted. Under "list of subscribers" job seekers can view all the recruiting organizations that have listed openings here.

JOBIsland.com

www.jobisland.com

Xandei Tena
Tena Technologies, 8164 Yarmouth Avenue, Reseda, CA 91335
Ph: 818-343-6239   E-mail: info@jobisland.com

JOBS	100,000s	RESUMES	100s
Cost to post	Cost to see	Cost to post	Cost to see
Free	Free	Free	Free
DISCIPLINE		LOCATION	
ALL		USA	
SPECIALTY		FEATURE	
ALL		Gateway	
AGENT: Job Seeker			

JOBIsland is the gateway to a network that seemed to include the USA, UK, Canada and the Pacific Rim (Australia, Phillipines, Malaysia, New Zealand and Singapore) Actually, the owners create websites for a living, and this is their live demo. During our visit there were 182,310 jobs (almost all USA) that could be searched by keyword, job type, date or location. Openings are in numerous areas but we found them in:engineering (36,629), programming (4,459) and teaching (1,334) in the tests we ran. Recruiters can post positions for free for 60 days and have access to the site's resume database. Jobs are automatically deleted after the posting period is over. A message board allows employers and recruiters to share information. Banners can be purchased for $50-$200 for employer visibility. The site's owners ask for voluntary contributions to keep the site afloat.

Job Launch

www.joblaunch.com

Tim Coy
P.O. Box 1276, Pflugerville, TX 78691
Ph: 512-990-0733   E-mail: jobs@joblaunch.com

JOBS	100s		RESUMES	100s
Cost to post	Cost to see		Cost to post	Cost to see
Free	Free		Free	Free
DISCIPLINE			LOCATION	
ALL			USA	
SPECIALTY			FEATURE	
ALL			N/A	
AGENT: N/A				

Job Launch continues its free service for companies wishing to fill staffing needs at all levels. Employers, employment agencies and recruiters are invited; multi-level marketing folks are not. After registering, companies are able to post as many positions as needed or review resumes for free. Recruiters get a password to access the site immediately after they register. Job seekers can view openings by category, location, or keyword and all are date posted. Resumes can be searched in a similar fashion, as well as by years of experience and all have contact information. Jobs are deleted after 60 day. Postings have links to the corporation's web site for additional information. Openings run the gamut from accounting to travel services.

Job Link For Journalists

ajr.org

Ernest Durso
1117 Journalism Building, College Park, MD 20742
Ph: 301-405-8803   Fax: 301-405-8323   E-mail: advertising@ajr.org

JOBS	10s		RESUMES	100s
Cost to post	Cost to see		Cost to post	Cost to see
Fee	Free		Free	Fee
DISCIPLINE			LOCATION	
Communications			USA	
SPECIALTY			FEATURE	
Writing/Journalism			N/A	
AGENT: Job Seeker				

American Journalism Review is a national magazine that covers all aspects of print, television, radio and online media. The site launched in 1997 offers employers the ability to access a resume database for free. The cost to post a job is $65 for a 5 week run. Job seekers who register their email may have their "job wish" emailed directly to their PC. Resumes can be blocked from specific employers by job seekers (no one wants the boss knowing they are in the hunt). The site has developed a very specific classification system relevant to this specialty. A well-designed resource for the journalism community.

JobMagic

www.jobmagic.net

Simon Hersh
Rexonline PLC, Garden House, London Road, Sunningdale, Berkshire, SL5 OLE United Kingdom
Ph: 084-513-04422   Fax. 084-513-04433   E-mail: sales@jobmagic.net

JOBS	10,000s	RESUMES	10,000s
Cost to post	Cost to see	Cost to post	Cost to see
Fee	Free	Free	Fee
DISCIPLINE		LOCATION	
ALL		INTL/Europe/UK	
SPECIALTY		FEATURE	
ALL		Gateway	
AGENT: Job Seeker			

Employers who subscribe to JobMagic (JB) can post a position for £375, and it will also be emailed to their 125,000 registered candidates. Jobs posted on one site are advertised on all 30 job-related sites that JB manages. Examples are www.jobtrack.co.uk (directed to third-party recruiters) and two other niche sites in the network, www.absolute-comms.co.uk-for the telecommunications industry, and www.rex.co.uk (for information technology contractors, etc.. The site claims to have tens of thousands of resumes in the database, and will provide services for online skill testing, psychometric testing and a career central zone that allows candidates to review articles relevant to recruitment. Recruiters should bookmark this site if only because the "recruitahead" section listed 759 openings for recruiters.

JobMonkey

www.jobmonkey.com

Mathew Lucas
PO Box 3956, Seattle, WA 98124
Ph: 800-230-1095   Fax: 707-221-1418   E-mail: admin@jobmonkey.com

JOBS	1,000s	RESUMES	10,000s
Cost to post	Cost to see	Cost to post	Cost to see
Fee	Free	Free	Fee
DISCIPLINE		LOCATION	
Hospitality /Retail/ Trades/Miscellaneous		USA	
SPECIALTY		FEATURE	
Resorts		N/A	
AGENT: N/A			

JobMonkey focuses on telling visitors about the "coolest jobs on earth." Launched in March 1999, Job Monkey includes opportunities with the Alaska fisheries, beach resorts, airlines, landtours, parks and forests, cruise lines, ski resorts and more. Many industries that hire seasonal employees can be found here. Openings for English schools in Asia and Europe can also be found. Recruiters pay $90 to post a job for 30 days and $75-$250 to search the resume database. The cost to view resumes depends on the number of people hired. Job seekers can post anonymous profiles of their resumes. A message board connects folks with similar interests. The owners claim to have over 2,000 pages of proprietary content to assist job seekers in finding employment. Job seekers need to check out the job hunting tips as the links offer extensive information.

JobNet Australia
www.jobnet.com.au

Henry Talbot
PO Box 500, St. Leonards, New South Wales Australia
Ph: 612-843-76388   Fax: 612-843-76399   E-mail: sales@jobnet.com.au

JOBS	1,000s	RESUMES	10,000s
Cost to post	Cost to see	Cost to post	Cost to see
Fee	Free	Free	Fee
DISCIPLINE		LOCATION	
IT		INTL/Pacific Rim/Australia/New Zealand	
SPECIALTY		FEATURE	
Communications		N/A	
AGENT: Both Recruiters & Jobseekers			

JobNet Australia specializes in the IT and communications arenas. The site discloses metrics about job postings on its home page (4,018 jobs listed). Recruiters pay $90 to post a job for a 28 days and $200 to view resume profiles for two weeks. Jobs can be searched by date of posting, title, skills or location. All jobs are date posted and have direct contact information. Job seekers register their email and matching openings will be pushed to them on a daily basis. Resumes are stored without contact data. Job seekers must indicate they are willing to start a new job in six weeks or their profile cannot be placed in the database. A recruitment agency listing with 100s of contacts can also be viewed. Job seekers should check out "job trends" to learn about what's hot and what's not in the job market.

Jobnet.com
www.jobnet.com

Don Kane
1700 Paoli Pike, Malvern, PA 19355
Ph: 888-562-6382   Fax: 610-296-9181   E-mail: recruit@jobnet.com

JOBS	1,000s	RESUMES	100,000s
Cost to post	Cost to see	Cost to post	Cost to see
Fee	Free	Free	Fee
DISCIPLINE		LOCATION	
ALL		USA/MDA/PA/NJ	
SPECIALTY		FEATURE	
ALL		N/A	
AGENT: Both Recruiters & Jobseekers			

Jobnet.com, launched in 1992, pioneered bulletin boards before switching to the web in 1994. The site offers top of the line services to recruiters and job seekers in the Delaware Valley. Recruiters can post a position for $125 for a 30 day run. Job seekers are advised about the number of job matches in a search's results, and search terms are highlighted in the text. The database contains over 100,000+ resumes, and can be searched for $595 per month. Job seekers are advised every six months to update their resumes before they are deleted. A job search service matches skills with the newest postings and emails them weekly to registered job seekers. All new resumes are pushed to subscribing employers daily. A monthly newsletter can also be found on the site. Information on living in and around Philadelphia, virtual job fairs, a unique approach to web hosting that is especially valuable for smaller employers, and an applicant tracking system (resume tracker) are features worth exploring.

jobpilot.com
www.jobpilot.com

Siemensstrasse 15-17, D-61352, Bad Homburg, Germany
Ph: 496-171-5069260 E-mail: international@jobpilot.com

JOBS	10,000s	RESUMES	100,000s
Cost to post	Cost to see	Cost to post	Cost to see
Fee	Free	Free	Free
DISCIPLINE		LOCATION	
ALL		INTL/Europe	
SPECIALTY		FEATURE	
ALL		N/A	
AGENT: Job Seeker			

Jobpilot.com, recently acquired by Adecco, was launched in 1995 as Jobs & Adverts, and is the gateway to a strong niche network in 19 countries in Europe as well as the Pacfic Rim. Positions are returned in order of the date of posting, with detailed job descriptions and contact information. Openings can be searched by location, language, or specific job categories for ease of access. Select a country at jobpilot's portal, but be prepared, you'll need additional language skills. Recruiters pay 300 - 400 euro's to post a position for a 4 week run. Resume profiles can be viewed for free as recruiters will need to register to obtain contact infor mation. The site claims 26,871 job listings and 150,000 resumes. Internships, thesis or student jobs can be posted for free. This site is well known in Europe and has excellent disclosure that now includes pricing.

Jobscience.com
www.jobscience.com

Ted Elliott
85 Bluxome Street, Suite 201, San Francisco, CA 94107
Ph: 877-298-6598   Fax: 510-208-5044   E-mail: sales@jobscience.com

JOBS	1,000s	RESUMES	10,000s
Cost to post	Cost to see	Cost to post	Cost to see
Fee	Free	Free	Fee
DISCIPLINE		LOCATION	
Science		USA	
SPECIALTY		FEATURE	
Research		N/A	
AGENT: Job Seeker			

Jobscience.com, launched in June 1999, assists recruiters in the healthcare and life sciences areas. The site specializes in physician and dental office, university/research, biotech/pharmaceuticals and medical devices positions. The owners have over 350 url's that lead back to job postings in specific niches. Recruiters pay $65 per week or $250 for 30 days to post a position, and all show title, location and date of posting. The site's search engine allows job seekers to browse openings by industry or keyword search. Searches can be narrowed by region, field, position or company. A "go" button next to each category allows jobseekers to find results quickly. Job seekers must register with the site to obtain contact information on job openings. The site's agent will push positions to job seekers who register. The resume database can be accessed for $1,500 for 90 days. The privacy statement is well written and easily understood. The owners are the Tribune, Kaplan Ventures, BrassRing and CNI Ventures, a division of Gannett.

259

Job Serve:Accountancy Vacancies in the UK

www.jobserve.com

Kelvedon Road, Tiptree, Colchester, Essex United Kingdom
Ph: 016-218-17335   Fax: 016-218-13357   E-mail: sales@jobserve.com

JOBS	1,000s	RESUMES	1,000s
Cost to post	Cost to see	Cost to post	Cost to see
Fee	Free	Free	Fee
DISCIPLINE		LOCATION	
ALL		INTL/Europe/UK	
SPECIALTY		FEATURE	
ALL		N/A	
AGENT: Jobseeker			

Job Serve was launched May, 1994 and is still a "list" service (it's IT version has been around for years). Site claims that it pushes thousands of UK vacancies a month to registered accountants. Site has 10% of its openings overseas. Positions are e-mailed daily to subscribers from the recruitment agencies that use this site. The agencies pay for each CV. To register:send a blank e-mail message to:subscribe@jobserve.com. Job seekers can browse using the site's search engine to check postings from within the last 5 days. Categories provide instant information about the number of openings. All "assignments" have salary ranges listed and direct contact information. A lengthy recruitment agency list with site links is also available.

JobShark

www.jobshark.com

William Bell
365 Bloor Street East, Suite 1902, Toronto, M4W 3L4 Canada
Ph: 800-304-7573   Fax: 416-944-3371   E-mail: wbell@jobshark.com

JOBS	1,000s	RESUMES	100,000s
Cost to post	Cost to see	Cost to post	Cost to see
Fee	Free	Fee	Free
DISCIPLINE		LOCATION	
ALL		INTL	
SPECIALTY		FEATURE	
ALL		N/A	
AGENT: Both Recruiters & Jobseekers			

JobShark was launched in 1997 and is the gateway to nine countries (Canada, Mexico, Peru, Columbia, Brasil, Chile, Argentina, Uruguay, El Salavador and USA-Miami). The owners claim 581,000 registered job seekers in Canada alone. Recruiters pay $575 for a single job posting for a 30 day run. Resumes can be accessed for $575 a day or $2,000 per month. Additional services allow recruiters to post pre-interview questions. Recruiters and job seekers must register to utilize the site so that matching jobs can be emailed. Job seekers view date-posted positions, but cannot respond automatically unless they have a resume posted at JobShark. CXR was impressed with the Shark's displauy of the number of registered job seekers by job category. The owners are also in the headhunting business. Each site is in the language of it's country. Miami is in spanish.

jobsite.com

www.jobsite.com/

Nancy Giles
239 Fort Pitt Boulevard, Pittsburgh, PA 15222
Ph: 877-256-2748   Fax: 412-566-1256   E-mail: info@jobsite.com

JOBS	100s		RESUMES	10,000s
Cost to post	Cost to see		Cost to post	Cost to see
Fee	Free		Free	Fee
DISCIPLINE			LOCATION	
Retail Sales & Services/Trades			USA	
SPECIALTY			FEATURE	
Construction/Finance/Real estate			N/A	
AGENT: Employer				

Jobsite.com is a niche site specializing in the real estate and construction industries. All resumes are industry specific and none are older than 90 days. An employer agent will match the job posting and forward any new resumes received by the job site. Employers may access a personal account to gain information about the number of individuals viewing job postings, the number of responses, how often the company profile page is viewed, and how many professionals have responded to each job posting. Recruiters pay $400 per job posting for a 90-day run, which includes access to the resume database. Recruiters and job seekers can check the site's metrics of current candidates and open jobs listed on the bottom of each page. Job seekers must go through registration before viewing openings. Direct contact is available for all posted jobs.

JobStreet

www.jobstreet.com

Priya
India Pvt. Ltd, 409 Midas Sahar Plaza, Kurla Road, Mumbai, 400059 India
Ph: 011-604-6445912 Fax: 011-604-6428653 E-mail: ads-in@jobstreet.com

JOBS	10,000s		RESUMES	1,000,000s
Cost to post	Cost to see		Cost to post	Cost to see
Fee	Free		Free	Fee
DISCIPLINE			LOCATION	
ALL			INTL/Pacific Rim	
SPECIALTY			FEATURE	
ALL			N/A	
AGENT: Both Recruiters & Jobseekers				

JobStreet is the gateway to a niche network of sites in India, Malaysia, Philippines and Singapore. The site also tracks openings in Australia, China (Hong Kong), Indonesia and Thailand. Jobs are listed by title, name of posting organization, location and date of posting. Jobseekers must register or be limited to ten job responses per search. Openings can also be emailed to the job seeker's desktop. The site has a matching agent called "LiNA" that connects employer requirements with the candidates' resumes. Recruiters pay $200 per job posting for a one-month run, which includes the resume database. CXR is a little nervous about sites whose metrics have not changed since our last visit. The owners are also in the headhunting business.

Job Toaster

www.jobtoaster.com/

Jens Frandsen
68 Blythwood Road, Waterloo, Ontario, Canada
Ph: 519-746-1113   E-mail: admin@jobtoaster.com

JOBS	1,000s	RESUMES	1,000s
Cost to post	Cost to see	Cost to post	Cost to see
Free	Free	Free	Free
DISCIPLINE		LOCATION	
ALL		USA	
SPECIALTY		FEATURE	
ALL		N/A	
AGENT: N/A			

Job Toaster.com, launched in August 1999, is located in Canada, but the majority of the jobs and resumes are USA based. The site allows job seekers to view openings by keyword, date of posting, job category, industry, education, location and salary required. The site has an agent so job seekers can register an email address and job preferences to have the information sent to their desktops. The site claims to have over 8,487 date-posted jobs and 2,769 resumes listed. Links to corporations' home pages are also available. Openings marked "new" signify recently posted opportunities. The price is right so see what pops up.

Job Village

www.jobvillage.com

Tripp Castell
1333 2nd ST NE, Suite 300, Hickory, NC 28601
Ph: 828-324-9054   Fax: 828-267-2622   E-mail: sales@jobvillage.com

JOBS	10,000s	RESUMES	10,000s
Cost to post	Cost to see	Cost to post	Cost to see
Free	Free	Free	Free
DISCIPLINE		LOCATION	
ALL		USA	
SPECIALTY		FEATURE	
ALL		N/A	
AGENT: N/A			

The Job Village home page says it all as the site has 75,218 jobs, 62,348 candidates and 18,347 employers. Recruiters can post jobs and review the resume database for free. The owners understand privacy issues and all visitors are offered privacy highlights about the disclosure of personal information prior to registering with the site. Resumes/jobs can be viewed by industry, are date posted and can be contacted through the site or directly. Employers and job seekers can access how many times their resumes or jobs were viewed. Job seekers can email their resume to thousands of targeted recruiters. Owners claim to receive 10,000 new resumes per month.

Jobware

www.jobware.com

Katja Rust
Technologiepark 13, D-33100, Paderborn, Germany
Ph: 495-251-54010   Fax: 495-251-540111 E-mail: info@jobware.net

JOBS	1,000s	RESUMES	N/A
Cost to post	Cost to see	Cost to post	Cost to see
Fee	Free	N/A	N/A
DISCIPLINE		LOCATION	
ALL		INTL/	
SPECIALTY		FEATURE	
ALL		Gateway	
AGENT: N/A			

Jobware is an international site with a German flair. Site publishes jobs for 29 countries. Recruiters need to complete a detailed form before cost information will be forwarded. Cost topost a job is Euro 250 for an 8 week run. The focus of this site is IT, business/administration, research and technology jobs. Job seekers will have difficulty since job search capability is limited to years of professional experience, job function (4 broad choices), college degree and language. Search results are easily broken out by country. Hope your German is up to date.

JobWarehouse

www.jobwarehouse.com

Malek Tawil
17 South Orange Ave., Orlando, FL 32801
Ph: 407-649-1224   Fax: 407-650-2607   E-mail: webmaster@jobwarehouse.com

JOBS	10,000s	RESUMES	1,000,000s
Cost to post	Cost to see	Cost to post	Cost to see
Fee	Free	Free	Fee
DISCIPLINE		LOCATION	
Engineering		USA	
SPECIALTY		FEATURE	
Software		N/A	
AGENT: Both Recruiters & Jobseekers			

JobWarehouse, launched in 1997, provides opportunities in many different fields. CXR found over 10,000 engineering jobs listed. Openings can be searched by keyword, location or employment type (contract or direct). Jobs are date posted and search criteria are highlighted for ease of viewing. Job seekers who input their resumes can have their skills matched against current openings. Recruiters pay $1,095 per quarter to post jobs and view the site's resume database. At "Midnight Match" each user can put criteria in a set of ten search strings and have results emailed every morning. Ask for a trial. The site claims 1.3 million passive resumes (stored for 180 days), 107,000 active resumes and 98,227 jobs posted. Owners claim to receive 900-1,100 new resumes a day.

Job.com

www.job.com

Alex Murphy
Job.com, Inc., 100 Riverside Parkway, Suite 201, Fredericksburg, VA 22406
Ph: 800-609-3900   Fax: 372 3010   E-mail: sales@job.com

JOBS	1,000s	RESUMES	10,000s
Cost to post	Cost to see	Cost to post	Cost to see
Fee	Free	Free	Fee
DISCIPLINE		LOCATION	
ALL		USA/	
SPECIALTY		FEATURE	
ALL		Career Hub	
AGENT: N/A			

The latest version of Job.com was launched at the end of 2001. With a Url to die for, it is no wonder this site is able to attract a heavy flow of traffic without having to rely on competitive advertising. Job.com claims nearly 60,000 postings a month and a resume database greater than 1/2 million. eQuest helps to distribute postings to this site.The site offers employers job postings for 60 days for $149. Access to the resume database is $999. Packages start at $399. A full array of services can be found including company research, salary reports, assessment tests, relocation services, and career related content.

Jobing.com

www.jobing.com

Randy Anderson
3550 N. Central #910, Phoenix, AZ 85012
Ph: 602-200-6800   Fax: 602-200-6804   E-mail: clients@jobing.com

JOBS	100s	RESUMES	1,000s
Cost to post	Cost to see	Cost to post	Cost to see
Fee	Free	Free	Fee
DISCIPLINE		LOCATION	
ALL		USA/SOW/AZ, NM	
SPECIALTY		FEATURE	
ALL		N/A	
AGENT: Both Recruiters & Jobseekers			

Jobing.com, launched in 2000, offers highly focused local services and content for employers and job-seekers throughout Arizona (New Mexico is next). A full range of services for employers are easily installed and logically presented. A single posting is $199. Tracking tools and virtual fairs are designed for the smaller employer as well. The strength of this site is how well it understands its customer base (the founder has an HR background). Job seekers are quickly able to evaluate positions based on their commute. Openings can also be searched by keyword, field of work, location, company, salary and date of posting. This is one site that is digging into its market.

Jobs for Programmers

www.prgjobs.com

Eric Shannon
JFP Resources, 1085 South 124th Street, Brookfield, WI 53005
Ph: 262-782-0072   Fax: 262-782-6444   E-mail: prgjobs@jfpresources.com

JOBS	1,000s	RESUMES	1,000s
Cost to post	Cost to see	Cost to post	Cost to see
Fee	Free	Free	Fee
DISCIPLINE		LOCATION	
IT		USA	
SPECIALTY		FEATURE	
Software		N/A	
AGENT: Both Recruiters & Jobseekers			

Jobs for Programmers (JP) continues to shine in the crowded information technology recruitment field. This site claims over 50,000 resumes and 5,000 programming jobs online at any time. The site offers recruiters a 30-day free trial to post up to 100 jobs or view the resume database. Recruiters can have a report pushed daily summarizing the resumes received by the site. The owners receive 1,800 new resumes per month. After the trial, recruiters are charged $149 per quarter to view resumes and post unlimited jobs. A resume matching service is also available. (The site will match employer specifications against its database and email recruiters everything that hits the mark). Job seekers can view openings by keyword and location. Site agent sends daily matches to job seekers. Candidates can choose buttons such as:"must have health insurance," "casual dress", "four day work week,""will hire part-time," etc. Each job posting advises job restrictions ("only considering local candidates"). The site also owns Jobs for Networkers (www.network-careers.com). JP continues to raise the bar for IT sites.

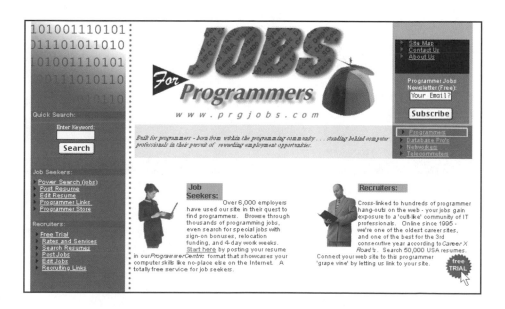

Jobsinlogistics
www.jobsinlogistics.com

Don Firth
PO Box 611297, Miami Beach, FL 33261
Ph: 877-562-7678   Fax: 305-940-9234   E-mail: don@jobsinlogistics.com

JOBS	1,000s	RESUMES	10,000s
Cost to post	Cost to see	Cost to post	Cost to see
Fee	Free	Free	Fee
DISCIPLINE		LOCATION	
Business		USA	
SPECIALTY		FEATURE	
Operations/Manufacturing/Logistics/Distribution		Gateway	
AGENT: Job Seeker			

Jobsinlogistics.com, started in February 2000, is one more niche site to add to a recruiter's kitbag. A gateway to purchasingjobs.com, jobsintransportation.com and jobsindistribution.com has also been added. The site offers discounted prices for multiple postings in logistics, distribution, warehousing and transportation. Recruiters pay $185 per posting for 60 days and $195 to search the resume database for a month. Jobs can be searched by job category, location, compensation or keyword. Job seekers can apply directly to the job opening or through the website once they register. Contact information can be kept confidential if the job seeker chooses. Resumes stay on the site for six months and are then deleted. Ask for a trial.

jobsinthemoney
www.jobsinthemoney.com

Paul Forster
7300 West Rim, Austin, TX 78731
Ph: 800-943-4592   Fax: 775-416-6157   E-mail: sales@jobsinthemoney.com

JOBS	1,000s	RESUMES	10,000s
Cost to post	Cost to see	Cost to post	Cost to see
Fee	Free	Free	Fee
DISCIPLINE		LOCATION	
Business		USA	
SPECIALTY		FEATURE	
Finance/Accounting		N/A	
AGENT: Both Recruiters & Jobseekers			

Jobsinthemoney invites job seekers to peruse opportunities in finance, banking, accounting, insurance or investments. Essentially designed for mid-level management professionals, the owners also host the career areas of 25 affiliate sites such as:auditnet.org, taxsites.com, smartpros. Job seekers can view positions by keyword, job category, state or country. Jobs are date posted, have key job requirements next to most postings which can be reviewed witha detailed job description. Job seekers can respond via the site or directly to the employer. Job seekers can post their resumes anonymously, register and have matching jobs pushed to their desktops. Recruiters pay $175 per posting and $495 for three months access to the resume database. Check out the "Company Gallery" for all the corporations that currently have open positions. With the financial world in turmoil, there is still a lot of opportunity on Wall Street.

Jobvertise

www.jobvertise.com

John Tate
2102 Rodney Drive, Champaign, IL 61821
Ph: 217-390-7793   Fax: 702-975-7318   E-mail: samr@cu-online.com

JOBS	10,000s	RESUMES	100,000s
Cost to post	Cost to see	Cost to post	Cost to see
Free	Free	Free	Free
DISCIPLINE		LOCATION	
ALL		USA	
SPECIALTY		FEATURE	
ALL		N/A	
AGENT: N/A			

Jobvertise, launched in August 1998, invites recruiters to post jobs and view the site's resume database for free. CXR loves metrics and this homepage says it all. Job stats show 60,000 openings with 11,674 posted this week. The site advises it has 100,000 resumes with 1,708 fresh ones posted. Openings are listed for 60 days and resumes for 120. Employers have the option of paying $50 to upgrade their jobs to the featured section of the search results. The site obtains 5,000 new resumes per month and states it does not acquire them from other sites. The jobs page is customizable to match the employer's existing website. The Jobvertise search engine allows the job seeker to view openings by keyword, location or choose a radius in miles. Many job postings have salary ranges listed.

Joint Service Academy Alumni Organizations

www.JSAJE.com

Bill Gross
JSAJE, 300 Steam Boat Rd. Babson Ctr., Kings Point, NY 11024
Ph: 516-487-1141   Fax: 516-482-5308   E-mail: jsaje@ix.netcom.com

JOBS	100s	RESUMES	N/A
Cost to post	Cost to see	Cost to post	Cost to see
Fee	Free	N/A	N/A
DISCIPLINE		LOCATION	
Business/Engineering		USA/	
SPECIALTY		FEATURE	
ALL		Military Transition	
AGENT: N/A			

Attention! Joint Service Academy Alumni Organizations assists graduates of one of the five Federal Service Academies, who are transitioning from military service to the commercial workforce. Launched in the summer of 2001, the site plans a resume database for 2003. Employers can post for a modest $60.

JournalismJobs.com

journalismjobs.com

Berkeley, CA
Ph: 510-524-2007   E-mail: jjobads@aol.com

JOBS	100s		RESUMES	10,000s
Cost to post	Cost to see		Cost to post	Cost to see
Fee	Free		Free	Fee
DISCIPLINE			LOCATION	
Communications			USA/	
SPECIALTY			FEATURE	
Journalism/Writing			Contingent	
AGENT: Jobseeker				

Great resource for writers and journalists, JournalismJobs.com offers positions for permanent, freelance and internships organized by newspapers and wire services, TV & radio, magazines & publishing, online newsletters and more. Content includes events, surveys, media happenings and extensive links. Employers pay $50 for a 5 week posting and $50 for the resume database of 15,000.

JustMyJobs.com

www.justmyjobs.com

Randi Curtis
5277 Manhattan Circle, Suite 250, Boulder, CO 80303
Ph: 877-906-6373   Fax: 888-808-6373   E-mail: sales@justmyjobs.com

JOBS	1,000s		RESUMES	1,000s
Cost to post	Cost to see		Cost to post	Cost to see
Free	Free		Free	Free
DISCIPLINE			LOCATION	
ALL			USA	
SPECIALTY			FEATURE	
ALL			Gateway	
AGENT: Both Recruiters & Jobseekers				

JustTECHJobs.com and JustMyJobs.com serve as the gateways to 41 niche information technology skill sites (type format:just"SKILLSET"jobs.com, i.e. justJAVAjobs.com) and 34 skill-specific jobsites (justac-countingjobs.com, justbiotechjobs.com etc). Recruiters must register and post a job in order to search a resume database. Recruiters are given a free test drive and at some point this site will start charging for posting and resume access. Up to 200 job postings can be listed for free and job seekers can apply direct or thru the site. On each site's home page is an excellent skill-based salary survey. While not perfectly valid, the data is right on the money.

Just Sales

www.justsales.com

2929-T Eskridge Road, Fairfax, VA 22031
Ph: 703-204-0930   Fax: 703-783-8357   E-mail: recruiting@justsell.com

JOBS	1,000s	RESUMES	1,000s
Cost to post	Cost to see	Cost to post	Cost to see
Free	Free	Free	Free
DISCIPLINE		LOCATION	
Prof. Sales & Marketing		USA	
SPECIALTY		FEATURE	
ALL		N/A	
AGENT: Job Seeker			

Just sales was launched February 1998, and advises all who enter that this is a free site. Recruiters can post jobs and view the resume database for free. Openings are listed by state, are date posted and many show salary range. Jobs are posted for 60 days. Owners claim to reach 45,000 subscribers through a twice monthly newsletter. Job seekers should check out the "just sell" career section which gives resume, cover letter and sales campaign advice. Great sample documents can be found. A discussion forum for sales professionals looking to share industry "tips and tricks" is also available.

JV Search

www.orasearch.com

Advanced Data, 11164 Yellow Leaf Way, Germantown, MD
Ph: 301-528-0777   E-mail: adi@jvasearch.com

JOBS	100s	RESUMES	1,000s
Cost to post	Cost to see	Cost to post	Cost to see
Fee	Free	Free (See Notes)	Fee
DISCIPLINE		LOCATION	
IT		USA	
SPECIALTY		FEATURE	
Java		Gateway	
AGENT: Job Seeker			

JV search serves as the gateway to a small network of mostly information technology sites (also includes hrstaffsearch.com site). After a 30 day free job posting trial, recruiters are asked to pay $95 for a three-month membership to view resumes and post unlimited jobs. Resumes profiles can be viewed for free but contact information costs $10 each. Openings can be pushed to registered job seekers via email for $39. Positions are posted by location, jobtitle and company but job seekers must post a resume to the site to review job listings. The minimum requirement for job seekers is that they have one year of experience in the specialty they are applying for. Job seekers who want their resume to get to the top of the charts pay $9 per month.The site network includes:www.orasearch.com, www.c++search.com www.unixadminsearch.com and www.vbasicsearch. com.

Eric Shannon
8551 W. Broward Blvd., Suite 302, Plantation, FL 33322
Ph: 954-474-6880   Fax: 954-474-4760   E-mail: 2sales@latpro.com

JOBS	1,000s		RESUMES	100,000s
Cost to post	Cost to see		Cost to post	Cost to see
Fee	Free		Fee	Fee
DISCIPLINE			LOCATION	
ALL			INTL/Latin America/	
SPECIALTY			FEATURE	
ALL			Diversity	
AGENT: Job Seeker				

LatPRO, launched in 1997, is an international job site for the USA, Latin and South American markets. This tri-lingual site targets professionals who speak English and Spanish or Portuguese. Frequently upgraded, the resume database has 220,000 (51,000 are less then 3 months old) and is free to view but candidate contact information costs $300 per month. The site offers hundreds of targeted job mailing lists. Employers pay $175 per job posting for 60 days. The site will email positions that match a candidate's skills. Job seekers can have free trial subscriptions as membership fees range from a minimum of $45 to $250. Only registered members can respond to job openings. Candidates can post up to six versions of their resume in any of the three languages, depending on the package. Recruiters can receive a monthly newsletter targeted to diversity recruiting issues that will be emailed to their PC. Articles and forums provide useful job-related information for professionals throughout the Americas. The International resources and the links to headhunters, newspapers, universities, etc. make this a CXR top pick.

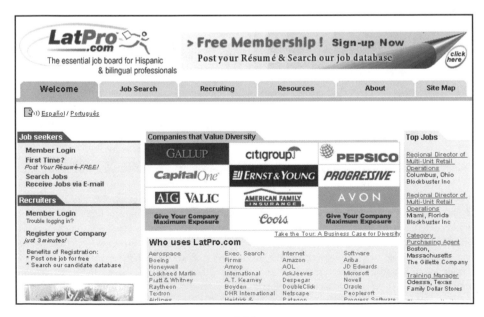

LavaTech's - Lotus Notes Jobs

www.lotusnotes.com

Jim Knight
827 Bow Lake Place, Leesburg, VA 20176
Ph: 800-437-6391   Fax: 703-579-1090   E-mail: sales@lavatech.com

JOBS	10s		RESUMES	10s
Cost to post	Cost to see		Cost to post	Cost to see
Free	Free		Free	Free
DISCIPLINE			LOCATION	
IT			USA	
SPECIALTY			FEATURE	
Lotus Notes			N/A	
AGENT: N/A				

Lotus Notes Jobs owner, LavaTech, has made it easy for recruiters to post jobs and view resume profiles for free. While few postings and resumes reside here, they are on target. Jobs/resumes can be viewed by date of posting with location and title of opening. Resumes from all over the world can be found. They now have direct contact information. In the past the site had to be contacted. Statistics on the number of times a resume or job has been viewed are also available. Jobs that have been filled are highlighted in yellow. An international jobs section has been created with Australia, Canada, Equador, France, Germany, India, KSA, Malaysia, Pakistan, Pichincha, Singapore, Thailand, The Netherlands, and the UK.

Law Jobs

www.lawjobs.com/

James Beckner
153 Kearny Street, 5th Floor, San Francisco, CA 94108
Ph: 800-628-1160   Fax: 415-352-5287   E-mail: ibedgood@corp.law.com

JOBS	1,000s		RESUMES	N/A
Cost to post	Cost to see		Cost to post	Cost to see
Fee	Free		N/A	N/A
DISCIPLINE			LOCATION	
Law & Order			USA	
SPECIALTY			FEATURE	
Attorney/Paralegal/Secretaries			N/A	
AGENT: N/A				

Law.com's law jobs offers job postings for the legal profession. It is a subsidiary of American Lawyer Media. Stats on the homepage advise that there are attorney (1,711), paralegal (114), secretarial (142), management & tech (28), and admin/support staff (38) openings listed. A news section includes links to career articles. Listings are acquired from legal newspapers and journals. The problem is (surprisingly) that the site avoids disclosing job posting pricing ($500 for one month or $300 per week) and simply offers to quote you a price when you call customer service. Links to the recruiting pages of law firms, temporary and search firm listings gives this site added value. The site's career center has taken a turn for the worst as articles and career advice can no longer be found. It must be all of those fees not collected from Enron that have made this site scrimp.

Layover.com

www.layover.com

Bruce Martin
240 North 7th Street, Suite 600, Akron, PA 17501
Ph: 717-481-5511   Fax: 717-481-5517   E-mail: sales@layover.com

JOBS	1,000s		RESUMES	10,000s
Cost to post	Cost to see		Cost to post	Cost to see
Fee	Free		Free	Fee

DISCIPLINE		LOCATION
Trades, Non-exempt & Hourly		USA

SPECIALTY		FEATURE
Transportation/Truck Driver		N/A

AGENT: Both Recruiters & Jobseekers

Layover.com, launched in October 1996, has been a CXR favorite and well deserved stop on the virtual highway. This site is a great example of how deeply the Internet is entrenched. Drivers enter the site and complete an application. Behind the scenes, the hiring company requirements are matched to the applications, and the trucker is advised as well as the recruiter. The site lists all hiring companies A-Z, and links back to their recruiting page so applicants can apply directly. Drivers learn where to pick up their next load, read well-written articles on what is happening in the trucking industry, link to online maps in order to plot the shortest routes, etc. The cost to post a job is $129 for a 30 day haul across the USA. The sites resume database can be viewed for free but contact information costs $7 each. Drivers can hitch a ride in the "drivers corner" for Q & A career advice. Not to be outdone "women in trucking" provides articles on the fender bender set. Everyone should catch the article on "OneWoman's Journey" for a true picture of the "day in the life" of a trucker. Layover has come a long way and ranks right up there with some of the best jobsites on the web.

Lee Hecht Harrison

www.lhh.com

David Estrada
200 Park Avenue, Suite 2600, NY, NY 10016
Ph: 212-455-8584   Fax: 212-455-8505   E-mail: info@lhh.com

JOBS	100s	RESUMES	1,000s
Cost to post	Cost to see	Cost to post	Cost to see
Free	Fee	Fee	Free
DISCIPLINE		LOCATION	
ALL		USA/	
SPECIALTY		FEATURE	
ALL		Executive	
AGENT: N/A			

Free for employers, Lee Hecht Harrison, one of the major players in the "Corporate Outplacement" world, offers a simple, direct and targeted service for its clients (the newly downsized employee) and an opportunity for companies seeking this pool of applicants. Job seekers must be clients to access the jobs. Recruiters can post and see resumes for free.

TIP FOR RECRUITERS

If your applicant tracking system is slow, do not blame the software.

It is an internal problem and the
IT department needs to be notified.

Legalstaff.com
www.legalstaff.com

Richard Hackett
4250 Executive Square, Suite 520, La Jolla, CA 92037
Ph: 858-587-9877   Fax: 858-587-0518   E-mail: info@legalstaff.com

JOBS	1,000s		RESUMES	1,000s
Cost to post	Cost to see		Cost to post	Cost to see
Fee	Free		Free	Fee

DISCIPLINE		LOCATION
Law & Order		USA
SPECIALTY		FEATURE
Attorney/Paralegal		Gateway
AGENT: Both Recruiters & Jobseekers		

Launched in late 98, Legalstaff has taken a niche market and literally rolled it up. By creating individual career sites for (54) county and state bar associations and various national associations as partners, the site network reaches nearly every lawyer and paralegal in the US from their local connection. Sites in the network charge $95 for a posting. Various packages allow for local or full network distribution. Corporate postings and agencies are differentiated. Site has tools for managing resumes and communication. A directory feature offers employers a free profile. Content includes training and association links. Network also includes Law Portals such as The New Jersey Law Network, LawGuru, Attorney.com, and LawStar.com. National sites include the Nat'l Federation of Paralegal Associations, The NationalParalegal Assoc. and NALS. This model is one of the most dominant niches we've seen.

LenderCareers

www.lendercareers.com

Lender Technologies Corporation, 1919 Pennsylvania Ave. NW, Washington, DC 20006
Ph: 202-557-2820   Fax: 202-833-1608   E-mail: sales@lenderCareers.com

JOBS	100s		RESUMES	1,000s	
Cost to post	Cost to see		Cost to post	Cost to see	
Fee	Free		Free	Fee	
DISCIPLINE			LOCATION		
Business			USA/		
SPECIALTY			FEATURE		
Finance/Banking/Mortgage			N/A		
AGENT: Jobseeker					

The official job board and a subsidiary of the heavyweight Mortgage Bankers Association, www.mbaa.org, LenderCareers aims to be a definitive site for the lending industry. Site is powered by CareerSite and as a result offers multiple levels of service starting with $185 per posting. Access to the resume database is $895 which includes 5 postings. Costs rapidly escalate as do services that include access to and simple management of resumes as well as cross posting to about 20 other sites.

LocalCareers.com

www.localcareers.com

Brian Weis
5464 N.Port Washington Rd, Suite 196, Milwaukee, WI 53217
Ph: 800-223-3080   Fax: 414-540-6610   E-mail: info@localcareers.com

JOBS	1,000s		RESUMES	10,000s	
Cost to post	Cost to see		Cost to post	Cost to see	
Fee	Free		Free	Fee	
DISCIPLINE			LOCATION		
ALL			USA		
SPECIALTY			FEATURE		
ALL			N/A		
AGENT: Both Recruiters & Jobseekers					

Launched in 1998, LocalCareers.com is the gateway to a network of 17+ location specific and specialty sites, including Jobs4Sales.com, Jobs4HR.com, WiJobs.com, ArizonaJobs.com, CaliforniaJobs.com, ChicagoJobs.com, NYCareers.com, OhioJobs.com and TexasJobs.com. Employers pay $100 to post an opening and $100 to access the site's resume database. Jobs are posted for 60 days. Other deals are available. Jobs are date-posted with company, title and location easy to view. Job seekers will appreciate the company profiles and the number of openings posted by category while doing a search. The site has a resume distribution tool, connections for contractors and freelancers as well as helpful links and resources.

MacTalent.com
www.mactalent.com

Doug Noble
15321 South Dixie Hwy,, Suite 306, Miami, FL 33157
Ph: 305-256-7575   Fax: 305-256-7768   E-mail: info@mactalent.com

JOBS	10s		RESUMES	100s
Cost to post	Cost to see		Cost to post	Cost to see
Free	Free		Fee	Free
DISCIPLINE			LOCATION	
IT			USA	
SPECIALTY			FEATURE	
Macintosh			N/A	
AGENT: N/A				

MacTalent.com is one of the few sites we know that caters to Apple geeks. Recruiters can post jobs and view resumes for free. Corporations who hire people from this site are asked to make a voluntary contribution. Job seekers pay $29 to post their resumes for three months. The site willl also give job seekers a lifetime membership for $89. Resumes can also be posted "MacAnonymously", and owners advise there are 800 in the database. Openings can be searched by keyword or location, and are listed by title, company, state and date of job posting. Resumes are easy to view and have direct contact information. If you love those funky colored imacs this is your place.

MarketingJobs.com
www.marketingjobs.com

Woody Haskins
PO Box 800, Hamburg, MI 48139
Ph: 877-348-5627   Fax: 810-231-2597   E-mail: sales@marketingjobs.com

JOBS	1,000s		RESUMES	10,000s
Cost to post	Cost to see		Cost to post	Cost to see
Fee	Free		Free	Fee
DISCIPLINE			LOCATION	
Prof. Sales & Marketing			USA	
SPECIALTY			FEATURE	
Marketing/Advertising			Gateway	
AGENT: Both Recruiters & Jobseekers				

MarketingJobs.com, launched in 1996, is the gateway to a regional network (Atlanta, Boston, California, Chicago, Washington DC, Detroit, New York and Texas) of sites for sales and marketing professionals. Jobs are viewed by company name or through the site's search engine by keyword, job category, or location. Job seekers will appreciate that job search terms are posted at the top of their results page for ease of viewing. Recruiters pay $150 to post a position for 30 days. Access to the resume database costs $395 per month. Job seekers must apply through the site for all openings.

MBA Jungle

www.mbajungle.com

James Winter
632 Broadway, 7th Floor, New York, NY 10012
Ph: 212-352-0840   Fax: 212-352-9282   E-mail: customerservice@mbajungle.com

JOBS	100s	RESUMES	10,000s
Cost to post	Cost to see	Cost to post	Cost to see
Fee	Free	N/A	N/A
DISCIPLINE		LOCATION	
Business		USA	
SPECIALTY		FEATURE	
MBA		Gateway	
AGENT: Job Seeker			

MBA Jungle, launched in September 2000, also publishes a print magazine. The sight is also a gateway to jdjungle.com launched in April 2001. Job seekers can view openings (237) by keyword, industry, location, date of posting or search employers by name. Applying for openings can now be done either directly to employers or thru the site. Job seekers can obtain interview feedback by logging in. CXR wonders how many corporations will comply? MBAs can use the site to find colleagues who attended the same school. Well-written, career articles posted from the print publication can be viewed online. Recruiters pay $95 per job posting for a 90 day run. A message board allows MBAs to share job-seeking war stories. An emailed weekly newsletter contains job postings for all who register.

MD Direct.com

www.mddirect.com

Allison Werthheimer
324 Hydesmere Drive, Sugar Hill, GA 30518
Ph: 888-633-4732   Fax: 770-271-9805   E-mail: mddirect@pol.net

JOBS	1,000s	RESUMES	1,000s
Cost to post	Cost to see	Cost to post	Cost to see
Fee	Free	Free	Fee
DISCIPLINE		LOCATION	
Health Care		USA	
SPECIALTY		FEATURE	
MD		N/A	
AGENT: Both Recruiters & Jobseekers			

MD Direct.com, launched in June 1996, claims to provide a confidential, secure environment in which hospitals, physician practices and medical organizations gain access to thousands of doctors seeking employment. The site has over 1,500 posted openings and 6,000 resumes listed. Recruiters pay $100 to post an opening for 1 month. The site gets its connection from PHYSICIANS ONLINE (POL), a medical information and communication network connecting its 230,000 physician members. Members can search through physician profiles at POL. Members must register to gain access to the site.

MDjobsite.com

Jay Overman
O.I.S.Media, Inc., 2929 Langley Avenue, Suite, Suite 203, Pensacola, FL 32504
Ph: 877-506-5627   E-mail: william@oismedia.com

JOBS	1,000s		RESUMES	1,000s
Cost to post	Cost to see		Cost to post	Cost to see
Fee	Free		Free	Fee
DISCIPLINE			LOCATION	
Health Care			USA	
SPECIALTY			FEATURE	
MD			N/A	
AGENT: Job Seeker				

MDjobsite, launched in 1999, offers an interesting alternative to the MD staffing industry. For $199.95 employers can post up to 150 openings from 1 location and view CVs (2,693 listed). A single job posting for 60 days is $74.95. The resume database alone for 1 month costs $99.95 for access. Next to each state MDjobsite displays the number of openings posted. Jobs are searched by specialty or state, but can only be replied to through the website. Doctors who register their email addresses and specialties can have openings pushed to their desktop.

MedBulletin

Paul Lukey
216 West Allen Street, Suite 124, Bloomington, IN 47403
Ph: 800-598-8044   Fax: 312-577-0467   E-mail: medbulletin@medbulletin.com

JOBS	10,000s		RESUMES	1,000s
Cost to post	Cost to see		Cost to post	Cost to see
Free (See Note)	Free		Free	Fee
DISCIPLINE			LOCATION	
Health Care			USA	
SPECIALTY			FEATURE	
MD			N/A	
AGENT: Job Seeker				

First launched in 1996, MedBulletin now has 15,000 jobs in the database. They offer exceptional services and an interesting pricing option where positions are free if posted under an employer name and cost $200 otherwise. This is a unique way to limit third-party recruiters. Job seekers can search openings by specialty, organization, or recruiter. Some job postings have direct contact information while others job seekers must register with the site. A CV database is now available.

MedCAREERS

Sharon Tappouni
4780 Ashford, Dunwoody Road Suite A-475, Atlanta, GA 30338
Ph: 800-307-1038   Fax: 678-424-3050   E-mail: sales@medcareers.com

JOBS	10,000s	RESUMES	10,000s
Cost to post	Cost to see	Cost to post	Cost to see
Fee	Free	Free	Fee

DISCIPLINE	LOCATION
Health Care	USA

SPECIALTY	FEATURE
Allied Health/Nursing	Gateway

AGENT: Job Seeker

MedCAREERS, launched February, 2000, is a gateway to a network of 16 partner sites as well as their own, which include:GovMedCareers.com, Nursingcenter.com, Salu.net and MomMd.com. Recruiters can post to most of these network sites for no additional charge. Employers pay $140 to post a position for 30 days. Resume access costs $250 per month. The site claims 10,183 jobs and 28,000 resumes in the total network. Statistics on open positions are displayed next to each job category. Job seekers can search openings by specialty and only the underlined job categories have live openings (great service). Job seekers can use a personalized profile to indicate how long their resume will remain active. Many other preference and privacy options are also available. Openings are shown via a short profile and more info is available with a click of the mouse. MC has great design features and other sites should take notice.

Medhunters

www.medhunters.com

Adele Mirabelli
180 Dundas Street West, Suite 2403, Toronto, ON, M5G 1Z8 Canada
Ph: 800-664-0278   Fax: 416-977-6128   E-mail: info@medhunters.com

JOBS	10,000s	RESUMES	10,000s
Cost to post	Cost to see	Cost to post	Cost to see
Fee	Free	Free	Fee
DISCIPLINE		LOCATION	
Health Care		INTL/Canada	
SPECIALTY		FEATURE	
Pharmacy/MD/Nursing		N/A	
AGENT: Both Recruiters & Jobseekers			

Nurses, pharmacists, technologists and many other health care professionals can find jobs posted on Medhunters. Recruiters can post a position for 60 days for $350. The number of job openings is posted next to each job group. The site claims over 11,298 posted openings from 373 hospital/employers in 528 locations, and over 40,000 resumes. Resume access with up to 50 job postings costs $4,500 for 6 months. After job seekers complete pre-employment questions, the site matches their responses against open jobs on a weekly basis. The site emails/phones job seekers to confirm their interest before information is forwarded to the recruiter. This is part of the site's standard service for job posting. Job seekers must register with the site to obtain contact information. The owners are in the headhunting business and do not allow other third-party recruiters access to this site.

medjump

www.medjump.com

Mark Yawitz
7119 E. Shea Blvd. #109-535, Scottsdale, AZ 85254
Ph: 877-863-9526   Fax: 630-839-2278   E-mail: info@medjump.net

JOBS	1,000s	RESUMES	10,000s
Cost to post	Cost to see	Cost to post	Cost to see
Fee	Free	Fee	Free
DISCIPLINE		LOCATION	
Health Care		USA	
SPECIALTY		FEATURE	
MD/Nursing/Allied Health		N/A	
AGENT: Both Recruiters & Jobseekers			

Medjump, launched in November 1999, targets the medical and pharmaceutical industries. Recruiters can post up to 25 jobs and access the resume database for $199 a month. Included in the $199 is the ability to email openings to registered members and receive resumes. An individual job posting is $50. Job seekers can view positions by keyword, job category or location. All openings are date posted with company, title and location listed. The total number of openings is posted by function. Job seekers can apply directly to the employer or through the site. Job seekers can view company profiles can by "clicking" on a map of the USA. The site's resource center offers helpful career links for additional information.

media bistro.com

www.mediabistro.com

Laurel Touby
494 Broadway, 4th Floor, New York, NY 10012
Ph. 212-929-2588   E-mail: sales@mediabistro.com

JOBS	100s	RESUMES	N/A
Cost to post	Cost to see	Cost to post	Cost to see
Fee	Free	N/A	N/A
DISCIPLINE		LOCATION	
Communications/Entertainment & Media		USA/MDA/NY/NYC	
SPECIALTY		FEATURE	
Graphic Arts/Writing/Advertising/ Public Relations		N/A	
AGENT: Job Seeker			

Media bistro.com offers creative designers, writers, advertising agency representatives, public relations folks and more a place to schmooze. The owners hold wine and cheese parties where members gather. Recruiters can post a position for $199 for 30 days or post plural titles for $275. The site claims over 425,000 unique visitors a month. Jobs can be searched by industry, location, keyword or, visitors can just browse the entire database. The site now requires job seekers to log in to see openings. A check box model allows job seekers to view selected positions in detail. Resumes can be posted, but there is no resume database. The site will also offer clients full placement services for a fee. This community oriented model also has a bulletin board for industry discussions. Committed ownership and focused efforts on city-based professionals make this a solid site you'll want to consider.

Medical DeviceLink.com

www.devicelink.com

Jason Barlow
Canon Communications, 11444 W. Olympic Blvd, Suite 900, Los Angeles, CA 90064
Ph: 310-445-4200   Fax: 310-445-4299   E-mail: sales@devicelink.com

JOBS	100s	RESUMES	1,000s
Cost to post	Cost to see	Cost to post	Cost to see
Fee	Free	Free	Fee
DISCIPLINE		LOCATION	
Science/Engineering		USA	
SPECIALTY		FEATURE	
Biomedical/Medical Device		N/A	
AGENT: N/A			

Medical Device Link provides well written career management articles from their medical device and diagnostic industry magazine. Recruiters pay $300 per job posting for 30 days. The site has a resume database that can be searched by categories for a fee. Daily industry news coverage, and a careers discussion forum keep this site ahead of the industry. Job seekers may view profiles of openings but they must register to view contact information.

MedZilla

www.medzilla.com

Frank Heasley, Ph.D.
PO Box 1710, Marysville, WA 98270
Ph: 425-742-4292   Fax: 425-742-2172   E-mail: sales@medzilla.com

JOBS	10,000s		RESUMES	1,000s
Cost to post	Cost to see		Cost to post	Cost to see
Fee (See Notes)	Free		Free	Fee
DISCIPLINE			LOCATION	
Science/Health Care			USA	
SPECIALTY			FEATURE	
Bio/ Pharmaceutical/MD/Clinical Research			N/A	
AGENT: Both Recruiters & Jobseekers				

MedZilla was launched in August 1994 to assist biotechnology, pharmaceutical, science, medicine, and health care candidates find their next employment opportunity. An extensive database of job listings (10,185) and resumes (10,000) is available. Job seekers can search the site by keyword or by corporate logo. Employers may query the candidate database at no charge and then pay to obtain contact information. Recruiters can list one job for $95 or pay $250 per month for up to 100 positions. Resumes older then four months are deleted. Resumes that match the employers job specifications can be pushed to recruiters via email. The resume database can be accessed for $275 per month. Annual clients can have their jobs wrapped from their jobs pages to Medzilla. A career forum and salary survey (2 years old) rounds out a site that has made a consistent contribution to the online employment space.

Military.com
www.military.com

Ralf Jeworowski
544 Pacific Avenue, Suite 300, San Francisco, CA 94133
Ph: 415-433-0999   Fax: 415-433-1277   E-mail: sales@military-inc.com

JOBS	1,000s	RESUMES	N/A
Cost to post	Cost to see	Cost to post	Cost to see
Free	Free	N/A	N/A
DISCIPLINE		LOCATION	
ALL		USA	
SPECIALTY		FEATURE	
ALL		Military Transition/Military	
AGENT: Both Recruiters & Jobseekers			

Military.com launched February 2001 is not just another site in a long line of military transition sites. Extensive content and services make this a viable portal. The site also offers Military recruiters the capability to attract recruits. Job seekers must register to view openings. Employer name is shown with a detailed job description. Job postings are free for the first 10. Recruiters can post predesigned questions tailored to each position. Job seekers can view all open positions or use the profile they have created to match openings. Job seekers who complete the profile are automatically emailed matched positions. Staffing organizations cannot search the site's resume database. Site claims over 1 million members. Recruiters must email the site for additional costs and services. Check out the "recruiter's corner".

MilwaukeeJobs.com
www.milwaukeejobs.com

Scott Molitor
Infosoft Group, 1123 N. Water Street, Suite 400, Milwaukee, WI 53202
Ph: 800-278-0700   Fax: 414-224-6099   E-mail: sales@milwaukeejobs.com

JOBS	1,000s	RESUMES	10,000s
Cost to post	Cost to see	Cost to post	Cost to see
Fee	Free	Free	Fee
DISCIPLINE		LOCATION	
ALL		USA/MDW/WI/	
SPECIALTY		FEATURE	
ALL		Gateway	
AGENT: Jobseeker			

MilwaukeeJobs.com was launched in 1994 and is a network of 26 Wisconsin city/location sites. Job postings are maintained for 60 days at a cost of $150. Resume database access and unlimited job posting charges are $550 per month. Small companies can obtain a discount. Site also includes ATS tools for employers

MinnesotaJobs.com
www.minnesotajobs.com

Sam Morse
Trumor Inc., 607 Highway 10, Suite 204, Blaine, MN 55434
Ph: 763-753-5050   Fax: 763-753-4430   E-mail: sam@minnesotajobs.com

JOBS	1,000s		RESUMES	1,000s
Cost to post	Cost to see		Cost to post	Cost to see
Fee	Free		Free	Fee

DISCIPLINE		LOCATION	
ALL		USA/MDW/MN	
SPECIALTY		FEATURE	
ALL		N/A	

AGENT: Both Recruiters & Jobseekers

MinnesotaJobs.com was launched in May 1995. The site is filled with salary surveys, relocation advice, career management articles, links to assessment programs and other content to aid in the employment process. MinnesotaJobs.com offers a wide range of options for employers which can be viewed on the site's resources pages. Company profiles are well laid out and easy to read. The basic cost to post a job is $60 which includes access to the resume database. Believe it or not, a $100 bonus is paid to job seekers if they are hired for jobs posted. Job seekers can register their email addresses and the site will push keyword descriptions to their desktops. Employers are pushed new resumes. Recruiters need to view the "site metrics" to understand the value of keeping track of job seekers preferences. Job seekers should click the "boss button" to stay out of trouble.

Mojolin
mojolin.com

Dan Barber
1489 Landings Run, Mt. Pleasant, SC 29464
Ph: 843-971-6268   E-mail: info@mojolin.com

JOBS	100s		RESUMES	1,000s
Cost to post	Cost to see		Cost to post	Cost to see
Free	Free		Free	Free
DISCIPLINE			LOCATION	
IT			USA	
SPECIALTY			FEATURE	
Linux/Internet			N/A	
AGENT: Both Recruiters & Jobseekers				

Mojolin and Mojosco were launched in September 1999. Both are free sites for recruiters to view resumes and post jobs all over the world (13 countries). The first is a niche for linux, unix and embedded community experts. Mojosco.com is a niche for network engineers. Jobs will be posted for 60 days and resumes are date posted (they remain on the site indefinitely). Job seekers can post their resumes in confidence or leave them open. A well-designed search engine includes keyword, location (telecommute, USA or state), discipline (25 are listed), type of position (called "tax term" i.e. contract - W2, contract - independent, contract-corp, full-time, etc.) and salary. The site pushes out the latest jobs and resumes to registered members daily. Openings are posted weekly to newsgroups for wider exposure. Email agents send out jobs and resumes each day. Corporations that wish to be in the company directory and have their logo here pay $50.

TIP FOR RECRUITERS

When interviewing a hiring manager, make them a partner...

...rather than giving them promises you cannot fulfill. Ask them for their rolodex, ask them to review online resumes with you. Ask them for contacts they know at other corporations and any vendors they work with. Good candidates are not always looking for a job.

Monster.com
www.monster.com

Kevin Mullins
5 Clock Tower Place, Suite 500, Maynard, MA 01754
Ph: 800-666-7837   Fax: 978-461-8100   E-mail: ae@monster.com

JOBS	1,000,000s	RESUMES	10,000,000s
Cost to post	Cost to see	Cost to post	Cost to see
Fee	Free	Free	Fee

DISCIPLINE	LOCATION
ALL	USA

SPECIALTY	FEATURE
ALL	Career Hub

AGENT: Both Recruiters & Jobseekers

There is no other king of the mountain. From their forward thinking management to their extensive study of job seeker behavior, Monster.com has more marbles in play (and plays them better) than anyone. Their willingness to invest in their brand is a challenge unmet by the entire newspaper industry. Don't get us wrong, job seekers and recruiters will always search for an extra edge and the bigger a site gets the more we look for an alternative. We just don't live in a society that rewards limited choice and we doubt that the largest board will ever contribute more than 5% of a corporation's hires. Monster is active in at least 25 countries and if they can't develop their presence, they buy it - aka Jobline. With over 1 million jobs and 18 million resumes the site is the runaway leader. Recruiters pay $305 to post an opening for 60 days. Access to the resume database (for local access to candidates) runs $400 for 2 weeks. Nationwide access starts at $8,500 per year. Preimum services include a "career fit" indicator, resume enhancement ($75 - $395), job file, job search tutorial and more. Corporate pricing packages and extensive added value services can reach the stratosphere. Interesting projects with the department of labor regarding the standardization of job descriptions has given Monster a potential edge for the future.

Job seekers can have their skills matched and jobs pushed to their desktops by registering their email addresses. Unfortunately, job seekers must return to the site to gain contact information. The logic behind the inconvenient agent approach is simple to continue to cook the traffic numbers. Monster.com is divided into communities, administration, campus, executive, finance, health care, human resources, international, retail, sales, technology, work abroad and self-employment. Interesting articles can be found in each of these niches. The Monster Talent Market pioneered the concept of auctioning independent professionals for contract assignments. Chief Monster.com focuses on the executive world. Monstertrak, (formerly JobTrak) brings the college market into the sandbox. HMonster focuses on the healthcare marketplace. Message boards and chatrooms keep the job seeker coming back for more. The biggest question as CXR goes to press is will Monster advertise in the 2003 Superbowl or not ? Without a doubt this site leads the pack and as of now everyone else is a follower.

Monstertrak.com (formerly JobTrak)
www.jobtrak.com

5 Clock Tower Place, Suite 500, Maynard, MA 01754
Ph: 800-999-8725   E-mail: sales@monster.com

JOBS	100,000s	RESUMES	100,000s
Cost to post	Cost to see	Cost to post	Cost to see
Fee	Free	Free	Fee
DISCIPLINE		LOCATION	
ALL		USA	
SPECIALTY		FEATURE	
ALL		College	
AGENT: N/A			

Monstertrak, (formerly JobTrak) remains a leader in the college marketplace with agreements with over 1,500 career counseling offices. Only students and alumni with a password can access posted openings from their schools. The site offers companies the ability to target specific schools' students and alumni. Job postings range from $25 for one college to $395 to blanket the nation. Monster will allow public, government and nonprofit schools to post openings for free. InterviewTrak allows recruiters self-service management of their on-campus interviews and the opportunity to view resumes to pre-select students and coordinate their schedules. "Jobtalk" is a message board for student job seeker issues

My Career.com.au
mycareer.com.au

Ben Mckenna
GPO Box 506, NSW 2001, Sydney, Australia
Ph: 039-601-4238   Fax: 039-601-2170   E-mail: sales@mycareer.com.au

JOBS	1,000s	RESUMES	N/A
Cost to post	Cost to see	Cost to post	Cost to see
Fee	Free	N/A	N/A
DISCIPLINE		LOCATION	
IT		INTL/Pacific Rim/Australia	
SPECIALTY		FEATURE	
ALL		Gateway	
AGENT: Jobseeker			

Mycareer.com.au is a viable Australian job site owned by a publishing company. Jobs can be viewed by keyword search, location or job category. All openings are date posted and each shows the publication date that the ad was placed. Job seekers can register their skills and have openings emailed to their PC. "Casual" advertisers pay $99 Au to post a job for a 28 day run. Package includes click-through email address and unlimited job description space. Site has video's on career management that are excellent. Owners also have www.itjobs.com.au in their network of sites and jobs appear on the mycareer site under the IT industry sector.

The Nat'l Assembly

www.nassembly.org

Todd Christensen
1319 F Street, Suite 601, Washington, DC 20004
Ph: 202-347-2080   Fax: 202-393-4517   E-mail: todd@nassembly.org

JOBS	1,000s	RESUMES	N/A
Cost to post	Cost to see	Cost to post	Cost to see
Free	Free	N/A	N/A

DISCIPLINE	LOCATION
Non-profit	USA

SPECIALTY	FEATURE
ALL	College/Intern

AGENT: N/A

The National Assembly of Health and Human Service Organizations is an association of nonprofits. This site has over 2,000 paid and unpaid internship listings in more than 500 organizations nationwide. Recruiters can post internship positions for free. Positions can be searched by state or city. All job postings have detailed descriptions and direct contact information.

Nat'l. Assoc. of Black Accountants

www.nabainc.org

Charles Quinn
7249-A Hanover Parkway, Greenbelt, MD 20770
Ph: 301-474-6222   Fax: 301-474-3114   E-mail: nabapobox@nabainc.org

JOBS	1,000s	RESUMES	1,000s
Cost to post	Cost to see	Cost to post	Cost to see
Fee	Free	Free	Fee

DISCIPLINE	LOCATION
Business	USA

SPECIALTY	FEATURE
Finance/Accounting	Diversity

AGENT: Both Recruiters & Jobseekers

National Association of Black Accountants was created in 1969 to expand the influence of 100,000 African-American professionals in accounting and finance. Recruiters can post a job and access the site's resume database for $285 per month. Unlimited job posting and resume database access costs $750 per month. Job seekers who save a targeted search will be notified of any new openings that fit their criteria. Openings can be searched by keyword, job category, level or location. There were 1,873 jobs posted and many have salary ranges listed. Recruiters can list all of their openings and have links to their job pages. Job seekers should check out the "FAQ Library" to answer their questions. This site is one of the best association job board designs on the web today.

Nat'l. Assoc. of Broadcasters

www.nab.org

Chris Vane
NAB,
Ph: 202-429-5300   Fax: 202-429-4199   E-mail: CareerCenter@nab.org

JOBS	100s		RESUMES	1,000s
Cost to post	Cost to see		Cost to post	Cost to see
Free	Free		Free	Free
DISCIPLINE			LOCATION	
Entertainment & Media			USA/WEST	
SPECIALTY			FEATURE	
Broadcasting/Radio & TV			N/A	
AGENT: N/A				

The Nat'l. Broadcasters Association is the source of 1000s of opportunities obtained via their state organizations. Created to promote professional services to commercial radio and television stations, the job bank allows free posting of opportunities and viewing of resumes.

Nat'l. Assoc. of Social Workers

www.socialworkers.org

Cathy Talley
700 First Street NE, Suite 700, Washington, DC 20002
Ph: 888-261-2265   E-mail: website@naswdc.org

JOBS	100s		RESUMES	100s
Cost to post	Cost to see		Cost to post	Cost to see
Fee	Free		Free	Fee
DISCIPLINE			LOCATION	
Non-Profit/Government			USA	
SPECIALTY			FEATURE	
Social Services			N/A	
AGENT: N/A				

National Association of Social Workers (NASW) claims to have over 150,000 members. Assoc. has partnered with Applied Recruitment Technologies to provide JobLink. Recruiters can usually post positions for $195 for a 30-day run. Searching the resume database is included in the job posting price. Jobs are date posted and can be searched by specialty or location. Resumes can be sent through the site or direct

Nat'l. Black MBA Assoc.

www.nbmbaa.org

1800 N. Michigan Avenue, Suite 1400, Chicago, IL 60601
Ph: 312-236-2622   Fax: 312-236-4131   E-mail: jobmatch@nbmbaa.org

JOBS	100s	RESUMES	100s
Cost to post	Cost to see	Cost to post	Cost to see
Fee	Free	Free	Fee
DISCIPLINE		LOCATION	
Business		USA	
SPECIALTY		FEATURE	
Finance/MBA		DIVERSITY	
AGENT: Both Recruiters & Jobseekers			

National Black MBA Association (NBMBAA) has over 7,800 members and chapters across the USA. Openings can be searched by keyword, location, job function, salary range or date of posting. Fortunately, there were over 147 jobs listed. Recruiters pay $3,500 to search the resume database for 6 months. The cost to post one job is $250 for a 60-day run. NBMBAA hosts an annual job fair that is attended by hundreds of companies during their national conference. The cost to access the conference resume database is $1,500. Job seekers can also view all of the listed openings by each employer or sort their searches by position or location. Job search results can be saved to view at a later date.

Nat'l. Gerontological SOA - AgeWork

www.agework.com

Melanie Radkiewicz
Gerontological Society of America, 1030 15th St. NW, Suite 250, Washington, DC 20005
Ph: 202-842-1275   Fax: 202-842-1150   E-mail: jobs@agework.com

JOBS	10s	RESUMES	N/A
Cost to post	Cost to see	Cost to post	Cost to see
Fee	Free	N/A	N/A
DISCIPLINE		LOCATION	
Science/Health Care/Education		USA/	
SPECIALTY		FEATURE	
Aging		N/A	
AGENT: N/A			

People who ask us why we would include a review of AgeWork in our database when it only had 4 openings posted on our visit are just old fuddy duddies. Postings cost $100 each for 60 days.

Nat'l. Soc. of Collegiate Scholars

www.nscs.org

Steve Loflin
NSCS, 1701 Pennsylvania Avenue NW, Suite 1000, Washington, DC 20006
Ph: 202-265-9000   Fax: 202-265-9200   E-mail: nscs@nscs.org

JOBS	10s	RESUMES	100s
Cost to post	Cost to see	Cost to post	Cost to see
Fee	Fee	Free	Free
DISCIPLINE		LOCATION	
ALL		USA	
SPECIALTY		FEATURE	
ALL		College/Intern	
AGENT: N/A			

The National Society of Collegiate Scholars (NSCS) is a nonprofit organization founded to recognize students who do well academically during their first or second year in college. Their job pages were launched in September 2001. NSCS has 300,000 lifetime members and 200 active chapters. Only members have access to the job openings. At CXR press time recruiters could have a 45-day free job posting trial. At some later point recruiters will pay $150 and internships will cost $50. Non-profits will be allowed to post for $50 and internships can be posted for free. A free resume database can be searched. Recruiters have to register and are checked that they are with a corporation (rather than an agency) before being granted access. Many Ivy League schools have chapters. CXR continues to feel that this could be a gold mine for companies capable of building relationships with college students earlier in their academic careers.

Nat'l. Society of Hispanic MBAs (BrassRing)

www.nshmba.org

Ana Herrera-Malone
1303 Walnut Hill Lane, Irving, TX 75038
Ph: 214-596-9338   Fax: 214-596-9325   E-mail: agoddard@brassring.com

JOBS	10s	RESUMES	10s
Cost to post	Cost to see	Cost to post	Cost to see
Fee	Fee	Fee	Fee
DISCIPLINE		LOCATION	
Business		USA	
SPECIALTY		FEATURE	
Finance/Accounting/MBA		DIVERSITY	
AGENT: N/A			

The National Society of Hispanic MBAs claims to have 4000 resumes. Site provides a job posting service and resume database. Site is now hosted by BrassRing but the resumes and jobs are not comingled with other BrassRing databases. Recruiters pay $150 to post a position for 30 days. Minimum package allowing resume access is $500. This association has 16 chapters in the US and Puerto Rico-some with independent web sites. Recruiters should look into this professional niche.

Nat'l. Society of Professional Engineering

www.nspe.org

1420 King Street, Alexandria, VA 22314
Ph: 703-684-2800   Fax: 703-836-4875   E-mail: jobboard@nspe.org

JOBS	10s	RESUMES	100s
Cost to post	Cost to see	Cost to post	Cost to see
Fee	Free	Free	Free
DISCIPLINE		LOCATION	
Engineering		USA	
SPECIALTY		FEATURE	
Construction/Civil/PE		N/A	
AGENT: N/A			

National Society of Professional Engineers (NSPE) has 60,000 members, with 500 chapters including every state and some territories. NSPE accepts positions for certified professional engineers in many disciplines. Recruiters pay $50 to post a job (members $40) for a 30-day run. Job listings can be searched by category, region or state and the number of jobs and resumes posted in each category is displayed. Recruiters can view resumes for free. Positions are posted with lengthy job descriptions and contact information. Internship positions are posted in a separate section for interested students. Getting a PE license is a major factor in an engineers career.

Nat'l. Technical Services Assoc.

www.ntsa.com/

Carolyn Kelley
NTSA, Eisenhower Center 1, 2121 Eisenhower Ave. Suite 604, Alexandria, VA
Ph: 703-684-4722   Fax: 703-684-7627   E-mail: ckelley@ntsa.com

JOBS	N/A	RESUMES	1,000s
Cost to post	Cost to see	Cost to post	Cost to see
N/A	N/A	Free	Fee
DISCIPLINE		LOCATION	
IT/Engineering		USA	
SPECIALTY		FEATURE	
ALL		3rd Party Staffing Exchange	
AGENT: N/A			

NTSA, the National Technical Services Association brings together over 250 temporary and contract recruitment agencies from 1,700 offices nationwide. The search engine allows job seekers to target an agency in their specialty. A resume database is available for members to share.

NationJob Network

www.nationjob.com

Bob Levinstein
601 SW 9th Street, Suite J&K, Des Moines, IA 50309
Ph: 800-292-7731   Fax: 515-283-1223   E-mail: njlistings@nationjob.comnjsales@nationjo...

JOBS	10,000s		RESUMES	100,000s
Cost to post	Cost to see		Cost to post	Cost to see
Fee	Free		Free	Fee (See Notes)

DISCIPLINE		LOCATION
ALL		USA

SPECIALTY		FEATURE
ALL		N/A

AGENT: Job Seeker

NationJob Network, launched in the early 1990s, quietly manages its business as a solid national site with extensive community alliances, especially in the Midwest. This site's agent (PJ Scout) pushes complete job information matching the interests of the nearly 800,000 registered job seekers. NationJob will post employer openings for 30 days for $150. For an additional $45 recruiters receive a company profile and links to openings. Think of the posting price as a potential direct email, which includes all the job content and contact information. Job seekers can be very specific in their search, leading to excellent results. Specialty pages focus attention on 28 key areas:health care, engineering, education, finance and more. Recruiters need to access the site's statistics & diversity pages to truly understand how powerful this job board is. Ease of access, skill-matching agent capability that really works, and local connections keep this site on top. The owners have partnerships with chambers of commerce across the USA to gain local access. The owners have been active since the early days and offer significant privacy and value for recruiters and job seekers

Ben Crowe
345 Park Avenue South, 10th Floor, New York, NY 10010
Ph: 800-989-7718   Fax: 800-989-7103   E-mail: b.crowe@natureny.com

JOBS	100s	RESUMES	N/A
Cost to post	Cost to see	Cost to post	Cost to see
Fee	Free	N/A	N/A
DISCIPLINE		LOCATION	
Science		INTL	
SPECIALTY		FEATURE	
Bio/Life Sciences		N/A	
AGENT: N/A			

Naturejobs, the website of the magazine, Nature, is a weekly journal that serves the scientific community, particularly the pharmaceutical and biotechnology areas. All of the classified ads are published on the web. The site search engine indexes jobs by keyword, location, company, position, subject or distance. A recent partnership with the Royal Society of Chemistry will be bringing additional job seekers and content to the site. Opening search terms are highlighted for ease of viewing. Jobs are date posted with contact information. Job seekers can also find similar jobs with the click of the mouse. Recruiters pay $350 to post a jobto the web. Ads placed in Nature are also listed in Scientific American. Recruiters and job seekers should also check out www.medicine.nature.com. Job seekers need to explore the extensive listing of career articles.

TIP FOR RECRUITERS

Understand that recruiting is a 24/7 position.

Most telephone interviews are done in the evenings or over the weekend. To be an effective recruiter this is what it takes.

Netshare.com
www.netshare.com

Kathy Simmons
2 Commerical Blvd.,, Suite 200, Novato, CA 94949
Ph: 800-241-5642   Fax: 415-883-1799   E-mail: netshare@netshare.com

JOBS	100s		RESUMES	1,000s
Cost to post	Cost to see		Cost to post	Cost to see
Free	Fee		Fee (See Notes)	Fee
DISCIPLINE			LOCATION	
ALL			USA	
SPECIALTY			FEATURE	
ALL			EXECUTIVE	
AGENT: N/A				

Netshare.com is an executive networking organization that launched its first site in November 1995. If you are a $100,000 job seeker or recruiter or employer, you need to be aware of this online job lead service. Job seekers pay $135 for 90 days of access and can have skill-matched positions pushed to their desktops. Other packages are available. Senior positions at $100,000 and up are listed here. Recruiters pay $250 per month for access to the resume database. Companies can post openings at no cost. The owners advise CXR that even though they are California based, the jobs listed are from across the USA. This site posted 24,000 six-figure openings in 2002. A free monthly newsletter and resume critique service are also available. This is an executive life raft that all should know about.

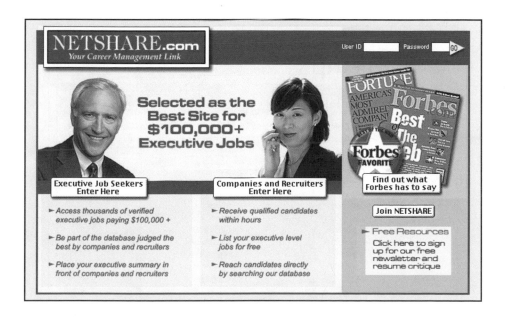

Net-Temps
www.net-temps.com

PJ
55 Middlesex Road, Suite 220, N. Chelmsford, MA 01863
Ph: 800-307-0062   Fax: 978-251-7250   E-mail: pj@net-temps.com

JOBS	10,000s	RESUMES	1,000,000s
Cost to post	Cost to see	Cost to post	Cost to see
Fee	Free	Free	Fee

DISCIPLINE	LOCATION
ALL	USA & INTL/Canada

SPECIALTY	FEATURE
ALL	Contingent/3rd Party Staffing Exchange

AGENT: Both Recruiters & Jobseekers

Net-Temps is primarily focused on serving the contract/temp marketplace within the staffing industry although they accept corporate clients. With 25,368 contract positions and 19,139 direct jobs posted each month in accounting, administration, engineering, executive, healthcare, legal, information technology, human resources, sales and marketing, this site is worth a close look. Recruiters pay $95 to post an opening for a 30 day run. NT is venturing into Canada and had 247 jobs posted. Access to the resume database costs $1,190 for 90 days. Jobs can be searched by category, location, type of job (contract or full-time) or keyword. NT claims it cross-posts its jobs to over 5000 Internet sites, including Lycos, LookSmart, Excite and AltaVista. The site provides additional services to recruiters that include a hosting capability, a talent center (where staffing firms showcase their candidates) and a daily resume hotlist that is automatically emailed to recruiters. Recruiters need to check out the site's statistics. The site's owners are always looking for new "toys" to place in the hands of recruiters and job seekers.

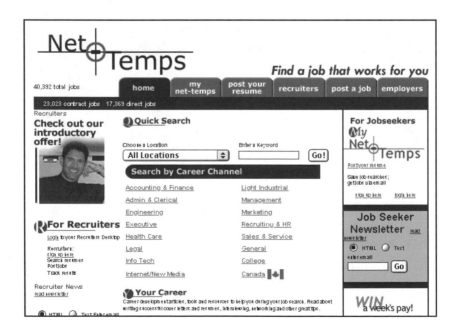

New England Journal of Medicine

www.nejm.org

860 Winter Street, Waltham, MA 02451
Ph: 800-635-6991   Fax: 781-895-1045   E mail: careerlinks@nejm.org

JOBS	1,000s	RESUMES	N/A
Cost to post	Cost to see	Cost to post	Cost to see
Fee	Free	N/A	N/A
DISCIPLINE		LOCATION	
Health Care		USA	
SPECIALTY		FEATURE	
MD		N/A	
AGENT: Job Seeker			

The New England Journal of Medicine reaches 200,000 physicians per week through its print publication. Their classified print ads are placed on this website. The site's search engine displayed 1,054 positions. Job seekers search by specialty, position title, practice type or location. Job seekers will not be happy with the site's newest changes because they must now apply to any job through the site. Job seekers who register can receive new openings every other week via email. Recruiters pay $5.65 per word to place an ad. CXR preferred the old approach.

newmonday.com

jobworld.co.uk

Ian Aitken
32-34 Broadwick Street, London, W1A 2HG United Kingdom
Ph: 080-009-20300   Fax: 020-731-69868   E-mail: help@vnu.co.uk

JOBS	1,000s	RESUMES	10,000s
Cost to post	Cost to see	Cost to post	Cost to see
Fee	Free	Free	Fee
DISCIPLINE		LOCATION	
ALL		INTL/Europe	
SPECIALTY		FEATURE	
ALL		N/A	
AGENT: Job Seeker			

Newmonday.com is a joint venture between VNU, an international publishing group and Randstad Holding, a headhunter. Site asks job seekers to register their email & skills and then pushes matching positions on a daily basis. Openings can be searched by keyword, profession (any, IT, finance), location or salary. Salary ranges are displayed in most instances. Owners also have sites in Belgium, France, Germany, Italy, Netherlands, and Spain. Recruitment agencies pay 5 pounds per week to post an opening. Site will email openings to it's members at 1,000 pounds per campaign. For 150 pounds a "job of the day" will be featured on the entry page of each of the subsections and then emailed to job seekers. Ad agencies (corporate jobs) pay 500 pounds for "job of the day" or 250 pounds for a 30-day posting.

Nokri.com
www.nokri.com

847A 2nd Avenue #277, New York, NY 10017
Ph: 212-560-5119   E-mail: info@nokri.com

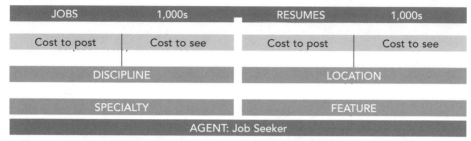

JOBS	1,000s		RESUMES	1,000s
Cost to post	Cost to see		Cost to post	Cost to see
DISCIPLINE			LOCATION	
SPECIALTY			FEATURE	
AGENT: Job Seeker				

Nokri.com would like to bill itself as the world's leading recruitment site, but our searches continue to only turn up openings in the USA. Recruiters can post 20 jobs for free for one month as a site trial. Openings run $79 for a 1 month run. For $2,109 recruiters can post five jobs and search the resume database for six months. The site offers three job search levels basic, advanced and experienced. In the advanced search, job seekers can search by location, job function, keyword, salary and benefits desired (health plans, bonus, stock options, etc.). Job seekers can save keyword searches for future use. A detailed guide prevents job seekers from coming up empty on a search. Job seekers must register to utilize the site. Limited disclosure, no metrics and with the trouble it took to find the telephone number and contact address, Nokri is hard to fathom.

Nurse Practitioners Central - NPJobs
www.npjobs.com

Mary Kozy
10024 S.E., 240th Street, Suite 102, Kent, WA 98031
Ph: 253-852-9042   Fax: 253-852-7725   E-mail: info@npcentral.net

JOBS	100s		RESUMES	100s
Cost to post	Cost to see		Cost to post	Cost to see
Fee	Free		Fee	Fee
DISCIPLINE			LOCATION	
Health Care			USA	
SPECIALTY			FEATURE	
Nursing			N/A	
AGENT: N/A				

Nurse Practitioners Central (NP Central) is a growing center of helpful content for the nursing rofession. Jobs can be searched by specialty, state, region or date of posting. Resume profiles can be viewed by recruiters but contact data must be obtained from the site. With no seach engine for viewing resumes this is going to be an arduous selection task. Job seekers pay $10 for posting a two page resume and cover letter. Recruiters pay $85-185 to post an opening for 3 months which is also emailed to all 6,000 advanced practice nurses on the sites mailing list. Resumes can be viewed for $75 per month.

Nursing Spectrum Career Fitness Online

www.nursingspectrum.com

David Patrick
2353 Hassell Rd #110, Hoffman Estates, IL 60564
Ph: 888-206-3791   Fax: 849-490-0429   E-mail: saleshelp@nursingspectrum.com

JOBS	1,000s	RESUMES	N/A
Cost to post	Cost to see	Cost to post	Cost to see
Fee	Free	N/A	N/A

DISCIPLINE	LOCATION
Health Care	USA

SPECIALTY	FEATURE
Nursing	N/A

AGENT: Both Recruiters & Jobseekers

Nursing Spectrum claims that it reaches 1.8 million RNs nationally through its print publication and its website. Nursing Spectrum is part of the Gannett publishing Co. The site search engine can sort openings by specialty, region or keyword, and had 2,451 jobs posted on our last visit.The display of job openings is arguably the best of any site on the web. Employers pay $150 to post a job for 2 weeks. Nurses can post their resumes to the site, but it is only a holding tank. Recruiters cannot access the database because it is only for job seekers to forward when they choose. The site's services include extensive career articles ("dear donna", a career management expert and "brent's law" for legal issues) along with continuing education content, employer profiles, a relocation network and hosted nurse-to-nurse chat room discussions. A special section for students who can obtain career advice is also available. One of the best in its class for the health care niche.

NY New Media Assoc. The Silicon Alley Job Board

www.nynma.org

55 Broad Street 3rd Floor, New York, NY 10004
Ph: 212-785-7898   Fax: 212-785-7963   E-mail: jobsboard@nynma.org

JOBS	10s	RESUMES	100s
Cost to post	Cost to see	Cost to post	Cost to see
Fee (See Notes)	Free	Free	Fee (See Notes
DISCIPLINE		LOCATION	
IT		USA/MDA/NY	
SPECIALTY		FEATURE	
New Media/Internet		N/A	
AGENT: N/A			

NY New Media Association, The Silicon Alley Job Board, is a nonprofit association founded in 1994 that has 8,500 members in 4,500 companies. Only members can post postiions which cost $50 for a 2 week run, which includes access to the resume database. Membership is $150 per year. Positions can be viewed by categories such as administrative, business development, education, executive, information architecture, interactive design, internships, production engineer, management, research, sales visual design and writer/editor. Openings can be keyword searched. Jobs are posted with direct contact information. Jobs must be based in the New York tri-state area. Job seekers should check out "Navigating the Alley" which provides career advice articles.

NY Times Job Market

www.nytimes.com

Ellen Dobrin
229 W. 43rd Street, New York, NY
Ph: 212-556-1598   E-mail: onlinejobs@nytimes.com

JOBS	1,000s	RESUMES	1,000s
Cost to post	Cost to see	Cost to post	Cost to see
Fee	Free	Free	Fee
DISCIPLINE		LOCATION	
ALL		USA/MDA/NY	
SPECIALTY		FEATURE	
ALL		N/A	
AGENT: Jobseeker			

The Times is intent on recovering their former glory (remember "I Got My Job Through The NY Times"? Top left of the home page flashes to advertise the site "job market". Recruiting is now powered by CareerCast which is a step in the right direction along with the ability to combine with other papers. Resumes are being collected on this site and recruiters can post a single opening for $275. Events and alliances are regularly announced. Jobs can be viewed by category or keyword search. An advanced search feature allows viewing by keyword, location, distance, company or category. Keywords are then highlighted in the text. Job seekers can register for skill matched openings to be sent to their PC.

OperationIT

www.operationit.com

Mat Arnell
295 Madison Avenue, 22nd Floor, New York, NY 10017
Ph: 888-338-9595   Fax: 212-338-0909   E-mail: info@operation.com

JOBS	1,000s	RESUMES	100,000s
Cost to post	Cost to see	Cost to post	Cost to see
Fee	Free	Fee	Free
DISCIPLINE		LOCATION	
IT		USA/MDA/NY/NYC	
SPECIALTY		FEATURE	
ALL		N/A	
AGENT: Both Recruiters & Jobseekers			

The OperationIT.com business center brings together clients' project needs with information technology specialty firms. These are mainly independent contractors looking for their next project. The site claims to have a national prominence but it's main forte is in the NYC area. Recruiters can post a position for 30 days for $195 and view resumes for an additional $262. Job seekers can either use a quick search engine or use the site's advanced features to search by keyword, job category, location or salary level. Resumes can be e-mailed through the site directly to the hiring corporation. Job seekers must have a resume registered with the site to apply for openings. Staffing firms can post their 100 top candidates and interact with corporate recruiters.

Opportunity Nocs

www.opportunitynocs.org

Laura Marett
870 Market Street, Suite #360, San Francisco, CA 94102
Ph: 415-362-9735   Fax: 415-394-0160   E-mail: nocs@tmcenter.org

JOBS	1,000s	RESUMES	N/A
Cost to post	Cost to see	Cost to post	Cost to see
Fee	Free	N/A	N/A
DISCIPLINE		LOCATION	
Non-Profit		USA	
SPECIALTY		FEATURE	
ALL		N/A	
AGENT: N/A			

Opportunity Nocs was launched in 1998, and has an online newsletter that mirrors its print cousin. The print edition claims a readership of 150,000 with an average of 1,100 job listings per month. Nonprofit organizations post positions to the website for $80 for a 30-day run. Jobs can be viewed by keyword, organization type, position, location or job freshness. There were 548 jobs posted on our visit, and all are date posted. Regional editions of the print version can be found in Northern CA, Atlanta, Boston, Dallas, Los Angeles, and Philadelphia. Print ads cost $180. Openings are date posted with direct contact information. A long list of helpful career and job links is also available under the resources link.

optics.org

Chris Kendall
Institute of Physics, Dirac House, Temple Back, Bristol, BS1 6BE United Kingdom
E-mail: info@optics.org

JOBS	10s	RESUMES	10s
Cost to post	Cost to see	Cost to post	Cost to see
Fee	Free	Free (See Notes)	Fee
DISCIPLINE		LOCATION	
Science		INTL	
SPECIALTY		FEATURE	
Optical Physics		Gateway	
AGENT: Job Seeker			

The Institute of Physics acquired Optics.org from the Society of Photo-optical Instrument Engineers in November 2000. IP also supports 9 sites such as physicsweb.org, compoundsemiconductor.net, fibers.org and nanotechweb.org. The site claims over 40,000 photonics professionals receive their newsletter. Recruiters post jobs for $500 for a 1 month run on all sites. Resumes and job listings are date posted. Recruiters also gain access to the resume database (max 20 cv's) when placing an ad. We only found eight job listings on our last visit, which proves that even with the right product, you have to advertise.

OutdoorNetwork

Bryan Buikema
PO Box 1928, Boulder, CO 80306
Ph: 303-444-7117   Fax: 303-447-8322   E-mail: info@outdoornetwork.com

JOBS	100s	RESUMES	100s
Cost to post	Cost to see	Cost to post	Cost to see
Fee	Free	Free	Free
DISCIPLINE		LOCATION	
Education		USA	
SPECIALTY		FEATURE	
Sports/Recreation/Teaching		N/A	
AGENT: N/A			

The OutdoorNetwork, launched in 1995, is the site for the true outdoor lover. Job seekers can post their resumes and view jobs for free. Resumes (311) or jobs (214) can be viewed via a specific checklist of skills, or through a keyword search. Jobs can also be searched by date for those who return to the wilderness often. Job seekers have a shopping cart feature to narrow their choices. Jobs may be posted for free if recruiters subscribe to the print publication ($85 per year), otherwise the price is $20 per posting. Openings include adventure trip and wilderness leader opportunities. The owners have thought the technology through in this site's design. Given the stress of living in cities these days, a job as a park ranger sounds better and better..

Pharmacy Week

www.pharmacyweek.com

Rebecca Polk
7 N. Pinckney Street, Suite 200, Madison, WI 53703
Ph: 608 251-1112   Fax: 608-251-1155   E-mail: sales@pharmacyweek.com

JOBS	100s	RESUMES	100s
Cost to post	Cost to see	Cost to post	Cost to see
Fee	Free	Free	Fee
DISCIPLINE		LOCATION	
Health Care		USA	
SPECIALTY		FEATURE	
Pharmacy		N/A	
AGENT: Recruiter			

Pharmacy Week is a trade magazine that displays the number of jobs posted on its website right on the homepage (171). Recruiters can post in print/web with access to the resume database for $1,050 for two weeks. Other packages are available. Job seekers can search by category and location and each is displayed by title, employer, and location with direct contact information. Job categories display the number of openings that are posted. Discussion forums for job seekers and recruiters are an added bonus. Job seekers who place their resume on this site can "invite" posted employers to view their background. Headhunter and temporary openings are separated from company listings. Candidate discussion boards are an added feature.

Philanthropy Journal Online

www.philanthropyjournal.org

Suzie Koonce
PO Box 12800, Raleigh, NC 27605
Ph: 804-342-7665   Fax: 804-342-8015   E-mail: ads@philanthropyjournal.org

JOBS	10s	RESUMES	N/A
Cost to post	Cost to see	Cost to post	Cost to see
Fee	Free	N/A	N/A
DISCIPLINE		LOCATION	
Non-Profit		USA	
SPECIALTY		FEATURE	
ALL		N/A	
AGENT: Job Seeker			

The Philanthropy Journal Online hosts information and jobs for nonprofit organizations. This site is updated on a daily basis and the newsletter is published every Monday. Openings can be viewed by selecting a region from a map of the USA. Job seekers can search by job title or field of interest. Lengthy job descriptions are provided with links to the employer's site for additional information. Direct contact data is supplied. Recruiters pay $50 to post a job for a 30-day run. Job seekers can register for an email newsletter that will be pushed to their PC. For those who want to work for firms that give more than they take, this might be the place to look.

Physics Today Online

www.aip.org/pt

Richard Kobel

American Institute of Physics, Ste 1NO1, 2 Huntington Quadrangle, Melville, NY 11747

Ph: 800-247-2242   Fax: 301-209-0841   E-mail: advtsg@aip.org

JOBS	100s	RESUMES	1,000s
Cost to post	Cost to see	Cost to post	Cost to see
Fee	Free	Free	Fee
DISCIPLINE		LOCATION	
Science		USA	
SPECIALTY		FEATURE	
Physics		N/A	
AGENT: N/A			

The American Institute of Physics (AIP) reaches 120,000 physicists and engineers worldwide. The cost of posting a job online on "Career Services" is $21.50 per line with an 8 line minimum - $172. Access to the site's resume database is $160 for 30 days. Job seekers search by keyword, job category (e.g. industry, optics, academic, computing, government, federally funded, R&D, etc.) or location. Job seekers can also search jobs through a list of posting organizations. There were 333 positions listed on our visit. The site also posts a listing of upcoming job fairs across the USA. Many of the posted positions are for teachers at the university level. Job seekers can apply with the direct contact information or through the website.

Plastic Careers.com

www.ejnetwork.com

Elayne West

EJ Network, Inc., PO Box 147, 419 E. Main Street, Plymouth, WI 53073

Ph: 920-893-5544   Fax: 920-893-5460   E-mail: ejn@ejnetwork.com

JOBS	100s	RESUMES	100s
Cost to post	Cost to see	Cost to post	Cost to see
Fee	Free	Free	Fee
DISCIPLINE		LOCATION	
Science/Engineering/Trades		USA/	
SPECIALTY		FEATURE	
Chemistry/Plastics		N/A	
AGENT: Jobseeker			

Posting positions cost $150 on Plastic Careers.com but the resume database is connected to the company's third party contingency model. Site provides links to relevant plastic industry publications, schools, professional organizations, and technical sites, as well as links to relocation services and useful employment information.

Playbill

www.playbill.com

Robert Simonson
E-mail: jobpost@playbill.com

JOBS	100s	RESUMES	N/A
Cost to post	Cost to see	Cost to post	Cost to see
Free	Free	N/A	N/A
DISCIPLINE		LOCATION	
Entertainment & Media		USA	
SPECIALTY		FEATURE	
Theatre		N/A	
AGENT: N/A			

Playbill is the casting call to the theatre that many young thesbians heed. Jobs can be viewed via the site's search engine or by category. Openings include:performer, technical, design, administrative and academic. Jobs are posted by date, title and state so prepare to scroll. 100s of opportunities are posted here.

PMjobs.com

www.pmjobs.com

Jonathan Grant
127 South Main Street, Suite 3, Plymouth, MI 48170
Ph: 877-682-6200   Fax: 734-737-0658   E-mail: jgrant@apartmentgear.com

JOBS	100s	RESUMES	1,000s
Cost to post	Cost to see	Cost to post	Cost to see
Fee	Free	Free	Fee
DISCIPLINE		LOCATION	
Retail Sales & Services		USA	
SPECIALTY		FEATURE	
Real Estate		N/A	
AGENT: Job Seeker			

PMjobs.com (property management) targets real estate professionals. Recruiters can post jobs for $45 each for a 1 month run. Access to the resume database and unlimited job postings is $1,500 per month. Job seekers search openings by selecting a state on a map of the USA. The jobs listed range from accounting and groundskeepers to leasing agents and vice presidents. Job descriptions with direct contact information are available. All jobs are deleted after 30 days. The position benefits for each position are listed next to the opening, with the ones an organization offers clearly marked. Job seekers who register their skills can have openings sent to their PC's. Simple, excellent design makes this site a pleasure for recruiters and job seekers to use.

PortaJobs

www.portajobs.com

Fran Carnevale
6039 Redwood Lane, Alexandria, VA 22310
Ph: 703-960-1461   E-mail: webmaster@portajobs.com

JOBS	100s		RESUMES	1,000s
Cost to post	Cost to see		Cost to post	Cost to see
Fee	Free		Free	Free
DISCIPLINE			LOCATION	
ALL			USA	
SPECIALTY			FEATURE	
ALL			Telecommuting/Telework/Home	
AGENT: Job Seeker				

PortaJobs intends to serve the overlapping interests of the telework (telecommuting), technology and transportation communities in the Baltimore–Washington, DC region. Employers can post telework positions for any of their locations, just as long as the job permits teleworking or the employer's posting states that telework will be considered for the right candidate. Recruiters pay $100 to post a job for one month. The site's resume database with contact information can be accessed for free. Recruiters who need to justify telework positions can link to a "cost/benefit" article on Cisco's corporate site.

PracticeChoice/Link

www.practicechoice.com

Ken Allman
Allman & Company, 312 2nd Avenue, PO Box 100, Hinton, WV 25951
Ph: 800-776-8383   E-mail: comments@practicelink.com

JOBS	1,000s		RESUMES	1,000s
Cost to post	Cost to see		Cost to post	Cost to see
Fee	Free		Free	Fee
DISCIPLINE			LOCATION	
Health Care			USA	
SPECIALTY			FEATURE	
MD/Nursing			N/A	
AGENT: Both Recruiters & Jobseekers				

PracticeChoice (PC-headhunters) was launched November 1995, and is affiliated with PracticeLink (PL-corporate recruiters). PracticeChoice caters to recruitment firms that go after doctors and nurses, while PracticeLink is geared to corporate recruiters.Site owners claim that more than 12,000 physicians, 700 hospitals and medical groups use this site on an annual basis. PC charges $950 to post ten job slots per year. PL charges recruiters $2,950 for five job posting slots. Job seekers search by profession, specialty, state, region or country. Next to each profession is the current number of openings posted. Every job profile includes contact information and offers job seekers the ability to send their resumes out with one click. Jobs posted here range from lab technicians to physicians. Headhunters cannot access the site's resume database. Resumes are deleted after 1 year. Recruiters are sent new job seeker profiles via email. MedJobs.net is a new site catering to nursing and allied health fields. Well designed and easy to use.

Private School Employment Network

www.privateschooljobs.com

Mary-Kay Rath
17618 College Road, Hagerstown, MD 21740
Fax: 301-766-0349   E-mail: schooljobs@aol.com

JOBS	100s	RESUMES	100s
Cost to post	Cost to see	Cost to post	Cost to see
Fee	Free	Fee	Free
DISCIPLINE		LOCATION	
Education		USA	
SPECIALTY		FEATURE	
Teaching, k-12		N/A	
AGENT: N/A			

The Private School Employment Network posts vacancies in administration and teaching for private and independent schools. Positions and resumes can be viewed for free by the type of experience (most have direct contact information). Coded jobs or resumes have a number next to their title, and you need to go back to the site for the contact data. Recruiters pay $80 to post an opening which runs indefinitely. Job seekers pay $25 to list their resumes which are from all over the USA. Schools can purchase banner ads for $75 per month to drive traffic to their site.

Professionals in Human Resources Assoc.

www.pihra.org

Iris Samayoa
888 South Figueroa Street, #1050, Los Angeles, CA 90017
Ph: 213-622-7472   Fax: 213-622-7450   E-mail: iris@pihra.org

JOBS	10s	RESUMES	100s
Cost to post	Cost to see	Cost to post	Cost to see
Fee	Free	Free	Free
DISCIPLINE		LOCATION	
Human Resources		USA/WEST/CA	
SPECIALTY		FEATURE	
ALL		N/A	
AGENT: N/A			

Professionals in Human Resources Association (PIHRA) is a large California based HR organization affilliated with SHRM. Recruiters pay $225 to post a position for 30 days. Openings are viewed by over 4,000 members. Openings are listed by job function:Sr. HR, generalist, training, admin., comp. benefits and HRIS, staffing or other. Profiles with contact information can only be posted if you are a PIRHA member. Agents email postings and resumes to job seekers and recruiters respectively. Cross posting to other sites is an added benefit.

ProgrammingJobs.com

www.programmingjobs.com

Walt Fischer
5144 N. Academy Blvd. #446, Colorado Springs, CO 80917
Ph: 314-609-6530   E-mail: webmaster@ProgrammingJobs.com

JOBS	1,000s	RESUMES	1,000s
Cost to post	Cost to see	Cost to post	Cost to see
Free	Free	Free	Fee
DISCIPLINE		LOCATION	
IT		USA	
SPECIALTY		FEATURE	
Software Programming		N/A	
AGENT: N/A			

ProgrammingJobs.com was launched February 2000, and charges $99 to access resumes for computer programmers/software engineers for 30 days. Each additional month access to resumes is $50. Jobs can be posted for free. A map of the USA offers openings by location. Date of posting and direct contact are available. The database includes 1,000+ jobs and over 4,000 resumes. Job seekers will appreciate the job location maps that are boldly colored (for us old guys) to find their way to their next gig.

Programming-Services.com

www.programming-services.com

Don Kennedy
E-mail: webmaster@programming-services.com

JOBS	1,000s	RESUMES	100s
Cost to post	Cost to see	Cost to post	Cost to see
Free	Free	Free	Free
DISCIPLINE		LOCATION	
IT		USA	
SPECIALTY		FEATURE	
Tandem/IBM/Unix/Windows NT/Web		N/A	
AGENT: Both Recruiters & Jobseekers			

Programming-Services.com hosts the equivalent of multiple job-related email discussion groups. Anyone can post a job or a resume profile for free. The site is broken into sections for the information technology world - Tandem, IBM, Unix, NT or Web Boards. Thousands of jobs and hundreds of resume profiles were available for free viewing.

Project Connect

careers.education.wisc.edu/projectconnect/MainMenu.cfm

Steve Head
University of Wisconsin-Madison
Ph: 608-262-1755   E-mail: projectconnect@educagtion.wisc.edu

JOBS	1,000s	RESUMES	N/A
Cost to post	Cost to see	Cost to post	Cost to see
Free	Free	N/A	N/A
DISCIPLINE		LOCATION	
Education		USA	
SPECIALTY		FEATURE	
Teaching, University, K-12		N/A	
AGENT: N/A			

Project Connect is a national cooperative effort between school districts and universities to get educational staffing on the Internet. In 1992, this program began to set standards for vacancy and candidate information. Job openings are transmitted to students and alumni via an online database through registered university career service departments. Registration information is available at this site.

Project Management Insititute

www.pmi.org

Darah L. Filidore
4 Campus Boulevard, Newtown Square, PA 19073
Ph: 610-356-4600   Fax: 610-356-4647   E-mail: careerhq@pmi.org

JOBS	10s	RESUMES	100s
Cost to post	Cost to see	Cost to post	Cost to see
Fee	Free	Free	Fee
DISCIPLINE		LOCATION	
Business		USA	
SPECIALTY		FEATURE	
Operations/Project Management		N/A	
AGENT: N/A			

The Project Management Institute's Career Headquarters (more than 80,000 members worldwide) establishes project management standards, provides seminars, educational programs and professional certification. PMI has over 170 chapters in 45 countries. Chapters contact information can be found via this website. Members pay $125 (non-members $250) to post positions for 30 days in the association's career headquarters and access a resume database. Openings can be viewed through the site's search engine and many have salary ranges posted.

PsycCareers

www.psyccareers.com

Freda Gibson
American Psycological Association, 750 First Street, NE, Washington, DC 20002
Ph: 202-336-5564   Fax: 202-336-5500   E-mail: advertising@apa.org

JOBS	100s	RESUMES	1,000s
Cost to post	Cost to see	Cost to post	Cost to see
Fee	Free	Free	Fee
DISCIPLINE		LOCATION	
Science/Health Care/Education		USA/	
SPECIALTY		FEATURE	
Psychology/Counseling/Teaching		N/A	
AGENT: N/A			

PsycCareers is work for headcases. CXR wonders if applicants at this site will be able to get through the online screening tools. Employers pay $9.75 a line (figures) and 6 lines are minimum. Resume access is $149 for 90 days. Hundreds of corporate, government, non-profit,health care positions are listed. Survey showing where 1999 graduates went and how they got there is interesting but needs updating.

Public Relations Soc. of America (PRSA)

www.prsa.org

Gale spreter
33 Irving Place, New York, NY
Ph: 212-460-1433   E-mail: lisa.granoff@prsa.org

JOBS	100s	RESUMES	10s
Cost to post	Cost to see	Cost to post	Cost to see
Fee	Free	Fee	Free
DISCIPLINE		LOCATION	
Communications		USA	
SPECIALTY		FEATURE	
Public Relations		N/A	
AGENT: N/A			

The Public Relations Society of America (PRSA) has 120 chapters, 25,000+ members and offers a careers section for individuals interested in the profession. Recruiters can post positions for $155 for the first five lines. Each additional line is $20. Jobs are posted each Friday, and are live for one month. Resumes can be viewed for free, but are in no particular order. Members of PRSA can post their resume for one month for free. Non-members pay $40. Job seekers view a map of the USA to select a location. All openings are date posted, and contact information is provided. A contact list for local chapters is available on the site, and should be checked, as many chapters run their own job boards. A membership directory is free to members or can be purchased for $75.

Pure Power's Database Jobs.com

www.databasejobs.com/

Michael Brown
Pure Power, PO Box 17001, Raleigh, NC 27619
Ph: 800-603-0030   Fax: 919-844-0080   E-mail: anyreason@purepowersites.com

JOBS	1,000s		RESUMES	1,000s
Cost to post	Cost to see		Cost to post	Cost to see
Fee	Free		Free	Fee
DISCIPLINE			LOCATION	
IT			USA	
SPECIALTY			FEATURE	
Database			Gateway	
AGENT: N/A				

Pure Power's sites are a network of nine information technology niche job boards. Recruiters can obtain a 30-day free trial on any of these sites. Initial pricing is $79 to post unlimited jobs on any of the sites for a month (the resume database is included). Individual jobs can be posted for $49 which includes access to the resume database. The ERPJobs site is free to post and view resumes. Jobs are listed by location and job title, date and source. Many come from other websites. Openings have direct contact information and brief job descriptions. Skill sites include cobol, C++, Database, Delphi, ERP, LAN, Lotus Notes, PowerBuilder, Visual Basic and Web Programming. There were over 5,700 openings posted from 1,700 employers.

QA-jobs.com

www.qa-jobs.com

JOBS	100s		RESUMES	100s
Cost to post	Cost to see		Cost to post	Cost to see
Free	Free		Free	Free
DISCIPLINE			LOCATION	
Business			USA	
SPECIALTY			FEATURE	
Operations/Manufacturing/QA			N/A	
AGENT: Both Recruiters & Jobseekers				

QA-Jobs.com allows employers to search and respond to resume postings on-line for free. When a recruiter responds to a resume posting, the applicant is immediately notified. QA-Jobs.com can also find applicants automatically with an agent matching capability All job seekers and recruiters must register to utilize the site. Site specializes in the medical and technical fields of QA. Resumes and jobs can be searched by category, country, state, salary range, employer, school or keyword. Openings are date posted and can be added to an inbox for later viewing. CXR still wonders why the site offers so little disclosure but so far (2 years) they seem to deliver.

Radio Online

www.radioonline.com

Ph: 806-352-7503   Fax: 806-352-3677   E-mail: customer.service@radio-online.com

JOBS	100s		RESUMES	10s
Cost to post	Cost to see		Cost to post	Cost to see
Free	Fee		Free	Free
DISCIPLINE			LOCATION	
Entertainment & Media			USA	
SPECIALTY			FEATURE	
Broadcasting			N/A	
AGENT: N/A				

Radio Online targets broadcast professionals in career transition. Job seekers pay $15 per month to become members and access posted job openings, but a 10-day free trial is available and recommended. Employers post positions and search the resume database for free. Recruiters will really have a blast with the email directory to radio station personalities (individuals can be looked up by alpha). For recruiters in need of a break, check out the hilarious clips of movie and TV sound bites. The Flintstones was a CXR favorite.

Radiology & Oncology JOBS (RTjobs.com)

www.rtjobs.com

Julie Morris
2193 Corte Limon, Carlsbad, CA 92009
Ph: 760-753-1399   Fax: 760-436-9147   E-mail: julie@rtjobs.com

JOBS	100s		RESUMES	100s
Cost to post	Cost to see		Cost to post	Cost to see
Fee	Free		Fee	Free
DISCIPLINE			LOCATION	
Health Care			USA	
SPECIALTY			FEATURE	
MD/Radiology/Oncology			N/A	
AGENT: Job Seeker				

Radiology and Oncology JOBS (RT Jobs.com) was launched in January 1998, and its target is hospitals, clinics and companies. Recruiters pay $175 to post a job for a 60-day run which is also emailed to all registered job seekers. Access to the resume database costs $175 per month with other packages available. The owners advise that they have 5,325 registered job seekers, and that a detailed breakdown of the job categories can be viewed on the site. Jobs can be viewed by category, location or by hospital or organization. Openings are date posted and include direct contact information. Recruiters can view resume content for free but must pay for contact data. CXR would like to see more sites disclose their active job seeker stats.

Real Jobs - Real Estate
www.real-jobs.com

Dr. Norm Miller
Ph: 513-556-7088   E-mail: norm.miller@uc.edu

JOBS	100s	RESUMES	100s
Cost to post	Cost to see	Cost to post	Cost to see
Free	Free	Free	Free
DISCIPLINE		LOCATION	
Retail Sales & Services		USA	
SPECIALTY		FEATURE	
Real estate		College	
AGENT: N/A			

Real-Jobs has provided services for the real estate community for years. Dr. Norm has recently decided that the site should be totally free. Over 712 resumes, all with contact information, can be found. Resumes can be viewed by location, job category or education and all have a completed skills evaluation. The site caters to recent college graduates with an interest in the real estate field. Job seekers can post their resumes for 90 days. Recruiters post jobs (157) ranging from sales agents to land barons. Jobs can be searched by company name, location, job category and education. Job seekers need to register to view job openings. CXR was advised that over 20% of the posted openings come from 3rd party recruiters.

RecruitMilitary
www.recruitmilitary.com

Drew Myers
4520 Cooper Road, Suite 304, Cincinnati, OH 45242
Ph: 513-621-5349   Fax: 513-621-9356   E-mail: customerservice@recruitmilitary.com

JOBS	100s	RESUMES	100s
Cost to post	Cost to see	Cost to post	Cost to see
Fee	Free	Fee	Free
DISCIPLINE		LOCATION	
IT/Engineering		USA	
SPECIALTY		FEATURE	
ALL		Military Transition	
AGENT: Both Recruiters & Jobseekers			

RecruitMilitary (formerly MilitaryHeadhunter.com), launched in 1998, allows recruiters to post jobs for $100 for 60-days and $2500 to view the resume database for a year. The site emphasizes opportunities for veterans, retirees, transitioning military personnel, veterans with business experience and military spouses. Jobs can be searched by location and job category. Job seekers can use all of the site's functionality after first completing a lengthy application process (fortunately the owners allow you to skip many sections). Jobs are listed by date of posting, title and company name (most are technical fields). A search by Military Occupational Specialty (MOS) and/or Military Schoolsgraduated from is extremely helpful. Several opt in newsletters and a military to civilian pay calculator are worth the trip.

Recruit USA

www.recruitusa.com

Doug Ries
12 South Sixth Street, Suite 730, Minneapolis, MN 55402
Ph: 612-278-0000   E-mail: info@recruitusa.com

JOBS	10,000s		RESUMES	10,000s	
Cost to post	Cost to see		Cost to post	Cost to see	
Fee	Free		Free	Free	
DISCIPLINE			LOCATION		
ALL			USA		
SPECIALTY			FEATURE		
ALL			Job Distribution Services		
AGENT: N/A					

Recruit USA is a clearinghouse for job postings. The owners also provide web recruiting strategies for corporate clients. Recruiters can post a position for $125 for 60 days to the 3,000 free sites and also cross-post to a network of fee sites. This sounds great, but be sure these are the places where you want your jobs to be listed. For $12,000-24,000 per year corporations can have their billing managed, ad responses tracked. Customer services are offered to insure ads are placed correctly. The resume database is free to view and can be searched by state and keyword. Recruiters who lack cross-posting alternatives are increasingly looking at services like Recruit USA that blend recruitment advertising firm features with job board capabilities.

Recruiter Seek

www.recruiterseek.com

Tony Bengston
PO Box 461804, Aurora, CO 80046
Ph: 303-627-9189   E-mail: info@recruitseek.com

JOBS	10s		RESUMES	1,000s	
Cost to post	Cost to see		Cost to post	Cost to see	
Free	Free		Free	Fee	
DISCIPLINE			LOCATION		
Human Resources			USA		
SPECIALTY			FEATURE		
Employment			N/A		
AGENT: Recruiter					

Recruiter Seek offers employers and recruiters the ability to connect via the web. The owners claim 6,549 employers and recruiters are currently registered. The site targets recruiting professionals and posts contract and fulltime openings. There were a handful of openings here when we visited- all were less than 60 days old. Jobs can be searched by location, industry, title, experience level or employer name. All who enter the site must register. A recruiting salary survey is available as the data is collected from all site registrants. A map of the USA contains the url's to recruiting associations.

Recruiters Online Network

www.recruitersonline.com

Tony Rossi
947 Essex Lane, Medina, OH 44256
Ph: 888-821-2490   Fax: 972-725-8425   E-mail: info@recruitersonline.com

JOBS	10,000s		RESUMES	100,000s
Cost to post	Cost to see		Cost to post	Cost to see
Fee	Free		Free	Fee

DISCIPLINE	LOCATION
ALL	USA

SPECIALTY	FEATURE
ALL	3rd Party Staffing Exchange

AGENT: Employer

The Recruiter's Online Network (RON) positions itself as a worldwide community of placement firms (8,000 3rd party registered recruiters). Bill Vick, the original founder sold his interest to his business partner in 2002. CXR will miss Bill's flare for the recruiting industry. Candidate resumes are shared, and commissions are split. Recruiters can join for a 30-day free trial. Membership is $995 per year for unlimited job postings to be broadcast to 3,000 sites. The price includes resume access. Job seekers can post their resumes and view openings at no charge. Corporate recruiters can find agencies in their particular field through SmartMATCH. Resumes (500,000) are active for 90 days. Staffing professionals gather in the "recruiters coffeeshop" discussion forums. RON has been around since the beginning of the web, and along with similar sites should be considered by agencies as a supplement to their individual strategy

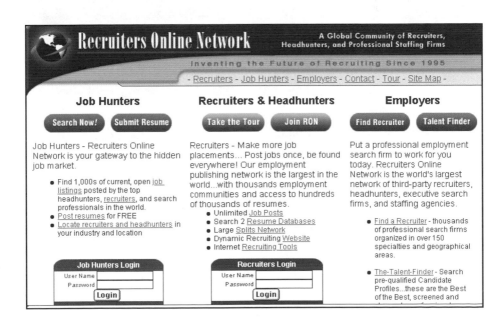

Recruiters World

www.recruitersworld.com

Christine Hirsch
HRT Internet LLC, PO Box 14261, Chicago, IL 60614-0261
Ph: 214-696-4845   E-mail: Feedback@RecruitersWorld.com

JOBS	100s		RESUMES	N/A
Cost to post	Cost to see		Cost to post	Cost to see
Fee	Free		N/A	N/A
DISCIPLINE			LOCATION	
Human Resources			USA	
SPECIALTY			FEATURE	
Employment			N/A	
AGENT: Jobseeker				

Recruiters World is a solid source of information for professionals in employment. Recruiters pay one of several subscription levels i.e. $99 per year but featured jobs are accessible from the home page and a "priceless" subscription will also get you in.. Posting costs $150 "a la carte" for a non-subscriber and $75 for a subscriber (although free postings come with subscriptions). A recruiting resource catalog provides a long list of job site links, a database of recruiters/firms, human resource consulting firms and individuals who provide services to major employers and recruiting organizations. Their online virtual job fair service, talent.event.com is still searching for its legs but these are folks that know how to persist.

Recruitment Exchange Online

www.rex.co.uk

hotgroup Plc., Garden House, London Road, Sunningdale, Berkshire, SL5 OLE United Kingdom
Ph: 084-513-04422   Fax: 084-513-04433   E-mail: sales@jobmagic.net

JOBS	1,000s		RESUMES	10,000s
Cost to post	Cost to see		Cost to post	Cost to see
Fee	Free		Free	Fee
DISCIPLINE			LOCATION	
IT			INTL/Europe/UK	
SPECIALTY			FEATURE	
ALL			Gateway	
AGENT: Job Seeker				

Recruitment Exchange is part of a network of career sites. Employers who subscribe to the site can post a position for £375. Recruiters can have unlimited resume and job posting access for 3,850 GBP per year. (The positions will also be emailed to their 125,000 registered candidates). Rex was created in 1996 to bring IT contractors together with agencies and corporations in the UK and Europe. Jobs posted on one site are also advertised on 30 other job-related sites that Rex manages. Examples are www.jobtrack.co.uk (directed to third-party recruiters), www.absolute-comms.co.uk (for the telecommunications industry), hotrecruit.co.uk (16-28 year olds), www.rex.co.uk (for information technology contractors, etc.). Recruiters can sponsor the site's daily email for a fee.

Regional Help Wanted.com
www.regionalhelpwanted.com

1 Civic Center Plaza, Ste 506, Poughkeepsie, NY 12601
Ph: 800-365-8630   Fax: 845-485-8398   E-mail: customerservice@regionalhelpwanted.com

JOBS	1,000s		RESUMES	10,000s
Cost to post	Cost to see		Cost to post	Cost to see
Fee	Free		Free	Fee
DISCIPLINE			LOCATION	
ALL			INTL/Canada/USA	
SPECIALTY			FEATURE	
ALL			Gateway	
AGENT: Job Seeker				

RegionalHelpWanted.com launched May 1999, is a gateway that offers links to 252 niche, city-location sites. Employers pay $78 to post a job for 30 days which includes resume access. Each site posts the number of employers and resumes for that url. Recruiters who only want resume access pay $78 for a 30 day run. Sixteen of the 252 sites are in Canada. Each site typically has less than 100 jobs posted and all have direct contact information. The site claims that resumes that have not been updated after 90 days are deleted. The site produces radio spots customized to local area recruiter markets to promote job postings.

Regulatory Affairs Professionals Society
www.careerconnections.raps.org/

Hillary Ross
RAPS, 11300 Rockville Pike, Suite 10, Rockville, MD 20852
Ph: 3017702920   Fax: 3017702924   E-mail: raps@raps.org

JOBS	100s		RESUMES	100s
Cost to post	Cost to see		Cost to post	Cost to see
Fee	Free		Free	Fee
DISCIPLINE			LOCATION	
Science			USA	
SPECIALTY			FEATURE	
Regulatory Affairs			N/A	
AGENT: Jobseeker				

The Regulatory Affairs Professionals Society's CareerConnections area offers employers a 30 day posting for $250. Resume access is free with the posting. The site was around for several years but outsourced to Boxwood in 2002. Job seekers can see how often their resume was viewed. The site also offers salary info, graduate program info, professional development advice, and other career related info specifically geared toward a target RA audience.

Rent-a-Geek

www.rentageek.com

Kathleen E. Dodge
250 Major Street, Toronto, M5S 2L6 Canada
E-mail: info@rentageek.com

JOBS	N/A		RESUMES	1,000s
Cost to post	Cost to see		Cost to post	Cost to see
N/A	N/A		Free	Free
DISCIPLINE			LOCATION	
IT			INTL/Canada/USA	
SPECIALTY			FEATURE	
ALL			Contingent	
AGENT: N/A				

Rent-a-Geek offers recruiters an interactive directory to thousands of computer industry professionals. Employers can search by location, specialization, platforms, keywords or new listings. What you'll see, however, is a limited profile with contact data. There is no cost to view the data. The site has opportunities for advertisers, and recruiters should take advantage of this space. Not much new since CXR's last review.

Resunet

www.resunet.com

Jeff Williams
Ph: 800-266-0101   E-mail: resunet@resunet.com

JOBS	100s		RESUMES	10,000s
Cost to post	Cost to see		Cost to post	Cost to see
Free	Free		Free	Free
DISCIPLINE			LOCATION	
ALL			USA	
SPECIALTY			FEATURE	
ALL			N/A	
AGENT: N/A				

Career World and Resume World are the names Resunet uses to direct visitors to the site. This general site allows recruiters to view resumes and post jobs for free. Unfortunately, resumes are not date posted so recruiters have no idea if these people are even remotely still on the market. Openings run the gamut from art/design to transporation. We found over 17 accounting openings and 380 resumes under this title alone. All openings and resumes provide direct contact information.

Right Management Consultants, Inc.

www.right.com

1818 Market Street, Thirty-third floor, Philadelphia, PA 19103
Ph: 800-237-4448   Fax: 215-988-0081   E-mail: contactus@right.com

JOBS	100s	RESUMES	100s
Cost to post	Cost to see	Cost to post	Cost to see
Free	Fee (See Notes)	Fee (See Notes)	Free
DISCIPLINE		LOCATION	
ALL		USA	
SPECIALTY		FEATURE	
ALL		N/A	
AGENT: N/A			

Right Management Consultants (RMC) is an outplacement firm that offers helpful content on its site. Recruiters need to click on the site map and then Right's "resume bank" to find out how to connect. Sorry, no headhunters allowed in the resume database. Only RMC clients can view the posted openings or post their resume. Openings can be posted here, but they can only be seen by RMC's clients. Corporations can view candidate resumes once they register and are approved. Excerpts from organization studies conducted by RMC can be found here. Recruiters should contact the firm for complete copies.

RxCareerCenter.com

www.pharmacychoice.com

Steve Croke
1666 Race Street, Denver, CO 80206
Ph: 720-941-0705   Fax: 720-941-8485   E-mail: scroke@rxcareercenter.com

JOBS	1,000s	RESUMES	1,000s
Cost to post	Cost to see	Cost to post	Cost to see
Fee	Free	Free	Fee
DISCIPLINE		LOCATION	
Science/Health Care		USA	
SPECIALTY		FEATURE	
Pharmacy		Gateway	
AGENT: Job Seeker			

RXCareerCenter is the gateway to a network of Pharmacy related sites including PharmacyChoice, RXimmigration and RPhRecruiter. Just know that a couple of these are geared to 3rd party contingency fees. Launched in November 1999 the site allows job seekers to search by category, keyword or location. Openings can be viewed by date of posting, location, title and company. Job seekers can apply through the site or directly to the employer. Recruiters can post a job for $250 for a 60-day run. Access to the resume database costs $800.

sales heads

www.salesheads.com

Todd Miller
5909 NW Expressway, Suite 480, Oklahoma City, OK 73132
Ph: 866-244-4323   Fax: 405-722-0088   E-mail: admin@salesheads.com

JOBS	10,000s		RESUMES	100s
Cost to post	Cost to see		Cost to post	Cost to see
Fee	Free		Free	Fee
DISCIPLINE			LOCATION	
Prof. Sales & Marketing			USA	
SPECIALTY			FEATURE	
ALL			N/A	
AGENT: Both Recruiters & Jobseekers				

Salesheads has a patter to match its name. The site sends interesting and quirky emails each week to visitors who register. Recruiters pay $150 to post a job for 60 days. Access to the resume database and unlimited job posting is $350 per month. Other packages are available. Jobs (68,196) can be searched by keyword, date of posting, location, distance from home, company name or job category. When we searched under sales, we found 13,299 jobs! Site uses CareerCast technology so each search term is highlighted in yellow. Openings are date posted with contact information and job seekers will appreciate a feature allowing them to find "similar" positions.

SalesJobs.com

www.salesjobs.com

Eric Martinez
1624 Franklin Street Penthouse, Oakland, CA 94612
Ph: 510-291-5300   Fax: 510-291-5360   E-mail: info@salesjobs.com

JOBS	100s		RESUMES	1,000s
Cost to post	Cost to see		Cost to post	Cost to see
Fee	Free		Free	Fee
DISCIPLINE			LOCATION	
Prof. sales & Marketing			USA/	
SPECIALTY			FEATURE	
Sales			N/A	
AGENT: Jobseeker				

Originally launched in 1997, SalesJobs.com claims 1000 new postings a month and several thousand new resumes. Employers pay $250 to post and $299 to view the resume database. Site is affiliated with Recruit USA and IQ Post for its distribution. Site offers video resumes and an example can be found at www.salesjobs.com/unregistered/Example_resume.html. Sales Job seekers have the ability to define their job search by industry, state, and area code. Sales Jobs also offer a key word search. Once a list of sales positions pop's up, the job seeker can define his or her job search even further by Base Salary, Total Compensation, Position Title, Name of Company, Most recent date posted, etc.

Sales Rep Central.com

www.salesrepcentral.com

Sharon Summerlin
1800 Peachtree Street, Suite 333, Atlanta, GA 30309
Ph: 404.603.9631   Fax: 404.355.4910   E-mail: sharon@salesrepcentral.com

JOBS	10s		RESUMES	N/A
Cost to post	Cost to see		Cost to post	Cost to see
Free (See Notes)	Free		N/A	N/A
DISCIPLINE			LOCATION	
Prof. Sales & Marketing			USA	
SPECIALTY			FEATURE	
ALL			N/A	
AGENT: Job Seeker				

Gone out of recruiting business.

SalesRepCentral.com was launched in January 1999 and still seems to be a work in progress. This site gets it when it comes to thinking about the customer. Everything is here to build a community of sales professionals. It is engaging and filled with helpful resources. The site advises that their job board is returning in January 2003. For now, job seekers and recruiters should tap into "the community" area where a discussion board has openings posted for free. The site advises it has over 200,000 registered sales reps. Sales training, resources, links to tools all focus on bringing the audience back again and again and again. We miss their large colorful ads in airports. We look forward to their return.

TIP FOR RECRUITERS

Know your company product line, marketing programs, sales projections cold.

As a recruiter you are the #1 salesperson for your organization. The more knowledge you possess regarding your company the easier it will be to convince a candidate to work for your corporation.

Saludos.com
www.saludos.com

Trina Rachal
73-121 Fred Waring Drive, Suite 100, Palm Desert, CA 92260
Ph: 800-371-4456   Fax: 760-776-1214   E-mail: info@saludos.com

JOBS	100s		RESUMES	1,000s
Cost to post	Cost to see		Cost to post	Cost to see
Fee	Free		Free	Fee

DISCIPLINE		LOCATION
ALL		USA/WEST/CA

SPECIALTY		FEATURE
ALL		Diversity

AGENT: Job Seeker

Saludos Web is supported by the Saludos Hispanos magazine and this site's job board design is a model for the industry. The site provides great navigation with drop down menus that add significantly to its user friendliness. Job seekers can post their resumes for free and search jobs by location, category, internship or company. Selected jobs are then viewed in alpha order. All posted openings have complete job descriptions and direct contact information. Job seekers who register their email addresses and skills will have matched positions sent to their desktops. The cost to post a job is $99. Access to the resume database plus five job postings is $995 for two months. Recruiters can post a job and receive matching resumes via email. The site keywords can be purchased for $199. The owner's clear instructions on how to use this site are a welcome addition. Online job fairs and career articles round out this well-designed effort.

SciJobs.org

Carol Plautz
Ph: 304-725-9241   Fax: 304-725-9463   E-mail: feedback@scijobs.org

JOBS	10,000s	RESUMES	100s
Cost to post	Cost to see	Cost to post	Cost to see
Fee	Free	Free	Fee
DISCIPLINE		LOCATION	
Science		USA	
SPECIALTY		FEATURE	
Research/Biology/Chemistry		N/A	
AGENT: Job Seeker			

SciJobs.org targets scientists with considerable skill. Recruiters can post 10 jobs for $500 per month. The site appears to prefer to link all search results by driving candidates to corporate sites' job pages (indexing the jobs). The owners advise that they also go out to university, nonprofit, corporate sites and pull down research job links to their site each week. Recruiters can access the site's resume bank for $25 a week. Access is only given to employers- not headhunters. Recruiters may want to think about becoming a preferred employer to get their postings better position. Jobs can be emailed to registered subscribers (10,000+) who have requested the information. Recruiters pay $150 per e-alert. Openings are for post doctorates, bioinformatics/LIMS, scientific writers and professors/lecturers. Job seekers can search jobs using the site's engine or select employers of choice and hyperlink to the company employment page. Job seekers can now also choose new links/postings to the site.

SciWeb Career Center

Edward Jakobovits
2934 Beverly Glen Circle, #403, Bel Air, CA 90077
Ph: 310-860-0431   Fax: 707-598-1405   E-mail: webmaster@sciweb.com

JOBS	100s	RESUMES	1,000s
Cost to post	Cost to see	Cost to post	Cost to see
Fee	Free	Free	Fee
DISCIPLINE		LOCATION	
Science		USA	
SPECIALTY		FEATURE	
Research		Gateway	
AGENT: N/A			

Launched in 1996, SciWeb's Career Center and network sites www.biocareer.com, www.scijobs.com and scitalk.com offer employers two-month job postings for $150 or 10 postings with resume database access for $2,000 per year. Other packages are confusing. Jobs can be searched by company, location, job discipline, keyword or field of science. Openings are listed with lengthy job descriptions and direct contact information. Owners claim to have 6,391 science resumes in the database. Discussion boards and access to career and industry information will encourage the job seeker to return. This is an easy-to-use site with large print job descriptions for us older guys. Interesting industry articles will keep job seekers returning.

Science Careers
www.sciencecareers.org

Beth Dwyer
1200 NY Avenue N.W., 9th Floor, Washington, DC 20005
Ph: 202-326-6722   Fax: 202-289-1451   E-mail: bdwyer@aaas.org

JOBS	1,000s	RESUMES	1,000s
Cost to post	Cost to see	Cost to post	Cost to see
Fee	Free	Free	Fee

DISCIPLINE	LOCATION
Science	USA

SPECIALTY	FEATURE
Research	N/A

AGENT: Job Seeker

Science Careers, launched in 1996, is an important benefit for members of the American Association for the Advancement of Science (AAAS). Employers can post openings for $400 for a 4 week run. Job seekers will appreciate that each discipline provides the number of openings posted and advanced search capability. Science Careers typically sponsors four career fairs a year to attract pharmaceutical and biotechnology talent for their advertisers. Access to the resume database costs $600 for 1 week or $1,000 to view the 8,000+ resumes for a month. Over 15,000 scientists receive job alerts via email, and recruiters can target specific segments of this group for $1,200 or spend $2,500 to send a posting to all. An AAAS salary calculator with excellent resume assistance and negotiating articles rounds out this site.Employers wanting to target the scientific community should consider this a layup addition to their strategy..

Sciencejobs.com
www.sciencejobs.com

Lauren Hoops
Reed Elsevier, 275 Washington Street, Newton, MA 02458
Ph. 617-558-4904   Fax: 617-558-4933   E-mail: sales@sciencejobs.com

JOBS	1,000s	RESUMES	N/A
Cost to post	Cost to see	Cost to post	Cost to see
Fee	Free	N/A	N/A
DISCIPLINE		LOCATION	
Science		INTL/Europe	
SPECIALTY		FEATURE	
Bio/Chemistry/Biology		N/A	
AGENT: Job Seeker			

Sciencejobs.com is owned by the publishers of ChemWeb.com, BioMedNet, Cell and the NewScientist. Job seekers need to tailor their search for either bioscience or chemistry opportunities when they enter the site. Job posting cost $275 for corporations and $175 for academic/non-profits. Jobs will also be listed in New Scientist magazine. Openings can be searched by sector (industry, academic, government), discipline, location, date of posting or keyword. Openings are date posted with detailed descriptions and direct contact information. Job seekers should register for weekly email updates to their desktop. A resume database may be in the cards for the near future.

Scientific American.com
www.sciam.com/jobs/

Mina Lux
415 Madison Avenue, New York, NY 10017
Ph: 212-451-8328   Fax: 212-832-2998   E-mail: mlux@sciam.com

JOBS	100s	RESUMES	N/A
Cost to post	Cost to see	Cost to post	Cost to see
Fee	Free	N/A	N/A
DISCIPLINE		LOCATION	
Science		INTL	
SPECIALTY		FEATURE	
ALL		N/A	
AGENT: Job Seeker			

ScientificAmerican.com was launched in 1996, and offers the latest developments in biotechnology and a broad range of information about most scientific disciplines. Recruiters pay $375 to post an opening for a 60 day run. Job seekers who register (65,000) can have openings pushed to their PC. Registrants can also sign up for an email alert, "techbiz", to keep up on new trends in the industry. Openings can be searched by keyword, location, company or subject. Owners utilize CareerCast technology as each job search keyword submitted is highlighted in yellow for ease of viewing. The site is International. The site collects resumes butCXR found no resume database for recruiters to access. A little disclosure and a few more metrics wouldn't hurt.

SearchEase
www.searchease.com

David Hirsch
SearchEase Corporation, 2 Commerce Way, Norwood, MA 02062
Ph: 781-255-1212   Fax: 781-255-1212   E-mail: sales@searchease.com

JOBS	1,000s	RESUMES	10,000s
Cost to post	Cost to see	Cost to post	Cost to see
Free	Free	Free	Free
DISCIPLINE		LOCATION	
ALL		USA	
SPECIALTY		FEATURE	
ALL		N/A	
AGENT: Jobseeker			

SearchEase, launched in 1997 is a general site that claims as many as 5000 new postings each month. Reason of course is the site is free and participates in job distribution networks -Allinonesubmit, datafrenzy and webhire.

Seasonal Employment
www.seasonalemployment.com

Debbie Murtagh
PMB #6350,, 163 Rainbow Dr., Livingston, TX 77399
Ph: 406-226-9165   E-mail: orders@seasonalemployment

JOBS	1,000s	RESUMES	N/A
Cost to post	Cost to see	Cost to post	Cost to see
Fee	Free	N/A	N/A
DISCIPLINE		LOCATION	
Hospitality & Food Services/Retail		USA	
SPECIALTY		FEATURE	
Retail/Sports/Outdoors		Contingent/Summer/Seasonal	
AGENT: N/A			

Launched March 1999, the positions at seasonal employment are categorized as summer, winter, careers, jobs by state, company listings, featured employers and Canada. All locations listed have openings otherwise they are absent (CXR appreciates this customer service touch). Openings have links to the recruiter's site and include contact information. Job postings cost $30-$50 and they remain on the site until they are filled. One problem is that you can't search by job titles. Happy trails.

Security Jobs Network

www.securityjobs.net

Joanne Brennan
344 Maple Avenue West #413, Vienna, VA 22180
Ph: 866-767-5627   Fax: 703-995-4343   E-mail: info@securityjobs.net

JOBS	100s	RESUMES	N/A
Cost to post	Cost to see	Cost to post	Cost to see
Free	Fee	N/A	N/A
DISCIPLINE		LOCATION	
Law & Order/Government		USA	
SPECIALTY		FEATURE	
Risk/Security		N/A	
AGENT: N/A			

Security Jobs Network is looking for a few good people to provide investigative, contract security, consulting, executive protection, senior law enforcement or other "james bond" types of assistance. Recruiters can post positions for free. Job seekers pay $25-160 (13-52 weeks) to view posted openings.

TIP FOR RECRUITERS

Positions need to be looked at for job sharing and or part-time fulfillment.

The graying of America is happening and there will be less qualified workers than jobs.

Seek (Australia)

Matthews Rockman
Seek Communications, 3 Wellington Street, Level 3, Windsor, VIC, 3181 Australia
Ph: 610-395-1000011 Fax: 610-395-105209 E-mail:

JOBS	10,000s		RESUMES	10,000s
Cost to post	Cost to see		Cost to post	Cost to see
Fee	Free		Free	Fee

DISCIPLINE		LOCATION
ALL		INTL/Pacific Rim/Australia

SPECIALTY		FEATURE
ALL		College/Executive

AGENT: Job Seeker

Seek, owned by a newspaper publisher also has Yahoo among its investors. The site is Australia's strongest job site and is divided into "zones":executive.seek.com.au, campus.seek.com.au, volunteerseek.com.au and it.seek.com.au. The site has over 35,000 jobs posted to the main website. Recruiters can post positions for $99-$250 (Australian), depending on which zone is selected. Executive is $250 to post. Job packs with resume search access start at $360. My seek gives job seekers access to an application that keeps track of job submissions and accompanying cover letters and resumes. A long list of local headhunters, and career tips are available. CXR especially appreciated the extensive list of articles on "Being your own Boss". Job search strategies, career transition information and an "experts" panel that gives career advice via a Q & A section.

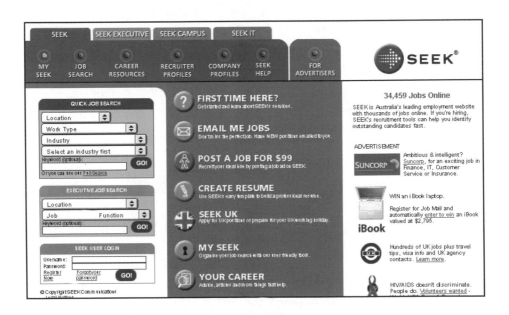

ShowBizJobs.com
www.showbizjobs.com

Jim Kocher
3579 E. Foothill Blvd PMB 526, Pasadena, CA 91107
Ph: 626-798-4533   E-mail: info@showbizjobs.com

JOBS	100s	RESUMES	1,000s
Cost to post	Cost to see	Cost to post	Cost to see
Fee	Free	Fee	Fee
DISCIPLINE		LOCATION	
Entertainment & Media		USA	
SPECIALTY		FEATURE	
ALL		N/A	
AGENT: N/A			

ShowBizJobs (SBJ) has a Hollywood set look to display its opportunities for the film, television, recording, multimedia and attractions job markets. Launched in 1995, SBJ only holds direct casting calls, no headhunters are allowed. Employers can post a job for $125 for a 30 day run. This includes access to the resume database and chat/message boards. Job seekers can select openings by company, job category, location, keyword, salary or posting date. Openings are distributed across many general categories that range from accounting to web development as well as all the jobs in the "biz." Job Seekers must pay ($35) to post their profiles for six months. Only in "show biz" would job seekers pay to play.

Smart Career Move
www.smartcareermove.com

Kerry Koonce
200 East Grand, Des Moines, IA 50309
Ph: 800-245-4692   Fax: 515-242-4776   E-mail: smartcareermove@ided.state.ia.us

JOBS	1,000s	RESUMES	1,000,000s
Cost to post	Cost to see	Cost to post	Cost to see
Fee	Free	Free	Fee
DISCIPLINE		LOCATION	
ALL		USA/MDW/IA	
SPECIALTY		FEATURE	
ALL		N/A	
AGENT: Job Seeker			

Smart Career Move gives job seekers access to Iowa corporations and information about work/life issues in the state. This site is a consortium of Iowa businesses, communities, educational institutions, professional associations and government. Thousands of jobs can be searched by keyword, community or company. Corporations pay $5,000-$10,000 per year for unlimited posting and access to the site's resume database. Job seekers can view openings by keyword, member company location or company name (great way for job seekers to get definite results). Check out the video on living, playing and working in Iowa. Internship links to corporations and career fair information is also available.

Snagajob.com

www.snagajob.com

Shawn Boyer
7151 Richmond Road, Williamsburg, VA 23188
Ph: 877-461-7624   Fax: 757-253-0672   E-mail: info@snagajob.com

JOBS	1,000s	RESUMES	100,000s
Cost to post	Cost to see	Cost to post	Cost to see
Fee	Free	Free	Fee (See Notes)
DISCIPLINE		LOCATION	
Hospitality & Food Services/Retail/		USA	
SPECIALTY		FEATURE	
ALL		College/Summer/High School	
AGENT: Both Recruiters & Jobseekers			

Snagajob.com targets high school and college students looking to find seasonal and part-time employment throughout the USA. Recruiters can post an opportunity for $175 for a one-month run. Pre-employment questions can be customized for each job opening. Recruiters can use an application manager capability of tracking applications for each location. The site has over 150,000 registered student emails to push jobs to with a sense of urgency. The owners do not have a searchable resume databas since part-timers and seasonal candidates are on the market for only a short period of time. Recruiters are notified when new students register at the site. Career counselors are also emailed when new employers come into their geographic area. Many of the fast food giants are featured employers on this site. Job seekers can search by commute distance.

Soc. for Automotive Engineers

www.sae.org

Jodie Mohnkern
400 Commonwealth Drive, Warrendale, PA
Ph: 724-776-4841   Fax: 724-776-5760   E-mail: advertising@sae.org

JOBS	1,000s	RESUMES	N/A
Cost to post	Cost to see	Cost to post	Cost to see
Fee	Free	N/A	N/A
DISCIPLINE		LOCATION	
Engineering		USA	
SPECIALTY		FEATURE	
Automotive		N/A	
AGENT: Jobseeker			

The Soc. for Automotive Engineers has nearly 80,000 members from 97 countries. Recruiters can post a position for $365 for 30 days. Access to the resume database costs $600 for 3 months. This organization will also provide recruiting inserts in related magazines. Recruiters can also email opportunities to members via the SAE monthly update newsletter. Only a handful of jobs were posted with direct contact information.

Society for Human Resource Management
www.shrm.org

1800 Duke Street, Alexandria, VA 22314
Ph: 800-283-7476   Fax: 703-535-6490   E-mail: hrjobs@shrm.org

JOBS	1,000s		RESUMES	N/A
Cost to post	Cost to see		Cost to post	Cost to see
Fee	Free		N/A	N/A
DISCIPLINE			LOCATION	
Human Resources			USA	
SPECIALTY			FEATURE	
ALL			N/A	
AGENT: Job Seeker				

The Society for Human Resource Management (SHRM) continues to lead the HR pack as a model for association sites on the web. The awards they've received, the results they achieve, and the site's Help Wanted contribution to SHRM's bottom line supports our opinion. Job listings that will eventually see print in the monthly tabloid HRNews are posted immediately to the Internet (few other print publications have yet to understand that sense of urgency). Positions can be viewed throughout the USA by location, keyword, or date of posting. Total openings by state can also be found. The cost to post a job is $20 per line, or $30 with a print version for a 30 day run. You do not have to be a member to view the job postings. However, only members can register to receive notification of new positions via email. Members have access to the membership directory, a great recruiting tool. With over 170,000 members, this is the first place to post a human resources opening. The second place is to check out the local chapter sites.

Software Contractors' Guild
www.scguild.com

David Keeney
PO Box 257, Nottingham, NH 03290
Ph: 603-895-9975   E-mail: admn@www.scguild.com

JOBS	100s		RESUMES	1,000s
Cost to post	Cost to see		Cost to post	Cost to see
Fee	Free		Fee	Free
DISCIPLINE			LOCATION	
IT			USA	
SPECIALTY			FEATURE	
Software/Programming			N/A	
AGENT: N/A				

The Software Contractor's Guild warehouses resumes of software contractors and claims close to 48,000 members worldwide. Job seekers pay $20 per year to post their resumes. For employers, resumes may be viewed for free, and the first two job postings after registration are free. Listing over two jobs costs $5 each for a 60-day run. Unlimited postings cost $200 per month. The site has chapters in Australia, Bulgaria, England, France, India and Israel, as well as seven in the US, but most jobs are US based (30 in Canada). Recruiters need to go where the job seekers meet and greet each other, this is the place.

Software Developer Careers (Dr Dobbs)
www.developercareers.com

CMP, 411 Borel Avenue, San Mateo, CA 94402
Ph: 650-513-4593   E-mail: jhamilton@cmp.com

JOBS	100s	RESUMES	1,000s
Cost to post	Cost to see	Cost to post	Cost to see
Fee	Free	N/A	N/A
DISCIPLINE		LOCATION	
IT		USA	
SPECIALTY		FEATURE	
Software/Developer		N/A	
AGENT: N/A			

Software Careers which includes CMP publications (Dr Dobbs Journal, MSDN Magazine, C/C++Users Journal, Software and Windows Developers Journals), have teamed up to post their combined positions on this site. Jobs can be searched by keyword and state. Positions are viewed by title, location and company name. For software professionals these are premier print publications. Online posting is $250. Recruiters should flock to post jobs here. Tech-engine is the host.

Space Careers
www.spacelinks.com/SpaceCareers/index.html

Pierre Oppetit
Les Terrasses du Golf 11, Suite A54 Rt. de Toulouse, Seilh, France
Ph: 440-149-1832671 Fax: 440-845-1274303 E-mail: webmaster@spacelinks.com

JOBS	100s	RESUMES	N/A
Cost to post	Cost to see	Cost to post	Cost to see
Free	Free	N/A	N/A
DISCIPLINE		LOCATION	
IT/Engineering		INTL/Europe/UK/Italy/France	
SPECIALTY		FEATURE	
Aerospace/Hardware		N/A	
AGENT: Job Seeker			

Space Careers was launched in August 1997. SC offers job opportunities and links to hundreds of corporation career pages. The site is designed to provide candidates with an opportunity to see openings worldwide in the space industry. Recruiters can post jobs for free, and all are date posted. The owners average 5,000 unique job seekers a month. Links to civil agencies, satellite manufacturers and operators, ground and launch systems, business services (financing, insurance etc.) and consulting/engineering services are available. The site's income is from selling banners, so services are free. Job seekers can register for a weekly job update emailed to their PC. Job seekers need to consider clicking the banners on this site as it is the space industry's who's who. "Beam me up, Scotty!".

Spacejobs

www.spacejobs.com

Jamie Hartling
84 Greenough Drive, Porters Lake, Nova Scotia B3E1L2 Canada
Ph: 888-366-6337   Fax: 902-827-4518   E-mail: sales@spacejobs.com

JOBS	1000s	RESUMES	1000s
Cost to post	Cost to see	Cost to post	Cost to see
Fee	Free	Free	Fee
DISCIPLINE		LOCATION	
Engineering		USA	
SPECIALTY		FEATURE	
Aerospace		N/A	
AGENT: Jobseeker			

Spacejobs.com (as well as aerojobs.com and aerospacejobs.com) claims to be a direct employment advertising channel to professionals in the aeronautics and space industries. SJ uses both e-mail and the World Wide Web to deliver employment ads straight to the desktops of potential employees. Site claims to have 12,000 job seeking subscribers. Employers are invited to fax, email or fill out an online form for $275. Demographics supplied suggest about 85% of the site's visitors and postings are from the USA. Job postings are limited to 300 words and posted for 60 days. Job seekers can search based on travel and salary as well as location and job criteria. Access to the site's resumé database costs $500 per month. Might as well shoot the moon..

StarChefs JobFinder

www.starchefs.com

Will Blunt
9 East 19th Street, 9th Floor, New York, NY 10003
Ph: 212-966-3775   Fax: 212-966-6644   E-mail: jobfinder@starchefs.com

JOBS	10s	RESUMES	100s
Cost to post	Cost to see	Cost to post	Cost to see
Fee	Free	Free	Fee
DISCIPLINE		LOCATION	
Hospitality & Food Services		USA	
SPECIALTY		FEATURE	
Restaurant/Chefs		N/A	
AGENT: Job Seeker			

StarChefs JobFinder, launched in 1997, is one of our four-star favorites. The site hosts delicious job opportunities in restaurants throughout the world. Executive chefs, pastry chefs, sous chefs and even culinary school instructors can all found here. Job listings are posted by date, as are resumes. Job seekers search by keyword, company, position or location but mustregister to obtain contact information. Recruiters pay $199 to post a position and obtain accessto the resume database for 45 days. The employer resource center serves up examples of theday-to-day human resources forms necessary to run any business. "Ask the Hospitality", a career expert feature, provides answers to employee questions. Everyone should check out the site's recipes, especially the 593 recipes for chocolate lovers.

StartupLynx

www.startuplynx.com

Martin Thisner
1036 Pinehurst Court, Concord, CA 94521
Ph: 510-388-5969   E-mail: info@startuplynx.com

JOBS	100s	RESUMES	1,000s
Cost to post	Cost to see	Cost to post	Cost to see
Fee	Free	Free	Fee
DISCIPLINE		LOCATION	
ALL		USA	
SPECIALTY		FEATURE	
ALL		Start-up	
AGENT: Job Seeker			

StartupLynx offers opportunities for entrepreneurs who like to work long hours, eat out of pizza boxes, and have IPO tattoos on various bodyparts. Oops, that was before the crash of 2,000. Actually, the site only includes companies that have recently received funding from an established VC firm. Recruiters can post an opening for 60 days for $75. Access to the resume database and unlimited postings start at $295 for 30 days. Openings can be searched by keyword, location, company, job category, investment stage, industry listing or age of company. Openings are date posted with contact information. Sample interview Q & A give job seekers an added edge. Job seekers can also take a "career quiz" to find out, what they want to do when they grow up.

StartupZone

www.startupzone.com

Charles Kim
26895 Aliso Creek Road, Suite, Aliso Viejo, CA 92656
Ph: 949-716-7535   Fax: 949-203-8594   E-mail: admin@startupzone.com

JOBS	100s	RESUMES	100s
Cost to post	Cost to see	Cost to post	Cost to see
Fee	Free	Free	Fee
DISCIPLINE		LOCATION	
Miscellaneous		USA	
SPECIALTY		FEATURE	
ALL		Start-ups	
AGENT: N/A			

Launched in 2000, StartupZone charges $75 to post a job and $150 to review resumes. Site has an additional service called "ListZone". ListZone is an extended database of VC funded startup companies in the technology industry. List Zone provides a platform through which startups can promote themselves to potential employees, job seekers can find thousands of VC backed startups. The company information is listed by industry, business type, location andfunding stage.

Stern Alumni Job Listings

www.stern.nyu.edu/alumni

44 West Fourth Street, Suite 10-190, New York, NY 10012
Ph: 212-998-4040   Fax: 212-995-4515   E-mail: alumni@stern.nyu.edu

JOBS	10s	RESUMES	N/A
Cost to post	Cost to see	Cost to post	Cost to see
Free	Free	N/A	N/A (See Notes)
DISCIPLINE		LOCATION	
ALL		USA	
SPECIALTY		FEATURE	
ALL		Executive	
AGENT: N/A			

NYU Stern School of Business serves 60,000 alumni in 98 countries. CXR continues to point to the Stern School's job pages and alumni career programs because they offer more value than most job boards. Where did you graduate? What is their alumni office doing for you - other than asking for the check?

Subcontract.com

www.subcontract.com

Ph: 888-754-1874   E-mail: customerservice@subcontract.com

JOBS	1,000s	RESUMES	1,000s
Cost to post	Cost to see	Cost to post	Cost to see
Fee	Fee	Fee	Fee
DISCIPLINE		LOCATION	
ALL		USA	
SPECIALTY		FEATURE	
ALL		3rd party staffing exchange	
AGENT: Jobseeker			

Subcontract.com's services provide a workable platform for 10,000 (claimed) suppliers and buyers of staffing talent and contingency labor. The site Staffing Exchange is offered primarily through the Applicant Tracking Systems of its partners which presently include Rezkeeper, Ecruiter, Icarian, Pure Carbon and SonicRecruit. The company recently reported that in excess of 20,000 candidates had been contracted through its services since 2001. The home page lists the number of candidates placed and positions filled for the previous week. "Buyers" and "Suppliers" are each charged $295 per quarter for the service. Definitely one to watch.

Systems Administration Guild

www.usenix.org/sage

Gale Berkowitz
2560 Ninth Street, Suite 215, Berkeley, CA 94710
Ph: 510-528-8649   Fax: 510-548-5738   E-mail: gale@usenix.org

JOBS	100s	RESUMES	100s
Cost to post	Cost to see	Cost to post	Cost to see
Free	Fee	Fee	Free
DISCIPLINE		LOCATION	
IT		USA	
SPECIALTY		FEATURE	
Systems Administration		N/A	
AGENT: N/A			

Systems Administration Guild allows recruiters to post jobs for free to this site. Job seekers have to be members of the guild to view opportunities. Members can post a brief profile with direct contact information which anyone can view. Membership to USENIX is $95 and SAGE is an additional $30. A list of local chapters can also be accessed. SAGE certification, conferences and print publications make this the place to be.

Talent4europe.com

www.talent4europe.com

Bernhard von WEYHE
c/o Cadres Online, 38, rue du Hameau, Paris, 75014 Paris
Ph: 003-314-4250682 E-mail: talent4europe@cadresonline.net

JOBS	1,000s	RESUMES	1,000s
Cost to post	Cost to see	Cost to post	Cost to see
Fee	Free	Free	Fee
DISCIPLINE		LOCATION	
ALL		INTL/Europe	
SPECIALTY		FEATURE	
ALL		N/A	
AGENT: N/A			

Talent4Europe is a pan-European recruitment portal consisting of a network of 15 jobsites and newspaper groups. Participating countries that Talent4Europe has allied itself with include:Belgian Vacature.com and Le Soir-References, sueddeutsche.de/jobcenter, Danish and Swedish Jobfinder, English Guardian Unlimited Jobs, French Cadres Online, Italian La Repubblica, Finnish Uratie, The Irish Independent, Luxemburgish Tageblatt Jobs, Spanish El Pais, Greek Ta Nea and Dutch ClickWork among others. All members of this network belong to national newspaper groups and play a key role in recruitment, both in print and online.

TaxTalent.com
www.tax-talent.com

John O'Neill
TaxTalent.com, Inc., 2205 Middle Street, Ste. 207, Sullivan's Island, SC 29482
Ph: 918-451-3360   Fax: 425-732-1882   E-mail: john@tax-talent.com

JOBS	10s	RESUMES	1,000s
Cost to post	Cost to see	Cost to post	Cost to see
Fee	Free	Free	Fee
DISCIPLINE		LOCATION	
Business		USA	
SPECIALTY		FEATURE	
Tax		Gateway	
AGENT: Jobseeker			

Launched early 2001, TaxTalent offers employers postings for $199 for 60 days. Salary comparisons, mentoring services, job agents and a career forum are available for job seekers. Openings are date posted. Site owns several other URLs including www.taxjobs.com; www.unclefed.com; www.ecommercetax.com; www.statetaxweb.com. eQuest, GoJobs, HodesIQ and WhotoChoose distribute jobs to the site. Only 50 jobs were posted at the time of our visit.

TCM's HR Careers
www.tcm.com

Eric Snyder
TCM Internet Services, 64 Thare Crescent, Nepean, Ontario, Canada K2J 2P6 Canada
Ph: 613-823-0244   Fax: 815-846-9367   E-mail: egs@TCM.com

JOBS	10s	RESUMES	1,000s
Cost to post	Cost to see	Cost to post	Cost to see
Fee	Free	Free	Free (See Notes)
DISCIPLINE		LOCATION	
Human Resources		USA & INTL/Canada	
SPECIALTY		FEATURE	
Training/Compensation		N/A	
AGENT: Job Seeker			

TCM's HR Careers was launched in 1995. It is a niche site for full-time and contract human resource, training, multimedia and instructional design professionals. Recruiters pay $100 per month to advertise a position that is also pushed to the site's 5,000 members. Subscriptions to TCM's 1,400+ resume database are available to employers for $200 per month. Recruiters who register can have resumes pushed to their desktops for free for human resources/TD professionals. (The resumes are from professionals who have paid for TCM's services). What makes TCM unique is the lengthy list of links to human resource/training and e-learning related resources. Hundreds of products and links are available. Job seekers can subscribe to an agent to receive email notification of new openings. TCM also provides resume services. JobGrabber will source 20+ sites for human resources openings for $25 per month. TCM is always looking for new technologies to add to this site.

Teachers Online

www.teachersonline.com

Jack Zaccaria
1700 Route 23 North, Wayne, NJ 07470
Ph: 877-832-2488   Fax: 732-282-1203   E-mail: sales@teachersonline.com

JOBS	100s	RESUMES	100s
Cost to post	Cost to see	Cost to post	Cost to see
Fee	Free	Free	Fee
DISCIPLINE		LOCATION	
Education		USA	
SPECIALTY		FEATURE	
Teaching/K-12		N/A	
AGENT: Both Recruiters & Jobseekers			

Teachers Online was launched in July 1999. Recruiters pay $49 to post a position for a 60-day run. A total of $99 buys a posting and access to the resume database for 60 days. Openings are for teachers, substitute teachers, teacher aids, tutors and home schooling personnel. The site claims over 7,000 registered teachers. Employers who post openings will be emailed when matching resumes are found in the database. Teachers are also emailed when posted jobs match their criterion. Jobs can be searched by keyword, date of posting, grade one wants to teach, salary, location or certification required. Job seekers can save searches for later viewing. This site deserves an apple.

Teachers-Teachers.com

www.teachers-teachers.com

P.O. Box 2519, Columbia, MD 21045
Ph: 877-812-4071   Fax: 509-752-6036   E-mail: schools@teacher-teachers.com

JOBS	1,000s	RESUMES	1,000s
Cost to post	Cost to see	Cost to post	Cost to see
Fee	Free	Free	Fee
DISCIPLINE		LOCATION	
Education		USA/	
SPECIALTY		FEATURE	
Teaching, K-12		N/A	
AGENT: N/A			

Teachers-Teachers.com charges schools $950 per year for unlimited jobs and access to resumes. Supported by several professional associations, this site has done its homework and offers the connections for those who seek to teach.

TechEmployment.com
www.techemployment.com

Matthew Hollingsworth
9775 Pawnee Pass, Dayton, OH 45458
Ph: 937-885-9339   E-mail: service@techemployment.com

JOBS	1,000s		RESUMES	10,000s
Cost to post	Cost to see		Cost to post	Cost to see
Fee	Free		Free	Fee
DISCIPLINE			LOCATION	
IT/Engineering			USA	
SPECIALTY			FEATURE	
ALL			N/A	
AGENT: Both Recruiters & Jobseekers				

Post your message or question on the discussion board at TechEmployment.com, or start your own discussion group. Chat in real time with colleagues at the community center. TechEmployment.com is building content for the information technology, information systems, technology development and computer engineering communities. Recruiters pay $120 to post a job and have resume access for 1 month. Employers can have a two week free trial offer to post up to 10 jobs and access the resume database 10 times. Jobs are date posted with job description and salary range. Added value includes an archive of professional tools, technical and even humorous content as well as the ability to research employers and technology subjects. Links to assessment, resume writing and other career skills are also available.

TIP FOR RECRUITERS

As a recruiter always be open to trying new technologies.

Recruiting has come a far stretch from paper resumes and in the near future they will totally disappear. Applicant profiles, agent technology, resume spiders are areas to embrace not hide from.

tech-engine.com
www.tech-engine.com

Will Warwick
Workstream, 352 Seventh Avenue, New York, NY 10001
Ph: 212-379-8300   Fax: 212-631-7542   E-mail: will.warwick@workstream.com

JOBS	1,000s		RESUMES	100,000s
Cost to post	Cost to see		Cost to post	Cost to see
Fee	Free		Free	Fee
DISCIPLINE			LOCATION	
IT			USA	
SPECIALTY			FEATURE	
ALL			N/A	
AGENT: Job Seeker				

Tech-Engine Career Network is a gateway to a family of sites all owned by Workstream. Recruiters pay $250 to own a job posting slot for 30 days. Openings will also be posted to 300 other affiliated sites in this network but the url's are not disclosed (If a job is filled before the period ends another can be put in its place for free). Recruiters pay $400 per month for 3 job slots and access to the resume database. Jobs can be searched by company, location, job title, industry, keyword or the use of boolean terms. Short cut searches can be done by pre-placed links to technical areas of interest. Jobs are date posted and the number of openings found is listed on each search page. Job seekers must register to apply for openings. A listing of IT user groups can be found for networking. Site receives 6-7,000 resumes a month but does not delete any of the resumes in the database. Company also does recruiting research but is not in the headhunting business. Tech-Engine with it's volume and connections to workstream is one to watch for the future.

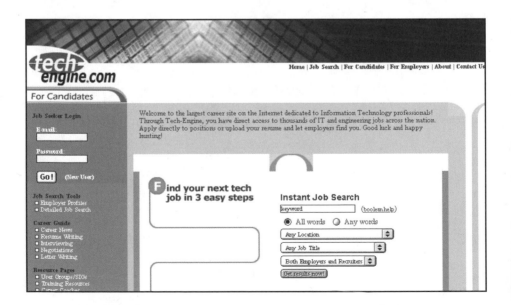

Techies .com

www.techies.com

Stan Berizzi
7580 Quattro Drive, Chanhassen, MN 55317
Ph: 800-829-3424   Fax: 952-253-5475   E-mail: mail@techies.com

JOBS	1,000s	RESUMES	10,000s
Cost to post	Cost to see	Cost to post	Cost to see
Fee	Free	Free	Fee
DISCIPLINE		LOCATION	
IT		USA	
SPECIALTY		FEATURE	
ALL		N/A	
AGENT: Both Recruiters & Jobseekers			

Techies.com would like to be in every major city in the USA, and claims to be in 39. The site claims 500,000 monthly unique IT visitors. Recruiters pay $295 for a single job posting in one job market and $695 to access the resume database for 60 days. Job seekers can view openings, but must register before they can apply for a position. Agent matching is the site's strength and its weakness. The site's "Hiring Alert" is an attempt to sell job seekers online self assessment at $74.99. Openings provide employer profiles with indepth information. Applicants can update their skills to fit the specific position. This is a niche site with strong potential that last its way on the road to IPO.

Teens4Hire

www.Teens4Hire.com

Renee Ward
The Forward Group, 7451 Warner Ave E245, Huntington Beach, CA 92647
Ph: 714-848-0996   Fax: 714-848-5445   E-mail: rbw@the4wardgroup.com

JOBS	1,000s	RESUMES	1,000s
Cost to post	Cost to see	Cost to post	Cost to see
Fee	Free	Free	Fee
DISCIPLINE		LOCATION	
ALL		USA	
SPECIALTY		FEATURE	
ALL		College/High School	
AGENT: Jobseeker			

Teens4Hire, a national online job matching service for U.S. teenagers and employers who hire them, launched in the summer of 2002. This is a free service for teenagers. It offers excellent disclosure and includes alliances with teen magazine publishers. Teenagers (14-19) can create a profile, search for job openings from local and national employers and apply directly online to employers of choice. Employers of teens are invited to advertise all suitable job openings for a $29 fee for 60 days. The site accepts all types of job openings; full-time, part-time, seasonal, temporary, vocational, apprentice, intern, volunteer, military etc. Site offers kids the basic career advice they really need to compete in todays cometpive job market.

telecomcareers.net
www.telecomcareers.net

Billy Trepagnier
2424 Edenborn Avenue, Suite 216, Metairie, LA 70001
Ph: 888-215-2537   Fax: 504-219-0098   E-mail: info@telecomcareers.net

JOBS	1,000s	RESUMES	10,000s
Cost to post	Cost to see	Cost to post	Cost to see
Fee	Free	Free	Fee
DISCIPLINE		LOCATION	
IT		USA	
SPECIALTY		FEATURE	
Communications/Telecom		N/A	
AGENT: Both Recruiters & Jobseekers			

Telecomcareers.net offers extensive capabilities for employers to post jobs, create agents that match resumes and track candidate activities. The site also has great links to telecom-related associations. Recruiters pay $125 to post a position and conduct 3 searches of the resume database. Access to the resume database for 3 months is $1250. Job seekers search by industry, location or by using keyword boolean logic. Openings are posted by date, company, title and location and have direct contact information. Job seekers can set up a search agent tohave openings sent to their PC. A telecom dictionary for lay persons who do not know the industry lingo is a super idea.

Telecommuting Jobs
www.tjobs.com

Sol Levine
126 Pinehurst Dr, Mundelein, IL
Ph: 847-835-2180   Fax: 847-835-2183   E-mail: contact@tjobs.com

JOBS	100s	RESUMES	1,000s
Cost to post	Cost to see	Cost to post	Cost to see
Free	Free	Fee	Free
DISCIPLINE		LOCATION	
ALL		USA	
SPECIALTY		FEATURE	
ALL		Telecommuting	
AGENT: N/A			

Launched in 1996, Telecommuting Jobs targets telecommuters and offsite workers. The site also suggests ways that workers can prepare themselves for telecommuting, and impress employers with their value as offsite workers. Solid content on how to profit by employing offsite workers is also available. Job seekers can post brief profiles with links to their site or online resumes for $10 per year. Recruiters can post positions for 60 days, and view job seekers' profiles for free. Resumes are coded, but recruiters can respond to candidates directly via email. Privacy is king. Resumes run the gamut and include:artists, data entry, desktop publishers, engineers, photographers, programmers, sales, web designers and writers.

TheSquare

www.thesquare.com

Joe Campanella
OurSquare, Inc., 24 W. 40th Street, 12th Floor, NY, NY 10018
Ph: 800-546-0816   Fax: 212-768-8309   E-mail: joec@thesquare.com

JOBS	10s	RESUMES	N/A
Cost to post	Cost to see	Cost to post	Cost to see
Fee	Free	N/A	N/A
DISCIPLINE		LOCATION	
ALL		USA/	
SPECIALTY		FEATURE	
ALL		Executive	
AGENT: Jobseeker			

Launched in late 1997, TheSquare is a premium priced product for what many perceive as a premium quality audience. TheSquare claims that nearly 70,000 alumni from 23 "tier 1" schools have registered for various opt in community networking services. The site's job board features an email alert. Employer posting packages start with 5 job postings for $1500 each. All members of this community have been veted as having graduated from the colleges they claim. TheSquare reaches the alumni through ads placed in the colleges' alumni magazines. Colleges include:Amherst, Berkeley, Brown, Caltech, Cambridge, Cornell, Dartmouth, Duke, Harvard, MIT, Northwestern, Oxford, Princeton, Stanford, Swarthmore, UChicago, UPenn, UVA, Welleseley, Williams and Yale.

Titleboard.com

www.titleboard.com

Julie Messina
3916 Sepuleeda Blvd., Culver City, CA 90230
Ph: 877-846-5478   Fax: 866-452-8799   E-mail: jobhelp@theboardnetwork.com

JOBS	1,000s	RESUMES	1,000,000s
Cost to post	Cost to see	Cost to post	Cost to see
Fee	Free	Free	Fee
DISCIPLINE		LOCATION	
Retail Sales & Services		USA	
SPECIALTY		FEATURE	
Real Estate/Mortgage/Escrow		N/A	
AGENT: Job Seeker			

Titleboard.com was launched in November 1999, and concentrates on title, escrow, mortgage and banking opportunities. The site is part of a small network that includes escrowboard.com, mortgageboard.net and bankingboard.com. The owners also have a third-party employment and temporary agency, and state that these are separate businesses. Job seekers need to register to view the site. Recruiters pay $179 to post a position for 60 days. Resume viewing and unlimited job posting packages run from $399 - $699 per month. Headhunters who purchase packages are limited to 250 resumes per day. Total openings by job function are posted for ease of viewing. The owners claim over 1,630 resumes. Job seekers submitting a resume should always check the privacy statement at a site owned by an agency (if not EVERY site where you provide personal information).

Top Echelon
www.topechelon.com

Toby Thomas
800 Market Avenue N., Canton, OH 44702
Ph: 330-455-1433   Fax: 330-455-8813   E-mail: info@TopEchelon.com

JOBS	100,000s		RESUMES	100,000s
Cost to post	Cost to see		Cost to post	Cost to see
Fee	Free		Free	Fee

DISCIPLINE		LOCATION
ALL		USA

SPECIALTY		FEATURE
ALL		3rd Party Staffing Exchange

AGENT: N/A

Top Echelon's network has 2,365 agency recruiters ready and willing to share resumes and split fees. This data is proudly displayed on the site's homepage. This service is only open to third-party recruiting firms. There are different levels of service from the web which start at $69 per month for an affiliate membership. The site claims to acquire 25,000-30,000 resumes a month via spider, and resumes are kept for six months. Corporate recruiters can search the resume database (46,044) for free, but candidate contact information is coded. Headhunters will be happy to help you. Members can utilize other web-based tools and job posting services to multiple sites. The site claims over 702,599 passive candidates in it's database (isn't everyone?). The owners claim to post jobs to as many as 5,718 websites. If a placement is made, the agency owes Top Echelon a fee. Job seekers must have an online profile prior to applyijng for an opening. Top Echelon has done well in continuing to build a viable model to support third-party recruiters on the web.

totaljobs.com
www.totaljobs.com

Andrew Griffin
Quadrant House, Sutton,, Surrey, SM2 5AS United Kingdom
Ph: 020-865-24535   E-mail: sales@totaljobs.com

JOBS	10,000s		RESUMES	10,000s
Cost to post	Cost to see		Cost to post	Cost to see
Fee	Free		Fee	Free
DISCIPLINE			LOCATION	
ALL			INTL/Europe/UK/Scotland/Wales	
SPECIALTY			FEATURE	
ALL			N/A	
AGENT: Both Recruiters & Jobseekers				

Totaljobs.com immediately advises job seekers that there are 29,606 openings posted. Employers can post jobs and retrieve resumes. Job seekers can view openings that range from accountants to travel agents. Each job category displays the number of openings by job function, and can also be searched by location. Jobs are date posted with contact information.Job seekers can add openings to their personal files for later viewing. an A-Z listing of headhunters is also available Recruiters pay £250 for one position or £2,000 for unlimited job postings per month. Access to the CV database is £2,000 per month. Job fairs and a lengthy list of hiring employers make this site one for job seekers to visit. Well designed and easy to navigate.

Trade Jobs Online
trades.buildfind.com/

Frederick Hornberger
3740 East Orchard Road, Littleton, CO 80121
Ph: 877-645-7730   Fax: 720-489-0556   E-mail: webmaster@aecjobbank.com

JOBS	100s		RESUMES	100s
Cost to post	Cost to see		Cost to post	Cost to see
Free	Free		Free	Free
DISCIPLINE			LOCATION	
Trades, Non-exempt & Hourly			INTL/Canada/USA	
SPECIALTY			FEATURE	
Construction/Mechanic/Electrician/Plumber			Hourly	
AGENT: N/A				

Trade Jobs Online remains a free site for job seekers and employers.. Employers can search resumes by job title, keyword, trade, experience, minimum hourly rate, location and or union membership. New listings can be found by clicking on the jobs link. Registration is simple, but this site provides a unique password (which no one will remember to view jobs or resumes). The site is part of industry portal "buildfind," and is managed by AEC Job Bank. Resumes and open jobs are all over the USA.

11600 Sallie Mae Drive, Reston, VA 20193
Ph: 800-441-4062   E-mail: truecareers@salliemae.com

JOBS	10,000s	RESUMES	100,000s
Cost to post	Cost to see	Cost to post	Cost to see
Fee	Free	Free	Fee

DISCIPLINE	LOCATION
ALL	USA

SPECIALTY	FEATURE
ALL	College

AGENT: Job Seeker

TrueCareers is the creation of Sallie Mae, a quasi-government service that manages student college loans. True careers logic stems from the fact that students who get jobs are more likely to pay off their loans. The logic stops there but the service has built a solid following in part based on access to millions of students during their senior year Launched in September 2001 recruiters pay $195 to post an opening for a 30-day run which includes access to the resume database. Openings can be viewed by job category, keyword, location, or date of posting. TC will also identify, pre screen and interview candidates for a fee. TC has partnered with wetfeet.com to provide career articles. The site claims to have over 1 million resumes. This site has ramped up quickly as a player and offers more than college opportunities since the average person in their database has at least 5 years experience.

TV Jobs

www.tvjobs.com

Mark C. Holloway
P.O.Box 4116, Oceanside, CA 92052
Ph: 760-754-8177   Fax: 760-754-2115   E-mail: markch@tvjobs.com

JOBS	1,000s		RESUMES	1,000s
Cost to post	Cost to see		Cost to post	Cost to see
Free	Fee		Fee	Free
DISCIPLINE			LOCATION	
Entertainment & Media/Communication			USA	
SPECIALTY			FEATURE	
Broadcasting			N/A	
AGENT: N/A				

Launched in 1995, TV Jobs keeps the airwaves humming for broadcast professionals. Openings include positions for associate producers, freelancers and researchers. Recruiters post positions and view the site resume database for free once they register. The site has 375 job bank links and 75 job line phone numbers. Job seekers must pay $50 (per year) to post their resumes. Access to view job posting is $20 per year. Students can view openings for free and are advised to save their money for beer. The site will monitor up to three job categories so that when a job seeker returns, he or she is advised of matching openings. We really do wish someone would replace the big 3 on the evening news.

TVSpy.com

www.tvspy.com

Ed Shen
Vault.com, 150 W. 22nd Street, 5th Floor, NY, NY 10011
Ph: 212-366-4212   Fax: 212-366-6117   E-mail: jobs@tvspy.com

JOBS	10s		RESUMES	100s
Cost to post	Cost to see		Cost to post	Cost to see
Free	Free		Free	Fee
DISCIPLINE			LOCATION	
Entertainment & Media			USA	
SPECIALTY			FEATURE	
Radio & TV Broadcast			N/A	
AGENT: Jobseeker				

Quirky network of Vault offers postings for $125 (2 weeks) and access to the resume database for $199 (3 months). Started as an underground newsletter before the web, the site launched a job board in 1997 and then partnered with vault.com to offer enhanced services including an audio resume. Content is the key to the attraction of pros in the business and opportunities here, while limited, are on target.

Ultrasoundjobs.com
www.ultrasoundjobs.com

George Junginger
1251 NW Maynard Road; #343, Cary, NC 27513
Ph: 410-628-5820   Fax: 410-628-0398   E-mail: ultrasoundjobs@networkpub.com

JOBS	100s	RESUMES	1,000s
Cost to post	Cost to see	Cost to post	Cost to see
Fee	Free	Free	Fee
DISCIPLINE		LOCATION	
Health Care		USA	
SPECIALTY		FEATURE	
Allied/Radiology		N/A	
AGENT: Jobseeker			

Ultrasoundjobs.com provides employers with postings for $200 and access to their resume database for $75 per resume. Ultrasoundjobs.com claims it is the exclusive internet recruitment partner to the ARDMS (American Registry of Diagnostic Medical Sonographers). This is the only organization that certifies ultrasound professionals. Out of the 36,000 certified ARDMS members, 24,300 are currently registered on Ultrasoundjobs.com. This would make it a dominant niche resource.

Unix Ugu Universe
www.ugu.com

Admin Labs, PO Box 802951, Santa Clarita, CA 91380
Fax: 801-469-6758   E-mail: info@ugu.com

JOBS	100s	RESUMES	100s
Cost to post	Cost to see	Cost to post	Cost to see
Free	Free	Free	Free
DISCIPLINE		LOCATION	
IT		USA	
SPECIALTY		FEATURE	
Unix		N/A	
AGENT: N/A			

Unix Ugu Universe is now a free site for the recruitment game. The site has been set up for Unix administrators to assist each other when seeking a new position. Recruiters can post as many positions for Unix professionals as they want for 30 days for free. Resumes by specialty or location can be viewed for free with contact information.

US Jobs.Com
www.usjobs.com

Thomas McGoldrick
PO Box 1287, Middleton, MA 01949
Ph: 978-750-9998   E-mail: tom@usjobs.com

JOBS	1,000s		RESUMES	100,000s
Cost to post	Cost to see		Cost to post	Cost to see
Fee	Free		Free	Fee
DISCIPLINE			LOCATION	
ALL			USA	
SPECIALTY			FEATURE	
ALL			N/A	
AGENT: Job Seeker				

US Jobs.com (formerly BostonSearch.com), if their name is any guide, plans to expand their niche location network. Recruiters pay $85 per job posting for a 45-day run. Resume database access is $100 per month. If the opening is filled before the time is up recruiters can add another job for the balance of the time. The price includes three categories on one specific regional site. The site has a presence in the following locations:Atlanta, Bay area, Boston, Chica go, Dallas, DC Metro area, Denver, Los Angeles, Minnesota/St. Paul, New York, Philadelphia and Seattle. Openings can be searched by type (regular/contract), category, location or keyword. All jobs are date posted with direct contact information. The owners are in the sourcing/headhunting business and they provide research services at $1,500 per assignment. CXR gives them credit as they fully disclose their business model

USA Today Careers Network
career.usatoday.com

Gannett, Ph: 888-533-4433   E-mail: help@usatodaycareers.com

JOBS	100,000s		RESUMES	100,000s
Cost to post	Cost to see		Cost to post	Cost to see
Fee	Free		Free	Fee
DISCIPLINE			LOCATION	
ALL			USA	
SPECIALTY			FEATURE	
ALL			N/A	
AGENT: Both Recruiters & Jobseekers				

Gannett, one of the country's largest publishers has now built its national network of job sites through its flagship property, USA Today. The owners have also invested $100 million in early Fall, 2002 in order to gain access to the CareerBuilder network of sites. A total of 90 newspapers are included within USA Today's network and with CB it will be over 130. Today,the USA Today Careers Network, ranges from the Arizona Republic to the West Virginia HeraldDispatch. Job seekers can roam the any of the network sites and search openings from the classified pages of every site. Jobs posted directly by an employer ($125 for 30 days) are posted to ALL sites. Serivces also include having jobs scraped from the company web pages. Openings are posted with title, company name, location and date. Jobs can be saved for futureviewing. A month of access to the resumes (200,000) is $300. Our view of the CB merger is that it will take some doing to resolve differences between the two models.

Vault.Com
www.vault.com

Thomas Nutt
150 W. 22nd Street, 5th Floor, NY, NY 10011
Ph: 888-562-82858   E-mail: marketing@staff.vault.com

JOBS	10,000s	RESUMES	100,000s
Cost to post	Cost to see	Cost to post	Cost to see
Fee	Free	Free	Fee
DISCIPLINE		LOCATION	
ALL		USA	
SPECIALTY		FEATURE	
ALL		N/A	
AGENT: Both Recruiters & Jobseekers			

VAULT.com is the "mosh pit" of the job board world (although "I resign" and another site we can't even spell here might give it a run for its money). Company gossip on the web is definitely a no holds barred experience. Employees (current and former) are encouraged to post comments (797,748 have) about what it is like to work in their company. Prospective candidates can research openings by location, industry, function or keyword. The site currently has 35,614 jobs posted. The minimum cost to recruiters is $75 to post 1 job for 60 days. Resume database access and 3 job slots costs $199 for 30 days. Industry-specific job boards have been created in consulting, finance, MBA and law. Vault will also cross-post openings to multiple sites. Ask the expert columns can be found for human resources professionals in many categories. Interesting career articles abound here, and the site sells career guides to job seekers and research reports to companies. CXR appreciated the "strange HR tales". Hopefully they will get rid of the annoying ads that continually pop-up. Site is well designed and continues to add new features.

Vet Jobs

www.vetjobs.com

Ted Daywalt
PO Box 71445, Marietta, GA 30007
Ph: 770-565-3221   Fax: 770-565-3238   E-mail: info@vetjobs.com

JOBS	10,000s		RESUMES	10,000s	
Cost to post	Cost to see		Cost to post	Cost to see	
Fee	Free		Free	Fee	
DISCIPLINE			LOCATION		
ALL			USA		
SPECIALTY			FEATURE		
ALL			Military Transition		
AGENT: N/A					

Vet Jobs was launched on Veterans Day 1999 by Ted Daywalt, a frequent contributor to employment discussion groups and a veteran himself. Corporations can access the resume database for $2,400. Individual job postings are listed for $150 for as long as an employer wishes. The site caters to transitioning military veterans and their spouses. Jobs can be searched by date of posting, keyword, category or location. All openings are date posted with links to the corporate site and multiple ways for job seekers to apply. Job seekers should check out "tips on conducting your search" for an excellent explanation on boolean operators. The site has excellent connections to the military transition market and strong staying power. Give Vet Jobs a try.

VolunteerMatch

www.volunteermatch.org

Jason Willett
385 Grove Street, San Francisco, CA 94102
Ph: 415-241-6868   Fax: 415-241-6869   E-mail: jwillett@volunteermatch.org

JOBS	1,000s		RESUMES	N/A	
Cost to post	Cost to see		Cost to post	Cost to see	
Free	Free		N/A	N/A	
DISCIPLINE			LOCATION		
Non-Profit			USA		
SPECIALTY			FEATURE		
ALL			N/A		
AGENT: N/A					

VolunteerMatch brings volunteers together with nonprofit organizations. If it is time to give something back, sign up online and check out the suggested assignments in cities throughout the U.S. Volunteers only need to input their zip code, the site does the rest. Opportunities are displayed by date of posting, with codes that reflect if they are for kids, teens, seniors or groups. There are over 22,588 organizations listed with over 42,000 opportunities. The site also has an email newsletter to keep you up-to-date on this organization. Entrepreneural owners of the site make their money by licensing a private version with their database of volunteer opportunities to large corporations.

Washington Post [Washington Jobs]

www.washingtonpost.com

Mary Mostlander
1515 North Courthouse Road, Arlington, VA 22201
Ph: 703-469-2676   E-mail: jobs@washingtonpost.com

JOBS	10,000s		RESUMES	10,000s
Cost to post	Cost to see		Cost to post	Cost to see
Fee	Free		Free	Fee

DISCIPLINE		LOCATION	
ALL		USA/MDA/DC	

SPECIALTY		FEATURE	
ALL		N/A	

AGENT: Both Recruiters & Jobseekers

The Washington Post (also www.washingtonjobs.com) continues to be one of the best designed recruiting sites on the web. Over 20,000 jobs are posted on this site from the newspaper in addition to the jobs directly posted here. Job seekers can register and save their favorite searches for future opportunities. They can also register their email address along with their skills and the site will push notification of matching local jobs to their PCs. Recruiters pay $225 to post a position, and access to the resume database costs $750 for one month. This is one of the few sites that work with corporate employers to determine the number of hires they have obtained from using this recruiting source. Openings posted by noon will be on the site by 5 p.m. Job seekers can participate in live video links to the site to ask career questions. Career message boards, salary surveys, and local company research make this more than just a job site. The Washington Post is one of the leaders in exploring the edges of the online job board market.

353

WEB Worldwide Employee Benefits Network
www.webenefits.org

21165 Whitfield Place, #105, Potomac Falls, VA 20165
Ph: 262-821-9080   Fax: 262-821-1275   E-mail: info@WEBnetwork.org

JOBS	10s	RESUMES	10s
Cost to post	Cost to see	Cost to post	Cost to see
Fee	Free	Fee	Free
DISCIPLINE		LOCATION	
Human Resources		USA	
SPECIALTY		FEATURE	
Benefits		N/A	
AGENT: N/A			

WEB Network of Benefit Professionals is a 16-year-old national organization committed to education and professionalism in the benefits field that has over 2,000 members. There are 25 chapters across the USA. Membership costs $125 per year. Members post for free. Non-member recruiters can post a position for $100 for a 60 day run. Brief resume skill profiles (positions wanted) can be viewed on the net for free. Only members can post a profile to this site.

Webgrrls
www.webgrrls.com

Ph: 212-535-2001   E-mail: webgrrls@cgim.com

JOBS	100s	RESUMES	100s
Cost to post	Cost to see	Cost to post	Cost to see
Fee	Free	Free	Fee
DISCIPLINE		LOCATION	
IT		USA/INTL	
SPECIALTY		FEATURE	
Web Design		Diversity	
AGENT: Jobseeker			

"Webgrrls International provides a forum for women in new media and technology to network, exchange job and business leads, form strategic alliances, mentor and teach, intern and learn the skills to help women succeed in an increasingly technical workplace and world." Webgrrls now offers an interactive JobBank. Members can create and maintain their resume online, search job postings, customize a job agent and much more. Employers pay $150 to post a single position and $750 to acces the resume database.

Westchester Job Central

www.westchesterteenjobs.com

Steve Sribnik
717 White Plains Road, Scarsdale, NY 10583
Ph: 914-725-3494   Fax: 914-725-4460   E-mail: steve@westchesterteenjobs.com

JOBS	100s		RESUMES	N/A
Cost to post	Cost to see		Cost to post	Cost to see
Fee	Free		N/A	N/A
DISCIPLINE			LOCATION	
ALL			USA/MDA/NY/Westchester	
SPECIALTY			FEATURE	
ALL			College/High School/Summer/Gateway	
AGENT: N/A				

Westchester Job Central (formerly westchester teen jobs) posts local part, full time, seasonal or volunteer openings for this local area. Recruiters pay $75 to post a position for 45 days. In the job corner teens can find resume and job search tips. Links to get working papers are also available. Resumes that are posted on the site are forwarded to employers. Everyone should check out the homeroom and play the online games. This fabulous local template has expanded to Orange and Rockland Counties (NY).

Womans-Work

www.womans-work.com

Kirsten Ross
PO Box 1913, Warren, MI 48093
Ph: 810-751-6767   E-mail: sales@womans-work.com

JOBS	10,000s		RESUMES	1,000s
Cost to post	Cost to see		Cost to post	Cost to see
Fee	Free		Free	Fee
DISCIPLINE			LOCATION	
ALL			USA	
SPECIALTY			FEATURE	
ALL			Diversity/Telecommunting/Home	
AGENT: N/A				

Womens-work.com offers employers the ability to post jobs based on their alternative work arrangements (job sharing, part-time, flex scheduling, telecommuting, work from home). A job can be posted for 60 days for $70 (resume access and unlimited posting cost $3,500 per year). A separate section for freelancers is available for job seekers to view. Job seekers who wish to job share can view potential partners for free (very unique) but the contact information is $9.95 each. The site has 30,000 full-time positions and a database of about 6,000 resumes. Corporate recruiters should read the articles on becoming a family friendly company. The owners offer consultative services to organizations intent on becoming more family friendly.

Women in Higher Education

www.wihe.com

Mary Dee Wenniger
1934 Monroe Street, Madison, Wisconsin 53711
Ph: 608-251-3232   Fax: 608-284-0601   E-mail: women@wihe.com

JOBS	100s	RESUMES	N/A
Cost to post	Cost to see	Cost to post	Cost to see
Fee	Free	N/A	N/A
DISCIPLINE		LOCATION	
Education		USA	
SPECIALTY		FEATURE	
Teaching/Administration, University		Diversity	
AGENT: N/A			

Women in Higher Education offers serious information to its constiutents. Site is small, well designed, professionally presented and personable. It claims to provide recruiters access to 12,000 women who work (or have aspirations) as administrators and educators in higher ed.. Recruiters can post their ads to the website for $180. Positions can be viewed by title, function and region of the US. Listings here include President, Chancellor, VP, Provost and Dean. The big deal here is that these job listings are fresh jobs, quality jobs and a lot of them. (Men, you might consider sneaking a peek if you need a few leads.)

Women In Technology International

www.witi.com

Cynthia Roe
6345 Balboa Blvd., #257, Encino, CA 91316
Ph: 800-342-9746   Fax: 818-342-9891   E-mail: membership@corp.witi.com

JOBS	100s	RESUMES	1,000s
Cost to post	Cost to see	Cost to post	Cost to see
Fee	Free	Free	Fee
DISCIPLINE		LOCATION	
Business/IT		USA	
SPECIALTY		FEATURE	
ALL		Diversity/Executive	
AGENT: N/A			

Women in Technology International (WITI) offers exceptional content for women looking to break through the glass ceiling in corporate America. WITI has 37 regional chapters and holds three national conferences. The cost to become a member is $150 per year. Recruiters pay $150 to post a position and $195 for access to the resume database for a 1 month run. Other packages are available. Jobs (551) can be searched by location, job category or keyword. This organization is dedicated to increasing the number of women in executive roles, helping women become more financially independent and technologically literate and encouraging young women to choose careers in science and technology.

The Work Circuit (EETimes)

www.theworkcircuit.com

Lynette Hodge
901 MoPac Expressway South, Barton Oaks Plaza 4, Ste.250, Austin, TX 78746
Ph: 530.344.0215   E-mail: lhodge@cmp.com

JOBS	1,00s	RESUMES	1,000s
Cost to post	Cost to see	Cost to post	Cost to see
Fee	Free	Free	Fee
DISCIPLINE		LOCATION	
Engineering		USA	
SPECIALTY		FEATURE	
Electrical/Electronic		N/A	
AGENT: Both Recruiters & Jobseekers			

The Work Circuit is the newest offering from EETimes (CMP publications). CMP includes several publication such as Electronic Engineering Times and Embedded. They created The Work Circuit to highlight its US and Int'l. opportunities. Recruiters pay $150 to post online or, for approximately $1500 per month there is a package allowing search and connection direct to the employer site. Employers do not have to post in the publication to get an online ad. A separate headhunter database is available. This is still a work in progress but the improvements should be acknowledged. 130 jobs were listed in the US on our visit. Great content for engineers. We hope this model will stay connected as CMP has been through more cycles than the profession they represent.

workinpr.com

www.workinpr.com

Allison May
121 Stewart Street, Suite 205, Seattle, WA 98101
Ph: 877 625-9125   Fax: 206-956-1986   E-mail: sales@workinpr.com

JOBS	10s	RESUMES	1,000s
Cost to post	Cost to see	Cost to post	Cost to see
Fee	Free	Free	Fee
DISCIPLINE		LOCATION	
Entertainment & Media/Communications		USA	
SPECIALTY		FEATURE	
Public Relations		N/A	
AGENT: Job Seeker			

Workinpr.com launched in June, 2000. The site targets public relations professionals. Recruiters pay $325 for a full-time opening ($275 for freelance) for a 60 day listing. This cost includes access to the resume database. Job seekers can see positions by location, title, industry, area of expertise, salary range or years of experience. The site will review a job seekers resume for $100. Openings can be applied to directly or via an online resume builder. The site has aligned itself with the Council of Public Relations Firms and the Public Relations Society of America. Owners are also in the candidate research and contingency headhunting business.

WorkinSports
www.workinsports.com

John Mellor
Work In Sports, LLC, 7335 E. Acoma Drive, Suite 201, Scottsdale, AZ 85260
Ph: 480-905-7221   Fax: 480-905-7231   E-mail: info@workinsports.com

JOBS	1,000s	RESUMES	1,000s
Cost to post	Cost to see	Cost to post	Cost to see
Free	Fee	Fee	Free

DISCIPLINE	LOCATION
Retail Sales & Services/Communicatons/Misc.	USA

SPECIALTY	FEATURE
Sports/Public Relations	N/A

AGENT: N/A

WorkinSports.com allows job seekers access to search hundreds of jobs in the sports industry and access contact information for hundreds of professional teams. Job seekers pay $24.95 for access to the site for 1 month. Openings are primarily in media/pr/broadcasting, sales/mktg/advt/promotions and finance/admin/mgmt. Employers post openings for free and can access the resume database. Jobs are online for a 3-4 week run with direct contact information. We're not fans of charging the job seekers but there appears to be a strong enough attraction to this industry that many are willing.

Work LP.com (Loss Prevention)
www.worklp.com

4804 Arlington Avenue, Riverside, CA 92504
Ph: 866-968-7562   Fax: 909-785-0951   E-mail: customerservice@worklp.com

JOBS	10s	RESUMES	100s
Cost to post	Cost to see	Cost to post	Cost to see
Fee	Free	Free	Fee

DISCIPLINE	LOCATION
Law & Order/Business	USA

SPECIALTY	FEATURE
Insurance/Security	N/A

AGENT: Both Recruiters & Jobseekers

WorkLP.com would like to make the world a better, safer place. Openings target security professionals. Positions can be posted for $55 for a 60-day run (this includes access to the resume database). The site also offers background and credit checks on potential employees. A map of the USA allows job seekers to search by state. An advanced search feature includes job category, location, salary range, company or keyword. Openings include detailed descriptions, a link to the corporate site and direct contact information. The site primarily attracts retail loss prevention positions at all levels.

WorkInsight

www.workinsight.com

David Perry
333 Preston Street, 11th Floor, Ottawa, Canada
Ph: 613-236-6995   E-mail: marketing@workinsight.com

JOBS	10,000s		RESUMES	N/A
Cost to post	Cost to see		Cost to post	Cost to see
Free	Free		N/A	N/A
DISCIPLINE			LOCATION	
ALL			INTL/Canada/USA	
SPECIALTY			FEATURE	
ALL			N/A	
AGENT: N/A				

WorkInsight.com proves the adage, "what goes around comes around". An older part of the net - newsgroups (can.jobs, ad.jobs. etc.) serves as the backdrop for this story. Workinsight crossposts automatically to 400+ newsgroups. All of the major distribution services also do this (or have workinsight do it for them) and the main reason is that it supports their ever increasing claims to crosspost to "1000s" of free sites. Workinsight offers job seekers another way to scan the postings being delivered to multiple websites from one source.

WorkLife Network

www.worklife.com

Dan Cahn
WorkLife Solutions, 15015 Main Street Suite 210, Bellevue, WA 98052
Ph: 800-488-2208   Fax: 425-643-3120   E-mail: megan@worklife.com

JOBS	100,000s		RESUMES	100,000s
Cost to post	Cost to see		Cost to post	Cost to see
Free	Free		Free	Free
DISCIPLINE			LOCATION	
ALL			USA	
SPECIALTY			FEATURE	
ALL			N/A	
AGENT: Jobseeker				

WorkLife Network has hung in there far longer than most thought. Slowly acquiring a huge network of small micro niche site addresses, portal affilliations and more, they may finally break through. Employers pay $100 to post and either $350 to access the resumes or, The WorkLife Network will allow recruiters to view resumes without contact information for free. Employers are charged $9.95 per resume after the candidate has indicated that they are interested and available. This is a good deal.

Workopolis.com
www.workopolis.com

Kim Peters
720 King Street West, Toronto, Ontario, Canada M5V 2T3 Canada
Ph: 888-641-4047   E-mail: sales@workopolis.com

JOBS	1,000s	RESUMES	10,000s
Cost to post	Cost to see	Cost to post	Cost to see
Fee	Free	Free	Fee
DISCIPLINE		LOCATION	
ALL		INTL/Canada	
SPECIALTY		FEATURE	
ALL		N/A	
AGENT: Employer			

Workopolis.com is a well-designed Canadian site with excellent content. Well supported and funded, Workopolis is highly effective in nearly every category. The site has forums, employer and applicant services and great navigation. Job seekers can view the number of openings after each search. A long listing of hiring corporations with the number of openings listed is a great asset. Recruiters will have to pay $595 Canadian to post one job. This price includes pre-employment questions and access to an applicant tracking system. Unlimited postings are $1,650 per month. Access to the resume database costs $2,000 per month, or $6,000 per year. Workopoliscampus.com costs $20 to post a job (30 days) for one campus. The owners have worked hard on their privacy and disclosure policy. The site is affiliated with The TorontoGlobe and Mail and The Toronto Star.

Worldatwork Job Links

www.worldatwork.org/joblinks

Tony Robson
WorldatWork, 14040 N. Northsight Blvd., Scottsdale, AZ 85260 joblinks@WorldatWork.org
Ph: 877-951-9191   Fax: 480-922-8352   E-mail: customerrelations@worldatwork

JOBS	10s	RESUMES	N/A
Cost to post	Cost to see	Cost to post	Cost to see
Fee	Free	N/A	N/A
DISCIPLINE		LOCATION	
Human Resources		USA	
SPECIALTY		FEATURE	
Compensation/Benefits		N/A	
AGENT: N/A			

Worldatwork Job links, formerly The American Compensation Association, allows recruiters to post positions for $175 for a four week run. The site earch engine allows the job seeker to view openings by location, title or keyword. This association has great potential and the name change is something CXR just does not get. Survey results available here are definitely worth a read.

World Workz

www.worldworkz.com

Michael King
Infinity Consulting Group, 1128 Royal Palm Beach Blvd., #412, Royal Palm Beach, FL 33411
Ph: 888-414-5023   Fax: 561-333-4546   E-mail: info@worldworkz.com

JOBS	1,000s	RESUMES	1,000s
Cost to post	Cost to see	Cost to post	Cost to see
Free	Free	Free	Free
DISCIPLINE		LOCATION	
ALL		USA	
SPECIALTY		FEATURE	
ALL		N/A	
AGENT: Both Recruiters & Jobseekers			

World Workz was launched in September 2000 with a "Boss Coming" button in the lower right hand corner of the home page. The owners also oversee salesworkz.com which holds its postings for a month and its resumes for a year. Recruiters register for a resume agent that will email skill-matched paper to their PCs. Job seekers who register their email addresses and skills will have positions forwarded to their desktops. Employers can post openings for free and access the resume database. Worldworkz.com is a general site that also sells online screening, testing and resume services.

The Write Jobs
www.writerswrite.com/jobs

Greg Knollenberg
8214 Westchester, Suite 500, Dallas, TX 75225
Ph: 214-353-9015   Fax: 214-853-5192   E-mail: jobs@writerswrite.com

JOBS	100s	RESUMES	100s
Cost to post	Cost to see	Cost to post	Cost to see
Fee	Free	N/A	N/A
DISCIPLINE		LOCATION	
Entertainment & Media/Communications		USA	
SPECIALTY		FEATURE	
Writing		N/A	
AGENT: N/A			

The Write Jobs is part of writerswrite.com, a niche audience that includes editors, journalists and writers. Recruiters pay $45 for a five-week run. Corporate profiles are also available for purchase by employers. Positions include freelance writing assignments, technical writing, media and publishing. About 50 new postings are received each month. The site also has a section with career advice, offers links to other job-related websites and has newsgroup search capability. All openings are date posted with detailed descriptions and direct contact information. The Editorial Dead Zone provides information on layoffs and industry news. Job seekers should check out resume and cover letter articles by Tracy Laswell. This site gets a lot of traffic for the niche.

Y-axis.com
www.y-axis.com

Xavier Augustin
Y-Axis Global Careers LLC, 1098 Foster City Blvd.,, Foster City, CA 94404
E-mail: customerservice@y-axis.com

JOBS	100s	RESUMES	1,000s
Cost to post	Cost to see	Cost to post	Cost to see
Free (See Notes)	Free	Free (See Notes)	Free
DISCIPLINE		LOCATION	
IT/Health Care Education		INTL/	
SPECIALTY		FEATURE	
ALL		Emmigration	
AGENT: N/A			

Y-Axis is one of the most practical sites we've seen to offer advice and guidance to the milliions of job-seekers asking questions about emigration/immigration and all that entails. The site offers 100s of low cost services to individuals seeking to move from point A to point B. For the employer, the site offers a leg up on incoming sources for IT, Teaching, Nursing and other professional positions. A resume database is available for $250 per month and posting jobs is a nominal fee.

Youth Specialties
www.youthspecialties.com

Mike Yaconelli
300 South Pierce Street, El Cajon, CA 92020
E-mail: jobs@youthspecialties.com

JOBS	100s		RESUMES	100s
Cost to post	Cost to see		Cost to post	Cost to see
Free	Free		Free	Free
DISCIPLINE			LOCATION	
Non-Profit			USA	
SPECIALTY			FEATURE	
ALL			N/A	
AGENT: N/A				

Youth Specialties offers opportunities for church and other nonprofit organizations in search of youth workers. Positions (494) ranged from youth pastors and ministers to directors of various ministries (these can be searched by denomination, and title). Resumes (643) can be searched by various categories such as "new resumes", "this week", "this month" or "all". Results are presented in the form of long lists. Career articles and hundreds of links to other organization sites for youth ministry add value. CXR appreciated the article "Should I Stay or Should I Go?" Email discussion groups, message boards and a chatroom make this free site a ministry all by itself.

JOB SEEKER TIP

Find a map of where you live.

Draw a commutable circle. Call your local library to obtain a list of the corporations within your circle and find their URL. Of the Fortune 500, 498 have websites and most post job openings.

CROSS REFERENCE INDEX

More than 2500 job and resume sites with their URLs are listed on the following pages (another 500 corporate sites are also listed elsewhere in the indices). Separate breakouts follow for: Associations; The Best of the Best (Top 50 sites); Career Management; College; Corporation Staffing Sites; Diversity; Job and Resumes (FEE or FREE); Location; and, Specialty and Industry.

CareerXroads includes over 3000 reviews and, while only 500 reviews are published in the directory each year, we invite you to email us to receive a free review for any site listed here (or any site at all).

Note: The sites in **Bold** are among the 500 Best and their reviews can be found in the main body of this edition. A Bold **(T)** indicates we consider the site among the "Top 50". The thousands of sites in plain text listed here were reviewed but, their reviews are not published (we promise to send you any review on request). All Web site URLs (web addresses) can be found in the Master List. A parentheses ( ) designates the "gateway" site that we reviewed. Brackets [ ] are used for clarification.

123 Charlotte.com
www.123charlotte.com
123 Jax.com
www.123Norfolk.com
123 Raleigh.com
www.123raleigh.com
123 USA hire.com
www.123USAhire.com
1800Drivers
www.1800drivers.com
1st 4 UK HR Jobs
www.1st4ukhrjobs.co.uk
3D Cafe
www.3dcafe.com
3D Site
www.3dsite.com/#jobs
3rd-level.com
www.3rd-level.com
3sectorsjob
www.3sectorsjob.com
4 Allied Health Jobs Online (HospitalJobsOnl...
www.4alliedhealthjobsonline.com
4 MD Jobs Online (HospitalJobsOnline)
www.4mdjobsonline.com
4 Nursing Jobs Online (HospitalJobsOnline)
www.4nursingjobsonline.com
4Labors Of Love
www.4laborsoflove.org
4weeks.com
www.4weeks.com
4Work
www.4work.com
6 FigureJobs
www.sixfigurejobs.com
6 FigureMBA.com
www.6figuremba.com
A Job4Accountants (Employmax)
www.ajob4accountants.com
A Job4Engineers (Employmax)
www.ajob4engineers.com
A Job4Programmers (Employmax)
www.ajob4programmers.com
A Job4Scientists (Employmax)
www.ajob4scientists.com

A1A Computer Jobs
www.a1acomputerpros.net
a1jobindia.com
www.a1jobindia.com
A2Z Moonlighter
www.a2zmoonlighter.com
AACI Israel Jobnet
www.jobnet.co.il
Aberdeen American News (CareerBuilder)
www.southdakota.com
About Jobs.com
www.aboutjobs.com
Abracat
www.abracat.com
Absolute-Comms
www.absolute-comms.co.uk
Absolutely Health Care
www.healthjobsusa.com
Academic Career Services in Finland
www.aarresaari.net/
Academic Employment Network
www.academploy.com
Academic Physician & Scientist
www.acphysci.com/aps.htm
Academic Position Network
www.apnjobs.com
Academy Grad.com (MMR)
www.academygrad.com
Academy Grads (The Destiny Group)
www.academy-grads.com
Access Dubuque (Telegraph Herald)
www.accessdubuque.com
Access: Networking in the Public Interest
www.accessjobs. org
Accessalesjobs.com
www.accesalesjobs.com
Account Manager.com (Career Marketplace)
www.accountmanager.com
Accountant Jobs (eJob Stores)
www.accountantjobs.com
Accountants World.com (Career Engine)
www.accountantsworld.com
Accounting Classifieds (Career Engine)
www.accountingclassifieds.com

366

Accounting Jobs Online
www.accountingjobonline.com
Accounting Professional.com (Career Marke...
www.accountingprofessional.com
Accounting.com
www.accounting.com
AccountingWEB.co.uk
www.accountingweb.co.uk
Aces-US
www.aces-fr.com
ActionJobs
www.actionjobs.com
Activate.co.uk
www.activate.co.uk
Actor's Worldlink
members.aol.com/aworldlink
ActualJobs
www.actualjobs.com
Ad Age
www.adage.com
ad world
www.adworld.ie
Adjunctopia
www.adjunctopia.com
Advance Careers (T)
www.advancecareers.com/
ADVANCE for Careers
www.advanceforcareers.com
Adventures in Hospitality Careers
www.hospitalityadventures.com
Adventures in Hospitality Careers
www.hospitalityadventures.com
Advertising Job Bank
www.pwr.com/adjobbank
Advertising Job Store (eJob Stores)
www.advertisingjobstore.com
Advertising Media Internet Center
www.amic.com
Advertising Research Foundation
www.arfsite.org
Adweek Online
www.adweek.com
AEC Job Bank
www.aecjobbank.com
AEC WorkForce
www.aecworkforce.com
Aeroindustryjobs.com
www.aeroindustryjobs.com
Aerospace Engineer.com (Career Marketpla...
www.aerospaceengineer.com
AfriCareers.com (Hire-Power)
www.africareers.com
After College (T)
www.aftercollege.com
Agricultural Labour Pool
www.agri-labourpool.com
Agricultural MVP.com (CareerMVP)
www.agriculturalmvp.com
Agricultural Technology Information Network
www.atinet.org
AIRS - Advanced Internet Recruitment Strat...
www.airsdirectory.com
AJCJobs.com (Atlanta Journal Constitution)
www.ajcjobs.com
Akron Beacon Journal (CareerBuilder)
www.beaconjournal.com
Alabama Computer Jobs.com
www.alabama.computerjobs.com
Alabama Live (Advance Careers)
www.al.com
Alabama State Jobs
www.personnel.state.al.us/
Alaska Job Center Network
www.jobs.state.ak.us/

Albany Times Union (CareerBuilder)
www.timesunion.com
Alberta jobs.com (Canjobs)
www.albertajobs.com
Albuquerque Journal (abracat)
localnet.abracat.com/abqjournal/
Aldaba
www.aldaba.org
All County Jobs.com
www.allcountyjobs.com
All Energy Jobs
www.allenergyjobs.com
All Jobz
www.alljobz.com
All Retail jobs.com
www.allretailjobs.com
AllEnergyJobs
www.energycentral.com/
Allentown Morning Call (CareerBuilder)
www.mcall.com
Allied Health Employment (HealthCareJobStore)
www.alliedhealthemployment.com
Allied Health Opportunities
www.gvpub.com
Almogordo Daily News (Employment Wizard)
www.almogordonews.com
AM FMJobs
www.amfmjobs.com
American Academy of Audiology
www.audiology.org/hearcareers
American Academy of Cosmetic Dentistry
www.aacd.com
American Academy of Forensic Sciences
www.aafs.org
American Accounting Assoc.
accounting.rutgers.edu/raw/aaa/index.html
American Advertising Federation
www.aaf.org
American Agricultural Economics Assoc.
www.aaea.org
American Anthropological Assoc.
www.aaanet.org
American Assoc. for Budget & Program Ana...
www.aabpa.org
American Assoc. for Respiratory Care
www.aarc.org
American Assoc. of Clinical Chemistry
www.aacc.org
American Assoc. of Collegiate Registrars

American Assoc. of Community Colleges
www.aacc.nche.edu
American Assoc. of Critical-Care Nurses
www.aacn.org
American Assoc. of Finance and Accounting
www.aafa.com
American Assoc. of People with Disabilities
www.aapd.com
American Assoc. of School Administrators
www.assa.org
American Assoc. of University Women
www.aauw.org
American Astronomical Society
www.aas.org
American Ceramic Society
www.acers.org
American Chamber of Commerce Execs
www.acce.org
American Chemical Society - JobSpectrum.org
www.acs.org
American College of Cardiology
www.acc.org
American College of Healthcare Executives
www.ache.org

American College of Radiology
www.acr.org
American College Personnel Assoc.
www.acpa.nche.edu
American Corporate Counsel Assoc.
www.acca.com
American Counseling Assoc.
www.counseling.org
American Culinary Federation
www.acfchefs.org
American Design Drafting Assoc.
www.adda.org/
American Fisheries Society
www.fisheries.org
American Health Lawyers Assoc.
www.healthlawyers.org
American Industrial Hygiene Assoc.
www.aiha.org
American Institute of Architects Career Center
www.aia.org
American Institute of Biological Sciences (A...
www.aibs.org
American Institute of Chemical Engineers

American Institute of CPA's
www.aicpa.org/
American Institute of Physics (AIP)
www.aip.org
American Jobs.com
www.americanjobs.com
American Lighting Assoc. (FlipDog)
www.americanlightingassoc.com
American Marketing Assoc.
www.ama.org
American Massage Therapy Assoc.
www.amtamassage.org
American Mathematical Society
www.ams.org
American Meteorological Society
www.ametsoc.org/AMS/pubs/index.html
American Music Therapy Assoc.
www.musictherapy.org
American Nuclear Society
www.ans.org
American Oil chemists' Society
www.aocs.org
American Physical Therapy Assoc.
www.apta.org
American Planning Assoc.
www.planning.org
American Public Health Assoc.
www.apha.org
American Public Works Assoc.
www.apwa.net
American Risk & Insurance Assoc.
www.aria.org
American School Counselor Assoc.
www.schoolcounselor.org
American Soc. for Engineering Education (...
www.asee.org
American Soc. for Quality
www.asq.org/net/career
American Soc. for Training & Development
www.astd.org
American Soc. of Agricultural Engineering
www.asae.org
American Soc. of Assoc. Executives (T)
www.asaenet.org/careers
American Soc. of Civil Engineers
www.asce.org
American Soc. of Echocardiography
www.echo-web.com
American Soc. of Limnology and Oceanogr...
www.aslo.org

American Soc. of Mech. Engineering
www.asme.org/jobs
American Soc. of Women Accountants
www.aswa.org/wanted.html
American Society fo P&E Nutrition
www.nutritioncare.org
American Society for Clinical Laboratory Sc...
www.ascls.org
American Society for Public Administration
www.aspanet.org
American Society of Crime Lab Directors
www.ascld.org
American Society of Gene Therapy
www.asgt.org
American Society of Health-System Pharma...
www.ashp.org
American Society of Interior Designers
www.asid.org
American Speech-Language-Hearing Assoc.
www.professional.asha.org
American Statistical Association
www.amstat.org
American Urological Assoc. Job Finder

American Urological Assoc.
www.auanet.org
American Water Works Assoc.
www.awwa.org
American Welding Society
www.aws.org/jobfind
American Zoo & Aquarium Assoc.
www.aza.org
America's Job Bank (T)
www.ajb.dni.us
America's Preferred Jobs
www.preferredjobs.com
Anchorage Daily News (Employment Wizard)
www.alaska.com
Anchorage HelpWanted (Reg.HelpWanted)
www.anchoragehelpwanted.com
Apartment Careers
www.apartmentcareers.com
Aquatic Network
www.aquanet.com
Arbetsformedlingen
www.ams.se
Archaeological Fieldwork Opportunities
www.cincpac.com/afos/testpit.html
Architect jobs.com (eJob Stores)
www.architectjobs.com
Architects Online
www.architects-online.org
Areo Ad's
aeroads.ca
Arizona Jobs.com (LocalCareers)
www.arizonajobs.com
Arizona Republic (USA Today Careers)
www.arizonarepublic.com
Army Career & Alumni Program
www.acap.army.mil
Art Deadlines List
www.xensei.com/users/adl/
Art Directors Club of Metro. Washington
www.adcmw.org
Art Hire
www.arthire.com
art jobonline
www.artjob.com
Asbury Park Press (USA Today Careers))
www.app.com
Asheville Area Talent Bank (NationJob)
www.ashevillechamber.org
Asheville Citizen-Times (USA Today Careers))
www.citizen-times.com

Ashland Daily Tidings (Employment Wizard)
www.dailytidings.com
Asiaco Jobs Center
jobs.asiaco.com
Asiadragons.com (Asiaco)
www.asiadragons.com/employment/home.shtml
Asia-Links
www.asia-links.com
Asian American Economic Dev. Enterprises
www.aaede.org
Asian American Journalists Assoc.
www.aaja.org
Asian Careers.com (Hire-Power)
www.asiancareers.com
Asia-Net
www.asia-net.com
ASP Computer work.com
www.asp.computerwork.com
Aspirasi Graduan
www.graduan.com.my
Assoc. for Advancement of Computing in Ed.
www.aace.org
Assoc. for Computing Machinery
www.acm.org
ASsoc. for Facilities Engineering

Assoc. for Financial Professionals
www.afponline.org
Assoc. for Fundraising Professionals
www.nsfre.org
Assoc. for Institutional Research
www.airweb.org/jobs.html
Assoc. for Interactive Marketing (CareerBuil...
www.imarketing.org
Assoc. for Investment Mgmt. & Research
www.aimr.org
Assoc. for Library and Information Science ...
www.alise.org
Assoc. for Telecom. in Higher Ed.
www.acuta.org
Assoc. for Women in Communications
www.womcom.org
Assoc. for Women in Mathematics
www.awm-math.org
Assoc. for Women in Sports Media
www.awsmonline.org
Assoc. of Clinical Research Professionals
www.acrpnet.org
Assoc. of eX-Lotus Employees
www.axle.org
Assoc. of Latino Professionals in Fin. & Acc.
www.aahcpa.org
Assoc. of Metropolitan Water Agencies
www.amwa.net
Assoc. of Perioperative Registered Nurses
www.aorn.org
Assoc. of Research Libraries
db.arl.org/careers/index.html
Assoc. of Women Surgeons
www.womensurgeons.org
Atlanta Computer Jobs.com
www.atlanta.computerjobs.com
Atlanta Computer work.com
www.atlanta.computerwork.com
Atlanta ContractJobs
www.atlantacontractjobs.com
Atlanta Smart City
www.atlantasmartcity.com
Atlantic Jobs.com (Canjobs)
www.atlanticjobs.com
Attorney Jobs Online
www.attorneyjobs.com
Attorney.com (Legal Staff)
www.attorney.com

Audit Net
www.auditnet.org
Augusta Chronicle (Employment Wizard)
www.augustachronicle.com
AuntMinnie.com (T)
www.auntminnie.com
Austin American Statesman
www.statesmanclassifieds.com
Austin Employment.com (Employocity)
www.austinemployment.com
Australian Careers Directory
www.careers.gov.au
Australian Job Search
jobsearch.gov.au
Author link
www.authorlink.com
Auto careers
www.autocareers.com
Auto Jobs.com
www.autodealerjobs.com
Autobody Online
www.autobodyonline.com
AutoCAD Job Network (Mercury Enterprises)
www.acjn.com
AutoHeadHunter.net
www.autoheadhunter.net
Automation Jobs
www.automationtechies.com
Automation Techies

Automotive Aftermarket Industry Asoc.
www.aftermarket.org
Automotive Techs.Com
www.automotivetechs.com
AutoTechs USA
www.autotechsusa.com
AV Canada
www.avcanada.ca
Av Crew.com
www.avcrew.com
AV Jobs
www.avjobs.com
Avenue J.com
www.avenueJ.com
Aviation Employment.com
www.aviationemployment.com
Aviation Job Search.com
www.aviationjobsearch.com
Aviation Jobs Online
www.aviationjobsonline.com
Aviation Now
jobs.aviationnow.com/Main/Default.asp
Awesome Accountants
www.awesomeaccountants.com
aztechjobs.com
www.aztechjobs.com
BA Jobs (T)
www.bajobs.com
BAAN Fanclub and User Forum (Fanclub)
www.baanfans.com
Back Door Jobs
www.backdoorjobs.com
Backstagejobs.com
www.backstagejobs.com
Bakery-Net
www.bakery-net.com
Baltimore Computerwork.com
www.baltimore.computerwork.com
Baltimore Sun (CareerBuilder)
www.sunspot.net
BaltimoreWanted (Reg.HelpWanted)
www.baltimorehelpwanted.com
Bank Connect.com
www.bankconnect.com

Bank Job Search (BAI)
www.bankjobsearch.com
bank jobs.com
www.bankjobs.com
Bank Talent.com
www.banktalent.com
Banking Job Store.com (eJob Stores)
www.bankingjobstore.com
bankingboard.com (TheBoardNetwork)
www.escrowboard.com
bankrole.com
www.bankrole.com
Baton Rouge Advocate
www.theadvocate.com
Baton Rouge Careers Online (Employment P...
www.batonrougecareersonline.com
Baton Rouge HelpWanted.com (Reg.HelpW...
www.batonrougehelpwanted.com
Battle Creek Enquirer (USA Today Careers)
www.battlecreekenquirer.com
Bay AreaHelpWanted (Reg.HelpWanted)
www.BayAreahelpwanted.com
Bay Recruiter.com
www.bayrecruiter.com
Be An Actuary
www.beanactuary.org
Be the Boss (Monster.com)
www.betheboss.com
Bellingham Herald (USA Today Careers))
www.bellinghamherald.com
Benefit News Online
www.benefitnews.com
Benefits Link (T)
www.benefitslink.com
Bergen Daily Record (USA Today Careers))
www.dailyrecord.com
Best Jobs California (Best Jobs)
www.bestjobscalifornia.com
Best Jobs Florida (Best Jobs)
www.bestjobsflorida.com
Best Jobs Illinois (Best Jobs)
www.bestjobsillinois.com
Best Jobs Massachusetts (Best Jobs)
www.bestjobsmassachusetts.com
Best Jobs New York (Best Jobs)
www.bestjobsnewyork.com
Best Jobs Texas (Best Jobs)
www.bestjobstexas.com
Best Jobs USA.com
www.bestjobsusa.com
Best Jobs Washington (Best Jobs)
www.bestjobswashington.com
Better Job Network (CareerLINK)
www.betterjobnetwork.com
better jobs KC.com (CareerLink)
www.betterjobsKC.com
BharatCareers.com
www.bharatcareers.com
Big FiveTalent.com
www.bigfivetalent.com
BigAppleHead.com
www.BigAppleHead.com
bigcountryjobs.com (Employment Wizard)
www.bigcountryjobs.com
Bilingual-Jobs
www.bilingual-jobs.com
Bilingualxpress.ca
www.bilingualexpress.ca
Billings Gazette (Employment Wizard)
www.billingsgazette.com
BillingsHelpWanted (Reg.HelpWanted)
www.billingshelpwanted.com
Bio Array News (GenomeWeb)
www.bioarraynews.com

Bio career.com (SciWeb)
www.biocareer.com
Bio Exchange.com
www.bioexchange.com
Bio find
www.biofind.com
Bio Inform (GenomeWeb)
www.bioinform.com
Bio Research Online (WorkLife)
www.bioresearchonline.com
Bio Snail
www.BioSnail.com
Bio Space.com
www.biospace.com
Bio Statistician Jobs (HealthCareJobStore)
www.biostatisticianjobs.com
Bio View (Monster)
www.bioview.com
Bio.com
www.bio.com
Bioinformatics Resource
www.hgmp.mrc.ac.uk/CCP11
Biomedical Engineer.com (Career Marketplace)
www.BiomedicalEngineer.com
Biomedical Engineering Society
www.bmes.org
Bioplanet
www.bioplanet.com
Bioscience and Medicine (HUM-MOLGEN)
hum-molgen.de/positions/
BioSnail.com
www.biosnail.com
Biotech Careers.com
www.Biotechcareers.com
Biotechnology Human Resource Counsel
www.bhrc.ca
Birchin Lane
www.birchinlane.com
Birmingham Employment.com (Employocity)
www.birminghamemployment.com
Birmingham HelpWanted (Reg.HelpWanted)
www.birminghamhelpwanted.com
Birmingham Online (Employment Partner)
www.birminghamcareersonline.com
Bismark Tribune (Employment Wizard)
www.jobs.bismarktribune.com
Biz Moonlighter
www.a2zmoonlighter.com
Black Career Women
www.bcw.org
Black Culinarians Alliance
www.blackculinarians.com
Black Data Processing Assoc.
www.bdpa.org
Black E.O.E Journal
www.blackeoejournal.com
Black Voices.com (CareerBuilder)
www.blackvoices.com
Black World Today (Career Engine)
www.tbwcareers.com
Blinks Magazine (FlipDog)
www.blinks.net
Blood Center Jobs (HealthCareJobStore)
www.bloodcenterjobs.com
Bloomberg.com (CareerBuilder)
www.bloomberg.com
Blue To Gray (Corporate Gray Online)
www.bluetogray.com
Boiler Room
www.boilerroom.com
BoiseHelpWanted (Reg.HelpWanted)
www.boisehelpwanted.com
Boldface Jobs
www.boldfacejobs.com

Book People
www.book-people.net
Boston Computer Jobs.com
www.boston.computerjobs.com
Boston Hire.com
www.bostonhire.com
Boston Job Bank
www.bostonjobs.com
Boston Job Source (Internet Job Source)
bostonjobsource.com
Boston Works- Boston Globe (T)
bostonworks.com
Boulder Daily Camera (Employment Wizard)
www.thedailycamera.com
Brain bench
www.brainbench.com
Brain Bid.com
www.brainbid.com
Brainhunter.com
www.brainhunter.com
Brainpower
www.brainpower.com
Brains Talent.com
www.brainstalent.com/
Branch Staff Online.com
www.branchstaffonline.com
Brass Ring.com (T)
www.brassring.com
Bread Bakers Guild of America
www.bbga.org
Bridgewater News-Courier (USA Today Ca...
www.c-n.com
Bright & Professional
www.brightrays.com
British Columbia Jobs.com (Canjobs)
www.britishcolumbiajobs.com
British Columbia Library Assoc.
www.bcla.bc.ca
British Columbia Water & Waste Assoc.
www.bcwwa.org
British Jobs
www.britishjobs.net
Broadband Careers Network
www.broadbandcareers.com
BroadbandCareers.Com
www.broadbandcareers.com
Broker hunter.com
www.brokerhunter.com
BuffaloHelpWanted (Reg.HelpWanted)
www.buffalohelpwanted.com
Buffalojobfinder.com (Employment Wizard)
www.buffalojobfinder.com
Building Industry Consulting Service Int'l.
www.bicsi.org
Bumeran
www.bumeran.com
Burlington Free-Press (USA Today Careers))
www.burlingtonfreepress.com
Business Analyst.com (Career Marketplace)
www.BusinessAnalyst.com
business financemag.com
businessfinancemag.com
Butte Montana Standard (Employment Wizard)
www.mtstandard.com
Buying Jobs.com (NicheJobs)
www.buyingjobs.com
C++ (JV Search)
www.cplusplussearch.com
C++ Computer work.com
www.cplusplus.computerwork.com
C++ Jobs.com (Pure Power)
www.cplusplusjobs.com/
Cable & Telecommunications Assoc. for Ma...
www.ctam.com

Cabletelevision Advertising Bureau
www.cabletvadbureau.com
cache mirror
www.cachemirror.com
CAD jobs.net
cadjobs.net
CAD Operators Online
seekworld.com/acadteam.htm
CADD Jobs.com
www.caddjobs.com
cal career.com
www.calcareer.com
CalgaryJobShop (Reg.HelpWanted)
www.calgaryjobshop.ca
Cali Careers.com (CareerMVP)
www.calicareers.com
California Agricultural Technology Institute
www.atinet.org
California Computerwork.com
www.california.computerwork.com
California HelpWanted.com (Reg. HelpWanted)
www.californiacoasthelpwanted.com
California Job Journal
www.jobjournal.com
California Job Source (Internet Job Source)
cajobsource.com
California Jobs.com (LocalCareers)
www.californiajobs.com
California Journalism Job Bank
www.csne.org/jobs/postings.html
California Soc. of Prof. Engineers (CareerBui...
www.cspe.com
Californian (USA Today Careers)
www.californianonline.com
Call Center Careers
www.callcentercareers.com
Call Center Jobs.com
www.callcenterjobs.com
Call CenterOps
www.callcenterops.com
Campus CareerCenter.com
www.campuscareercenter.com
Canada Computerwork.com
www.canada.computerwork.com
Canada IT.com
www.canadait.com
Canada Jobs.com
www.canadajobs.com
Canadian Bar Assoc.
www.cba.org/career/careersite.asp
Canadian Institue of Quantity Surveyors
www.ciqs.org
Canadian Mgmt. Accountants Society
www.cma-canada.org
Canadian Restaurant & Foodservices Assoc.
www.crfa.ca
Candidate Seeker
www.candidateseeker.com
Canjobs.com
www.canjobs.com
Cape Cod Online (Employment Wizard)
www.capecodonline.com
cardiac nurse jobs.com (HealthCareJobs)
www.cardiacnursejobs.com
Career Age
www.careerage.com
Career Bahrain (CareerMidEast)
www.careerbahrain.com
Career Bank
www.careerbank.com
Career Beacon.com
www.atlanticcanadacareers.com
Career Board
www.careerboard.com

Career Builder (T)
www.careerbuilder.com
Career Buzz
www.careerbuzz.com
Career Chase
www.careerchase.net
Career Click
www.careerclick.com
Career Connector
www.careerconnector.com
Career Consulting Corner
www.careercc.com
Career Cross Japan
www.careercross.com
Career Edge
www.careeredge.org
Career Egypt.com (CareerMidEast)
www.careeregypt.com
Career Emirates.com (CareerMidEast)
www.careeremirates.com
Career Engine Network
www.careerengine.com
Career Espresso/Emory University
www.sph.emory.edu/studentservice/Career.html
Career Exchange.com
www.careerexchange.com/
Career Exposure
www.careerexposure.com
Career Fables.com
www.careerfables.com
Career File
www.careerfile.com
Career Giant
www.careergiant.com
Career Gram
www.careergram.com
Career Guidance.com
www.careerguidance.com
Career Hunters.com
www.careerhunters.com
Career India
www.careerindia.com
Career Information Exchange
www.careerinfoexchange.com
Career Innovator
www.netjobsexpress.com
Career Jordan.com (CareerMidEast)
www.careerjordan.com
Career Journal Asia.com (CareerJournal)
www.careerjournalasia.com
Career Journal Europe.com (CareerJournal)
www.careerjournaleurope.com
Career Journal.com (T)
www.careerjournal.com
Career Junction
www.careerjunction.co.za
career key
www.careerkey.com
Career Kuwait.com (CareerMidEast)
www.careerkuwit.com
Career Lebanon.com (CareerMidEast)
www.careerlebanon.com
Career Link- Applied Info. Mgm't Institute
www.careerlink.org
Career Local Net
www.careerlocal.net
Career Machine
www.careermachine.com
Career Mag.com
www.careermag.com
Career Marketplace
www.careermarketplace.com
Career Mart
www.careermart.com

Career Matrix.com
www.careermatrix.com
Career MidEast.com
www.careermideast.com
Career Morocco.com (CareerMidEast)
www.careermorocco.com
Career Mosaic India
www.careermosaicindia.com
Career MVP.com
www.CareersMVP.com
Career Net
www.careernet.com
Career NJ.com (CareerMVP)
www.careernj.com
Career Oman.com (CareerMidEast)
www.careeroman.com
Career One
www.careerone.com.au
Career Owl
www.careerowl.com
Career Pal
www.careerpal.com
Career Park
www.careerpark.com
Career PLACE
www.careerplace.com
Career Plus
www.career-plus.com
Career Qtar.com (CareerMidEast)
www.careerqtar.com
Career Saudi.com (CareerMidEast)
www.careersaudi.com
Career Search America
www.careersearchamerica.com
Career Shop.com
www.careershop.com
Career Site.com
www.careersite.com
Career span
www.careerspan.com
Career Surf.com
www.careersurf.com
Career Tunis.com (CareerMidEast)
www.careertunis.com
Career Woman2000.com (Hire-Power)
www.careerwoman2000.com
Career Women (Career Exposure)
www.careerwomen.com
Career Yemen.com (CareerMidEast)
www.careeryemen.com
Career.com
www.career.com
CareerAnalog
www.careeranalog.com
CareerHut.com
www.CareerHut.com
Careers 2000.net
www.careers2000.net
Careers in Construction
www.careersinconstruction.com
Careers in Food.com
www.careersinfood.com
Careers in Government
www.careersingovernment.com
Careers in Recruitment
www.careersinrecruitment.com
Car-eers.com
www.car-eers.com
CareersColorado.com
www.careerscolorado.com
Carolina Computer Jobs.com
www.carolina.computerjobs.com
Casino Careers Online (T)
www.casinocareers.com

Casino Employment Guide
www.casinoemployment.com
Casting America
www.casting-america.com
Casting Daily
www.castingnet.com
Castingpro.com (Staffingpro)
www.castingpro.com
Casualty Actuarial Society
www.casact.org
Catho Online
www.catho.com.br
CATIA Job Network (Mercury Enterprises)
www.catjn.com
ccJobsOnline.com
www.ccjobsonline.com
CCollegeJobs.com
www.CCollegeJobs.com
Cellular Telecom. & Internet Assoc. (Job Opt...
www.wow-com.com
Center Watch
www.centerwatch.com
Certified Management Assoc. of Canada
www.cma-canada.org
CFO Asia
www.cfoasia.com/_others/job.htm
CFO Postions.com (Career Engine)
www.cfopositions.com
Charity JOB
www.charityjob.co.uk
Charity Village.com
www.charityvillage.com
Charityopps.com
www.charityopps.com
Charleston Daily Mail (Employment Wizard)
www.dailymail.com
CharlestonHelpWanted (Reg.HelpWanted)
www.charlestonhelpwanted.com
CharlestonJobMarket
www.charlestonjobmarket.com
Charlotte Observer (CareerBuilder)
www.charlotte.com
CharlotteHelpWanted (Reg.HelpWanted)
www.charlottehelpwanted.com
Chattanooga Times (Employment Wizard)
www.timesfreepress.com
Chef Job.com
www.chefjob.com
Chef Jobs Network (Escoffier On Line)
chefjobsnetwork.com
Chem Jobs
www.chemjobs.net
Chemical Engineer.com (Career Marketplace)
www.ChemicalEngineer.com
Chemistry Jobs.com (NicheJobs)
www.chemistryjobs.com
Cherry Hill Courier-Post (USA Today Careers)
www.courierpostonline.com
Chesapeake Human Resources Assoc.
www.chra.com
Chicago Careers Online (Employment Partner)
www.chicagocareersonline.com
Chicago Computer Jobs.com
www.chicago.computerjobs.com
Chicago Employment.com (Employocity)
www.chicagoemployment.com
Chicago HelpWanted.com (Reg. HelpWanted)
www.suburbanchicagohelpwanted.com
Chicago Job Network (Chicago Sun Times)
www.chicagojobnetwork.com
Chicago Jobs.com (LocalCareers)
www.chicagojobs.com
Chicago Tribune (CareerBuilder)
www.chicago.tribune.com

Chicano/a Latino/a NET
latino.sscnet.ucla.edu/
Chico Enterprise Record (Employment Wizard)
www.chicoer.com
Chief Financial Officer.com
www.cfo.com
CHOICE Career
www.choicecareer.com
Christian Career Center
www.ChristianCareerCenter.com
Christian Jobs Online
www.christianjobs.com
Christian Placements.com
www.christianplacements.com
Chronicle of Higher Education
www.chronicle.com
Chronicle of Philanthropy
philanthropy.com
Cincinatti Career Board
www.cincinatti.careerboard.com
Cincinatti Careers (Employment Partner)
www.gcincinatticareers.com
Cincinnati Enquirer (USA Today Careers))
enquirer.com/today
CIO Council.com (Career Marketplace)
www.CIOCouncil.com
CIO Magazine (ITCareers)
www.cio.com
Ciol Jobs
www.cioljobs.com
Circulation Jobs.com
www.circjobs.com
City Jobs
www.cityjobs.com
City Search.com (CareerBuilder)
www.citysearch.com
Civic Action in Eurasia
www.friends-partners.org/ccsi
Civil Engineering Jobs
www.civilengineeringjobs.com
CIVIL Jobs.com
www.civiljobs.com
Clarksville Leaf-Chronicle (USA Today Care...
www.theleafchronicle.com
Classic Web
www.classicweb.com
Classified Employment Web Site (CLEWS)
www.yourinfosource.com/clews
Classifieds 2000 (CareerBuilder)
www.classifieds2000.com
Classifieds For Women (Career Engine)
www.classifiedsforwomen.com
Clear Star
www.clearstar.com
Clearance Jobs.com
www.clearancejobs.com
Cleveland Career Board
www.cleveland.careerboard.com
Cleveland Live (Cleveland Plain Dealer)
www.cleveland.com/careers
Click4Talent
WWW.click4talent.it
Clinical Laboratory Management Assoc.
www.clma.org
CNC Machines Job Network (Mercury Enter...
www.acjn.com
COACH's Job Board
www.coachhelp.com
Coastal Bend Careers (Employment Wizard)
www.coastalbendcareers.com
Cobol Computer work.com
www.cobol.computerwork.com
Cobol Jobs.com (Pure Power)
www.coboljobs.com/

Coderider- VIC Job Board
www.coderider.com/jobs
Cold Fusion Advisor (CF Advisor)
www.cfadvisor.com
CollectionIndustry.com
www.collectionindustry.com
College & University Personnel Assoc.
www.cupahr.org
College & University Prof. Assoc. for HR
tcurtis@cupahr.org
College Central Network (T)
www.collegecentral.com
College Grad Job Hunter
www.collegegrad.com
College Job Board
www.collegejobboard.com
College of Healthcare Infor. Mgmt. Exec.
www.cio-chime.org/default.html
College Recruiter
www.collegerecruiter.com
CollegeJournal.com (Career Journal)
www.collegejournal.com
Colorado Alive (Employment Wizard)
www.coloradoalive.com
Colorado Careers Online (Employment Partner)
www.coloradospringscareersonline.com
Colorado Computerwork.com
www.colorado.computerwork.com
Colorado Guide
www.coloradoguide.com
Colorado Human Resources Assoc.
www.chra.org
Colorado Online Job Connection
www.coloradojobs.com
Colorado Software & Internet Assoc.
www.coloradosoftware.org
Coloradoan (USA Today Careers)
www.coloradoan.com
Columbia Today (CareerBuilder)
www.columbiatoday.com
Columbia-Williamette Compensation Group
www.cwcg.org
Columbus Career Board
www.columbus.careerboard.com
Columbus Careers Online (Employment Part...
www.columbuscareersonline.com
ColumbusHelpWanted (Reg.HelpWanted)
www.columbushelpwanted.com
ColumbusJobs.com (Employment Wizard)
www.columbusjobs.com
Communications Roundtable
www.roundtable.org
Community Career Center
www.nonprofitjobs.org/
Computational Fluid Dynamics Jobs Database
www.cfd-online.com/Jobs
Computer Jobs AS/400
www.as400.computerjobs.com
Computer Jobs Data Warehousing
www.datawarehousing.computerjobs.com
Computer Jobs Database Systems
www.databasesystems.computerjobs.com
Computer Jobs E-Commerce
www.ecommerce.computerjobs.com
Computer Jobs Entry Level
www.entrylevel.computerjobs.com
Computer Jobs ERP
www.erp.computerjobs.com
Computer Jobs Executive Level
www.executive.computerjobs.com
Computer Jobs H-1B
www.h1b.computerjobs.com
Computer Jobs Hardware
www.engineering.computerjobs.com

Computer Jobs Help Desk
www.helpdesk.computerjobs.com
Computer Jobs in Israel
www.cji.co.il
Computer Jobs Legacy Systems
www.legacysystems.computerjobs.com
Computer Jobs Networking
www.networking.computerjobs.com
Computer Jobs New Media
www.newmedia.computerjobs.com
Computer Jobs Project Management
www.projectmanagement.computerjobs.com
Computer Jobs Quality Assurance
www.qualityssurance.computerjobs.com
Computer Jobs Technical Recruiting
www.technicalrecruiting.computerjobs.com
Computer Jobs Technical Sales
www.technicalsales.computerjobs.com
Computer Jobs Technical Writing
www.technicalwriting.computerjobs.com
Computer Jobs Unix
www.unix.computerjobs.com
Computer Jobs Windows Development
www.windowsdevelopment.computerjobs.com
Computer Jobs.com (T)
www.computerjobs.com
Computer Weekly.com
www.computerweekly.com
Computer work.com (T)
www.computerwork.com
Computer World (ITCareers)
www.computerworld.com
Configuration Management (CM Today)
www.cmtoday.com
Connecticut Jobs Online (CTJobs.com)
www.ctjobs.com
Connecticut Jobs.com (LocalCareers)
www.connecticutjobs.com
Connecticut Post (Employment Wizard)
www.connpost.com
Construction Executives.com
www.constructionexecutives.com
Construction Financial Mgmt. Assoc.
www.cfma.org
Construction Gigs
www.constructiongigs.com/
Construction Job Store (eJob Stores)
www.constructionjobstore.com
Construction Jobs.com
www.constructionjobs.com
Construction.com
www.construction.com/CareerCenter
ConstructionJobsites.com (Geojobsites)
www.constructionjobsites.com
Construction-net
www.construction-net.co.uk
ConstructionOnly.Com
www.constructiononly.com/
ConsultantTV.com
www.consultanttv.com
Contact Point Career Development
www.contactpoint.ca
Contract Employment Connection
www.ntes.com
Contract Engineering
www.contractengineering.com
Contract JobHunter
www.cjhunter.com
Contracts247
www.contracts247.co.uk
Cool Jobs.com
www.cooljobs.com
Cool Works - Jobs in Great Places
www.coolworks.com

374

CareerXroads 2003

Copy Editor Job Board
www.copyeditorjobs.com
coroflot
www.coroflot.com
Corporate Gray Online
www.corporategrayonline.com
Corporate Gray
www.bluetogray.com
Corporate Skills (Irish Jobs)
www.irishjobs.com
Corrections Connection
www.corrections.com
Corridor Careers
www.corridorcareers.com
Council for Advancement & Support od Ed.
www.case.org
Council of Logistics Management
www.clm1.org
Council on Employee Benefits
www.ceb.org
Council on Foundations
www.cof.org
Counsel.net
www.counsel.net
CPA jobs.com
www.cpajobs.com
CPA net
www.cpanet.com
CPA2bizcareers.com
www.cpa2biz.com
CPACareerNet
www.cpacareernet.com
Craigs List [Atlanta]
atlanta.
Craigs List [Austin]
Austin
Craigs List [Boston]
boston.craigslist.org
Craigs List [Chicago]
chicago.craigslist.org
Craigs List [Denver]
Denver.
Craigs List [Los Angeles]
LosAngeles
Craigs List [New York]
newyork.
Craigs List [Portland]
portland.
Craigs List [Sacramento]
sacramento.
Craigs List [San Diego]
sandiego.
Craigs List [Seattle]
seattle.
Craigs List [Vancouver]
vancouver.
Craigs List [Washington DC]
washingtondc.
Craigs List
www.craigslist.org
Crains New York (Career Engine)
www.crainsny.com
Creative Central.com
www.creativecentral.com
Creative Freelancers Online
www.freelancers.com
Creative Hotlist
www.creativehotlist.com
Creative Moonlighter
www.a2zmoonlighter.com
Credit Jobs Today
www.creditjobstoday.com
Credit Union Executives Society
www.cuews.org

Creditjobs.com
www.creditjobs.com
Crew Net
www.crewnet.com
Crhurch Jobs.com
www.Churchjobsonline.com
crmXchange
www.telemkt.com
Crystallography Worldwide
www.iucr.org
CT Health Careers.com (All County Jobs)
www.cthealthcareers.com
CT High Tech.com (All County Jobs)
www.cthightech.com
Ct. Business & Industry Assoc. (CTJobs.com)
www.cbia.com
CTJob Search (CareerLINK)
www.ctjobsearch.com
Curriculum Vitae Online
www.cuvitae.com
Customer Service Job Stores (eJob Stores)
www.customerservicejobstore.com
CV Europe
www.cveurope.com
CV Index Directory
www.cvindex.com
CV Online- Czech (CV Europe)
www.cvonline.cz
CV Online- Estonia (CV Europe)
www.vv.ee
CV Online- Finland (CV Europe)
www.cvonline.net
CV Online- Hungary (CV Europe)
www.cvonline.hu
CV Online- Latvia (CV Europe)
www.cv.lv
CV Online- Lithuania (CV Europe)
www.cvonline.lt
CV Online- Poland (CV Europe)
www.cvonline.pl
CV Online- Romania (CV Europe)
www.cvonline.ro
CV Online- Russia (CV Europe)
www.cvonline.ru
Cyber KingEmployment
www.cyberkingemployment.com
Cyber-Sierra
www.cyber-sierra.com/nrjobs/
DaiJob
www.daijob.com
Dallas HR Jobs
www.dallashr.org
Dallas Morning News (Employment Wizard)
www.dallasnews.com
Database Analyst.com (Career Marketplace)
www.databaseanalyst.com
Dave's ESL Cafe (English as a Second Lan...
www.eslcafe.com
daVinci Times (T)
www.davincitimes.org
Davjobs.com (The Destiny Group)
www.davjobs.com
Daytona HelpWanted.com (Reg. HelpWanted)
www.daytonahelpwanted.com
DC AccountingJobs
www.dcaccountingjobs.com
DC Computer Jobs.com
www.dc.computerjobs.com
DC Computerwork.com
www.dc.computerwork.com
DC Job Source.com (Internet Job Source)
dcjobsource.com
Decatur Herald & Review (Employment Wiza...
www.herald-review.com

Degree Hunter.com
www.degreehunter.com
Delphi Jobs.com (Pure Power)
www.delphijobs.com/
Delphi World.com
www.delphiworld.com
Dent Search.com
www.dentsearch.com
Dental Hygienist Jobs (HealthCareJobStore)
www.dentalhygienistjobs.com
Dentist Jobs.com (HealthCare Job Store)
www.dentistjobs.com
Denver Computer Jobs.com
www.denver.computerjobs.com
Denver Post (Employment Wizard)
www.careers.post-newsclassified.com
Desert Sun (USA Today Careers)
www.thedesertsun.com
Designer Max.com
www.designermax.com
Desktop Publishing.com JobBank
desktoppublishing.com/employ.html
DesMoines Register (USA Today Careers))
www.desmoinesregister.com
Destiny Group-Military Transition Center (T)
www.destinygroup.com
Detroit Computer Jobs.com
www.detroit.computerjobs.com
Detroit Employment.com (Employocity)
www.detroitEmployment.com
Detroit News (USA Today Careers))
www.detnews.com
Developers.net (Tapestry.net)
www.tapestry.net
DFW Employment.com (Employocity)
www.dallasemployment.com
DFWHelpWanted. (Reg.HelpWanted)
www.DFWhelpwanted.com
DICE High Tech Jobs Online (T)
www.dice.com
Dietician Jobs (HealthCareJobStore)
www.dieticianjobs.com
Direct Employers (T)
www.DirectEmployers.com
direct marketingcareers.com
www.directmarketingcareers.com
direct-jobs.com
www.direct-jobs.com
Distr. of Columbia Bar Career Center (Legal...
www.dcbar.org
Diversilink
www.diversilink.com
Diversity Careers Online
www.diversitycareers.com
Diversity Employment
www.diversityemployment.com
Diversity Inc.com
www.diversityinc.com
Diversity Job Fairs.com
www.americanjobfairs.com
Diversity Job Network
diversityjobnetwork.com
Diversity Link.com
www.diversitylink.com
Diversity Recruiting.com
www.diversityrecruiting.com/index2.html
Diversity Search (Career Exposure)
www.diversitysearch.com
Diversityforhire.Com
www.diversityforhire.com
Diversityinc.com
www.diversityinc.com
Do A Project.com
www.doaproject.com

doctorjob.com
www.doctorjob.com
DOD Job Search (America's Job Bank)
dod.jobsearch.org
DOE-JOBBS
www.doejobbs.com
Donohue's RS/6000 Employment Page
www.s6000.com
dot Jobs
www.dotjobs.co.uk/
Dragon Surf
www.dragonsurf.com/careerwise
Dream Construction Jobs
www.dreamconstructionjobs.co.uk/
Drillers Job Center
www.drillers.com
Drug Information Association
www.diahome.org
Dubuque- AccessSuccess
www.accessdubuque.com/jobs
Dubuque Telegraph Herald
www.thonline.com
Duluth News Tribune (CareerBuilder)
www.duluthsuperior.com
Earthworks
www.earthworks-jobs.com
East Valley Tribune (CareerCast)
www.eastvalleytribune.com
Eat up drink up.com
www.eatupdrinkup.com
eAttorney
www.eattorney.com
ecampus recruiter
www.ecampusrecruiter.com
eCommerce Computer work.com
ecommerce.computerwork.com
Econ Jobs.com (NicheJobs)
www.econjobs.com
Ed Jobs U Seek
education.umn.edu/jobs/
Ed Physician.com
www.edphysician.com/
Edie's Environmental Job Centre
www.on-edie.net/fr_jobs.htm
Editor & Publisher
www.mediainfo.com
EDN Magazine CarEEr Zone (CareerBuilder)
www.ednmag.com/
Education Jobs
www.education-jobs.co.uk
Education Week
www.edweek.org
Education-jobs.com
www.education-jobs.com
EDUCAUSE
www.educause.edu/jobpost/jobpost.asp
EE Times (The Work Circuit)
www.eetimes.com
EE-Link/North American Assoc. for Env. Ed.
eelink.net
eFinancialCareers
www.efinancialcareers.com
EFLWeb
www.eflweb.com
e-itwizards.com
e-itwizards.com
eJob Stores
www.eJobStores.com
e-Job
www.e-job.com
El Paso Times (USA Today Careers))
www.elpasotimes.com
elance
www.elance.com

Electric job.com
www.electricjob.com
Electrical Employment
www.cossin.com
Electrical Engineer.com (Career Marketplace)
www.ElectricalEngineer.com
Electrical World (McGraw-Hill)
www.electricalworld.com
Electrician Job Store (eJob Stores)
www.electricianjobstore.com
Electronic Labour Exchange
www.ele-spe.org
Electronic News OnLine
www.electronicnews.com
Electronics Engineer.com (Career Marketplace)
www.ElectronicsEngineer.com
Elf Network.com
www.elfnetwork.com
Elmira Star Gazette (USA Today Careers)
www.star-gazette.com
Embedded.com (The Work Circuit)
www.embedded.com
Emplawyernet
www.employernet.com
Empleos Web
www.empleosweb.com.ar
Employ China
www.epchina.net
Employ U.com
www.employu.com
Employee Assistance Professionals Assoc.
www.eapassn.org
Employee Relocation Council
www.erc.org
Employers Online
www.employersonline.com
employMAX
www.employmax.com
EmployMED
www.employmed.com
Employment 2000
www.employment2000.net
Employment 411
www.employment411.com
Employment 911
www.employment911.com
Employment Avenue.com
www.employmentavenue.com
Employment Guide.com
www.employmentguide.com
Employment Information in the Mathematical ...
www.asm.org/eims
Employment Partner
www.employmentpartner.com
Employment Weekly (IN)
www.employmentweekly.com
Employment Wizard (Career Site) (T)
www.jobexchange.com
Employxpress
www.employxpress.com
Empty.net
www.empty.net
ENDS Environmental Jobs
www.ends.co.uk/jobs
Energy Career Network
www.energycareernetwork.com
Energy Jobs Network
www.energyjobsnetwork.com
Energy jobs.com
www.energyjobs.com
Energy Vortex.com
www.energyvortex.com
Engineer 500.com
www.engineer500.com

Engineer Employment (eJob Stores)
www.engineeremployment.com
Engineer jobs.com
www.engineerjobs.com
Engineer.net
www.engineer.net
Engineer-Cad.com
www.engineer-cad.com
Engineering Central
www.engcen.com
Engineering Institute of Canada
www.eic-ici.ca
Engineering News Record
www.enr.com
Engineeringj.Jobsites.com (Gcojobsites)
www.engineeringjobsites.com
EngineerMax.com
www.engineermax.com
ENT Careers
www.entnet.org/careers
Entertainment Careers.Net
www.entertainmentcareers.net
Entertainment Jobs.com
www.eej.com
Entomology Society of America
www.entsoc.org
Entry Level Job Seeker Assistant
www.dnaco.net/~dantassi/jobhome.html
Enviro Network.com
www.environetwork.com
Environmental Career Opportunities
www.ecojobs.com
Environmental Career.com
www.environmentalcareer.com
Environmental Career.com
www.environmental-jobs.com
Environmental Careers Org. (Eco.org)
www.eco.org
Environmental Engineer.com (Career Market...
www.EnvironmentalEngineer.com
Environmental Expert
www.environmental-expert.com/
Environmental Jobs and Careers
www.ejobs.org
EnvJobs-L Archives
environment.harvard.edu/lists/archives/envjobs-l/
ePro Net (Experience.com)
www.epronet.com
Equal Opportunity Publications
www.eop.com
Equimax
www.equimax.com
ER Exchange
www.erexchange.com/
Erie Jobs
www.eriejobs.com
ERP Fan Club and User Forum (Fanclub)
www.erpfans.com
Erp Professional.com (Career Marketplace)
www.erpprofessional.com
ERPJobs.com (Pure Power)
www.erpjobsites.com
Erp-Jobs.com
www.erp-jobs.com
Escape Artist.com
www.escapeartist.com
Escoffier On Line - Employment Resources (T)
www.escoffier.com
Escrowboard.com (TheBoardNetwork)
www.escrowboard.com
ESL Worldwide.com
www.eslworldwide.com
Estimator Jobs (eJob Stores)
www.estimatorjobs.com

eteach.com
www.eteach.com
EveryTruckJob.com
www.everytruckjob.com
eWork Exchange
www.ework.com
exBigFive.com
www.exbigfive.com
Exec Searches.com
www.execsearches.com
ExecGlobalNet
www.ExecGlobalNet.com
Execs on the Net (UK)
www.eotn.co.uk
ExecuCentral.com
www.execucentral.com
ExecuClassifieds.com (Career Engine)
www.ExecuClassifieds.com
ExecuNet (T)
www.execunet.com
Executive Registry.com
www.executiveregistry.com
ExecutivesOnly
www.executivesonly.com/
Expatica Jobs
www.expatica.com/jobs
experience.com
www.experience.com
Experimental Medicine Job Listing
www.medcor.mcgill.ca/EXPMED/DOCS/jobs.html
Fairbanks Daily Miner (Employment Wizard)
www.newsminer.com
FairfieldCounty Jobs.com (All County Jobs)
www.fairfieldcountyjobs.com
FargoHelpWanted (Reg.HelpWanted)
www.fargohelpwanted.com
Farms.com
www.farms.com/careers
Fashion Career Center.com
www.fashioncareercenter.com
Fat Job.com
www.fatjob.com
Fed World.gov Federal Jobs
www.fedworld.gov
Federal Jobs Central
www.fedjobs.com
Federal Jobs Digest
www.jobsfed.com
Federation of American Soc. for Exp. Biology
www.faseb.org
Feminist Career Center
www.feminist.org
Feminist Majority Foundation Online
www.feminist.org
FetchMeAJob.com
www.fetchmeajob.com
Film TV Production Jobs (Mandy.com)
www.mandy.com
Film, TV, & Commercial Employment Network
www.employnow.com
Finance Mag.com (Job Mag)
www.jobmag.com
Finance MVP.com (CareerMVP)
www.financemvp.com
Finance-Jobs
www.finance-jobs.com
FinanceJobsites.com (Geojobsites)
www.financejobsites.com
Financial Executives Institute
www.fei.org
Financial Executives Networking Group
www.thefeng.org
Financial Job Network
www.fjn.com

Financial Jobfinder.com
www.financialjobfinder.com
Financial jobs.com
www.financialjobs.com
Financial Positions (Career Engine)
www.financialpositions.com
Financial Times Career Point (T)
www.ftcareerpoint.com
Financial Women International
www.fwi.org/
Find a job in Africa
www.findajobinafrica.com
Find A Pilot
www.findapilot.com
Find Florida Jobs
www.findfloridajobs.com
Find Law
www.findlaw.com
Find-A-Job-Canada
www.find-a-job-canada.com
Finishing.com
www.finishing.com
First Coast Jobs
www.firstcoastjobs.com
First Jobs (Advance Careers)
www.firstjobs.com
fish 4 Jobs
www.jobhunter.co.uk/
Fish jobs
www.fishjobs.com
Fitness Link
www.fitnesslink.com
FlintWanted (Reg.HelpWanted)
www.flinthelpwanted.com
Flip Dog (Monster)
www.flipdog.com
Florida Computer Jobs.com
www.florida.computerjobs.com
Florida Computerwork.com
www.florida.computerwork.com
Food and Drink Jobs.com
www.foodanddrinkjobs.com
Food and Drug Law Institute
www.fdli.org
Food Industry Jobs.com
www.foodindustryjobs.com
Food Job Source
www.foodjobsource.com
food service.com
www.foodservice.com
Food Supplier.com
www.foodsupplier.com
ForContractRecruiters.com
www.forcontractrecruiters.com
Fort Bend Jobs
www.fortbendjobs.com
Fort Wayne News Sentinel (CareerBuilder)
www.fortwayne.com
Fort Worth Star-Telegram (CareerBuilder)
www.dfw.com
Free Agent
www.freeagent.com
Free JobFinder
www.freejobfinder.com
Freelance Work Exchange
www.freelanceworkexchange.com
Freetime Jobs.com
www.freetimejobs.com
Fresh Jobs
www.freshjobs.com
Fresno Bee (Employment Wizard)
www.fresnobee.com
Frontiers in Bioscience
www.bioscience.org

Ft. Myers News-Press (USA Today Careers)
www.news-press.com
Ft. Worth Star-Telegram (CareerBuilder)
www.star-telegram.com
Funeral Net
www.funeralnet.com
funjobs.com
www.funjobs.com
Future Access Employment Guide
www.futureaccess.com
GasJobs.com
www.gasjobs.com
GasWork.com
www.gaswork.com
Gay Work.com
www.gaywork.com
Genome Web
www.genomeweb.com
Geo HealthJobsites.com (Geojobsites)
www.geohelthjobsite.som
Geo Job Source
www.geojobsource.com
Geo Jobsites.com
www.grojobsites.com
Geo Place.com
www.geoplace.com
Geo Search
www.geosearch.com
Geo TechJobs.com
www.geotechjobs.com
GeoCommunity Career Center
careers.geocomm.com
Georgia Careers.com (LocalCareers)
www.georgiacareers.com
Georgia Jobs.com
www.georgiajobs.com
Georgia Jobs.net (LocalCareers)
www.georgiajobs.net
GeoSearch, Inc.
www.geosearch.com
Geospatial Information & Technology Assoc.
www.gita.org
GeoWeb Interactive
www.ggrweb.com
get a govjob.com
www.getagovjob.com
Get Jobs.com
www.getjobs.com
Get Me A Job
www.getmeajob.com
Get Work.com
www.getwork.com
GIS careers.com
www.giscareers.com
GIS Jobs Clearinghouse
www.gjc.org
GIS-A-Job
www.gisajob.com
GISjobs.com
www.gisjobs.com
Global Wrokplace
www.global-workplace.com
Go Erie.com (Employment Wizard)
www.goerie.com
Go Ferret Go
www.goferretgo.com
GO Jobs
www.gojobs.com
Go Jobsite-France
www.gojobsite.fr
Go Jobsite-Germany
www.gojobsite.de
Go Jobsite-Ireland
www.gojobsite.ie

Go Jobsite-Italy
www.gojobsite.it
Go Jobsite-Spain
www.gojobsite.es
Go Jobsite-UK
www.gojobsite.co.uk
Go SanAngelo (Standard-Times)
www.gosanangelo.com
GOJobs.com
www.gojobs.com
Golf Surfin
www.golfsurfin.com
Golfing Careers
www.golfingcareers.com
gomemphis.com (Employment Wizard)
www.gomemphis.com
Good Works
www.essential.org/goodworks/
Government Classifieds (Career Engine)
www.governmentclassifieds.com
GovernmentJobs.com
www.governmentjobs.com/
GovMed CAREERS (MedCareers)
www.govmedcareers.com
Graduate Nurse
www.GraduateNurse.com
graduate-jobs.com
www.graduate-jobs.com
Graduating Engineer & Computer Careers O...
www.graduatingengineer.com
Gradunet
www.gradunet.co.uk
Grand Forks.com (CareerBuilder)
www.grandforks.com
Grand Rapids Careers (Employment Partner)
www.grandrapidscareers.com
Graphic Artists Guild
www.gag.org
Graphic Arts Information Network
www.gain.org
Grass Is Greener.com (Employon.com)
www.grassisgreener.com
Great Falls Tribune (USA Today Careers))
www.greatfallstribune.com
Great Insurance Jobs
www.GreatInsuranceJobs.com
Great Nurse.com
www.greatnurse.com
Great Summer Jobs/Misc
www.greatsummerjobs.com
Great Teacher.net
greatteacher.net
Gree To Gray (Corporate Gray Online)
www.greentogray.com
Green Dream Jobs
www.sustainablebusiness.com/jobs
Green Energy Jobs
www.greenenergyjobs.com
Greensboro News & Record
www.greensboro.com/
Greenville News (USA Today Careers))
www.greenvilleonline.com
Greenwich Time (CareerBuilder)
www.greenwichtime.com
GrooveJob.com
www.groovejob.com
Guardian Unlimited Jobs
www.jobsunlimited.co.uk
Gulf Coast Sun-Herald (CareerBuilder)
www.mississippicoast.com
Gulf Live (Advance Careers)
www.gulflive.com
Guru.com
www.guru.com

H Careers
www.hcareers.com
H Monster.com (Monster.com)
www.hmonster.com
H1B Sponsors
www.h1bsponsors.com
H1Maia.com
www.corp2corp.com
Hampton Roads Daily Press (CareerBuilder)
www.hamptonroadscareers.com
Hanap-Buhay.com.ph
www.hanap-buhay.com
Hartford County Jobs.com (All County Jobs)
www.hartfordcountyjobs.com
Hartford Courant (CareerBuilder)
www.ctnow.com
HartfordHelpWanted (Reg.HelpWanted)
www.hartfordhelpwanted.com
Hattiesburg American (USA Today Careers)
www.hattiesburgamerican.com
HeadHunt (Counsel Network)
www.headhunt.com
Health Care Job Store
www.healthcarejobstore.com
Health Care Jobs Online
www.hcjobsonline.com
Health Care Recruitment Online
www.healthcareers-online.com
Health Care Source
www.healthcaresource.com
Health Care Talents
www.healthcaretalents.com
Health CareerWeb.com (Employment Guide)
www.healthcareerweb.com
Health Jobsite.com
www.healthjobsite.com
Healthcare Employment.com (Career Market...
www.healthcareprofessional.com
Healthcare Financial Management Assoc.
www.hfma.org
HealthCare Hub.com (Nursing Spectrum)
www.healthcarehub.com
HEALTHeCareers (T)
www.healthecareers.com
Help Desk Institute
www.thinkhdijobdesk.com
Help Wanted.com
www.helpwanted.com
HelpWanted Boston (Reg.HelpWanted)
www.helpwantedboston.com
Help-Wanted.Net
www.help-wanted.net/
HelpWantedDC.com (Reg.HelpWanted)
www.helpwantedDC.com
hi techclub.com
www.hitechclub.com
Higher EdJobs.com
www.higheredjobs.com
Hilton Head Island Packet (Employment Wizard)
www.islandpacketonline.com
Hire A Vet (The Destiny Group)
www.hireavet.com
Hire Abilitiy.com
www.hireability.com
Hire Albany.com
www.hirealbany.com
Hire Asian
www.hireasian.com
Hire Atlanta.com
www.hireatlanta.com
Hire Austin.com
www.hireaustin.com
Hire Buffalo.com
www.hirebuffalo.com

Hire Charlotte.com
www.hirecharlotte.com
Hire Cincinnatti.com
www.hirecincinatti.com
Hire Columbus.com
www.hirecolumbus.com
Hire Dayton.com
www.hiredayton.com
Hire Deaf.com
www.hiredeaf.com
Hire Denver.com
www.hiredenver.com
Hire Diversity.com
www.hirediversity.com
Hire GreaterWashington.com
www.hiregreaterwashington.com
hire health.com
www.hirehealth.com
Hire Honolulu.com
www.hirehonolulu.com
Hire houston.com
www.hirehouston.com
Hire hub
www.hirehub.com
Hire in a Click
www.hireinaclick.com
Hire Jacksonville.com
www.hirejacksonville.com
Hire KansasCity.com
www.hirekansascity.com
Hire Loisville.com
www.hirelouisville.com
Hire Memphis.com
www.hirememphis.com
Hire Milwaukee.com
www.hiremilwaukee.com
Hire Nashville.com
www.hirenashville.com
Hire Orlando.com
www.hireorlando.com
Hire Philadelphia.com
www.hirephiladelphia.com
Hire Phoenix.com
www.phoenix.com
Hire Pittsburgh.com
www.hirepittsburgh.com
Hire Sacramento.com
www.hiresacramento.com
Hire San Antonio.com
www.sanantonio.com
Hire SanFrancisco.com
www.hiresanfrancisco.com
Hire SanJose.com
www.hiresanjose.com
Hire Seattle.com
www.hireseattle.com
Hire Skills.com
www.hireskills.com
Hire StLouis.com
www.hirestlouis.com
Hire Tampa Bay.com
www.hiretampabay.com
Hire Texas
www.twc.state.tx.us/jobs/job.html
Hire the Triad
www.hirethetriad.com
Hire the Triangle
www.hirethetriangle.com
Hire Top Talent
www.hiretoptalent.com
Hire TwinCities.com
www.hiretwincities.com
Hire Wichita.com
www.hiregreaterwichita.com

HireBaltimore.com
www.hireBaltimore.com
HireBio
www.hirebio.com
HireGate
www.hiregate.com
HireMass.com
www.hiremass.com
hireMedical
www.hiremedical.com
HireNursing
www.hirenursing.com
Hiring Network
www.hiringnetwork.com
Hispania Net
www.hispanianet.com
Hispanic Alliance for Career Enhancement
www.hace.org
Hispanic Business.com)
www.hispanicbusiness.com
Hispanic Nat'l Bar Association
www.hnba.com
Hispanic Online (Monster)
www.hispaniconline.com
Hispanicareers.com (Hire-Power)
www.hispanicareers.com
Historically Black Colleges and Universities
HBCUCareerCenter.com
Hollywood MVP.com (CareerMVP)
www.hollywoodmvp.com
Hollywood Web
www.hollywoodweb.com
Home Jobs Plus.com
www.homejobsplus.com
Honolulu Advertiser (USA Today Careers))
www.honoluluadvertiser.com
Honolulu Star Bulletin
starbulletin.com
HonoluluHelpWanted (Reg.HelpWanted)
www.honoluluhelpwanted.com
Horticultural Jobs
www.horticulturaljobs.com
Hospital Hub UK.com
www.hospitalhubuk.com
Hospital Jobs Online
www.hospitaljobsonline.com
hospitality careernet.com
www.hospitalitycareernet.com
Hospitality Careers.net
www.hospitalitycareers.net
Hospitality Financial & Technology Professi...
www.iaha.org
Hospitality Jobs Online
www.hospitalityonline.com
Hospitality Jobs Online
www.hotel-jobs.com
Hospitality jobz.net
www.hospitalityjobz.net
Hospitality Link
www.hospitalitylink.com
Hospitality MVP.com (CareerMVP)
www.hospitalitymvp.com
Hospitality Net
www.hospitalitynet.org
Hot Jobs.com (T)
www.hotjobs.com
Hot Nurse Jobs
www.hotnursejobs.com
Hot resumes.com
www.hotresumes.com
hotauditjobs.com
www.hotauditjobs.com
Hotel Jobs- Ireland
www.hoteljobs.ie

Hotel Jobs.com
www.hoteljobs.com
Hotel Online
www.hotel-online.com
HotelJobsites.com (Geojobsites)
www.geohoteljobsites.com
HotJobs.ca (HotJobs.com)
www.hotjobs.ca
House of Fusion
www.houseoffusion.com
Houston Geological Society
www.hgs.org
Houston Chronicle
www.chron.com
Houston Employment.com (Employocity)
www.employocity.com
HR Connections Direct
www.hrjobs.com
HR Job Net
www.hrjobnet.com/
HR Junction
www.hrjunction
HR Next
www.hrnext.com
HR Pal
www.hrpal.com
HR Staffing Search (JV Search)
www.hrstaffingsearch.com
HR World
www.hrworld.com
HR.com
www.hr.com
HRIM Mall
www.hrimmall.com
HRM Jobs (NicheJobs)
www.hrmjobs.com
HRMed.com
www.hrmed.com
HRMVP MVP.com (CareerMVP)
www.hrmvp.com
hs people (Human Services)
www.hspeople.com
HTML Writers Guild Job List
www.hwg.org
Human Factors and Ergonomics Society
www.hfes.org
Human Resource Assoc. of the Nat'l. Capital...
www.hra-nca.org
Human Resources Job Store (eJob Stores)
www.humanresourcesjobstore.com
Human Resources Online
www.hro.ru/
Human Services Career Network
www.HSCareers.com
Humanlinks.com
www.humanlinks.com
Huntington Herald-Disp. (USA Today Careers))
www.info@hdonline.com
HVAC Careers (CareerMVP)
www.hvaccareers.com
HVAC job.com (Electric Job)
www.havacjob.com
HVAC Mall
www.hvacmall.com
Hydrocarbon Online (VerticalNet)
www.hydrocarbononline.com/
i -street
www.i-street.com
Iamable.com (Hire-Power)
www.iamable.com
Idaho Press-Tribune (Employment Wizard)
www.idahopress.com
Idaho State Jobs
www.labor.state.id.us/

Idaho Statesman (USA Today Careers))
www.idahostatesman.com
idealist.org
www.idealist.org
IDEAS Job Network (Mercury Enterprises)
www.ideasjn.com
iHire Job Network
www.ihirejobnetwork.com
ihispano.com
www.ihispano.com
IL Careers.com (CareerMVP)
www.ilcareers.com
Illinois Jobs.com (LocalCareers)
www.illinoisjobs.com
IMdiversity.com (T)
www.imdiversitycom
Impact Online
www.impactonline.org
Independent Press Assoc.
www.indypress.org
Independent School Management (ISM)
www.isminc.com/pubs/mart/mm.html
Independent Sector Job Link
www.independentsector.org
Indian Jobs
www.indianjobs.com
Indianapolis Star (USA Today Careers)
www.indystar.com
Industrial Designers Society of America
www.idsa.org
Industrial Engineer.com (Career Marketplace)
www.industrialengineer.com
Infectious Disease Soc. of America
www.idsociety.org
Info Jobs.net (Bolsa de Trabajo)
www.infojobs.net
Info Mine
www.infomine.com
InhouseCounsel (Counsel Network)
www.inhousecounsel.ca
Inner City Jobs.com(NicheJobs)
www.innercityjobs.com
Inomics
www.inomics.com
InPharm.com
www.inpharm.com
InRetail
www.inretail.co.uk
Inside Careers
www.insidecareers.co.uk
Inside Careers
www.insidecareers.co.uk
InspectionJobs.com
www.inspectionjobs.com
Institute for Professionals in Taxation
www.ipt.org
Institute for Supply Management
www.ism.ws
Institute of Certified Travel Agents
www.icta.com
Institute of Electrical and Electronics Engineers
www.ieee.org
Institute of Food Technologists
www.ift.org
Institute of Industrial Engineers
www.iienet.org
Institute of Internal Auditors
www.theiia.org/careercenter
Institute of Packaging Professionals
www.iopp.org
Institute of Store Planners
www.ispo.org
Institution of Professional Engineers
http://www.ipenz.org.nz/jobhunt

Instrumentation Soc. of America
www.isajobs.org/
Insurance File
www.insfile.com
Insurance National Search
www.insurancerecruiters.com
Intelligence & Defense Careers
www.intelligencecareers.com
InterEC.NET
www.interec.net
Interface JOBS.com
www.interfacejobs.com
Interior Design Jobs.com
www.interiordesignjobs.com
Intern Jobs.com (About Jobs.com)
www.internjobs.com
Intern Web.com
www.internweb.com
Internet Career Connection
www.iccweb.com
Internet Employment in New Mexico
www.internetjobs.org
Internet Job Locator
www.joblocator.com
Internet Jobs.com
www.internetjobs.com
Internship Programs.com (Wet Feet)
www.internshipprograms.com
Int'l Assoc. of Business Communicators
www.iabc.com
Int'l Customer Service Assoc.
www.icsa.com
Int'l Nortel Networks Meridian Users Group
www.innmug.org
Int'l Soc. for the Performing Arts
www.ispa.org
Int'l Tandem Users Group
www.itug.org
Int'l. Assoc. for HR Info Mgmt.
ihrim.org
Int'l. Assoc. of Amusement Parks and Attrac...
www.iaapa.org
Int'l. Assoc. of Conference Centers
www.iacconline.com
Int'l. Career Employment Center
www.internationaljobs.org
Int'l. Economic Development Council
www.iedconline.org
Int'l. Foundation of Employee Benefit Plans
www.ifebp.org/jobs
Int'l. Personnel Mgmt. Assoc. (CareerBuilder)
www.ipma-hr.org
Int'l. Pharmajobs
www.pharmajobs.com
Int'l. Seafarers Exchange
www.jobxchange.com
Int'l. Soc. of Logistics
www.sole.org
Int'l. Society For Performance Improvements
www.ispi.org
Iowa City Press-Citizen (USA Today Careers)
www.press-citizen.com
Iowa State Jobs
www.state.ia.us/jobs/index.htm
Ireland Hiring
www.irelandhiring
i-resign.com
www.i-resign.com
Irish Jobs.ie (T)
www.irishjobs.ie
Iron and Steel Society
www.iss.org
Ist Free Jobs
www.1stfreejobs.com

382

IT Careers.com
www.itcareers.com
IT Classifieds (Career Engine)
www.itclassifieds.com
IT Jobfinder.co.za (JobUniverse)
www.ITJobfinder.co.za
IT Jobs4.com
www.itjobs4.com
IT Moonlighter
www.a2zmoonlighter.com
IT Online Jobs
www.itonlinejobs.com
IT talent.com
www.ittalent.com
IT Toolbox Forums
www.ittoolbox.com
IT Toolbox's Baan Assist
baan.ittoolbox.com
IT Toolbox's CRM Assist
crm.ittoolbox.com
IT Toolbox's Data Warehousing Assist
dw.ittoolbox.com
IT Toolbox's EAI Assist
eai.ittoolbox.com
IT Toolbox's E-Business Assist
ebiz.ittoolbox.com
IT Toolbox's ERP Assist
erp.ittoolbox.com
IT Toolbox's Oracle Assist
oracle.ittoolbox.com
IT Toolbox's PeopleSoft Assist
peoplesoft.ittoolbox.com
IT Toolbox's SAP Assist
sap.ittoolbox.com
IT World (ITCareers)
www.itworld.com
Ithaca Cortland Careers (Employment Partner)
www.ithacacortlandcareers.com
ITonlinejobs
www.ITonlinejobs.com
It's Your Job Now
www.itsyourjobnow.com
ItsYourJobNow.com
www.itsyourjobnow.com
it-TEMP
it-temp.com
ITwow.com
www.itwow.com
iVillage (CareerBuilder)
www.ivillage.com
Jackson Clarion-Ledger (USA Today Careers))
www.clarionledger.com
Jackson Sun (USA Today Careers))
www.jacksonsun.com
JacksonvilleHelpWanted (Reg.HelpWanted)
www.jacksonvillehelpwanted.com
JamminJobs.com
www.jamminjobs.com
Japanese Jobs
www.japanesejobs.com
Java Computer work.com
www.java.computerwork.com
Java Jobs
www.javajobs.com/
Java World (ITCareers)
www.javaworld.com
Javajobsonline.com
www.javajobsonline.com
Jeff Gaulin's Canadian Journalism Job Board
www.jeffgaulin.com
Jersey Job Guide
www.jerseyjobguide.com
Jewish Camp Staff
www.jewishcampstaff.com

Jewish Vocational Services Career Moves
www.jvsjobs.org
JMO Jobs (MMR)
www.jmojobs.com
Job AA
www.jobaa.com
Job Access (CareerBuilder)
www.jobaccess.org
Job Ads
www.jobads.com
Job Asia
www.jobasia.com
Job Bank USA
www.jobbankusa.com
Job Boards.com
www.jobboards.com
Job Bright
www.jobbright.com
Job Cafe
www.jobcafe.co.za
Job Catalog
www.jobcatalog.com
Job Centro
www.jobcentro.com
job channel.tv
www.jobchannel.tv
Job Circle.com (T)
www.jobcircle.com
Job City USA.com (Spherion)
www.jobcityusa.com
Job Dig
www.jobdig.com
Job Easy
www.jobeasy.com
Job Factory
www.jobfactory.com
job find.com
www.jobfind.com
Job fly
www.jobfly.com
Job Folder.com
www.jobfolder.com
Job Food
www.jobfood.com
job force
www.jobforce.com
Job Gusher.com
www.Jobgusher.com
Job Hub
www.jobhub.com/
Job Index.co.za
www.thejobindex.co.za
Job Island.com
www.jobisland.com
job khoj
www.jobkhoj.com
Job Latino
www.joblatino.com
Job Launch
www.joblaunch.com
Job Link Asia
www.JobLinkAsia.com
Job Link For Journalists
ajr.org
Job Link-USA
www.joblink-usa.com
Job Listings.net
www.joblistings.net
Job Mag.com
www.jobmag.com
Job Magic
www.jobmagic.net
Job Master
www.jobmaster.com.sg

Job Monkey
www.jobmonkey.com
Job Navigator
www.jobs.co.za
Job Net Australia
www.jobnet.com.au
Job net.com
www.jobnet.com
Job Next Career Network
www.jobnext.com
Job Opps.net
www.jobopps.net
Job Penguin
www.jobpenguin.com
job pilot.com Austria
www.jobpilot.at
job pilot.com Belgium
www.jobpilot.be
job pilot.com Czech
www.jobpilot.cz
job pilot.com Denmark
www.jobpilot.dk
job pilot.com France
www.jobpilot.fr
job pilot.com Germany
www.jobpilot.de
job pilot.com Hungary
www.jobpilot.hu
job pilot.com Italy
www.jobpilot.it
job pilot.com Netherlands
www.jobpilot.nl
job pilot.com Norway
www.jobpilot.no
job pilot.com Poland
www.jobpilot.pl
job pilot.com Spain
www.jobpilot.es
job pilot.com Sweden
www.jobpilot.se
job pilot.com Switzerland
www.jobpilot.ch
job pilot.com Thailand
www.jobpilot.co.th
job pilot.com UK
www.jobpilot.co.uk
job pilot.com USA
www.usa.jobpilot.com
Job Postings
www.jobpostings.net
Job right.com
www.jobright.com
Job science.com
www.jobscience.com
Job Seekers Mailing List
www.met.rdg.ac.uk/~brugge/jobseekers.html
Job Serve: Accountancy Vacancies in the UK
www.jobserve.com
Job Shark
www.jobshark.com
Job Shark-Argentina
www.jobsharkargentina.com
Job Shark-Brasil
www.jobshark.com.br
Job Shark-Canada
www.jobshark.ca
Job Shark-Chile
www.jobshark.com.cl
Job Shark-Columbia
www.jobshark.com.co
Job Shark-Ireland
www.jobshark.ie
Job Shark-Mexico
www.jobshark.com.mx

Job Shark-Peru
www.jobshark.com.pe
Job Shark-UK
www.jobshark.co.uk
Job Shark-Uruguay
www.jobsharkuruguay.com
Job Shark-Venezuela
www.jobshark.com.ve
job site.com
www.jobsite.com/
Job Smack
www.jobsmack.com
Job Square
www.jobsquare.com
Job Street
www.jobstreet.com
Job Street-India
www.jobstreet.co.in
Job Toaster
www.jobtoaster.com/
Job Track Online (Job Magic)
www.jobtrack.co.uk
Job Universe
www.jobuniverse.com
Job Village
www.jobvillage.com
Job Ware
www.jobware.com
Job Warehouse
www.jobwarehouse.com
Job.com
www.job.com
Job2Teach
www.jobs2teach.doded.mil/
Jobbig
www.jobbig.com
JobDoggy
www.JobDoggy.com
JobExpo.com
www.americanjobfairs.com
JobGusher
www.JobGusher.com
job-hunt.org
www.job-hunt.org
Jobing.com
www.jobing.com
Jobline-Finland (Monster.com)
www.jobline.fi
Jobline-France (Monster.com)
www.jobline.fr
Jobline-Germany (Monster.com)
www.jobline.de
Jobline-Italy (Monster.com)
www.jobline.it
Jobline-Netherlands (Monster.com)
www.jobline.nl
Jobline-Norway (Monster.com)
www.jobline.no
Jobline-Spain (Monster.com)
www.jobline.es
Jobline-Sweden (Monster.com)
www.jobline.se
Jobline-Switzerland (Monster.com)
www.jobline.ch
Jobline-UK (Monster.com)
www.jobline.co.uk
jobpilot.com
www.jobpilot.com
JobRadio.com
www.JobRadio.com
Jobs 4 HR (LocalCareers)
www.jobs4hr.com
Jobs 4 Sales.com (LocalCareers)
www.jobs4sales.com

Jobs 4police
www.jobs4police.com
Jobs Bazaar.com
www.JobsBazaar.com
Jobs Bazaar.com
www.jobsbazaar.com
Jobs Canada
www.jobscanada.com
Jobs DB.com
www.jobsdb.com
Jobs for Colorado.com
www.jobsforcolorado.com
Jobs for Economists (JOE)
www.eco.utexas.edu/joe/
Jobs for Networkers (JobsforProgrammers)
www.network-careers.com
Jobs for Programmers (T)
www.prgjobs.com
Jobs Hawaii
www.jobshawaii.com
Jobs in Chicago
www.jobsinchicago.com
Jobs in Edinburgh.com
www.jobsinedinburgh.com
Jobs in Education
www.jobsineducation.com
Jobs in Entomology
www.colostate.edu/Depts/Entomology/jobs/jobs.html
Jobs in Fashion.com
www.jobsinfashion.com
Jobs in Horticulture
www.hortjobs.com
Jobs in Japan
www.jobsinjapan.com
Jobs in Journalism
eb.journ.latech.edu/jobs.html
Jobs in Logistics
www.jobsinlogistics.com
Jobs in Maine
www.jobsinme.com
Jobs in MFG.com (Jobs in Logistics)
www.allretailjobs.com
Jobs in Philosophy
www.sozialwiss.uni-hamburg.de/phil/ag/jobs
Jobs in Sports
www.jobsinsports.com
Jobs in the Biz
www.jobsinthebiz.com
jobs in the money
www.jobsinthemoney.com
Jobs in Therapy
www.jobsintherapy.com
Jobs Nation
www.jobsnation.co.uk
Jobs on Guam.com
www.jobsonguam.com
Jobs Online
www.jobsonline.com/
Jobs Plus.com.au
www.careersonline.com.au
Jobs Retail.com
www.jobsretail.com
Jobs tri-cities.com (Employment Wizard)
www.jobstri-cities.com
Jobs USA.co.uk (FlipDog)
www.JobsUSA.co.uk
Jobs.ac.uk
www.jobs.ac.uk
Jobs.com (Monster)
www.jobs.com
Jobs.in.York.com (CareerSite)
www.jobs.inyork.com
jobs.internet.com (DICE)
jobs.internet.com

Jobs.net
www.jobs.net
Jobs4Gems
www.jobs4gems.com
JOBSfront
www.jobsfront.com
Jobs-Ireland.com
www.jobs-ireland.com
Job-Sites.com
www.job-sites.com
Jobstor.com
www.jobstor.com
Jobvertise
www.jobvertise.com
Jobz
www.jobz.ozware.com
Joint Service Academy Alumni Organizations
www.JSAJE.com
Joint Service Academy Resume DBS (Desti...
www.jsards.com
Journal of Commerce (Career Engine)
www.journalofcommerce.com
Journalism and Women's Symposium
www.jaws.org
Journalism for journalists (UK)
www.journalism.co.uk
Journalism Jobs.com
journalismjobs.com
Jumbo Classifieds
www.jumboclassifieds.com
Just Access Jobs
www.justaccessjobs.com
Just Accounting Jobs.com
www.justaccountingjobs.com
Just AS400 Jobs
www.justas400jobs.com
Just ASP Jobs
www.justaspjobs.com
Just Baan Jobs
www.justbaanjobs.com
Just c Jobs
www.justcjobs.com
Just CAD Jobs
www.justCADjobs.com
Just Cobol Jobs
www.justcoboljobs.com
Just computerjobs.com
www.justcomputerjobs.com
Just DB2 Jobs
www.justDB2jobs.com
Just E-Commerce Jobs
www.juste-commercejobs.com
Just Engineering Jobs.com
www.justengineeringjobs.com
Just Entertainment Jobs.com
www.justentertainmentjobs.com
Just Health Care Jobs.com
www.justhealthcarejobs.com
Just Help Desk Jobs
www.justhelpdeskjobs.com
Just Hospitality Jobs.com
www.justhospitalityjobs.com
Just JAVA Jobs
www.justjavajobs.com
Just Manufacturing Jobs.com
www.justmanufacturingjobs.com
Just Marketing Jobs.com
www.justmarketingjobs.com
Just My Jobs.com
www.justmyjobs.com
Just Networking Jobs
www.justnetworkingjobs.com
Just Notes Jobs
www.justnotesjobs.com

Just NT Jobs
www.justntjobs.com
Just Oracle Jobs
www.justoraclejobs.com
Just PeopleSoft Jobs
www.justpeoplesoftjobs.com
Just Sales
www.justsales.com
Just Science Jobs.com
www.justsciencejobs.com
Just SQL Server Jobs
www.justsqlserverjobs.com
Just Sybase Jobs
www.justsybasejobs.com
Just Tech Jobs.com
www.justtechjobs.com
Just Telephony Jobs
www.justtelephonyjobs.com
Just Unix Jobs
www.justunixjobs.com
Just Visual Basic Jobs
www.justvisualbasicjobs.com
Just Writing Jobs.com
www.justwritingjobs.com
JV Search
www.orasearch.com
Kansas City Star (CareerBuilder)
www.kansascity.com
Kansas State Jobs
da.state.ks.us
Kansas.com (CareerBuilder)
www.kansas.com
KansasCityWanted (Reg.HelpWanted)
www.kansascityhelpwanted.com
KareerMakers.com
www.kareermakers.com
KARRIER Online
www.karrier.hu
Kenosha County.com (Employment Wizard)
www.kenoshacounty.com
Kentuckiana Jobs
www.kentuckianajobs.com/
Kentucky KY Direct
www.kydirect.net
Knox Careers.com (Employment Wizard)
www.knoxcareers.com
Knox News.com
www.knoxnews.com
Knoxville Careers Online (Employment Partner)
www.knoxvillecareersonline.com
LA Daily News (Employment Wizard)
www.dailynews.com
LA Employment.com (Employocity)
www.laemployment.com
LA Job Market (CareerLINK)
www.lajobmarket.com
LA Times.com (CareerBuilder)
www.latimes.com
Laborum.com
www.laborum.com
LaCrosse Tribune (Employment Wizard)
www.lacrossetribune.com
Lafayette Daily Advertiser (USA Today Car...
www.theadvertiser.com
Lafayette Journal & Courier (USA Today Ca...
www.jconline.com
Lan Jobs.com (Pure Power)
www.lanjobs.com
Lancaster Eagle-Gazette (USA Today Care...
www.lancastereaglegazette.com
Lancaster Sentinel Enterprise (Employment...
www.sentinelandenterprise.com
Lanka Web
www.lankaweb.com

Lansing State Journal (USA Today Careers)
www.lansingstatejournal.com
LasVegasHelpWanted (Reg.HelpWanted)
www.lasvegashelpwanted.com
Latin American Jobs.com
www.latinamericanjobs.com
Latino Web
www.latinoweb.com
LatPRO (T)
www.latpro.com
LavaTech's - Lotus Notes Jobs
www.lotusnotes.com
Law Bulletin
www.lawbulletin.com
law enforcementjobs.com
www.lawenforcementjobs.com
Law Forum
www.lawforum.net
Law Guru (Legal Staff)
www.lawguru.com
Law Guru.com (Legalstaff)
www.lawguru.com
Law Info.com
jobs.lawinfo.com
Law Jobs
www.lawjobs.com/
Law Listings (Career Engine)
www.lawlistings.com
Lawsonline.com (Legal Staff)
www.lawsonline.com
LawStar (Legal Staff)
www.lawstar.com
Lawyers Weekly
www.lawyersweeklyjobs.com
Layoff Lounge
www.layofflounge.com
Layover.com (T)
www.layover.com
Lebenon Daily News (Employment Wizard)
www.ldnews.com
Lee Hecht Harrison
www.lhh.com
Legal CV
www.legalcv.com
Legal Report
www.legalreport.com
Legal SecretariesUSA.com
www.legalsecretariesusa.com
Legal staff.com (T)
www.legalstaff.com
Lender Careers
www.lendercareers.com
Lexington Herald-Leader (CareerBuilder)
www.kentucky.com
LI jobs.com
www.lijobs.com
Lincoln Journal Star.com (Employment Wizard)
www.journalstar.com
Linux World (ITCareers)
www.linuxworld.com
Little Rock Careers Online (Employment Part...
www.littletockcareersonline.com
Little Rock Democart-Gazette
www.ardemgaz.com
LittleRock HelpWanted. (Reg.HelpWanted)
www.littlerockhelpwanted.com
Local Careers.com
www.localcareers.com
Local job Network
www.localjobnetwork.com
Locum Tenens.com
www.locumtenens.com
Long Beach Press-Telegram (Employment W...
www.newsminer.com

Los Angeles Computer Jobs.com
www.losangeles.computerjobs.com
LosAngelesHelpWanted (Reg.HelpWanted)
www.losangeleshelpwanted.com
Lotus Notes Jobs.com (Pure Power)
www.lotusnotesjobs.com
Lotus Professional.com (Career Marketplace)
www.lotusprofessional.com
Louisiana State Jobs
www.dscs.state.la.us/
Louisville Careers (Employment Partner)
www.ilouisvillecareers.com
Louisville Courier Jrnl (USA Today Careers))
www.courier-journal.com
LouisvilleWanted (Reg.HelpWanted)
www.louisvillehelpwanted.com
Lowell Sun (Employment Wizard)
www.lowellsun.com
LPN Jobs.com (HealthCareJobStore)
www.lpnjobs.com
MA Careers.com (CareerMVP)
www.macareers.com
Mac Talent.com
www.mactalent.com
Macon Telegraph (CareerBuilder)
www.macon.com
Madison Newspapers (Employment Wizard)
www.madison.com
Magazine Publishers of America
www.magazine.org
Manitoba jobs.com (Canjobs)
www.manitobajobs.com
Mansfield News Journal (USA Today Careers)
www.mansfieldnewsjournal.com
Manufacturing MVP.com (CareerMVP)
www.manufacturingmvp.com
Marion Star(USA Today Careers)
www.marionstar.com
Marketing Dreamjobs
www.rosengren.net
Marketing Jobs.com
www.marketingjobs.com
Marketing JobStore.com (eJob Stores)
www.marketingjobstore.com
Marketing Manager.com (Career Marketplace)
www.MarketingManager.com
Marketing MVP.com (CareerMVP)
www.marketingmvp.com
Mass Live (Advance Careers)
www.masslive.com/careers
Massachusetts Biotechnology Council
www.massbio.org
Material Information Society
www.asminternational.org
Materials Jobs.com (NicheJobs)
www.materialsjobs.com
MBA Careers (Career Exposure)
www.mbacareers.com
MBA GlobalNet
www.mbaglobalnet.com
MBA Jungle
www.mbajungle.com
MD Direct.com
www.mddirect.com
MD Jobsite.com
www.mdjobsite.com
MD Recruitment Online (HC Recruitment Onli...
www.mdrecruitmentonline.com
Mechanical Contractors Asso. of America
www.mcaa.org
Mechanical Engineer.com (Career Marketpla...
www.mechanicalengineer.com
Mechanical Engineers Magazine Online (AS...
www.memagazine.org/

Med BizPeople.com
www.medbizpeople.com
Med Bulletin
www.medbulletin.com
Med CAREERS (T)
www.medcareers.com
Med Hunters
www.medhunters.com
med jump
www.medjump.com
Med Options (Absolutely Health Care)
www.medoptions.com
med2020
www.med2020.com
media bistro.com
www.mediabistro.com
Media Jobz.Com
www.mediajobz.com
Media Line.com
www.medialine.com
Media Recruiter.com
www.mediarecruiter.com
Medical DeviceLink.com
www.devicelink.com
Medical MVP.com (CareerMVP)
www.medicalmvp.com
Medical Records Jobs.com (HealthCareJobS...
www.medicalrecordsjobs.com
Medical Reps.com
www.medicalreps.com
Medical Researcher.com (Career Marketplace)
www.medicalresearcher.com
Medical Transition for Veteran Health Care
www.medicaltransition.com
Medicats
www.medicats.com
MediCenter.com (TheBoardNetwork)
www.medicenter.com
MediCentral.com
www.medicentral.com
MedZilla (T)
www.medzilla.com
Meeting Professionals Int'l
www.mpiweb.org
Mega Job Sites (Worklife)
www.megajobsites.com
Memphis Commercial Appeal (Employment W...
www.commercialappeal.com
MemphisComputer work.com
www.memphis.computerwork.com
MemphisHelpWanted (Reg.HelpWanted)
www.memphishelpwanted.com
Mental Web.com
www.mentalweb.com
Mercury Enterprises Job Network
www.acjn.com
Meteorological Employment Journal
www.swiftsite.com/mejjobs/
Mexican American Eng. and Scientists Soc.
www.maes-natl.org
Mexico Online
www.mexonline.com/classifd.htm
Miami Herald (CareerBuilder)
www.herald.com
Michigan Job Hunter.com (Detroit Free Press)
www.MichiganJobHunter.com
Michigan Jobs.com (LocalCareers)
www.michiganjobs.com
Michigan Live (Advance Careers)
www.michiganlive.com/careers
Mid Wife Jobs.com
www.midwifejobs.com
Midwest Computerwork.com
www.midwest.computerwork.com

MASTER LIST

Mil 2Civ.com (The Destiny Group)
mil2civ.com
Military spouses.com (The Destiny Group)
militaryspouses.com
Military.com
www.military.com
Milwaukee Career Board
www.milwaukee.careerboard.com
Milwaukee Journal Sentinel (Employment Wi...
www.onwisconsin.com
Milwaukee Naturally
www.milwaukee-naturally.com
MilwaukeeJobs.com
www.milwaukeejobs.com
Mining USA
www.miningusa.com
Ministry Careers.com
www.ministrycareers.com
Ministry Connect
www.ministryconnect.org
Ministry Jobs.com
www.ministryjobs.com
ministry search.com
www.ministrysearch.com
MinistryEmployment.Com
ministryemployment.com
Minneapolis Star Tribune
www.startribune.com
Minnesota Council of Nonprofits
www.mncn.org
Minnesota Jobs.com (T)
www.minnesotajobs.com
Minority Career Network
www.minoritycareernet.com/
Minority Nurse.com (CASS)
www.minoritynurse.com
Mississippi Coast.com (CareerBuilder)
www.mississippicoast.com
Modern Language Association of America
www.mla.org
Modern Machine Shop Online
www.mmsonline.com
Modesto Bee (Employment Wizard)
www.modbee.com
Mojolin
mojolin.com
Money Making Mommy
moneymakingmommy.com
Monitor
www.monitordaily.com
Monroe News-Star (USA Today Careers)
www.thenewsstar.com
Monster International Zone
international.monster.com
Monster Retail.com
retail.monster.com
Monster Talent Market
talentmarket.monster.com
Monster.com (T)
www.monster.com
Monstertrak.com (formerly JobTrak)
www.jobtrak.com
Montana Society of CPAs
www.mscpa.org
Montana State Jobs
jsd.dli.state.mt.us/
Monterey County Herald (CareerBuilder)
www.montereyca.com
Montgomery Advertiser (USA Today Careers)
career.montgomeryadvertiser.com
mortgage career.com
www.mortgagecareer.com
Mortgage Mag.com (Job Mag)
www.jobmag.com

MortgageJobsites.com (Geojobsites)
www.mortgagejobsites.com
MortgageJobStore.com (eJob Stores)
www.mortgagejobstore.com
Motor Careers
www.motorcareers.com
Mountainjobs.com
www.mountainjobs.com
Muncie Star-Press (USA Today Careers)
www.thestarpress.com
Musicians Network
www.bytes4u.ca
Must Jobs.com
www.mustjobs.com
My Career.com.au
mycareer.com.au
My JobCafe
www.jobcafe.ca
MyRGV.com
jobs.myrgv.com
Myrtle Beach Sun News (CareerBuilder)
www.myrtlebeachonline.com
MyrtleBeachHelpWanted (Reg.HelpWanted)
www.myrtlebeachhelpwanted.com
Nace Web
www.naceweb.org
NACELink
www.Nacelink.org
NALS (Legal staff.)
www.nals.org
Nashville Careers Online (Employment Partner)
www.nashvillecareersonline.com
Nashville Tennesean (USA Today Careers))
www.tennesean.com
Nation Job Network (T)
www.nationjob.com
Native American Jobs.com
www.nativeamericanjobs.com
Native Jobs.com
www.nativejobs.com
Nat'l. Academies Career Center
www4.nationalacademies.org/osep/cpc.nsf
Nat'l. Accrediting Commission of Cosmetolo...
www.naccas.org
Nat'l. Alliance of Black School Educators
www,nabse.org
Nat'l. Assoc of Credit Management.
www.nacm.org
Nat'l. Assoc of Student Personnel Administr...
www.naspa.org
Nat'l. Assoc. for Home Care
www.nahc.org
Nat'l. Assoc. of African Americans in HR
www.naaahr.org
Nat'l. Assoc. of Black Accountants
www.nabainc.org
Nat'l. Assoc. of Black Journalists
nabj.org
Nat'l. Assoc. of Broadcasters
www.nab.org
Nat'l. Assoc. of Corp. Real Estate Exec's.
www.nacore.com
Nat'l. Assoc. of Development Organizations
www.nado.org
Nat'l. Assoc. of Educational Buyers
www.naeb.org
Nat'l. Assoc. of Elevator Contractors
www.naec.org
Nat'l. Assoc. of Environmental Profesionals
www.naep.org
Nat'l. Assoc. of Federal Credit Unions
www.nafcu.org
Nat'l. Assoc. of Hispanic Journalists
www.nahj.org

Nat'l. Assoc. of Ind. & Office Properties
www.naiop.com
Nat'l. Assoc. of Independent Schools
www.nais.org
Nat'l. Assoc. of Industrial Technology
www.nait.org
Nat'l. Assoc. of Manufacturers
www.nam.org
Nat'l. Assoc. of Personal Financial Advisors
www.napfa.org
Nat'l. Assoc. of Sales Professionals
www.nasp.com
Nat'l. Assoc. of Social Workers
www.socialworkers.org
Nat'l. Assoc. of Student Financial Aid
www.nasfaa.org
Nat'l. Assoc. of Women In Construction (Fli...
www.nawic.org/
Nat'l. Assoc. Recording Merchandisers
www.narm.com
Nat'l. Athletic Trainers' Assoc.
www.nata.org
Nat'l. Banking & Financial Services Network
www.nbn-jobs.com
Nat'l. Black MBA Assoc. (NY Chapter)
www.nyblackmba.org
Nat'l. Black MBA Assoc.
www.nbmbaa.org
Nat'l. Business & Disibility Council   Able to ...
www.business-disability.com
Nat'l. Business Incubation Assoc.
www.nbia.org
Nat'l. Contract Management Association
www.NCMAjobs.com
Nat'l. Council of Teachers of Math Jobs Online
www.nctm.org
Nat'l. Directory of Emergency Services
www.policejobs.com
Nat'l. Diversity Newspaper Job Bank
www.newsjobs.com
Nat'l. Emergency Number Assoc.
www.nena9-1-1.org
Nat'l. Environmental Health Assoc.
www.neha.org
Nat'l. Fed. of Paralegal Assoc. (Legal staff.)
www.paralegals.com
Nat'l. FFA Organization
www.ffa.org
Nat'l. Fire & Protection Agency (Monster)
www.nfpa.org
Nat'l. Gerontological SOA - AgeWork
www.agework.com
Nat'l. Registry of Environmental Professionals
www.nrep.org
Nat'l. Soc. of Collegiate Scholars
www.nscs.org
Nat'l. Society of Black Engineers
www.nsbe.org
Nat'l. Society of Hispanic MBAs (BrassRing)
www.nshmba.org
Nat'l. Society of Professional Engineering
www.nspe.org
Nat'l. Teacher Recruitment Clearinghouse
www.recruitingteachers.org
Nat'l. Technical Services Assoc.
www.ntsa.com/
Nat'l. Weather Association
www.nwas.org/jobs.html
Nat'l. Youth Development Information Center
www.nydic.org
Nature Jobs.com
www.nature.com
Naukri
www.naukri.com

NBA Online (Nebraska Bankers Assoc.)
www.nebankers.org
NC Careers.com (CareerMVP)
www.NCCareers.com
NCAA Jobs in College Athletics
www.ncaa.org
NCO Jobs (MMR)
www.ncojobs.com
Nebraska Bankers Assoc.
www.nebankers.org
Nebraska has jobs.com
www.nebraskahasjobs.com
Need Techs.com
www.needtechs.com
Net Empleo.com
www.netempleo.com
Net Jobs
www.netjobs.com
Net share.com (T)
www.netshare.com
Net Staff
www.netstaff.co.za
Net work and Systems Profesionals Assoc.
www.naspa.com
NetEmpleo
www.netempleo.com
Net-Temps (T)
www.net-temps.com
Network Engineer.com (Career Marketplace)
www.nctworkengineer.com
Network of Commercial Real Estate Women
www.nncrew.org
Network World (ITCareers)
www.networkworld.com
Networking Computer work.com
www.networking.computerwork.com
Nevada JobConnect
www.nevadajobconnect.com
Nevada Jobs.com (LocalCareers)
www.Nevadajobs.com
Nevada State Jobs
www.state.nv.us/personnel
New England Computerwork.com
www.newengland.computerwork.com
New England Employee Benefits Council
www.nebc.org
New England Human Resource Assoc.
www.nehra.com
New England Journal of Medicine
www.nejm.org
New England Telecommunications Assoc.
www.n-e-t-a.org/
New Hampshire Job Finder (Telegraph)
www.nhjobfinder.com
New Haven County Jobs.com (All County J...
www.newhavencountyjobs.com
New Jersey Technical Recruiters Alliance
www.njtra.org
New London Careers Online (Employment P...
www.newlondoncareersonline.com
New Media Assoc. of NJ
www.nmanj.com
New Mexico Careers Online (Employment P...
www.newmexicocareersonline.com
New Mexico High Tech Job Forum
www.internetjobs.org
New Mexico State Jobs
www.state.nm.us
new monday.com
jobworld.co.uk
New Orleans Live (Advance Careers)
www.nola.com/careers
New OrleansHelpWanted. (Reg.HelpWanted)
www.neworleanshelpwanted.com

New York Computer Jobs.com
www.newyork.computerjobs.com
New York Computer work.com
www.newyork.computerwork.com
New York Post (CareerBuilder)
www.nypost.com
Newark Advocate (USA Today Careers)
www.newarkadvocate.com
NewHampshireHelpWanted (Reg.HelpWanted)
www.newhapshirehelpwanted.com
Newsday.com (CareerBuilder)
www.newsday.com
NewsOK.com (Employment Wizard)
www.newsok.com
Newspaper Assoc. of America
http://www.naa.org
NH Careers Online (Employment Partner)
www.NHcareersonline.com
NI Jobs.com (Irish Jobs)
www.nijobs.com
NicheJobs.com
www.jobsinaclick.com
NJ Careers
www.njcareers.com
NJ Hire
www.njhire.com
NJ JOBS
www.njjobs.com
NJ Law Network (Legal Staff)
www.njlawnet.com
NJ Online (Advance Careers)
www.nj.com/careers
NJParalegal.com
www.paralegal.com
Nokri.com
www.nokri.com
Non Profit Career.com
www.nonprofitcareer.com
NonprofitOyster
www.nonprofitoyster.com
North Dakota State Jobs
www.state.nd.us
North Jersey HelpWanted.com (Reg. HelpW...
www.northjerseyhelpwanted.com
North Jersey.com (Bergen Record)
www.bergen.com
NorthCountryHelpWanted (Reg.HelpWanted)
www.northcountryhelpwanted.com
Northeast Human Resources Association
www.nehra.com
Northwest Arkansas Times
www.nwarktimes.com
Northwest Recruiters Association
www.nwrecruit.org
Norwich Bulletin (USA Today Careers)
www.norwichbulletin.com
NPO .NET
www.npo.net
Nuke Worker.com
www.nukeworker.com/
Nurse Aid Jobs (HealthCareJobStore)
www.nurseaidjobs.com
Nurse Options (Absolutely Health Care)
www.nurseoptions.com
Nurse Practitioners Central - NPJobs
www.npjobs.com
Nurse-Recruiter
www.nurse-recruiter.com
Nursing Spectrum Career Fitness Online (T)
www.nursingspectrum.com
NW Classifieds (Seattle Times)
www.snwclassifieds.com
NY Careers.com (LocalCareers)
www.NYCareers.com

NY Daily News (Abracat)
www.mostnewyork.com
NY Job Source (Internet Job Source)
nyjobsource.com
NY New Media Assoc. The Silicon Alley Job...
www.nynma.org
NY Newsday.com (CareerBuilder)
www.newsday.com
NY Times Job Market
www.nytimes.com
NYC Employment.com (Employocity)
www.nycemployment.com
NYC Workforce 1
www.nyc.gov/html/wia/home.html
NZ Jobs.co
www.nzjobs.co.nz
Occupational Therapist Jobs (HealthCareJo...
www.occupationaltherapistjobs.com
Office Moonlighter
www.officemoonlighter.com
Offshore Guides
www.offshoreguides.com
O-Hayo Sensei
www.ohayosensei.com
Ohio Jobs.com (LocalCareers)
www.ohiojobs.com
Ohio.com (CareerBuilder)
www.ohio.com
Oil Careers
www.oilcareers.com
Oil Directory.com
www.oildirectory.com
Oil job.com
www.oiljob.com
Oil Online
www.oilonline.com/
OK City Careers (Employment Partner)
www.okcitycareers.com
Oklahoma State Jobs
www.state.ok.us/~opm/
Olympia Olympian (USA Today Careers))
www.theolympian.com
Omaha World Herald (Employment Wizard)
www.omaha.com
OmahaHelpWanted (Reg.HelpWanted)
www.omahahelpwanted.com
one world.net
www.oneworld.net/jobs
Online-Jobs.com
www.online-jobs.com
Ontario Assoc. of Architects
www.oaa.on.ca
Ontario jobs.com (Canjobs)
www.ontariojobs.com
OnWisconsinJobs.com (Employment Wizard)
www.onwisconsin.com
Operation IT
www.operationit.com
Opportunity Nocs
www.opportunitynocs.org
Optical Engineer.com (Career Marketplace)
www.OpticalEngineer.com
optics.org
optics.org/employment
ORA Search (JV Search)
www.jvsearch.com
Oracle Computer work.com
www.oracle.computerwork.com
Oracle Fanclub and User Forum (Fanclub)
www.oraclefans.com
Oracle Job Network
www.oracjobs.com/
Oracle Professional.com (Career Marketplace)
www.oracleprofessional.com

Orajobs.com
www.orajobs
Orange County Register (CareerCast)
www.ocjobfinder.com
Oregon Jobs.com (LocalCareers)
www.oregonjobs.com
Oregon Live (Advance Careers)
www.oregonlive.com/careers
Oregon State Jobs
www.dashr.state.or.us/jobs/
Organic Chemistry Jobs Worldwide
http://organicworldwide.net/jobs/
Orlando Careers Online (Employment Partner)
www.orlandocareersonline.com
Orlando Sentinel (CareerBuilder)
www.orlandosentinel.com
OrlandoHelpWanted (Reg.HelpWanted)
www.orlandohelpwanted.com
OT JobLink
www.otjoblink.org
OttawaJobShop (Reg HelpWanted)
www.ottowajobshop.ca
Out Professionals
www.outprofessionals.org
Outdoor Network
www.outdoornetwork.com
Overseas Jobs.com (About Jobs.com)
www.overseasjobs.com
Packaging Business
www.packagingbusiness.com
Passing Notes.com (jobvertise)
www.passingnotes.com
Pediatric Nurse Jobs (HealthCareJobStore)
www.pediatricnursejobs.com
Penn Live (Advance Careers)
www.pennlive.com/careers
Pennsylvania Computerwork.com
www.pennsylvannia.computerwork.com
Pennsylvania Jobs.com
www.pennsylvaniajobs.com
Pensacola News Journal (USA Today Care...
www.pensacolanewsjournal.com
pensacolajobs.com
www.pensacolajobs.com
People Bank
www.peoplebank.com
People Online
www.peopleonline.com.br
People Soft Developer.com (Career Marketp...
www.peoplesoftdeveloper.com
Perl Computer work.com
www.perl.computerwork.com
Petroleum Engineer.com (Career Marketplace)
www.PetroleumEngineer.com
Petroleum Services Assoc. of Canada
www.psac.ca
Pharm Web
www.pharmweb.net
Pharmacy Jobs Online (HC Recruitment Onli...
www.pharmacyjobsonline.com
Pharmacy Week
www.pharmacyweek.com
Philadelphia Computer Jobs.com
www.philadelphia.computerjobs.com
Philadelphia Inquirer (CareerBuilder)
www.phillynews.com
PhiladelphiaHelpWanted (Reg.HelpWanted)
www.philadelphiahelpwanted.com
Philanthropy Journal Online
www.philanthropyjournal.org
Philly Jobs.com
www.phillyjobs.com
Philly.com (CareerBuilder)
www.philly.com

Phoenix Computerwork.com
www.phoenix.computerwork.com
Phoenix Employment.com (Employocity)
www.phoenixemployment.com
Physician Board
www.physicianboard.com
Physicians Employment
www.physemp.com
Physics Today Online
www.aip.org/pt
Physics World Jobs
physicsweb.org
Pick ajob.com
www.pickajob.com
Pilot Jobs
www.pilot-jobs.com
Pittsburgh Live.com (Employment Wizard)
www.pittsburghlive.com
P-Jobs
www.pjobs.org
Placement India
www.placementindia.com
Plan Ahead- Soc. For College & University P...
www.scup.org
Planet Recruit UK
www.planetrecruit.com
Planet SAP.com
www.planetsap.com
Plastic Careers.com
www.ejnetwork.com
Plastic Pro (staffingpro)
www.staffingpro.com
Plastics News
www.plasticnews.com
Play Bill
www.playbill.com
Plumbjob.com (Electric Job)
www.plumbjob.com
Plus (+) Jobs America
www.us.plusjobs.com
Plus (+) Jobs Australia
www.au.plusjobs.com
Plus (+) Jobs Canada
www.canada.plusjobs.com
Plus (+) Jobs Denmark
www.denmark.plusjobs.com
Plus (+) Jobs U.K.
www.uk.plusjobs.com
PMjobs.com
www.pmjobs.com
Police Employment.com
www.policeemployment.com
Police Executive
www.thepoliceexecutive.com
Political Resources
politicalresources.com
Polk Job Finder (Lakeland FL Ledger)
www.polkjobfinder.com
PolySort
www.polysort.com
PortaJobs
www.portajobs.com
Portland Computer Jobs.com
www.portland.computerjobs.com
Position Watch
www.positionwatch.com
Poughkeepsie Journal (USA Today Careers)
www.poughkeepsiejournal.com
Power Builder Jobs.com (Pure Power)
www.powerbuilderjobs.com
Power Builder Journal
www.sys-con.com/pbdj
Power Highway
www.powerhighway.com

Power Mag (McGraw-Hill)
www.powermag.com
PR Soc. of America [LA]
www.prsa-la.org/jobs.htm
PR WeekJobs
www.prweek.com
Practice Choice/Link
www.practicechoice.com
Pre-Cast Stressed Convrete Assoc.
www.pci.org
Prime JobSite.com
www.primejobsite.com
princeton info.com (U.S. 1)
www.princetoninfo.com
Privacy Job Opportunity Boards
www.pjobs.org
Private School Employment Network
www.privateschooljobs.com
Prized Jobs
www.prizedjobs.com
Pro GayJobs.com
www.progayjobs.com
Pro Hire
www.prohire.com
Pro/E Job Network (Mercury Enterprises)
www.pejn.com
Procruit
www.procruit.com
Product Manager.com (Career Marketplace)
www.ProductManager.com
Professional Exchange
www.professional-exchange.com/
Professionals in Human Resources Assoc.
www.pihra.org
Programmer Analyst.com (Career Marketplace)
www.programmeranalyst.com
Programming Jobs.com
www.programmingjobs.com
Programming-Services.com
www.programming-services.com
Project Connect
careers.education.wisc.edu/projectconnect/MainMenu.cf
m
Project Management Insititute
www.pmi.org
Project Manager.com (Career Marketplace)
www.projectmanager.com
ProMatch
www.promatch.org
Providence Journal (Employment Wizard)
www.projo.com
Psyc Careers
www.psyccareers.com
Public Health Nurse.com (HealthCareJobStore)
www.publichealthnursejobs.com
Public Relations Soc. of America (PRSA)
www.prsa.org
PugetSoundHelpWanted (Reg.HelpWanted)
www.pugetsoundhelpwanted.com
Pure Power's Database Jobs.com
www.databasejobs.com/
QA-jobs.com
www.qa-jobs.com
QC Employ Me (CareerLINK)
www.qcemployme.com
Quad City Times (Employment Wizard)
www.qctimes.com
Quebec jobs.com (Canjobs)
www.quebecjobs.com
Qworx.com
www.qworx.com
Racine Journal Times (Employment Wizard)
www.journaltimes.com
Rad Working.com
www.radworking.com

Radio & Records Online
www.rronline.com
Radio Online
www.radioonline.com
Radiology & Oncology JOBS (RTjobs.com)
www.rtjobs.com
Radiology Jobs (HC Recruitment Online))
www.radiologyjobs.com
Raleigh News Observer (Employment Wizard)
www.triangle.com
RE Buz
www.rebuz.com
Real Columbus.com (CareerBuilder)
www.realcolumbus.com.com
Real Estate Best Jobs
www.realestatebestjobs.com
Real Estate Job Store
www.realestatejobstore.com
Real Estate Jobs.com
www.realestatejobs.com
Real Jobs - Real Estate
www.real-jobs.com
RealEstateJobsites.com (Geojobsites)
www.realestatejobsites.com
Recruit Ireland
www.recruitireland.com
Recruit Military
www.recruitmilitary.com
Recruit USA
www.recruitusa.com
Recruit
www.recruit.com
Recruitaly
www.recruitaly.it
Recruiter Connection
www.recruiterconnection.com
Recruiter Networks
www.recruiternetworks.com
Recruiter Seek
www.recruiterseek.com
Recruiters Cafe.com
www.recruiterscafe.com
Recruiters Dream
www.recruitersdream.com
Recruiters Forum
www.recruitersforum.com
Recruiters Online Network (T)
www.recruitersonline.com
Recruiters World
www.recruitersworld.com
Recruitex
www.recruitex.com/
Recruitment Exchange Online
www.rex.co.uk
recruitment JOBZ.com
www.recruitmentjobz.com
Redding Searchlight (Employment Wizard)
www.reding.com
Refrigeration-engineer.com
www.refrigeration-engineer.com
Regional Help Wanted.com
www.regionalhelpwanted.com
Regulatory Affairs Professionals Society
www.careerconnections.raps.org/
Rehab Options (Absolutely Health Care)
www.rehaboptions.com
Reno Careers Online (Employment Partner)
www.renocareersonline.com
Reno Gazette-Observer Today Careers)
www.rgj.com
Rent-a-Geek
www.rentageek.com
Research Network
www.researchnetwork.com

Resort Jobs (About Jobs.com)
www.resortjobs.com
Resort Professional.com (Career Marketplace)
www.resortprofessional.com
Restaurant Job Store (eJob Stores)
www.restaurantjobstore.com
Restaurant Jobs
www.restaurantjobs.com
Restaurant News
www.restaurantnews.com
Restaurant Recruit.com
www.restaurantrecruit.com
ResuMate2002
www.resumate2002.com
Resume Depot
www.theresumedepot.com
Resume Detector
www.resumedetector.com
Resunet
www.resunet.com
Retail Classifieds (Career Engine)
www.retailclassifieds.com
Retail Job Store (eJob Stores)
www.retailjobstore.com
Retail Seek.com
www.retailseek.com
RF Global Net (Verticalnet)
www.rfglobalnet.com
RF Job Network (Mercury Enterprises)
www.rfjn.com
Rhinomite
www.rhinomite.com
Rhode Island Jobs.com (LocalCareers)
www.connecticutjobs.com
Richmond Careers Online (Employment Part...
www.richmondcareersonline.com
Richmond Times-Dispatch (CareerBuilder)
www.timesdispatch.com
RichmondHelpWanted (Reg.HelpWanted)
www.richmondhelpwanted.com
Right Management Consultants, Inc.
www.right.com
Rising Star Internships
www.rsinternships.com
Risk & Insurance Management Society
www.rims.org
Riverside Press-Enterprise (Employment Wi...
www.pe.com
RN Jobs (HC Recruitment Online))
www.rnjobs.com
Rochester Democrat (USA Today Careers))
www.democratandchronicle.com
Rochester jobFinder (Employment Wizard)
www.rochesterjobfinder.com
Rock Hill Herald(Employment Wizard)
www.heraldonline.com
Rockford Register Star (USA Today Careers))
www.rrstar.com
Rocky Mountain Jobs
www.rockymountainjobs.com
Rocky Mountain Water Environment Assoc.
www.rmwea.org
Rocky MountainNews.com
www.denver-rmn.com
RockyMountainHelpWanted (Reg.HelpWanted)
www.losangeleshelpwanted.com
Royal Society of Chemistry
chemistry.rsc.org/siteguide/careers.htm
RRT Jobs.com (HC Recruitment Online))
www.rrtjobs.com
RxCareerCenter.com
www.pharmacychoice.com
RxImmigration.com
www.RxImmigration.com

Sacramento Bee (Employment Wizard)
www.sacbee.com
Safety Online (Vertical Net)
www.safetyonline.com
Salary.com (CareerBuilder)
www.salary.com
Salem Statesman Journal (USA Today Care...
www.staesmanjournal.com
Sales Classifieds (Career Engine)
www.salesclassifieds.com
Sales Engineer.com (Career Marketplace)
www.SalesEngineer.com
sales heads
www.salesheads.com
Sales Job Store.com (eJob Stores)
www.Salesjobstore.com
Sales Jobs.com
www.salesjobs.com
Sales Rep Central.com
www.salesrepcentral.com
Sales Workz (World Workz)
www.salesworkz.com
salestrax.com
www.salestrax.com
Salisbury Daily Times (USA Today Careers)
www.delmarvanow.com
Salt Lake City Deseret News (Employment W...
www.desnews.com
Saludos.com (T)
www.saludos.com
San Antonio Job Network
www.sajobnet.com
San Bernadino Sun (Employment Wizard)
www.sbsun.com
San Francisco Chronicle Gate
www.sfgate com/classifieds/
San Jose Mercury News (CareerBuilder)
www.bayarea.com
San Louis Obispo Tribune News (CareerBui...
www.sanlouisobispo.com
Santa Barbara News-Press (Employment W...
www.newspress.com
SAP Club
www.sapclub.com
SAP Computer work.com
www.SAP.computerwork.com
Sap Developer.com (Career Marketplace)
www.sapdeveloper.com
SAP Fanclub and User Forum (Fanclub)
www.sapfans.com
Sask jobs.com (Canjobs)
www.saskjobs.com
Sci Jobs.com
www.scijobs.com
Sci Jobs.org
www.scijobs.org
Sci Web Career Center
www.scijobs.com
Science Careers (T)
www.sciencecareers.org
Science jobs.com
www.sciencejobs.com
Scientific American.com
www.sciam.com/jobs/
Scientific Researcher.com (Career Marketpl...
www.scientificresearcher.com
SCJobMarket.com
www.charlestonjobmarket.com
SE Missourian (Employment Wizard)
www.semissourian.com
Search Security
www.searchsecurity.com
SearchEase
www.searchease.com

Seasonal Employment
www.seasonalemployment.com
Seattle Computer Jobs.com
www.seattle.computerjobs.com
Seattle Computer work.com
www.seattle.computerwork.com
Security Clearance ComputerJobs.com
www.SecurityClearance.ComputerJobs.com
Security Jobs Network
www.securityjobs.net
Seek (Australia) (T)
www.seek.com.au
Selling Jobs.com (NicheJobs)
www.Sellingjobs.com
Senior Techs
www.seniortechs.com/
SensorJobs
www.sensorjobs.com
SF Bay Employment.com (Employocity)
www.sfbayemployment.com
ShowBizJobs.com
www.showbizjobs.com
Shreveport Times (USA Today Careers)
www.nwlouisiana.com
SignOn SanDiego (Union-Tribune)
www.signonsandiego.com
Silicon Valley Computer Jobs.com
www.siliconvalley.computerjobs.com
Silicon Valley.com (CareerBuilder)
www.siliconvalley.com
Sioux Falls Argus Leader (USA Today Car...
www.argusleader.com
Skiing the Net
www.skiingthenet.com
Skillogic
www.skillogic.com
Smart Career Move
www.smartcareermove.com
SmartPros
www.SmartPros.com
Snagajob.com
www.snagajob.com
Soc. for Adv. of Chicanos & Native Amer. in...
www.sacnas.org
Soc. for Automotive Engineers
www.sae.org
Soc. for Industrial & Org. Psychology
www.siop.org
Soc. for Technical Communication
www.stc.org
Soc. of Broadcast Engineers
www.sbe.org
Soc. of Cable Telecommunications Eng.
www.scte.org
Soc. of Hispanic Prof. Engineers (BrassRing)
www.resume-link.com/society/shpewebportal.htm
Soc. of Women Engineers (BrassRing)
www.swe.org
Social Service.Com
www.socialservice.com
Social Work & Services Jobs Online
gwbweb.wustl.edu/jobs/index.html
Social Work JobBank
www.socialworkjobbank.com
Society for Foodservice Management
www.sfm-online.org
Society for Human Resource Management
www.shrm.org
Society of Actuaries
www.soa.org
Society of Automotive Engineers
www.sae.org
Society of Competitive Intelligence Porf.
www.scip.org

Society of Consuler Affairs Prof. in Bus.
www.socap.org
Society of Environ. Toxicology & Chemistry
www.setac.org
Society of Manufacturing Engineers
www.sme.org
Software Contractors' Guild
www.scguild.com
Software Developer Careers (Dr Dobbs)
www.developercareers.com
Software Developer Jobs.com (eJob Stores)
www.softwaredeveloperjobs.com
Software Developer.com (Career Marketplace)
www.softwaredeveloper.com
Software Engineer.com (Career Marketplace)
www.softwareengineer.com
Software Jobs.com (Tech-Engine.com)
www.softwarejobs.com
SoftwareSalesJobs.com
www.SoftwareSalesJobs.com
Solid Edge Job Network (Mercury Enterprises)
www.sejn.com
Solid Works Job Network (Mercury Enterpri...
www.swjn.com
Sologig.com (CareerBuilder)
www.sologig.com
South Carolina State Jobs
www.state.sc.us/jobs
South Coast JobMart.com (The Standard-Ti...
www.southcoastjobmart.com
South Dakota State Jobs
www.state.sd.us
South Jersey Careers Online (Employment ...
www.southjerseycareersonline.com
SouthBendWanted (Reg.HelpWanted)
www.southbendhelpwanted.com
Southern California EDI Roundtable
www.scedir.org
Southern Illinoisian (Employment Wizard)
www.southerillinoisian.com
SouthernMaineWanted (Reg.HelpWanted)
www.southernmainehelpwanted.com
SouthSoundJobs (Tacoma News Tribune)
www.tribnet.com
Southwest-Online (Employment Wizard)
www.southwest-online.com
Space Careers
www.spacelinks.com/SpaceCareers/index.html
Space Jobs
www.spacejobs.com
Spanishjobs.com
www.spanishjobs.com
Special Library Association
www.sla.org
Speech Therapist Jobs (HealthCareJobStore)
www.speechtherapistjobs.com
SPIEWorks- Int'l Society for Optical Engineering
www.spieworks.com
Splitit.com
www.splitit.com
Spokane Careers Online (Employment Partner)
www.spokanecareersonline.com
sports employment.com
www.sportsemployment.com
Springfield NewsLdr (USA Today Careers)
wwwozarksnow.com
SQL Computer work.com
www.SQL.computerwork.com
St. Cloud Times (USA Today Careers))
www.sctimes.com
St. George Spectrum (USA Today Careers))
www.thespectrum.com
St. Louis Computer Jobs.com
www.stlouis.computerjobs.com

St. Louis Metro (CareerBuilder)
www.stlouismetro.com
St. Louis Today (Post Dispatch- CareerBuilder)
www.stlouistoday.com
St. Petersburg Times (CareerBuilder)
www.sptimes.com
Staffing World
www.staffingworld.com
Stamfordadvocate.com (CareerBuilder)
www.stamfordadvocate.com
Star Chefs JobFinder
www.starchefs.com
Startup Lynx
www.startuplynx.com
Startup Zone.com
www.startupzone.com
StartupZone
www.startupzone.com
Staten Island Live (Advance Careers)
www.silive.com/careers
Step Beyond
www.stepbeyond.com
Stern Alumni Job Listings
www.stern.nyu.edu/alumni
Strategic Account Mgmt. Association (SAMA)
www.strategicaccounts.org
Student Affairs Administrators in Higher Ed
www.naspa.org
Subcontract.com
www.subcontract.com
SuburbanChicagoHelpWanted (Reg.HelpWa...
www.suburbanchicagohelpwanted.com
Summer Clerk
www.summerclerk.com
Summer Jobs (About Jobs.com)
www.summerjobs.com
Sun Guru
www.sunguru.com
Sunoasis Jobs
www.sunoasis.com
Superintendent jobs.com (eJob Stores)
www.superintendentjobs.com/
SuperJobs.net
www.superjobs.net
Supermarket News
www.supermarketnews.com
Supply Jobs.com (NicheJobs)
www.supplyjobs.com
Support Analyst.com (Career Marketplace)
www.supportanalyst.com
Sustainable Business.com
www.sustainablebusiness.com
Swap jobs.com
www.swapjobs.com
SwiftJobs
www.swiftjobs.com
Syracuse Careers Online (Employment Part...
www.syracusecareersonline.com
Syracuse Online (Advance Careers)
www.syracuse.com/careers
System Administrator.com (Career Marketpl...
www.systemadministrator.com
Systems Administration Guild
www.usenix.org/sage
Systems Analyst.com (Career Marketplace)
www.systemsanalyst.com
Talent Campus
www.talentcampus.com
Talent rock
www.talentrock.com
Talent Works: The Online Casting Source
www.talentworks.com
Talent4europe.com
www.talent4europe.com

Tallahasse.com (CareerBuilder)
www.tallahassee.com
Tampa Bay Online (Tampa Bay Tribune)
www.tbo.com
Tax Talent.com
www.tax-talent.com
Tax-Jobs.Com
www.tax-jobs.com
TC Theatre and Film
www.tctheatreandfilm.org
TCM's HR Careers
www.tcm.com
Teachers of English to Speakers of Other L...
www.tesol.org
Teachers Online
www.teachersonline.com
teachersplanet.com
www.teachersplanet.com
Teachers-Teachers.com
www.teachers-teachers.com
Tech Employment.com
www.techemployment.com
Tech Profiles
www.techprofiles.com
tech-engine.com (T)
www.tech-engine.com
Techies .com
www.techies.com
Technical Assoc. of Pulp & Paper (TAPPI)
www.tappi.org
Technical Assoc. of the Graphic Arts
www.taga.org
Technical Communicator.com (Career Marke...
www.technicalcommunicator.com
Technical Recruiter.com (Career Marketplace)
www.technicalrecruiter.com/
Technical Trainer.com (Career Marketplace)
www.technicaltrainer.com
Technical Writer Jobs (eJob Stores)
www.technicalwriterjobs.com
TechnoCentral.com
www.technocentral.com
Technojobs.co.uk
www.technojobs.co.uk
Technology MVP.com (CareerMVP)
www.technolgymvp.com
Teens4Hire
www.Teens4Hire.com
telecom careers.net
www.telecomcareers.net
Telecom Engineer.com (Career Marketplace)
www.telecomengineer.com
Telecommunications Computer work.com
www.telecommunications.computerwork.com
Telecommunications Industry Assoc. B2B
www.getcommstuff.com
Telecommuter's Digest
www.tdigest.com
Telecommuting Jobs
www.tjobs.com
TeleJob Academic Job Exchange
www.telejob.ch
Television Bureau of Advertising
www.tvb.org
Teller Jobs (eJob Stores)
www.tellerjobs.com
Tenn Careers.com (CareerMVP)
www.tenncareers.com
Tennessee State Jobs
www.state.tn.us/personnel/
Terre Haute Tribune Star (Employment Wizard)
www.tribstar.com
Texan Careers.com (CareerMVP)
www.texancareers.com

Texas Computer Jobs.com
www.texas.computerjobs.com
Texas Computerwork.com
www.texas.computerwork.com
Texas Jobs.com (LocalCareers)
www.texasjobs.com
Texas Workforce
www.twc.state.tx.us/
The Black Collegian Online
www.blackcollegian.com
The Blue Line
www.theblueline.com
The Board Network
www.theboardnetwork.com
The Financial Planning Association
www.fpanet.org
The Internet Job Source
www.statejobs.com
The Job Seeker
www.thejobseeker.net
The Jobs Site
www.the-jobs-site.com
The Multicultural Advantage
www.tmaonline.net
The Nat'l Assembly
www.nassembly.org
The Retired Officers Assoc. (TROA)
www.troa.org
The Work Circuit (EETimes)
www.theworkcircuit.com
The Write Jobs
www.writerswrite.com/jobs
TheSquare
www.thesquare.com
Thingamajob
www.thingamajob.com
This is Jobs
www.thisisjobs.co.uk
Tiger Jobs
www.tigerjobs.com/
TimberSite.com
www.timbersite.com
Title board.com (TheBoardNetwork)
www.titleboard.com
Todays Job Market.com
www.todaysjobmarket.com
Toledo Beacon Journal (CareerBuilder)
www.ohio.com
Toledo Career Board
toledo.careerboard.com
Top Contracts
www.topcontracts.com
Top Echelon
www.topechelon.com
Top Jobs.co.uk
www.topjobs.co.uk
Top Money Jobs
www.topmoneyjobs.com
Top Sales Positions
www.topsalespositions.com
Top StartUps.com
www.topstartups.com
Topeka Capital Journal (Employment Wizard)
www.cjonline.com
TopekaWanted (Reg.HelpWanted)
www.topekahelpwanted.com
Toronto Job Shop (Reg. HelpWanted)
www.Torontojobshop.ca
Torrence Daily Breeze (Employment Wizard)
www.dailybreeze.com
total jobs.com (T)
www.totaljobs.com
Total Telecom
www.totaltele.com

Town Online (JobFind)
www.townonline.com/working
Trabajo.org
www.trabajo.org
Trade Jobs Online
trades.buildfind.com/
Training Resource Network
www.trninc.com
TrainMark.com
www.trainmark.com/tm/
trans-ACTION Classified Website
www.trans-action.com
Transition Assistance Online
www.taonline.com
Transportation Engineer.com (Career Marke...
www.transportationengineer.com
travel jobs (Australia/New Zealand)
www.traveljobs.com.au
Travel jobz.net
www.traveljobz.net
Travel Nurse Jobs (HealthCareJobStore)
www.travelnursejobs.com
Tri StateJobs.com
www.tristatejobs.com
Triangle.com (Raleigh News & Observer)
www.nando.net
Truck Driver
www.truckdriver.com
Truck Net
www.truck.net
TruckinJobs.com
truckinjobs.com
True Careers (T)
www.truecareers.com
Tucson Careers Online (Employment Partner)
www.tucsoncareersonline.com
Tucson Citizen (USA Today Careers)
www.tucsonCitizen.com
TucsonHelpWanted (Reg.HelpWanted)
www.tucsonhelpwanted.com
TulsaHelpWanted (Reg.HelpWanted)
www.tulsahelpwanted.com
TV Jobs
www.tvjobs.com
TVandRadioJobs.com
www.tvandradiojobs.com
TVSpy.com
www.tvspy.com
Twin Cities Computer Jobs.com
www.twincities.computerjobs.com
Twin Cities Pioneer Press (CareerBuilder)
www.fortwayne.com
TwinCitiesWanted (Reg.HelpWanted)
www.twincitieshelpwanted.com
UBidContract.com
www.UBidContract.com
UG Job Network (Mercury Enterprises)
www.ugjn.com
Ultrasoundjobs.com
www.ultrasoundjobs.com
Underwriter Employment (eJob Stores)
underwriteremployment.com
underwriting Jobs.com
www.uwjobs.com
unicru
www.unicru.com
UniversoE.com
www.universoe.com
Unix Admin (JV Search)
www.unixadminsearch.com
Unix Computer work.com
www.unix.computerwork.com
Unix Ugu Universe
www.ugu.com

US Exec Jobs (Job Network)
www.usexecjobs.com
US Internet Industry Association
www.usiia.org
US Jobs.Com
www.usjobs.com
US Law Jobs (Job Network)
www.uslawjobs.com
US Med Jobs (Job Network)
www.usmedjobs.com
US Tech Jobs (Job Network)
www.ustechjobs.com
US TECH JOBS
www.ustechjobs.net
USA Today Careers Network
career.usatoday.com
USHOTJOBS.com
www.ushotjobs.com
Utah Careers Online (Employment Partner)
www.utahcareersonline.com
Utah State Jobs
www.state.ut.us
Utica Observer-Dispatch (USA Today Caree...
www.info@uticaod.com
Vallejo Times-Herald (Employment Wizard)
www.timesheraldonline.com
VancouverJobShop (Reg.HelpWanted)
www.vancouverjobshop.ca
Vault.Com (T)
www.vault.com
Vermont State Jobs
www.state.vt.us/pers/
Vet Jobs
www.vetjobs.com
Veterinary Jobs.com
www.veterinaryjobs.com
VeterinaryLife.com
www.veterinarylife.com/
Vets 4 Hire.com (The Destiny Group)
vets4hire.com
Vice President Jobs.com (eJob Stores)
www.vicepresidentjobs.com
Vineland Daily Journal (USA Today Careers)
www.thedailyjournal.com
Virginia Computerwork.com
www.virginia.computerwork.com
Virtual Jobs.com
info@virtualjobs.com
Visual Basic Computer work.com
www.visualbasic.computerwork.com
Visual Basic Jobs.com (Pure Power)
www.visualbasicjobs.com
Visual Basic Search (JV Search)
www.vbasicsearch.com
Volunteer Match
www.volunteermatch.org
WA Careers.com (CareerMVP)
www.wacareers.com
Washington DC Area SGML/XML Users Group
www.eccnet.com/xmlug
Washington Post [Washington Jobs] (T)
www.washingtonpost.com
Web Food Pros (Escoffier On Line)
www.webfoodpros.com
Web Jobs USA.com (eJob Stores)
www.webjobsusa.com
Web Programming Jobs.com (Pure Power)
www.webprogrammingjobs.com
WEB Worldwide Employee Benefits Network
www.webenefits.org
Webgrrls
www.webgrrls.com
Website Builder.com (Career Marketplace)
www.websitebuilder.com

Weed Jobs (Positions in Weed Science)
www.nrcan.gc.ca/~bcampbel/
Welding Jobs.com (Hire in a Click)
www.weldingjobs.com
West Virginia State Jobs
www.state.wv.us/admin/personnel/jobs
Westchester Job Central
www.westchesterteenjobs.com
Westchester Jrnl News (USA Today Careers)
www.thejournal.com
Western NY Jobs
www.wnyjobs.com
Wi Jobs.com (LocalCareers)
www.wijobs.com
Wichita Eagle (CareerBuilder)
www.kansas.com
Wichita Falls Times Record (Employment Wi...
www.trnonline.com
Wilmington News Journal (USA Today Care...
career.delawareonline.com
Windows Computer work.com
www.windows.computerwork.com
Wireless Design (VeticalNet)
www.wirelessdesignonline.com
Wireless Developer Network
www.wirelessdevnet.com/career
Wireless Engineer.com (Career Marketplace)
www.WirelessEngineer.com
Wisconsin Jobs.com (LocalCareers)
www.wisconsinjobs.com
Wisconsin's Gannet Newspapers (USA To...
www.info@wisinfo.com
Womans-Work
www.womans-work.com
Women in Higher Education
www.wihe.com
Women In Technology International
www.witi.com
Women Sports Jobs
www.womensportsjobs.com
Worcester Careers Online (Employment Par...
www.worcestercareersonline.com
Worcester Works (Boston Works)
www.worcesterworks.com
work in pr.com
www.workinpr.com
Work in Sports
www.workinsports.com
Work LP.com (Loss Prevention)
www.worklp.com
WorkInsight
www.workinsight.com
WorkLife Network
www.worklife.com
Workopolis.com (T)
www.workopolis.com
WorkopolisCampus.com (Workopolis)
www.campusworklink.com
Workplace Diversity.com (Career Engine)
www.workplacediversity.com
workthing.com
www.workthing.com
World at Work Job Links
www.worldatwork.org/joblinks
World Org. of Webmasters
www.joinwow.org
World Workz
www.worldworkz.com
Worldwideworker.com
www.worldwideworker.com
Wow-com: World of Wireless Communications
www.wow-com.com
Wyoming Job Quest (Star-Tribune)
www.wyomingjobquest.com

Wyoming State Jobs
  personnel.state.wy.us/
WyomingJobs.com (LocalCareers)
  www.wyomingjobs.com
XML Computer work.com
  www.xml.computerwork.com
Y-axis.com
  www.y-axis.com
yourEEcareer.com
  www.youreecareer.com
Youth Specialties
  www.youthspecialties.com
Youth@Work
  www.youthatwork.org/
Zanesville Times Rec. (USA Today Careers)
  www.zanesvilletimesrecorder.com
Zillion Resumes.com
  www.zillionresumes.com

Presented in this edition for the first time, associations have come into their own. Large and small we have always emphasized this niche because it has what all employers want — the means to reach a targeted audience.

Note: The sites in **Bold** are among the 500 Best and their reviews can be found in the main body of this edition. A Bold **(T)** indicates we consider the site among the "Top 50". The thousands of sites in plain text listed here were reviewed but, their reviews are not published (we promise to send you any review on request). All Web site URLs (web addresses) can be found in the Master List. A parentheses ( ) designates the "gateway" site that we reviewed. Brackets [ ] are used for clarification.

Academic Physician & Scientist
  www.acphysci.com/aps.htm
Advertising Research Foundation
  www.arfsite.org
American Academy of Audiology
  www.audiology.org/hearcareers
American Academy of Cosmetic Dentistry
  www.aacd.com
American Academy of Forensic Sciences
  www.aafs.org
American Accounting Assoc.
  accounting.rutgers.edu/raw/aaa/index.html
American Advertising Federation
  www.aaf.org
American Agricultural Economics Assoc.
  www.aaea.org
American Anthropological Assoc.
  www.aaanet.org
American Assoc. for Budget & Program Analysts
  www.aabpa.org
American Assoc. for Respiratory Care
  www.aarc.org
American Assoc. of Clinical Chemistry
  www.aacc.org
American Assoc. of Collegiate Registrars
  www.aacrao.org
American Assoc. of Community Colleges
  www.aacc.nche.edu
American Assoc. of Critical-Care Nurses
  www.aacn.org
American Assoc. of People with Disabilities
  www.aapd.com
American Assoc. of School Administrators
  www.assa.org
American Assoc. of University Women
  www.aauw.org
American Astronomical Society
  www.aas.org
American Ceramic Society
  www.acers.org
American Chamber of Commerce Execs
  www.acce.org
American Chemical Society - JobSpectrum.org
  www.acs.org
American College of Cardiology
  www.acc.org
American College of Healthcare Executives
  www.ache.org
American College of Radiology
  www.acr.org
American College Personnel Assoc.
  www.acpa.nche.edu

American Corporate Counsel Assoc.
  www.acca.com
American Counseling Assoc.
  www.counseling.org
American Culinary Federation
  www.acfchefs.org
American Design Drafting Assoc.
  www.adda.org/
American Fisheries Society
  www.fisheries.org
American Health Lawyers Assoc.
  www.healthlawyers.org
American Industrial Hygiene Assoc.
  www.aiha.org
American Institute of Architects Career Center
  www.aia.org
American Institute of Biological Sciences (A...
  www.aibs.org
American Institute of Chemical Engineers
  www.aiche.org
American Institute of CPA's
  www.aicpa.org/
American Institute of Physics (AIP)
  www.aip.org
American Lighting Assoc. (FlipDog)
  www.americanlightingassoc.com
American Marketing Assoc.
  www.ama.org
American Massage Therapy Assoc.
  www.amtamassage.org
American Mathematical Society
  www.ams.org
American Meteorological Society
  www.ametsoc.org/AMS/pubs/index.html
American Music Therapy Assoc.
  www.musictherapy.org
American Nuclear Society
  www.ans.org
American Oil chemists' Society
  www.aocs.org
American Physical Therapy Assoc.
  www.apta.org
American Planning Assoc.
  www.planning.org
American Public Works Assoc.
  www.apwa.net
American Risk & Insurance Assoc.
  www.aria.org
American School Counselor Assoc.
  www.schoolcounselor.org
American Soc. for Engineering Education
  www.asee.org

American Soc. for Quality
www.asq.org/net/career
American Soc. for Training & Development
www.astd.org
American Soc. of Agricultural Engineering
www.asae.org
American Soc. of Civil Engineers
www.asce.org
American Soc. of Echocardiography
www.echo-web.com
American Soc. of Limnology and Oceanography
www.aslo.org
American Soc. of Mech. Engineering
www.asme.org/jobs
American Soc. of Women Accountants
www.aswa.org/wanted.html
American Society fo P&E Nutrition
www.nutritioncare.org
American Society for Clinical Laboratory Sc...
www.ascls.org
American Society for Public Administration
www.aspanet.org
American Society of Crime Lab Directors
www.ascld.org
American Society of Gene Therapy
www.asgt.org
American Society of Interior Designers
www.asid.org
American Speech-Language-Hearing Assoc.
www.professional.asha.org
American Statistical Association
www.amstat.org
American Urological Assoc.
www.auanet.org
American Water Works Assoc.
www.awwa.org
American Welding Society
www.aws.org/jobfind
American Zoo & Aquarium Assoc.
www.aza.org
Art Directors Club of Metro. Washington
www.adcmw.org
Asian American Journalists Assoc.
www.aaja.org
Assoc. for Computing Machinery
www.acm.org
Assoc. for Facilities Engineering
www.afe.org
Assoc. for Financial Professionals
www.afponline.org
Assoc. for Institutional Research
www.airweb.org/jobs.html
Assoc. for Interactive Marketing (CareerBuilder)
www.imarketing.org
Assoc. for Investment Mgmt. & Research
www.aimr.org
Assoc. for Library and Information Science ...
www.alise.org
Assoc. for Women in Sports Media
www.awsmonline.org
Assoc. of Clinical Research Professionals
www.acrpnet.org
Assoc. of eX-Lotus Employees
www.axle.org
Assoc. of Latino Professionals in Fin. & Acc.
www.aahcpa.org
Assoc. of Metropolitan Water Agencies
www.amwa.net
Assoc. of Perioperative Registered Nurses
www.aorn.org
Assoc. of Research Libraries
db.arl.org/careers/index.html
Assoc. of Women Surgeons
www.womensurgeons.org

Automotive Aftermarket Industry Asoc.
www.aftermarket.org
Bank Job Search (BAI)
www.bankjobsearch.com
Be An Actuary
www.beanactuary.org
Biomedical Engineering Society
www.bmes.org
Black Data Processing Assoc.
www.bdpa.org
Bread Bakers Guild of America
www.bbga.org
British Columbia Library Assoc.
www.bcla.bc.ca
British Columbia Water & Waste Assoc.
www.bcwwa.org
California Journalism Job Bank
www.csne.org/jobs/postings.html
Canadian Bar Assoc.
www.cba.org/career/careersite.asp
Canadian Mgmt. Accountants Society
www.cma-canada.org
Canadian Restaurant & Foodservices Assoc.
www.crfa.ca
Career Link- Applied Info. Mgm't Institute
www.careerlink.org
Casualty Actuarial Society
www.casact.org
Cellular Telecom. & Internet Assoc. (Job Opt...
www.wow-com.com
Certified Management Assoc. of Canada
www.cma-canada.org
Chesapeake Human Resources Assoc.
www.chra.com
COACH's Job Board
www.coachhelp.com
College & University Personnel Assoc.
www.cupahr.org
College & University Prof. Assoc. for HR
tcurtis@cupahr.org
Colorado Human Resources Assoc.
www.chra.org
Colorado Software & Internet Assoc.
www.coloradosoftware.org
Council of Logistics Management
www.clm1.org
Council of Public Relations Firms
www.prfirms.org
Council on Employee Benefits
www.ceb.org
Council on Foundations
www.cof.org
Credit Union Executives Society
www.cuews.org
Ct. Business & Industry Assoc. (CTJobs.com)
www.cbia.com
EDUCAUSE
www.educause.edu/jobpost/jobpost.asp
EE-Link/North American Assoc. for Env. Ed.
eelink.net
Employee Assistance Professionals Assoc.
www.eapassn.org
Employee Relocation Council
www.erc.org
Engineering Institute of Canada
www.eic-ici.ca
ENT Careers
www.entnet.org/careers
Entomology Society of America
www.entsoc.org
Environmental Careers Org. (Eco.org)
www.eco.org
Feminist Majority Foundation Online
www.feminist.org

Financial Women International
www.fwi.org/
Food and Drug Law Institute
www.fdli.org
Frontiers in Bioscience
www.bioscience.org
Geospatial Information & Technology Assoc.
www.gita.org
Good Works
www.essential.org/goodworks/
Graphic Artists Guild
www.gag.org
Healthcare Financial Management Assoc.
www.hfma.org
HEALTHeCareers (T)
www.healthecareers.com
Help Desk Institute
www.thinkhdijobdesk.com
Hispanic Nat'l Bar Association
www.hnba.com
Hospitality Financial & Technology Professionals
www.iaha.org
hotauditjobs.com
www.hotauditjobs.com
Human Factors and Ergonomics Society
www.hfes.org
Human Resource Assoc. of the Nat'l. Capital...
www.hra-nca.org
Independent Press Assoc.
www.indypress.org
Independent Sector Job Link
www.independentsector.org
Industrial Designers Society of America
www.idsa.org
Institute of Certified Travel Agents
www.icta.com
Institute of Food Technologists
www.ift.org
Institute of Industrial Engineers
www.iienet.org
Institute of Internal Auditors
www.theiia.org/careercenter
Institute of Store Planners
www.ispo.org
Institution of Professional Engineers
http://www.ipenz.org.nz/jobhunt
Int'l Assoc. of Business Communicators
www.iabc.com
Int'l Nortel Networks Meridian Users Group
www.innmug.org
Int'l Tandem Users Group
www.itug.org
Int'l. Assoc. for HR Info Mgmt.
ihrim.org
Int'l. Assoc. of Amusement Parks and Attractions
www.iaapa.org
Int'l. Assoc. of Conference Centers
www.iacconline.com
Int'l. Economic Development Council
www.iedconline.org
Int'l. Personnel Mgmt. Assoc. (CareerBuilder)
www.ipma-hr.org
Int'l. Society For Performance Improvements
www.ispi.org
Iron and Steel Society
www.iss.org
Massachusetts Biotechnology Council
www.massbio.org
Mechanical Contractors Asso. of America
www.mcaa.org
Mechanical Engineers Magazine Online (ASME)
www.memagazine.org/
Meeting Professionals Int'l
www.mpiweb.org

Mexican American Eng. and Scientists Soc.
www.maes-natl.org
Modern Language Association of America
www.mla.org
Montana Society of CPAs
www.mscpa.org
NALS (Legal staff.)
www.nals.org
Nat'l. Academies Career Center
www4.nationalacademies.org/osep/cpc.nsf
Nat'l. Accrediting Commission of Cosmetolo...
www.naccas.org
Nat'l. Alliance of Black School Educators
www.nabse.org
Nat'l. Assoc of Credit Management.
www.nacm.org
Nat'l. Assoc of Student Personnel Administr...
www.naspa.org
Nat'l. Assoc. for Home Care
www.nahc.org
Nat'l. Assoc. of African Americans in HR
www.naaahr.org
Nat'l. Assoc. of Black Journalists
nabj.org
Nat'l. Assoc. of Corp. Real Estate Exec's.
www.nacore.com
Nat'l. Assoc. of Development Organizations
www.nado.org
Nat'l. Assoc. of Educational Buyers
www.naeb.org
Nat'l. Assoc. of Elevator Contractors
www.naec.org
Nat'l. Assoc. of Hispanic Journalists
www.nahj.org
Nat'l. Assoc. of Ind. & Office Properties
www.naiop.com
Nat'l. Assoc. of Independent Schools
www.nais.org
Nat'l. Assoc. of Industrial Technology
www.nait.org
Nat'l. Assoc. of Manufacturers
www.nam.org
Nat'l. Assoc. of Personal Financial Advisors
www.napfa.org
Nat'l. Assoc. of Sales Professionals
www.nasp.com
Nat'l. Assoc. of Student Financial Aid
www.nasfaa.org
Nat'l. Assoc. of Women In Construction (Fli...
www.nawic.org/
Nat'l. Assoc. Recording Merchandisers
www.narm.com
Nat'l. Athletic Trainers' Assoc.
www.nata.org
Nat'l. Black MBA Assoc. (NY Chapter)
www.nyblackmba.org
Nat'l. Business Incubation Assoc.
www.nbia.org
Nat'l. Council of Teachers of Math Jobs Online
www.nctm.org
Nat'l. Emergency Number Assoc.
www.nena9-1-1.org
Nat'l. Environmental Health Assoc.
www.neha.org
Nat'l. Fed. of Paralegal Assoc. (Legal staff.)
www.paralegals.com
Nat'l. FFA Organization
www.ffa.org
Nat'l. Fire & Protection Agency (Monster)
www.nfpa.org
Nat'l. Registry of Environmental Professionals
www.nrep.org
Nat'l. Society of Black Engineers
www.nsbe.org

ASSOCIATIONS

Nat'l. Weather Association
www.nwas.org/jobs.html
Nat'l. Youth Development Information Center
www.nydic.org
NBA Online (Nebraska Bankers Assoc.)
www.nebankers.org
Net work and Systems Profesionals Assoc.
www.naspa.com
Network of Commercial Real Estate Women
www.nncrew.org
New England Employee Benefits Council
www.nebc.org
New England Human Resource Assoc.
www.nehra.com
New England Telecommunications Assoc.
www.n-e-t-a.org/
New Media Assoc. of NJ
www.nmanj.com
New Mexico High Tech Job Forum
www.internetjobs.org
Newspaper Assoc. of America
http://www.naa.org
Northeast Human Resources Association
www.nehra.com
Northwest Recruiters Association
www.nwrecruit.org
Ontario Assoc. of Architects
www.oaa.on.ca
OT JobLink
www.otjoblink.org
Petroleum Services Assoc. of Canada
www.psac.ca
Plan Ahead- Soc. For College & University P...
www.scup.org
Pre-Cast Stressed Convrete Assoc.
www.pci.org
Risk & Insurance Management Society
www.rims.org
Rocky Mountain Water Environment Assoc.
www.rmwea.org
Royal Society of Chemistry
chemistry.rsc.org/siteguide/careers.htm
Science Careers (T)
www.sciencecareers.org
Soc. for Adv. of Chicanos & Native Amer. in...
www.sacnas.org
Soc. for Industrial & Org. Psychology
www.siop.org
Soc. of Broadcast Engineers
www.sbe.org
Soc. of Cable Telecommunications Eng.
www.scte.org
Soc. of Hispanic Prof. Engineers (BrassRing)
www.resume-link.com/society/shpewebportal.htm
Soc. of Women Engineers (BrassRing)
www.swe.org
Society for Foodservice Management
www.sfm-online.org
Society of Competitive Intelligence Porf.
www.scip.org
Society of Consumer Affairs Prof. in Bus.
www.socap.org
Society of Environ. Toxicology & Chemistry
www.setac.org
Society of Manufacturing Engineers
www.sme.org
Special Library Association
www.sla.org
SPIEWorks- Int'l Society for Optical Engineering
www.spieworks.com
Strategic Account Mgmt. Association (SAMA)
www.strategicaccounts.org
Student Affairs Administrators in Higher Ed
www.naspa.org

Technical Assoc. of Pulp & Paper (TAPPI)
www.tappi.org
Technical Assoc. of the Graphic Arts
www.taga.org
Telecommunications Industry Assoc. B2B
www.getcommstuff.com
Television Bureau of Advertising
www.tvb.org
The Financial Planning Association
www.fpanet.org
US Internet Industry Association
www.usiia.org
Weed Jobs (Positions in Weed Science)
www.nrcan.gc.ca/~bcampbel/
World Org. of Webmasters
www.joinwow.org
Wow-com: World of Wireless Communications
www.wow-com.com

The (50) sites listed below are our picks for the Best of the Best in 2003. Some were picked for their marketing prowess, impact on an industry or ability to reach a targeted population. Others were chosen for their commitment to a profession or in recognition of a unique community. When you see these sites listed in other sections of these indices, they will be listed in **BOLD** with the designation **(T)** after the web site name. What works for us may work for you but without experimenting you'll never find your own best sites.

Advance Careers
www.advancecareers.com/
After College
www.aftercollege.com
America's Job Bank
www.ajb.dni.us
American Soc. of Assoc. Executives
www.asaenet.org/careers
AuntMinnie.com
www.auntminnie.com
BA Jobs
www.bajobs.com
Benefits Link
www.benefitslink.com
Boston Works- Boston Globe
bostonworks.com
Brass Ring.com
www.brassring.com
Career Builder
www.careerbuilder.com
Career Journal.com
www.careerjournal.com
Casino Careers Online
www.casinocareers.com
College Central Network
www.collegecentral.com
Computer Jobs.com
www.computerjobs.com
Computer work.com
www.computerwork.com
daVinci Times
www.davincitimes.org
Destiny Group-Military Transition Center
www.destinygroup.com
DICE High Tech Jobs Online
www.dice.com
Direct Employers
www.DirectEmployers.com
Employment Wizard (Career Site)
www.jobexchange.com
Escoffier On Line - Employment Resources
www.escoffier.com
ExecuNet
www.execunet.com
Financial Times Career Point
www.ftcareerpoint.com
HEALTHeCareers
www.healthecareers.com
Hot Jobs.com
www.hotjobs.com

IMdiversity.com
www.imdiversitycom
Irish Jobs.ie
www.irishjobs.ie
Job Circle.com
www.jobcircle.com
Jobs for Programmers
www.prgjobs.com
LatPRO
www.latpro.com
Layover.com
www.layover.com
Legal staff.com
www.legalstaff.com
Med CAREERS
www.medcareers.com
MedZilla
www.medzilla.com
Minnesota Jobs.com
www.minnesotajobs.com
Monster.com
www.monster.com
Nation Job Network
www.nationjob.com
Net share.com
www.netshare.com
Net-Temps
www.net-temps.com
Nursing Spectrum Career Fitness Online
www.nursingspectrum.com
Recruiters Online Network
www.recruitersonline.com
Saludos.com
www.saludos.com
Science Careers
www.sciencecareers.org
Seek (Australia)
www.seek.com.au
tech-engine.com
www.tech-engine.com
total jobs.com
www.totaljobs.com
True Careers
www.truecareers.com
Vault.Com
www.vault.com
Washington Post [Washington Jobs]
www.washingtonpost.com
Workopolis.com
www.workopolis.com

CAREER MANAGEMENT RESOURCES

Nearly every job site offers "career management" content. Unfortunately, most of it is generic, misleading advice, limited tactics or simply a teaser to get you to pay for services. The sad fact is that guarantees of jobs and offers to send your resume to thousands of recruiters and firms in return for $$$ are the worst types of abuse. They offer hope and cannot possibly deliver. The sites below might be controversial to some but each offers interesting content that can be used in exploring or managing a career. We've only included sites that offer enough free value that it is worth a trip. Check out the Resources section for more explanation.

10 Minute Resume
  www.10minuteresume.com
Be An Actuary
  www.beanactuary.com
Business Week Online Career Center
  www.businessweek.com
Canadian Careers.com
  www.canadiancareers.com
CareerBabe
  www.careerbabe.com
Career Consulting Corner
  www.careercc.com
Career Hunters.com
  www.careerhunters.com
Career Profiles
  icpac.indiana.edu/career_profiles/
Career Way
  www.careerway.com
Careers-Internet.org
  www.careers-internet.org
disAbility.gov
  www.disability.gov
fuc*ed company.com
  www.fuckedcompany.com
Go Army
  www.goarmy.com
GradSchools.com
  www.gradschools.com
Hard@Work
  www.hardatwork.com
iResign
  www.iresign.com
Job Bus (Canadajobs)
  www.jobbus.com
Job Star: California Job Search Guide
  www.jobstar.org

Jobs and moms.com
  www.jobsandmoms.com
Military Careers
  www.militarycareers.com
My Future
  www.myfuture.com
Nat'l. Academies Career Center
  www4.nationalacademies.org/osep/cpc.nsf
Navyjobs.com
  www.navyjobs.com
Nevada JobConnect
  www.nevadajobconnect.com
Operation ABLE of Michigan
  www.OperationABLE.org
ProMatch
  www.promatch.org
Quintessential Career
  www.quintcareers.com
Retailology
  Retailology.com
Salary.com (CareerBuilder)
  www.salary.com
The Riley Guide
  www.rileyguide.com
Troops to Teachers
  www.jobs2teach.doded.mil/
Vault
  www.vault.com
Virtual Interviewing Assistant
  www.ukans.edu/cwis/units/coms2/via/index.html
WetFeet
  www.wetfeet.com
Working Woman
  www.workingwoman.com

The sites below offer leads to jobs for college graduates, interns, and coops. Summer jobs and offer opportunity for high school students can be found here as well.

Note: The sites in **Bold** are among the 500 Best and their reviews can be found in the main body of this edition. A Bold **(T)** indicates we consider the site among the "Top 50". The thousands of sites in plain text listed here were reviewed but, their reviews are not published (we promise to send you any review on request). All Web site URLs (web addresses) can be found in the Master List. A parentheses ( ) designates the "gateway" site that we reviewed. Brackets [ ] are used for clarification.

3rd-level.com
www.3rd-level.com
6 FigureMBA.com
www.6figuremba.com
About Jobs.com
www.aboutjobs.com
Academic Career Services in Finland
www.aarresaari.net/
Academic Employment Network
www.academploy.com
Activate.co.uk
www.activate.co.uk
After College (T)
www.aftercollege.com
American Advertising Federation
www.aaf.org
American Soc. of Agricultural Engineering
www.asae.org
Aspirasi Graduan
www.graduan.com.my
Black E.O.E Journal
www.blackeoejournal.com
Campus CareerCenter.com
www.campuscareercenter.com
Career Chase
www.careerchase.net
Career Connector
www.careerconnector.com
Career Edge
www.careeredge.org
Career Espresso/Emory University
www.sph.emory.edu/studentservice/Career.html
Career Guidance.com
www.careerguidance.com
Career Owl
www.careerowl.com
College Central Network (T)
www.collegecentral.com
College Grad Job Hunter
www.collegegrad.com
College Job Board
www.collegejobboard.com
College Recruiter
www.collegerecruiter.com
CollegeJournal.com (Career Journal)
www.collegejournal.com
Computer Jobs Entry Level
www.entrylevel.computerjobs.com
Cool Jobs.com
www.cooljobs.com
Cool Works - Jobs in Great Places
www.coolworks.com
doctorjob.com
www.doctorjob.com

Drug Information Association
www.diahome.org
eAttorney
www.eattorney.com
ecampus recruiter
www.ecampusrecruiter.com
eFinancialCareers
www.efinancialcareers.com
Emplawyernet
www.employernet.com
Employ U.com
www.employu.com
Empty.net
www.empty.net
Engineering Central
www.engcen.com
Entry Level Job Seeker Assistant
www.dnaco.net/~dantassi/jobhome.html
Environmental Careers Org. (Eco.org)
www.eco.org
ePro Net (Experience.com)
www.epronet.com
experience.com
www.experience.com
funjobs.com
www.funjobs.com
Global Wrokplace
www.global-workplace.com
Go Ferret Go
www.goferretgo.com
graduate-jobs.com
www.graduate-jobs.com
Graduating Engineer & Computer Careers
www.graduatingengineer.com
Gradunet
www.gradunet.co.uk
Great Summer Jobs
www.greatsummerjobs.com
GrooveJob.com
www.groovejob.com
Hispanic Alliance for Career Enhancement
www.hace.org
IMdiversity.com (T)
www.imdiversitycom
Inside Careers
www.insidecareers.co.uk
Intern Jobs.com (About Jobs.com)
www.internjobs.com
Intern Web.com
www.internweb.com
Internship Programs.com (Wet Feet)
www.internshipprograms.com
Irish Jobs.ie (T)
www.irishjobs.ie

Jewish Camp Staff
  www.jewishcampstaff.com
Job Easy
  www.jobeasy.com
Job Gusher.com
  www.Jobgusher.com
Job Postings
  www.jobpostings.net
JobGusher
  www.JobGusher.com
Massachusetts Biotechnology Council
  www.massbio.org
MBA Careers (Career Exposure)
  www.mbacareers.com
Mechanical Contractors Asso. of America
  www.mcaa.org
Nat'l. Academies Career Center
  www4.nationalacademies.org/osep/cpc.nsf
Nat'l. Youth Development Information Center
  www.nydic.org
Overseas Jobs.com (About Jobs.com)
  www.overseasjobs.com
Pre-Cast Stressed Convrete Assoc.
  www.pci.org
Recruitaly
  www.recruitaly.it
Resort Jobs (About Jobs.com)
  www.resortjobs.com
Rising Star Internships
  www.rsinternships.com
Seek (Australia) (T)
  www.seek.com.au
Social Work & Services Jobs Online
  gwbweb.wustl.edu/jobs/index.html
Summer Jobs (About Jobs.com)
  www.summerjobs.com
The Black Collegian Online
  www.blackcollegian.com
True Careers (T)
  www.truecareers.com
WorkopolisCampus.com (Workopolis)
  www.campusworklink.com
Youth@Work
  www.youthatwork.org/

CORPORATION STAFFING PAGES

These addresses are for the home pages of the companies listed on *Fortune* Magazine's annual FORTUNE 500 list for 2002. Nearly every site includes openings that can be reached from the home page via a "career" or "job" button. We rated each of these sites during the summer of 2002 on a scale ranging from "0" or "Offline" (because their online presence was useless) to "Best of Class". The 25 best sites are **BOLDED** and the worst still have a "0" next to their names. Keep in mind that this doesn't mean they aren't a good place to work. They simply don't know how to get their message out. Our detailed report can be found on our website.

Abbott
www.abbott.com
Adams Resources & Energy (0)
No Web Site
Adelphia Communications
www.adelphia.net
Administaff Inc
www.administaff.com
Advanced Micro Devices, Inc.
www.amd.com
Advancepcs
www.advparadigm.com
AES Corporation (0)
www.aesc.com
Aetna
www.aetna.com
AFLAC, Inc.
www.aflac.com
Agilent Technologies
www.agilent.com
Aid Association for Lutherans
www.aal.org
Air Products & Chemicals
www.airproducts.com
Airborne Freight Corporation
www.airborne.com
AK Steel Holding
www.aksteel.com
Albertson's, Inc.
www.albertsons.com
Alcoa, Inc.
www.alcoa.com
Allegheny Energy
www.alleghenyenergy.com
Allied Waste Industries, Inc.(0)
www.awin.com
Allmerica Financial Corporation
www.allmerica.com
ALLSTATE
www.allstate.com
ALLTEL Corporation
www.alltel.com
Amazon
www.amazon.com
Amerada Hess Corporation
www.hess.com
Ameren Corporation
www.ameren.com
American Axle & MFG
www.aam.com
American Electric Power Company, Inc.
www.aep.com
American Express Company
www.americanexpress.com
American Family Mutual Insurance Company
www.amfam.com/

American Financial Group, Inc. (0)
www.amfnl.com
American International Group,Inc.
www.aig.com
American Standard Companies, Inc. (0)
www.americanstandard.com
AmeriSource Health Corporation
www.amerisource.com
Ames Department Stores, Inc.
www.amesstores.com
Amgen, Inc.
www.amgen.com
AMR Corporation
www.amrcorp.com
Amsouth Bancorporation
www.amsouth.com
Anadarko Petroleum Corp.
www.anadarko.com
Anheuser-Busch Companies, Inc.
www.anheuser-busch.com
Anixter International Inc.
www.anixter.com
Anthem Insurance Companies, Inc.
www.anthem-inc.com
AOL Time Warner
www.aoltimewarner.com
Aon Corporation
www.aon.com
Apple Computer, Inc.
www.apple.com
Applied Materials, Inc.
www.appliedmaterials.com
Aquila
www.aquila.com
ARAMARK Corporation
www.aramark.com
Archer Daniels Midland Company
www.admworld.com
Armstrong World Industries, Inc.
www.armstrong.com
Arrow Electronics
www.arrow.com
Arvin Meritor
www.arvinmeritor.com
Ashland Inc.
www.ashland.com
AT&T Corp.
www.att.com
Autoliv, Inc.
www.autoliv.com
Automatic Data Processing, Inc.
www.adp.com
AutoNation, Inc.
www.autonation.com
AutoZone, Inc.
www.autozone.com

Avaya
www.avaya.com
Avery Dennison Corporation
www.averydennison.com
Avista Corp.
www.avistacorp.com
Avnet, Inc.
www.avnet.com
Avon Products, Inc.
www.avon.com
Baker Hughes Incorporated
www.bakerhughes.com
Ball Corporation
www.ball.com
Bank of America Corporation
www.bankofamerica.com
Bank of New York Co.
www.bankofny.com
Bank One Corporation
www.bankone.com
Barnes & Noble Inc. (0)
www.bn.com
Baxter International Inc.
www.baxter.com
BB&T Corp
www.bbandt.com
Bear Stearns
www.bearsterns.com
Becton, Dickinson and Company
www.bd.com
BellSouth Corporation
www.bellsouthcorp.com
Berkshire Hathaway Inc. (0)
www.berkshirehathaway.com
Best Buy Co. Inc.
www.bestbuy.com
Bethlehem Steel Corporation
www.bethsteel.com
Big Lots
www.biglots.com
BJ's Wholesale Club, Inc.
www.bjs.com
Black & Decker (0)
www.blackanddecker.com
Boeing
www.boeing.com
Boise Cascade Corporation
www.bc.com
Borders Group, Inc.
www.bordersgroupinc.com
Bristol-Myers Squibb Company
www.bms.com
Brunswick Corporation
www.brunswickcorp.com
Burlington Northern Santa Fe Corp.
www.bnsf.com
Burlington Resources
www.br-inc.com
Cablevision Systems Corp.
www.cablevision.com
Calpine
www.calpine.com
Campbell Soup Company
www.campbellsoups.com
Capital One Financial Corporation
www.capitalone.com
Cardinal Health, Inc.
www.cardinal-health.com
Caremark Rx, Inc.
www.caremark.com
Caterpillar, Inc.
www.cat.com
CDW Computer Centers, Inc.
www.cdw.com

Cendant
www.cendant.com
Cenex Harvest States Cooperatives
www.cenexharveststates.com
Centex Corporation
www.centex.com
Charter Communications, Inc.
www.chartercom.com
Chevron Corporation
www.chevron.com
Chubb Corporation
www.chubb.com
CIGNA Corporation
www.cigna.com
Cinergy Corp.
www.cinergy.com
Circuit City Stores, Inc.
www.circuitcity.com
Cisco Systems, Inc.
www.cisco.com
Citigroup, Inc.
www.citigroup.com
Claiborne
www.lizclaiborne.com
Clear Channel Communications, Inc.
www.clearchannel.com
Clorox
www.clorox.com
CMS Energy Corporation
www.cmsenergy.com
CNF Transportation Inc.
www.cnf.com
Coca-Cola
www.cocacola.com
Coca-Cola Enterprises, Inc.
www.cokecce.com
Colgate-Palmolive Company
www.colgate.com
Comcast Corporation
www.comcast.com
Comdisco, Inc.
www.comdisco.com
Comerica Incorporated (0)
www.comerica.com
Compaq Computer Corporation
www.compaq.com
Computer Associates International, Inc.
www.cai.com
Computer Sciences Corporation
www.csc.com
ConAgra
www.conagra.com
Conectiv
www.conectiv.com
Conoco
www.conoco.com
Conseco, Inc.
www.conseco.com
Consolidated Edison, Inc.
www.conedison.com
Constellation Energy Group, Inc.
www.constellation.com
Continental Airlines
www.continental.com
Cooper Industries
www.cooperindustries.com
Cooper Tire & Rubber Company
www.coopertire.com
Core-Mark International
www.core-mark.com
Corning Inc.
www.corning.com
Costco Wholesale Corporation (0)
www.costco.com

CORPORATION STAFFING PAGES

Countrywide Credit Industries
www.countrywide.com
Coventry Health Care
www.coventryhealth.com
Cox Communications, Inc.
www.cox.com
Crown Cork & Seal Company, Inc.
www.crowncork.com
CSX Corporation
www.csx.com
Cummins Engine Company, Inc.
www.cummins.com
CVS Corporation
www.cvs.com
Dana Corporation
www.dana.com
Danaher Corporation
www.danaher.com
Darden Restaurants, Inc.
www.darden.com
Dean Foods Company
www.deanfoods.com
Deere & Company
www.deere.com
Dell Computer Corporation
www.dell.com
Delphi Automotive Systems Corporation
www.delphiauto.com
Delta Air Lines, Inc.
www.delta.com
Devon Energy
www.devonenergy.com
Dillard's Inc.
www.dillards.com
Disney (2-3)
www.disney.com
Dole Food Company, Inc.
www.dole.com
Dollar General Corporation
www.dollargeneral.com
Dominion Resources, Inc.
www.domres.com
Donnelley (R.R.) & Sons
www.rrdonnelley.com
Dover Corporation (0)
www.dovercorporation.com
Dow Chemical
www.dowchemical.com
DTE Energy Company
www.dteenergy.com
Duke Energy Corporation
www.dukenergy.com
Du Pont De Memours (E.I.)
www.dupont.com
Dynegy Inc.
www.dynegy.com
Eastman Chemical Company
www.eastman.com
Eastman Kodak Company
www.kodak.com
Eaton Corporation
www.eaton.com
Echostar Communications
www.dishnetwork.com
Edison International
www.edison.com
Electronic Data Systems Corporation
www.eds.com
El Paso Energy Corporation
www.elpaso.com
EMC Corporation
www.emc.com
Emcor Group, Inc.
www.emcorgroup.com

Emerson Electric Co.
www.emersonelectric.com
Encompass Services Corporation
www.encompserv.com
Energy East
www.energyeast.com
Engelhard Corporation (0)
www.engelhard.com
Enron
www.enron.com
Entergy Corporation Standard
www.entergy.com
Enterprize Products (0)
www.epplp.com
Equity Office Properties
www.equityoffice.com
Exelon
www.exeloncorp.com
Express Scripts Inc
www.express-scripts.com
Exxon Mobil Corporation
www.exxon.mobil.com
Family Dollar Stores
www.familydollar.com
Fannie Mae
www.fanniemae.com
Farmland Industries, Inc.
www.farmland.com
Federal-Mogul Corporation
WWW.federal-mogul.com
Federated Department Stores, Inc.
www.federated-fds.com
FedEx Corporation
www.fedexcorp.com
Fidelity National Financial (0)
www.fnf.com
Fifth Third Bancorp
www.53.com
First American Corporation
www.firstarn.com
First Data Corporation (0)
www.firstdatacorp.com
First Energy
www.firstenergycorp.com
FleetBoston Financial
www.fleet.com
Fleming Companies, Inc.
www.fleming.com
Fluor Corporation
www.fluor.com
FMC Corporation
www.fmc.com
Foot Locker
www.footlocker-inc.com
Ford Motor Company
www.ford.com
Fortune Brands, Inc.
www.fortunebrands.com
Foster Wheeler Corporation
www.fwc.com
FPL Group, Inc.
www.fplgroup.com
Freddie Mac
www.freddiemac.com
Gannett Co., Inc.
www.gannett.com
Gap
www.gapinc.com
Gateway, Inc.
www.gateway.com
General Dynamics Corporation
www.generaldynamics.com
General Electric Company
www.ge.com

General Mills, Inc.
www.generalmills.com
General Motors Corporation
www.gm.com
Genuine Parts Company
www.genpt.com
Georgia-Pacific Corporation
www.gp.com
Gillette Company
www.gillette.com
Golden State Bancorp (0)
www.goldenstatebancorp.com
Golden West Financial Corporation
www.worldsavings.com
Goldman Sachs Group, Inc.
www.gs.com
Goodrich (B.F.)
www.goodrich.com
Goodyear Tire & Rubber
www.goodyear.com
GPU (First Energy)
www.gpu.com
Grainger (W.W.)
www.grainger.com
Graybar Electric Company, Inc.
www.graybar.com
Group 1 Automotive Inc. (0)
www.group1auto.com
Guardian Life Insurance Co. of America
www.glic.com
Halliburton Company
www.halliburton.com
Harley-Davidson
www.harleydavidson.com
Harrah's Entertainment, Inc.
www.harrahs.com
Hartford Financial Services Group Inc.
www.thehartford.com
HCA
www.hcahealthcare.com
Health Net
www.health.net
HEALTHSOUTH Corporation
www.healthsouth.com
Heinz (H.J.)
www.heinz.com
Hershey Foods Corporation
www.hersheys.com
Hewlett-Packard Company
www.hp.com
Hilton Hotels Corporation
www.hilton.com
Home Depot
www.homedepot.com
Honeywell International Inc.
www.honeywell.com
Hormel Foods Corporation
www.hormel.com
Host Marriott (0)
www.hostmarriott.com
Horton (D.R.) (0)
www.horton.com
Household International, Inc.
www.household.com
Humana Inc.
www.humana.com
IDA Corporation (0)
www.idacorpinc.com
Ikon Office Solutions, Inc.
www.ikon.com
Illinois Tool Works, Inc. (0)
www.itwinc.com
Ingram Micro, Inc.
www.ingrammicro.com

Intel Corporation
www.intel.com
International Business Machines Corporation
www.ibm.com
International Paper Company
www.internationalpaper.com
Interpublic Group of Companies, Inc. (0)
www.interpublic.com
Interstate Bakeries Corporation (0)
No web site
ITT Industries, Inc.
www.ittind.com
Jabil Circuit
www.jabil.com
Jacobs Engineering Group Inc.
www.jacobs.com
JDS Uniphase
www.jdsuniphase.com
Jefferson-Pilot Corporation
www.jpfinancial.com
John Hancock Financial Services Inc.
www.johnhancock.com
Johnson & Johnson
www.jnj.com
Johnson Controls, Inc.
www.johnsoncontrols.com
Jones Apparel Group, Inc.
www.jny.com
KB Home
www.kbhome.com
Kellogg Company
www.kelloggs.com
Kelly Services, Inc.
www.kellyservices.com
Kerr-McGee Corporation (0)
www.Kerr-McGee.com
KeyCorp
www.key.com
KeySpan Corporation
www.keyspanenergy.com
Kiewit (Peter) Sons'
www.kiewit.com
Kimberly-Clark Corporation
www.kimberly-clark.com
Kindred Healthcare
www.kindredhealthcare.com
Kmart Corporation
www.bluelight.com
Kohl's Corporation
www.kohls.com
Kroger
www.kroger.com
Lauder (Estee)
www.elcompanies.com
Lear Corporation
www.lear.com
Leggett & Platt, Incorporated
www.leggett.com
Lehman Brothers Holdings, Inc.
www.lehman.com
Lennar Corporation
www.lennar.com
Lennox International, Inc. (0)
www.lennoxinternational.com
Lexmark International Group, Inc.
www.lexmark.com
Liberty Mutual Insurance Group
www.libertymutual.com
Lilly (ELI)
www.lilly.com
Limited
www.limited.com
Lincoln National Corporation
www.lnc.com

Lockheed Martin Corporation
www.lockheedmartin.com
Loews Corporation
www.loews.com
Longs Drug Stores Corporation
www.longs.com
Lowe's Companies, Inc.
www.lowes.com
LTV (0) Bankrupt
www.ltvsteel.com
Lucent Technologies
www.lucent.com
Lyondell Chemical Company
www.lyondell.com
Manpower Inc.
www.manpower.com
Marathon Oil
www.marathon.com
Marriott International, Inc.
www.marriott.com
Marsh & McLennan Companies, Inc. (0)
www.mmc.com
Masco Corporation
www.masco.com
Massachusetts Mutual Life Insurance
www.massmutual.com
Maxtor
www.maxtor.com
Mattel, Inc.
www.mattel.com
May Department Stores
www.maydepartmentstores.com
Maytag Corporation
www.maytagcorp.com
MBNA Corporation
www.mbna.com
McDonald's Corporation
www.mcdonalds.com
McGraw-Hill
www.mcgraw-hill.com
McKesson HBOC Inc.
www.mckhboc.com
MEAD (0)
www.mead.com
Medtronic, Inc.
www.medtronic.com
Mellon Financial Corp.
www.mellon.com
Merck & Co., Inc.
www.merck.com
Merrill Lynch & Co., Inc.
www.ml.com
Metropolitan Life Insurance Co.
www.metlife.com
MGM Mirage
www.mgmgrand.com
Micron Technology, Inc.
www.micron.com
Microsoft Corporation
www.microsoft.com
Minnesota Mining and Manufacturing Company
www.3m.com
Mirant
www.mirant.com
Mohawk Industries, Inc. (0)
www.mohawkcarpet.com
Morgan (J.P.) Chase
www.jpmorgan.com
Morgan Stanley Dean Witter & Co.
www.msdw.com
Motorola, Inc.
www.motorola.com
Murphy Oil Corporation
www.murphyoilcorp.com

Mutual of Omaha Insurance Companies
www.mutualofomaha.com
Nash Finch Company
www.nashfinch.com
National City Corporation
www.national-city.com
Nationwide Insurance Enterprise
www.nationwide.com
Navistar International Corporation
www.navistar.com
NCR Corporation
www.ncr.com
New York Life Insurance Company
www.newyorklife.com
New York Times
www.nytco.com
Newell Rubbermaid Inc.
www.newellco.com
Nextel Communications, Inc.
www.nextel.com
Nike, Inc.
www.nike.com
NiSource Inc.
www.nisource.com
Nordstrom, Inc.
www.nordstrom.com
Norfolk Southern Corporation
www.nscorp.com
Northeast Utilities
www.nu.com
Northern Trust Corporation
www.northerntrust.com
Northrop Grumman Corporation
www.northgrum.com
Northwest Airlines Corporation
www.nwa.com
NorthWestern Corporation
www.northwestern.com
Northwestern Mutual Life Insurance Company
www.northwesternmutual.com
Nstar
www.nstaronline.com
NTL
www.ntl.com
Nucor Corporation (0)
www.nucor.com
Occidental Petroleum Corporation
www.oxy.com
Office Depot, Inc.
www.officedepot.com
OfficeMax, Inc.
www.officemax.com
OGE Energy Corp
www.oge.com
Omnicom Group Inc. (0)
www.omnicomgroup.com
ONEOK Inc. (0)
www.oneok.com
Oracle Corporation
www.oracle.com
Owens & Minor, Inc.
www.owens-minor.com
Owens Corning
www.owenscorning.com
Owens-Illinois, Inc.
www.o-i.com
Oxford Health Plans, Inc.
www.oxhp.com
Paccar Inc.
www.paccar.com
Pacific Life Insurance Company
www.pacificlife.com
PacifiCare Health Systems, Inc.
www.pacificare.com

CORPORATION STAFFING PAGES

Park Place Entertainment Corp.
www.parkplace.com
Parker Hannifin Corporation
www.parker.com
Pathmark Stores, Inc.
www.pathmark.com
Penney (J.C.)
www.jcpenney.com
PepsiAmericas
www.pepsiamericas.com
Pepsi Bottling
www.pbg.com
PepsiCo, Inc.
www.pepsico.com
Performance Food Group
www.pfgc.com
Pfizer Inc.
www.pfizer.com
PG&E Corporation
www.pgecorp.com
Pharmacia
www.pnu.com
Phelps Dodge Corporation
www.phelpsdodge.com
Philip Morris Companies Inc.
www.philipmorris.com
Phillips Petroleum
www.phillips66.com
Pinnacle West Capital Corporation
www.pinnaclewest.com
Pitney Bowes, Inc.
www.PB.com
Pittston
www.pittston.com
Plains All American Resources
www.paalp.com
PNC Financial Services Group
www.pncbank.com
PPG Industries, Inc.
www.ppg.com
PPL Corporation
www.pplresources.com
Praxair, Inc.
www.praxair.com
Premcor
www.premcor.com
Principal Financial Group
www.principal.com
Proctor & Gamble
www.pg.com
Progress Energy
www.progress-energy.com
Progressive
www.progressive.com
Providian Financial Corporation (0)
www.providian.com
Prudential Insurance Company of America
www.prudential.com
Public Service Enterprise Group, Inc.
www.pseg.com
Publix Super Markets, Inc.
www.publix.com
Puget Sound Energy, Inc.
www.psechoice.com
Pulte Corporation
www.pulte.com
Quantum Corporation
www.quantum.com
Quest Diagnostics Incorporated
www.questdiagnostics.com
Qwest Communications International Inc.
www.qwest.com
Radio Shack
www.tandy.com

Raytheon Company
www.raytheon.com
Regions Financial
www.regionsbank.com
Reliant Energy, Incorporated
www.reliantenergy.com
Reynolds (R.J.) Tobacco
www.rjr.com
Rite Aid Corporation
www.riteaid.com
Robinson (C.H.)
www.chrobinson.com
Rockwell Automation
www.rockwell.com
Rohm and Haas Company
www.rohmhaas.com
Roundy's
www.roundys.com
Ryder System, Inc.
www.ryder.com
Safeco Corporation
www.safeco.com
Safeway Inc.
www.safeway.com
Saks, Incorporated
www.saksincorporated.com
Sanmina Corporation
www.sanmina.com
Sara Lee Corporation
www.saralee.com
SBC Communications, Inc.
www.sbc.com
SCANA Corporation
www.scana.com
Schering-Plough Corporation
www.schering-plough.com
Schwab (Charles)
www.schwab.com
Science Applications International Corporation
www.saic.com
SCI Systems, Inc.
www.sci.com
Sealed Air
www.sealedair.com
Sears, Roebuck and Co.
www.sears.com
Sempra Energy
www.sempra.com
Service Master
www.servicemaster.com
Sherwin Williams
www.sherwin.com
Shopko Stores, Inc.
www.shopko.com
Smithfield Foods, Inc. (0)
www.smithfield.com
Smith International
www.smith.com
Smurfit-Stone Container Corporation (0)
www.smurfit-stone.com
Solectron Corporation
www.solectron.com
Sonic Automotive Inc.
www.sonicautomotive.com
Southern Company
www.southernco.com
SouthTrust Corporation
www.southtrust.com
Southwest Airlines Co.
www.southwest.com
Spartan Stores
www.spartanstores.com
Sprint Corporation
www.sprint.com

412

SPX
www.spx.com
Staff Leasing
www.gevityhr.com
Staples, Inc.
www.staples.com
Starwood Hotels & Resorts Worldwide, Inc.
www.starwood.com
State Farm Insurance Companies
www.statefarm.com
State Street Corporation
www.statestreet.com
Steelcase, Inc.
www.steelcase.com
St. Paul Cos.
www.stpaul.com
Strauss (Levi)
www.levistrauss.com
Sun Microsystems, Inc.
www.sun.com
Sunoco, Inc.
www.sunocoinc.com
SunTrust Banks, Inc.
www.suntrust.com
Supervalu Inc.
www.supervalu.com
Sysco Corporation
www.sysco.com
Target
www.target.com
Tech Data Corporation
www.techdata.com
Temple-Inland Inc.
www.templeinland.com
Tenet Healthcare Corporation
www.tenethealth.com
Tenneco Automotive
www.tenneco-automotive.com
Tesoro Petroleum Corporation
www.tesoropetroleum.com
Texas Instruments Incorporated
www.ti.com
Textron Inc.
www.textron.com
TIAA-CREF
www.tiaa-cref.org
Tjx
www.tjx.com
Toys `R' Us, Inc.
www.toysrus.com
Transmontaigne Inc. (0)
www.transmontaigne.com
Tribune Company
www.tribune.com
Tricon Global Restaurants, inc.
www.triconglobal.com
TRW Inc.
www.trw.com
TXU
www.txu.com
Tyson Foods, Inc.
www.tyson.com
UAL Corporation
www.ual.com
Union Pacific
www.up.com
Union Planters
www.unionplanters.com
Unisys Corporation
www.unisys.com
United Auto Group, Inc. (0)
www.unitedauto.com
United Parcel Service of America, Inc.
www.ups.com

United Stationers Inc.
www.unitedstationers.com
United Technologies Corporation
www.utc.com
UnitedHealth Group, Incorporated
www.unitedhealthgroup.com
Unocal Corporation
www.unocal.com
UnumProvident Corporation
www.unum.com
US Airways Group, Inc.
www.usairways.com
USAA
www.usaa.com
USA Education
www.salliemae.com
USA Networks, Inc.
www.usanetwork.com
US Bancorp
www.usbancorp.com
USG
www.usg.com
Valero Energy Corporation
www.valero.com
Verizon Communications
www.verizon.com
VF Corporation
www.vfc.com
Viacom Inc.
www.viacom.com
Visteon
www.visteon.com
Wachovia Corporation
www.wachovia.com
Walgreen Co.
www.walgreens.com
Wal-Mart Stores, Inc.
www.walmartstores.com
Washington Mutual, Inc.
www.wamu.com
Waste Management Inc.
www.wm.com
WellPoint Health Networks, Inc.
www.wellpoint.com
Wells Fargo & Co.
www.wellsfargo.com
Wesco International, Inc.
www.wescodist.com
Western Gas Resources, Inc.
www.westerngas.com
Weyerhaeuser Company
www.weyerhaeuser.com
Whirlpool Corporation
www.whirlpoolcorp.com
Willamette Industries, Inc.
www.wii.com
Williams
www.williams.com
Winn-Dixie Stores, Inc.
www.winn-dixie.com
Wisconsin Energy Corporation (0)
www.wisenergy.com
Worldcom
www.worldcom.com
Wyeth
www.wyeth.com
Xcel Energy (0)
www.excelenergy.com
Xerox Corporation
www.xerox.com
Yellow Corporation
www.yellowcorp.com
York International Corporation
www.york.com

DIVERSITY

The niche sites listed here are as diverse as you will find anywhere. Many more career hubs and general sites offer diversity content, partnerships and connections.

Note: The sites in **Bold** are among the 500 Best and their reviews can be found in the main body of this edition. A Bold **(T)** indicates we consider the site among the "Top 50". The thousands of sites in plain text listed here were reviewed but, their reviews are not published (we promise to send you any review on request). All Web site URLs (web addresses) can be found in the Master List. A parentheses ( ) designates the "gateway" site that we reviewed. Brackets [ ] are used for clarification.

AfriCareers.com (Hire-Power)
  www.africareers.com
American Assoc. of People with Disabilities
  www.aapd.com
American Soc. of Women Accountants
  www.aswa.org/wanted.html
Asian American Economic Dev. Enterprises
  www.aaede.org
Asian American Journalists Assoc.
  www.aaja.org
Asian Careers.com (Hire-Power)
  www.asiancareers.com
Asia-Net
  www.asia-net.com
Assoc. for Women in Communications
  www.womcom.org
Assoc. for Women in Mathematics
  www.awm-math.org
Assoc. for Women in Sports Media
  www.awsmonline.org
Assoc. of Latino Professionals in Fin. & Acc.
  www.aahcpa.org
Assoc. of Women Surgeons
  www.womensurgeons.org
Bilingual-Jobs
  www.bilingual-jobs.com
Bilingualxpress.ca
  www.bilingualexpress.ca
Black Career Women
  www.bcw.org
Black Culinarians Alliance
  www.blackculinarians.com
Black Data Processing Assoc.
  www.bdpa.org
Black E.O.E Journal
  www.blackeoejournal.com
Black Voices.com (CareerBuilder)
  www.blackvoices.com
Black World Today (Career Engine)
  www.tbwcareers.com
Blinks Magazine (FlipDog)
  www.blinks.net
Career Engine Network
  www.careerengine.com
Career Exposure
  www.careerexposure.com
Career Fables.com
  www.careerfables.com
Career PLACE
  www.careerplace.com
Career Woman2000.com (Hire-Power)
  www.careerwoman2000.com
Career Women (Career Exposure)
  www.careerwomen.com
Chicano/a Latino/a NET
  latino.sscnet.ucla.edu/

Classifieds For Women (Career Engine)
  www.classifiedsforwomen.com
Developers.net (Tapestry.net)
  www.tapestry.net
Diversilink
  www.diversilink.com
Diversity Careers Online
  www.diversitycareers.com
Diversity Employment
  www.diversityemployment.com
Diversity Inc.com
  www.diversityinc.com
Diversity Job Fairs.com
  www.americanjobfairs.com
Diversity Job Network
  diversityjobnetwork.com
Diversity Link.com
  www.diversitylink.com
Diversity Recruiting.com
  www.diversityrecruiting.com/index2.html
Diversity Search (Career Exposure)
  www.diversitysearch.com
Diversityforhire.Com
  www.diversityforhire.com
Diversityinc.com
  www.diversityinc.com
Equal Opportunity Publications
  www.eop.com
Feminist Career Center
  www.feminist.org
Feminist Majority Foundation Online
  www.feminist.org
Financial Women International
  www.fwi.org/
Gay Work.com
  www.gaywork.com
Hire Deaf.com
  www.hiredeaf.com
Hire Diversity.com
  www.hirediversity.com
Hispania Net
  www.hispanianet.com
Hispanic Alliance for Career Enhancement
  www.hace.org
Hispanic Business.com)
  www.hispanicbusiness.com
Hispanic Nat'l Bar Association
  www.hnba.com
Hispanicareers.com (Hire-Power)
  www.hispanicareers.com
Historically Black Colleges and Universities
  HBCUCareerCenter.com
Iamable.com (Hire-Power)
  www.iamable.com
ihispano.com
  www.ihispano.com

IMdiversity.com (T)
www.imdiversitycom
iVillage (CareerBuilder)
www.ivillage.com
Job Access (CareerBuilder)
www.jobaccess.org
Job Centro
www.jobcentro.com
Job City USA.com (Spherion)
www.jobcityusa.com
Job Factory
www.jobfactory.com
Job Latino
www.joblatino.com
Latino Web
www.latinoweb.com
LatPRO (T)
www.latpro.com
Mexican American Eng. and Scientists Soc.
www.maes-natl.org
Minority Career Network
www.minoritycareernet.com/
Minority Nurse.com (CASS)
www.minoritynurse.com
Native American Jobs.com
www.nativeamericanjobs.com
Native Jobs.com
www.nativejobs.com
Nat'l. Alliance of Black School Educators
www.nabse.org
Nat'l. Assoc. of African Americans in HR
www.naaahr.org
Nat'l. Assoc. of Black Accountants
www.nabainc.org
Nat'l. Assoc. of Black Journalists
nabj.org
Nat'l. Assoc. of Hispanic Journalists
www.nahj.org
Nat'l. Black MBA Assoc.
www.nbmbaa.org
Nat'l. Business & Disbility Council - Able to ...
www.business-disability.com
Nat'l. Diversity Newspaper Job Bank
www.newsjobs.com
Nat'l. Society of Black Engineers
www.nsbe.org
Nat'l. Society of Hispanic MBAs (BrassRing)
www.nshmba.org
Network of Commercial Real Estate Women
www.nncrew.org
Out Professionals
www.outprofessionals.org
Pro GayJobs.com
www.progayjobs.com
Saludos.com (T)
www.saludos.com
Soc. for Adv. of Chicanos & Native Amer. in...
www.sacnas.org
Soc. of Hispanic Prof. Engineers (BrassRing)
www.resume-link.com/society/shpewebportal.htm
Soc. of Women Engineers (BrassRing)
www.swe.org
Spanishjobs.com
www.spanishjobs.com
The Black Collegian Online
www.blackcollegian.com
The Multicultural Advantage
www.tmaonline.net
Training Resource Network
www.trninc.com
Webgrrls
www.webgrrls.com
Womans-Work
www.womans-work.com

Women in Higher Education
www.wihe.com
Women In Technology International
www.witi.com
Women Sports Jobs
www.womensportsjobs.com
Workplace Diversity.com (Career Engine)
www.workplacediversity.com

Looking for a free site where you can post your jobs? Want a few free resumes? Sometimes you get exactly what you pay for. Occasionally you'll find much more- even a gem or two. Use this list with other indices to narrow your choices.

Note: The sites in **Bold** are among the 500 Best and their reviews can be found in the main body of this edition. A Bold **(T)** indicates we consider the site among the "Top 50". The thousands of sites in plain text listed here were reviewed but, their reviews are not published (we promise to send you any review on request). All Web site URLs (web addresses) can be found in the Master List. A parentheses ( ) designates the "gateway" site that we reviewed. Brackets [ ] are used for clarification.

RECRUITERS
Post your jobs for FEE (+) OR FREE (0)
See resumés for FEE (+) OR FREE (0)

EXAMPLE ... Job/Resumé
JobResuméSite ... 0/+

(This means it is free to post a job to this site, but requires a fee to view resumés)

123 Charlotte.com....................................+/+
123 Jax.com..+/+
123 Raleigh.com.......................................+/+
123 USA hire.com.................................+/+
1800Drivers..+/+
1st 4 UK HR Jobs ....+/+
3D Cafe...+/0
3D Site 0/nla
3rd-level.com...0/nla
3sectorsjob...+/nla
4 Allied Health Jobs Online (HospitalJobsOnline) ....+/+
4 MD Jobs Online (HospitalJobsOnline)...................+/+
4 Nursing Jobs Online (HospitalJobsOnline)...............+/+
4Labors Of Love.......................................0/0
4weeks.com...+/+
4Work ....+/nla
6 FigureJobs ....+/+
6 FigureMBA.com......................................0/+
A Job4Accountants (Employmax).......................0/+
A Job4Engineers (Employmax).........................0/0
A Job4Programmers (Employmax) 0/0
A Job4Scientists (Employmax).........................0/0
A1A Computer Jobs ....+/nla
a1jobindia.com...0/0
A2Z Moonlighter 0/0
AACI Israel Jobnet.....................................+/nla
Aberdeen American News (CareerBuilder)......................+/+
About Jobs.com....................................+/nla
Abracat ....+/+
Absolute-Comms.......................................+/+
Absolutely Health Care ....+/+
Academic Career Services in Finland........................0/0
Academic Employment Network....................+/+
Academic Physician & Scientist...................+/nla
Academic Position Network........................+/nla
Academy Grad.com (MMR)..............................+/+
Academy Grads (The Destiny Group) ....+/+
Access Dubuque (Telegraph Herald) ....+/nla
Access: Networking in the Public Interest ....+/+
Accessalesjobs.com................................+/+
Account Manager.com (Career Marketplace)...................+/+
Accountant Jobs (eJob Stores) ....+/+
Accountants World.com (Career Engine).........../+/+
Accounting Classifieds (Career Engine) ....+/+

Accounting Jobs Online ....+/nla
Accounting Professional.com (Career Marketplace) ....+/+
Accounting.com ....+/+
AccountingWEB.co.uk....................................+/+
Aces-US...+/0
ActionJobs..0/nla
Activate.co.uk ....+/0
Actor's Worldlink....................................nla/0
ActualJobs..+/nla
Ad Age..+/nla
ad world 0/0
Adjunctopia ....+/+
Advance Careers (T) ....+/+
ADVANCE for Careers ....+/nla
Adventures in Hospitality Careers..............+/+
Adventures in Hospitality Careers.......................+/+
Advertising Job Bank...................................+/0
Advertising Job Store (eJob Stores) ....+/+
Advertising Media Internet Center 0/0
Advertising Research Foundation ....+/nla
Adweek Online...+/+
AEC Job Bank ....+/+
AEC WorkForce ....+/+
Aeroindustryjobs.com ....+/nla
Aerospace Engineer.com (Career Marketplace).................+/nla
AfriCareers.com (Hire-Power)...........................+/nla
After College (T) ....+/+
Agricultural Labour Pool...............................+/nla
Agricultural MVP.com (CareerMVP).....................+/nla
Agricultural Technology Information Network...............+/nla
AIRS - Advanced Internet Recruitment Strategies.......0/0
AJCJobs.com (Atlanta Journal Constitution)..............+/+
Akron Beacon Journal (CareerBuilder)....................+/+
Alabama Computer Jobs.com ....+/+
Alabama Live (Advance Careers)...........................+/+
Alabama State Jobs 0/nla
Alaska Job Center Network 0/nla
Albany Times Union (CareerBuilder)......................+/nla
Alberta jobs.com (Canjobs).............................+/0
Albuquerque Journal (abracat)...........................+/+
Aldaba 0/0
All County Jobs.com ....+/nla
All Energy Jobs ....+/+
All Jobz...0/nla
All Retail jobs.com ....+/+
AllEnergyJobs ....+/+
Allentown Morning Call (CareerBuilder) ....+/+
Allied Health Employment (HealthCareJobStore)........... +/+
Allied Health Opportunities.......................+/nla
Almogordo Daily News (Employment Wizard)..................+/+
AM FMJobs 0/0
American Academy of Audiology ....+/+
American Academy of Cosmetic Dentistry.......................+/0
American Academy of Forensic Sciences ....+/nla

American Accounting Assoc ....+/0
American Advertising Federation ....+/nla
American Agricultural Economics Assoc.......................+/nla
American Antropological Assoc ....+/+
American Assoc. for Budget & Program Analysis 0/nla
American Assoc. for Respiratory Care.........................+/+
American Assoc. of Clinical Chemistry ....+/+
American Assoc. of Collegiate Registrars.....................+/nla
American Assoc. of Community Colleges......................+/+
American Assoc. of Critical-Care Nurses...................+/nla
American Assoc. of Finance and Accounting ....+/+
American Assoc. of People with Disabilities....................+/+
American Assoc. of School Administrators....................+/nla
American Assoc. of University Women ....+/nla
American Astronomical Society ....+/nla
American Ceramic Society 0/nla
American Chamber of Commerce Execs......................+/nla
American Chemical Society - JobSpectrum.org ....+/+
American College of Cardiology..................................+/+
American College of Healthcare Executives 0/0
American College of Radiology ....+/nla
American College Personnel Assoc.............................+/nla
American Corporate Counsel Assoc 0/0
American Counseling Assoc......................................+/+
American Culinary Federation 0/0
American Design Drafting Assoc................................+/0
American Fisheries Society ....+/nla
American Health Lawyers Assoc ....+/+
American Industrial Hygiene Assoc ....+/nla
American Institue of Architects Career Center............+/0
American Institute of Biological Sciences (AIBS) ....+/nla
American Institute of Chemical Engineers.......................+/+
American Institute of CPA's ....+/nla
American Institute of Physics (AIP) ....+/+
American Jobs.com ....+/+
American Lighting Assoc. (FlipDog).............................+/+
American Marketing Assoc ....+/1
American Massage Therapy Assoc ....+/+
American Mathematical Society...................................+/nla
American Meteorological Society................................+/nla
American Music Therapy Assoc 0/nla
American Nuclear Society ....+/+
American Oil chemists' Society ....+/0
American Physical Therapy Assoc ....+/nla
American Planning Assoc..+/nla
American Public Health Assoc ....+/nla
American Public Works Assoc...................................+/nla
American Risk & Insurance Assoc 0/0
American School Counselor Assoc 0/0
American Soc. for Engineering Education (ASEE)......+/None
American Soc. for Quality ....+/+
American Soc. for Training & Development.................+/+
American Soc. of Agricultural Engineering ....+/0
American Soc. of Assoc. Executives (T).......................+/+
American Soc. of Civil Engineers ....+/nla
American Soc. of Echocardiography.............................0/0
American Soc. of Limnology and Oceanography 0/nla
American Soc. of Mech. Engineering ....+/+
American Soc. of Women Accountants ....+/nla
American Society fo P&E Nutrition..............................+/nla
American Society for Clinical Laboratory Science ....+/nla
American Society for Public Administration....................+/+
American Society of Crime Lab Directors 0/nla
American Society of Gene Therapy ....+/nla
American Society of Health-System Pharmacists............+/nla
American Society of Interior Designers..........................+/+
American Speech-Language-Hearing Assoc....................+/+
American Statistical Association ....+/+
American Urological Assoc. Job Finder ....+/+
American Urological Assoc.......................................+/+
American Water Works Assoc ....+/nla
American Welding Society ....+/+
American Zoo & Aquarium Assoc..............................+/nla
America's Job Bank (T) 0/0
America's Preferred Jobs ....0/+

Anchorage Daily News (Employment Wizard) ....+/+
Anchorage HelpWanted (Reg.HelpWanted) ....+/+
Apartment Careers..+/+
Aquatic Network 0/0
Arbetsformedlingen 0/0
Archaeological Fieldwork Opportunities ....+/nla
Architect jobs.com (eJob Stores) ....+/+
Architects Online..+/nla
Areo Ad's 0/0
Arizona Jobs.com (LocalCareers) ....+/+
Arizona Republic (USA Today Careers) ....+/1
Army Career & Alumni Program 0/nla
Art Deadlines List..+/nla
Art Directors Club of Metro. Washington ....+/+
Art Hire ....+/0
art jobonline ....+/+
Asbury Park Press (USA Today Careers)) ....+/+
Asheville Area Talent Bank (NationJob).........................+/nla
Asheville Citizen-Times (USA Today Careers))...................+/+
Ashland Daily Tidings (Employment Wizard) ....+/+
Asiaco Jobs Center..0/+
Asiadragons.com (Asiaco) ....+/nla
Asia-Links ....+/+
Asian American Economic Dev. Enterprises.................nla/nla
Asian American Journalists Assoc 0/nla
Asian Careers.com (Hire-Power)................................+/nla
Asia-Net ....+/+
ASP Computer work.com...+/+
Aspirasi Graduan ....+/+
Assoc for Advancement of Computing in Ed...............+/nla
Assoc. for Computing Machinery.................................+/+
ASsoc. for Facilities Engineering ....+/nla
Assoc. for Financial Professionals..............................+/+
Assoc. for Fundraising Professionals............................+/+
Assoc. for Institutional Research...............................0/nla
Assoc. for Interactive Marketing (CareerBuilder) ....+/+
Assoc. for Investment Mgmt. & Research ....+/+
Assoc. for Library and Information Science Educ.........+/nla
Assoc. for Telecom. in Higher Ed 0/nla
Assoc. for Women in Communications ....+/+
Assoc. for Women in Mathematics ....+/nla
Assoc. for Women in Sports Media.............................0/nla
Assoc. of Clinical Research Professionals ....+/nla
Assoc. of eX-Lotus Employees................................0/0
Assoc. of Latino Professionals in Fin. & Acc..................0/nla
Assoc. of Metropolitan Water Agencies.........................0/nla
Assoc. of Perioperative Registered Nurses....................+/nla
Assoc. of Research Libraries ....+/nla
Assoc. of Women Surgeons 0/nla
Atlanta Computer Jobs.com ....+/+
Atlanta Computer work.com ....+/+
Atlanta ContractJobs 0/0
Atlanta Smart City..0/nla
Atlantic Jobs.com (Canjobs) ....+/0
Attorney Jobs Online ....0/+
Attorney.com (Legal Staff) ....+/+
Audit Net ....+/nla
Augusta Chronicle (Employment Wizard) ....+/+
AuntMinnie.com (T)...+/nla
Austin American Statesman ....+/nla
Austin Employment.com (Employocity) ....+/NA
Australian Careers Directory 0/0
Australian Job Search ....+/nla
Author link ....+/0
Auto careers ....+/+
Auto Jobs.com ....+/0
Autobody Online 0/0
AutoCAD Job Network (Mercury Enterprises) ....+/nla
AutoHeadHunter.net ....+/+
Automation Jobs...+/+
Automation Techies..+/+
Automotive Aftermarket Industry Assoc......................+/Nla
Automotive Techs.Com ....+/0
AutoTechs USA..+/+
AV Canada 0/0

Av Crew.com .... +/0
AV Jobs **0/0**
Avenue J.com 0/0
Aviation Employment.com .... +/+
Aviation Job Search.com .... **+/+**
Aviation Jobs Online 0/0
Aviation Now .... +/nla
Awesome Accountants 0/0
aztechjobs.com .... nla/+
BA Jobs (T) .... **+/+**
BAAN Fanclub and User Forum (Fanclub) 0/nla
Back Door Jobs .... **+/nla**
Backstagejobs.com **0/0**
Bakery-Net .... **+/0**
Baltimore Computerwork.com .... +/+
Baltimore Sun (CareerBuilder) .... +/+
BaltimoreWanted (Reg.HelpWanted) .... +/+
Bank Connect.com .... 0/+
Bank Job Search (BAI) **0/nla**
bank jobs.com .... **+/+**
Bank Talent.com .... nla/+
Banking Job Store.com (eJob Stores) .... +/+
bankingboard.com (TheBoardNetwork) .... +/+
bankrole.com .... +/+
Baton Rouge Advocate .... +/nla
Baton Rouge Careers Online (Employment Partner) .... +/+
Baton Rouge HelpWanted.com (Reg.HelpWanted) .... +/+
Battle Creek Enquirer (USA Today Careers) .... +/+
Bay AreaHelpWanted (Reg.HelpWanted) .... +/+
Bay Recruiter.com .... **+/nla**
Be An Actuary .... +/nla
Be the Boss (Monster.com) .... +/nla
Bellingham Herald (USA Today Careers)) .... +/+
Benefit News Online **0/0**
Benefits Link (T) .... **+/+**
Bergen Daily Record (USA Today Careers)) .... +/+
Best Jobs California (Best Jobs) .... +/+
Best Jobs Florida (Best Jobs) .... +/+
Best Jobs Illinois (Best Jobs) .... +/+
Best Jobs Massachusetts (Best Jobs) .... +/+
Best Jobs New York (Best Jobs) .... +/+
Best Jobs Texas (Best Jobs) .... +/+
Best Jobs USA.com .... +/+
Best Jobs Washington (Best Jobs) .... +/+
Better Job Network (CareerLINK) .... +/+
better jobs KC.com (CareerLink) .... +/+
BharatCareers.com .... +/+
Big FiveTalent.com .... **+/+**
BigAppleHead.com 0/nla
bigcountryjobs.com (Employment Wizard) .... +/+
Bilingual-Jobs .... +/+
Bilingualxpress.ca .... +/+
Billings Gazette (Employment Wizard) .... +/+
BillingsHelpWanted (Reg.HelpWanted) .... +/+
Bio Array News (GenomeWeb) .... +/nla
Bio career.com (SciWeb) .... +/+
Bio Exchange.com .... **+/+**
Bio find .... **+/0**
Bio Inform (GenomeWeb) .... +/nla
Bio Research Online (WorkLife) .... +/+
Bio Snail .... +/+
Bio Space.com .... **+/nla**
Bio Statistician Jobs (HealthCareJobStore) .... +/+
Bio View (Monster) .... **+/+**
Bio.com .... **+/nla (See Notes)**
Bioinformatics Resource 0/nla
Biomedical Engineer.com (Career Marketplace) .... +/+
Biomedical Engineering Society .... +/nla
Bioplanet 0/nla
Bioscience and Medicine (HUM-MOLGEN) 0/nla
BioSnail.com .... +/+
Biotech Careers.com .... +/nla
Biotechnology Human Resource Counsel .... +/nla
Birchin Lane 0/nla
Birmingham Employment.com (Employocity) ...... +/NA

Birmingham HelpWanted (Reg.HelpWanted) ...... +/+
Birmingham Online (Employment Partner) .... +/+
Bismark Tribune (Employment Wizard) .... +/+
Biz Moonlighter .... +/nla (See Notes)
Black Career Women 0/nla
Black Culinarians Alliance .... +/nla
Black Data Processing Assoc 0/nla
Black E.O.E Journal .... +/+
Black Voices.com (CareerBuilder) .... **+/+**
Black World Today (Career Engine) .... +/+
Blinks Magazine (FlipDog) .... +/+
Blood Center Jobs (HealthCareJobStore) .... +/+
Bloomberg.com (CareerBuilder) .... +/+
Blue To Gray (Corporate Gray Online) .... +/+
Boiler Room 0/nla
BoiseHelpWanted (Reg.HelpWanted) .... +/+
Boldface Jobs .... +/0
Book People 0/0
Boston Computer Jobs.com .... +/+
Boston Hire.com .... +/+
Boston Job Bank .... **+/0**
Boston Job Source (Internet Job Source) .... +/+
Boston Works- Boston Globe (T) .... **+/+**
Boulder Daily Camera (Employment Wizard) ...... +/+
Brain bench .... **nla/+**
Brain Bid.com 0/0
Brainhunter.com .... **+/+**
Brainpower .... +/+
Brains Talent.com .... +/nla
Branch Staff Online.com .... +/+
Brass Ring.com (T) .... **+/+**
Bread Bakers Guild of America .... +/nla
Bridgewater News-Courier (USA Today Careers) .... +/+
Bright & Professional 0/nla
British Columbia Jobs.com (Canjobs) .... +/0
British Columbia Library Assoc 0/nla
British Columbia Water & Waste Assoc 0/nla
British Jobs .... +/nla
Broadband Careers Network .... +/+
BroadbandCareers.Com .... **+/+**
Broker hunter.com .... +/+
BuffaloHelpWanted (Reg.HelpWanted) .... +/+
Buffalojobfinder.com (Employment Wizard) .... +/+
Building Industry Consulting Service Int'l .... +/0
Bumeran .... +/+
Burlington Free-Press (USA Today Careers) .... +/+
Business Analyst.com (Career Marketplace) .... +/+
business financemag.com .... +/+
Butte Montana Standard (Employment Wizard) .... +/+
Buying Jobs.com (NicheJobs) .... +/nla
C++ (JV Search) .... 0/+
C++ Computer work.com .... +/+
C++ Jobs.com (Pure Power) .... +/nla
Cable & Telecommunications Assoc. for Marketi .... +/nla
Cabletelevision Advertising Bureau .... +/nla
cache mirror .... +/+
CAD jobs.net 0/nla
CAD Operators Online 0/nla
CADD Jobs.com .... +/0
cal career.com 0/0
CalgaryJobShop (Reg.HelpWanted) .... +/+
Cali Careers.com (CareerMVP) .... +/nla
California Agricultural Technology Institute 0/nla
California Computerwork.com .... +/+
California HelpWanted.com (Reg. HelpWanted) .... +/+
California Job Journal .... +/nla
California Job Source (Internet Job Source) .... +/+
California Jobs.com (LocalCareers) .... +/+
California Journalism Job Bank .... +/nla
California Soc. of Prof. Engineers (CareerBuilder) .... +/+
Californian (USA Today Careers) .... +/+
Call Center Careers .... **+/+**
Call Center Jobs.com .... **+/+**
Call CenterOps **0/0**
Campus CareerCenter.com .... **+/+**

Canada Computerwork.com ....+/+
Canada IT.com...**0/nla**
Canada Jobs.com...**+/nla**
Canadian Bar Assoc ....+/nla
Canadian Institue of Quantity Surveyors ....+/0
Canadian Mgmt. Accountants Society..........................+/nla
Canadian Restaurant & Foodservices Assoc ....+/0
Candidate Seeker..+/nla
Canjobs.com...**+/nla**
Cape Cod Online (Employment Wizard)..........................+/+
cardiac nurse jobs.com (HealthCare.Jobs) ....+/+
Career Age ....+/+
Career Bahrain (CareerMidEast) ....+/+
Career Bank ....**+/+**
Career Beacon.com ....+/nla
Career Board...**+/+**
Career Builder (T)..**+/+**
Career Buzz...**+/nla**
Career Chase...0/0
Career Click ....+/+
Career Connector ....**0/+**
Career Consulting Corner..0/0
Career Consulting Corner..0/0
Career Cross Japan ....**+/+**
Career Edge ....+/nla
Career Egypt.com (CareerMidEast)..............................+/+
Career Emirates.com (CareerMidEast) ....+/+
Career Engine Network ....**+/+**
Career Espresso/Emory University **0/nla**
Career Exchange.com ....**+/+**
Career Exposure...**+/+**
Career Fables.com...**0/+**
Career File...**0/+**
Career Giant ....+/+
Career Gram ....+/+
Career Guidance.com ....nla/+
Career Hunters.com nla/0
Career India ....+/+
Career Information Exchange ....+/nla
Career Innovator 0/0
Career Jordan.com (CareerMidEast) ....+/+
Career Journal Asia.com (CareerJournal)........................+/+
Career Journal Europe.com (CareerJournal).....................+/+
Career Journal.com (T) ....**+/+**
Career Junction ....+/+
career key...+/nla
Career Kuwait.com (CareerMidEast) ....+/+
Career Lebanon.com (CareerMidEast) ....+/+
Career Link- Applied Info. Mgm't Institute ....**+/+**
Career Local Net ....+/nla
Career Machine ....0/+
Career Mag.com ....+/+
Career Marketplace...**+/+**
Career Mart...**+/+**
Career Matrix.com ....+/+
Career MidEast.com ....**+/+**
Career Morocco.com (CareerMidEast) ....+/+
Career Mosaic India ....+/+
Career MVP.com ....**+/nla**
Career Net..+/+
Career NJ.com (CareerMVP)......................................+/nla
Career Oman.com (CareerMidEast) ....+/+
Career One...**+/0**
Career Owl...**+/+**
Career Pal ....0/+
Career Park ....+/nla
Career PLACE..+/+
Career Plus ....+/nla
Career Qtar.com (CareerMidEast) ....+/+
Career Saudi.com (CareerMidEast) ....+/+
Career Search America 0/0
Career Shop.com...**+/+**
Career Site.com...**0/+**
Career span...0/+
Career Surf.com ....+/+

Career Tunis.com (CareerMidEast)................................+/+
Career Woman2000.com (Hire-Power) ....+/nla
Career Women (Career Exposure)..................................+/+
Career Yemen.com (CareerMidEast) ....+/+
Career.com ....+/+
CareerAnalog ....+/nla
CareerHut.com ....+/+
Careers 2000.net...**+/+**
Careers in Construction...**+/+**
Careers in Food.com...**+/0**
Careers in Government ....**+/0**
Careers in Recruitment ....+/+
Car-eers.com ....+/+
CareersColorado.com ....+/+
Carolina Computer Jobs.com ....+/+
Casino Careers Online (T)...**+/+**
Casino Employment Guide ....+/+
Casting America 0/0
Casting Daily 0/0
Castingpro.com (Staffingpro) ....+/+
Casualty Actuarial Society ....+/+
Catho Online 0/0
CATIA Job Network (Mercury Enterprises) ....+/nla
ccJobsOnline.com ....+/+
CCollegeJobs.com ....+/+
Cellular Telecom. & Internet Assoc. (Job Options)..........+/+
Center Watch ....**+/+**
Certified Management Assoc. of Canada ....+/+
CFO Asia ....+/nla
CFO Postions.com (Career Engine)................................+/+
Charity JOB 0/nla
Charity Village.com...**+/nla**
Charityopps.com ....+/+
charityopps.com ....+/nla
Charleston Daily Mail (Employment Wizard)....................+/+
CharlestonHelpWanted (Reg.HelpWanted).......................+/+
CharlestonJobMarket ....+/+
Charlotte Observer (CareerBuilder).................................+/+
CharlotteHelpWanted (Reg.HelpWanted) ....+/+
Chattanooga Times (Employment Wizard) ....+/+
Chef Job.com...0/0
Chef Jobs Network (Escoffier On Line) ....+/+
Chem Jobs ....+/+
Chemical Engineer.com (Career Marketplace)..................+/+
Chemistry Jobs.com (NicheJobs)..................................+/nla
Cherry Hill Courier-Post (USA Today Careers)..................+/+
Chesapeake Human Resources Assoc ....+/nla
Chicago Careers Online (Employment Partner)................+/+
Chicago Computer Jobs.com ....+/+
Chicago Employment.com (Employocity) ....+/NA
Chicago HelpWanted.com (Reg. HelpWanted) ....+/+
Chicago Job Network (Chicago Sun Times) ....+/nla
Chicago Jobs.com (LocalCareers)..................................+/+
Chicago Tribune (CareerBuilder).....................................+/+
Chicano/a Latino/a NET 0/nla
Chico Enterprise Record (Employment Wizard)................+/+
Chief Financial Officer.com ....+/nla
Christian Career Center..+/+
Christian Jobs Online ....**+/0**
Christian Placements.com ....+/+
Chronicle of Higher Education ....**+/nla**
Chronicle of Philanthropy ....**+/nla**
Cincinatti Career Board ....+/+
Cincinatti Careers (Employment Partner) ....+/+
Cincinnati Enquirer (USA Today Careers)).......................+/+
CIO Council.com (Career Marketplace) ....+/+
CIO Magazine (ITCareers)...+/nla
Ciol Jobs ....+/nla
Circulation Jobs.com ....+/nla
City Jobs...+/+
City Search.com (CareerBuilder) ....+/+
Civic Action in Eurasia 0/nla
Civil Engineering Jobs ....+/+
CIVIL Jobs.com..+/0

Clarksville Leaf-Chronicle (USA Today Careers)) ....+/+
Classic Web..+/nla
Classified Employment Web Site (CLEWS)...................+/+
Classifieds 2000 (CareerBuilder).......................................+/+
Classifieds For Women (Career Engine)............................+/+
Clear Star...0/0
Clearance Jobs.com..+/+
Cleveland Career Board ....+/+
Cleveland Live (Cleveland Plain Dealer).........................+/nla
Click4Talent ....+/+
Clinical Laboratory Management Assoc............................+/+
CNC Machines Job Network (Mercury Enterprises) ....+/nla
COACH's Job Board 0/0
Coastal Bend Careers (Employment Wizard) ....+/+
Cobol Computer work.com...+/+
Cobol Computerwork.com..+/+
Cobol Jobs.com (Pure Power)...+/nla
Coderider- VIC Job Board...0/nla
Cold Fusion Advisor (CF Advisor) 0/0
CollectionIndustry.com...+/+
College & University Personnel Assoc ....+/nla
College & University Prof. Assoc. for HR ....+/nla
College Central Network (T) ....+/nla
College Grad Job Hunter...+/+
College Job Board ....+/+
College of Healthcare Infor. Mgmt. Exec 0/0
College Recruiter ....+/+
CollegeJournal.com (Career Journal)..................................+/+
Colorado Alive (Employment Wizard)................................+/+
Colorado Careers Online (Employment Partner) ....+/+
Colorado Computerwork.com ....+/+
Colorado Guide...0/nla
Colorado Human Resources Assoc...................................+/nla
Colorado Online Job Connection...................................+/+
Colorado Software & Internet Assoc................................+/+
Coloradoan (USA Today Careers).....................................+/+
Columbia Today (CareerBuilder) ....+/+
Columbia-Williamette Compensation Group.....................0/nla
Columbus Career Board ....+/+
Columbus Careers Online (Employment Partner) ....+/+
Columbus Ledger-Enquirer (CareerBuilder).......................+/+
ColumbusHelpWanted (Reg.HelpWanted)........................+/+
ColumbusJobs.com (Employment Wizard) ....+/+
Communications Roundtable...0/nla
Community Career Center ....+/+
Computational Fluid Dynamics Jobs Database..............+/nla
Computer Jobs AS/400..+/+
Computer Jobs Data Warehousing.....................................+/+
Computer Jobs Database Systems ....+/+
Computer Jobs E-Commerce...+/+
Computer Jobs Entry Level..+/+
Computer Jobs ERP ....+/+
Computer Jobs Executive Level...+/+
Computer Jobs H-1B ....+/+
Computer Jobs Hardware..+/+
Computer Jobs Help Desk ....+/+
Computer Jobs in Israel 0/nla
Computer Jobs Legacy Systems ....+/+
Computer Jobs Networking..+/+
Computer Jobs New Media ....+/+
Computer Jobs Project Management.................................+/+
Computer Jobs Quality Assurance ....+/+
Computer Jobs Technical Recruiting ....+/+
Computer Jobs Technical Sales ....+/+
Computer Jobs Technical Writing ....+/+
Computer Jobs Unix ....+/+
Computer Jobs Windows Development..............................+/+
Computer Jobs.com (T)...+/+
Computer Weekly.com..+/nla
Computer work.com (T) ....+/+
Computer World (ITCareers)..+/nla
Configuration Management (CM Today) ....+/nla
Connecticut Jobs Online (CTJobs.com)...........................+/+
Connecticut Jobs.com (LocalCareers)..............................+/+
Connecticut Post (Employment Wizard)...........................+/+

Construction Executives.com ....+/+
Construction Financial Mgmt. Assoc................................+/+
Construction Gigs 0/0
Construction Job Store (eJob Stores) ....+/+
Construction Jobs.com..+/+
Construction.com...+/+
ConstructionJobsites.com (Geojobsites)............................+/+
Construction-net 0/0
ConstructionOnly.Com...+/+
ConsultantTV.com ....nla/+
Contact Point Career Development 0/nla
Contract Employment Connection.....................................+/+
Contract Engineering 0/0
Contract JobHunter ....+/+
Contracts247..+/+
Cool Jobs.com 0/nla
Cool Works - Jobs in Great Places ....+/+
Copy Editor Job Board 0/nla
coroflot...+/0
Corporate Gray Online...+/+
Corporate Gray ....0/+
Corporate Skills (Irish Jobs) ....+/+
Corrections Connection 0/0
Corridor Careers ....+/+
Council for Advancement & Support od Ed.................+/nla
Council of Logistics Management....................................nla/0
Council of Public Relations Firms....................................nla/+
Council on Employee Benefits...+/nla
Council on Foundations...+/0
Counsel.net 0/nla
CPA jobs.com ....+/nla
CPA net ....+/nla
CPA2bizcareers.com..+/+
CPACareerNet..+/+
Craigs List [Atlanta] 0/0
Craigs List [Austin]..0/0
Craigs List [Boston] 0/0
Craigs List [Chicago]...+/0
Craigs List [Denver] 0/0
Craigs List [Los Angeles] 0/0
Craigs List [New York] 0/0
Craigs List [Portland] 0/0
Craigs List [Sacramento]...0/0
Craigs List [San Diego] 0/0
Craigs List [Seattle]...0/0
Craigs List [Vancouver]...0/0
Craigs List [Washington DC] 0/0
Craigs List...+/0
Crains New York (Career Engine) ....+/+
Creative Central.com 0/nla
Creative Freelancers Online ....+/+
Creative Hotlist..0/0
Creative Moonlighter 0/0
Credit Jobs Today ....+/+
Credit Union Executives Society.......................................+/0
Creditjobs.com ....+/+
Crew Net ....+/+
Crhurch Jobs.com ....+/+
crmXchange 0/0
Crystallography Worldwide 0/nla
CT Health Careers.com (All County Jobs) ....+/nla
CT High Tech.com (All County Jobs).............................+/nla
Ct. Business & Industry Assoc. (CTJobs.com)................+/+
CTJob Search (CareerLINK)..+/+
Curriculum Vitae Online 0/0
Customer Service Job Stores (eJob Stores)....................+/+
CV Europe 0/0
CV Index Directory ....+/+
CV Online- Czech (CV Europe) 0/0
CV Online- Estonia (CV Europe) 0/0
CV Online- Finland (CV Europe) 0/0
CV Online- Hungary (CV Europe) 0/0
CV Online- Latvia (CV Europe)...0/0
CV Online- Lithuania (CV Europe)....................................0/0
CV Online- Poland (CV Europe)..0/0

CV Online- Romania (CV Europe) 0/0
CV Online- Russia (CV Europe) 0/0
Cyber KingEmployment ....+/+
Cyber-Sierra...+/nla
DaiJob..nla/+
Dallas HR Jobs ....+/nla
Dallas Morning News (Employment Wizard).................+/+
Database Analyst.com (Career Marketplace) ....+/+
Dave's ESL Cafe (English as a Second Language).........+/0
daVinci Times (T) ....+/+
Davjobs.com (The Destiny Group) ....+/+
Daytona HelpWanted.com (Reg. HelpWanted) ,.............+/+
DC AccountingJobs ....+/+
DC Computer Jobs.com ....+/+
DC Computerwork.com ....+/+
DC Job Source.com (Internet Job Source).....................+/0
Decatur Herald & Review (Employment Wizard) ....+/+
Degree Hunter.com ....+/+
Delphi Jobs.com (Pure Power).....................................+/nla
Delphi World.com 0/nla
Dent Search.com ....+/+
Dental Hygienist Jobs (HealthCareJobStore)..................+/+
Dentist Jobs.com (HealthCare Job Store)........................+/+
Denver Computer Jobs.com ....+/+
Denver Post (Employment Wizard) ....+/+
Desert Sun (USA Today Careers)...................................+/+
Designer Max.com ....+/+
Desktop Publishing.com JobBank..................................0/nla
DesMoines Register (USA Today Careers)).......................+/+
Destiny Group-Military Transition Center (T)..................+/+
Detroit Computer Jobs.com ....+/+
Detroit Employment.com (Employocity) ....+/NA
Detroit News (USA Today Careers)) ....+/+
Developers.net (Tapestry net)......................................0/+
DFW Employment.com (Employocity) ....+/NA
DFWHelpWanted. (Reg.HelpWanted)............................+/+
DICE High Tech Jobs Online (T) ....+/+
Dietician Jobs (HealthCareJobStore)..............................+/+
Direct Employers (T) ....+/nla
direct marketingcareers.com ....+/+
direct-jobs.com ....+/+
Distr. of Columbia Bar Career Center (LegalStaff) ....+/+
Diversilink ....+/+
Diversity Careers Online ....nla/+
Diversity Employment ....+/+
Diversity Inc.com ....+/+
Diversity Job Fairs.com ....0/+
Diversity Job Network.......................nla/nla (See Notes)
Diversity Link.com ....+/+
Diversity Recruiting.com ....+/nla
Diversity Search (Career Exposure) ....+/+
Diversityforhire.Com ....+/+
Diversityinc.com ....+/+
Do A Project.com 0/0
doctorjob.com ....+/nla
DOD Job Search (America's Job Bank).........................0/0
DOE-JOBBS 0/0
Donohue's RS/6000 Employment Page ....+/nla
dot Jobs ....+/nla
Dragon Surf 0/nla
Dream Construction Jobs...+/+
Drillers Job Center..+/nla
Drug Information Association 0/nla
Dubuque- AccessSuccess ....+/+
Dubuque Telegraph Herald ....+/nla
Duluth News Tribune (CareerBuilder)............................+/+
Earthworks ....+/0
East Valley Tribune (CareerCast) ....+/+
Eat up drink up.com 0/nla
eAttorney ....0/+
ecampus recruiter ....+/+
eCommerce Computer work.com...................................+/+
Econ Jobs.com (NicheJobs)..+/nla
Ed Jobs U Seek 0/nla
Ed Physician.com...0/nla

Edie's Environmental Job Centre ....+/+
Editor & Publisher ....+/0
EDN Magazine CarEEr Zone (CareerBuilder)...................+/+
Education Jobs ....+/nla
Education Week ....+/nla
Education-jobs.com...+/+
EDUCAUSE ....+/nla
EE Times (The Work Circuit) ....+/nla
EE-Link/North American Assoc. for Env. Ed..................0/nla
eFinancialCareers...+/nla
EFLWeb ....1/+
e-itwizards.com ....+/+
eJob Stores ....+/+
e-Job ....+/nla
El Paso Times (USA Today Careers)) ....+/+
elance 0/0
Electric job.com ....+/+
Electrical Employment 0/0
Electrical Engineer.com (Career Marketplace) ....+/+
Electrical World (McGraw-Hill) ....+/nla
Electrician Job Store (eJob Stores) ....+/+
Electronic Labour Exchange..0/nla
Electronic News OnLine..+/nla
Electronics Engineer.com (Career Marketplace) ....+/+
Elf Network.com ....+/nla
Elmira Star Gazette (USA Today Careers)......................+/+
Embedded.com (The Work Circuit) ....+/nla
Emplawyernet ....0/+
Empleos Web 0/nla
Employ China ....+/+
Employ U.com ....+/+
Employee Assistance Professionals Assoc ....+/nla
Employee Relocation Council.......................................+/0
Employers Online ....+/+
employMAX ....+/+
EmployMED ....+/nla
Employment 2000 ....+/nla
Employment 411 ....+/+
Employment 911 ....+/+
Employment Avenue.com 0/0
Employment Guide.com...+/+
Employment Information in the Mathematical Science ....+/nla
Employment Partner ....+/+
Employment Weekly (IN) ....+/nla
Employment Wizard (Career Site) (T)..........................+/+
Employxpress ....+/+
Empty.net 0/0
ENDS Environmental Jobs...+/nla
Energy Career Network 0/nla
Energy Jobs Network ....+/+
Energy jobs.com..+/+
Energy Vortex.com ....+/+
Engineer 500.com ....+/+
Engineer Employment (eJob Stores)..............................+/+
Engineer jobs.com ....+/+
Engineer.net ....+/nla
Engineer-Cad.com ....+/nla
Engineering Central ....+/+
Engineering Institute of Canada ....+/+
Engineering News Record ....+/nla
EngineeringjJobsites.com (Geojobsites)..........................+/+
EngineerMax.com ....+/+
ENT Careers ....+/+
Entertainment Careers.Net ....0/+
Entertainment Jobs.com..+/nla
Entomology Society of America....................................0/nla
Entry Level Job Seeker Assistant nla/0
Enviro Network.com..+/0
Environmental Career Opportunities ....+/nla
Environmental Career.com ....+/+
Environmental Career.com ....+/0
Environmental Careers Org. (Eco.org) ....+/nla
Environmental Engineer.com (Career Marketplace).........+/+
Environmental Expert..+/nla
Environmental Jobs and Careers ....+/nla

Great Falls Tribune (USA Today Careers)) ....+/+
Great Insurance Jobs ....**+/+**
Great Nurse.com...+/nla
Great Summer Jobs/Misc...**+/+**
Great Teacher.net..0/0
Gree To Gray (Corporate Gray Online) ....+/+
Green Dream Jobs...**+/nla**
Green Energy Jobs ....**+/nla**
Greensboro News & Record ....+/+
Greenville News (USA Today Careers)) ....+/+
Greenwich Time (CareerBuilder) ....+/+
GrooveJob.com ....+/nla
Guardian Unlimited Jobs ...., ...+/nla
Gulf Coast Sun-Herald (CareerBuilder) ....+/+
Gulf Live (Advance Careers)...+/+
Guru.com...+/+
H Careers ....**+/+**
H Monster.com (Monster.com) ....**+/+**
H1B Sponsors..**0/+**
H1Maia.com ....+/+
Hampton Roads Daily Press (CareerBuilder) ....+/+
Hanap-Buhay.com.ph ....+/+
Hartford County Jobs.com (All County Jobs) ....+/nla
Hartford Courant (CareerBuilder) ....+/+
HartfordHelpWanted (Reg.HelpWanted) ....+/+
Hattiesburg American (USA Today Careers)) ....+/+
Head Hunt (Counsel Network) 0/nla
headhunt.com (Counsel Network)...................................0/+
Health Care Job Store...**+/+**
Health Care Jobs Online..+/nla
Health Care Recruitment Online ....**+/+**
Health Care Source ....**+/+**
Health Care Talents ....+/nla
Health CareerWeb.com (Employment Guide) ....+/+
Health Jobsite.com ....+/+
Healthcare Employment.com (Career Marketplace) ....+/+
Healthcare Financial Management Assoc......................+/nla
HealthCare Hub.com (Nursing Spectrum)........................+/+
HEALTHeCareers (T) ....**+/+**
Help Desk Institute ....+/+
Help Wanted.com ....+/+
HelpWanted Boston (Reg.HelpWanted) ....+/+
Help-Wanted.Net 0/0
HelpWantedDC.com (Reg.HelpWanted) ....+/+
hi techclub.com ....+/+
Higher EdJobs.com ....**+/+**
Hilton Head Island Packet (Employment Wizard) ....+/+
Hire A Vet (The Destiny Group)..+/+
Hire Abilitiy.com ....**+/+**
Hire Albany.com ....+/+
Hire Asian...0/+
Hire Atlanta.com ....+/+
Hire Austin.com ....+/+
Hire Buffalo.com ....+/+
Hire Charlotte.com ....+/+
Hire Cincinnatti.com ....+/+
Hire Columbus.com ....+/+
Hire Dayton.com ....+/+
Hire Deaf.com...**+/nla**
Hire Denver.com ....+/+
Hire Diversity.com ....**+/+**
Hire GreaterWashington.com...+/+
hire health.com ....**+/+**
Hire Honolulu.com ....+/+
Hire houston.com ....+/+
Hire hub ....nla/+
Hire in a Click...**+/nla**
Hire Jacksonville.com...+/+
Hire KansasCity.com...+/+
Hire Loisville.com ....+/+
Hire Memphis.com ....+/+
Hire Milwaukee.com...+/+
Hire Nashville.com ....+/+
Hire Orlando.com...+/+
Hire Philadelphia.com ....+/+

Hire Phoenix.com ....+/+
Hire Pittsburgh.com...+/+
Hire Sacramento.com ....+/+
Hire San Antonio.com ....+/+
Hire SanFrancisco.com ....+/+
Hire SanJose.com...+/+
Hire Seattle.com ....+/+
Hire Skills.com..**0/nla**
Hire StLouis.com ....+/+
Hire Tampa Bay.com ....+/+
Hire Texas 0/nla
Hire the Triad...+/+
Hire the Triangle..+/+
Hire Top Talent ....+/+
Hire TwinCities.com ....+/+
Hire Wichita.com ....+/+
HireBaltimore.com ....+/+
HireBio..+/+
HireGate ....+/+
HireMass.com ....+/+
hireMedical ....+/+
HireNursing ....+/+
Hiring Network ....+/+
Hispania Net ....+/nla
Hispanic Alliance for Career Enhancement......................+/+
Hispanic Business.com) ....+/+
Hispanic Nat'l Bar Association ....+/nla
Hispanic Online (Monster)...+/+
Hispanicareers.com (Hire-Power)....................................+/nla
Historically Black Colleges and Universities ....**+/+**
Hollywood MVP.com (CareerMVP)....................................+/nla
Hollywood Web...**0/+**
Home Jobs Plus.com 0/0
Honolulu Advertiser (USA Today Careers))........................+/+
Honolulu Star Bulletin ....+/nla
HonoluluHelpWanted (Reg.HelpWanted) ....+/nla
Horticultural Jobs..**+/0**
Hospital Hub UK.com ....+/nla
Hospital Jobs Online...**+/+**
hospitality careernet.com ....+/+
Hospitality Careers.net...+/nla
Hospitality Financial & Technology Professionals 0/0
Hospitality Jobs Online ....+/+
Hospitality Jobs Online..**+/nla**
Hospitality jobz.net ....+/+
Hospitality Link..**+/0**
Hospitality MVP.com (CareerMVP) ....+/nla
Hospitality Net 0/0
Hot Jobs.com (T)...**+/+**
Hot Nurse Jobs...**+/+**
Hot resumes.com ....+/+
hotauditjobs.com ....+/0
Hotel Jobs- Ireland...+/+
Hotel Jobs.com ....+/+
Hotel Online ....+/0
HotelJobsites.com (Geojobsites) ....+/+
HotJobs.ca (HotJobs.com) ....+/+
House of Fusion 0/0
Houston Geological Society...0/nla
Houston Chronicle ....+/nla
Houston Employment.com (Employocity) ....**+/+**
HR Connections Direct..+/nla
HR Job Net...+/+
HR Junction..**+/nla**
HR Next ....+/0
HR Pal ....+/+
HR Staffing Search (JV Search) ....0/+
HR World ....0/+
HR.com..**0/+**
HRIM Mall...**0/nla**
HRM Jobs (NicheJobs)...+/nla
HRMed.com ....+/nla
HRMVP MVP.com (CareerMVP) ....+/nla
hs people (Human Services) ....**+/+**
HTML Writers Guild Job List ....**0/+**

Human Factors and Ergonomics Society	+/+
Human Resource Assoc. of the Nat'l. Capital Area	0/nla
Human Resources Job Store (eJob Stores)	+/+
Human Resources Online	+/+
Human Services Career Network	+/+
Humanlinks.com	0/+
Huntington Herald-Disp. (USA Today Careers))	+/+
HVAC Careers (CareerMVP)	+/nla
HVAC job.com (Electric Job)	+/+
HVAC Mall	0/0
Hydrocarbon Online (VerticalNet)	+/+
i -street	+/nla
Iamable.com (Hire-Power)	+/nla
Idaho Press-Tribune (Employment Wizard)	+/+
Idaho State Jobs	0/nla
Idaho Statesman (USA Today Careers))	+/+
idealist.org	**+/nla**
IDEAS Job Network (Mercury Enterprises)	+/nla
iHire Job Network	**+/+**
ihispano.com	**+/+**
IL Careers.com (CareerMVP)	+/nla
Illinois Jobs.com (LocalCareers)	+/+
IMdiversity.com (T)	**+/+**
Impact Online	0/nla
Independent Press Assoc	+/+
Independent School Management (ISM)	**+/nla**
Independent Sector Job Link	+/nla
Indian Jobs	0/0
Indianapolis Star (USA Today Careers)	+/+
Industrial Designers Society of America	+/0
Industrial Engineer.com (Career Marketplace)	+/+
Infectious Disease Soc. of America	**0/0**
Info Jobs.net (Bolsa de Trabajo)	0/0
Info Mine	**+/0**
InhouseCounsel (Counsel Network)	0/+
Inner City Jobs.com (NicheJobs)	+/nla
Inomics	0/nla
InPharm.com	+/+
InRetail	+/0
Inside Careers	**+/nla**
Inside Careers	+/nla
InspectionJobs.com	+/+
Institute for Professionals in Taxation	+/+
Institute for Supply Management	**0/0**
Institute of Certified Travel Agents	0/nla
Institute of Electrical and Electronics Engineers	**+/+**
Institute of Food Technologists	+/+
Institute of Industrial Engineers	+/+
Institute of Internal Auditors	0/nla
Institute of Packaging Professionals	0/0
Institute of Store Planners	0/0
Institution of Professional Engineers	+/nla
Instrumentation Soc. of America	**+/0**
Insurance File	+/nla
Insurance National Search	+/nla
Intelligence & Defense Careers	**+/+**
InterEC.NET	**0/0**
Interface JOBS.com	0/0
Interior Design Jobs.com	**+/0**
Intern Jobs.com (About Jobs.com)	+/nla
Intern Web.com	0/nla
Internet Career Connection	**0/0**
Internet Employment in New Mexico	+/0
Internet Job Locator	+/+
Internet Jobs.com	+/+
Internship Programs.com (Wet Feet)	0/nla
Int'l Assoc. of Business Communicators	nla/+
Int'l Customer Service Assoc	**0/0**
Int'l Nortel Networks Meridian Users Group	+/+
Int'l Soc. for the Performing Arts	0/nla
Int'l Tandem Users Group	+/+
Int'l Tandem Users Group	+/+
Int'l. Assoc. for HR Info Mgmt	+/+
Int'l. Assoc. of Amusement Parks and Attractions	+/nla
Int'l. Assoc. of Conference Centers	+/0

Int'l. Career Employment Center	+/nla
Int'l. Economic Development Council	+/nla
Int'l. Foundation of Employee Benefit Plans	**+/0**
Int'l. Personnel Mgmt. Assoc. (CareerBuilder)	+/+
Int'l. Pharmajobs	+/+
Int'l. Seafarers Exchange	**0/0**
Int'l. Soc. of Logistics	+/+
Int'l. Society For Performance Improvements	+/+
Iowa City Press-Citizen (USA Today Careers)	+/+
Iowa State Jobs	0/nla
Ireland Hiring	+/+
i-resign.com	**+/nla**
Irish Jobs.ie (T)	**+/+**
Iron and Steel Society	+/0
Ist Free Jobs	0/0
IT Careers.com	**+/nla**
IT Classifieds (Career Engine)	+/+
IT Jobfinder.co.za (JobUniverse)	+/nla
IT Jobs4.com	+/+
IT Moonlighter	+/nla (See Notes)
IT Online Jobs	+/+
IT talent.com	0/0
IT Toolbox Forums	**0/nla**
IT Toolbox's Baan Assist	0/nla
IT Toolbox's CRM Assist	0/nla
IT Toolbox's Data Warehousing Assist	0/nla
IT Toolbox's EAI Assist	0/nla
IT Toolbox's E-Business Assist	0/nla
IT Toolbox's ERP Assist	0/nla
IT Toolbox's Oracle Assist	0/nla
IT Toolbox's PeopleSoft Assist	0/nla
IT Toolbox's SAP Assist	0/nla
IT World (ITCareers)	+/nla
Ithaca Cortland Careers (Employment Partner)	+/+
ITonlinejobs	**+/+**
It's Your Job Now	+/+
ItsYourJobNow.com	+/+
it-TEMP	0/0
ITwow.com	0/0
iVillage (CareerBuilder)	+/+
Jackson Clarion-Ledger (USA Today Careers))	+/+
Jackson Sun (USA Today Careers))	+/+
JacksonvilleHelpWanted (Reg.HelpWanted)	+/+
JamminJobs.com	+/+
Japanese Jobs.	+/+
Java Computer work.com	+/+
Java Jobs	0/0
Java World (ITCareers)	+/nla
Javajobsonline.com	+/0
Jeff Gaulin's Canadian Journalism Job Board	+/0
Jersey Job Guide	+/+
Jewish Camp Staff	+/+
Jewish Vocational Services Career Moves	0/0
JMO Jobs (MMR)	+/+
Job AA	0/0
Job Access (CareerBuilder)	+/+
Job Ads	**+/+**
Job Asia	**+/nla**
Job Bank USA	**+/+**
Job Boards.com	**+/+**
Job Bright	+/+
Job Cafe	+/+
Job Catalog	0/0
Job Centro	**+/+**
job channel.tv	+/+
Job Circle.com (T)	**+/0**
Job City USA.com (Spherion)	+/+
Job Dig	+/+
Job Easy	0/+
Job Factory	**+/nla**
job find.com	**+/+**
Job fly	0/+
Job Folder.com	+/0
Job Food	+/+
job force	+/+

Job Gusher.com	+/nla
Job Hub	0/nla
Job Index.co.za	**+/+**
Job Island.com	**0/0**
job khoj	nla/+
Job Latino	+/+
Job Launch	**0/0**
Job Link Asia.com	+/+
Job Link For Journalists	**+/+**
Job Link-USA	+/+
Job Listings.net	+/nla
Job Mag.com	+/+
Job Magic	**+/+**
Job Master	0/+
Job Monkey	**+/+**
Job Navigator	+/+
Job Net Australia	**+/+**
Job net.com	**+/+**
Job Next Career Network	+/+
Job Opps.net	+/+
Job Penguin	+/+
job pilot.com Austria	+/+
job pilot.com Belgium	+/+
job pilot.com Czech	+/+
job pilot.com Denmark	+/+
job pilot.com France	+/+
job pilot.com Germany	+/+
job pilot.com Hungary	+/+
job pilot.com Italy	+/+
job pilot.com Netherlands	+/+
job pilot.com Norway	+/+
job pilot.com Poland	+/+
job pilot.com Spain	+/+
job pilot.com Sweden	+/+
job pilot.com Switzerland	+/+
job pilot.com Thailand	+/+
job pilot.com UK	+/+
job pilot.com USA	+/+
Job Postings	+/+
Job right.com	0/nla
Job science.com	**+/+**
Job Seekers Mailing List	0/nla
Job Serve: Accountancy Vacancies in the UK	**+/+**
Job Shark	**+/0**
Job Shark-Argentina	+/0
Job Shark-Brasil	+/0
Job Shark-Canada	+/0
Job Shark-Chile	+/0
Job Shark-Columbia	+/0
Job Shark-Ireland	+/0
Job Shark-Mexico	+/0
Job Shark-Peru	+/0
Job Shark-UK	+/0
Job Shark-Uruguay	+/0
Job Shark-Venezuela	+/0
job site.com	**+/+**
Job Smack	+/+
Job Square	+/+
Job Street	**+/+**
Job Street-India	+/+
Job Toaster	**0/0**
Job Track Online (Job Magic)	+/+
Job Universe (Canada)	+/nla
Job Universe (IT Careers-IDG)	+/nla
Job Universe (New Zealand)	+/nla
Job Village	**0/0**
Job Ware	**+/nla**
Job Warehouse	**+/+**
Job.com	**+/+**
Job2Teach	0/nla
Jobbig	+/+
JobDoggy.com	+/0
JobExpo.com	0/+
JobGusher	+/+
job-hunt.org	nla/nla

Jobing.com	**+/+**
Jobline-Finland (Monster.com)	+/+
Jobline-France (Monster.com)	+/+
Jobline-Germany (Monster.com)	+/+
Jobline-Italy (Monster.com)	+/+
Jobline-Netherlands (Monster.com)	+/+
Jobline-Norway (Monster.com)	+/+
Jobline-Spain (Monster.com)	+/+
Jobline-Sweden (Monster.com)	+/+
Jobline-Switzerland (Monster.com)	+/+
Jobline-UK (Monster.com)	+/+
jobpilot.com	**+/0**
JobRadio.com	+/+
Jobs 4 HR (LocalCareers)	+/+
Jobs 4 Sales.com (LocalCareers)	+/+
Jobs 4police	+/0
Jobs Bazaar.com	+/+
Jobs Bazaar.com	0/+
Jobs Canada	+/+
Jobs DB.com	0/+
Jobs for Colorado.com	+/+
Jobs for Economists (JOE)	0/nla
Jobs for Networkers (JobsforProgrammers)	+/+
Jobs for Programmers (T)	**+/+**
Jobs Hawaii	+/nla
Jobs in Chicago	+/nla
Jobs in Edinburgh.com	+/nla
Jobs in Education	+/nla
Jobs in Entomology	0/nla
Jobs in Fashion.com	+/nla
Jobs in Horticulture	+/0
Jobs in Japan	0/0
Jobs in Journalism	0/nla
Jobs in Logistics	**+/+**
Jobs in Maine	+/+
Jobs in MFG.com (Jobs in Logistics)	+/+
Jobs in Philosophy	0/nla
Jobs in Sports	0/nla
Jobs in the Biz	+/0
jobs in the money	**+/+**
Jobs in Therapy	+/nla
Jobs Nation	+/+
Jobs on Guam.com	0/nla
Jobs Online	0/nla
Jobs Plus.com.au	+/nla
Jobs Retail.com	+/+
Jobs tri-cities.com (Employment Wizard)	+/+
Jobs USA.co.uk (FlipDog)	+/+
Jobs.ac.uk	+/nla
Jobs.com (Monster)	+/+
Jobs.in.York.com (CareerSite)	+/+
jobs.internet.com (DICE)	+/+
Jobs.net	0/0
Jobs4Gems	+/+
JOBSfront	+/+
Jobs-Ireland.com	+/nla
Job-Sites.com	+/nla
Jobstor.com	+/nla
Jobvertise	**0/0**
Jobz	+/0
Joint Service Academy Alumni Organizations	**+/nla**
Joint Service Academy Resume DBS (Destiny Gr	+/+
Journal of Commerce (Career Engine)	+/+
Journalism and Women's Symposium	+/nla
Journalism for journalists (UK)	+/nla
Journalism Jobs.com	**+/+**
Jumbo Classifieds	+/+
Just Access Jobs	+/+
Just Accounting Jobs.com	+/+
Just AS400 Jobs	+/+
Just ASP Jobs	+/+
Just Baan Jobs	+/+
Just c Jobs	+/+
Just CAD Jobs	+/+

Just Cobol Jobs ....+/+
Just computerjobs.com...................................+/+
Just DB2 Jobs ....+/+
Just E-Commerce Jobs ....+/+
Just Engineering Jobs.com..............................+/+
Just Entertainment Jobs.com............................+/+
Just Health Care Jobs.com ....+/+
Just Help Desk Jobs.......................................+/+
Just Hospitality Jobs.com ....+/+
Just JAVA Jobs..+/+
Just Manufacturing Jobs.com ....+/+
Just Marketing Jobs.com ....+/+
Just My Jobs.com..**0/0**
Just Networking Jobs......................................+/+
Just Notes Jobs...+/+
Just NT Jobs ....+/+
Just Oracle Jobs..+/+
Just PeopleSoft Jobs......................................+/+
Just Sales..**0/0**
Just Science Jobs.com ....+/+
Just SQL Server Jobs ....+/+
Just Sybase Jobs ....+/+
Just Tech Jobs.com ....+/+
Just Telephony Jobs.......................................+/+
Just Unix Jobs ....+/+
Just Visual Basic Jobs.....................................+/+
Just Writing Jobs.com.....................................+/+
JV Search ....**+/+**
Kansas City Star (CareerBuilder).......................+/+
Kansas State Jobs...0/nla
Kansas.com (CareerBuilder) ....+/+
KansasCityWanted (Reg.HelpWanted)..................+/+
KareerMakers.com..+/+
KARRIER Online ....+/nla
Kenosha County.com (Employment Wizard).........+/+
Kentuckiana Jobs ....+/+
Kentucky KY Direct.......................................0/nla
Knox Careers.com (Employment Wizard)............+/+
Knox News.com ....+/nla
Knoxville Careers Online (Employment Partner)...........+/+
LA Daily News (Employment Wizard)..................+/+
LA Employment.com (Employocity) ....+/NA
LA Job Market (CareerLINK) ....+/+
LA Times.com (CareerBuilder)...........................+/+
Laborum.com ....+/+
LaCrosse Tribune (Employment Wizard) ....+/+
Lafayette Daily Advertiser (USA Today Careers) ....+/+
Lafayette Journal & Courier (USA Today Careers) ....+/+
Lan Jobs.com (Pure Power)..............................+/nla
Lancaster Eagle-Gazette (USA Today Careers) ....+/+
Lancaster Sentinel Enterprise (Employment Wizard) ....+/+
Lanka Web 0/0
Lansing State Journal (USA Today Careers) ....+/+
LasVegasHelpWanted (Reg.HelpWanted)..........................+/+
Latin American Jobs.com ....0/+
Latino Web...+/nla
LatPRO (T) ....**+/+**
LavaTech's - Lotus Notes Jobs **0/0**
Law Bulletin..+/0
law enforcementjobs.com..............................+/nla
Law Forum ....+/0
Law Guru (Legal Staff) ....+/+
Law Guru.com (Legalstaff)...............................+/+
l aw Info.com...0/0
Law Jobs ....**+/nla**
Law Listings (Career Engine) ....+/+
Lawsonline.com (Legal Staff) ....+/+
LawStar (Legal Staff) ....+/+
Lawyers Weekly...+/nla
Layoff Lounge...0/0
Layover.com (T) ....**+/+**
Lebenon Daily News (Employment Wizard)..................+/+
Lee Hecht Harrison **0/0**
Legal CV ....+/+
Legal Report...+/nla

Legal SecretariesUSA.com ....+/+
Legal staff.com (T).......................................**+/+**
Lender Careers...**+/+**
Lexington Herald-Leader (CareerBuilder) ....+/+
LI jobs.com ....+/+
Lincoln Journal Star.com (Employment Wizard)..............+/+
Linux World (ITCareers)..................................+/nla
Little Rock Careers Online (Employment Partner)..........+/+
Little Rock Democart-Gazette ....+/nla
LittleRock HelpWanted. (Reg.HelpWanted) ....+/+
Local Careers.com ....**+/+**
Local job Network ....+/+
Locum Tenens.com ....+/+
Long Beach Press-Telegram (Employment Wizard) ....+/+
Los Angeles Computer Jobs.com......................+/+
LosAngelesHelpWanted (Reg.HelpWanted) ....+/+
Lotus Notes Jobs.com (Pure Power)...................+/nla
Lotus Professional.com (Career Marketplace)..................+/+
Louisiana State Jobs.......................................0/nla
Louisville Careers (Employment Partner)...........+/+
Louisville Courier Jrnl (USA Today Careers))....................+/+
LouisvilleWanted (Reg.HelpWanted) ....+/+
Lowell Sun (Employment Wizard)......................+/+
LPN Jobs.com (HealthCareJobStore)..................+/+
MA Careers.com (CareerMVP) ....+/nla
Mac Talent.com..**0/0**
Macon Telegraph (CareerBuilder) ....+/+
Madison Newspapers (Employment Wizard) ....+/+
Magazine Publishers of America........................+/nla
Manitoba jobs.com (Canjobs)...........................+/0
Mansfield News Journal (USA Today Careers) ....+/+
Manufacturing MVP.com (CareerMVP).............................+/+
Marion Star(USA Today Careers)........................+/+
Marketing Dreamjobs......................................0/nla
Marketing Jobs.com.....................................**+/+**
Marketing JobStore.com (eJob Stores).................+/+
Marketing Manager.com (Career Marketplace)..................+/+
Marketing MVP.com (CareerMVP).......................+/nla
Mass Live (Advance Careers)..............................+/+
Massachusetts Biotechnology Council...............+/nla
Material Information Society ....+/nla
Materials Jobs.com (NicheJobs) ....+/nla
MBA Careers (Career Exposure).........................+/+
MBA GlobalNet...+/+
MBA Jungle ....**+/nla**
MD Direct.com ....**+/+**
MD Jobsite.com ....**+/+**
MD Recruitment Online (HC Recruitment Online))........+/nla
Mechanical Contractors Asso. of America 0/nla
Mechanical Engineer.com (Career Marketplace)..............+/+
Mechanical Engineers Magazine Online (ASME)...........+/nla
Med BizPeople.com ....+/+
Med Bulletin ....**0/+**
Med CAREERS (T)..**+/+**
Med Hunters ....**+/+**
med jump ....**+/0**
Med Options (Absolutely Health Care) ....+/+
med2020 ....+/+
media bistro.com ....**+/nla**
Media Jobz.Com 0/nla
Media Line.com ....0/+
Media Recruiter.com.......................................0/+
Medical DeviceLink.com...............................**+/+**
Medical MVP.com (CareerMVP) ....+/nla
Medical Records Jobs.com (HealthCareJobStore)...........+/+
Medical Reps.com..+/nla
Medical Researcher.com (Career Marketplace)..................+/+
Medical Transition for Veteran Health Care ....+/+
Medicats..0/0
MediCenter.com (TheBoardNetwork)............................**+/+**
MediCentral.com..0/nla
MedZilla (T) ....**+/+**
Meeting Professionals Int'l ....+/+
Mega Job Sites (Worklife)................................+/nla
Memphis Commercial Appeal (Employment Wizard) ....+/ɪ

MemphisComputer work.com..+/+
MemphisHelpWanted (Reg.HelpWanted)........................+/+
Mental Web.com..+/nla
Mercury Enterprises Job Network ....+/nla
Meteorological Employment Journal..............................0/0
Mexican American Eng. and Scientists Soc 0/nla
Mexico Online..0/0
Miami Herald (CareerBuilder)..+/+
Michigan Job Hunter.com (Detroit Free Press) ....+/+
Michigan Jobs.com (LocalCareers)................................+/+
Michigan Live (Advance Careers) ....+/+
Mid Wife Jobs.com ....+/nla
Midwest Computerwork.com ....+/+
Mil 2Civ.com (The Destiny Group) ....+/+
Military spouses.com (The Destiny Group) ....+/+
Military.com..0/0
Milwaukee Career Board..+/+
Milwaukee Journal Sentinel (Employment Wizard)..........+/+
Milwaukee Naturally 0/nla
MilwaukeeJobs.com ....+/+
Mining USA...0/nla
Ministry Careers.com ....+/0
Ministry Connect...+/0
Ministry Jobs.com ....+/nla
ministry search.com ....+/0
MinistryEmployment.Com 0/nla
Minneapolis Star Tribune...+/+
Minnesota Council of Nonprofits.................................+/nla
Minnesota Jobs.com (T) ....+/+
Minority Career Network..+/+
Minority Nurse.com (CASS)...+/nla
Mississippi Coast.com (CareerBuilder) ....+/+
Modern Language Association of America ....+/nla
Modern Machine Shop Online.......................................0/0
Modesto Bee (Employment Wizard) ....+/+
Mojolin...0/0
Money Making Mommy 0/nla
Monitor...+/nla
Monroe News-Star (USA Today Careers)........................+/+
Monster International Zone..1/1
Monster Retail.com 1/1
Monster Talent Market ....+/+
Monster.com (T) ....+/+
Monstertrak.com (formerly JobTrak)...........................+/+
Montana Society of CPAs...0/0
Montana State Jobs 0/0
Monterey County Herald (CareerBuilder)........................+/+
Montgomery Advertiser (USA Today Careers) ....+/+
mortgage career.com ....+/+
Mortgage Mag.com (Job Mag).....................................+/+
MortgageJobsites.com (Geojobsites) ....+/+
MortgageJobStore.com (eJob Stores) ....+/+
Motor Careers ....+/+
Mountainjobs.com ....+/nla
Muncie Star-Press (USA Today Careers) ....+/+
Musicians Network 0/0
Must Jobs.com 0/0
My Career.com.au ....+/nla
My JobCafe 0/0
MyRGV.com...+/+
Myrtle Beach Sun News (CareerBuilder) ....+/+
MyrtleBeachHelpWanted (Reg.HelpWanted)....................+/+
Nace Web ....+/nla
NACELink..+/+
NALS (Legal staff.) ....+/+
Nashville Careers Online (Employment Partner)...............+/+
Nashville Tennesean (USA Today Careers))......................+/+
Nation Job Network (T) ....+/+
Native American Jobs.com ....+/+
Native Jobs.com 1/nla
Nat'l. Academies Career Center 0/nla
Nat'l. Accrediting Commission of Cosmetology Art 0/0
Nat'l. Alliance of Black School Educators 0/nla
Nat'l. Assoc of Credit Management................................+/+
Nat'l. Assoc of Student Personnel Administrators ....+/+

Nat'l. Assoc. for Home Care ....+/nla
Nat'l. Assoc. of African Americans in HR......................+/nla
Nat'l. Assoc. of Black Accountants..............................+/+
Nat'l. Assoc. of Black Journalists ....+/+
Nat'l. Assoc. of Broadcasters......................................0/0
Nat'l. Assoc. of Corp. Real Estate Exec's......................+/0
Nat'l. Assoc. of Development Organizations.................+/nla
Nat'l. Assoc. of Educational Buyers..............................+/0
Nat'l. Assoc. of Elevator Contractors ....+/+
Nat'l. Assoc. of Environmental Profesionals ....+/nla
Nat'l. Assoc. of Federal Credit Unions...........................0/0
Nat'l. Assoc. of Hispanic Journalists 0/nla
Nat'l. Assoc. of Ind. & Office Properties.......................+/+
Nat'l. Assoc. of Independent Schools ....+/nla
Nat'l. Assoc. of Industrial Technology ....+/nla
Nat'l. Assoc. of Manufacturers ....+/nla
Nat'l. Assoc. of Personal Financial Advisors ....+/nla
Nat'l. Assoc. of Sales Professionals............................+/nla
Nat'l. Assoc. of Social Workers ....+/+
Nat'l. Assoc. of Student Financial Aid ....+/nla
Nat'l. Assoc. of Women In Construction (FlipDog).........+/nla
Nat'l. Assoc. Recording Merchandisers..........................+/+
Nat'l. Athletic Trainers' Assoc 0/nla
Nat'l. Banking & Financial Services Network ....+/+
Nat'l. Black MBA Assoc. (NY Chapter)...........................+/+
Nat'l. Black MBA Assoc..+/+
Nat'l. Business & Disbility Council - Able to Work ....+/+
Nat'l. Business Incubation Assoc ....+/nla
Nat'l. Contract Management Association......................+/nla
Nat'l. Council of Teachers of Math Jobs Online ....+/0
Nat'l. Directory of Emergency Services........................0/nla
Nat'l. Diversity Newspaper Job Bank 0/0
Nat'l. Emergency Number Assoc ....+/nla
Nat'l. Environmental Health Assoc ....+/nla
Nat'l. Fed. of Paralegal Assoc. (Legal staff.) ....+/+
Nat'l. FFA Organization ....+/nla
Nat'l. Fire & Protection Agency (Monster) ....+/nla
Nat'l. Gerontological SOA - AgeWork......................+/nla
Nat'l. Registry of Environmental Professionals.................+/+
Nat'l. Soc. of Collegiate Scholars ....+/0
Nat'l. Society of Black Engineers ....+/+
Nat'l. Society of Hispanic MBAs (BrassRing) ....+/+
Nat'l. Society of Professional Engineering ....+/0
Nat'l. Teacher Recruitment Clearinghouse....................0/nla
Nat'l. Technical Services Assoc ....nla/+
Nat'l. Weather Association 0/nla
Nat'l. Youth Development Information Center 0/nla
Nature Jobs.com...+/nla
Naukri ....+/0
NBA Online (Nebraska Bankers Assoc.).......................+/nla
NC Careers.com (CareerMVP).....................................+/nla
NCAA Jobs in College Athletics ....+/0
NCO Jobs (MMR)...+/+
Nebraska Bankers Assoc 0/nla
Nebraska has jobs.com ....+/+
Need Techs.com...+/+
Net Empleo.com ....+/+
Net Jobs..+/+
Net share.com (T) ....0/+
Net Staff ....+/+
Net work and Systems Profesionals Assoc ....+/nla
NetEmpleo..+/+
Net-Temps (T)...+/+
Network Engineer.com (Career Marketplace) ....+/nla
Network of Commercial Real Estate Women................0/nla
Network World (ITCareers)...+/nla
Networking Computer work.com ....+/+
Nevada JobConnect 0/0
Nevada Jobs.com (LocalCareers)..................................+/+
Nevada State Jobs 0/nla
New England Computerwork.com ....+/+
New England Enployee Benefits Council ....+/nla
New England Human Resource Assoc ....+/0
New England Journal of Medicine...........................+/nla
New England Telecommunications Assoc ....+/nla

New Hampshire Job Finder (Telegraph) ....+/+
New Haven County Jobs.com (All County Jobs)............+/nla
New Jersey Technical Recruiters Alliance 0/nla
New London Careers Online (Employment Partner)..........+/+
New Media Assoc. of NJ 0/0
New Mexico Careers Online (Employment Partner) ....+/+
New Mexico High Tech Job Forum ....+/0
New Mexico State Jobs 0/nla
new monday.com ....**+/+**
New Orleans Live (Advance Careers)...............................+/+
New OrleansHelpWanted. (Reg.HelpWanted)...................+/+
New York Computer Jobs.com ....+/+
New York Computer work.com ....+/+
New York Post (CareerBuilder) ....+/+
Newark Advocate (USA Today Careers)............................+/+
NewHampshireHelpWanted (Reg.HelpWanted) ....+/+
Newsday.com (CareerBuilder)..+/+
NewsOK.com (Employment Wizard)..................................+/+
Newspaper Assoc. of America.......................................+/nla
NH Careers Online (Employment Partner).........................+/+
NI Jobs.com (Irish Jobs) ....+/+
NicheJobs.com ....+/nla
NJ Careers ....+/0
NJ Hire 0/nla
NJ JOBS ....+/0
NJ Law Network (Legal Staff) ....+/+
NJ Online (Advance Careers)..+/+
NJParalegal.com ....+/nla
Nokri.com...**+/+**
Non Profit Career.com ....+/+
NonprofitOyster ....+/+
North Dakota State Jobs..0/nla
North Jersey HelpWanted.com (Reg. HelpWanted) ....+/+
North Jersey.com (Bergen Record) ....+/nla
NorthCountryHelpWanted (Reg.HelpWanted)...................+/+
Northeast Human Resources Association.........................+/0
Northwest Arkansas Times..+/nla
Northwest Recruiters Association ....+/0
Norwich Bulletin (USA Today Careers) ....+/+
NPO .NET..0/nla
Nuke Worker.com..0/0
Nurse Aid Jobs (HealthCareJobStore) ....+/+
Nurse Options (Absolutely Health Care)............................+/+
Nurse Practitioners Central - NPJobs ....**+/+**
Nurse-Recruiter..+/+
Nursing Spectrum Career Fitness Online (T)..............**+/nla**
NW Classifieds (Seattle Times)..+/+
NY Careers.com (LocalCareers)...+/+
NY Daily News (Abracat)..+/nla
NY Job Source (Internet Job Source)..................................+/+
NY Job Source.com...+/0
NY New Media Assoc. The Silicon Alley Job Board.....+/+
NY Newsday.com (CareerBuilder).....................................+/+
NY Times Job Market ....**+/+**
NYC Employment.com (Employocity) ....+/NA
NYC Workforce 1..0/nla
NZ Jobs.co..+/nla
Occupational Therapist Jobs (HealthCareJobStore)..........+/+
Office Moonlighter..+/+
Offshore Guides..0/0
O-Hayo Sensei..0/nla
Ohio Jobs.com (LocalCareers) ....+/+
Ohio.com (CareerBuilder)..+/+
Oil Careers ....+/+
Oil Directory.com..0/nla
Oil job.com...+/+
Oil Online ....+/+
OK City Careers (Employment Partner).............................+/+
Oklahoma State Jobs..0/nla
Olympia Olympian (USA Today Careers)) ....+/+
OmahaHelpWanted (Reg.HelpWanted) ....+/+
one world.net ....+/nla
Online-Jobs.com ....+/0
Ontario Assoc. of Architects ....+/nla

Ontario jobs.com (Canjobs)..+/0
OnWisconsinJobs.com (Employment Wizard) ....+/+
Operation IT...**+/0**
Opportunity Nocs ....**+/nla**
Optical Engineer.com (Career Marketplace)......................+/+
optics.org...**+/+**
ORA Search (JV Search) ....+/+
Oracle Computer work.com...+/+
Oracle Fanclub and User Forum (Fanclub)......................0/nla
Oracle Job Network ....0/+
Oracle Professional.com (Career Marketplace).................+/+
Orajobs.com...+/+
Orange County Register (CareerCast)...............................+/+
Oregon Jobs.com (LocalCareers) ....+/+
Oregon Live (Advance Careers) ....+/+
Oregon State Jobs 0/nla
Organic Chemistry Jobs Worldwide.................................0/+
Orlando Careers Online (Employment Partner) ....+/+
Orlando Sentinel (CareerBuilder)......................................+/+
OrlandoHelpWanted (Reg.HelpWanted)...........................+/+
OT JobLink...+/+
OttawaJobShop (Reg.HelpWanted) ....+/+
Out Professionals 0/0
Outdoor Network...**+/0**
Overseas Jobs.com (About Jobs.com) ....+/nla
Packaging Business ....+/nla
Passing Notes.com (jobvertise) 0/nla
Pediatric Nurse Jobs (HealthCareJobStore).....................+/+
Penn Live (Advance Careers)...+/+
Pennsylvania Computerwork.com.....................................+/+
Pennsylvania Jobs.com ....+/+
Pensacola News Journal (USA Today Careers)...................+/+
pensacolajobs.com ....+/+
People Bank ....+/+
People Online 0/0
People Soft Developer.com (Career Marketplace)............+/+
Perl Computer work.com...+/+
Petroleum Engineer.com (Career Marketplace) ....+/+
Petroleum Services Assoc. of Canada ....+/nla
Pharm Web...0/nla
Pharmacy Jobs Online (HC Recruitment Online))............+/nla
Pharmacy Week..**+/+**
Philadelphia Computer Jobs.com.....................................+/+
Philadelphia Inquirer (CareerBuilder) ....+/+
PhiladelphiaHelpWanted (Reg.HelpWanted) ....+/+
Philanthropy Journal Online ....**+/nla**
Philly Jobs.com ....0/+
Philly.com (CareerBuilder)..+/+
Phoenix Computerwork.com..+/+
Phoenix Employment.com (Employocity).......................+/NA
Physician Board ....+/+
Physicians Employment...+/+
Physics Today Online..**+/+**
Physics World Jobs ....+/nla
Pick ajob.com..nla/+
Pilot Jobs...0/0
Pittsburgh Live.com (Employment Wizard) ....+/+
P-Jobs...+/nla
Placement India ....0/+
Plan Ahead- Soc. For College & University Planning......0/nla
Planet Recruit UK...+/nla
Planet SAP.com 0/0
Plastic Careers.com ....**+/+**
Plastic Pro (staffingpro)..+/+
Plastics News ....+/nla
Play Bill...**0/nla**
Plumbjob.com (Electric Job) ....+/+
Plus (+) Jobs America...+/+
Plus (+) Jobs Australia..+/+
Plus (+) Jobs Canada...+/+
Plus (+) Jobs Denmark...+/+
Plus (+) Jobs U.K ....+/+
PMjobs.com...**+/+**
Police Employment.com ....+/nla
Police Executive ....+/nla

Political Resources...0/0
Polk Job Finder (Lakeland FL Ledger).................+/+
PolySort..0/nla
PortaJobs ....**+/0**
Portland Computer Jobs.com.............................+/+
Position Watch ....+/nla
Poughkeepsie Journal (USA Today Careers)........+/+
Power Builder Jobs.com (Pure Power)...............+/nla
Power Builder Journal ....+/nla
Power Highway..+/+
Power Mag (McGraw-Hill) ....+/nla
PR Soc. of America [LA] ....+/nla
PR WeekJobs ....+/nla
Practice Choice/Link...................................**+/+**
Pre-Cast Stressed Convrete Assoc nla/0
Prime JobSite.com...+/+
princeton info.com (U.S. 1) ....+/nla
Privacy Job Opportunity Boards ....+/+
Private School Employment Network ....**+/0**
Prized Jobs..+/+
Pro GayJobs.com..+/0
Pro Hire..+/+
Pro/E Job Network (Mercury Enterprises).........+/nla
Procruit...0/0
Product Manager.com (Career Marketplace) ....+/+
Professional Exchange ....nla/+
Professionals in Human Resources Assoc .....**+/0**
Programmer Analyst.com (Career Marketplace) ....+/+
Programming Jobs.com...............................**0/+**
Programming-Services.com **0/0**
Project Connect..**0/nla**
Project Management Insititute.....................**+/+**
Project Manager.com (Career Marketplace).......+/+
ProMatch...nla/0
Providence Journal (Employment Wizard) ....+/+
Psyc Careers...**+/+**
Public Health Nurse.com (HealthCareJobStore).........+/+
Public Relations Soc. of America (PRSA) ....**+/0**
PugetSoundHelpWanted (Reg.HelpWanted) ....+/nla
Pure Power's Database Jobs.com ....**+/+**
QA-jobs.com...**0/0**
QC Employ Me (CareerLINK)...............................+/+
Quad City Times (Employment Wizard) ....+/+
Quebec jobs.com (Canjobs) ....+/0
Qworx.com..0/0
Racine Journal Times (Employment Wizard)........+/+
Rad Working.com..+/+
Radio & Records Online......................................0/0
Radio Online...**0/0**
Radiology & Oncology JOBS (RTjobs.com) ....**+/0**
Radiology Jobs (HC Recruitment Online) ....+/nla
Raleigh News Observer (Employment Wizard) ....+/+
RE Buz ....+/+
Real Columbus.com (CareerBuilder) ....+/0
Real Estate Best Jobs ....+/+
Real Estate Job Store ....+/+
Real Estate Jobs.com.......................................+/nla
Real Jobs - Real Estate **0/0**
RealEstateJobsites.com (Geojobsites) ....+/+
Recruit Ireland..+/nla
Recruit Military ....**+/0**
Recruit USA ....**+/0**
Recruit ....+/+
Recruitaly..+/+
Recruiter Connection 0/0
Recruiter Networks ....+/+
Recruiter Seek...**0/+**
Recruiters Cafe.com ....+/+
Recruiters Dream 0/nla
Recruiters Forum ....+/nla
Recruiters Online Network (T).......................**+/+**
Recruiters World ....**+/nla**
Recruitex ....0/+
Recruitment Exchange Online.......................**+/+**
recruitment JOBZ.com.......................................+/nla

Redding Searchlight (Employment Wizard) ....+/+
Refrigeration-engineer.com................................0/nla
Regional Help Wanted.com............................**+/+**
Regulatory Affairs Professionals Society ....**+/+**
Rehab Options (Absolutely Health Care) ....+/+
Reno Careers Online (Employment Partner) ....+/+
Reno Gazette-Observer Today Careers).............+/nla
Rent-a-Geek **nla/0**
Research Network..0/nla
Resort Jobs (About Jobs.com).........................+/nla
Resort Professional.com (Career Marketplace) ....+/+
Restaurant Job Store (eJob Stores) ....+/+
Restaurant Jobs..+/+
Restaurant News ....+/nla
Restaurant Recruit.com ....+/+
ResuMate2002..+/+
Resume Depot ....0/+
Resume Detector...+/+
Resunet..**0/0**
Retail Classifieds (Career Engine).....................+/+
Retail Job Store (eJob Stores).............................+/+
Retail Seek.com...+/+
RF Global Net (Verticalnet)...............................+/+
RF Job Network (Mercury Enterprises) ....+/nla
Rhinomite ....+/nla
Rhode Island Jobs.com (LocalCareers) ....+/+
Richmond Careers Online (Employment Partner) ....+/+
Richmond Times-Dispatch (CareerBuilder) ....+/+
RichmondHelpWanted (Reg.HelpWanted).........+/+
Right Management Consultants, Inc **0/0**
Rising Star Internships ....+/nla
Risk & Insurance Management Society 0/nla
Riverside Press-Enterprise (Employment Wizard).............+/+
RN Jobs (HC Recruitment Online)) ....+/nla
Rochester Democrat (USA Today Careers)) ....+/+
Rochester jobFinder (Employment Wizard)........+/+
Rock Hill Herald(Employment Wizard) ....+/+
Rockford Register Star (USA Today Careers))......+/+
Rocky Mountain Jobs...+/+
Rocky Mountain Water Environment Assoc 0/0
Rocky MountainNews.com.................................+/+
RockyMountainHelpWanted (Reg.HelpWanted) ....+/+
Royal Society of Chemistry.................................0/nla
RRT Jobs.com (HC Recruitment Online)) ....+/nla
RxCareerCenter.com ....**+/+**
RxImmigration.com ....+/+
Sacramento Bee (Employment Wizard)..............+/+
Safety Online (Vertical Net) ....+/+
Salary.com (CareerBuilder) ....+/+
Salem Statesman Journal (USA Today Careers)) ....+/+
Sales Classifieds (Career Engine) ....+/+
Sales Engineer.com (Career Marketplace)............+/+
sales heads ....**+/+**
Sales Job Store.com (eJob Stores).....................+/+
Sales Jobs.com..**+/+**
Sales Rep Central.com **0/nla**
Sales Workz (World Workz) ....+/nla
salestrax.com...+/+
Salisbury Daily Times (USA Today Careers).......+/+
Salt Lake City Deseret News (Employment Wizard).........+/+
Saludos.com (T)..**+/+**
San Antonio Job Network..................................+/+
San Bernadino Sun (Employment Wizard) ....+/+
San Francisco Chronicle Gate.............................+/0
San Jose Mercury News (CareerBuilder) ....+/+
San Louis Obispo Tribune News (CareerBuilder) ....+/+
Santa Barbara News-Press (Employment Wizard).............+/+
SAP Club ....+/+
SAP Computer work.com....................................+/+
Sap Developer.com (Career Marketplace) ....+/+
SAP Fanclub and User Forum (Fanclub)................0/nla
Sask jobs.com (Canjobs).....................................+/0
Sci Jobs.com ....+/+
Sci Jobs.org..**+/+**
Sci Web Career Center...................................**+/+**

Science Careers (T)..+/+
Science jobs.com ....+/nla
Scientific American.com...+/nla
Scientific Researcher.com (Career Marketplace) ....+/+
SCJobMarket.com..+/+
SE Missourian (Employment Wizard)................................+/+
Search Security ....+/+
SearchEase..0/0
Seasonal Employment...+/nla
Seattle Computer Jobs.com ....+/+
Seattle Computer work.com ....+/+
Security Clearance ComputerJobs.com........................+/+
Security Jobs Network...0/nla
Seek (Australia) (T) ....+/+
Selling Jobs.com (NicheJobs)......................................+/nla
Senior Techs ....nla/+
SensorJobs ....+/+
SF Bay Employment.com (Employocity).......................+/NA
ShowBizJobs.com...+/+
Shreveport Times (USA Today Careers) ....+/+
SignOn SanDiego (Union-Tribune)................................+/+
Silicon Valley Computer Jobs.com.................................+/+
Silicon Valley.com (CareerBuilder)...............................+/+
Sioux Falls Argus Leader (USA Today Careers)) ....+/+
Skiing the Net...+/0
SkiingtheNet ....+/0
Skillogic ....+/+
Smart Career Move ....+/+
SmartPros ....+/+
Snagajob.com..+/+
Soc. for Adv. of Chicanos & Native Amer. in Sci ....+/nla
Soc. for Automotive Engineers.................................+/nla
Soc. for Industrial & Org. Psychology ....+/+
Soc. for Technical Communication 0/nla
Soc. of Broadcast Engineers...0/+
Soc. of Cable Telecommunications Eng ....+/nla
Soc. of Hispanic Prof. Engineers (BrassRing).................+/+
Soc. of Women Engineers (BrassRing)...........................0/+
Social Service.Com ....+/nla
Social Work & Services Jobs Online 0/0
Social Work JobBank..+/+
Society for Foodservice Management 0/nla
Society for Human Resource Management...............+/nla
Society of Actuaries...+/+
Society of Automotive Engineers ....+/nla
Society of Competitive Intelligence Porf......................+/0
Society of Consuler Affairs Prof. in Bus.......................+/+
Society of Environ. Toxicology & Chemistry ....+/nla
Society of Manufacturing Engineers 0/nla
Software Contractors' Guild.......................................+/0
Software Developer Careers (Dr Dobbs) ....+/nla
Software Developer Jobs.com (eJob Stores)..................+/+
Software Developer.com (Career Marketplace) ....+/+
Software Engineer.com (Career Marketplace)................+/+
Software Jobs.com (Tech-Engine.com) ....+/+
SoftwareSalesJobs.com ....+/+
Solid Edge Job Network (Mercury Enterprises).............+/nla
Solid Works Job Network (Mercury Enterprises) ....+/nla
Sologig.com (CareerBuilder)..0/0
South Carolina State Jobs 0/nla
South Coast JobMart.com (The Standard-Times)...........+/+
South Dakota State Jobs...0/nla
South Jersey Careers Online (Employment Partner)........+/+
SouthBendWanted (Reg.HelpWanted).........................+/+
Southern California EDI Roundtable...........................+/nla
Southern Illinoisian (Employment Wizard)....................+/+
SouthernMaineWanted (Reg.HelpWanted) ....+/+
SouthSoundJobs (Tacoma News Tribune).....................+/nla
Southwest-Online (Employment Wizard) ....+/+
Space Careers 0/nla
Space Jobs ....+/+
Spanishjobs.com ....+/+
Special Library Association ....+/nla
Speech Therapist Jobs (HealthCareJobStore) ....+/+
SPIEWorks- Int'l Society for Optical Engineering.............+/0

Splitit.com ....+/+
Spokane Careers Online (Employment Partner) ....+/+
sports employment.com 0/0
Springfield NewsLdr (USA Today Careers))...................+/+
SQL Computer work.com ....+/+
St. Cloud Times (USA Today Careers)) ....+/+
St. George Spectrum (USA Today Careers))....................+/+
St. Louis Computer Jobs.com..+/+
St. Louis Metro (CareerBuilder) ....+/+
St. Louis Today (Post Dispatch- CareerBuilder) ....+/nla
St. Petersburg Times (CareerBuilder) ....+/+
Staffing World..0/nla
Stamfordadvocate.com (CareerBuilder) ....+/+
Star Chefs JobFinder ....+/+
Startup Lynx ....+/+
Startup Zone.com...+/+
StartupZone ....+/+
Staten Island Live (Advance Careers) ....+/+
Step Beyond..+/+
Stern Alumni Job Listings.......................0/nla (See Notes)
Strategic Account Mgmt. Association (SAMA)...............0/nla
Student Affairs Administrators in Higher Ed ....+/nla
Subcontract.com..+/+
SuburbanChicagoHelpWanted (Reg.HelpWanted) 0/0
Summer Clerk...0/0
Summer Jobs (About Jobs.com)....................................+/nla
Sun Guru 0/0
Sunoasis Jobs ....+/+
Superintendent jobs.com (eJob Stores).........................+/+
SuperJobs.net ....+/+
Supermarket News...+/nla
Supply Jobs.com (NicheJobs)......................................+/nla
Support Analyst.com (Career Marketplace) ....+/+
Sustainable Business.com...0/nla
Swap jobs.com ....+/+
SwiftJobs ....+/+
Syracuse Careers Online (Employment Partner) ....+/+
Syracuse Online (Advance Careers) ....+/+
System Administrator.com (Career Marketplace)............+/+
Systems Administration Guild.................................0/0
Systems Analyst.com (Career Marketplace) ....+/+
Talent Campus..+/+
Talent rock 0/0
Talent Works: The Online Casting Source 0/0
Talent4europe.com..+/+
Tallahasse.com (CareerBuilder) ....+/+
Tampa Bay Online (Tampa Bay Tribune) ....+/nla
Tax Talent.com ....+/+
Tax-Jobs.Com ....+/nla
TC Theatre and Film...+/+
TCM's HR Careers...+/0
Teachers of English to Speakers of Other Langua.................
+/+
Teachers Online..+/+
teachersplanet.com..+/nla
Teachers-Teachers.com ....+/+
Tech Employment.com ....+/+
Tech Profiles ....+/+
tech-engine.com (T)...+/+
Techies .com..+/+
Technical Assoc. of Pulp & Paper (TAPPI) ....+/nla
Technical Assoc. of the Graphic Arts.............................0/0
Technical Communicator.com (Career Marketplace).........+/+
Technical Recruiter.com (Career Marketplace) ....+/+
Technical Trainer.com (Career Marketplace)......................+/+
Technical Writer Jobs (eJob Stores) ....+/+
TechnoCentral.com..0/nla
Technojobs.co.uk..+/+
Technology MVP.com (CareerMVP).............................+/nla
Teens4Hire ....+/+
telecom careers.net..+/+
Telecom Engineer.com (Career Marketplace) ....+/+
Telecommunications Computer work.com.......................+/+
Telecommunications Industry Assoc. B2B......................+/+
Telecommuter's Digest 0/nla

JOBS & RESUMES FOR FEE (+) AND FOR FREE (0)

Telecommuting Jobs 0/0
TeleJob Academic Job Exchange............................+/nla
Television Bureau of Advertising...............................+/nla
Teller Jobs (eJob Stores) ....+/+
Tenn Careers.com (CareerMVP) ....+/nla
Tennessee State Jobs...0/nla
Terre Haute Tribune Star (Employment Wizard)...............+/+
Texan Careers.com (CareerMVP)...........................+/nla
Texas Computer Jobs.com..+/+
Texas Computerwork.com...+/+
Texas Jobs.com (LocalCareers) ....+/+
Texas Workforce..0/0
The Black Collegian Online ....+/+
The Blue Line..0/nla
The Board Network..+/+
The Financial Planning Association ....+/0
The Internet Job Source...+/0
The Job Seeker...+/nla
The Jobs Site ....+/+
The Multicultural Advantage.................................+/nla
The Nat'l Assembly..0/nla
The Retired Officers Assoc. (TROA) ....+/+
The Work Circuit (EETimes)......................................+/+
The Write Jobs..+/nla
TheSquare ....+/nla
Thingamajob ....+/+
This is Jobs..+/nla
Tiger Jobs...+/+
TimberSite.com ....+/nla
Title board.com (TheBoardNetwork)........................+/+
Todays Job Market.com ....+/+
Toledo Beacon Journal (CareerBuilder) ....+/+
Toledo Career Board ....+/+
Top Contracts..+/+
Top Echelon...+/+
Top Jobs.co.uk ....+/+
Top Money Jobs ....+/+
Top Sales Positions..+/+
Top StartUps.com 0/0
Topeka Capital Journal (Employment Wizard)..................+/+
TopekaWanted (Reg.HelpWanted) ....+/+
Toronto Job Shop (Reg. HelpWanted)........................+/+
Torrence Daily Breeze (Employment Wizard) ....+/+
total jobs.com (T) ....+/0
Total Telecom nla/0
Town Online (JobFind) ....+/+
Trabajo.org..0/+
Trade Jobs Online..0/0
Training Resource Network ....+/nla
TrainMark.com nla/0
trans-ACTION Classified Website ....+/nla
Transition Assistance Online....................................+/+
Transportation Engineer.com (Career Marketplace)..........+/+
travel jobs (Australia/New Zealand) ....+/nla
Travel jobz.net ....+/+
Travel Nurse Jobs (HealthCareJobStore) ....+/+
Tri StateJobs.com...+/+
Triangle.com (Raleigh News & Observer) ....+/+
Truck Driver ....nla/+
Truck Net ....0/+
TruckinJobs.com ....+/nla
True Careers (T)..+/+
Tucson Careers Online (Employment Partner) ....+/+
Tucson Citizen (USA Today Careers) ....+/+
TucsonHelpWanted (Reg.HelpWanted)...........................+/+
TulsaHelpWanted (Reg.HelpWanted)...........................+/+
TV Jobs..0/0
TVandRadioJobs.com 0/0
TVSpy.com...0/+
Twin Cities Computer Jobs.com ....+/+
Twin Cities Pioneer Press (CareerBuilder) ....+/+
TwinCitiesWanted (Reg.HelpWanted) ....+/+
UBidContract.com ....+/+
UG Job Network (Mercury Enterprises) ....+/nla
Ultrasoundjobs.com ....+/+

Underwriter Employment (eJob Stores).........................+/nla
underwriting Jobs.com...+/+
unicru...0/0
UniversoE.com ....+/+
Unix Admin (JV Search) ....0/+
Unix Computer work.com ....+/+
Unix Ugu Universe 0/0
US Exec Jobs (Job Network).....................................+/+
US Internet Industry Association 0/nla
US Jobs.Com...+/+
US Law Jobs (Job Network) ....+/+
US Med Jobs (Job Network) ....+/+
US Tech Jobs (Job Network)......................................+/+
US TECH JOBS 0/0
USA Today Careers Network....................................+/+
USHOTJOBS.com 0/0
Utah Careers Online (Employment Partner).....................+/+
Utah State Jobs 0/nla
Utica Observer-Dispatch (USA Today Careers) ....+/+
Vallejo Times-Herald (Employment Wizard) ....+/+
VancouverJobShop (Reg.HelpWanted)...........................+/+
Vault.Com (T)..+/+
Vermont State Jobs...0/nla
Vet Jobs..+/+
Veterinary Jobs.com...+/+
VeterinaryLife.com..0/nla
Vets 4 Hire.com (The Destiny Group).............................+/+
Vice President Jobs.com (eJob Stores)............................+/+
Vineland Daily Journal (USA Today Careers)....................+/+
Virginia Computerwork.com......................................+/+
Virtual Jobs.com...+/+
Visual Basic Computer work.com................................+/+
Visual Basic Jobs.com (Pure Power)............................+/nla
Visual Basic Search (JV Search) ....0/+
Volunteer Match..0/nla
WA Careers.com (CareerMVP) ....+/nla
Washington DC Area SGML/XML Users Group....0/nla
Washington Post [Washington Jobs] (T) ....+/+
Web Food Pros (Escoffier On Line)............................+/+
Web Jobs USA.com (eJob Stores) ....+/+
Web Programming Jobs.com (Pure Power).....................+/nla
WEB Worldwide Employee Benefits Network.............+/0
Webgrrls ....+/+
Website Builder.com (Career Marketplace).......................+/+
Weed Jobs (Positions in Weed Science)............................0/0
Welding Jobs.com (Hire in a Click).............................+/+
West Virginia State Jobs 0/nla
Westchester Job Central ....+/nla
Westchester Jrnl News (USA Today Careers)....................+/+
Western NY Jobs...+/+
Wi Jobs.com (LocalCareers) ....+/+
WI Jobs.com..+/+
Wichita Eagle (CareerBuilder) ....+/+
Wichita Falls Times Record (Employment Wizard)............+/+
Wilmington News Journal (USA Today Careers))..............+/+
Windows Computer work.com....................................+/+
Wireless Design (VeticalNet).....................................+/+
Wireless Developer Network ....+/nla
Wireless Engineer.com (Career Marketplace) ....+/+
Wisconsin Jobs.com (LocalCareers) ....+/+
Wisconsin Jobs.com (LocalCareers) ....+/+
Wisconsin's Gannet Newspapers (USA Today Ca .... +/+
Womans-Work...+/+
Women in Higher Education ....+/nla
Women In Technology International............................+/+
Women Sports Jobs 0/nla
Worcester Careers Online (Employment Partner).............+/+
Worcester Works (Boston Works).............................+/+
work in pr.com ....+/+
Work in Sports..0/0
Work LP.com (Loss Prevention) ....+/+
WorkInsight...0/nla
WorkLife Network 0/0
Workopolis.com (T) ....+/+

431

WorkopolisCampus.com (Workopolis) 0/0
Workplace Diversity.com (Career Engine) ....+/+
workthing.com ....+/nla
World at Work Job Links ....+/nla
World Org. of Webmasters ....+/+
World Workz...0/0
Worldwideworker.com......................................+/+
Wow-com: World of Wireless Communications................+/+
Wyoming Job Quest (Star-Tribune)..............................+/nla
Wyoming State Jobs 0/nla
WyomingJobs.com (LocalCareers) ....+/+
XML Computer work.com ....+/+
Xml Computerwork.com ....+/+
Y-axis.com 0/0
yourEEcareer.com...+/+
Youth Specialties 0/0
Youth@Work 0/nla
Zanesville Times Rec. (USA Today Careers) ....+/+
Zillion Resumes.com ....nla/+

JOB SEEKERS

*The sites below require membership fees or
other related fees in order to see the positions on the site.*

ActionJobs
American College of Healthcare Executives
American College of Radiology
American Counseling Assoc.
American Culinary Federation
American Soc. for Quality
Art Directors Club of Metro. Washington
art jobonline
Assoc. for Financial Professionals
Assoc. for Interactive Marketing (CareerBuilder)
Assoc. for Investment Mgmt. & Research
Attorney Jobs Online
Auto Jobs.com
AV Jobs
Aviation Jobs Online
Birchin Lane
Black Culinarians Alliance
Canadian Mgmt. Accountants Society
Casting America
Casting Daily
Catho Online
Chronicle of Philanthropy
Clinical Laboratory Management Assoc.
Columbia-Williamette Compensation Group
Contract JobHunter
CPA2bizcareers.com
Crew Net
Do A Project.com
Emplawyernet
Escoffier On Line (T)
ExecuNet (T)
ExecutivesOnly
Federal Jobs Central
Freelance Work Exchange
Freetime Jobs.com
Geo Search
Geospatial Information & Technology Assoc.
Graphic Artists Guild
Grass Is Greener.com (Employon.com)
H1Maia.com
Home Jobs Plus.com
Hospitality Financial & Technology Professi...........................
Hotel Jobs- Ireland
HTML Writers Guild Job List
Infectious Disease Soc. of America
Info Jobs.net (Bolsa de Trabajo)
Info Mine
Institute for Supply Management

Institute of Internal Auditors
Institute of Packaging Professionals
Int'l. Career Employment Center
Int'l. Seafarers Exchange
i-resign.com
Jobs 4police
Jobs in Sports
Lee Hecht Harrison
Media Line.com
Media Recruiter.com
Meteorological Employment Journal
Minnesota Council of Nonprofits
Modern Language Association of America
Nat'l. Assoc. of Black Journalists
Nat'l. Athletic Trainers' Assoc.
Nat'l. Black MBA Assoc. (NY Chapter)
Nat'l. Directory of Emergency Services
Nat'l. Soc. of Collegiate Scholars
Nat'l. Society of Hispanic MBAs (BrassRing)
Netshare.com (T)
Network of Commercial Real Estate Women
NY Job Source.com
Radio Online
Recruiters Cafe.com
Right Management Consultants, Inc.
Risk & Insurance Management Society
Security Jobs Network
Soc. of Broadcast Engineers
Society of Manufacturing Engineers
Sologig.com (CareerBuilder)
sports employment.com
Subcontract.com
Systems Administration Guild
Talent Works: The Online Casting Source
Telecommuter's Digest
The Blue Line
The Internet Job Source
The Job Seeker
TV Jobs
US Internet Industry Association
Work in Sports

JOB SEEKERS:

*The sites below require membership fees or other related fees to post a
resume on the site.*

Academic Employment Network
Actor's Worldlink
Advertising Job Bank
AM FMJobs
American Accounting Assoc.
American Chemical Society - JobSpectrum.org
American College of Healthcare Executives
American Corporate Counsel Assoc.
American Counseling Assoc.
American Culinary Federation
American Oil chemists' Society
American Soc. for Quality
Art Directors Club of Metro. Washington
art jobonline
Assoc. for Computing Machinery
Assoc. for Financial Professionals
Assoc. for Investment Mgmt. & Research
Author link
Auto Jobs.com
AV Canada
AV Jobs
Aviation Employment.com
Aviation Jobs Online
Bank Talent.com
CADD Jobs.com
Canadian Institue of Quantity Surveyors
Career One
Careers in Food.com
Casting America

432

Casting Daily
Catho Online
CHOICE Career
CIVIL Jobs.com
Clinical Laboratory Management Assoc.
College of Healthcare Infor. Mgmt. Exec.
Community Career Center
Construction Gigs
ConsultantTV.com
Council on Foundations
CPA2bizcareers.com
Do A Project.com
Editor & Publisher
Film, TV, & Commercial Employment Network
Financial Executives Institute
Find A Pilot
Freelance Work Exchange
Freetime Jobs.com
Geospatial Information & Technology Assoc.
GISjobs.com
H1Maia.com
Hospitality Financial & Technology Professionals
Hotel Jobs- Ireland
Hotel Online
HTML Writers Guild Job List
Info Mine
Institute for Supply Management
Institute of Electrical and Electronics Engineers
Instrumentation Soc. of America
Internet Employment in New Mexico
Int'l. Foundation of Employee Benefit Plans
Int'l. Seafarers Exchange
Job Shark
LatPRO (T)
Law Bulletin
Law Forum
Lee Hecht Harrison
Mac Talent.com
MBA GlobalNet
med jump
Meteorological Employment Journal
Ministry Careers.com
Ministry Connect
ministry search.com
Nat'l. Assoc. of Black Journalists
Nat'l. Assoc. of Corp. Real Estate Exec's.
Nat'l. Society of Hispanic MBAs (BrassRing)
Naukri
NCAA Jobs in College Athletics
Netshare.com (T)
New England Human Resource Assoc.
New Mexico High Tech Job Forum
NJ JOBS
Non Profit Career.com
Northeast Human Resources Association
Northwest Recruiters Association
Nurse Practitioners Central - NPJobs
NY Job Source.com
Offshore Guides
Online-Jobs.com
Operation IT
Pilot Jobs
Plus (+) Jobs America
Plus (+) Jobs Australia
Plus (+) Jobs Canada
Plus (+) Jobs Denmark
Plus (+) Jobs U.K.
Private School Employment Network
Public Relations Soc. of America (PRSA)
Radiology & Oncology JOBS (RTjobs.com)
Recruit Military
Recruiter Connection
Right Management Consultants, Inc.
San Francisco Chronicle Gate
ShowBizJobs.com

Soc. of Broadcast Engineers
Social Work & Services Jobs Online
Society of Consuler Affairs Prof. in Bus.
Software Contractors' Guild
Sologig.com (CareerBuilder)
Splitit.com
sports employment.com
Subcontract.com
Systems Administration Guild
Talent Works: The Online Casting Source
Telecommuting Jobs
The Internet Job Source
total jobs.com (T)
TrainMark.com
TV Jobs
TVandRadioJobs.com
WEB Worldwide Employee Benefits Network
Work in Sports

LOCATION

Location matters. While many job boards offer positions and candidates from every point on the compass, sites specific to a country, region, state, city- even a neighborhood offer a powerful attraction. The more targeted the better but they can only succeed when they can demonstrate a unique understanding of their locale. Too often a niche location site in one location is simply a mirror of another location.

Note: The sites in **Bold** are among the 500 Best and their reviews can be found in the main body of this edition. A Bold **(T)** indicates we consider the site among the "Top 50". The thousands of sites in plain text listed here were reviewed but, their reviews are not published (we promise to send you any review on request). All Web site URLs (web addresses) can be found in the Master List. A parentheses ( ) designates the "gateway" site that we reviewed. Brackets [ ] are used for clarification.

INTERNATIONAL SITES (330)

GENERAL (34)

Bio find
Bioscience and Medicine (HUM-MOLGEN)
Career Journal.com (T)
Crystallography Worldwide
Cyber KingEmployment
Drillers Job Center
EDUCAUSE
Engineering News Record
Environmental Expert
Escape Artist.com
Frontiers in Bioscience
graduate-jobs.com
Green Energy Jobs
H Careers
H1B Sponsors
InPharm.com
Int'l. Career Employment Center
Int'l. Pharmajobs
Job Shark
Job Ware
Jobs Bazaar.com
Jobs for Economists (JOE)
Jobs in Philosophy
Monster International Zone
Nature Jobs.com
one world.net
optics.org
Organic Chemistry Jobs Worldwide
Overseas Jobs.com (About Jobs.com)
Pharm Web
Physics World Jobs
Qworx.com
Scientific American.com
Talent4europe.com
Webgrrls
Y-axis.com

AFRICA (7)

Career Junction [South Africa]
Find a job in Africa
IT Jobfinder.co.za (JobUniverse) [South Africa]
Job Café [South Africa]
Job Food [South Africa]
Job Index.co.za [South Africa]
Job Navigator [South Africa]
Net Staff

CANADA (80)

Agricultural Labour Pool
Alberta jobs.com (Canjobs)
Areo Ad's
Atlantic Jobs.com (Canjobs)
AV Canada
Bilingualxpress.ca [Toronto]
Biotechnology Human Resource Counsel
Brain Bid.com
Brainhunter.com
Brains Talent.com
British Columbia Jobs.com (Canjobs)
British Columbia Library Assoc.
British Columbia Water & Waste Assoc.
CalgaryJobShop (Reg.HelpWanted)
Canada Computerwork.com
Canada IT.com
Canada Jobs.com
Canadian Bar Assoc.
Canadian Institue of Quantity Surveyors
Canadian Mgmt. Accountants Society
Canadian Restaurant & Foodservices Assoc.
Canjobs.com
Career Beacon.com
Career Click
Career Edge
career key
Career Machine [British Columbia]
Career Owl
Certified Management Assoc. of Canada
Charity Village.com
Contact Point Career Development
CPA2bizcareers.com
Craigs List Vancouver]
Electronic Labour Exchange
Employxpress
Engineering Institute of Canada
Erp-Jobs.com
Experimental Medicine Job Listing
Get Me A Job
headhunt.com (Counsel Network)
Hire Top Talent

Home Jobs Plus.com
Hot Nurse Jobs
HotJobs.ca (HotJobs.com)
Info Mine
InhouseCounsel (Counsel Network)
Int'l. Assoc. for HR Info Mgmt.
Jeff Gaulin's Canadian Journalism Job Board
Job Postings
Job Shark-Canada
Job Universe (Canada)
Jobs Canada
Manitoba jobs.com (Canjobs)
Med Hunters
Musicians Network
My JobCafe
Net Jobs
Net-Temps (T)
Oil Directory.com
Ontario Assoc. of Architects
Ontario jobs.com (Canjobs)
OttawaJobShop (Reg.HelpWanted)
Petroleum Services Assoc. of Canada
Plus (+) Jobs
Position Watch
Quebec jobs.com (Canjobs)
Recruiters Cafe.com
Recruitex
Regional Help Wanted.com
Rent-a-Geek
Sask jobs.com (Canjobs)
TCM's HR Careers
Toronto Job Shop (Reg. HelpWanted)
Trade Jobs Online
Vancouver.JobShop (Reg.HelpWanted)
VeterinaryLife.com
Weed Jobs (Positions in Weed Science)
WorkInsight
Workopolis.com (T)
WorkopolisCampus.com (Workopolis)

EUROPE (119)

ALL EUROPE

Aces-US
Academic Career Services
Career Journal Europe.com (CareerJournal)
Career Plus
City Jobs
Classic Web
Computational Fluid Dynamics Jobs Database
CV Europe
eFinancialCareers
Expatica Jobs
Financial Times Career Point (T)
Go Jobsite
i-resign.com
JobUniverse (IT Careers-IDG)
jobpilot.com
Monster.com/jobline
new monday.com
Oil Careers
Science jobs.com
Talent Campus
TeleJob Academic Job Exchange
Top Jobs.co.uk

DENMARK

Plus (+) Jobs Denmark

FRANCE

Space Careers

GERMANY

Inomics
job force

HUNGARY

KARRIER Online

IRELAND

3rd-level.com
ad world
All Jobz
Corporate Skills (Irish Jobs)
Go Jobsite
Ireland Hiring
Irish Jobs.ie (T)
Job Shark
Jobs Nation
Jobs-Ireland.com
NI Jobs.com (Irish Jobs)
Recruit Ireland
Technojobs.co.uk

ITALY

Recruitaly
Go Jobsite
Space Careers

RUSSIA

Human Resources Online

SPAIN

Go Jobsite
Info Jobs.net (Bolsa de Trabajo)
Trabajo.org

SWEDEN

Arbetsformedlingen

SWITZERLAND

Top Contracts

UNITED KINGDOM

1st 4 UK HR Jobs
3sectorsjob
Absolute-Comms
AccountingWEB.co.uk
Activate.co.uk
Architects Online
Aviation Job Search.com
bankrole.com
Bioinformatics Resource
Book People
British Jobs

Careers in Construction
Careers in Recruitment
Charity JOB
charityopps.com
Charityopps.com
Chem Jobs
Computer Weekly.com
Construction-net
Contracts247
CV Index Directory
doctorjob.com
dot Jobs
Dream Construction Jobs
Earthworks
Edie's Environmental Job Centre
Education Jobs
e-Job
ENDS Environmental Jobs
eteach.com
Execs on the Net (UK)
fish 4 Jobs
GIS-A-Job
Go Jobsite
Gradunet
Guardian Unlimited Jobs
Hospital Hub UK.com
InRetail
Inside Careers
Inside Careers
IT Jobs4.com
job channel.tv
job force
Job Magic
job pilot.com UK
Job Seekers Mailing List
Job Serve: Accountancy Vacancies in the UK
Job Shark-UK
Job Track Online (Job Magic)
Jobline-UK (Monster.com)
Jobs in Edinburgh.com [Scotland]
Jobs.ac.uk
JOBSfront [West Midlands]
Legal CV
People Bank
Planet Recruit UK
Plus (+) Jobs U.K.
Recruitment Exchange Online
recruitment JOBZ.com
Refrigeration-engineer.com
Royal Society of Chemistry
Space Careers
Technojobs.co.uk
The Jobs Site
This is Jobs
total jobs.com (T)
Total Telecom
workthing.com

INDIA (15)

a1jobindia.com
BharatCareers.com
Career Age
Career India
Career Mosaic India
Ciol Jobs
Hire Asian
Indian Jobs
job khoj
Job Street
Jobs Bazaar.com
Lanka Web [Sri Lanka]
Naukri
Placement India

Prized Jobs

LATIN & SOUTH AMERICA (13)

Aldaba
Bumeran
Catho Online [Brasil]
Curriculum Vitae Online
Empleos Web [Argentina]
Job Shark
Latin American Jobs.com
LatPRO (T)
Mexico Online [Mexico]
NetEmpleo
People Online [Brasil]
UniversoE.com [Mexico]
Venezuela]Job Shark-Venezuela

MIDDLEAST (20)

AACI Israel Jobnet
Career Bahrain (CareerMidEast)
Career Egypt.com (CareerMidEast)
Career Emirates.com (CareerMidEast)
Career Jordan.com (CareerMidEast)
Career Kuwait.com (CareerMidEast)
Career Lebanon.com (CareerMidEast)
Career MidEast.com
Career Morocco.com (CareerMidEast)
Career Oman.com (CareerMidEast)
Career Qtar.com (CareerMidEast)
Career Saudi.com (CareerMidEast)
Career Tunis.com (CareerMidEast)
Career Yemen.com (CareerMidEast)
Computer Jobs in Israel
Earthworks
Offshore Guides
Oil job.com
Procruit [Egypt]
Worldwideworker.com

PACIFIC RIM (42)

Asiaco Jobs Center
Asiadragons.com (Asiaco)
Asia-Links
Asia-Net
Aspirasi Graduan [Malasia]
Australian Careers Directory
Career Cross Japan
Career Journal Asia.com (CareerJournal)
Career One [Australia]
CFO Asia
Civic Action in Eurasia
DaiJob [Japan]
Dave's ESL Cafe [Korea]
Dragon Surf [China]
Employ China
Hanap-Buhay.com.ph [Philippines]
Institution of Professional Engineers [New Zealand]
Japanese Jobs
Job AA
Job Asia [Hong Kong]
Job Easy [Japan/Hong Kong]
Job Link Asia.com [Malasia]
Job Master [Singapore]
Job Net Australia
job pilot.com [Thailand]
Job Street

Job Universe [Australia/New Zealand]
Jobs DB.com
Jobs in Japan
Jobs on Guam.com
Jobs Plus.com.au [Austrailia]
Jobs.net [Philippines]
Jobz [Australia]
Monster International
My Career.com.au [Australia]
NZ Jobs.com [New Zealand]
O-Hayo Sensei [Japan]
Plus (+) Jobs Australia
Recruit.com [Japan]
Seek [Australia] (T)
Top Money Jobs
travel jobs [Australia/New Zealand]

UNITED STATES REGIONAL SITES (717)

NORTH EAST STATES (73)
CT, MA, ME, NY, VT, NH, RI

Albany Times Union (CareerBuilder) [NY/Albany]
All County Jobs.com [USA/NOE/CT]
Best Jobs Massachusetts (Best Jobs) [MA]
Boston Computer Jobs.com [MA/Boston]
Boston Hire.com [MA/Boston]
Boston Job Bank [MA/Boston]
Boston Job Source (Internet Job Source) [MA/Boston]
BuffaloHelpWanted (Reg.HelpWanted) [NY/Buffalo]
Buffalojobfinder.com (Employment Wizard) [NY/Buffalo]
Burlington Free-Press (USA Today Careers) [VT/Burlington]
Candidate Seeker
Cape Cod Online (Employment Wizard) [MA/Cape Cod]
Connecticut Jobs Online (CTJobs.com) [CT]
Connecticut Jobs.com (LocalCareers) [CT]
Connecticut Post (Employment Wizard) [CT/Bridgeport]
Craigs List [Boston] [MA/Boston]
CT Health Careers.com (All County Jobs) [CT]
CT High Tech.com (All County Jobs) [CT]
CTJob Search (CareerLINK) [CT/Hartford]
Diversity Job Fairs.com [NJ/NY/PA]
Elmira Star Gazette (USA Today Careers) [NY/Elmira]
Erie Jobs [PA/Erie]
FairfieldCounty Jobs.com (All County Jobs) [CT]
Freetime Jobs.com [NY]
Go Erie.com (Employment Wizard) [PA/Erie]
Greenwich Time (CareerBuilder) [CT/Greewhich]
Hartford County Jobs.com (All County Jobs) [CT]
Hartford Courant (CareerBuilder) [CT/Hartford]
HartfordHelpWanted (Reg.HelpWanted) [CT/Hartford]
HelpWanted Boston (Reg.HelpWanted) [MA]
Hire Albany.com [NY/Albany]
Hire Buffalo.com [NY/Buffalo]
HireMass.com [MA/Boston]
hspeople (Human Services) [CT/ME/MA]
Interface JOBS.com
Ithaca Cortland Careers (Employment Partner) [NY/Ithaca]
Jewish Vocational Services Career Moves [MA/Boston]
jobfind.com [MA/Boston]
JobExpo.com [NJ/NY/PA]
Jobs in Maine [ME]
Lancaster Sentinel Enterprise (Employment Wizard) [MA/Lancaster]
Lowell Sun (Employment Wizard) [MA/Lowell]
MA Careers.com (CareerMVP) [MA]
Mass Live (Advance Careers) [MA]
Massachusetts Biotechnology Council [MA]
New England Computerwork.com
New England Enployee Benefits Council
New England Human Resource Assoc. [MA]
New England Telecommunications Assoc.
New Hampshire Job Finder (Telegraph) [NH]

New Haven County Jobs.com (All County Jobs) [CT]
New London Careers Online (Employment Partner) [CT/New London]
NewHampshireHelpWanted (Reg.HelpWanted) [NH]
NH Careers Online (Employment Partner) [NH]
NorthCountryHelpWanted (Reg.HelpWanted) [VT]
Norwich Bulletin (USA Today Careers) [CT/Norwich]
Poughkeepsie Journal (USA Today Careers) [NY/Poughkeepsie]
Providence Journal (Employment Wizard) [RI/Providence]
Rhode Island Jobs.com (LocalCareers) [RI]
Rochester Democrat (USA Today Careers) [NY/Rochester]
South Coast JobMart.com (The Standard-Times) [MA]
SouthernMaineWanted (Reg.HelpWanted) [ME]
Stamfordadvocate.com (CareerBuilder) [CT/Stamford]
Syracuse Careers Online (Employment Partner) [NY/Syracuse]
Syracuse Online (Advance Careers) [Syracuse]
Talent rock [MA/Boston]
Town Online (JobFind) [MA]
Utica Observer-Dispatch (USA Today Careers) [NY/Utica]
Vermont State Jobs [VT]
Western NY Jobs [NY/Rochester]
Worcester Careers Online (Employment Partner) [MA/Worcester]
Worcester Works (Boston Works) [MA/Worcester]

MIDDLE ATLANTIC STATES (83)
DC, DE, MD, NY (NYC), NJ, PA, VA (NORTH)

Allentown Morning Call (CareerBuilder) [PA]
Art Directors Club of Metro. Washington [DC]
Baltimore Computerwork.com [MD/Baltimore]
Baltimore Sun (CareerBuilder) [MD/Baltimore]
BaltimoreWanted (Reg.HelpWanted) [MD/Baltimore]
Bergen Daily Record (USA Today Careers) [NJ]
Best Jobs New York (Best Jobs) [NY]
Better Job Network (CareerLINK) [MD/Baltimore]
BigApplcHead.com [NY/NYC]
Bridgewater News-Courier (USA Today Careers) [NJ/Bridgewater]
Career Local Net [NJ]
Career NJ.com (CareerMVP) [NJ]
Cherry Hill Courier-Post (USA Today Careers) [NJ/Cherry Hill]
Craigs List [New York] [NY/NYC]
Craigs List [Washington DC] [DC]
Crains New York (Career Engine) [New York]
Creative Freelancers Online [NY/NYC]
Ct. Business & Industry Assoc. (CTJobs.com) [CT]
DC AccountingJobs [DC]
DC Computer Jobs.com [DC]
DC Computerwork.com [DC]
DC Job Source.com (Internet Job Source) [DC]
Fashion Career Center.com [NY]
Feminist Majority Foundation Online [Washington DC]
Financial Executives Networking Group [CT/NJ/NY]
HelpWantedDC.com (Reg.HelpWanted) [DC]
Hire GreaterWashington.com [DC]
hire health.com [NJ]
Hire Philadelphia.com [PA/Philadelphia]
Hire Pittsburgh.com [PA/Pittsburgh]
HireBaltimore.com [MD/Baltimore]
Jersey Job Guide [NJ]
Job Circle.com (T) [PA]
Job City USA.com (Spherion)
Job net.com [PA/NJ]
Jobs Retail.com [VA/Richmond]
Jobs.in.York.com (CareerSite) [PA/York]
Lebenon Daily News (Employment Wizard) [PA/Lebenon]
Legal SecretariesUSA.com [NY]
LI jobs.com [NY/Long Island]
media bistro.com [NY/NYC]
New Jersey Technical Recruiters Alliance [NJ]
New Media Assoc. of NJ [NJ]

437

New York Computer Jobs.com [NY/NYC]
New York Computer work.com [NY/NYC]
New York Post (CareerBuilder) [NY/NYC]
Newsday.com (CareerBuilder) [NY/Long Island]
NJ Careers [NJ]
NJ Hire [NJ]
NJ JOBS [NJ]
NJ Law Network (Legal Staff) [NJ]
NJ Online (Advance Careers) [NJ]
NJParalegal.com [NJ]
North Jersey HelpWanted.com (Reg. HelpWanted) [NJ]
North Jersey.com (Bergen Record) [NJ/Bergen County]
NY Careers.com (LocalCareers) [NY]
NY Daily News (Abracat) [NY/NYC]
NY Job Source (Internet Job Source) [NY/New York]
NY Job Source.com [NY/NY]
NY New Media Assoc. The Silicon Alley Job Board [NY]
NY Newsday.com (CareerBuilder) [NY/LI/NYC]
NY Times Job Market [NY]
NYC Employment.com (Employocity) [NY/NYC]
NYC Workforce 1 [NY/New York]
Operation IT [NY/NYC]
Out Professionals [NY]
Penn Live (Advance Careers) [PA]
Pennsylvania Computerwork.com [PA]
Pennsylvania Jobs.com [PA]
Philadelphia Computer Jobs.com [PA/Philadelphia]
Philadelphia Inquirer (CareerBuilder) [PA]
PhiladelphiaHelpWanted (Reg.HelpWanted) [PA/Philadelphia]
Philly.com (CareerBuilder) [PA/Philadelphia]
Pittsburgh Live.com (Employment Wizard) [PA/Pittsburgh]
princeton info.com (U.S. 1) [NJ/Princeton]
Salisbury Daily Times (USA Today Careers) [MD/Salisbury]
South Jersey Careers Online (Employment Partner) [NJ]
Staten Island Live (Advance Careers) [NY/Staten Island]
Tri StateJobs.com
Vineland Daily Journal (USA Today Careers) [NJ/Vineland]
Washington DC Area SGML/XML Users Group [DC]
Washington Post [Washington Jobs] (T) [DC]
Westchester Job Central [NY/Westchester]
Westchester Jrnl News (USA Today Careers) [NY/Westchester]
Wilmington News Journal (USA Today Careers) [DE/Wilmington]

SOUTH EAST STATES (70)
VA, GA, FL, NC, SC

123 Charlotte.com [NC/Charlotte]
123 Jax.com [FL/Jacksonville]
123 Raleigh.com [NC/Raleigh]
123 USA hire.com
Advertising Job Bank [FL]
Asheville Area Talent Bank (NationJob) [NC/Asheville]
Asheville Citizen-Times (USA Today Careers) [NC/Asheville]
Atlanta Computer Jobs.com [GA/Atlanta]
Atlanta Computer work.com [GA/Atlanta]
Atlanta ContractJobs [GA Atlanta]
Atlanta Smart City [GA, Atlanta]
Augusta Chronicle (Employment Wizard) [GA/Augusta]
Best Jobs Florida (Best Jobs) [FL]
Carolina Computer Jobs.com [NC,SC]
CharlestonJobMarket [SC/Charleston]
Charlotte Observer (CareerBuilder) [NC/Charlotte]
CharlotteHelpWanted (Reg.HelpWanted) [NC/Charlotte]
CJobs.com (Atlanta Journal Constitution) [GA, Atlanta]
Columbia Today (CareerBuilder) [SC/Columbia]
Communications Roundtable [NC]
Craigs List [Atlanta] [GA/Atlanta]
Daytona HelpWanted.com (Reg. HelpWanted) [FL]
Find Florida Jobs [FL]
First Coast Jobs [FL/Jacksonville]
Florida Computer Jobs.com [FL]

Florida Computerwork.com [FL]
Ft. Myers News-Press (USA Today Careers) [FL/Ft. Myers]
Georgia Careers.com (LocalCareers) [GA]
Georgia Jobs.com [Georgia]
Georgia Jobs.net (LocalCareers) [GA]
Greensboro News & Record [NC/Greensboro]
Greenville News (USA Today Careers) [SC/Greenville]
Hampton Roads Daily Press (CareerBuilder) [VA/HamptonRoads]
Hilton Head Island Packet (Employment Wizard) [SC/Hilton Head]
Hire Atlanta.com [GA/Atlanta]
Hire Charlotte.com [NC/Charlotte]
Hire Jacksonville.com [FL/Jacksonville]
Hire Orlando.com [FL/Orlando]
Hire Tampa Bay.com [FL/TampaBay]
Hire the Triad [NC/Winston-Salem]
Hire the Triangle [NC/Raleigh-Durham]
JacksonvilleHelpWanted (Reg.HelpWanted) [FL/Jacksonville]
Lawyers Weekly [MDA/]
Macon Telegraph (CareerBuilder) [GA/Macon]
Miami Herald (CareerBuilder) [FL/Miami]
Myrtle Beach Sun News (CareerBuilder) [FL/MyrtleBeach]
MyrtleBeachHelpWanted (Reg.HelpWanted) [SC/Myrtle Beach]
NC Careers.com (CareerMVP) [NC]
Orlando Careers Online (Employment Partner) [FL/Orlando]
Orlando Sentinel (CareerBuilder) [FL/Orlando]
OrlandoHelpWanted (Reg.HelpWanted) [FL/Orlando]
Pensacola News Journal (USA Today Careers) [FL/Pensacola]
pensacolajobs.com [FL/Pensacola]
Polk Job Finder (Lakeland FL Ledger) [FL]
Raleigh News Observer (Employment Wizard) [NC/Raleigh]
Real Columbus.com (CareerBuilder) [GA/Columbus]
Rhinomite [FL]
Richmond Careers Online (Employment Partner) [VA/Richmond]
Richmond Times-Dispatch (CareerBuilder) [VA/Richmond]
RichmondHelpWanted (Reg.HelpWanted) [VA/Richmond]
Rock Hill Herald(Employment Wizard) [SC/Rock Hill]
SCJobMarket.com [SC]
Sioux Falls Argus Leader (USA Today Careers) [SC/Sioux Falls]
South Carolina State Jobs [SC]
St. Petersburg Times (CareerBuilder) [FL/St. Petersburg]
Tallahasse.com (CareerBuilder) [FL/Tallahassee]
Tampa Bay Online (Tampa Bay Tribune) [FL/Tampa]
Triangle.com (Raleigh News & Observer) [NC/Raleigh]
Virginia Computerwork.com [VA]

MID-WEST STATES (116)
IA, IL, IN, KS, NE, OH, MI, MN, ND, SD, WI

Aberdeen American News (CareerBuilder) [SD/Aberdeen]
Access Dubuque (Telegraph Herald) [IA/Dubuque]
Battle Creek Enquirer (USA Today Careers) [MI/Battle Creek]
Bismark Tribune (Employment Wizard) [ND/Bismark]
Black Career Women
Career Board
Career Connector [IL/Chicago]
Career LinkApplied Info. Mgm't Institute [NE]
Career Matrix.com [MI]
Chicago Careers Online (Employment Partner) [IL/Chicago]
Chicago Computer Jobs.com [IL/Chicago]
Chicago Employment.com (Employocity) [IL/Chicago]
Chicago HelpWanted.com (Reg. HelpWanted) [IL]
Chicago Jobs.com (LocalCareers) [IL/Chicago]
Chicago Tribune (CareerBuilder) [IL/Chicago]
Chicago Job Network (Chicago Sun Times) [IL/Chicago]
Cincinatti Career Board [OH/Cincinatti]
Cincinatti Careers (Employment Partner) [OH/Cincinatti]
Cincinnati Enquirer (USA Today Careers) [OH/Cincinnati]
Cleveland Career Board [OH/Cleveland]
Cleveland Live (Cleveland Plain Dealer) [OH/Cleveland]

College Recruiter [MN]
Columbus Career Board [OH/Columbus]
Columbus Careers Online (Employment Partner)
[OH/Columbus]
Columbus Ledger-Enquirer (CareerBuilder) [OH/Columbus]
ColumbusHelpWanted (Reg.HelpWanted) [OH/Columbus]
ColumbusJobs.com (Employment Wizard) [OH/Columbus]
Craigs List [Chicago] [IL/Chicago]
Decatur Herald & Review (Employment Wizard) [IL/Decatur]
DesMoines Register (USA Today Careers) [IA/DesMoines]
Detroit Computer Jobs.com [MI/Detroit]
Detroit Employment.com (Employocity) [MI/Detroit]
Detroit News (USA Today Careers) [MI/Detroit]
DubuqueAccessSuccess [IA/]
Dubuque Telegraph Herald [IA/Dubuque]
Duluth News Tribune (CareerBuilder) [MN/Duluth]
Employment Weekly (IN) [IN]
FargoHelpWanted (Reg.HelpWanted) [ND/Fargo]
FetchMeAJob.com
FlintWanted (Reg.HelpWanted) [MI/Flint]
Fort Wayne News Sentinel (CareerBuilder) [IN/FtWayne]
Get Work.com [MN]
Grand Forks.com (CareerBuilder) [ND/Grand Forks]
Grand Rapids Careers (Employment Partner) [MI/Grand
Rapids]
Hire Cincinnatti.com [OH/Cincinnatti]
Hire Columbus.com [OH/Columbus]
Hire Dayton.com [OH/Dayton]
Hire Milwaukee.com [WI/Milwaukee]
Hire TwinCities.com [MN/Minneapolis-St. Paul]
istreet [IL/Chicago]
IL Careers.com (CareerMVP) [IL]
Illinois Jobs.com (LocalCareers) [IL]
Indianapolis Star (USA Today Careers) [IN/Indianapolis]
Iowa City Press-Citizen (USA Today Careers) [IA/Iowa City]
Iowa State Jobs [IA]
Job Boards.com [OH/IN/KY]
Jobs in Chicago [IL/Chicago]
Kenosha County.com (Employment Wizard) [WI/Kenosha]
LaCrosse Tribune (Employment Wizard) [WI/Lacrosse]
Lafayette Journal & Courier (USA Today Careers)
[IN/Lafayette]
Lancaster Eagle-Gazette (USA Today Careers) [OH/Lancaster]
Lansing State Journal (USA Today Careers) [MI/Lansing]
Law Bulletin
Lincoln Journal Star.com (Employment Wizard) [NE]
Local job Network [MI/Detroit]
Madison Newspapers (Employment Wizard) [WI/Madisson]
Mansfield News Journal (USA Today Careers) [OH/Mansfield]
Marion Star(USA Today Careers) [OH/Marion]
Michigan Job Hunter.com (Detroit Free Press) [MI/Detroit]
Michigan Jobs.com (LocalCareers) [MI]
Michigan Live (Advance Careers) [MI]
Midwest Computerwork.com
Milwaukee Career Board [WI/Milwaukee]
Milwaukee Journal Sentinel (Employment Wizard)
[WI/Milwaukee]
Milwaukee Naturally [WI/Milwaukee]
MilwaukeeJobs.com [WI/]
Minneapolis Star Tribune [MN/Minneapolis]
Minnesota Council of Nonprofits [MN]
Minnesota Jobs.com (T) [MN]
Muncie Star-Press (USA Today Careers) [IN/Muncie]
NBA Online (Nebraska Bankers Assoc.) [Nebraska]
Nebraska Bankers Assoc. [NE]
Newark Advocate (USA Today Careers) [OH/Newark]
North Dakota State Jobs [ND]
NPO .NET [IL/Chicago]
Ohio Jobs.com (LocalCareers) [OH]
Ohio.com (CareerBuilder) [OH/Akron & Cleveland]
Omaha World Herald (Employment Wizard) [NE/Omaha]
OmahaHelpWanted (Reg.HelpWanted) [NE/Omaha]
OnWisconsinJobs.com (Employment Wizard) [WI/Milwaukee]
QC Employ Me (CareerLINK) [IA/Davenport]
Quad City Times (Employment Wizard) [IA/Quad Cities]

Racine Journal Times (Employment Wizard) [WI/Racine]
Rochester jobFinder (Employment Wizard) [MN/Rochester]
Rockford Register Star (USA Today Careers) [IL/Rockford]
Salem Statesman Journal (USA Today Careers) [OH/Salem]
Smart Career Move [IA]
South Dakota State Jobs [SD]
SouthBendWanted (Reg.HelpWanted) [IN/Sout Bend]
Southern Illinoisian (Employment Wizard) [IL]
St. Cloud Times (USA Today Careers) [MN/St. Cloud]
SuburbanChicagoHelpWanted (Reg.HelpWanted)
[IL/Chicago]
TC Theatre and Film [MN/Twin Cities]
Terre Haute Tribune Star (Employment Wizard) [IN/Terre
Haute]
The Blue Line
Toledo Beacon Journal (CareerBuilder) [OH/Toledo]
Toledo Career Board [OH/Toledo]
Twin Cities Computer Jobs.com [MN/Twin Cities]
Twin Cities Pioneer Press (CareerBuilder) [IN/FtWayne]
TwinCitiesWanted (Reg.HelpWanted) [MN/Twin Cities]
Wi Jobs.com (LocalCareers) [WI]
WI Jobs.com [WI]
Wisconsin Jobs.com (LocalCareers) [WI]
Wisconsin Jobs.com (LocalCareers) [WI]
Wisconsin's Gannet Newspapers (USA Today Careers) [WI]
Zanesville Times Rec. (USA Today Careers) [OH/Zanesville]

SOUTHERN STATES (74)
AL, AR, KS, KY, LA, MS, MO, OK TN, WV

Alabama Computer Jobs.com [AL]
Alabama Live (Advance Careers) [AL]
Alabama State Jobs [AL]
Asbury Park Press (USA Today Careers) [AL/Montgomery]
Baton Rouge Advocate [LA/Baton Rouge]
Baton Rouge Careers Online (Employment Partner)
[LA/Baton Rouge]
Baton Rouge HelpWanted.com (Reg.HelpWanted) [LA]
better jobs KC.com (CareerLink) [MO/Kansas City]
Birmingham Employment.com (Employocity)
[AL/Birmingham]
Birmingham HelpWanted (Reg.HelpWanted)
[AL/Birmingham]
Birmingham Online (Employment Partner) [AL/Birmingham]
Charleston Daily Mail (Employment Wizard) [WV/Charleston]
CharlestonHelpWanted (Reg.HelpWanted) [WV/Charleston]
Chattanooga Times (Employment Wizard) [TN/Chattanooga]
Clarksville Leaf-Chronicle (USA Today Careers)
[TN/Clarksville]
Go Ferret Go [MO/Kansas City]
gomemphis.com (Employment Wizard) [TN/Memphis]
Gulf Coast Sun-Herald (CareerBuilder) [MS]
Hattiesburg American (USA Today Careers) [MS/Hattiesburg]
Hire KansasCity.com [KS/Kansas City]
Hire Loisville.com [KY/Louisville]
Hire Memphis.com [TN/Memphis]
Hire Nashville.com [TN/Nashville]
Hire StLouis.com [MO/St. Louis]
Hire Wichita.com [KS/Wichita]
Huntington Herald-Disp. (USA Today Careers)
[WV/Huntington]
Jackson Clarion-Ledger (USA Today Careers) [MS/Jackson]
Jackson Sun (USA Today Careers) [TN/Jackson]
Kansas City Star (CareerBuilder) [KS & MO/KansasCity]
Kansas State Jobs [KS]
Kansas.com (CareerBuilder) [KS/Wichita]
KansasCityWanted (Reg.HelpWanted) [MO/Kansas City]
Kentuckiana Jobs [KY, IN]
Kentucky KY Direct [KY]
Knox Careers.com (Employment Wizard) [TN/Knoxville]
Knox News.com [TN/Knoxville]
Knoxville Careers Online (Employment Partner)
[TN/Knoxville]
LA Job Market (CareerLINK) [LA/Baton Rouge]

LOCATION

Lafayette Daily Advertiser (USA Today Careers) [LA/Lafayette]
Lexington Herald-Leader (CareerBuilder) [KY/Lexington]
Little Rock Careers Online (Employment Partner) [AR/Little Rock]
Little Rock Democart-Gazette [AR/Little Rock]
LittleRock HelpWanted. (Reg.HelpWanted) [AR/Little Rock]
Louisiana State Jobs [LA]
Louisville Careers (Employment Partner) [KY/Louisville]
Louisville Courier Jrnl (USA Today Careers) [KY/Louisville]
LouisvilleWanted (Reg.HelpWanted) [KY/Louisville]
Memphis Commercial Appeal (Employment Wizard) [TN/Memphis]
MemphisComputer work.com [TN/Memphis]
MemphisHelpWanted (Reg.HelpWanted) [TN/Memphis]
Mississippi Coast.com (CareerBuilder) [MI/Biloxi]
Monroe News-Star (USA Today Careers) [LA/Monroe]
Montgomery Advertiser (USA Today Careers) [AL/Montgomery]
Nashville Careers Online (Employment Partner) [TN/Nashville]
Nashville Tennesean (USA Today Careers) [TN/Nashville]
New Orleans Live (Advance Careers) [LA/New Orleans]
New OrleansHelpWanted. (Reg.HelpWanted) [LA/NewOrleans]
NewsOK.com (Employment Wizard) [OK/Oklahoma City]
Northwest Arkansas Times [AR/Fayettville]
OK City Careers (Employment Partner) [OK/Oklahoma City]
Oklahoma State Jobs [OK]
SE Missourian (Employment Wizard) [MO]
Shreveport Times (USA Today Careers) [LA/Shreveport]
Springfield NewsLdr (USA Today Careers) [MO/Springfield]
St. Louis Computer Jobs.com [MO/St. Louis]
St. Louis Metro (CareerBuilder) [MO/St Louis]
St. Louis Today (Post DispatchCareerBuilder) [MO/St. Louis]
Tenn Careers.com (CareerMVP) [TN]
Tennessee State Jobs [TN]
Topeka Capital Journal (Employment Wizard) [KS/Topeka]
TopekaWanted (Reg.HelpWanted) [KS/Topeka]
TulsaHelpWanted (Reg.HelpWanted) [OK/Tulsa]
West Virginia State Jobs [WV]
Wichita Eagle (CareerBuilder) [KS/Wichita]

SOUTH WEST STATES (69)
AZ, CO, NM, TX

4Labors Of Love [CO/Denver]
Albuquerque Journal (abracat) [NM/Abuquerque]
Almogordo Daily News (Employment Wizard) [NM/Almogordo]
Arizona Jobs.com (LocalCareers) [AZ]
Arizona Republic (USA Today Careers) [AZ/Phoenix]
Austin American Statesman [TX/Austin]
Austin Employment.com (Employocity) [TX/Austin]
Best Jobs Texas (Best Jobs) [TX]
bigcountryjobs.com (Employment Wizard) [TX/Abilene]
Boulder Daily Camera (Employment Wizard) [CO/Boulder]
Career Consulting Corner [TX]
CareersColorado.com [CO]
Coastal Bend Careers (Employment Wizard) [TX/Corpus Christi]
Colorado Alive (Employment Wizard) [CO/Aspen]
Colorado Careers Online (Employment Partner) [CO/Colorado Springs]
Colorado Computerwork.com [CO]
Colorado Guide [CO]
Colorado Human Resources Assoc. [CO]
Colorado Online Job Connection [CO]
Colorado Software & Internet Assoc. [CO]
Coloradoan (USA Today Careers) [CA/Ft. Collins]
Craigs List [Austin] [TX/Austin]
Craigs List [Denver] [CO/Denver]
Dallas Morning News (Employment Wizard) [TX/Dallas]
Denver Computer Jobs.com [CO/Denver]

Denver Post (Employment Wizard) [CO/Denver]
DFW Employment.com (Employocity) [TX/Dallas]
DFWHelpWanted. (Reg.HelpWanted) [TX/Dallas]
East Valley Tribune (CareerCast) [AZ/Mesa]
El Paso Times (USA Today Careers)) [TX/El Paso]
Fort Bend Jobs [TX/Houston]
Fort Worth Star-Telegram (CareerBuilder) [TX/FtWorth]
Ft. Worth Star-Telegram (CareerBuilder) [TX/Ft. Worth]
Go SanAngelo (Standard-Times) [TX/San Antonio]
Gulf Live (Advance Careers) [TX]
Hire Austin.com [TX/Austin]
Hire Denver.com [CO/Denver]
Hire houston.com [TX/Houston]
Hire Phoenix.com [AZ/Phoenix]
Hire San Antonio.com [TX/San Antonio]
Houston Geological Society [TX/Houston]
Houston Chronicle [TX/Houston]
Internet Employment in New Mexico [NM]
Internet Jobs.com [TX]
Jobfly [TX]
Jobing.com [AZ, NM]
Jobs for Colorado.com [CO]
MyRGV.com [TX]
New Mexico Careers Online (Employment Partner) [NM]
New Mexico High Tech Job Forum [NM]
New Mexico State Jobs [NM]
Phoenix Computerwork.com [AZ]
Phoenix Employment.com (Employocity) [AZ/Phoenix]
Recruiters Dream [TX/Dallas]
Rocky Mountain Jobs [CO]
Rocky Mountain Water Environment Assoc. [CO]
Rocky MountainNews.com [CO/Boulder/Denver]
RockyMountainHelpWanted (Reg.HelpWanted) [CO]
San Antonio Job Network [TX/San Antonio]
Southwest-Online (Employment Wizard) [NM/Las Cruces]
Texan Careers.com (CareerMVP) [TX]
Texas Computer Jobs.com [TX]
Texas Computerwork.com [TX]
Texas Jobs.com (LocalCareers) [TX]
Tucson Careers Online (Employment Partner) [AZ/Tucson]
Tucson Citizen (USA Today Careers) [AZ/Tucson]
TucsonHelpWanted (Reg.HelpWanted) [AZ/Tucson]
Wichita Falls Times Record (Employment Wizard) [TX/Wichita Falls]

WESTERN STATES (92)
CA, NV, UT, HI

Agricultural Technology Information Network [CA]
Asian American Journalists Assoc. [CA]
aztechjobs.com [CA]
BA Jobs (T) [CA/San Francisco]
Bay AreaHelpWanted (Reg.HelpWanted) [CA/SanFrancisco]
Bay Recruiter.com [CA/San Francisco]
Best Jobs California (Best Jobs) [CA]
Best Jobs Illinois (Best Jobs) [CA]
cal career.com [CA]
Cali Careers.com (CareerMVP) [CA]
California Agricultural Technology Institute [CA]
California Computerwork.com [CA]
California HelpWanted.com (Reg. HelpWanted) [CA]
California Job Journal [CA]
California Job Source (Internet Job Source) [CA]
California Jobs.com (LocalCareers) [CA]
California Journalism Job Bank
California Soc. of Prof. Engineers (CareerBuilder) [CA]
Californian (USA Today Careers) [CA/Salinas]
Career Giant [CA/HI]
Chicano/a Latino/a NET [CA]
Chico Enterprise Record (Employment Wizard) [CA/Chico]
Clear Star [CA]
CoderiderVIC Job Board [CA/LA]
Craigs List [Los Angeles] [CA/Los Angeles]
Craigs List [Sacramento] [CA/Sacramento]

Craigs List [San Diego] [CA/San Diego]
Craigs List [San Francisco]
Desert Sun (USA Today Careers) [CA/PalmSprings]
Entertainment Careers.Net [CA]
Fat Job.com [CA/San Francisco]
Fresno Bee (Employment Wizard) [CA/Fresno]
Hire Honolulu.com [HI/Honolulu]
Hire Sacramento.com [CA/Sacramento]
Hire SanFrancisco.com [CA/SanFrancisco]
Hire SanJose.com [CA/SanJose]
Honolulu Advertiser (USA Today Careers)) [HI/Honolulu]
Honolulu Star Bulletin [HI/Honolulu]
HonoluluHelpWanted (Reg.HelpWanted) [HI/Honolulu]
Internet Jobs.com [CA]
ITwow.com [CA]
Job Hub [CA/San Francisco]
Job right.com [CA/San Diego]
Jobfly [CA]
Jobs Hawaii [HI]
Jobs in the Biz [CA]
LA Daily News (Employment Wizard) [CA/Los Angeles]
LA Employment.com (Employocity) [CA/LA]
LA Times.com (CareerBuilder) [CA/Los Angeles]
LasVegasHelpWanted (Reg.HelpWanted) [NV/Las Vegas]
Latino Web [CA]
Legal Report [CA]
Long Beach Press-Telegram (Employment Wizard) [CA/Long Beach]
Los Angeles Computer Jobs.com [CA/Los Angeles]
LosAngelesHelpWanted (Reg.HelpWanted) [CA/Los Angeles]
Modesto Bee (Employment Wizard) [CA/Modesto]
Monterey County Herald (CareerBuilder) [CA/Monterey]
Nat'l. Assoc. of Broadcasters
Nevada JobConnect [NV]
Nevada Jobs.com (LocalCareers) [NV]
Nevada State Jobs [NV]
Orange County Register (CareerCast) [CA/Santa Ana]
PR Soc. of America [CA/LA]
Professionals in Human Resources Assoc. [CA]
ProMatch [CA/San Francisco]
Recruiters Forum [CA]
Redding Searchlight (Employment Wizard) [CA/Redding]
Reno Careers Online (Employment Partner) [NV/Reno]
Reno Gazette-Observer Today Careers) [NV/Reno]
Restaurant Jobs [CA]
Riverside Press-Enterprise (Employment Wizard) [CA/Riverside]
Sacramento Bee (Employment Wizard) [CA/Sacramento]
Salt Lake City Deseret News (Employment Wizard) [UT/Salt Lake City]
Saludos.com (T) [CA]
San Bernadino Sun (Employment Wizard) [CA/San Bernadino]
San Francisco Chronicle Gate [CA/San Francisco]
San Jose Mercury News (CareerBuilder) [CA/San Jose]
San Louis Obispo Tribune News (CareerBuilder) [CA/SanLouisObispo]
Santa Barbara News-Press (Employment Wizard) [CA/Santa Barbara]
SF Bay Employment.com (Employocity) [CA/San Francisco]
SignOn SanDiego (Union-Tribune) [CA/San Diego]
Silicon Valley Computer Jobs.com [CA/SanFrancisco]
Soc. for Adv. of Chicanos & Native Amer. in Sci. [CA]
Southern California EDI Roundtable [CA]
St. George Spectrum (USA Today Careers)) [UT/St. George]
Torrence Daily Breeze (Employment Wizard) [CA/Torrence]
Utah Careers Online (Employment Partner) [UT]
Utah State Jobs [UT]
Vallejo Times-Herald (Employment Wizard) [CA/Vallejo]
Youth@Work [CA/Santa Clara]

NORTH WEST STATES (40)
AK, ID, MT, OR, WA, WY

Alaska Job Center Network [AK]
Anchorage Daily News (Employment Wizard) [AK/Anchorage]
Anchorage HelpWanted (Reg.HelpWanted) [AK/Anchorage]
Ashland Daily Tidings (Employment Wizard) [OR/Ashland]
Bellingham Herald (USA Today Careers)) [WA/Bellingham]
Best Jobs Washington (Best Jobs) [WA]
Billings Gazette (Employment Wizard) [MT/Billings]
BillingsHelpWanted (Reg.HelpWanted) [MT/Billings]
BoiseHelpWanted (Reg.HelpWanted) [ID/Boise]
Butte Montana Standard (Employment Wizard) [MT/Butte]
Columbia-Williamette Compensation Group [WA/OR]
Craigs List [Portland] [OR/Portland]
Craigs List [Seattle] [WA/Seattle]
Fairbanks Daily Miner (Employment Wizard) [AK/Fairbanks]
Great Falls Tribune (USA Today Careers)) [MT/Great Falls]
Hire Seattle.com [WA/Seattle]
HireGate [OR/Eugene]
Idaho Press-Tribune (Employment Wizard) [ID/Nampa]
Idaho State Jobs [ID]
Idaho Statesman (USA Today Careers)) [ID/Boise]
Jobs tri-cities.com (Employment Wizard) [WA]
Marketing Dreamjobs [WA/Seattle]
Montana Society of CPAs [MT]
Montana State Jobs [MT]
Northwest Recruiters Association
NW Classifieds (Seattle Times) [WA/Seattle]
Olympia Olympian (USA Today Careers)) [WA/Olympia]
Oregon Jobs.com (LocalCareers) [OR]
Oregon Live (Advance Careers) [OR]
Oregon State Jobs [OR]
Portland Computer Jobs.com [OR/Portland]
PugetSoundHelpWanted (Reg.HelpWanted) [WA/Seattle]
Seattle Computer Jobs.com [WA/Seattle]
Seattle Computer work.com [WA/Seattle]
SouthSoundJobs (Tacoma News Tribune) [WA/Tacoma]
Spokane Careers Online (Employment Partner) [WA/Spokane]
WA Careers.com (CareerMVP) [WA]
Wyoming Job Quest (Star-Tribune) [WY/Casper]
Wyoming State Jobs [WY]
WyomingJobs.com (LocalCareers) [WY]

441

SPECIALTY & INDUSTRY

Business, Communications & Media, Contract, Customer Service & Technical Support, Education, Engineering, Entertainment & Media, Executive Health Care, Hospitality & Food Services, Human Resource, Information Technology, Law & Order, Military Transition, Non-Profit, Public Sector, Retail Sales & Services, Professional Sales & Marketing, Science, Trade & Hourly, Miscellaneous.

Many job and resume sites narrow their coverage to one or two specialties, disciplines or industries. Critical to the success of these sites is being able to reach the people who have these specialties.

Note: The sites in **Bold** are among the 500 Best and their reviews can be found in the main body of this edition. A Bold **(T)** indicates we consider the site among the "Top 50". The thousands of sites in plain text listed here were reviewed but, their reviews are not published (we promise to send you any review on request). All Web site URLs (web addresses) can be found in the Master List. A parentheses ( ) designates the "gateway" site that we reviewed. Brackets [ ] are used for clarification.

BUSINESS (162)

ACCOUNTING, BANKING, FINANCE, INSURANCE, MANU-
FACTURING, MBA, OPERATIONS

3sectorsjob
6 FigureMBA.com
A Job4Accountants (Employmax)
Accountant Jobs (eJob Stores)
Accountants World.com (Career Engine)
Accounting Classifieds (Career Engine)
Accounting Jobs Online
Accounting Professional.com (Career Marke...
Accounting.com
AccountingWEB.co.uk
American Accounting Assoc.
American Assoc. for Budget & Program Ana...
American Assoc. of Finance and Accounting
American Industrial Hygiene Assoc.
American Institute of CPA's
American Lighting Assoc. (FlipDog)
American Planning Assoc.
American Soc. for Quality
American Soc. of Women Accountants
American Statistical Association
Arbetsformedlingen
Asian American Economic Dev. Enterprises
Assoc. for Financial Professionals
Assoc. for Investment Mgmt. & Research
Assoc. of Latino Professionals in Fin. & Acc.
Audit Net
Awesome Accountants
Bank Connect.com
Bank Job Search (BAI)
bank jobs.com
Bank Talent.com
Banking Job Store.com (eJob Stores)
bankrole.com
Be An Actuary
Big FiveTalent.com

Biz Moonlighter
Bloomberg.com (CareerBuilder)
Broker hunter.com
Building Industry Consulting Service Int'l.
Business Analyst.com (Career Marketplace)
business financemag.com
Buying Jobs.com (NicheJobs)
Canadian Mgmt. Accountants Society
Career Bank
Career Consulting Corner
Career Journal Asia.com (CareerJournal)
Career Journal Europe.com (CareerJournal)
Career Journal.com   **(T)**
Casualty Actuarial Society
CFO Asia
CFO Postions.com (Career Engine)
Chief Financial Officer.com
City Jobs
CollectionIndustry.com
CollegeJournal.com (Career Journal)
Construction Financial Mgmt. Assoc.
Council of Logistics Management
CPA jobs.com
CPA net
CPA2bizcareers.com
CPACareerNet
Crains New York (Career Engine)
Credit Jobs Today
Credit Union Executives Society
Creditjobs.com
Ct. Business & Industry Assoc. (CTJobs.com)
DC AccountingJobs
Econ Jobs.com (NicheJobs)
eFinancialCareers
Estimator Jobs (eJob Stores)
exBigFive.com
Execs on the Net (UK)
ExecuCentral.com
Finance Mag.com (Job Mag)

Finance MVP.com (CareerMVP)
Finance-Jobs
FinanceJobsites.com (Geojobsites)
Financial Executives Institute
Financial Executives Networking Group
Financial Job Network
Financial Jobfinder.com
Financial jobs.com
Financial Positions (Career Engine)
Financial Times Career Point   (T)
Financial Women International
Finishing.com
Great Insurance Jobs
Healthcare Financial Management Assoc.
Hispanic Business.com
Hospitality Financial & Technology Professi...
hotauditjobs.com
Inomics
Inside Careers
InspectionJobs.com
Institute for Professionals in Taxation
Institute for Supply Management
Institute of Internal Auditors
Institute of Store Planners
Insurance File
Insurance National Search
Intelligence & Defense Careers
Int'l. Economic Development Council
Job Mag.com
Jobs for Economists (JOE)
Jobs In Logistics
Jobs in MFG.com (Jobs in Logistics)
Jobs in the money
Job-Sites.com
Joint Service Academy Alumni Organizations
Journal of Commerce (Career Engine)
Just Accounting Jobs.com
Just Manufacturing Jobs.com
Lender Careers
Manufacturing MVP.com (CareerMVP)
MBA Careers (Career Exposure)
MBA GlobalNet
MBA Jungle
Monitor
Montana Society of CPAs
mortgage career.com
Mortgage Mag.com (Job Mag)
MortgageJobsites.com (Geojobsites)
MortgageJobStore.com (eJob Stores)
Mountainjobs.com
Nat'l. Assoc of Credit Management
Nat'l. Assoc of Credit Management.
Nat'l. Assoc. of Black Accountants
Nat'l. Assoc. of Educational Buyers
Nat'l. Assoc. of Federal Credit Unions
Nat'l. Assoc. of Manufacturers
Nat'l. Assoc. of Personal Financial Advisors
Nat'l. Assoc. of Student Financial Aid
Nat'l. Banking & Financial Services Network
Nat'l. Black MBA Assoc.
Nat'l. Black MBA Assoc. (NY Chapter)
Nat'l. Contract Management Asscoiation
Nat'l. Fire & Protection Agency (Monster)
Nat'l. Society of Hispanic MBAs (BrassRing)
NBA Online (Nebraska Bankers Assoc.)
Nebraska Bankers Assoc.
Net Staff
Office Moonlighter
Packaging Business
Project Management Insititute
QA-jobs.com
Risk & Insurance Management Society
Safety Online (Vertical Net)
SmartPros
Society of Competitive Intelligence Porf.

Supply .Jobs.com (NicheJobs)
Tax Talent.com
Tax-Jobs.Com
Teller Jobs (eJob Stores)
The Financial Planning Association
Thingamajob (3rd Party)
Top Money Jobs
Town Online (JobFind)
Underwriter Employment (eJob Stores)
underwriting Jobs.com
Women In Technology International
Work LP.com [Loss Prevention]
WorkopolisCampus.com (Workopolis)

COMMUNICATIONS (70)

ADVERTISING, GRAPHIC ARTS, JOURNALISM
PUBLIC RELATIONS, WRITING

3D Cafe
3D Site
Ad Age
ad world
Advertising Job Bank
Advertising Job Store (eJob Stores)
Advertising Media Internet Center
Adweek Online
American Advertising Federation
American Soc. of Assoc. Executives (T)
Art Directors Club of Metro. Washington
Art Hire
art jobonline
Asian American Journalists Assoc.
Assoc. for Women in Communications
Author link
Cabletelevision Advertising Bureau
California Journalism Job Bank
Career NJ.com (CareerMVP)
Communications Roundtable
Computer Jobs Technical Writing
Copy Editor Job Board
coroflot
Council of Public Relations Firms
Creative Central.com
Creative Freelancers Online
Creative Hotlist
Desktop Publishing.com JobBank
Editor & Publisher
e-Job
Graphic Artists Guild
Graphic Arts Information Network
IL Careers.com (CareerMVP)
Independent Press Assoc.
Int'l Assoc. of Business Communicators
Jeff Gaulin's Canadian Journalism Job Board
Job Link For Journalists
Jobs in Journalism
Journalism and Women's Symposium
Journalism for journalists (UK)
Journalism Jobs.com
Just Writing Jobs.com
MA Careers.com (CareerMVP)
Magazine Publishers of America
media bistro.com
Media Jobz.Com
Media Line.com
Nat'l. Assoc. of Black Journalists
Nat'l. Assoc. of Hispanic Journalists
Nat'l. Diversity Newspaper Job Bank
NC Careers.com (CareerMVP)
Newspaper Assoc. of America
PR Soc. of America [LA]
PR WeekJobs

SPECIALTY & INDUSTRY

Privacy Job Opportunity Boards
Public Relations Soc. of America (PRSA)
Soc. for Technical Communication
Society of Consumer Affairs Prof. in Bus.
Special Library Association
Sunoasis Jobs
Technical Communicator.com (Career Marke...
Technical Writer Jobs (eJob Stores)
Television Bureau of Advertising
Tenn Careers.com (CareerMVP)
Texan Careers.com (CareerMVP)
The Write Jobs
TV Jobs
WA Careers.com (CareerMVP)
Website Builder.com (Career Marketplace)
work in pr.com

CONTRACT (CONTINGENT)/PROJECT (46)

A2Z Moonlighter
Agricultural Labour Pool
Art Hire
Atlanta ContractJobs
Biz Moonlighter
Brain Bid.com
Career Gram
ConsultantTV.com
Contract Employment Connection
Contract Engineering
Contract JobHunter
Contracts247
DICE High Tech Jobs Online (T)
Do A Project.com
elance
Employee Assistance Professionals Assoc.
eWork Exchange
ForContractRecruiters.com
Free Agent
Freelance Work Exchange
Freetime Jobs.com
Graphic Artists Guild
Guru.com
Hire Abilitiy.com
Hire Skills.com
Independent Press Assoc.
IT Moonlighter
it-TEMP
Jeff Gaulin's Canadian Journalism Job Board
jobs.internet.com (DICE)
Journalism Jobs.com
MBA GlobalNet
Mechanical Contractors Asso. of America
Money Making Mommy
Monster Talent Market
Must Jobs.com
Net-Temps (T)
Office Moonlighter
Rent-a-Geek
Seasonal Employment
Software Contractors' Guild
Sologig.com (CareerBuilder)
Subcontract.com
Top Contracts
TrainMark.com
UBidContract.com

CUSTOMER SERVICE & TECH. SUPPORT (8)

Call Center Careers
Call Center Jobs.com
Call CenterOps

Creative Moonlighter
CRM Exchange
Customer Service Job Stores (eJob Stores)
Help Desk Institute
Int'l Customer Service Assoc.
Need Techs.com

EDUCATION (94)

Academic Employment Network
Academic Physician & Scientist
Academic Position Network
Adjunctopia
American Accounting Assoc.
American Agricultural Economics Assoc.
American Assoc. of Collegiate Registrars
American Assoc. of Community Colleges
American Assoc. of School Administrators
American Assoc. of University Women
American Astronomical Society
American College Personnel Assoc.
American Mathematical Society
American Risk & Insurance Assoc.
American School Counselor Assoc.
American Soc. for Engineering Education (ASEE)
Archaeological Fieldwork Opportunities
Assoc. for Advancement of Computing in Ed.
Assoc. for Computing Machinery
Assoc. for Institutional Research
Assoc. for Library and Information Science Education
Assoc. for Women in Mathematics
Assoc. of Research Libraries
Assoc. of Women Surgeons
Bioscience and Medicine (HUM-MOLGEN)
ccJobsOnline.com
CCollegeJobs.com
Chronicle of Higher Education
Civic Action in Eurasia
COACH's Job Board
College & University Personnel Assoc.
Computational Fluid Dynamics Jobs Database
Council for Advancement & Support od Ed.
Crystallography Worldwide
Dave's ESL Cafe (English as a Second Language)
Ed Jobs U Seek
Education Jobs
Education-jobs.com
EDUCAUSE
EE-Link/North American Assoc. for Env. Ed.
EFLWeb
Employment Information in the Mathematical Sciences
Entomology Society of America
ESL Worldwide.com
eteach.com
Great Teacher.net
Higher EdJobs.com
Independent School Management (ISM)
Inomics
Job2Teach
Jobs for Economists
Jobs in Education
Jobs in Entomology
Nat'l. Gerontological SOA - AgeWork
Outdoor Network
Private School Employment Network
Project Connect
PsycCareers
Teachers Online
Teachers-Teachers.com
Women in Higher Education
Y-axis.com
Jobs in Philosophy
Mechanical Engineers Magazine Online (ASME)

Mexican American Eng. and Scientists Society
Milwaukee Naturally
Minority Nurse.com (CASS)
Modern Language Association of America
Nat'l. Alliance of Black School Educators
Nat'l. Assoc of Student Personnel Administration

ENGINEERING (196)

A Job4Engineers (Employmax)
AEC Job Bank
AEC WorkForce
Aeroindustryjobs.com
Aerospace Engineer.com (Career Marketplace)
All Energy Jobs
AllEnergyJobs
American Ceramic Society
American Chemical Society - JobSpectrum.org
American Institute of Architects Career Center
American Institute of Chemical Engineers
American Lighting Assoc. (FlipDog)
American Nuclear Society
American Oil chemists' Society
American Soc. for Engineering Education (ASEE)
American Soc. of Agricultural Engineering
Society of Automotive Engineers
American Soc. of Civil Engineers
American Soc. of Mech. Engineering
American Statistical Association
American Water Works Assoc.
Architect jobs.com (eJob Stores)
Architects Online
Assoc. for Facilities Engineering
Assoc. of Metropolitan Water Agencies
AutoCAD Job Network (Mercury Enterprises)
Automation Jobs
Automation Techies
AV Jobs
Aviation Jobs Online
Aviation Now
aztechjobs.com
Biomedical Engineer.com (Career Marketplace)
British Columbia Water & Waste Assoc.
California Soc. of Prof. Engineers (CareerBuilder)
Canadian Institue of Quantity Surveyors
Career Mag.com
Career NJ.com (CareerMVP)
CareerAnalog
Careers in Construction
Car-eers.com
Castingpro.com (Staffingpro)
CATIA Job Network (Mercury Enterprises)
Chemical Engineer.com (Career Marketplace)
Chemistry Jobs.com (NicheJobs)
Civil Engineering Jobs
CIVIL Jobs.com
Classified Employment Web Site (CLEWS)
CNC Machines Job Network (Mercury Enterprises)
Computational Fluid Dynamics Jobs Database
Computer Jobs Hardware
Construction Executives.com
Construction Gigs
Construction Job Store (eJob Stores)
Construction Jobs.com
Construction.com
ConstructionJobsites.com (Geojobsites)
Construction-net
Contract Engineering
Curriculum Vitae Online
Cyber KingEmployment
daVinci Times (T)
Designer Max.com
Diversilink

Diversity Careers Online
Dream Construction Jobs
Drillers Job Center
Edie's Environmental Job Centre
EDN Magazine CarEEr Zone (CareerBuilder)
Electrical Engineer.com (Career Marketplace)
Electrical World (McGraw-Hill)
Electronic News OnLine
Electronics Engineer.com (Career Marketplace)
Empty.net
ENDS Environmental Jobs
Energy Career Network
Energy Jobs Network
Energy jobs.com
Engineer 500.com
Engineer Employment (eJob Stores)
Engineer jobs.com
Engineer.net
Engineer-Cad.com
Engineering Central
Engineering Institute of Canada
Engineering News Record
EngineeringJobsites.com (Geojobsites)
EngineerMax.com
EnviroNetwork.com
Environmental Career Opportunities
Environmental Career.com
Environmental Engineer.com (Career Marketplace)
Environmental Jobs and Careers
EnvJobs-L Archives
Geo Job Source
Geo Job Source & GIS Jobs
Geo TechJobs.com
GooSearch, Inc.
Geospatial Information & Technology Assoc.
GeoWeb Interactive
GISjobs.com
Graduating Engineer & Computer Careers Online
Green Dream Jobs
Green Energy Jobs
Houston Geological Society
Human Factors and Ergonomics Society
Hydrocarbon Online (VerticalNet)
IDEAS Job Network (Mercury Enterprises)
IL Careers.com (CareerMVP)
Industrial Designers Society of America
Industrial Engineer.com (Career Marketplace)
Info Mine
Inside Careers
Institute of Electrical and Electronics Engineers
Institute of Industrial Engineers
Institute of Packaging Professionals
Institution of Professional Engineers
Instrumentation Soc. of America
Intelligence & Defense Careers
InterEC.NET
Iron and Steel Society
Job Circle.com (T)
Job Warehouse
JobRadio.com
Job-Sites.com
Joint Service Academy Alumni Organizations
Just Engineering Jobs.com
MA Careers.com (CareerMVP)
Mechanical Contractors Asso. of America
Mechanical Engineer.com (Career Marketplace)
Mechanical Engineers Magazine Online (ASME)
Med BizPeople.com
Medical DeviceLink.com
Mercury Enterprises Job Network
Mexican American Eng. and Scientists Soc.
Mining USA
Nat'l. Academies Career Center
Nat'l. Assoc. of Manufacturers
Nat'l. Registry of Environmental Professionals

Nat'l. Society of Black Engineers
Nat'l. Society of Professional Engineering
Nat'l. Technical Services Assoc.
NC Careers.com (CareerMVP)
New Mexico High Tech Jobs Forum
NI Jobs.com (Irish Jobs)
Nuke Worker.com
Oil Careers
Oil Directory.com
Oil job.com
Oil Online
Optical Engineer.com (Career Marketplace)
Packaging Business
Petroleum Engineer.com (Career Marketplace)
Petroleum Services Assoc. of Canada
Physics World Jobs
Plastic Careers.com
Plastic Pro (staffingpro)
Plastics News
Power Highway
Power Mag (McGraw-Hill)
Pre-Cast Stressed Convrete Assoc.
Pro/E Job Network (Mercury Enterprises)
Procruit
Project Manager.com (Career Marketplace)
Recruit Military
Refrigeration-engineer.com
RF Global Net (Verticalnet)
RF Job Network (Mercury Enterprises)
Rocky Mountain Water Environment Assoc.
Safety Online (Vertical Net)
Sales Engineer.com (Career Marketplace)
SensorJobs
Soc. for Automotive Engineers
Soc. of Cable Telecommunications Eng.
Soc. of Hispanic Prof. Engineers (BrassRing)
Soc. of Women Engineers (BrassRing)
Society of Manufacturing Engineers
Solid Edge Job Network (Mercury Enterprises)
Solid Works Job Network (Mercury Enterprises)
Space Careers
Space Jobs
SPIEWorks- Int'l Society for Optical Engineering
Step Beyond
Talent rock
Tech Employment.com
Telecom Engineer.com (Career Marketplace)
TeleJob Academic Job Exchange
Tenn Careers.com (CareerMVP)
Texan Careers.com (CareerMVP)
The Work Circuit (EETimes)
Transportation Engineer.com (Career Marketplace)
UG Job Network (Mercury Enterprises)
WA Careers.com (CareerMVP)
Wireless Engineer.com (Career Marketplace)
Workplace Diversity.com (Career Engine)
Worldwideworker.com
yourEEcareer.com

ENTERTAINMENT & MEDIA (47)

Actor's Worldlink
AM FMJobs
Art Directors Club of Metro. Washington
Art Hire
Assoc. for Women in Communications
Assoc. for Women in Sports Media
Backstagejobs.com
Casino Employment Guide
Casting America
Casting Daily
Classic Web
Communications Roundtable

Cool Jobs.com
Cool Works - Jobs in Great Places
Creative Freelancers Online
Crew Net
Editor & Publisher
Entertainment Careers.Net
Entertainment Jobs.com
Film TV Production Jobs (Mandy.com)
Film, TV, & Commercial Employment Network
Hollywood MVP.com (CareerMVP)
Hollywood Web
Int'l Soc. for the Performing Arts
Int'l. Assoc. of Amusement Parks and Attractions
Jobs in the Biz
Just Entertainment Jobs.com
media bistro.com
Media Jobz.Com
Media Line.com
Musicians Network
Nat'l. Assoc. of Broadcasters
Nat'l. Assoc. Recording Merchandisers
Play Bill
Radio & Records Online
Radio Online
ShowBizJobs.com
Soc. of Broadcast Engineers
Talent Works: The Online Casting Source
TC Theatre and Film
Television Bureau of Advertising
The Write Jobs
TV Jobs
TVandRadioJobs.com
TVSpy.com
Women Sports Jobs
workinpr.com

EXECUTIVE (52)

1st 4 UK HR Jobs
6 FigureJobs
American Chamber of Commerce Execs
American College of Healthcare Executives
American Soc. of Assoc. Executives (T)
Asia-Links
Assoc. for Financial Professionals
Big FiveTalent.com
Bloomberg.com (CareerBuilder)
business financemag.com
Career Journal Asia.com (CareerJournal)
Career Journal Europe.com (CareerJournal)
Career Journal.com (T)
Career Link- Applied Info. Mgm't Institute
CFO Postions.com (Career Engine)
Chief Financial Officer.com
Chronicle of Philanthropy
CIO Magazine (ITCareers)
College of Healthcare Infor. Mgmt. Exec.
Crains New York (Career Engine)
Credit Union Executives Society
exBigFive.com
Exec Searches.com
ExecGlobalNet
Execs on the Net (UK)
ExecuCentral.com
ExecuClassifieds.com (Career Engine)
ExecuNet (T)
Executive Registry.com
ExecutivesOnly
Financial Executives Institute
Financial Executives Networking Group
Financial Job Network
Global Wrokplace
Health Care Talents

Int'l. Assoc. of Amusement Parks and Attractions
Irish Jobs.ie (T)
Journal of Commerce (Career Engine)
Lee Hecht Harrison
Nat'l. Assoc. of Corp. Real Estate Exec's.
Nat'l. Business Incubation Assoc.
Net Jobs
Net share.com (T)
Police Executive
Seek (Australia) (T)
Stern Alumni Job Listings
TheSquare
Top Money Jobs
US Exec Jobs (Job Network)
US Internet Industry Association
Vice President Jobs.com (eJob Stores)
Women In Technology International

HEALTH CARE (126)

4 Allied Health Jobs Online (HospitalJobsOnl...
4 MD Jobs Online (HospitalJobsOnline)
4 Nursing Jobs Online (HospitalJobsOnline)
Absolutely Health Care
Academic Physician & Scientist
ADVANCE for Careers
Allied Health Employment (HealthCareJobStore)
Allied Health Opportunities
American Academy of Audiology
American Academy of Cosmetic Dentistry
American Assoc. for Respiratory Care
American Assoc. of Critical-Care Nurses
American College of Cardiology
American College of Healthcare Executives
American College of Radiology
American Counseling Assoc.
American Massage Therapy Assoc.
American Physical Therapy Assoc.
American Public Health Assoc.
American Soc. of Echocardiography
American Society fo P&E Nutrition
American Society of Health-System Pharma...
American Speech-Language-Hearing Assoc.
American Urological Assoc.
American Urological Assoc. Job Finder
American Zoo & Aquarium Assoc.
Assoc. of Perioperative Registered Nurses
Assoc. of Women Surgeons
AuntMinnie.com (T)
Bio Statistician Jobs (HealthCareJobStore)
Bioscience and Medicine (HUM-MOLGEN)
Blood Center Jobs (HealthCareJobStore)
cardiac nurse jobs.com (HealthCareJobs)
College of Healthcare Information Mgmt. Exec.
CT Health Careers.com (All County Jobs)
Dent Search.com
Dental Hygienist Jobs (HealthCareJobStore)
Dentist Jobs.com (HealthCare Job Store)
Dietician Jobs (HealthCareJobStore)
Ed Physician.com
EmployMED
ENT Careers
GasJobs.com
GasWork.com
Geo HealthJobsites.com (Geojobsites)
GovMed CAREERS (MedCareers)
Graduate Nurse
Great Nurse.com
H Monster.com (Monster.com)
Health Care Job Store
Health Care Jobs Online
Health Care Recruitment Online

Health Care Source
Health Care Talents
Health CareerWeb.com (Employment Guide)
Health Jobsite.com
Healthcare Employment.com (Career Market...
Healthcare Financial Management Assoc.
HealthCare Hub.com (Nursing Spectrum)
HEALTHeCareers (T)
hire health.com
hireMedical
HireNursing
Hospital Hub UK.com
Hospital Jobs Online
Hot Nurse Jobs
HRMed.com
Infectious Disease Soc. of America
Jobs in Therapy
Just Health Care Jobs.com
Locum Tenens.com
LPN Jobs.com (HealthCareJobStore)
MD Direct.com
MD Jobsite.com
MD Recruitment Online (HC Recruitment Onli...
Med Bulletin
Med CAREERS (T)
Med Hunters
med jump
Med Options (Absolutely Health Care)
med2020
Medical MVP.com (CareerMVP)
Medical Records Jobs.com (HealthCareJobS...
Medical Reps.com
Medical Researcher.com (Career Marketplace)
Medicats
MediCentral.com
MedZilla (T)
Mental Web.com
Mid Wife Jobs.com
Minority Nurse.com (CASS)
Nat'l. Assoc. for Home Care
Nat'l. Athletic Trainers' Assoc.
Nat'l. Gerontological SOA - AgeWork
New England Journal of Medicine
Nurse Aid Jobs (HealthCareJobStore)
Nurse Options (Absolutely Health Care)
Nurse Practitioners Central - NPJobs
Nurse-Recruiter
Nursing Spectrum Career Fitness Online (T)
Occupational Therapist Jobs (HealthCareJo...
OT JobLink
Pediatric Nurse Jobs (HealthCareJobStore)
Pharmacy Jobs Online (HC Recruitment Onli...
Pharmacy Week
Physician Board
Physicians Employment
Practice Choice/Link
Psyc Careers
Public Health Nurse.com (HealthCareJobStore)
Rad Working.com
Radiology & Oncology JOBS (RTjobs.com)
Radiology Jobs (HC Recruitment Online))
Rehab Options (Absolutely Health Care)
RN Jobs (HC Recruitment Online))
RRT Jobs.com (HC Recruitment Online))
RxCareerCenter.com
RxImmigration.com
Speech Therapist Jobs (HealthCareJobStore)
Travel Nurse Jobs (HealthCareJobStore)
Ultrasoundjobs.com
US Med Jobs (Job Network)
Veterinary Jobs.com
VeterinaryLife.com
Y-axis.com

SPECIALTY & INDUSTRY

HOPITALITY & FOOD SERVICES (71)

CHEF/HOTEL/RESORT/RESTAURANT/SUPERMARKET

ActionJobs
Adventures in Hospitality Careers
Adventures in Hospitality Careers
American Culinary Federation
Bakery-Net
Black Culinarians Alliance
Black World Today (Career Engine)
Bread Bakers Guild of America
Canadian Restaurant & Foodservices Assoc.
Careers in Food.com
Casino Careers Online (T)
Casino Employment Guide
Chef Job.com
Chef Jobs Network (Escoffier On Line)
Cool Jobs.com
Cool Works - Jobs in Great Places
Eat up drink up.com
Escoffier On Line - Employment Resources (T)
Food and Drink Jobs.com
Food Industry Jobs.com
Food Job Source
food service.com
Food Supplier.com
funjobs.com
Golf Surfin
H Careers
hospitality careernet.com
Hospitality Careers.net
Hospitality Financial & Technology Professi...
Hospitality Jobs Online
Hospitality Jobs Online
Hospitality jobz.net
Hospitality Link
Hospitality MVP.com (CareerMVP)
Hospitality Net
Hotel Jobs- Ireland
Hotel Jobs.com
Hotel Online
HotelJobsites.com (Geojobsites)
Inner City Jobs.com   (NicheJobs)
Institute of Certified Travel Agents
Int'l. Assoc. of Amusement Parks and Attrac...
Int'l. Assoc. of Conference Centers
Job Monkey
Jobs in Sports
Jobs Retail.com
Just Hospitality Jobs.com
Meeting Professionals Int'l
Monster Retail.com
Mountainjobs.com
NCAA Jobs in College Athletics
Net Empleo.com
Resort Jobs (About Jobs.com)
Resort Professional.com (Career Marketplace)
Restaurant Job Store (eJob Stores)
Restaurant Jobs
Restaurant News
Restaurant Recruit.com
Retail Classifieds (Career Engine)
Retail Job Store (eJob Stores)
Retail Seek.com
Seasonal Employment
Skiing the Net
Snagajob.com
Society for Foodservice Management
sports employment.com
Star Chefs JobFinder
Supermarket News
Travel jobz.net
Web Food Pros (Escoffier On Line)

HUMAN RESOURCES (59)

1st 4 UK HR Jobs
A1A Computer Jobs
AIRS - Advanced Internet Recruitment Strategy
American Soc. for Training & Development
Benefit News Online
Benefits Link (T)
Branch Staff Online.com
Careers in Recruitment
Chesapeake Human Resources Assoc.
College & University Personnel Assoc.
College & University Prof. Assoc. for HR
Colorado Human Resources Assoc.
Columbia-Williamette Compensation Group
Computer Jobs Technical Recruiting
Contact Point Career Development
Council on Employee Benefits
Dallas HR Jobs
Employee Assistance Professionals Assoc.
Employee Relocation Council
ER Exchange
ForContractRecruiters.com
HR Connections Direct
HR Job Net
HR Junction
HR Next
HR World
HR.com
HRIM Mall
HRM Jobs (NicheJobs)
HRMVP MVP.com (CareerMVP)
Human Factors and Ergonomics Society
Human Resource Assoc. of the Nat'l. Capital...
Human Resources Job Store (eJob Stores)
Int'l. Assoc. for HR Info Mgmt.
Int'l. Foundation of Employee Benefit Plans
Int'l. Personnel Mgmt. Assoc. (CareerBuilder)
Int'l. Society For Performance Improvements
Jobs 4 HR (LocalCareers)
Nat'l. Assoc. of African Americans in HR
New England Enployee Benefits Council
New England Human Resource Assoc.
New Jersey Technical Recruiters Alliance
Northeast Human Resources Association
Northwest Recruiters Association
Passing Notes.com (jobvertise)
Professionals in Human Resources Assoc.
Recruiter Seek
Recruiters Dream
Recruiters Forum
Recruiters World
Recruitex
Soc. for Industrial & Org. Psychology
Society for Human Resource Management
Staffing World
TCM's HR Careers
Technical Recruiter.com (Career Marketplace)
Technical Trainer.com (Career Marketplace)
WEB Worldwide Employee Benefits Network
World at Work Job Links

INFORMATION TECHNOLOGY (409)

3D Cafe
3D Site
3sectorsjob
4weeks.com
A Job4Programmers (Employmax)
A1A Computer Jobs
Absolute-Comms
Alabama Computer Jobs.com
ASP Computer work.com

Assoc. for Advancement of Computing in Ed.
Assoc. for Computing Machinery
Assoc. for Telecom. in Higher Ed.
Assoc. of eX-Lotus Employees
Atlanta Computer Jobs.com
Atlanta Computer work.com
Atlanta ContractJobs
AutoCAD Job Network (Mercury Enterprises)
Automation Techies
Avenue J.com
aztechjobs.com
BAAN Fanclub and User Forum (Fanclub)
Baltimore Computerwork.com
BioSnail.com
Black Data Processing Assoc.
Blinks Magazine (FlipDog)
Boston Computer Jobs.com
Brain bench
Brainpower
Brass Ring.com (T)
Broadband Careers Network
BroadbandCareers.Com
Building Industry Consulting Service Int'l.
C++ (JV Search)
C++ Computer work.com
C++ Jobs.com (Pure Power)
Cable & Telecommunications Assoc. for Ma...
CAD jobs.net
CAD Operators Online
CADD Jobs.com
California Computerwork.com
Canada Computerwork.com
Canada IT.com
Career Consulting Corner
Career Gram
Career India
Career Junction
Career Link- Applied Info. Mgm't Institute
Career Mag.com
Career N.I com (CareerMVP)
Car-eers.com
Carolina Computer Jobs.com
CATIA Job Network (Mercury Enterprises)
Cellular Telecom. & Internet Assoc. (Job Opt...
Chicago Computer Jobs.com
CIO Council.com (Career Marketplace)
CIO Magazine (ITCareers)
Ciol Jobs
Classified Employment Web Site (CLEWS)
CNC Machines Job Network (Mercury Enter...
Cobol Computer work.com
Cobol Computerwork.com
Cobol Jobs.com (Pure Power)
Coderider- VIC Job Board
Cold Fusion Advisor (CF Advisor)
College of Healthcare Infor. Mgmt. Exec.
Colorado Computerwork.com
Colorado Software & Internet Assoc.
Computer Jobs AS/400
Computer Jobs Data Warehousing
Computer Jobs Database Systems
Computer Jobs E-Commerce
Computer Jobs Entry Level
Computer Jobs ERP
Computer Jobs Executive Level
Computer Jobs H-1B
Computer Jobs Hardware
Computer Jobs Help Desk
Computer Jobs in Israel
Computer Jobs Legacy Systems
Computer Jobs Networking
Computer Jobs New Media
Computer Jobs Project Management
Computer Jobs Quality Assurance
Computer Jobs Technical Recruiting

Computer Jobs Technical Sales
Computer Jobs Technical Writing
Computer Jobs Unix
Computer Jobs Windows Development
Computer Jobs.com (T)
Computer Weekly.com
Computer work.com (T)
Computer World (ITCareers)
Configuration Management (CM Today)
ConsultantTV.com
Contract Employment Connection
Contract JobHunter
Contracts247
Craigs List
Craigs List [Atlanta]
Craigs List [Austin]
Craigs List [Boston]
Craigs List [Chicago]
Craigs List [Denver]
Craigs List [Los Angeles]
Craigs List [New York]
Craigs List [Portland]
Craigs List [Sacramento]
Craigs List [San Diego]
Craigs List [Seattle]
Craigs List [Vancouver]
Craigs List [Washington DC]
Creative Freelancers Online
Creative Moonlighter
CT High Tech.com (All County Jobs)
Curriculum Vitae Online
CV Europe
CV Online- Czech (CV Europe)
CV Online- Estonia (CV Europe)
CV Online- Finland (CV Europe)
CV Online- Hungary (CV Europe)
CV Online- Latvia (CV Europe)
CV Online- Lithuania (CV Europe)
CV Online- Poland (CV Europe)
CV Online- Romania (CV Europe)
CV Online- Russia (CV Europe)
Database Analyst.com (Career Marketplace)
daVinci Times (T)
DC Computer Jobs.com
DC Computerwork.com
Delphi Jobs.com (Pure Power)
Delphi World.com
Denver Computer Jobs.com
Detroit Computer Jobs.com
Developers.net (Tapestry.net)
DICE High Tech Jobs Online (T)
Diversity Careers Online
Do A Project.com
Donohue's RS/6000 Employment Page
eCommerce Computer work.com
EDN Magazine CarEEr Zone (CareerBuilder)
EDUCAUSE
EE Times (The Work Circuit)
e-itwizards.com
e-Job
elance
Embedded.com (The Work Circuit)
ERP Fan Club and User Forum (Fanclub)
Erp Professional.com (Career Marketplace)
Erp-Jobs.com
ERPJobs.com (Pure Power)
eWork Exchange
ExecuCentral.com
Florida Computer Jobs.com
Florida Computerwork.com
Geo Job Source
Geo Job Source & GIS Jobs
Geo Place.com
Geo Search
Geo TechJobs.com

GeoCommunity Career Center
GeoSearch, Inc.
GeoWeb Interactive
GIS careers.com
GIS Jobs Clearinghouse
GIS-A-Job
GISjobs.com
Graduating Engineer & Computer Careers O...
Graphic Artists Guild
Graphic Arts Information Network
Guru.com
H1B Sponsors
H1Maia.com
hi techclub.com
Hire Abilitiy.com
Hospitality Financial & Technology Professi...
House of Fusion
HR Staffing Search (JV Search)
HTML Writers Guild Job List
i -street
IDEAS Job Network (Mercury Enterprises)
IL Careers.com (CareerMVP)
Info Jobs.net (Bolsa de Trabajo)
Institute of Electrical and Electronics Engineers
Internet Employment in New Mexico
Internet Jobs.com
Int'l Nortel Networks Meridian Users Group
Int'l Tandem Users Group
Int'l Tandem Users Group
Int'l. Assoc. for HR Info Mgmt.
Ist Free Jobs
IT Careers.com
IT Classifieds (Career Engine)
IT Jobfinder.co.za (JobUniverse)
IT Jobs4.com
IT Moonlighter
IT Online Jobs
IT talent.com
IT Toolbox Forums
IT Toolbox's Baan Assist
IT Toolbox's CRM Assist
IT Toolbox's Data Warehousing Assist
IT Toolbox's EAI Assist
IT Toolbox's E-Business Assist
IT Toolbox's ERP Assist
IT Toolbox's Oracle Assist
IT Toolbox's PeopleSoft Assist
IT Toolbox's SAP Assist
IT World (ITCareers)
ITonlinejobs
it-TEMP
ITwow.com
Java Computer work.com
Java Jobs
Java World (ITCareers)
Javajobsonline.com
Job Bright
Job Cafe
Job Circle.com (T)
Job Easy
job force
Job Hub
job khoj
Job Net Australia
Job Penguin
Job Smack
Job Universe (Canada)
Job Universe (IT Careers-IDG)
Job Universe (New Zealand)
JobRadio.com
Jobs DB.com
Jobs for Networkers (JobsforProgrammers)
Jobs for Programmers (T)
jobs.internet.com (DICE)
Jobstor.com

Just Access Jobs
Just AS400 Jobs
Just ASP Jobs
Just Baan Jobs
Just c Jobs
Just CAD Jobs
Just Cobol Jobs
Just computerjobs.com
Just DB2 Jobs
Just E-Commerce Jobs
Just Help Desk Jobs
Just JAVA Jobs
Just Networking Jobs
Just Notes Jobs
Just NT Jobs
Just Oracle Jobs
Just PeopleSoft Jobs
Just SQL Server Jobs
Just Sybase Jobs
Just Telephony Jobs
Just Unix Jobs
Just Visual Basic Jobs
JV Search
KareerMakers.com
Lan Jobs.com (Pure Power)
LavaTech's - Lotus Notes Jobs
Linux World (ITCareers)
Los Angeles Computer Jobs.com
Lotus Notes Jobs.com (Pure Power)
Lotus Professional.com (Career Marketplace)
MA Careers.com (CareerMVP)
Mac Talent.com
Marketing Dreamjobs
MemphisComputer work.com
Mercury Enterprises Job Network
Midwest Computerwork.com
Mojolin
Mountainjobs.com
Must Jobs.com
My Career.com.au
My JobCafe
Nat'l. Technical Services Assoc.
Naukri
NC Careers.com (CareerMVP)
Net Staff
Net work and Systems Profesionals Assoc.
Network Engineer.com (Career Marketplace)
Network World (ITCareers)
Networking Computer work.com
New England Computerwork.com
New England Telecommunications Assoc.
New Media Assoc. of NJ
New Mexico High Tech Jobs Forum
New Mexico Hight Tech Job Forum
New York Computer Jobs.com
New York Computer work.com
NI Jobs.com (Irish Jobs)
NY New Media Assoc. The Silicon Alley Job...
Operation IT
ORA Search (JV Search)
Oracle Computer work.com
Oracle Fanclub and User Forum (Fanclub)
Oracle Job Network
Oracle Professional.com (Career Marketplace)
Orajobs.com
Pennsylvania Computerwork.com
People Online
People Soft Developer.com (Career Marketp...
Perl Computer work.com
Philadelphia Computer Jobs.com
Phoenix Computerwork.com
Planet SAP.com
Portland Computer Jobs.com
Position Watch
Power Builder Jobs.com (Pure Power)

Power Builder Journal
Pro Hire
Pro/E Job Network (Mercury Enterprises)
Procruit
Programmer Analyst.com (Career Marketplace)
Programming Jobs.com
Programming-Services.com
Project Manager.com (Career Marketplace)
ProMatch
Pure Power's Database Jobs.com
Recruit Military
Recruitment Exchange Online
Rent-a-Geek
RF Global Net (Verticalnet)
RF Job Network (Mercury Enterprises)
SAP Club
SAP Computer work.com
Sap Developer.com (Career Marketplace)
SAP Fanclub and User Forum (Fanclub)
Search Security
Seattle Computer Jobs.com
Seattle Computer work.com
Security Clearance ComputerJobs.com
Senior Techs
SensorJobs
Silicon Valley Computer Jobs.com
Silicon Valley.com (CareerBuilder)
Soc. of Cable Telecommunications Eng.
Software Contractors' Guild
Software Developer Careers (Dr Dobbs)
Software Developer Jobs.com (eJob Stores)
Software Developer.com (Career Marketplace)
Software Engineer.com (Career Marketplace)
Software Jobs.com (Tech-Engine.com)
SoftwareSalesJobs.com
Solid Edge Job Network (Mercury Enterprises)
Solid Works Job Network (Mercury Enterpri...
Southern California EDI Roundtable
Space Careers
SQL Computer work.com
St. Louis Computer Jobs.com
Sun Guru
Support Analyst.com (Career Marketplace)
SwiftJobs
System Administrator.com (Career Marketpl...
Systems Administration Guild
Systems Analyst.com (Career Marketplace)
Talent rock
Tech Employment.com
Tech Profiles
tech-engine.com (T)
Techies .com
Technical Assoc. of the Graphic Arts
Technical Communicator.com (Career Marke...
Technical Trainer.com (Career Marketplace)
TechnoCentral.com
Technojobs.co.uk
Technology MVP.com (CareerMVP)
telecom careers.net
Telecom Engineer.com (Career Marketplace)
Telecommunications Computer work.com
Telecommunications Industry Assoc. B2B
Tenn Careers.com (CareerMVP)
Texan Careers.com (CareerMVP)
Texas Computer Jobs.com
Texas Computerwork.com
Thingamajob (3rd Party)
Top Contracts
Total Telecom
TrainMark.com
Twin Cities Computer Jobs.com
UG Job Network (Mercury Enterprises)
UniversoE.com
Unix Admin (JV Search)
Unix Computer work.com

Unix Ugu Universe
US Internet Industry Association
US TECH JOBS
US Tech Jobs (Job Network)
Virginia Computerwork.com
Virtual Jobs.com
Visual Basic Computer work.com
Visual Basic Jobs.com (Pure Power)
Visual Basic Search (JV Search)
WA Careers.com (CareerMVP)
Washington DC Area SGML/XML Users Group
Web Jobs USA.com (eJob Stores)
Web Programming Jobs.com (Pure Power)
Webgrrls
Website Builder.com (Career Marketplace)
Windows Computer work.com
Wireless Design (VeticalNet)
Wireless Developer Network
Wireless Engineer.com (Career Marketplace)
World Org. of Webmasters
Wow-com: World of Wireless Communications
XML Computer work.com
Xml Computerwork.com
Y-axis.com
yourEEcareer.com

LAW & ORDER (46)

POLICE/FIRE/SECURITY/LEGAL

American Academy of Forensic Sciences
American Corporate Counsel Assoc.
American Health Lawyers Assoc
American Society of Crime Lab Directors
Attorney Jobs Online
Attorney.com (Legal Staff)
Canadian Bar Assoc.
Corrections Connection
Counsel net
Distr. of Columbia Bar Career Center (Legal...
eAttorney
Emplawyernet
Find Law
Food and Drug Law Institute
Head Hunt (Counsel Network)
headhunt.com (Counsel Network)
Hispanic Nat'l Bar Association
InhouseCounsel (Counsel Network)
Jobs 4police
Law Bulletin
law enforcementjobs.com
Law Forum
Law Guru (Legalstaff)
Law Guru.com (Legalstaff)
Law Info.com
Law Jobs
Law Listings (Career Engine)
Lawsonline.com (Legalstaff)
LawStar (Legalstaff)
Lawyers Weekly
Legal CV
Legal Report
Legal SecretariesUSA.com
Legalstaff.com (T)
NALS (Legalstaff.)
Nat'l. Directory of Emergency Services
Nat'l. Fed. of Paralegal Assoc. (Legal staff.)
NJ Law Network (Legal Staff)
NJParalegal.com
Police Employment.com
Police Executive
Security Jobs Network
Summer Clerk

SPECIALTY & INDUSTRY

The Blue Line
US Law Jobs (Job Network)
Work LP.com (Loss Prevention)

MILITARY TRANSITION/SECURITY CLEARANCE (32)

Academy Grad.com (MMR)
Academy Grads (The Destiny Group)
Army Career & Alumni Program
Blue To Gray (Corporate Gray Online)
Classified Employment Web Site (CLEWS)
Clearance Jobs.com
Computer Jobs (T)
Corporate Gray
Corporate Gray Online
Davjobs.com (The Destiny Group)
Destiny Group-Military Transition Center (T)
DOD Job Search (America's Job Bank)
DOE-JOBBS
Gree To Gray (Corporate Gray Online)
Hire A Vet (The Destiny Group)
Intelligence & Defense Careers
JMO Jobs (MMR)
Job Circle.com (T)
Job2Teach
Joint Service Academy Alumni Organizations
Joint Service Academy Resume DBS (Destiny Group)
Medical Transition for Veteran Health Care
Mil 2Civ.com (The Destiny Group)
Military spouses.com (The Destiny Group)
Military.com
NCO Jobs (MMR)
Recruit Military
Skillogic
The Retired Officers Assoc. (TROA)
Transition Assistance Online
Vet Jobs
Vets 4 Hire.com (The Destiny Group)
Washington Post (T)

NON-PROFIT (89)

4Labors Of Love
Access: Networking in the Public Interest
AEC Job Bank
Agricultural Labour Pool
American Chamber of Commerce Execs
American Design Drafting Assoc.
American Soc. of Assoc. Executives (T)
American Welding Society
Archaeological Fieldwork Opportunities
art jobonline
Assoc. for Fundraising Professionals
Career Connector
Careers in Construction
Charity JOB
Charity Village.com
charityopps.com
Charityopps.com
Christian Jobs Online
Chronicle of Philanthropy
Civic Action in Eurasia
Clear Star
Community Career Center
ConstructionOnly.Com
Contact Point Career Development
Council on Foundations
Cyber-Sierra
Electric job.com
Electrical Employment
Electrician Job Store (eJob Stores)

Elf Network.com
Engineering News Record
Environmental Career.com
Environmental Career.com
Environmental Jobs and Careers
EveryTruckJob.com
Exec Searches.com
Feminist Majority Foundation Online
Find-A-Job-Canada
Golfing Careers
Good Works
Great Summer Jobs/Misc
Hire Skills.com
HS People
hs people (Human Services)
Human Services Career Network
HVAC Careers (CareerMVP)
HVAC job.com (Electric Job)
HVAC Mall
idealist.org
Impact Online
Independent Sector Job Link
Int'l. Career Employment Center
Int'l. Economic Development Council
Jewish Camp Staff
Jewish Vocational Services Career Moves
Layover.com (T)
Ministry Careers.com
Ministry Connect
Ministry Jobs.com
ministry search.com
MinistryEmployment.Com
Minnesota Council of Nonprofits
Modern Machine Shop Online
Nat'l. Assoc. of Elevator Contractors
Nat'l. Assoc. of Social Workers
Nat'l. Assoc. of Women In Construction (Fli...
Nat'l. Youth Development Information Center
Non Profit Career.com
NonprofitOyster
NPO.NET
one world.net
Opportunity Nocs
Philanthropy Journal Online
Plumbjob.com (Electric Job)
Social Service.Com
Social Work & Services Jobs Online
Social Work JobBank
Superintendent jobs.com (eJob Stores)
Sustainable Business.com
The Job Seeker
The Nat'l Assembly
Trade Jobs Online
Training Resource Network
Truck Driver
Truck Net
Volunteer Match
Welding Jobs.com (Hire in a Click)
WorkopolisCampus.com (Workopolis)
Youth Specialties

PUBLIC SECTOR (59)

STATE & FEDERAL GOVERNMENT JOBS

Alabama State Jobs
American Assoc. for Budget & Program Ana...
American Planning Assoc.
American Public Health Assoc.
American Public Works Assoc.
American Society for Public Administration
Boston Job Source (Internet Job Source)
California Job Source (Internet Job Source)

452

Career Espresso/Emory University
Careers in Government
Contact Point Career Development
Cyber-Sierra
DC Job Source.com (Internet Job Source)
DOE-JOBBS
Fed World.gov Federal Jobs
Federal Jobs Central
Federal Jobs Digest
get a govjob.com
Government Classifieds (Career Engine)
GovernmentJobs.com
GovMed CAREERS (MedCareers)
Hire Texas
HS People
Human Services Career Network
Idaho State Jobs
Intelligence & Defense Careers
Int'l. Career Employment Center
Int'l. Economic Development Council
Int'l. Personnel Mgmt. Assoc. (CareerBuilder)
Iowa State Jobs
Kansas State Jobs
Kentucky KY Direct
Louisiana State Jobs
Montana State Jobs
Nat'l. Assoc. of Development Organizations
Nat'l. Assoc. of Social Workers
Nevada State Jobs
New Mexico State Jobs
North Dakota State Jobs
NY Job Source (Internet Job Source)
NY Job Source.com
NYC Workforce 1
Oklahoma State Jobs
Oregon State Jobs
Political Resources
Security Jobs Network
Social Service.Com
South Carolina State Jobs
South Dakota State Jobs
Special Library Association
Sustainable Business.com
Tennessee State Jobs
Texas Workforce
The Internet Job Source
Training Resource Network
Utah State Jobs
Vermont State Jobs
West Virginia State Jobs
Wyoming State Jobs

SALES – RETAIL SALES & SERVICES (51)

AUTO/ REAL ESTATE/ STORE/TRAVEL

All Retail jobs.com
Apartment Careers
Auto careers
Auto Jobs.com
AutoHeadHunter.net
Automotive Aftermarket Industry Asoc.
Automotive Techs.Com
AutoTechs USA
Casino Careers Online (T)
Cool Jobs.com
funjobs.com
Go Ferret Go
Golf Surfin
Inner City Jobs.com (NicheJobs)
InRetail
job site.com
Jobs Retail.com

Jobs in Sports
Jobs4Gems
Media Recruiter.com
Monster Retail.com
Motor Careers
Mountainjobs.com
Nat'l. Assoc. of Corp. Real Estate Exec's.
Nat'l. Assoc. of Ind. & Office Properties
Nat'l. Assoc. Recording Merchandisers
Need Techs.com
Net Empleo.com
Network of Commercial Real Estate Women
PMJobs.com
RE Buz
Real Estate Best Jobs
Real Estate Job Store
Real Estate Jobs.com
Real Jobs - Real Estate
RealEstateJobsites.com (Geojobsites)
Retail Classifieds (Career Engine)
Retail Job Store (eJob Stores)
Retail JobNet.com
Retail Seek.com
Sales Job Store.com (eJob Stores)
Sales Workz (World Workz)
salestrax.com
Seasonal Employment
Snagajob.com
sports employment.com
Television Bureau of Advertising
Tiger Jobs
Title board.com
trans-ACTION Classified Website
travel jobs (Australia/New Zealand)
Travel jobz.net
Women Sports Jobs
Work in Sports

SALES – PROFESSIONAL SALES & MARKETING (43)

3sectorsjob
Accessalesjobs.com
Account Manager.com (Career Marketplace)
Ad Age
Advertising Research Foundation
Adweek Online
AM FMJobs
American Lighting Assoc. (FlipDog)
American Marketing Assoc.
Assoc. for Interactive Marketing (CareerBuil...
Aviation Now
Cable & Telecommunications Assoc. for Ma...
Career Journal Europe.com (CareerJournal)
CareerJournal.com (T)
ExecuCentral.com
Insurance File
job force
Jobs 4 Sales.com (LocalCareers)
Just Marketing Jobs.com
Just Sales
Marketing Dreamjobs
Marketing Jobs.com
Marketing JobStore.com (eJob Stores)
Marketing Manager.com (Career Marketplace)
Marketing MVP.com (CareerMVP)
Medical Reps.com
Nat'l. Assoc. of Sales Professionals
Net Staff
Pharm Web
PolySort
Pro Hire
Product Manager.com (Career Marketplace)
Sales Engineer.com (Career Marketplace)

sales heads
Sales Jobs.com
Sales Rep Central.com
SalesWorkz (World Workz)
salestrax.com
Selling Jobs.com (NicheJobs)
Society of Automotive Engineers
SoftwareSalesJobs.com
Strategic Account Mgmt. Association (SAMA)
Top Money Jobs

SCIENCE (152)

A Job4Scientists (Employmax)
American Academy of Forensic Sciences
American Agricultural Economics Assoc.
American Anthropological Assoc.
American Assoc. of Clinical Chemistry
American Astronomical Society
American Ceramic Society
American Chemical Society - JobSpectrum.org
American Fisheries Society
American Institute of Biological Sciences
American Institute of Physics
American Mathematical Society
American Meteorological Society
American Nuclear Society
American Oil chemists' Society
American Soc. of Agricultural Engineering
American Soc. of Limnology and Oceanography
American Society for Clinical Laboratory Sciences
American Society of Gene Therapy
American Speech-Language-Hearing Assoc.
American Statistical Association
American Water Works Assoc.
Aquatic Network
Assoc. of Clinical Research Professionals
Assoc. of Metropolitan Water Agencies
Assoc. of Research Libraries
Bio Array News (GenomeWeb)
Bio career.com (SciWeb)
Bio Exchange.com
Bio find
Bio Inform (GenomeWeb)
Bio Research Online (WorkLife)
Bio Snail
Bio Space.com
Bio Statistician Jobs (HealthCareJobStore)
Bio View (Monster)
Bio.com
Bioinformatics Resource
Biomedical Engineer.com (Career Marketplace)
Biomedical Engineering Society
Bioplanet
Bioscience and Medicine (HUM-MOLGEN)
BioSnail.com
Biotech Careers.com
Biotechnology Human Resource Counsel
British Columbia Library Assoc.
Career Mag.com
Careers in Food.com
Car-eers.com
Castingpro.com (Staffingpro)
Center Watch
Chem Jobs
Chemistry Jobs.com (NicheJobs)
Clinical Laboratory Management Assoc.
Computational Fluid Dynamics Jobs Database
Crystallography Worldwide
Cyber-Sierra
Drillers Job Center
Drug Information Association
Earthworks

Edie's Environmental Job Centre
Empty.net
ENDS Environmental Jobs
Energy Jobs Network
Entomology Society of America
Environmental Career.com
Environmental Career.com
Environmental Careers Org. (Eco.org)
Environmental Expert
Environmental Jobs and Careers
EnvJobs-L Archives
Experimental Medicine Job Listing
Federation of American Soc. for Exp. Biology
Food and Drug Law Institute
Frontiers in Bioscience
Genome Web
Geospatial Information & Technology Assoc.
Green Dream Jobs
Green Energy Jobs
hire health.com
HireBio
Horticultural Jobs
Houston Geological Society
Hydrocarbon Online (VerticalNet)
Industrial Designers Society of America
InPharm.com
Institute of Food Technologists
Intelligence & Defense Careers
Int'l. Pharmajobs
Job science.com
Job Seekers Mailing List
Jobs in Entomology
Jobs in Horticulture
Jobs.ac.uk
Job-Sites.com
Just Science Jobs.com
Massachusetts Biotechnology Council
Materials Jobs.com (NicheJobs)
Med BizPeople.com
Medical DeviceLink.com
Medical Reps.com
Medical Researcher.com (Career Marketplace)
MedZilla (T)
Meteorological Employment Journal
Mexican American Eng. and Scientists Society
Milwaukee Naturally
Nat'l. Academies Career Center
Nat'l. Assoc. of Environmental Profesionals
Nat'l. Council of Teachers of Math Jobs Online
Nat'l. Environmental Health Assoc.
Nat'l. Gerontological SOA - AgeWork
Nat'l. Registry of Environmental Professionals
Nat'l. Weather Association
Nature Jobs.com
Nuke Worker.com
Oil Careers
Oil Directory.com
Oil job.com
Oil Online
one world.net
optics.org
Organic Chemistry Jobs Worldwide
Pharm Web
Physics Today Online
Physics World Jobs
Plastic Careers.com
Plastic Pro (staffingpro)
Plastics News
PolySort
Psyc Careers
Regulatory Affairs Professionals Society
Research Network
Rocky Mountain Water Environment Assoc.
Royal Society of Chemistry
RxCareerCenter.com

454

Sci Jobs.com
Sci Jobs.org
Sci Web Career Center
Science Careers (T)
Science jobs.com
Scientific American.com
Scientific Researcher.com (Career Marketplace)
Soc. for Adv. of Chicanos & Native Amer. in Science
Society of Environ. Toxicology & Chemistry
SPIEWorks- Int'l Society for Optical Engineering
Talent rock
Technical Assoc. of Pulp & Paper (TAPPI)
TeleJob Academic Job Exchange
The Job Seeker
Thingamajob
Weed Jobs (Positions in Weed Science)
Worldwideworker.com

TRADE, NON-EXEMPT & HOURLY (85)

1800Drivers
AEC Job Bank
AEC WorkForce
Agricultural Labour Pool
American Design Drafting Assoc.
American Welding Society
Apartment Careers
Arbetsformedlingen
Areo Ad's
Auto Jobs.com
Autobody Online
Automation Jobs
Automation Techies
Automotive Aftermarket Industry Assoc.
Automotive Techs.Com
AutoTechs USA
AV Canada
Av Crew.com
AV Jobs
Aviation Employment.com
Aviation Job Search.com
Aviation Jobs Online
Backstagejobs.com
Boiler Room
Career Connector
Career NJ.com (CareerMVP)
Careers in Construction
Castingpro.com (Staffingpro)
Clear Star
Construction Gigs
Construction Job Store (eJob Stores)
Construction Jobs.com
Construction.com
ConstructionJobsites.com (Geojobsites)
Construction-net
ConstructionOnly.Com
Curriculum Vitae Online
Electric job.com
Electrical Employment
Electrician Job Store (eJob Stores)
Engineering News Record
EveryTruckJob.com
Find A Pilot
Find-A-Job-Canada
Finishing.com
Go Ferret Go
Golfing Careers
Great Summer Jobs/Misc
Hire Skills.com
HVAC Careers (CareerMVP)
HVAC job.com (Electric Job)
HVAC Mall
IL Careers.com (CareerMVP)

Info Mine
Inner City Jobs.com   (NicheJobs)
InspectionJobs.com
Interior Design Jobs.com
Int'l. Seafarers Exchange
job site.com
Jobs in Horticulture
Layover.com (T)
MA Careers.com (CareerMVP)
Mining USA
Modern Machine Shop Online
Motor Careers
Nat'l. Assoc. of Elevator Contractors
Nat'l. Assoc. of Women In Construction (Fli...
NC Careers.com (CareerMVP)
Need Techs.com
Nuke Worker.com
Offshore Guides
Oil Careers
Plastic Careers.com
Plastic Pro (staffingpro)
Plumbjob.com (Electric Job)
Refrigeration-engineer.com
Superintendent jobs.com (eJob Stores)
Tenn Careers.com (CareerMVP)
Texan Careers.com (CareerMVP)
Trade Jobs Online
Truck Driver
Truck Net
TruckinJobs.com
Unicru
WA Careers.com (CareerMVP)
Welding Jobs.com (Hire in a Click)

MISCELLANEOUS (60)

AGRICULTURE/ AVIATION/OUTDOORS/SPORTS

1800Drivers
Agricultural Labour Pool
Agricultural MVP.com (CareerMVP)
Agricultural Technology Information Network
American Society of Interior Designers
American Zoo & Aquarium Assoc.
Archaeological Fieldwork Opportunities
Areo Ad's
Art Deadlines List
AV Canada
Av Crew.com
AV Jobs
Aviation Employment.com
Aviation Job Search.com
Back Door Jobs
Book People
Branch Staff Online.com
California Agricultural Technology Institute
Casino Careers Online (T)
Circulation Jobs.com
Colorado Guide
Cool Jobs.com
Cool Works - Jobs in Great Places
dot Jobs
Equimax
Escape Artist.com
Farms.com
Fashion Career Center.com
Find A Pilot
Fish jobs
Fitness Link
Funeral Net
funjobs.com
Golf Surfin
Great Summer Jobs/Misc

SPECIALTY & INDUSTRY

H1B Sponsors
Institute of Store Planners
Interior Design Jobs.com
Int'l. Seafarers Exchange
Jewish Camp Staff
Job Monkey
Jobs in Fashion.com
Jobs in Sports
Mountainjobs.com
Nat'l. Accrediting Commission of Cosmetolo...
Nat'l. Athletic Trainers' Assoc.
Nat'l. Emergency Number Assoc.
NCAA Jobs in College Athletics
Offshore Guides
Pilot Jobs
P-Jobs
Resort Jobs (About Jobs.com)
Skiing the Net
SkiingtheNet
sports employment.com
StartupZone
TimberSite.com
Women Sports Jobs
Work in Sports
Worldwideworker.com

Order now and receive a
FREE DEMO
of *CareerXroads Online*

Visit www.careerxroads.com to order your book and database subscription
OR fax this short order form to 732-821-1343

CareerXroads 2003 Order Form

Name _____

Organization _____

Address _____

City _____ State _____ Zip _____

Phone_____Fax_____ Email____ _____

Quantity_____ @26.95   _____

NJ residents add 6% sales tax   _____

Shipping, add $5 for the first book
and $1 for each additional book   _____

Online access @19.95 per search   _____
Contact us for corporate search rates.

TOTAL   _____

Payment Method

_____Credit Card   ___Visa   ___MasterCard   ___AMEX

Card Number_____ Exp. Date _____

Name on card _____

Signature_____

_____Check or money order payable to **MMC Group**

MMC Group
P.O. Box 253
Kendall Park, NJ 08824
PH: **732-821-6652**   FAX: **732-821-1343**   www.careerxroads.com

Notes

Notes

Notes